SECOND EDITION

# The Great Writings in Management and Organizational Behavior

◆

## LOUIS E. BOONE

Ernest G. Cleverdon Chair of Business and Management
*University of South Alabama*

## DONALD D. BOWEN

Professor of Management
*The University of Tulsa*

McGRAW-HILL PUBLISHING COMPANY
New York   St. Louis   San Francisco
Auckland   Bogotá   Caracas   Hamburg
Lisbon   London   Madrid   Mexico
Milan   Montreal   New Delhi   Oklahoma City
Paris   San Juan   São Paulo   Singapore
Sydney   Tokyo   Toronto

*To our families*

Pat, Barry, and Christopher Boone
Polly, Mike, Ted, Tom, and Matt Bowen

The Great Writings in
Management and Organizational Behavior 2/e

Copyright © 1987 by McGraw-Hill, Inc. All rights reserved. Printed in the United
States of America. Except as permitted under the United States Copyright Act of
1976, no part of this publication may be reproduced or distributed in any form or
by any means, or stored in a data base or retrieval system, without the prior
written permission of the publisher.

10  9  8  7  6  5

**Library of Congress Cataloging-in-Publication Data**
The Great writings in management and organizational
   behavior.
   Bibliography: p.
   Includes indexes.
   1. Management.   2. Organizational behavior.
3. Industrial management.   I. Boone, Louis E.
II. Bowen, Donald D.
HD31.G74   1987          658          86-33900
ISBN 0-07-555030-X

Cover photo by Paul Silverman

# *Preface*

◆

*Taylor . . . Fayol . . . Follett . . . Drucker . . . Maslow . . . Mayo . . . Argyris . . . Schein . . . Simon . . . Mintzberg . . . Likert. . . .* These writers are among the giants of twentieth century management thought. Their contributions—*scientific management, Theory X* and *Theory Y, the needs hierarchy, path-goal theory, the Vroom-Yetton model*—have become cornerstones in guiding management professionals in the performance of management tasks.

*The Great Writings in Management and Organizational Behavior* brings together in one volume the classic writings of our era. But the book is more than a collection of classic writings; it is a complete teaching/learning package. Each selection in the book is preceded by a comprehensive preview for the reader and is followed by a self-scoring learning review of each major point. The accompanying *Instructor's Manual* contains detailed summaries of each selection and a series of objective and discussion questions and answers to facilitate class use.

## How the Book was Developed

We faced two major issues in the development of *The Great Writings*. First, there was the problem of which selections to choose as representative of the entire fields of management and organizational behavior. The final selections were chosen on the following bases: (1) fundamental contributions; (2) reflections of the views of influential scholars and practitioners; (3) ability to stimulate thought and new research; and (4) skill in presentation of ideas and concepts. In a discipline as diverse and rich as management and organizational behavior, it would be presumptuous to state that this volume contains all of the classic writings. Nevertheless, the selections contained in *The Great Writings* are works with which every serious student of management and organizational behavior should be familiar. *The Great Writings* belongs in the library of all managers who consider themselves professionals with a heritage of classical management literature.

A second problem was how to bring the time-honored and widely quoted writings up to date. Many of them were written several decades ago. An exciting solution was chosen: *ask the authors to update their articles.* A number of the authors are no longer living or could not be contacted; their updates have been written by others chosen for their interest and acknowledged expertise in that specific area of management and organizational behavior. The inclusion of *Retrospective Commentaries* adds a fascinating dimension to *The Great Writings.*

*PREFACE*

## Developing the Second Edition

The decision to revise *The Great Writings* was a difficult one; a decision we postponed for almost seven years. After all, how does one revise a book with a title such as ours? Correspondence with adopters revealed that the book is used in a diverse variety of courses, ranging from introductory management and organizational behavior to doctoral-level seminars in a variety of colleges and universities in the United States, Canada, and Europe. Over the years a number of our colleagues have provided input, including suggestions for including new works and commenting on some current selections that are not frequently assigned to students.

A second major input was comprised of the responses received from our questionnaire mailed to colleagues in the discipline. Over 100 educators offered their suggestions for improving the new edition.

The end result of these inputs is the new second edition of *The Great Writings*. The 27 selections include several new articles that have stood the test of time. In addition, a few classics were deleted on the basis of our survey of adopters and other professional educators.

## Organizational Structure

The outline of *The Great Writings* is straightforward and roughly chronological. The introductory section focuses on the writings of Weber, Fayol, Taylor, Follett, and Sheldon—five pioneers of management thought. Part 2, *The Second Generation,* spans the era between 1920 and 1945. Its selections reveal a sharpening focus on the human problems of organization, thereby laying the framework for the discipline. In Part 3, *The Paradigm Creators,* selections from the period between 1945 and 1960 are included. In this section the reader is exposed to the definers of the issues, variables, and values influencing the scientific investigation of management and organizational issues for the next two decades. The final part, *Major Current Contributions,* includes several writings since 1965 that focus on such important issues as goal-setting, job design, managerial roles, leadership, contingency approaches, decision making, culture, and organizational effectiveness.

*The Great Writings* is a complete teaching/learning package that can be used in management and organizational behavior courses at the undergraduate and graduate level. It is a book to which every serious student of management should be exposed.

## Acknowledgments

We have been fortunate in obtaining the assistance of a number of colleagues in making suggestions and reviewing our preliminary selections. Special thanks must go to our colleagues Edward L. Harrison, Donald C. Mosley, Paul H. Pietri, Jr., and Terrell F. Pike of the University of South Alabama, and to Joe

Wolfe and Conrad Jackson of The University of Tulsa for their recommendations for improving the new edition. We are particularly appreciative of the comments and suggestions offered by the following colleagues at other colleges and universities.

Steven H. Appelbaum
Concordia University

Achilles Armenakis
Auburn University

Arthur G. Bedeian
Louisiana State University

Lee Bolman
Harvard University

Robert W. Boozer
Memphis State University

David Bradford
Stanford University

Karen Brown
Seattle University

Edgar T. Busch
Western Kentucky University

James G. Clawson
University of Virginia

Keith Davis
Arizona State University

W. Jack Duncan
University of Alabama—
   Birmingham

C. Patrick Fleenor
Seattle University

John J. Gabarro
Harvard University

Sam Gould
University of Dayton

Walter E. Greene
Pan American University

Douglas T. Hall
Boston University

Francine S. Hall
University of New Hampshire

Don Hellriegel
Texas A & M University

Donald C. King
Purdue University

Bruce A. Kirchoff
Babson College

Janina C. Latack
Ohio State University

Roy J. Lewicki
Ohio State University

William W. McCartney
University of Central Florida

Joseph W. McGuire
University of California, Irvine

Leon C. Megginson
Mobile College

R. Henry Migliore
Oral Roberts University

R. Wayne Mondy
McNeese State University

David P. Rutenberg
Queen's University

Larry Pate
University of Kansas

Charles E. Woodfill
Franklin University

Jacob P. Siegel
University of Toronto

Betty Yantis
University of Nevada, Las Vegas

Henry Tosi
University of Florida

G. Lawrence Zahn
University of California,
    Riverside

Peter B. Vaill
George Washington University

Thomas W. Zimmerer
Clemson University

Paul J. Wolff II
Dundalk Community College

Appreciation is also expressed to the dozens of anonymous reviewers who provided us with invaluable inputs. We would particularly like to thank our executive editor June Smith, Susan Badger, Acquiring Editor, and Anne Mahoney, Development Editor, for their insights, suggestions, and good humor and patience.

Special thanks must go to Professors Rogene Bucholz, Janice Beyer, Henry L. Tosi, Daniel A. Wren, Robert A. Russell, George F. F. Lombard, William B. Wolf, Raymond E. Miles, John R. Schermerhorn, Jr., the late M. M. Hargrove, and Robert Duncan for their *Great Expert's Note* on specific selections. The real credit, of course, goes to the 35 authors whose works are included in the book. They alone have made *The Great Writings* possible.

*January 1987*                                                    LOUIS E. BOONE

                                                                  DONALD D. BOWEN

# Contributors

✦

Chris Argyris
Chester I. Barnard
Peter F. Drucker
Henri Fayol
Fred E. Fiedler
Mary Parker Follett
J. Richard Hackman
Frederick Herzberg
Robert J. House
Robert Janson
Steven Kerr
Harold Koontz
Gary P. Latham
Edward E. Lawler, III
Rensis Likert
Edwin A. Locke
Jay W. Lorsch
James G. March

Abraham H. Maslow
Elton Mayo
David C. McClelland
Douglas M. McGregor
Henry Mintzberg
Terence R. Mitchell
Greg Oldham
Lyman W. Porter
Kenneth Purdy
Edgar H. Schein
Warren H. Schmidt
Oliver Sheldon
Herbert A. Simon
Robert Tannenbaum
Frederick W. Taylor
Victor H. Vroom
Max Weber

# Contents

✦

## Part 1
## The Pioneers  1

## Part 2
## The Second Generation  75

## CONTENTS

## Part 3

# The Paradigm Creators   123

## Part 4
## Major Current Contributions  279

# CONTENTS

# Contents

## (Organized by Managerial Functions)

# MOTIVATION

# LEADERSHIP

# CONTROL AND DECISION MAKING

# Part 1
# THE PIONEERS

◆

The need to organize and manage human efforts in order to achieve the goals of groups of people undoubtedly goes back to virtually the beginning of human existence. Hunting and foraging parties, mutual defense activities and even the family all call for some provisions for coordinating and motivating the efforts of individual members of the group. Wherever we find such a need, we inevitably find some form of organization; a degree of task specialization and an arrangement whereby decisions can be made on behalf of the group.

While the need for organization and management is as old as the human race, attempts to systematically study these important social phenomena are relatively new. George (1968) reports that the earliest written records of managerial activity date from the Sumerians in about 5000 B.C. Up to the beginning of the twentieth century, there was a steady but slow development of written materials dealing with the topic with little systematic accumulation of knowledge.

In the last few years of the nineteenth century, things began to change dramatically. The industrial revolution had proceeded to the point where business organizations of heretofore undreamt of size and power developed to satisfy the seemingly endless demand for new goods, products, and services. With increasing size came a trend toward urbanization of the workforce and an emerging labor movement to counter the harsh managerial practices of the day. With the growth of cities and towns came a need for large non-business organizations to provide for the needs of the population: universities, hospitals, schools, social service agencies, and governmental agencies—each presenting its own unique problems of organization and management.

Another parallel force operating simultaneously to encourage a more systematic study of organization and management was the development of modern scientific

1

method. In the Western world, science had achieved spectacular gains in the physical sciences, medicine, and technology. By the mid-nineteenth century, attempts were being made to turn the same techniques to the study of social phenomena and the earliest psychological and sociological studies began to appear.

And thus we find at the beginning of the twentieth century, three separate major figures, each in his own way *and without knowledge of the work of the others,* making an initial attempt at what he saw to be the crucial need for launching a systematic and scientific study of organization and management. None of the three, Fayol, Weber, and Taylor, was the first to write about management. But their efforts gave impetus to a rapid expansion of our codified knowledge of the field. Today, the academic disciplines of management and organizational behavior are accepted components of most university curricula. Academic programs at both the undergraduate and graduate levels train thousands of business students and budding social scientists every year. Moreover, practicing managers spend millions on management development programs and consulting services to keep themselves abreast of new developments.

It all began with the three men whose works are excerpted in this section.

Of the three, Taylor was initially the most influential. He was also a controversial figure—in his own day and today. His new approaches to managing work, which he called "scientific management," aroused distrust and suspicion among workers who feared the potential for exploitation. Management was much more friendly to ideas that promised to increase worker productivity, but public furor led to Congressional investigations of the application of Taylor's ideas to government workers.

In the 1920's, the "efficiency expert," with stopwatch in hand, became the symbol of all that both clerical and blue-collar workers feared most from the "dehumanizing" effects of scientific management techniques. It was no accident that the American labor movement grew strongest in those industries where mass production and scientific management techniques were most prevalent.

Today, there is some evidence that Taylor may have fabricated some of his evidence (e.g., his famous story of how he taught the laborer, "Schmidt," to increase his productivity several-fold in the loading of pig-iron) and may have used the work of an associate (Morris Cooke) without appropriate credit in his most famous work, *The Principles of Scientific Management* (Wrege & Perroni, 1974; Wrege & Stotka, 1978). Whatever shortcomings Taylor may have exhibited in his integrity, however, the fact remains that his work continues to be immensely influential in modern management practice and thought.

Fayol, like Taylor, was a practitioner of management first and foremost. Rising from engineer to managing director of a French mining firm, Fayol felt a need to distill his knowledge for the benefit of managers of the future. His viewpoint was very different from Taylor's, however. While Taylor was primarily concerned with issues of planning, organizing and supervising the work at the lowest levels of the organization, Fayol wrote from the perspective of the top managers of the organization. He deals with topics such as planning and forecasting for the firm, developing its organization and control systems, and achieving overall coordination of efforts at all levels.

The selection reprinted here provides a good example of Fayol's approach to the topic of planning even if it does not do justice to the breadth of his interests in all aspects of the managerial job.

Weber, the German sociologist, had the least impact on practitioners of management; his influence was primarily on academicians in the early years. Weber was a great admirer of the "bureaucratic" form of organization which was developing in German governmental circles in the nineteenth century. For Weber, the term bureaucracy has none of the critical implications which usually accompany our use of the term; a bureaucracy was simply an organization with the following characteristics (based on Weber, 1946):

1. Each office has fixed official duties.
2. Impersonal rules and regulations apply to governing conduct.
3. A hierarchy of offices with graduated levels of authority coordinates efforts.
4. Reliance is placed on written communication and files of documents.
5. Employment is a full time career for the members of the organization.
6. Officials are appointed to office by their superiors.
7. Promotion is based on merit.

Clearly, the bureaucracy Weber described is not far from the ideal that most organizations of today strive to achieve. For this reason, Weber's "model" has provided several generations of sociologists and students of organizations with a powerful perspective for understanding how organizations function and what they try to accomplish.

A key to Weber's case for bureaucracy is to be found in the piece in this section which deals with the concept of authority. Weber feared the dangers of social systems where the basis of authority was in tradition (as in feudalism) or charisma (as in religious cults). Again, these are attitudes that most of us today would endorse.

Taylor, Fayol, and Weber were followed closely by a number of theorists and practitioners expanding and further defining the new field of management. The Gilbreths, Gantt, Emerson, and other proponents of Taylor's industrial engineering approach were the most prominent. A few, like Oliver Sheldon and Mary Parker Follett, had interests more akin to those of Fayol in general management.

Chronologically, Sheldon and Follett were contemporaries of what we have called "The Second Generation"—especially Elton Mayo and Chester I. Barnard. Intellectually, however, Sheldon and Follett were direct descendants of the practicing managers like Taylor and Fayol, whose writings were a distillation of their observations from their personal experience, rather than descriptions of empirical studies of organizational phenomena such as those we find in Mayo's Hawthorne studies. As might be expected, Follett, Sheldon, and similar theorists seem to have had relatively little impact on the historical development of the scientific study of management and organizations as we know it today. It is unfortunate that their writings received so little attention during the early development of the field, since they foresaw many of the issues that later emerged as central to the discipline. As the selection from Sheldon's work illustrates, he identified the need for socially responsible management. It was not until the 1960's that social responsibility became a required course in U.S. business schools.

The ideas explored in Follett's article, if we could modernize the language a bit, would sound like a prescription for the proper management of a present-day, high-tech professional group. She clearly recognizes the interdependence between the components of an organization (as emphasized in contemporary systems theory). She argues for leadership founded upon expertise and gaining the commitment of one's followers, rather than dependence on authoritarian or bureaucratic means of influence. She urges participative management and the development of one's subordinates and the departmental team. Her prescription for leadership effectiveness, presented in 1933, would be heartily endorsed by contemporary proponents of managerial excellence (Peters & Waterman, 1982) and Japanese management techniques (Ouchi, 1981).

# REFERENCES

George, C. S., Jr., *The History of Management Thought*. Englewood Cliffs, NJ: Prentice-Hall, 1968.

Ouchi, W. *Theory Z: How American Business Can Meet the Japanese Challenge*. Reading, MA: Addison-Wesley, 1981.

Peters, T. J. & Waterman, R. H., Jr., *In Search of Excellence*. New York: Harper & Row, 1982.

Weber, M. "Bureaucracy" (excerpt from Max Weber, *Essays in Sociology*, 1946) in J. A. Litterer (Ed.) *Organizations: Structure and Behavior*. New York: Wiley, 1963. Pp. 40–50.

Wrege, C. D. & Perroni, A. G. "Taylor's pig-tale: A historical analysis of Frederick W. Taylor's pig-iron experiment." *Academy of Management Journal*, 1974, *17*, 6–27.

Wrege, C. D. & Stotka, A. M. "Cooke creates a classic: The story behind F. W. Taylor's Principles of Scientific Management." *Academy of Management Review*, 1978, *3*, 736–749.

# 1

# *Legitimate Authority and Bureaucracy*

## MAX WEBER

## *About the Author*

**Max Weber** (1864–1920) was a German sociologist, political scientist, and economist. Weber is perhaps best known for his extensive review of the relationship
between religious and economic systems. Weber argued that Protestantism
particularly favored the development of capitalism because the Protestant Ethic
encourages hard work, self-denial, and thrift.

For students of organizations, Weber's concepts of the organizational effects
of different types of authority were seminal. Weber was an unabashed admirer
of bureaucracy as a form of organization. His concept of bureaucratic organization
(impersonal rules, hierarchical design, promotion on the basis of merit, etc.)
provides a model which almost all private as well as public organizations still
emulate.

Reprinted with permission of The Free Press, a Division of Macmillan, Inc. from
Max Weber, *The Theory of Social and Economic Organization,* translated by A. M. Hender-
son and Talcott Parsons, edited by Talcott Parsons. Copyright 1947, renewed 1975 by
Talcott Parsons. (Footnotes abridged and renumbered). Photo courtesy of the German
Information Center.

# PREVIEW

A. The three pure types of legitimate authority may be based on:
1. *Rational grounds*—obedience is owed to the legally established impersonal order.
2. *Traditional grounds*—obedience is owed to the person or the chief who occupies the traditionally sanctioned position of authority and who is bound by tradition.
3. *Charismatic grounds*—obedience is owed to the charismatically qualified leader by virtue of personal trust, heroism, or exemplary character.
B. The effectiveness of legal authority rests on the acceptance of the validity of the following mutually inter-dependent ideas:
1. That any given legal norm may be established by agreement or by imposition, on grounds of expediency or rational values or both, with a claim to obedience at least on part of the members of the corporate group.
2. That in every body of law there is a system of abstract rules which have been intentionally established, and are applicable to particular cases.
3. That a person in authority occupies an "office".
4. That the persons obeying the authority do so only in their capacity as "members" of the corporate group and what they obey is only the law.
5. That the members of the corporate group, in so far as they obey a person in authority, do not owe this obedience to him or her as an individual, but to the impersonal order.
C. The fundamental categories of rational legal authority are:
1. A continuous organization of official functions bound by rules.
2. A specified sphere of competence that involves
   (a) a sphere of obligations to perform functions,
   (b) carrying out these functions with the necessary authority,
   (c) the necessary means of compulsion are clearly defined and their use is subject to definite conditions. Such a unit is called an "administrative organ".
3. The organization of offices follows the principle of hierarchy.
4. The rules which regulate the conduct of an office may be technical rules or norms.
5. It is a matter of principle that the members of the administrative staff should be completely separated from ownership of the means of production or administration.
6. There is also a complete absence of appropriation of his or her official position by the incumbent.
7. Administrative acts, decisions and rules are formulated and recorded in writing, even in cases where oral discussion is the rule or is even mandatory.
8. Legal authority can be exercised in a wide variety of different forms.
D. The purest type of exercise of legal authority is that which employs a bureaucratic administrative staff who function under the supreme authority, according to the following criteria:

1. They are personally free and subject to authority only with respect to their impersonal official obligations.
2. They are organized in a clearly defined sphere of competence in the legal sense.
3. Each office has a clearly defined sphere of competence in the legal sense.
4. The office is filled by a free contractual relationship.
5. Candidates are selected on the basis of technical qualifications.
6. They are paid fixed salaries with a right to pensions, according to rank in hierarchy, the responsibility of the position, and the requirements of the incumbent's social status.
7. The office is treated as the sole, or at least the primary, occupation of the incumbent.
8. It constitutes a career with promotions depending on seniority or achievement, and judgement of superiors.
9. The official works entirely separated from ownership of the means of administration and without appropriation of his or her position.
10. The official is subject to strict and systematic discipline and control in the conduct of the office.

E. The monocratic type of bureaucratic organization is superior to any other form of organization (a) from a technical point of view, (b) in precision, (c) in stability, (d) in the stringency of its discipline, (e) in its reliability, (f) in intensive efficiency, (g) in the scope of its operations and (h) in its application to all kinds of administrative tasks.

F. The primary source of the superiority of bureaucratic administration lies in the role of technical knowledge.

G. The characteristics of the "spirit" of rational bureaucracy are:
1. Formalism, which is promoted by all the interests which are concerned with the security of their own personal situation, whatever this may consist of.
2. Tendency of officials to treat their official function from what is substantively a utilitarian point of view in the interest of the welfare of those under their authority. This contradicts the above characteristic.

---

There are three pure types of legitimate authority. The validity of their claims to legitimacy may be based on:

1. Rational grounds—resting on a belief in the 'legality' of patterns of normative rules and the right of those elevated to authority under such rules to issue commands (legal authority).
2. Traditional grounds—resting on an established belief in the sanctity of immemorial traditions and the legitimacy of the status of those exercising authority under them (traditional authority); or finally,
3. Charismatic grounds—resting on devotion to the specific and exceptional sanctity, heroism or exemplary character of an individual person, and of the normative patterns or order revealed or ordained by him (charismatic authority).

In the case of legal authority, obedience is owed to the legally established impersonal order. It extends to the persons exercising the authority of office under it only by virtue of the formal legality of their commands and only within the scope of authority of the office. In the case of traditional authority, obedience is owed to the *person* of the chief who occupies the traditionally sanctioned position of authority and who is (within its sphere) bound by tradition. But here the obligation of obedience is not based on the impersonal order, but is a matter of personal loyalty within the area of accustomed obligations. In the case of charismatic authority, it is the charismatically qualified leader as such who is obeyed by virtue of personal trust in him and his revelation, his heroism or his exemplary qualities so far as they fall within the scope of the individual's belief in his charisma.

1. The usefulness of the above classification can only be judged by its results in promoting systematic analysis. The concept of 'charisma' ('the gift of grace') is taken from the vocabulary of early Christianity. For the Christian religious organization Rudolf Sohm, in his *Kirchenrecht,* was the first to clarify the substance of the concept, even though he did not use the same terminology. Others (for instance, Hollin, *Enthusiasmus und Bussgewalt*) have clarified certain important consequences of it. It is thus nothing new.

2. The fact that none of these three ideal types, the elucidation of which will occupy the following pages, is usually to be found in historical cases in 'pure' form, is naturally not a valid objection to attempting their conceptual formulation in the sharpest possible form. In this respect the present case is no different from many others. Later on the transformation of pure charisma by the process of routinization will be discussed and thereby the relevance of the concept to the understanding of empirical systems of authority considerably increased. But even so it may be said of every empirically historical phenomenon of authority that it is not likely to be 'as an open book.' Analysis in terms of sociological types has, after all, as compared with purely empirical historical investigation, certain advantages which should not be minimized. That is, it can in the particular case of a concrete form of authority determine what conforms to or approximates such types as 'charisma,' 'hereditary charisma,' 'the charisma of office,' 'patriarchy', 'bureaucracy', the authority of status groups,[1] and in doing so it can work with relatively unambiguous concepts. But the idea that the whole of concrete historical reality can be exhausted in the conceptual scheme about to be developed is as far from the author's thoughts as anything could be.

## Legal Authority with a Bureaucratic Administrative Staff [2]

*3:   Legal Authority: The Pure Type with Employment of a Bureaucratic Administrative Staff*

The effectiveness of legal authority rests on the acceptance of the validity of the following mutually inter-dependent ideas.

1. That any given legal norm may be established by agreement or by imposition, on grounds of expediency or rational values or both, with a claim to obedience at least on the part of the members of the corporate group. This is, however, usually extended to include all persons within the sphere of authority or of power in question—which in the case of territorial bodies is the territorial area—who stand in certain social relationships or carry out forms of social action which in the order governing the corporate group have been declared to be relevant.

2. That every body of law consists essentially in a consistent system of abstract rules which have normally been intentionally established. Furthermore, administration of law is held to consist in the application of these rules to particular cases; the administrative process in the rational pursuit of the interests which are specified in the order governing the corporate group within the limits laid down by legal precepts and following principles which are capable of generalized formulation and are approved in the order governing the group, or at least not disapproved in it.

3. That thus the typical person in authority occupies an 'office.' In the action associated with his status, including the commands he issues to others, he is subject to an impersonal order to which his actions are oriented. This is true not only for persons exercising legal authority who are in the usual sense 'officials,' but, for instance, for the elected president of a state.

4. That the person who obeys authority does so, as it is usually stated, only in his capacity as a 'member' of the corporate group and what he obeys is only 'the law.' He may in this connection be the member of an association, of a territorial commune, of a church, or a citizen of a state.

5. In conformity with point 3, it is held that the members of the corporate group, in so far as they obey a person in authority, do not owe this obedience to him as an individual, but to the impersonal order. Hence, it follows that there is an obligation to obedience only within the sphere of the rationally delimited authority which, in terms of the order, has been conferred upon him.

The following may thus be said to be the fundamental categories of rational legal authority:

(1) A continuous organization of official functions bound by rules.

(2) A specified sphere of competence. This involves (a) a sphere of obligations to perform functions which has been marked off as part of a systematic division of labor. (b) The provision of the incumbent with the necessary authority to carry out these functions. (c) That the necessary means of compulsion are clearly defined and their use is subject to definite conditions. A unit exercising authority which is organized in this way will be called an 'administrative organ.'

There are administrative organs in this sense in large-scale private organizations, in parties and armies, as well as in the state and the church. An elected president, a cabinet of ministers, or a body of elected representatives also in this sense constitute administrative organs. This is not, however, the place to discuss these concepts. Not every administrative organ is provided with compulsory powers. But this distinction is not important for present purposes.

(3) The organization of offices follows the principle of hierarchy; that is, each lower office is under the control and supervision of a higher one. There is a

right of appeal and of statement of grievances from the lower to the higher. Hierarchies differ in respect to whether and in what cases complaints can lead to a ruling from an authority at various points higher in the scale, and as to whether changes are imposed from higher up or the responsibility for such changes is left to the lower office, the conduct of which was the subject of complaint.

(4) The rules which regulate the conduct of an office may be technical rules or norms.[3] In both cases, if their application is to be fully rational, specialized training is necessary. It is thus normally true that only a person who has demonstrated an adequate technical training is qualified to be a member of the administrative staff of such an organized group, and hence only such persons are eligible for appointment to official positions. The administrative staff of a rational corporate group thus typically consists of 'officials,' whether the organization be devoted to political, religious, economic—in particular, capitalistic—or other ends.

(5) In the rational type it is a matter of principle that the members of the administrative staff should be completely separated from ownership of the means of production or administration. Officials, employees, and workers attached to the administrative staff do not themselves own the non-human means of production and administration. These are rather provided for their use in kind or in money, and the official is obligated to render an accounting of their use. There exists, furthermore, in principle complete separation of the property belonging to the organization, which is controlled within the sphere of office, and the personal property of the official, which is available for his own private uses. There is a corresponding separation of the place in which official functions are carried out, the 'office' in the sense of premises, from living quarters.

(6) In the rational type case, there is also a complete absence of appropriation of his official position by the incumbent. Where 'rights' to an office exist, as in the case of judges, and recently of an increasing proportion of officials and even of workers, they do not normally serve the purpose of appropriation by the official, but of securing the purely objective and independent character of the conduct of the office so that it is oriented only to the relevant norms.

(7) Administrative acts, decisions, and rules are formulated and recorded in writing, even in cases where oral discussion is the rule or is even mandatory. This applies at least to preliminary discussions and proposals, to final decisions, and to all sorts of orders and rules. The combination of written documents and a continuous organization of official functions constitutes the 'office'[4] which is the central focus of all types of modern corporate action.

(8) Legal authority can be exercised in a wide variety of different forms which will be distinguished and discussed later. The following analysis will be deliberately confined for the most part to the aspect of imperative co-ordination in the structure of the administrative staff. It will consist in an analysis in terms of ideal types of officialdom or 'bureaucracy.'

In the above outline no mention has been made of the kind of supreme head appropriate to a system of legal authority. This is a consequence of certain considerations which can only be made entirely understandable at a later stage in the analysis. There are very important types of rational imperative co-ordination which, with respect to the ultimate source of authority, belong to other categories. This is true of the hereditary charismatic type, as illustrated by hereditary monarchy and of the pure charismatic type of a president chosen by plebiscite. Other cases involve rational elements at important points, but are made up of a combination of bureaucratic and charismatic components, as is true of the cabinet form of government. Still others are subject to the authority of the chief of other corporate groups, whether their character be charismatic or bureaucratic; thus the formal head of a government department under a parliamentary regime may be a minister who occupies his position because of his authority in a party. The type of rational, legal administrative staff is capable of application in all kinds of situations and contexts. It is the most important mechanism for the administration of everyday profane affairs. For in that sphere, the exercise of authority and, more broadly, imperative co-ordination, consists precisely in administration.

### 4:   Legal Authority: The Pure Type with Employment of a Bureaucratic Administrative Staff—(Continued)

The purest type of exercise of legal authority is that which employs a bureaucratic administrative staff. Only the supreme chief of the organization occupies his position of authority by virtue of appropriation, of election, or of having been designated for the succession. But even *his* authority consists in a sphere of legal 'competence.' The whole administrative staff under the supreme authority then consists, in the purest type, of individual officials who are appointed and function according to the following criteria: [5]

(1) They are personally free and subject to authority only with respect to their impersonal official obligations.

(2) They are organized in a clearly defined hierarchy of offices.

(3) Each office has a clearly defined sphere of competence in the legal sense.

(4) The office is filled by a free contractual relationship. Thus, in principle, there is free selection.

(5) Candidates are selected on the basis of technical qualifications. In the most rational case, this is tested by examination or guaranteed by diplomas certifying technical training, or both. They are *appointed,* not elected.

(6) They are remunerated by fixed salaries in money, for the most part with a right to pensions. Only under certain circumstances does the employing authority, especially in private organizations, have a right to terminate the appointment, but the official is always free to resign. The salary scale is primarily graded according to rank in the hierarchy; but in addition to this criterion, the responsibility of the position and the requirements of the incumbent's social status may be taken into account.

(7) The office is treated as the sole, or at least the primary, occupation of the incumbent.

(8) It constitutes a career. There is a system of 'promotion' according to seniority or to achievement, or both. Promotion is dependent on the judgment of superiors.

(9) The official works entirely separated from ownership of the means of administration and without appropriation of his position.

(10) He is subject to strict and systematic discipline and control in the conduct of the office.

This type of organization is in principle applicable with equal facility to a wide variety of different fields. It may be applied in profit-making businesses or in charitable organizations, or in any number of other types of private enterprises serving ideal or material ends. It is equally applicable to political and to religious organizations. With varying degrees of approximation to a pure type, its historical existence can be demonstrated in all these fields.

1. For example, this type of bureaucracy is found in private clinics, as well as in endowed hospitals or the hospitals maintained by religious orders. Bureaucratic organization has played a major role in the Catholic Church. It is well illustrated by the administrative role of the priesthood in the modern church, which has expropriated almost all of the old church benefices, which were in former days to a large extent subject to private appropriation. It is also illustrated by the conception of the universal Episcopate, which is thought of as formally constituting a universal legal competence in religious matters. Similarly, the doctrine of Papal infallibility is thought of as in fact involving a universal competence, but only one which functions 'ex cathedra' in the sphere of the office, thus implying the typical distinction between the sphere of office and that of the private affairs of the incumbent. The same phenomena are found in the large-scale capitalistic enterprise; and the larger it is; the greater their role. And this is not less true of political parties, which will be discussed separately. Finally, the modern army is essentially a bureaucratic organization administered by that peculiar type of military functionary, the 'officer.'

2. Bureaucratic authority is carried out in its purest form where it is most clearly dominated by the principle of appointment. There is no such thing as a hierarchy of elected officials in the same sense as there is a hierarchical organization of appointed officials. In the first place, election makes it impossible to attain a stringency of discipline even approaching that in the appointed type. For it is open to a subordinate official to compete for elective honors on the same terms as his superiors, and his prospects are not dependent on the superior's judgment.

3. Appointment by free contract, which makes free selection possible, is essential to modern bureaucracy. Where there is a hierarchical organization with impersonal spheres of competence, but occupied by unfree officials—like slaves or dependents, who, however, function in a formally bureaucratic manner—the term 'patrimonial bureaucracy' will be used.

4. The role of technical qualifications in bureaucratic organizations is continually increasing. Even an official in a party or a trade-union organization is in need of specialized knowledge, though it is usually of an empirical character, developed by experience, rather than by formal training. In the modern state, the only 'offices' for which no technical qualifications are required are those of ministers and presidents. This only goes to prove that they are 'officials' only in a formal sense, and not substantively, as is true of the managing director or president

of a large business corporation. There is no question but that the 'position' of the capitalistic entrepreneur is as definitely appropriated as is that of a monarch. Thus at the top of a bureaucratic organization, there is necessarily an element which is at least not purely bureaucratic. The category of bureaucracy is one applying only to the exercise of control by means of a particular kind of administrative staff.

5. The bureaucratic official normally receives a fixed salary. By contrast, sources of income which are privately appropriated will be called 'benefices.' Bureaucratic salaries are also normally paid in money. Though this is not essential to the concept of bureaucracy, it is the arrangement which best fits the pure type. Payments in kind are apt to have the character of benefices, and the receipt of a benefice normally implies the appropriation of opportunities for earnings and of positions. There are, however, gradual transitions in this field with many intermediate types. Appropriation by virtue of leasing or sale of offices or the pledge of income from office are phenomena foreign to the pure type of bureaucracy.

6. 'Offices' which do not constitute the incumbent's principal occupation, in particular 'honorary' offices, belong in other categories, which will be discussed later.[6] The typical 'bureaucratic' official occupies the office as his principal occupation.

7. With respect to the separation of the official from ownership of the means of administration, the situation is essentially the same in the field of public administration and in private bureaucratic organizations, such as the large-scale capitalistic enterprise.

8. Collegial bodies will be discussed separately below.[7] At the present time they are rapidly decreasing in importance in favour of types of organization which are in fact, and for the most part formally as well, subject to the authority of a single head. For instance, the collegial 'governments' in Prussia have long since given way to the monocratic 'district president.' The decisive factor in this development has been the need for rapid, clear decisions, free of the necessity of compromise between different opinions and also free of shifting majorities.

9. The modern army officer is a type of appointed official who is clearly marked off by certain class distinctions. This will be discussed elsewhere.[8] In this respect such officers differ radically from elected military leaders, from charismatic condottieri, from the type of officers who recruit and lead mercenary armies as a capitalistic enterprise, and, finally, from the incumbents of commissions which have been purchased. There may be gradual transitions between these types. The patrimonial 'retainer,' who is separated from the means of carrying out his function, and the proprietor of a mercenary army for capitalistic purposes have, along with the private capitalistic entrepreneur, been pioneers in the organization of the modern type of bureaucracy. This will be discussed in detail below.[9]

*5: The Monocratic Type of Bureaucratic Administration*

Experience tends universally to show that the purely bureaucratic type of administrative organization—that is, the monocratic variety of bureaucracy—is, from a purely technical point of view, capable of attaining the highest degree of efficiency and is in this sense formally the most rational known means of carrying out imperative control over human beings. It is superior to any other form in precision, in stability, in the stringency of its discipline, and in its reliability. It thus makes possible a particularly high degree of calculability of results for the heads of the organization and for those acting in relation to it. It is finally superior both in intensive efficiency and in the scope of its operations, and is formally capable of application to all kinds of administrative tasks.

The development of the modern form of the organization of corporate groups in all fields is nothing less than identical with the development and continual spread of bureaucratic administration. This is true of church and state, of armies, political parties, economic enterprises, organizations to promote all kinds of causes, private associations, clubs, and many others. Its development is, to take the most striking case, the most crucial phenomenon of the modern Western state. However many forms there may be which do not appear to fit this pattern, such as collegial representative bodies, parliamentary committees, soviets, honorary officers, lay judges, and what not, and however much people may complain about the 'evils of bureaucracy,' it would be sheer illusion to think for a moment that continuous administrative work can be carried out in any field except by means of officials working in offices. The whole pattern of everyday life is cut to fit this framework. For bureaucratic administration is, other things being equal, always, from a formal, technical point of view, the most rational type. For the needs of mass administration to-day, it is completely indispensable. The choice is only that between bureaucracy and dilettantism in the field of administration.

The primary source of the superiority of bureaucratic administration lies in the role of technical knowledge which, through the development of modern technology and business methods in the production of goods, has become completely indispensable. In this respect, it makes no difference whether the economic system is organized on a capitalistic or a socialistic basis. Indeed, if in the latter case a comparable level of technical efficiency were to be achieved, it would mean a tremendous increase in the importance of specialized bureaucracy.

When those subject to bureaucratic control seek to escape the influence of the existing bureaucratic apparatus, this is normally possible only by creating an organization of their own which is equally subject to the process of bureaucratization. Similarly the existing bureaucratic apparatus is driven to continue functioning by the most powerful interests which are material and objective, but also ideal in character. Without it, a society like our own—with a separation of officials, employees, and workers from ownership of the means of administration, dependent on discipline and on technical training—could no longer function. The only exception would be those groups, such as the peasantry, who are still in possession of their own means of subsistence. Even in case of revolution by force or of occupation by an enemy, the bureaucratic machinery will normally continue to function just as it has for the previous legal government.

The question is always who controls the existing bureaucratic machinery. And such control is possible only in a very limited degree to persons who are not technical specialists. Generally speaking, the trained permanent official is more likely to get his way in the long run than his nominal superior, the Cabinet minister, who is not a specialist.

Though by no means alone, the capitalistic system has undeniably played a major role in the development of bureaucracy. Indeed, without it capitalistic production could not continue and any rational type of socialism would have simply to take it over and increase its importance. Its development, largely under capitalistic auspices, has created an urgent need for stable, strict, intensive, and calculable administration. It is this need which gives bureaucracy a crucial role in our society as the central element in any kind of large-scale administration. Only by reversion in every field—political, religious, economic, etc.—to small-scale organization would it be possible to any considerable extent to escape its influence. On the one hand, capitalism in its modern stages of development strongly tends to foster the development of bureaucracy, though both capitalism and bureaucracy have arisen from many different historical sources. Conversely, capitalism is the most rational economic basis for bureaucratic administration and enables it to develop in the most rational form, especially because, from a fiscal point of view, it supplies the necessary money resources.

Along with these fiscal conditions of efficient bureaucratic administration, there are certain extremely important conditions in the fields of communication and transportation. The precision of its functioning requires the services of the railway, the telegraph, and the telephone, and becomes increasingly dependent on them. A socialistic form of organization would not alter this fact. It would be a question whether in a socialistic system it would be possible to provide conditions for carrying out as stringent bureaucratic organization as has been possible in a capitalistic order. For socialism would, in fact, require a still higher degree of formal bureaucratization than capitalism. If this should prove not to be possible, it would demonstrate the existence of another of those fundamental elements of irrationality in social systems—a conflict between formal and substantive rationality of the sort which sociology so often encounters.

Bureaucratic administration means fundamentally the exercise of control on the basis of knowledge. This is the feature of it which makes it specifically rational. This consists on the one hand in technical knowledge which, by itself, is sufficient to ensure it a position of extraordinary power. But in addition to this, bureaucratic organizations, or the holders of power who make use of them, have the tendency to increase their power still further by the knowledge growing out of experience in the service. For they acquire through the conduct of office a special knowledge of facts and have available a store of documentary material peculiar to themselves. While not peculiar to bureaucratic organizations, the concept of 'official secrets' is certainly typical of them. It stands in relation to technical knowledge in somewhat the same position as commercial secrets do to technological training. It is a product of the striving for power.

Bureaucracy is superior in knowledge, including both technical knowledge and knowledge of the concrete fact within its own sphere of interest, which is usually confined to the interests of a private business—a capitalistic enterprise. The capitalistic entrepreneur is, in our society, the only type who has been able to maintain at least relative immunity from subjection to the control of rational bureaucratic knowledge. All the rest of the population have tended to be organized in large-scale corporate groups which are inevitably subject to bureaucratic control. This is as inevitable as the dominance of precision machinery in the mass production of goods.

The following are the principal more general social consequences of bureaucratic control:

(1) The tendency to 'levelling' in the interest of the broadest possible basis of recruitment in terms of technical competence.

(2) The tendency to plutocracy growing out of the interest in the greatest possible length of technical training. To-day this often lasts up to the age of thirty.

(3) The dominance of a spirit of formalistic impersonality, '*Sine ira et studio,*' without hatred or passion, and hence without affection or enthusiasm. The dominant norms are concepts of straightforward duty without regard to personal considerations. Everyone is subject to formal equality of treatment; that is, everyone in the same empirical situation. This is the spirit in which the ideal official conducts his office.

The development of bureaucracy greatly favours the levelling of social classes and this can be shown historically to be the normal tendency. Conversely, every process of social levelling creates a favourable situation for the development of bureaucracy; for it tends to eliminate class privileges, which include the appropriation of means of administration and the appropriation of authority as well as the occupation of offices on an honorary basis or as an avocation by virtue of wealth. This combination everywhere inevitably foreshadows the development of mass democracy, which will be discussed in another connection.

The 'spirit' of rational bureaucracy has normally the following general characteristics:

(1) Formalism, which is promoted by all the interests which are concerned with the security of their own personal situation, whatever this may consist in. Otherwise the door would be open to arbitrariness and hence formalism is the line of least resistance.

(2) There is another tendency, which is apparently in contradiction to the above, a contradiction which is in part genuine. It is the tendency of officials to treat their official function from what is substantively a utilitarian point of view in the interest of the welfare of those under their authority. But this utilitarian tendency is generally expressed in the enactment of corresponding regulatory measures which themselves have a formal character and tend to be treated in a formalistic spirit. This tendency to substantive rationality is supported by all those subject to authority who are not included in the class mentioned above as interested in the security of advantages already controlled. The problems which open up at this point belong in the theory of 'democracy.'

## FOOTNOTES

1.  *Ständische.* There is no really acceptable English rendering of this term. _____
_____Ed.

2. The specifically modern type of administration has intentionally been taken as a point of departure in order to make it possible later to contrast the others with it.

3. Weber does not explain this distinction. By a 'technical rule' he probably means a prescribed course of action which is dictated primarily on grounds touching efficiency of the performance of the immediate functions, while by 'norms' he probably means rules which limit conduct on grounds other than those of efficiency. Of course, in one sense all rules are norms in that they are prescriptions for conduct, conformity with which is problematical. _____Ed.

4. *Bureau.* It has seemed necessary to use the English word 'office' in three different meanings, which are distinguished in Weber's discussion by at least two terms. The first is *Amt,* which means 'office' in the sense of the institutionally defined status of a person. The second is the 'work premises' as in the expression 'he spent the afternoon in his office.' For this Weber uses *Bureau* as also for the third meaning which he has just defined, the 'organized work process of a group'. In this last sense an office is a particular type of 'organization', or *Betrieb* in Weber's sense. This use is established in English in such expressions as 'the District Attorney's Office has such and such functions.' Which of the three meanings is involved in a given case will generally be clear from the context. _____Ed.

5. This characterization applies to the 'monocratic' as opposed to the 'collegial' type, which will be discussed below [not included].

6. Not included _____Ed.

7. Not included _____Ed.

8. Refers to chapter iv in the original which Weber never completed _____ Ed.

9. The parts of Weber's work included in this translation contain only fragmentary discussions of military organization. It was a subject in which Weber was greatly interested and to which he attributed great importance for social phenomena generally. This factor is one on which, for the ancient world, he laid great stress in his important study, *Agrarverhältnisse im Altertum.* Though at various points in the rest of *Wirtschaft und Gesellschaft* the subject comes up, it is probable that he intended to treat it systematically but that this was never done. _____Ed.

---

## Learning Review

### Questions:

1. The validity of the three pure types of legitimate authority may be based on _____, _____, and _____ grounds.

2. One fundamental category of rational _____ authority is the organization of offices according to the principle of _____; that is each _____ office under the control and supervision of a _____ one.

3. The present type of exercise of legal authority is that which employs a _____administrative staff wherein only the _____ chief of the organization occupies his or her position of authority by virtue of _____, of _____, or having been designated for the _____.

4. In the modern state, only _____ for which no technical qualifications are required are those of _____ and _____.

5. The _____ type of bureaucratic administration is the _____ known means of carrying out imperative control over human beings.

*Answers:*

presidents 5. monocratic, rational.
cratic, supreme, appropriation, election, succession 4. offices, ministers,
1. rational, traditional, charismatic 2. legal, hierarchy, lower, higher 3. bureau-

---

# Retrospective Comment

## BY HENRY L. TOSI *

What a classic piece is this selection by Max Weber. It captures the very essence of complex bureaucratic organization in a way that later writers have failed to improve. There are several key points to which the reader should attend. The first is the concept of "ideal type." An "ideal type" is an analytical device in which a phenomenon, in this case organization, is caricatured as it would be in its most perfect form. It should not be confused with the reality of organizations. It is much like the description by a physiologist of the characteristics of the "perfectly healthy person." Few of us will achieve that state and many of us, though far from the ideals, may live very very long healthy lives. So also with organizations; just because an organization does not have these "ideal type" characteristics does not doom it to failure.

A major limitation in this selection (as well as in Weber's other work) is that the set of assumptions which underlie the ideal bureaucratic type are not clear. Recent approaches to organizational analysis have argued that there are several possible "ideal types", depending upon the environmental context within which the organization is embedded (See for instance Tosi 1984; Burns and Stalker, 1961; and Woodward, 1965). These current extensions of the "ideal type" concept provide a more fulsome understanding of variations from the bureaucratic model of organization.

A second major feature is the analysis of different types of authority which is at the cornerstone of most treatments of organizational control and influence. Weber makes a clear distinction between "charisma" (what most mean by the term *leadership*) and administration. According to Weber, to be effective an organization needs administrative competence perhaps more than charisma.

But, "charisma" is more exciting and administration requires technical expertise, which means competence. It is difficult indeed to be the "ideal" administrator as outlined by Weber. Because many managers lack technical competence it is easy to understand why members of organizations, and often the general public, have lost confidence in large organizations.

This selection should not be glossed over because it is difficult to read. Other, more easily read descriptions of the organization form lack the depth and comprehensiveness of analysis that is present here. After studying this selection, it is little wonder why Weber's work still remains in the bedrock of organizational studies.

---

\* Professor, Department of Management, University of Florida.

# REFERENCES

Burns, T. and G. M. Stalker. *The Management of Innovation.* London: Tavistock, 1961.

Tosi, H. *Theories of Organization.* New York: John Wiley, 1984.

Woodward, J. *Industrial Organization: Theory and Practice.* London: Oxford University Press, 1965.

# 2

# *Planning*

## HENRI FAYOL

## *About the Author*

**Henri Fayol** was the French counterpart of Frederick W. Taylor. Born in 1841, he was employed by the mining firm of S. A. Commentry-Fourchambault and rose to the position of managing director. Unlike Taylor, whose perspective was the shop, Fayol viewed management problems from the board of directors down. His management concepts, tested over the years, were compiled into an overall theory of management in the 1916 publication of *General and Industrial Management*. Publication of the book was a landmark of management thought since it was the first comprehensive theory of management. Fayol was also first to emphasize the concept of universality of management and to point out the need for teaching management in colleges and universities.

Reprinted by special permission of David Lake Publications from Henri Fayol, *General and Industrial Management,* translated by Constance Storrs (London: Pitman Books, Ltd., 1949), pp. 43–52. Photo Comité National de l'Organisation Française.

# PREVIEW

A. In the business world planning is an important and essential factor of management since it enables one to assess the future and make provision for it.
   1. The plan of action is the most effective instrument of planning, and rests on the firm's resources, the nature and importance of work in progress, and on future trends.
   2. The manager takes the initiative for preparing the plan of action by indicating its objective and scope, fixing the share of each department in the communal task, coordinating the parts and harmonizing the whole, and deciding the course of action that should be taken.
B. Although the true value of a plan is determined by experience, it is essential that the manager know what is possible and what is wanted before taking any action.
   1. Characteristics of a good plan of action are unity, continuity, flexibility, and precision.
   2. The methods that most experienced managers use to draw up their plans of action can be similar to those plans of action the author lists as followed in a large mining and metallurgical firm.
   3. The entire plan is made up of a series of separate plans called yearly, ten-year and special forecasts which, when merged into a single program, form an operating guide for the whole concern.
      a. Yearly forecasts deal with production, sales, technical, commercial, economic consequences, etc.
         (i) They are in the form of a general report, drawn up two months after the end of each budgetary period.
         (ii) The report is accompanied by forecasts, a kind of anticipatory summary of the activities and results of the new budgetary period.
      b. Ten-year forecasts are identical to the yearly forecasts in the matters they deal with.
         (i) The yearly forecasts merge into the first year of the ten-year forecasts. From the second year onwards there are wide divergencies.
         (ii) Ten-year forecasts must be reconciled with annual ones so that at the end of some years the ten-year forecasts do not need redrafting.
      c. Special forecasts include sudden activities that affect the conditions of business, or activities whose full cycle exceeds one or several ten-year periods.
C. The advantages and shortcomings of these forecasts are:
   1. They provide assurances that no resource shall be neglected; future possibilities shall be prudently and courageously assessed; and that means shall be appropriate to ends.
   2. There is increasing interest and usefulness in the annual plan because of

the attention demanded for executing the plan, the indispensable comparison between predicted and actual facts, the recognition of mistakes made and successes attained, the search for means of repeating the one and avoiding the other.

D. The reason why such a plan is neither used nor often developed to its extreme point is that its compilation demands of managerial personnel a required combination of qualities and conditions which are rarely found.

E. The conditions and qualities essential for drawing up a good plan of action are:
   1. The art of handling people—Managers should be able to get loyal and active cooperation from departmental heads without fear of trouble or responsibility.
   2. Energy—Constant vigilance on management's part for yearly, ten-year and special forecasts.
   3. Moral courage—Be able to face criticism for errors in forecasting or for not carrying out the plan according to schedule.
   4. Continuity of tenure—If at a particular moment, a new manager feels that he/she will not have sufficient time to complete the work, or have only enough time to put it into execution, or if he/she is convinced that the plan will only be criticized, then he/she should not undertake it, since there can be no good plan of action.
   5. Professional competence in the requirements of business.
   6. General business knowledge.

F. To safeguard business against a lack of plan or a bad plan:
   1. A plan must be compulsory.
   2. Good specimen plans of successful businesses must be easily available.
   3. Planning must be introduced into education.

---

The maxim, "managing means looking ahead," gives some idea of the importance attached to planning in the business world, and it is true that if foresight is not the whole of management at least it is an essential part of it. To foresee, in this context, means both to assess the future and make provision for it; that is, foreseeing is itself action already. Planning is manifested on a variety of occasions and in a variety of ways, its chief manifestation, apparent sign and most effective instrument being the plan of action. The plan of action is, at one and the same time, the result envisaged, the line of action to be followed, the stages to go through, and methods to use. It is a kind of future picture wherein proximate events are outlined with some distinctness, whilst remote events appear progressively less distinct, and it entails the running of the business as foreseen and provided against over a definite period.

The plan of action rests: (1) on the firm's resources (buildings, tools, raw materials, personnel, productive capacity, sales outlets, public relations, etc.). (2) on the nature and importance of work in progress. (3) on future trends which depend partly on technical, commercial, financial and other conditions, all subject to change, whose importance and occurrence cannot be pre-determined. The preparation of the plan of action is one of the most difficult and most important matters of every business and brings into play all departments and all functions, especially the management function. It is, in effect, in order to carry out his managerial function that the manager takes the initiative for the plan of action, that he indicates its objective and scope, fixes the share of each department in the communal task, co-ordinates the parts and harmonizes the whole; that he decides, in fine, the line of conduct to be followed. In this line of conduct it is not only imperative that nothing should clash with principles and rules of good management, but also that the arrangement adopted should facilitate application of these principles and rules. Therefore, to the diverse technical, commercial, financial and other abilities necessary on the part of a business head and his assistants, there must be added considerable managerial ability.

## General Features of a Good Plan of Action

No one disputes the usefulness of a plan of action. Before taking action it is most necessary to know what is possible and what is wanted. It is known that absence of plan entails hesitation, false steps, untimely changes of direction, which are so many causes of weakness, if not of disaster, in business. The question of and necessity for a plan of action, then, does not arise and I think that I am voicing the general opinion in saying that a plan of action is indispensable. But there are plans and plans; there are simple ones, complex ones, concise ones, detailed ones, long- or short-term ones; there are those studied with meticulous attention, those treated lightly; there are good, bad, and indifferent ones. How are the good ones to be singled out from among the others? Experience is the only thing that finally determines the true value of a plan, i.e. on the services it can render to the firm, and even then the manner of its application must be taken into account. There is both instrument and player. Nevertheless, there are certain broad characteristics on which general agreement may be reached beforehand without waiting for the verdict of experience.

Unity of plan is an instance. Only one plan can be put into operation at a time; two different plans would mean duality, confusion, disorder. But a plan may be divided into several parts. In large concerns, there is found alongside the general plan a technical, commercial, and a financial one, or else an overall one with a specific one for each department. But all these plans are linked, welded, so as to make up one only, and every modification brought to bear on any one of them is given expression in the whole plan. The guiding action of the plan must be continuous. Now the limitations of human foresight necessarily set bounds to the duration of plans, so, in order to have no break in the guiding action, a second plan must follow immediately upon the first, a third upon the second, and so on. In large businesses the annual plan is more or less in current use. Other plans of shorter or longer term, always in close accord with the annual plan, operate simultaneously with this latter. The plan should be flexible enough to bend before such adjustments, as it is considered well to introduce, whether from pressure of circumstances or from any other reason. First as last, it is the law to which one bows. Another good point about a plan is to have as much accuracy as is compatible with the unknown factors bearing on the fate of the concern. Usually it is possible to mark out the line of proximate action fairly accurately, while a simple general indication does for remote activities, for before the moment for their execution has arrived sufficient enlightenment will have been forthcoming to settle the line of action more precisely. When the unknown factor occupies a relatively very large place there can be no preciseness in the plan, and then the concern takes on the name of venture.

Unity, continuity, flexibility, precision: such are the broad features of a good plan of action.

As for other specific points which it should have, and which turn on the nature, importance and condition of the business for which the plan is drawn up, there could be no possibility of settling them beforehand save by comparison with other plans already recognized as effective in similar businesses. In each case, then, comparable elements and models must be sought in business practice, after the fashion of the architect with a building to construct. But the architect, better served than the manager, can call upon books, courses in architecture, whereas there are no books on plans of action, no lessons in foresight, for management theory has yet to be formulated.

There is no lack of good plans, they can be guessed at from the externals of a business but not seen at sufficiently close quarters to be known and judged. Nevertheless, it would be most useful for those whose concern is management to know how experienced managers go about drawing up their plans. By way of information or sample, I am going to set out the method which has long been followed in a great mining and metallurgical concern with which I am well acquainted.

**Method of Drawing up the Plan of Action in a Large Mining and Metallurgical Firm.** This company includes several separate establishments and employs about ten thousand personnel. The entire plan is made up of a series of separate plans called forecasts; and there are yearly forecasts, ten-yearly forecasts, monthly, weekly, daily forecasts, long-term forecasts, special forecasts, and all merge into a single programme which operates as a guide for the whole concern.

(i) *Yearly Forecasts.* Each year, two months after the end of the budgetary period, a general report is drawn up of the work and results of this period. The report deals especially with production, sales, technical, commercial, financial position, personnel, economic consequences, etc. The report is accompanied by forecasts dealing with those same matters, the forecasts being a kind of anticipatory summary of the activities and results of the new budgetary period. The two months of the new plan which have elapsed are not left without plan, because of provisional forecasts drawn up fifteen days before the end of the previous period. In a large mining and metallurgical firm not many activities are quite completed during the course of one year. Cooperative projects of a technical, commercial, and financial nature, which provide the business with its activities need more time for their preparation and execution. From another aspect, account must be taken of the repercussions which proximate activities must have on ultimate ones and of the obligation to prepare far ahead sometimes for a requisite state of affairs.

Finally, thought must be given to constant modifications operating on the technical, commercial, financial and social condition of the industrial world in general and of the business in particular, to avoid being overtaken by circumstances. These various considerations come outside the framework of yearly forecasts and lead on to longer-term ones.

(ii) *Ten-yearly Forecasts.* Ten-yearly forecasts deal with the same matters as yearly ones. At the outset these two types of forecast are identical, the yearly forecast merging into the first-year of the ten-yearly one, but from the second year onwards notable divergences make their appearance. To maintain unity of plan each year the ten-yearly forecasts must be reconciled with annual ones so that at the end of some years the ten-yearly forecasts are generally so modified and transformed as to be no longer clear and need re-drafting. In effect the custom of re-drafting every five years has become established. It is the rule that ten-yearly forecasts always embrace a decade, and that they are revised every five years. Thus there is always a line of action marked out in advance for five years at least.

## YEARLY AND TEN-YEARLY FORECASTS

### CONTENTS

#### Technical section

Mining rights. Premises. Plant.
Extraction. Manufacture. Output.
New workings. Improvements.
Maintenance of plant and buildings.
Production costs.

#### Commercial section

Sales outlets.
Marketable goods.
Agencies. Contracts.
Customers. Importance. Credit standing.
Selling price.

#### Financial section

Capital. Loans. Deposits.

Circulating assets
{ Supplies in hand.
Finished goods.
Debtors.
Liquid assets.

Available assets.
Reserves and sundry appropriations.

Creditors
{ Wages.
Suppliers.
Sundry.

Sinking funds. Dividends. Bankers.

*Accounting*

**Balance sheet. Profit and Loss account. Statistics.**

*Security*

**Accident precautions.**
**Works police. Claims. Health service.**
**Insurance.**

*Management*

**Plan of action.**
**Organization of personnel. Selection.**
**Command.**
**Co-ordination. Conferences.**
**Control.**

(iii) *Special Forecasts.* There are some activities whose full cycle exceeds one or even several ten-yearly periods, there are others which occurring suddenly, must sensibly affect the conditions of the business. Both the one and the other are the object of special forecasts whose findings necessarily have a place in the yearly and ten-yearly forecasts. But it must never be lost sight of that there is one plan only.

These three sorts of forecast, yearly, ten-yearly, and special, merged and harmonized, constitute the firm's general plan.

So, having been prepared with meticulous care by each regional management, with the help of departmental management, and then revised, modified, and completed by general management and then submitted for scrutiny and approval to the Board of Directors, these forecasts become the plan which, so long as no other has been put in its place, shall serve as guide, directive, and law for the whole staff.

Fifty years ago I began to use this system of forecasts, when I was engaged in managing a colliery, and it rendered me such good service that I had no hesitation in subsequently applying it to various industries whose running was entrusted to me. I look upon it as a precious managerial instrument and have no hesitation in recommending its use to those who have no better instrument available. It has necessarily some shortcomings, but its shortcomings are very slight compared with the advantages it offers. Let us glance at these advantages and shortcomings.

## Advantages and Shortcomings of Forecasts

(a) The study of resources, future possibilities, and means to be used for attaining the objective call for contributions from all departmental heads within the framework of their mandate, each one brings to this study the contribution of his experience together with recognition of the responsibility which will fall upon him in executing the plan.

Those are excellent conditions for ensuring that no resource shall be neglected and that future possibilities shall be prudently and courageously assessed and that means shall be appropriate to ends. Knowing what are its capabilities and its intentions, the concern goes boldly on, confidently tackles current problems and is prepared to align all its forces against accidents and surprises of all kinds which may occur.

(b) Compiling the annual plan is always a delicate operation and especially lengthy and laborious when done for the first time, but each repetition brings some simplification and when the plan has become a habit the toil and difficulties are largely reduced. Conversely, the interest it offers increases. The attention demanded for executing the plan, the indispensable comparison between predicted and actual facts, the recognition of mistakes made and successes attained, the search for means of repeating the one and avoiding the other—all go to make the new plan a work of increasing interest and increasing usefulness.

Also, by doing this work the personnel increases in usefulness from year to year, and at the end is considerably superior to what it was in the beginning. In truth, this result is not due solely to the use of planning but everything goes together, a well-thought-out plan is rarely found apart from sound organizational, command, co-ordination, and control practices. This management element exerts an influence on all the rest.

(c) Lack of sequence in activity and unwarranted changes of course are dangers constantly threatening businesses without a plan. The slightest contrary wind can turn from its course a boat which is unfitted to resist. When serious happenings occur, regrettable changes of course may be decided upon under the influence of profound but transitory disturbance. Only a programme carefully pondered at an undisturbed time permits of maintaining a clear view of the future and of concentrating maximum possible intellectual ability and material resources upon the danger.

It is in difficult moments above all that a plan is necessary. The best of plans cannot anticipate all unexpected occurrences which may arise, but it does include a place for these events and prepare the weapons which may be needed at the moment of being surprised. The plan protects the business not only against undesirable changes of course which may be produced by grave events, but also against those arising simply from changes on the part of higher authority. Also, it protects against deviations, imperceptible at first, which end by deflecting it from its objective.

## Conditions and Qualities Essential for Drawing up a Good Plan of Action

To sum up: the plan of action facilitates the utilization of the firm's resources and the choice of best methods to use for attaining the objective. It suppresses or reduces hesitancy, false steps, unwarranted changes of course, and helps to improve personnel. It is a precious managerial instrument.

The question may be asked as to why such an instrument is not in general use and everywhere developed to the farthest extent. The reason is that its compilation demands of managerial personnel a certain number of qualities and conditions rarely to be found in combination. The compilation of a good plan demands for the personnel in charge—

1. The art of handling men.
2. Considerable energy.
3. A measure of moral courage.
4. Some continuity of tenure.
5. A given degree of competence in the specialized requirements of the business.
6. A certain general business experience.

(i) *The Art of Handling Men.* In a large firm the majority of departmental managers take part in the compiling of the working arrangements. The execution of this task from time to time is in addition to ordinary everyday work and includes a certain responsibility and does not normally carry any special remuneration. So, to have in such conditions loyal and active co-operation from departmental heads an able manager of men is needed who fears neither trouble nor responsibility. The art of handling men is apparent from keenness of subordinates and confidence of superiors.

(ii) *Energy.* Yearly and ten-yearly forecasts and special forecasts demand constant vigilance on the part of management.

(iii) *Moral Courage.* It is well known that the best-thought-out plan is never exactly carried out. Forecasts are not prophecies, their function is to minimize the unknown factor. Nevertheless, the public generally, and even shareholders best informed about the running of a business, are not kindly disposed towards a manager who has raised unfulfilled hopes, or allowed them to be raised. Whence the need for a certain prudence which has to be reconciled with the obligation of making every preparation and seeking out optimum possible results.

The timid are tempted to suppress the plan or else whittle it down to nothing in order not to expose themselves to criticism, but it is a bad policy even from the point of view of self-interest. Lack of plan, which compromises smooth running, also exposes the manager to infinitely graver charges than that of having to explain away imperfectly executed forecasts.

(iv) *Continuity of Tenure.* Some time goes by before a new manager is able to take sufficient cognizance of the course of affairs, the usefulness of employees, the resources of the business, its general set-up and future possibilities, so as usefully to undertake the compiling of the plan. If, at such a moment, he feels that he will not have enough time to complete the work or only enough time to start putting it into execution, or if, on the other hand, he is convinced that such work, condemned to bear no fruit, will only draw criticism upon him, is it to be thought that he will carry it out enthusiastically or even undertake it unless obliged? Human nature must be reckoned with. Without continuity of tenure on the part of management personnel there can be no good plan of action.

(v and vi) *Professional Competence and General Business Knowledge.* These are abilities just as necessary for drawing up a plan as for carrying it out.

Such are the conditions essential for compiling a good plan. They presuppose intelligent and experienced management. Lack of plan or a bad plan is a sign of managerial incompetence. To safeguard business against such incompetence—

1. A plan must be compulsory.
2. Good specimen plans must be made generally available. (Successful businesses could be asked to furnish such specimens. Experience and general discussion would single out the best.)
3. Planning (as a subject) must be introduced into education.

Thus could general opinion be better informed and react upon management personnel, so that the latter's inefficiency would be less to be feared—a state of affairs which would in no wise detract from the importance of men of proven worth.

---

## *Learning Review*

*Questions:*

1. The _____ of _____ is a kind of future picture where _____ events are outlined with some distinctness, while _____ events appear progressively less distinct.

2. Although _____ is the only thing that finally determines the true _____ of a plan, there are certain broad characteristics such as _____, _____, _____, and _____ on which general agreement may be reached in advance.

3. Drawing up a plan of action involves preparation of _____, _____, and _____ forecasts; which when all merged into a single _____ act as a _____ for the whole concern.

4. One _____ of the plan is that it protects _____ from undesirable changes by grave events, and from changes on the part of _____ authorities.

5. To safeguard business against _____ from lack of a plan or a bad plan, a plan must be _____, good specimen plans must be _____, and planning must be introduced into _____.

*Answers:*

1. plan, action, proximate, remote   2. experience, value, unity, continuity, flexibility, precision   3. yearly, ten-year, special, program, guide   4. advantage, business, higher   5. incompetence, compulsory, available, education

# Retrospective Comment

✦

## BY DANIEL A. WREN *

This selection from Henri Fayol's *General and Industrial Management* on planning is indeed a classic. Fayol's discussion of the need for, the importance of, and the fundamental conception of the planning function is as current today as it was when it was originally published in 1916. So many of our modern management concepts find their origins in the writings of Fayol that we often overlook the seminal thinking of this great French pioneer in management. Fayol was a manager, the chief executive of a large mining and metallurgical group in central France, and he wrote from his experiences so that others might understand the job of the manager in complex organizations.

Central to Fayol's conception of the manager's job was *prevoyance* or the exercise of foresight and planning. Without sound plans and goals, Fayol saw that other managerial activities would be barren. Planning provided the foundation for organizing, for personnel selection, for leadership, for coordination, and for control. Fayol also pioneered the idea of *long range planning,* anticipating to whatever extent possible the future conditions of the organization in a changing environment. He realized that decisions made today shape the alternatives present in the future and that managers must constantly look ahead to prepare for changing economic conditions and technological developments. He wrote of the importance of *participation* in planning, a key concept for managers today. He also demonstrated how planning skills of managers can be improved by planning and re-planning as conditions changed and as the far distant future moved more closely to the present.

All of these ideas of Fayol apply to today's managers—any revisions to Fayol's thoughts to make them more applicable to the present would be in two areas: (1) the development of more sophisticated planning techniques; and (2) changes in the competitive environment in which the organization operates. In the interim between Fayol's writing and today, a host of planning aids and techniques have been developed. For example, the "Delphi" technique and the "Nominal Group Technique" are means of pooling judgments about future occurrences; quantitative techniques are available to simulate and to build "models" for decision making; and finally, computer technology facilitates data gathering, model building, and problem solving.

Fayol would also want to consider a more complex environment in which plans must be developed. The competitive world today is more likely to be affected by energy shortages, ecology considerations, balance of trade problems, changed social expectations about business performance, and a multitude of legislative enactments and administrative bodies which affect managerial planning. Technological advancements are more rapid today and are more costly, leading to the need to refine plans to a greater extent. Fayol would also want to mention planning by "project" as well as planning by business function; and he might consider "zero-based budgeting" as a recent development.

Today we know so much more than Fayol because he indicated the way for us to do research, to develop managers, and to sharpen our planning skills. In the seven decades since his writing, we have been able to advance our ability to plan because of his pioneering efforts which indicated the importance and role of this activity in goal seeking endeavors. We have sharpened and advanced our planning aids and we have become more aware of the impact of the environment and of technology on the organization. But Fayol provided the conceptual base and demonstrated the significance of planning long ago so that managers of today will be prepared for tomorrow.

---

* Professor of Management, The University of Oklahoma.

# 3

# *The Principles of Scientific Management*

## FREDERICK WINSLOW TAYLOR

## *About the Author*

**Frederick W. Taylor,** the "Father of Scientific Management," began his career with the Midvale Steel Company in Philadelphia in 1878. While at Midvale, Taylor served in succession as gang boss, assistant foreman, foreman of the machine shop, master mechanic, chief draftsman, and chief engineer. He was responsible for organizing the managements of such firms as Bethlehem Steel Company, Cramps Shipbuilding Company, and Midvale Steel Company. In 1900 Taylor received a personal gold medal from the Paris Exposition for his invention of the Taylor-White process for treating modern high speed tools. In all, he held nearly one hundred patents for various inventions. Taylor published five books of which two—*The Principles of Scientific Management* and *Shop Management*—earned him a place as a major contributor to management thought.

Reprinted by special permission of the Society for Advancement of Management from *Bulletin of the Taylor Society* (December 1916), pp. 13–23. Photo courtesy of Samuel C. Williams Library, Stevens Institute of Technology, Hoboken, New Jersey.

# PREVIEW

A. The most important fact facing the industries of the civilized world is that nineteen out of twenty workers firmly believe that it is better to adopt a "go slow" policy, rather than to go fast.

B. There are two reasons for this belief:

   1. The introduction of *labor-saving devices* which result in making less work for less people in that trade, rather than more work for more people.

   2. The development of *soldiering,* where workers are even less to blame than for their superiors; it is the employers who restrict increases in productivity by refusing to give adequate compensation.

C. The first step taken to remedy the above evils, especially of soldiering, was the development of scientific management.

D. The workers have been the chief beneficiaries from the introduction of scientific management.

E. Scientific management is neither an efficiency device nor a group of efficiency devices. It does not exist and cannot exist until there has been a complete mental revolution on the part of the people working under it, as to their duties toward themselves and toward their employers, and a complete mental revolution in the outlook of the employers—toward their duties, toward themselves, and toward their employees.

   1. The highest type of management is the case in which the managers deliberately set out to do something better for their workers than other people are doing, and to give them a special incentive, to which the workers respond by giving a share of their initiative.

F. The greatest source of gain under scientific management comes from the new and almost unheard-of-duties and burdens which are voluntarily assumed by the management, rather than by the workers.

G. These new duties and burdens undertaken by the management are called the *Principles of Scientific Management.*

   1. The first principle of scientific management is the deliberate gathering together of the great mass of traditional knowledge by the means of *time and motion study.*

   2. The second principle of scientific management is the scientific *selection* of the workers and then their progressive *development.*

   3. The third principle of scientific management is the bringing together of this science and the trained worker, by offering some *incentive* to the worker.

   4. The fourth principle of scientific management involves a complete *redivision of the work* of the establishment, to bring about democracy and cooperation between the management and the workers.

H. The proof of the theory is found in illustrations such as the handling of pig-iron (lowest form of work that is known) and the science of shoveling.

   1. Under the new system, if the person shoveling does not meet the manage-

ment's expectations, the presumption is that it is the management's fault for not showing the person how to do the work.

I. To make scientific management pay it is necessary for both sides to cooperate, since any business that cannot be done on a profitable basis ought not to be done on a philanthropic basis, for it will not last.

---

By far the most important fact which faces the industries of our country, the industries, in fact, of the civilized world, is that not only the average worker, but nineteen out of twenty workmen throughout the civilized world firmly believe that it is for their best interests to go slow instead of to go fast. They firmly believe that it is for their interest to give as little work in return for the money that they get as is practical. The reasons for this belief are two-fold, and I do not believe that the workingmen are to blame for holding these fallacious views.

If you will take any set of workmen in your own town and suggest to those men that it would be a good thing for them in their trade if they were to double their output in the coming year, each man turn out twice as much work and become twice as efficient, they would say, "I do not know anything about other people's trades; what you are saying about increasing efficiency being a good thing may be good for other trades, but I know that the only result if you come to our trade would be that half of us would be out of a job before the year was out." That to the average workman is an axiom, it is not a matter subject to debate at all. And even among the average business men of this country that opinion is almost universal. They firmly believe that that would be the result of a great increase in efficiency, and yet directly the opposite is true.

## The Effect of Labor-Saving Devices

Whenever any labor-saving device of any kind has been introduced into any trade—go back into the history of any trade and see it—even though that labor-saving device may turn out ten, twenty, thirty times that output that was originally turned out by men in that trade, the result has universally been to make work for more men in that trade, not work for less men.

Let me give you one illustration. Let us take one of the staple businesses, the cotton industry. About 1840 the power loom succeeded the old hand loom in the cotton industry. It was invented many years before, somewhere about 1780 or 1790, but it came in very slowly. About 1840 the weavers of Manchester, England, saw that the power loom was coming, and they knew it would turn out three times the yardage of cloth in a day that the hand loom turned out. And what did they do, these five thousand weavers of Manchester, England, who saw starvation staring them in the face? They broke into the establishments into which those machines were being introduced, they smashed them, they did everything possible to stop the introduction of the power loom. And the same result followed that follows every attempt to interfere with the introduction of any labor-saving device, if it is really a labor-saving device. Instead of stopping the introduction of the power loom, their opposition apparently accelerated it, just as opposition to scientific management all over the country, bitter labor opposition to-day, is accelerating the introduction of it instead of retarding it. History repeats itself in that respect. The power loom came right straight along.

And let us see the result in Manchester. Just what follows in every industry when any labor-saving device is introduced. Less than a century has gone by since 1840. The population of England in that time has now more than doubled. Each man in the cotton industry in Manchester, England, now turns out, at a restricted estimate ten yards of cloth for every yard of cloth that was turned out in 1840. In 1840 there were 5,000 weavers in Manchester. Now there are 265,000. Has that thrown men out of work? Has the introduction of labor-saving machinery, which has multiplied the output per man by ten-fold, thrown men out of work?

What is the real meaning of this? All that you have to do is to bring wealth into this world and the world uses it. That is the real meaning. The meaning is that where in 1840 cotton goods were a luxury to be worn only by rich people when they were hardly ever seen on the street, now every man, woman and child all over the world wears cotton goods as a daily necessity.

Nineteen-twentieths of the real wealth of this world is used by the poor people, and not the rich, so that the workingman who sets out as a steady principle to restrict output is merely robbing his own kind. That group of manufacturers which adopts as a permanent principle restriction of output, in order to hold up prices, is robbing the world. The one great thing that marks the improvement of this world is measured by the enormous increase in output of the individuals in this world. There is fully twenty times the output per man now that there was three hundred years ago. That marks the increase in the real wealth of the world; that marks the increase of the happiness of the world, that gives us the opportunity for shorter hours, for better education, for amusement, for art, for music, for everything that is worth while in this world—goes right straight back to this increase in the output of the individual. The workingmen of today live better than the king did three hundred years ago. From what does the progress the world has made come? Simply from the increase in the output of the individual all over the world.

## The Development of Soldiering

The second reason why the workmen of this country and of Europe deliberately restrict output is a very simple one. They, for this reason, are even less to blame than they are for the other. If, for example, you are manufacturing a pen, let us assume for simplicity that a pen can be made by a single man. Let us say that the workman is turning out ten pens per day, and that he is receiving $2.50 a day for his wages. He has a progressive foreman who is up to date, and that foreman goes to the workman and suggests, "Here, John, you are getting $2.50 a day, and you are turning out ten pens. I would suggest that I pay you 25 cents for making that pen." The man takes the job, and through the help of his foreman, through his own ingenuity, through the help of his friends, at the end of the year he finds himself turning out twenty pens instead of ten. He is happy, he is making $5, instead of $2.50 a day. His foreman is happy because, with the same room, with the same men he had before, he has doubled the output of his department, and the manufacturer himself is sometimes happy, but not often. Then someone on the board of directors asks to see the payroll, and he finds that we are paying $5 a day where other similar mechanics are only getting $2.50, and in no uncertain terms he announces that we must stop ruining the labor market. We cannot pay $5 a day when the standard rate of wages is $2.50; how can we hope to compete with surrounding towns? What is the result? Mr. Foreman is sent for, and he is told that he has got to stop ruining the labor market of Cleveland. And the foreman goes back to his workman in sadness, in depression, and tells his workman, "I am sorry, John, but I have got to cut the price down for that pen; I cannot let you earn $5 a day; the board of directors has got on to it, and it is ruining the labor market; you ought to be willing to have the price reduced. You cannot earn more than $3 or $2.75 a day, and I will cut your wages so that you will only get $3 a day." John, of necessity accepts the cut, but he sees to it that he never makes enough pens to get another cut.

## Characteristics of the Union Workman

There seem to be two divergent opinions about the workmen of this country. One is that a lot of the trade unions' workmen, particularly in this country, have become brutal, have become dominating, careless of any interests but their own, and are a pretty poor lot. And the other opinion which those same trade unionists hold of themselves is that they are pretty close to little gods. Whichever view you may hold of the workingmen of this country, and my personal view of them is that they are a pretty fine lot of fellows, they are just about the same as you and I. But whether you hold the bad opinion or the good opinion, it makes no difference. Whatever the workingmen of this country are or whatever they are not, they are not fools. And all that is necessary is for a workingman to have but one object lesson, like that I have told you, and he soldiers for the rest of his life.

There are a few exceptional employers who treat their workmen differently, but I am talking about the rule of the country. Soldiering is the absolute rule with all workmen who know their business. I am not saying it is for their interest to soldier. You cannot blame them for it. You cannot expect them to be large enough minded men to look at the proper view of the matter. Nor is the man who cuts the wages necessarily to blame. It is simply a misfortune in industry.

## The Development of Scientific Management

There has been, until comparatively recently, no scheme promulgated by which the evils of rate cutting could be properly avoided, so soldiering has been the rule.

Now the first step that was taken toward the development of those methods, of those principles, which rightly or wrongly have come to be known under the name of scientific management, the first step that was taken was taken in an earnest endeavor to remedy the evils of soldiering; an earnest endeavor to make it unnecessary for workmen to be hypocritical in this way, to deceive themselves, to deceive their employers, to live day in and day out a life of deceit, forced upon them by conditions—the very first step that was taken toward the development was to overcome that evil. I want to emphasize that, because I wish to emphasize the one great fact relating to scientific management the greatest factor, namely, that scientific management is no new set of theories that has been tried on by any one at every step. Scientific management at every step has been an evolution, not a theory. In all cases the practice has preceded the theory, not succeeded it. In every case one measure after another has been tried out, until the proper remedy has been found. That series of proper eliminations, that evolution, is what is called scientific management. Every element of it has had to fight its way against the elements that preceded it, and prove itself better or it would not be there to-morrow.

All the men that I know of who are in any way connected with scientific management are ready to abandon any scheme, any theory in favor of anything else that could be found that is better. There is nothing in scientific management that is fixed. There is no one man, or group of men, who has invented scientific management.

What I want to emphasize is that all of the elements of scientific management are an evolution, not an invention. Scientific management is in use in an immense range and variety of industries. Almost every type of industry in this country has scientific management working successfully. I think I can safely say that on the average in those establishments in which scientific management has been introduced, the average workman is turning out double the output he was before. I think that is a conservative statement.

## The Workmen the Chief Beneficiaries

Three or four years ago I could have said there were about fifty thousand men working under scientific management, but now I know there are many more. Company after company is coming under it, many of which I know nothing about. Almost universally they are working successfully. This increasing of the output per individual in the trade, results, of course, in cheapening the product; it results, therefore, in larger profit usually to the owners of the business; it results also, in many cases, in a lowering of the selling price, although that has not come to the extent it will later. In the end the public gets the good. Without any question, the large good which so far has come from scientific management has come to the worker. To the workman has come, practically right off as soon as scientific management is introduced, an increase in wages amounting from 33 to 100 per cent, and yet that is not the greatest good that comes to the workmen from scientific management. The great good comes from the fact that, under scientific management, they look upon their employers as the best friends they have in the world; the suspicious watchfulness which characterizes the old type of management, the semi-antagonism, or the complete antagonism between workmen and employers is entirely superseded, and in its place comes genuine friendship between both sides. That is the greatest good that has come under scientific management. As a proof of this in the many businesses in which scientific management has been introduced, I know of not one single strike of workmen working under it after it had been introduced, and only two or three while it was in process of introduction. In this connection I must speak of the fakers, those who have said they can introduce scientific management into a business in six months or a year. That is pure nonsense. There have been many strikes stirred up by that type of man. Not one strike has ever come, and I do not believe ever will come, under scientific management.

## What Scientific Management Is

What is scientific management? It is no efficiency device, nor is it any group or collection of efficiency devices. Scientific management is no new scheme for paying men, it is no bonus system, no piece-work system, no premium system of payment; it is no new method of figuring costs. It is no one of the various elements by which it is commonly known, by which people refer to it. It is not time study nor man study. It is not the printing of a ton or two of blanks and unloading them on a company and saying, "There is your system, go ahead and use it." Scientific management does not exist and cannot exist until there has been a complete mental revolution on the part of the workmen working under it, as to their duties toward themselves and toward their employers, and a complete mental revolution in the outlook of the employers, toward their duties, toward themselves, and toward their workmen. And until this great mental change takes place, scientific management does not exist. Do you think you can make a great mental revolution in a large group of workmen in a year, or do you think you can make it in a large group of foremen and superintendents in a year? If you do, you are very much mistaken. All of us hold mighty close to our ideas and principles in life, and we change very slowly toward the new, and very properly too.

Let me give you an idea of what I mean by this change in mental outlook. If you are manufacturing a hammer or a mallet, into the cost of that mallet goes a certain amount of raw materials, a certain amount of wood and metal. If you will take the cost of the raw materials and then add to it that cost which is frequently called by various names—overhead expenses, general expense, indirect expense; that is, the proper share of taxes, insurance, light, heat, salaries of officers and advertising—and you have a sum of money. Subtract that sum from the selling price, and what is left over is called the surplus. It is over this surplus that all of the labor disputes in the past have occurred. The workman naturally wants all he can get. His wages come out of that surplus. The manufacturer wants all he can get in the shape of profits, and it is from the division of this surplus that all the labor disputes have come in the past—the equitable division.

The new outlook that comes under scientific management is this: The workmen, after many object lessons, come to see, and the management come to see that this surplus can be made so great, providing both sides will stop their pulling apart, will stop their fighting and will push as hard as they can to get as cheap an output as possible, that there is no occasion to quarrel. Each side can get more than ever before. The acknowledgement of this fact represents a complete mental revolution.

## Intelligent Old-Style Management

There is one more illustration of the new and great change which comes under scientific management. I can make it clearer, perhaps, by contrasting it with what I look upon as the best of the older types of management. If you have a company employing five hundred or a thousand men, you will have in that company perhaps fifteen different trades. The workmen in those trades have learned absolutely all that they know, not from books, not by being taught, but they have learned it traditionally. It has been handed down to them, not even by word of mouth in many cases, but by seeing what other men do. One man stands alongside of another man and imitates him. That is the way the trades are handed down, and my impression is that trades are now picked up just as they were in the Middle Ages.

The manufacturer, the manager, or the foreman who knows his business realizes that his chief function as a manager—I am talking now of the old-fashioned manager—ought to be to get the true initiative of his workman. He wants the initiative of the workman, their hard work, their good will, their ingenuity, their determination to do all they can for the benefit of his firm. If he knows anything about human nature, if he has thought over the problems, he must realize that in order to get the initiative of his workman, in order to modify their soldiering, he must do something more for his men than other employers are doing for their men under similar circumstances. The wise manager, under the old type of management, deliberately sets out to do something better for his workmen than his competitors are doing, better than he himself has ever done before. It takes a good while for the workmen to stop (being suspicious) . . . but if the manager keeps at them for a sufficiently long time he will get the confidence of the men, and when he does workmen of all kinds will respond by giving a great increase in output. When he sets out to do better for his men than other people do for theirs, the workmen respond liberally when that time comes. I refer to this case as being the highest type of management, the case in which the managers deliberately set out to do something better for their workmen than other people are doing, and to give them a special incentive of some kind, to which the workmen respond by giving a share at least of their initiative.

## What Scientific Management Will Do

I am going to try to prove to you that even that type of management has not a ghost of a chance in competition with the principles of scientific management.

Why? In the first place, under scientific management, the initiative of the workmen, their hard work, their good-will, their best endeavors are obtained with absolute regularity. There are cases all the time where men will soldier, but they become the exception, as a rule, and they give their true initiative under scientific management. That is the least of the two sources of gain. The greatest source of gain under scientific management comes from the new and almost unheard-of-duties and burdens which are voluntarily assumed, not by the workmen, but by the men on the management side. These are the things which make scientific management a success. These new duties, these new burdens undertaken by the management have rightly or wrongly been divided into four groups, and have been called the principles of scientific management.

The first of the great principles of scientific management, the first of the new burdens which are voluntarily undertaken by those on the management side is the deliberate gathering together of the great mass of traditional knowledge which, in the past, has been in the heads of the workmen, recording it, tabulating it, reducing it in most cases to rules, laws, and in many cases to mathematical formulae, which, with these new laws, are applied to the co-operation of the management to the work of the workmen. This results in an immense increase in the output, we may say, of the two. The gathering in of this great mass of traditional knowledge, which is done by the means of motion study, time study, can be truly called the science.

Let me make a prediction. I have before me the first book, so far as I know, that has been published on motion study and on time study. That is, the motion study and time study of the cement and concrete trades. It contains everything relating to concrete work. It is of about seven hundred pages, and embodies the motions of men, the time and the best way of doing that sort of work. It is the first case in which a trade has been reduced to the same condition that engineering data of all kinds have been reduced, and it is this sort of data that is bound to sweep the world.

I have before me something which has been gathering for about fourteen years, the time or motion study of the machine shop. It will take probably four or five years more before the first book will be ready to publish on that subject. There is a collection of sixty or seventy thousand elements affecting machine-shop work. After a few years, say three, four or five years more, some one will be ready to publish the first book giving the laws of the movements of men in the machine shop—all the laws, not only a few of them. Let me predict, just as sure as the sun shines, that is going to come in every trade. Why? Because it pays, for no other reason. That results in doubling the output in any shop. Any device which results in an increased output, is bound to come in spite of all opposition, whether we want it or not. It comes automatically.

## The Selection of the Workman

The next of four principles of scientific management is the scientific selection of the workman, and then his progressive development. It becomes the duty under scientific management, of not one, but of a group of men on the management side, to deliberately study the workmen who are under them; study them in the most careful, thorough and painstaking way, and not just leave it to the poor, overworked foreman to go out and say, "Come on, what do you want? If you are cheap enough I will give you a trial."

That is the old way. The new way is to take a great deal of trouble in selecting the workmen. The selection proceeds year after year. And it becomes the duty of those engaged in scientific management to know something about the workmen under them. It becomes their duty to set out deliberately to train the workmen in their employ to be able to do a better and still better class of work than ever before, and to then pay them higher wages than ever before. This deliberate selection of the workmen is the second of the great duties that devolve on the management under scientific management.

## Bringing Together the Science and the Man

The third principle is the bringing together of this science of which I have spoken and the trained workmen. I say bringing because they don't come together unless some one brings them. Select and train your workmen all you may, but unless there is some one who will make the men and the science come together, they will stay apart. The "make" involves a great many elements. They are not all disagreeable elements. The most important and largest way of "making" is to do something nice for the man whom you wish to make come together with the science. Offer him a plum, something that is worth while. There are many plums offered to those who come under scientific management—better treatment, more kindly treatment, more consideration for their wishes, and an opportunity for them to express their wants freely. That is one side of the "make." An equally important side is, whenever a man will not do what he ought, to either make him do it or stop it. If he will not do it, let him get out. I am not talking of any mollycoddle. Let me disabuse your minds of any opinion that scientific management is a mollycoddle scheme.

I have a great many union friends. I find they look with especial bitterness on this word "make." They have been used to doing the "making" in the past. That is the attitude of the trade unions, and it softens matters greatly when you can tell them the facts, namely, that in our making the science and the men come together, nine-tenths of our trouble comes with the men on the management side in making them do their new duties. I am speaking of those who have been trying to change from the old system to the new. Nine-tenths of our troubles come in trying to make the men on the management side do what they ought to do, to make them do the new duties, and take on these new burdens, and give up their old duties. That softens this word "make."

## The Principle of the Division of Work

The fourth principle is the plainest of all. It involves a complete redivision of the work of the establishment. Under the old scheme of management, almost all of the work was done by the workmen. Under the new, the work of the establishment is divided into two large parts. All of that work which formerly was done by the workmen alone is divided into two large sections, and one of those sections is handed over to the management. They do a whole division of the work formerly done by the workmen. It is this real co-operation, this genuine division of the work between the two sides, more than any other element which accounts for the fact that there never will be strikes under scientific management. When the workman realizes that there is hardly a thing he does, that does not have to be preceded by some act of preparation on the part of the management, and when that workman realizes when the management falls down and does not do its part, that he is not only entitled to a kick, but that he can register that kick in the most forcible possible way, he cannot quarrel with the men over him. It is team work. There are more complaints made every day on the part of the workmen that the men on the management side fail to do their duties, than are made by the management that the men fail. Every one of the complaints of the men have to be heeded, just as much as the complaints from the management that the workmen do not do their share. That is characteristic of scientific management. It represents a democracy, co-operation, a genuine division of work which never existed before in this world.

## The Proof of the Theory

I am through now with the theory. I will try to convince you of the value of these four principles by giving you some practical illustrations. I hope that you will look for these four elements in the illustrations. I shall begin by trying to show the power of these four elements when applied to the greatest kind of work I know of that is done by man. The reason I have heretofore chosen pig-iron for an illustration is that it is the lowest form of work that is known.

A pig of iron weighs about ninety-two pounds on an average. A man stoops down, and with no implement than his hands, picks up a pig of iron, walks a few yards with it, and drops it on a pile. A large part of the community has the impression that scientific management is chiefly handling pig-iron. The reason I first chose pig-iron for an illustration is that, if you can prove to any one the strength, the effect, of those four principles when applied to such rudimentary work as handling pig-iron, the presumption is that it can be applied to something better. The only way to prove it is to start at the bottom and show those four principles all along the line. I am sorry I cannot, because of lack of time, give you the illustration of handling pig-iron. Many of you doubt whether there is much of any science in it. I am going to try to prove later with a high class mechanic, that the workman who is fit to work at any type of work is almost universally incapable of understanding the principles without the help of some one else. I will use shoveling because it is a shorter illustration, and I will try to show what I mean by the science of shoveling, and the power which comes to the man who knows the science of shoveling. It is a high art compared with pig-iron handling.

## The Science of Shoveling

When I went to the Bethlehem Steel Works, the first thing I saw was a gang unloading rice coal. They were a splendid set of fellows, and they shoveled fast. There was no loafing at all. They shoveled as hard as you could ask any man to work. I looked with the greatest of interest for a long time, and finally they moved off rapidly down in the yard to another part of the yard and went right at handling iron ore. One of the main facts connected with that shoveling was the work those men were doing was that, in handling the rice coal, they had on their shovels a load of 3¾ pounds, and when the same men went to handling ore with the same shovel, they had over 38 pounds on their shovels. Is it asking too much of any one to inquire whether 3¾ pounds is the right load for a shovel, or whether 38 pounds is the right load for a shovel? Surely if one is right the other must be wrong. I think that is a self-evident fact, and yet I am willing to bet that that is what workmen are doing right now in Cleveland.

That is the old way. Suppose we notice that fact. Most of us do not notice it because it is left to the foreman. At the Midvale works, we had to find out these facts. What is the old way of finding them out? The old way was to sit down and write one's friends and ask them the question. They got answers from contractors about what they thought it ought to be, and then they averaged them up, or took the most reliable man, and said, "That is all right; now we have a shovel load of so much." The more common way is to say, "I want a good shovel foreman." They will send for the foreman of the shovelers and put the job up to him to find what is the proper load to put on a shovel. He will tell you right off the bat. I want to show you the difference under scientific management.

Under scientific management you ask no one. Every little trifle,—there is nothing too small—becomes the subject of experiment. The experiments develop into a law; they save money; they increase the output of the individual and make the thing worth while. How is this done? What we did in shoveling experiments was to deliberately select two first class shovelers, the best we knew how to get. We brought them into the office and said, "Jim and Mike, you two fellows are both good shovelers. I have a proposition to make to you. I am going to pay you double wages if you fellows will go out and do what I want you to do. There will be a young chap go along with you with a pencil and a piece of paper, and he will tell you to do a lot of fool things, and you will do them, and he will write down a lot of fool things, and you will think it is a joke, but it is nothing of the kind. Let me tell you one thing; if you fellows think that you can fool that chap you are very much mistaken, you cannot fool him at all. Don't get it through your heads you can fool him. If you take this double wages, you will be straight and do what you are told." They both promised and did exactly what they were told. What we told them was this: "We want you to start in and do whatever shoveling you are told to do, and work at just the pace, all day long, that when it comes night you are going to be good and tired, but not tired out. I do not want you exhausted or anything like that, but properly tired. You know what a good day's work is. In other words, I do not want any loafing business or any overwork business. If you find yourself overworked and getting too tired, slow down." Those men did that, and did it in the most splendid kind of way day in and day out. We proved their co-operation because they were in different parts of the yard, and they both got near enough the same results. Our results were duplicated.

I have found that there are a lot of schemes among my working friends, but no more among them than among us. They are good, straight fellows if you only treat them right, and put the matter up squarely to them. We started in at a pile of material, with a very large shovel. We kept innumerable, accurate records of all kinds, some of them useless. Thirty or forty different items were carefully observed about the work of those two men. We counted the number of shovelfuls thrown in a day. We found with a weight of between thirty-eight and thirty-nine pounds on the shovel, the man made a pile of material of a certain height. We then cut off the shovel again and with a thirty-four pound load his pile went up and he shoveled more in a day. We again cut off the shovel to thirty pounds, and the pile went up again. With twenty-six pounds on the shovel, the pile again went up, and at twenty-one and one-half pounds the men could do their best. At twenty pounds the pile went down, at eighteen it went down, and at fourteen it went down, so that they were at the peak at twenty-one and one-half pounds. There is a scientific fact. A first class shoveler ought to take twenty-one and one-half pounds on his shovel in order to work to the best possible advantage. You are not giving that man a chance unless you give him a shovel which will hold twenty-one pounds.

The men in the yard were run by the old fashioned foreman. He simply walked about with them. We at once took their shovels away from them. We built a large labor tool room which held ten to fifteen different kinds of shoveling implements so that for each kind of material that was handled in that yard, all the way from rice coal, ashes, coke, all the way up to ore, we would have a shovel that would just hold twenty-one pounds, or average twenty-one. One time it would hold eighteen, the next twenty-four, but it will average twenty-one.

When you have six hundred men laboring in the yard, as we had there, it becomes a matter of quite considerable difficulty to get, each day, for each one of those six hundred men, engaged in a line one and one-half to two miles long and a half mile wide, just the right shovel for shoveling material. That requires organization to lay out and plan for those men in advance. We had to lay out the work each day. We had to have large maps on which the movements of the men were plotted out a day in advance. When each workman came in in the morning, he took out two pieces of paper. One of the blanks gave them a statement of the implements which they had to use, and the part of the yard in which they had to work. That required organization planning in advance.

One of the first principles we adopted was that no man in that labor gang could work on the new way unless he earned sixty per cent higher wages than under the old plan. It is only just to the workman that he shall know right off whether he is doing his work right or not. He must not be told a week or month after, that he fell down. He must know it the next morning. So the next slip that came out of the pigeon hole was either a white or yellow slip. We used the two colors because some of the men could not read. The yellow slip meant that he had not earned his sixty per cent higher wages. He knew that he could not stay in that gang and keep on getting yellow slips.

## Teaching the Men

I want to show you again the totally different outlook there is under scientific management by illustrating what happened when that man got his yellow slips. Under the old scheme, the foreman could say to him, "You are no good, get out of this; no time for you, you cannot earn sixty per cent higher wages; get out of this! Go!" It was not done politely, but the foreman had no time to palaver. Under the new scheme what happened? A teacher of shoveling went down to see that man. A teacher of shoveling is a man who is handy with a shovel, who has made his mark in life with a shovel, and yet who is a kindly fellow and knows how to show the other fellow what he ought to do. When that teacher went there he said, "See here, Jim, you have a lot of those yellow slips, what is the matter with you? What is up? Have you been drunk? Are you tired? Are you sick? Anything wrong with you? Because if you are tired or sick we will give you a show somewhere else." "Well, no, I am all right." Then if you are not sick, or there is nothing wrong with you, you have forgotten how to shovel. I showed you how to shovel. You have forgotten something, now go ahead and shovel and I will show you what is the matter with you." Shoveling is a pretty big science, it is not a little thing.

If you are going to use the shovel right you should always shovel off of an iron bottom; if not an iron bottom, a wooden bottom; and if not a wooden bottom a hard dirt bottom. Time and again the conditions are such that you have to go right into the pile. When that is the case, with nine out of ten materials it takes more trouble and more time and more effort to get the shovel into the pile than to do all the rest of the shoveling. That is where the effort comes. Those of you again who have taught the art of shoveling will have taught your workmen to do this. There is only one way to do it right. Put your forearm down onto the upper part of your leg, and when you push into the pile, throw your weight against it. That relieves your arm of work. You then have an automatic push, we will say, about eighty pounds, the weight of your body thrown on to it. Time and again we would find men whom we had taught to shovel right were going at it in the old way, and of course they could not do a day's work. The teacher would simply stand over that fellow and say, "There is what is the matter with you, Jim, you have forgotten to shovel into the pile."

You are not interested in shoveling, you are not interested in whether one way or the other is right, but I do hope to interest you in the difference of the mental attitude of the men who are teaching under the new system. Under the new system, if a man falls down, the presumption is that it is our fault at first, that we probably have not taught the man right, have not given him a fair show, have not spent time enough in showing him how to do his work.

Let me tell you another thing that is characteristic of scientific management. In my day, we were smart enough to know when the boss was coming, and when he came up we were apparently really working. Under scientific management, there is none of that pretense. I cannot say that in the old days we were delighted to see the boss coming around. We always expected some kind of a roast if he came too close. Under the new, the teacher is welcomed; he is not an enemy, but a friend. He comes there to try to help the man get bigger wages, to show him how to do something. It is the great mental change, the change in the outlook that comes, rather than the details of it.

## Does Scientific Management Pay?

It took the time of a number of men for about three years to study the art of shoveling in that yard at the Bethlehem Steel Works alone. They were carefully trained college men, and they were busy all the time. That costs money, the tool room costs money, the clerks we had to keep there all night figuring up how much the men did the day before cost money, the office in which the men laid out and planned the work cost money. The very fair and proper question, the only question to ask is "Does it pay?" because if scientific management does not pay, there is nothing in it; if it does not pay in dollars and cents, it the rankest kind of nonsense. There is nothing philanthropic about it. It has got to pay, because business which cannot be done on a profitable basis ought not to be done on a philanthropic basis, for it will not last. At the end of three and one-half years we had a very good chance to know whether or not it paid.

Fortunately in the Bethlehem Steel Works they had records of how much it cost to handle the materials under the old system, where the single foreman led a group of men around the works. It costs them between seven and eight cents a ton to handle materials, on an average throughout the year. After paying for all this extra work I have told you about, it cost between three and four cents a ton to handle materials, and there was a profit of between seventy-five and eighty thousand dollars a year in that yard by handling those materials in the new way. What the men got out of it was this: Under the old system there were between four and six hundred men handling the material in that yard, and when we got through there were about one hundred and forty. Each one was earning a great deal more money. We made careful investigation and found they were almost all saving money, living better, happier, they are the most contented set of laborers to be seen anywhere. It is only by this kind of justification, justification of a profit for both sides, an advantage to both sides, that scientific management can exist.

---

## *Learning Review*

*Questions:*

1. The most important fact facing the _____ of the civilized world is that _____ firmly believe that it is in their own interests to go _____ instead of going _____.

2.  The _____ of _____ is the second reason why workers believe in giving as little _____ in return for the _____ that they get as is practical.

3.  The greatest good under _____ _____ comes from the fact that workers look upon their _____ as the best friends they have in the world.

4.  The first _____ of scientific management is to gather a great mass of _____ _____ by the means of _____ and _____ study.

5.  The _____ of _____ which involves a complete _____ of the work between the management and the workers, is the _____ principle of scientific management.

*Answers:*

1. industries, workers, slow, fast, 2. development, soldiering, work, money 3. scientific management, employers 4. principle, traditional knowledge, time, motion 5. division, work, redivision, fourth

---

# Retrospective Comment

## BY ROBERT A. RUSSELL.*

Frederick Taylor is credited with being the father of scientific management. His idea of employing the scientific method in managerial problems was, however, controversial during most of his lifetime. Taylor's contribution to the era of scientific management can be summarized as four ideas which helped revolutionize management practice:

1.  The development of laws and scientific principles for work tasks to replace old-fashioned or traditional methods.
2.  The scientific selection and development of workers.
3.  The bringing together of science and the trained worker by offering better treatment and an opportunity for the expression of employee needs.
4.  The division of work into two equal sections, one section for the workers and one section for management, the total effort requiring a cooperation between the two parties.

The ideas had an effect on work methods and productivity during Taylor's time. However, he was somewhat disappointed in their general level of acceptance. Even though some of Taylor's ideas are considered passé in modern management theory, his ideas have had an enormous impact. His first idea above has developed into the fields of work measurement and human engineering. Ideas 2 and 3 have contributed significantly to the fields of personnel and industrial relations.

In spite of specific contributions, the single most important idea that Taylor left us with is the use of the scientific method in management. Both of the modern schools of management thought (the behavioral approach and the management science approach) are philosophically based on the scientific method. In this fundamental way, modern management is indebted to Frederick Taylor.

---

* Associate Professor of Quantitative Methods and Management Information Systems, The University of Tulsa.

# 4

# *The Essentials of Leadership*

## MARY PARKER FOLLETT

### *About the Author*

**Mary Parker Follett** (1868–1933) was born into an old New England family and spent most of her early working life as a social worker, serving the poor and underprivileged in Boston's Roxbury section. After graduating summa cum laude from Radcliffe College in 1898, Follett organized evening centers for young people and was elected vice president of the National Community Center Association.

From this unlikely beginning, she became a management pioneer who advised business people on organizational problems and made important contributions to the emerging profession of management. Even though she had never set foot in a factory except as an observer, and had never participated in the management of a company, Follett understood the important roles managers played in producing constructive change that enables an organization to function.

Follett focused on the cross-fertilization of thinking that occurs when people work together in groups. She believed that group members who communicate with one another begin to think in a more compatible and harmonious way. It is the role of the manager to cultivate this group interaction to improve decision making.

This selection, which anticipates the development of participative leadership and MBO programs a half-century later, is from a series of lectures Follett presented at the University of London a few months before her death in 1933.

Reprinted by special permission of the publisher from Mary Parker Follett, *Freedom and Coordination* (London: Pitman Publishing Corporation, 1949), pp. 47–60. Photo reproduced courtesy of Price Waterhouse Urwick from the collection of Mary Parker Follett papers at the Urwick Management Center. The editors gratefully acknowledge the assistance of Dr. Terrell F. Pike of the University of South Alabama in securing the photograph.

# PREVIEW

A. In progressively managed industries, functional leadership tends to carry more weight than leadership of position or personality.
  1. A leader leads, not by force of a dominating personality, but by superior knowledge of a situation.
  2. Leadership can be learned; it is not a quality with which one must be born.
B. Several requisites exist for successful leadership.
  1. A leader must have a thorough knowledge of the job.
  2. A leader must possess the ability to grasp the total situation in order to organize all the forces in the enterprise to pursue a common goal.
  3. A leader must possess the ability to see the evolving situation in order to direct the future.
  4. A leader should have a spirit of adventure.
C. Following is only a part of what other members of a group do; they must also keep the leader in control of a situation.
  1. Lower levels can send suggestions to higher levels.
  2. Followers can inform leaders of problems they are experiencing.
  3. Followers can point out orders that are wrong, so they can be corrected.
D. Leaders must teach their followers.
  1. Followers must be taught their part in the leadership situation.
  2. Followers must be taught how to control the situations for which they are responsible.

I have tried to show you certain changes which are creeping into our thinking on business management. As I have said, in the more progressively managed businesses an order was no longer an arbitrary command but—the law of the situation. A week ago I defined authority as something which could not really be conferred on someone, but as a power which inhered in the job. Now I want to show the difference between the theory of leadership long accepted and a conception which is being forced on our attention by the way in which business is today conducted.

What I call the old-fashioned theory of leadership is well illustrated by a study made a few years ago by two psychologists. They worked out a list of questions by which to test leadership ability. Here are some of the questions:

At a reception or tea, do you try to meet the important persons present?

At a lecture or entertainment, do you go forward and take a front seat?

At a hairdresser's, are you persuaded to try a new shampoo or are you able to resist?

If you make purchases at Woolworth's, are you ashamed to have your friends know it?

If you are at a stupid party, do you try to inject life into it?

If you hold an opinion, the reverse of which the lecturer has expressed, do you usually volunteer your opinion?

Do you find it difficult to say No when a salesman is trying to sell you something?

What do you do when someone tries to push in ahead of you in a line at the box office?

When you see someone in a public place whom you think you have met, do you go up to him and enquire whether you have met?

And so on—there were a good many more. But what on earth has all this to do with leadership? I think nothing whatever. These psychologists were making tests, they said, for aggressiveness, assuming that aggressiveness and leadership are synonymous, assuming that you cannot be a good leader unless you are aggressive, masterful, dominating. But I think, not only that these characteristics are not the qualities essential to leadership, but, on the contrary, that they often militate directly against leadership. I knew a boy who was very decidedly the boss of his gang all through his youthful days. That boy is now forty-eight years old. He has not risen in his business or shown any power of leadership in his community. And I do not think that this has been in spite of his dominating traits, but because of them.

But I cannot blame the psychologists too much, for in the business world too there has been an idea long prevalent that self-assertion, pugnacity even, are necessary to leadership. Or at any rate, the leader is usually supposed to be one who has a compelling personality, who can impose his own will on others, can make others do what he wants done.

One writer says that running a business is like managing an unruly horse, a simile I particularly dislike. Another writer says, "The successful business man feels at his best in giving orders. . . . The business man tends to lay down the law—he feels himself to be an individual source of energy." While this is undoubtedly true of many business men, yet there are many today of whom it is not true. It is no longer the universally accepted type of administrative leadership. We saw two weeks ago that in scientifically managed plants, with their planning departments, their experts, their staff officials, their trained managers of the line, few "orders" are given in the old sense of the word. When therefore we are told that large-scale ability means masterfulness and autocratic will, some of us wish to reply: But that is the theory of the past, it is not what we find today in the best-managed industries.

This does not however denote that less leadership is required than formerly, but a different kind. Let me take two illustrations, one of the foreman, one of the salesman. We find in those plants where there is little order-giving of the old kind, where the right order is found by research, that the foreman is not only as important but more important than formerly. He is by no means less of a leader; indeed he has more opportunities for leadership in the sense of that word which is now coming to be accepted by many. This is because his time is freed for more constructive work. With the more explicitly defined requirements made upon him—requirements in regard to time, quality of work and methods—he has a greater responsibility for group accomplishment, he is developing a technique very different from the old foreman technique. The foreman today does not merely deal with trouble, he forestalls trouble. In fact, we don't think much of a foreman who is always dealing with trouble; we feel that if he were doing his job properly, there wouldn't be so much trouble. The job of the head of any unit—foreman or head of department—is to see that conditions (machines, materials, etc.) are right, to see that instructions are understood, and to see that workers are trained to carry out the instructions, trained to use the methods which have been decided on as best. The test of a foreman now is not how good he is at bossing, but how little bossing he has to do, because of the training of his men and the organization of their work.

Now take the salesman. If the foreman was supposed to dominate by aggressiveness, the salesman was supposed to dominate by persuasiveness. Consider the different demand made on salesmen today. Salesmen are being chosen less and less for their powers of persuasion, but for their general intelligence, for their knowledge of the goods handled, and for their ability to teach prospective customers the best way to use the goods. A business man said to me: "The training of salesmen . . . is being carried on with increasing elaboration, and always with more emphasis on knowledge of the product and its uses, and distinctly less on the technique of persuasion. . . ." For the firms who sell production equipment, this means sending men who sometimes act as consulting engineers for their customers.

We find this same doctrine taught in the salesmanship classes held in the big shops. The shop assistants are told not to over-persuade a customer, else when the customer gets home she may be sorry she has bought that article and may not come to that shop again. The saleswoman may have made one sale and lost a dozen by her persuasiveness. Her job is to know her goods and to study the needs of her customer.

To dominate, either by a masterful or a persuasive personality, is going out of fashion. People advertise courses in what they call "applied psychology" and promise that they will teach you how to develop your personality and thus become leaders, but wiser teachers say to their students, "Forget your personality, learn your job."

What then are the requisites of leadership? First, a thorough knowledge of your job. And this fact is keenly appreciated today as business is becoming a profession and business management a science. Men train themselves to become heads of departments or staff officials by learning all that goes with the particular position they wish to attain.

Consider the influence which it is possible for the cost accountant to exercise because of his special knowledge. Where there is cost-accounting and unit budgeting, the cost accountant is in a position to know more about the effect of a change in price than anyone else. His analyses and his interpretations may dictate policy to the chief executive.

Moreover, we find leadership in many places besides these more obvious ones, and this is just because men are learning special techniques and therefore naturally lead in those situations. The chairman of a committee may not occupy a high official position or be a man of forceful personality, but he may know how to guide discussion effectively, that is, he may know the technique of *his* job. Or consider the industrial-relations-man now maintained in so many industries. This man is adept at conciliation. He has a large and elaborate technique for that at his command.

When it is a case of instruction, the teacher is the leader. Yet a good instructor may be a poor foreman. Again, some men can make people produce, and some are good at following up quality who could never make people produce.

There is also individual leadership which may come to the fore irrespective of any particular position; of two girls on a machine, one may be the leader. We often see individual leadership, that is, leadership irrespective of position, springing up in a committee. There was an instance of this in a sales committee. The chairman of the committee was the sales manager, Smith. Smith was narrow but not obstinate. Not being obstinate, Jones was able to get Smith to soften his opinion on the particular matter in question, and there was then an integration of the opinion of that committee around Jones' leadership.

I think it is of great importance to recognize that leadership is sometimes in one place and sometimes in another. For it tends to prevent apathy among under-executives. It makes them much more alert if they realise that they have many chances of leadership before they are advanced to positions which carry with them definitely, officially, leadership. Moreover, if such occasional leadership is exercised with moderation without claiming too much for oneself, without encroaching on anyone's official position, it may mean that person will be advanced to an official position of leadership.

But let us look further at the essentials of leadership. Of the greatest importance is the ability to grasp a total situation. The chief mistake in thinking of leadership as resting wholly on personality lies probably in the fact that the executive leader is not a leader of men only but of something we are learning to call the total situation. This includes facts, present and potential, aims and purposes and men. Out of a welter of facts, experience, desires, aims, the leader must find the unifying thread. He must see a whole, not a mere kaleidoscope of pieces. He must see the relation between all the different factors in a situation. The higher up you go, the more ability you have to have of this kind, because you have a wider range of facts from which to seize the relations. The foreman has a certain range—a comparatively small number of facts and small number of people. The head of a sub-department has a wider range; the head of a department a wider still, the general manager the widest of all. One of the principal functions of the general manager is to organize all the scattered forces of the business. The higher railway officials may not understand railway accounting, design of rolling stock, and assignment of rates as well as their expert assistants, but they know how to use their knowledge, how to relate it, how to make a total situation.

The leader then is one who can organize the experience of the group—whether it be the small group of the foreman, the larger group of the department, or the whole plant—can organize the experience of the group and thus get the full power of the group. The leader makes the team. This is pre-eminently the leadership quality—the ability to organize all the forces there are in an enterprise and make them serve a common purpose. Men with this ability create a group power rather than express a personal power. They penetrate to the subtlest connections of the forces at their command, and make all these forces available and most effectively available for the accomplishment of their purpose.

Some writers tell us that the leader should represent the accumulated knowledge and experience of his particular group, but I think he should go far beyond this. It is true that the able executive learns from everyone around him, but it is also true that he is far more than the depository where the wisdom of the group collects. When leadership rises to genius it has the power of transforming, of transforming experience into power. And that is what experience is for, to be made into power. The great leader creates as well as directs power. The essence of leadership is to create control, and that is what the world needs today, control of small situations or of our world situation.

I have said that the leader must understand the situation, must see it as a whole, must see the inter-relation of all the parts. He must do more than this. He must see the evolving situation, the developing situation. His wisdom, his judgment, is used, not on a situation that is stationary, but on one that is changing all the time. The ablest administrators do not merely draw logical conclusions from the array of facts of the past which their expert assistants bring to them, they have a vision of the future. To be sure, business estimates are always, or should be, based on the probable future conditions. Sales policy, for instance, is guided not only by past sales but by probable future sales. The leader, however, must see all the future trends and unite them. Business is always developing. Decisions have to anticipate the development. You remember how Alice in Wonderland had to run as fast as she could in order to stand still. That is a commonplace to every business man. And it is up to the general manager to see that his executives are running as fast as they can. Not, you understand, working as hard as they can—that is taken for granted—but anticipating as far as they can.

This insight into the future we usually call in business anticipating. But anticipating means more than forecasting or predicting. It means far more than meeting the next situation, it means making the next situation. If you will watch decisions, you will find that the highest grade decision does not have to do merely with the situation with which it is directly concerned. It is always the sign of the second-rate man when the decision merely meets the present situation. It is the left-over in a decision which gives it the greatest value. It is the carry-over in a decision which helps develop the situation in the way we wish it to be developed. In business we are always passing from one significant moment to another significant moment, and the leader's task is pre-eminently to understand the moment of passing. The leader sees one situation melting into another and has learned the mastery of that moment. We usually have the situation we make—no one sentence is more pregnant with meaning for business success. This is why the leader's task is so difficult, why the great leader requires great qualities—the most delicate and sensitive perceptions, imagination and insight, and at the same time courage and faith.

The leader should have the spirit of adventure, but the spirit of adventure need not mean the temperament of the gambler. It should be the pioneer spirit which blazes new trails. The insight to see possible new paths, the courage to try them, the judgment to measure results—these are the qualifications of the leader.

And now let me speak to you for a moment of something which seems to me of the utmost importance, but which has been far too little considered, and that is the part of the followers in the leadership situation. Their part is not merely to follow, they have a very active part to play and that is to keep the leader in control of a situation. Let us not think that we are either leaders or—nothing of much importance. As one of those led we have a part in leadership. In no aspect of our subject do we see a greater discrepancy between theory and practice than here. The definition given over and over again of the leader is one who can induce others to follow him. Or that meaning is taken for granted and the question is asked: "What is the technique by which a leader keeps his followers in line?" Some political scientists discuss why men obey or do not obey, why they tend to lead or to follow, as if leading and following were the essence of leadership. I think that following is a very small part of what the other members of a group have to do. I think that these authors are writing of theory, of words, of stereotypes of the past, that they are, at any rate, not noticing the changes that are going on in business thinking and business practice. If we want to treat these questions realistically, we shall watch what is actually happening, and what I see happening in some places is that the members of a group are not so much following a leader as helping to keep him in control of a situation.

How do we see this being done? For one thing, in looking at almost any business we see many suggestions coming up from below. We find sub-executives trying to get upper executives to install mechanical improvements, to try a new chemical process, to adopt a plan for increasing incentives for workers, and so on. The upper executives try to persuade the general manager and the general manager the board of directors. We have heard a good deal in the past about the consent of the governed; we have now in modern business much that might be called the consent of the governing, the suggestions coming from below and those at the top consenting. I am not trying to imitate Shaw and Chesterton and being paradoxical; there is actually a change going on in business practice in this respect which I want to emphasise to you at every point.

How else may a man help to keep those above him in control? He may, instead of trying to "get by" on something, instead of covering up his difficulties so that no one will know he is having any, inform his chief of his problems, tell him the things he is not succeeding in as well as all his wonderful achievements. His chief will respect him just as much for his failures as for his successes if he himself takes the right attitude towards them.

Another way is to take a wrong order back for correction. It may have been an error, or it may be that it was all right once, but that it must be changed to meet changing conditions. The worker has not met his responsibility by merely obeying. Many a worker thinks that the pointing out of a wrong order is a gratuitous thing on his part, a favor he generously confers but which he need not because it is not really his job, his job is to obey. As a matter of fact, however, obeying is only a small part of his job. One general manager told me that what they disliked in his factory was what they called there the yes, yes man. The intelligent leader, this man said, does not want the kind of follower who thinks of his job only in terms of passive obedience.

But there is following. Leader and followers are both following the invisible leader—the common purpose. The best executives put this common purpose clearly before their group. While leadership depends on depth of conviction and the power coming therefrom, there must also be the ability to share that conviction with others, the ability to make purpose articulate. And then that common purpose becomes the leader. And I believe that we are coming more and more to act, whatever our theories, on our faith in the power of this invisible leader. Loyalty to the invisible leader gives us the strongest possible bond of union, establishes a sympathy which is not a sentimental but a dynamic sympathy.

Moreover, when both leader and followers are obeying the same demand, you have instead of a passive, an active, self-willed obedience. The men on a fishing smack are all good fellows together, call each other by their first names, yet one is captain and the others obey him; but it is an intelligent, alert, self-willed obedience.

The best leaders get their orders obeyed because they too are obeying. Sincerity more than aggressiveness is a quality of leadership.

If the leader should teach his followers their part in the leadership situation, how to help keep their chief in control, he has another duty equally important. He has to teach them how to control the situations for which they are specifically responsible. This is an essential part of leadership and a part recognized today. We have a good illustration of this in the relation between upper executives and heads of departments in those firms where the Budget is used as a tool of control. Suppose an upper executive is dissatisfied with the work of a department. When this happens, it is either because quality is too poor or costs are too high. The old method of procedure was for the upper executive simply to blame the head of the department. But in a plant where the departments are budgeted, an upper executive can ask the head of a department to sit down with him and consider the matter. The Budget objectifies the whole situation. It is possible for an upper executive to get the head of the department to find out himself where the difficulty lies and to make him give himself the necessary orders to meet the situation.

Many are coming to think that the job of a man higher up is not to make decisions for his subordinates but to teach them how to handle their problems themselves, teach them how to make their own decisions. The best leader does not persuade men to follow his will. He shows them what it is necessary for them to do in order to meet their responsibility, a responsibility which has been explicitly defined to them. Such a leader is not one who wishes to do people's thinking for them, but one who trains them to think for themselves.

Indeed, the best leaders try to train their followers themselves to become leaders. A second-rate executive will often try to suppress leadership because he fears it may rival his own. I have seen several instances of this. But the first-rate executive tries to develop leadership in those under him. He does not want men who are subservient to him, men who render him an unthinking obedience. While, therefore, there are still men who try to surround themselves with docile servants—you all know that type—the ablest men today have a larger aim, they wish to be leaders of leaders. This does not mean that they abandon one iota of power. But the great leader tries also to develop power wherever he can among those who work with him, and then he gathers all this power and uses it as the energizing force of a progressing enterprise.

If any of you think I have underestimated the personal side of leadership, let me point out that I have spoken against only that conception which emphasizes the dominating, the masterful man. I most certainly believe that many personal qualities enter into leadership—tenacity, sincerity, fair dealings with all, steadfastness of purpose, depth of conviction, control of temper, tact, steadiness in stormy periods, ability to meet emergencies, power to draw forth and develop the latent possibilities of others, and so on. There are many more. There is, for instance, the force of example on which we cannot lay too great stress. If workers have to work overtime, their head should be willing to do the same. In every way, he must show that he is willing to do what he urges on others.

One winter I went yachting with some friends in the inland waterways of the southern part of the United States. On one occasion our pilot led us astray and we found ourselves one night aground in a Carolina swamp. Obviously, the only thing to do was to try to push the boat off, but the crew refused, saying that the swamps in that region were infested with rattlesnakes. The owner of the yacht offered not a word of remonstrance, but turned instantly and jumped overboard. Every member of the crew followed.

So please remember that I do not underestimate what is called the personal side of leadership, indeed there is much in this paper, by implication, on that side. And do not think that I underestimate the importance of the man at the top. No one could put more importance on top leadership than I do, as I shall try to show you next week when we consider the part of the chief executive in that intricate system of human relationship which business has now become.

I might say as a summary of this talk that we have three kinds of leadership: the leadership of position, the leadership of personality and the leadership of function. My claim for modern industry is that in the best managed plants the leadership of function is tending to have more weight and the leadership of mere position or of mere personality less.

Please note that I say only a tendency. I am aware how often a situation is controlled by a man either because his position gives him the whip hand and he uses it, or because he knows how to play politics. My only thesis is that in the more progressively managed businesses there is a tendency for the control of a particular situation to go to the man with the largest knowledge of that situation, to him who can grasp and organize its essential elements, who understands its total significance, who can see it through—who can see length as well as breadth—rather than to one with merely a dominating personality or in virtue of his official position.

And that thought brings me to my conclusion. The chief thing I have wanted to do in this hour is to explode a long-held superstition. We have heard repeated again and again in the past, "Leaders are born, not made." I read the other day, "Leadership is a capacity that cannot be acquired." I believe that leadership can, in part, be learned. I hope you will not let anyone persuade you that it cannot be. The man who thinks leadership cannot be learned will probably remain in a subordinate position. The man who believes it can be, will go to work and learn it. He may not ever be president of the company, but he can rise from where he is.

Moreover, if leadership could not be learned, our large, complex businesses would not have much chance of success, for they require able leadership in many places, not only in the president's chair.

Leadership is a part of business management and there is a rapidly developing technique for every aspect of the administration and management of a business.

I urge you then, instead of accepting the idea that there is something mysterious about leadership, to analyze it. I think that then you cannot fail to see that there are many aspects of it which can be acquired. For instance, a part of leadership is all that makes you get on most successfully in your direct contacts with people—how and when to praise, how and when to point out mistakes, what attitude to take toward failures. All this can of course be learned. The first thing to do is to discover what is necessary for leadership and then to try to acquire by various methods those essentials. Even those personal characteristics with which we were endowed by birth can often be changed. For instance, vitality, energy, physical endurance, are usually necessary for leadership, but even this is not always beyond us. Theodore Roosevelt was a delicate lad and yet became an explorer, a Rough Rider, a fighter, and by his own determined efforts. You have seen timid boys become self-confident. You have seen bumptious little boys have all that taken out of them by their schoolmasters.

Leadership is not the "intangible," the "incalculable" thing we have often seen it described. It is capable of being analyzed into its different elements, and many of these elements can be acquired and become part of one's equipment.

My paper has been concerned with functional leadership and with multiple leadership. Our present historians and biographers are strengthening the conception of multiple leadership by showing us that in order to understand any epoch we must take into account the lesser leaders. They tell us also that the number of these lesser leaders has been so steadily increasing that one of the most outstanding facts of our life today is a widely diffused leadership. Wells goes further and says that his hope for the future depends on a still more widely diffused leadership. In the past, he says, we depended on a single great leader . . . today many men and women must help to lead. In the past, he says, Aristotle led the world in science, today there are thousands of scientists each making his contribution.

Industry gives to men and women the chance for leadership, the chance to make their contribution to what all agree is the thing most needed in the world today.

Business used to be thought of as trading, managing as manipulating. Both ideas are now changing. Business is becoming a profession and management a science and an art. This means that men must prepare themselves for business as seriously as for any other profession. They must realize that they, as all professional men, are assuming grave responsibilities, that they are to take a creative part in one of the large functions of society, a part which, I believe, only trained and disciplined men can in the future hope to take with success.

---

## *Learning Review*

*Questions:*

1. The traditional view of leadership was that _____ was an important attribute of a leader.

2. The four leadership requisites are _____, _____, _____, and _____.

3. A major part of the job of followers is to _____.

4. Progressive leaders lead, not by domination by a forceful _____, but by _____.

5. Three types of leadership include (1) leadership of _____, (2) leadership of _____, and (3) leadership of _____.

6. Leaders must teach their followers _____ and _____.

7. The most important personal ability of a leader is his or her _____.

*Answers:*

1. aggressiveness;   2. thorough knowledge of the job, ability to grasp the total situation, ability to see the evolving situation, sense of adventure;   3. keep the leader in control of a situation;   4. personality, knowledge of the situation;   5. authority, personality, function;   6. their role in the leadership situation, how to control the situation for which they are responsible;   7. force of example.

---

## *Retrospective Comment*

◆

### BY JANICE M. BEYER *

Like many seminal thinkers, Mary Parker Follett had much to say that anticipated later developments in the field of management. By introducing the idea of the law of situation, she not only went beyond what she called the old-fashioned theory of leadership—the idea that leaders lead because they have certain personal qualities—but prefigured later contingency theories of leadership and power and of organizational design.

Her approach to leadership recognizes that different kinds of leadership must be exercised at different times, depending on the situation. The first contingency she emphasizes is the functional expertise of the leader. Those who lead should have the relevant expertise for the situation; this might be the line manager, but it might also be a staff expert or even a nonmanagerial employee, for leadership occurs "in many places." The latter idea recognizes that subordinates should be encouraged to participate in decision-making when they have relevant knowledge and skills.

But Follett is not advocating the cultivation of narrow expertise. On the contrary, she stresses that the general manager must be an integrator—someone who can "grasp a total situation" and "organize all the scattered forces of a business." To do this, managers must become professionals and the practice of management a science. This is what modern business or management education should be all about. I fear that sometimes it emphasizes the acquisition of specialized knowledge more than this ability to integrate knowledge and apply it. Students of business and management should recognize that most of their professors are specialists; therefore, they will need to integrate much of the knowledge they learn on their own. The single required policy or strategy course will hardly suffice. By the questions they ask, students can also press their professors to place their subject in a broad context and thereby integrate it with the others.

The second set of contingencies that Follett recognizes are the many impersonal modes of control and coordination that we now think of as part of organizational design. She reminds her audience that managers have budgets, procedures, and above all, the general way in which the work is organized, to assist them in maintaining control. In other words, leaders do not personally have to do all of the controlling. They can use the structure of the organization and of work processes to help them guide and direct the efforts of subordinates. Like present contingency theories of leadership, she is saying that leaders do not need to give lots of direction when the situation is structured to do it for them.

The third set of contingencies she discusses is the leader's vision of the future. She believes that leaders must have ideas about where they want to go and how to get there. She also believes that managers must make it happen—that they must act to create the future situations they want. Knowledge that helps predict the future scientifically should help managers develop ways to deal with it creatively. But here she is mostly talking of something that cannot be reduced to scientific principles. She recognizes that exceptional leaders do indeed have exceptional personal qualities, but suggests these are a rather different set from the old-fashioned idea of the dominant personality. The qualities she mentions— "delicate and sensitive perceptions, imagination and insight, and at the same time, courage and faith"—are not ones that can be taught in a course on leadership. They can only be cultivated through a more general process of personal development and education.

The final set of contingencies that Follett emphasizes are the behaviors and skills of followers. She recognizes that exercising leadership requires cooperative followers. Thus she urges managers to give their subordinates opportunities to contribute their expertise by originating suggestions and ideas. This particular idea is one for which Japanese management is well known. In the so-called *ringi* system of decision making, decisions originate at lower levels of management and move upward for consent and approval. Follett also stresses how important shared goals are to ensure that followers and leaders are headed in the same direction. By pointing out that it is important for leaders to articulate these goals and behave in accordance with them, she anticipates current ideas about the importance of symbolic or cultural leadership.

---

*Professor, New York University.

# 5

# A Professional Creed for Management

OLIVER SHELDON

## About the Author

**Oliver Sheldon** (1894–1951) presented a "suggested creed, as it were, by which the practice of management in the future shall be governed." His views of the social responsibilities of practicing managers are as relevant today as they were when he incorporated them in the closing chapter of his book, *The Philosophy of Management,* published in 1923.

Although Sheldon's manufacturing perspective of management can be traced to his own career with the British chocolate manufacturer Rowntree & Company Ltd. (today, Rowntree Mackintosh), his views transcend any single industry and are applicable to the overall professional responsibilities of managers everywhere.

Having served four years (1914–1918) in the First World War, Sheldon returned to Oxford, graduated, and joined Rowntree in 1919. He remained with the firm throughout his entire working life, holding a variety of positions, and becoming a member of the Board of Directors in 1931. In addition to his writings on management, Sheldon was also a poet and active in a number of civic endeavors including the founding of the University of York.

Reprinted by special permission of the publisher from Oliver Sheldon, *The Philosophy of Management* (London: Pitman Publishing Ltd., 1923), pp. 280–291. Photograph courtesy of Rowntree Mackintosh.

# PREVIEW

A. The present form of industry is determined, in a broad sense, by the interplay of both internal and external forces.
  1. External forces affecting industry include actions of the state, attitudes of the public, education, financing, and foreign competition and trade conditions.
  2. Internal forces consist of labor and science.
  3. Both types represent forces for change in industry. This is especially true of labor and science because of their insistence upon progress, growth, and innovation.
B. Management is the one stable element in the process of organizational evolution.
  1. Management is as inherent in the composition of industry as is labor.
  2. In all possible structures of society management performs the same basic functions.
  3. A firmly-established body of management is the greatest safeguard against disruptive change.
C. Management should be seen as a common body, pursuing a common end, with common motives, purposes, and laws to provide an assurance of stability.
  1. A need exists for a philosophy of management.
  2. A proposed philosophy of management is offered to form a concrete beginning for the development of a common creed.
D. A philosophy of management is codified in ten parts:
  1. Industry exists to provide and distribute necessary commodities at fair prices.
  2. The responsibility of industrial management is to direct industry to this end.
  3. Management is a separate division—distinguishable from capital and labor—and divisible into administration, management, and organization.
  4. Management should achieve its objectives by developing efficiency.
  5. Efficiency results from the use of scientific analysis and knowledge, and through development of human potential.
  6. Efficiency depends on the structure of the organization.
  7. Managerial functions can be divided into those functions that are essential to the inception of manufacture, production functions, activities facilitating manufacture, and distribution functions.
  8. Management must use the scientific method to ensure the most economical utilization of impersonal factors and those personal factors regarded purely as productive units.
  9. Proper practices should be followed in regard to the human agent in production—in relation to the community, industrial work, and industrial life.

10. Standards should be developed to generate a science of industrial management.

In a book of this character, it is not intended to analyse and weigh up the various schemes promulgated for the moulding of industry, either by means revolutionary or evolutionary, into a form fundamentally different from the shape it assumes at present. In any event, all such schemes must necessarily be largely manufactured of the tissue of dreams, since, though in some cases they may be based squarely enough upon the facts of to-day, they cannot by any conceivable means take adequately into account the circumstances and the influences which will affect our kaleidoscopic society as it moves forward towards the dawns of days to come. He who sets himself either to design a future form of industry or to conjure up a vision of what industry may yet become, faces a problem not of logical construction or of scientific planning, but of continual adjustment and adaptation to circumstances which cannot be foretold. The value of such schemes is rather that they may trace the outline of our ideals, and thus mayhap can guide our progress. But that our progress will lead us to any prefigured land of promise is as improbable as the existence of Utopia itself.

Therefore, though the thoughts of the more daring and speculative may fare ahead of the times, to set before us social systems wherein our present ills have vanished, the thoughts of others, who offer gifts of no less value to future generations, may well, whilst accepting the criticism of being opportunistic, take only into consideration the immediate tendencies in the area where forecasts bear some chance of realization. For such as these, the analysis of the present provides as large a scope as the uncharted future offers to others.

The present form of industry is determined, in a broad sense, by the interplay of forces and tendencies, both within and without industry. The main forces, outside industry, which today appear to be exercising the greatest effect upon the evolution of the industrial structure, may be summarized as, firstly, the action of the State, viewed not as the whole of organized society, but as one of several forms of social organization; secondly, the attitude of the general public in the capacity of consumers and critics; thirdly, education; fourthly, foreign competition and foreign trade conditions; and fifthly, finance. The main forces affecting industry from within are, firstly, the position and progress of Labour; secondly, the progress of science in management, organization and manufacturing technique.

With none of these are we immediately concerned, save one—the progress of science in management and organization. In management we have the one stable element in our process of evolution. Whether the State continues increasingly to circumscribe the activities of industry, or leaves it to shoulder its own way into the future; whether foreign competition overwhelms us or compels us radically to reconstruct the form of our industry; whether the consciousness, on the part of society, of its responsibility for those who toil for it develops, as education proceeds, or becomes less insistent as industry grows more complex;

whether, indeed, the means of production come to be owned by the State or continue in the hands of private Capital—no matter what the changes, management as a function remains constant. There is no conceivable structure of industry—whether we take the self-governing and self-ownership conception of Syndicalism, the State ownership and Government management of State Socialism, the Guild management and State ownership of Guild Socialism, or the Soviet system as exemplified in Russia to-day—there is no structure where management does not fulfil approximately the same functions as under the present system in this country. Every scheme for the reconstruction of industry is concerned primarily with the ownership of the means of production and, only as incidental to that, with the management of industry. Whether the managers of the factories are appointed, as on the Soviet model, by the Minister or local representative of the "Supreme Council of Political Economy"; or, as visualized by the Guild Socialists, by a National Guild composed of representatives of all those engaged, whether on manual, technical or intellectual work, in the particular industry; or, as under our present system, by the acting representatives of the private capitalistic owners, will not materially affect the duties they have to perform. Each system will, of course, occasion different relations between management and labour, management and ownership, management and State, management and the organized consumers, but the functions of management will remain much the same under each régime. Efficiency engineers will still be necessary, whether State, Guild or Syndicalist Committee is in supreme command. Management is as inherent in the composition of industry as Labour. By virtue of its functions, moreover, it is that element in industry which, whatever changes may come, will be charged with the piloting of the ship through the waters of change. A firmly established body of management, therefore, is the greatest safeguard against disruptive change.

Looking immediately ahead, the two major forces making for change, with which management has to deal, are Labour and Science. The greater the changes these forces portend, the greater the responsibility of management for the safe pilotage of the vessel. The activities of these two forces indicate most surely that the sea which has to be traversed in the years ahead will be far from placid. Labour, viewed either as an organized entity or as a heaving, throbbing movement of the times, is wedded to progress. Chafing at the restrictions of economic logic, it grounds its faith upon a profound moral reconstruction of society. It steps forward into the future, deeply assured that, despite the abstractions of economists, statisticians and politicians, the days to come will witness a revision of the ethical principles of our social order. It is convinced by neither argument nor experience. It clings to its faith in a new world of justice; it thinks upon the moral plane. It trusts to progress, primarily and fundamentally, not because progress means more material advantages and a wider and higher field for human intelligence, but rather because it promises a state of society in which the principles governing the form and conduct of society shall be founded upon neither expediency nor force but upon what is morally right. Amid the whirling of widely divergent movements and manifold philosophies, its ultimate goal is clearly established. Its discontent is neither of mind nor of body, but of spirit.

It demands a constant impulse to go forward, it resents every setback and hindrance.

Science is similarly imbued with the forward-looking mind. It subjects every established precedent to dispassionate research. It is continually amending our methods both of manufacture and of management. It impels us to a higher and still higher standard of efficiency. It installs method in the place of chaos, laws in the place of "rule-of-thumb," knowledge in the place of ignorance. It sifts our experience, analyses our practices, and puts to new purpose our energies. It devises machines for our manual work, new methods for our procedure in management, new forms of our organization. It experiments, compares, tests, standardizes, organizes and rebuilds. It regards no standard as final, no method as ideal, no sphere as sacred. It applies its analytical process to both the things and the men of production. Without partiality, it marshals facts, discovers principles, and unhesitatingly applies them. It improves quality, decreases cost, designs products, and effects economies. It holds efficiency to be not the negative virtue of eliminating what is wasteful, but the positive virtue of building up what is the best. In its own sphere, it spells as great an ear of change and progress as does the restless mentality of Labour in the sphere of human relations. Neither is content with the *status quo;* both insist upon growth and renovation.

As for the forces outside industry, a greater exercise of regulatory activity by the State, a greater concern on the part of all grades of the community in the conduct of industry, a steady uplift of the general intelligence, a more menacing assult upon our industrial supremacy as a nation, and a greater complication, or, alternatively, prodigious disruption of the powers of finance—these, in their effect upon industry, promise at least no stagnation, no respite from the strain of progressive change.

Amid the waters, blown stormy by the blast of all these forces, management stands at the helm of industry. Labour may bring about a change in its composition and relations; Science in its methods and materials, but neither can change its functions. The man at the wheel may be replaced, may be put under a new authority, may be regarded differently by the crew, and may work with different instruments in a different way, but the functions performed remain constant, essential under every conceivable circumstance. It is important, therefore, that we should devise a philosophy of management, a code of principles, scientifically determined and generally accepted, to act as a guide, by reason of its foundation upon ultimate things, for the daily practice of the profession. The adoption of this or that principle in this or that plant will avail but little. Management must link up all its practitioners into one body, pursuing a common end, conscious of a common purpose, actuated by a common motive, adhering to a corporate creed, governed by common laws of practice, sharing a common fund of knowledge. Without this not only have we no guarantee of efficiency, no hope of concerted effort, but also no assurance of stability.

It may be a fitting conclusion, therefore, to state as concisely as possible a suggested codification of such a philosophy, not with any hope that it will be adopted as it stands, but rather that it may form a concrete beginning, in the criticism and explanation, elaboration and amendment of which some acceptable creed may be ultimately arrived at which shall govern the practice of management in the future.

## A Philosophy of Industrial Management

### I

Industry exists to provide the commodities and services which are necessary for the good life of the community, in whatever volume they are required. These commodities and services must be furnished at the lowest prices compatible with an adequate standard of quality, and distributed in such a way as directly or indirectly to promote the highest ends of the community.

### II

Industrial management, in a broad sense, is the function, practised by whatever persons or classes, responsible for the direction of industry to the above end. It must, therefore, be governed by certain principles inherent in the motive of service to the community.

Such principles are—

*Firstly,* that the policies, conditions, and methods of industry shall conduce to communal well-being. It is therefore part of the task of management to value such policies, conditions, and methods, by an ethical measure.

*Secondly,* that, in this ethical valuation, management shall endeavour to interpret the highest moral sanction of the community as a whole, as distinct from any sanction resting upon group or class interests, or, in other words, shall attempt to give practical effect to those ideals of social justice which would generally be accepted by the most unbiased portion of communal opinion.

*Thirdly,* that, though the community, expressing itself through some representative organization, is, consequently, the ultimate authority in the determination of such matters as legitimate wages and profits, it is for management, as an integral and a highly trained part of the community, to take the initiative, so far as possible within its own sphere, in raising the general ethical standard and conception of social justice.

### III

Management, as a comprehensive division of industry, is to be distinguished on the one hand from Capital, and, on the other hand, from Labour. It is divisible into three main parts—

ADMINISTRATION, which is concerned in the determination of corporate policy, the coordination of finance, production and distribution, the settlement of the compass of the organization, and the ultimate control of the executive;

MANAGEMENT proper, which is concerned in the execution of policy, within the limits set up by Administration, and the employment of the organization for the particular objects set before it; and

ORGANIZATION, which is the process of so combining the work which individuals or groups have to perform with the faculties necessary for its execution that the duties, so formed, provide the best channels for the efficient, systematic, positive and coordinated application of effort.

## IV

It is for Management, while maintaining industry upon an economic basis, to achieve the object for which it exists by the development of efficiency—both personal or human efficiency, in the workers, in the managerial staff, and in the relations between the two, and impersonal efficiency, in the methods and material conditions of the factory.

## V

Such efficiency is, in general, to be developed by Management—
*Firstly,* through the treatment of all features in every field of industry by the scientific method of analysis and the synthetical use of established knowledge, with the object of determining standards of operative and managerial practice; the application of the accepted sciences to those features of industry to which they are applicable; and the gradual formation and subsequent elaboration of a science of management, as distinct from those accepted sciences which, in practice, it employs; and
*Secondly,* through the development of the human potentialities of all those who serve industry, in a cooperation consequent upon the common acceptance of a definite motive and ideal in industry, and through the pursuit of that policy, as affecting the human agent in production, which a social responsibility to the community imposes.

## VI

Efficiency in management by these general means is, in the first instance, dependent upon a structure of organization, based upon a detailed analysis of the work to be done and the faculties requisite for doing it, and built up on the principle of combining related activities in such a way as to allow for the economical practice, progressive development, and constant coordination of all such activities.

## VII

Apart from Finance, which is primarily concerned in the provision and usage of Capital, and Administration, which determines the field and ultimately controls and coordinates the activities of Management proper, the various activities of Management proper are divisible, on the above principle, into the following functions—
*Firstly,* those functions essential to the inception of manufacture—

DESIGN (Purchasing), or that group of activities which determines the final character of the product and specifies and provides the material for its manufacture; and

EQUIPMENT, or that group of activities which provides and maintains the necessary means of production.

*Secondly,* the function dealing with the actual production, i.e. with all those activities whereby skill and effort are applied to the transformation of the material into the finished product. This function may broadly be described as MANUFACTURE.

*Thirdly,* those functions comprising the work necessary to facilitate the manufacture of the product—

TRANSPORT, or that group of activities which connects up the various units of production, stores or moves the material between the processes of manufacture, and provides the means of transportation for each function;

PLANNING, or that group of activities which determines the volume and progress of work;

COMPARISON, or that group of activities which analyses the work of each function and compares the records of its activities with the scientific standards set up for each function;

LABOUR, or that group of activities concerned in the application and maintenance of the human agent in production, and the promotion of cooperation between all engaged in production.

*Fourthly,* those functions comprising the work necessary for the distribution of the product—

SALES PLANNING, or that group of activities which determines, according to the data available, the policy and methods of distribution; and

SALES EXECUTION, or that group of activities which disposes of and actually distributes the product.

## VIII

The use of the scientific method to ensure the most economical utilization of the impersonal factors—or, of the personal factors regarded purely as productive units—in industry, involves in particular—

*Firstly,* the development of research and accurate measurement in each branch of activity which management undertakes or controls, followed by experiments upon or deductions from the data established by such research;

*Secondly,* the preparation and use of precise definitions and statements of what actually constitutes each item of work in each function;

*Thirdly,* the determination, after the analysis of the constituent parts of any activity and their synthetical reconstruction, of reference and working standards, both for manufacture and for management, representing, for the present, a justifiable and precise appraisement of desirable achievement; and

*Fourthly,* the institution of the necessary supervision, authority, and machinery to ensure the application of, adherence to, and improvement upon such standards, the measurement of actual practice by such standards, and their utilization for planning the most economical mode of production and management.

## IX

The application of that policy, which responsibility to the community imposes, involves certain practices as regards the human agent in production, whether by hand or by brain. These may be enumerated as follows—

*Firstly,* in the relation of such human agent to the community—(*a*) the recognition of and cooperation with such forms of association as may be founded for the furtherance of the ends of those engaged in industry, provided such ends are not held, by the community, to be deleterious to communal well-being; and (*b*) the facilitation, within the necessary economic limits of the conduct of industry, of the exercise by the individual, in his own self-development, of his higher faculties for the better service of the community.

*Secondly,* in the relation of such human agent to his industrial work—the promotion of individual and corporate effectiveness of effort, by the stimulus of a compelling leadership and an equitable discipline, in turn developing a corporate spirit of loyalty and high endeavour; by the provision of such training as will qualify the individual effectively to carry out his work, whilst at the same time furthering his general mental capacity; by the provision for each individual of work as far as possible calling for the exercise of his best ability, and in any event suited to his type of mentality; by the provision of conditions, both material and spiritual, conducive to the highest working efficiency; by the provision of legitimate and equitable incentives to and opportunities for the exercise of interest, both in the particular task of the individual and the general policy and progress of the business; and by the cultivation of cooperation, as a working principle, among all concerned in the activities of production.

*Thirdly,* in the relation of such human agent to his life as an individual—(*a*) the provision of means whereby all concerned may share in the determination and maintenance of the conditions under which work is to be conducted; (*b*) the provision of the means requisite to furnish a standard of living appropriate to a civilized community; (*c*) an allowance of leisure adequate for the maintenance of bodily and mental health and the development of individual capacity both as workers and as citizens; (*d*) the provision of security for efficient workers from the hardships incidental to involuntary unemployment due to trade conditions or other unfavourable circumstances; (*e*) the provision of a share in industrial prosperity proportionate to the share taken in the promotion of such prosperity; and (*f*) the conduct of the relations arising in the course of industrial activities in a strict spirit of equity.

## X

By the elaboration of Standards, on the impersonal side of industry, through the analytical and synthetical methods of Science, and by the deductive determination of the principles and methods of management on the personal or human side, it is the aim of those practising management to evolve, by a sharing of knowledge and experience, irrespective of trade and business divisions, a Science of Industrial Management, distinct alike from the sciences it employs and the technique of any particular industry, for the several purposes of forming a code to govern the general conduct of industry, of raising the general level and providing a standard measure of managerial efficiency, of formulating the basis for further development and improvement, and of instituting a standard as a necessary qualification for the practice of the profession.

---

## Learning Review

### Questions:

1. External forces affecting industry include _____ _____, _____, _____, and _____ _____.

2. Internal forces affecting industry include _____ _____ and _____ _____.

3. The two major forces for change in industry are _____ and _____.

4. _____ is the one constant element amid the evolution of industry.

5. Standards for management of industry should be developed into a _____.

### Answers:

trial management
progress of science; 5. science of indus-
competition and trade conditions; 2. the position and progress of labor, the
1. actions by the state, attitudes of the public, education, finance, and foreign

---

## Retrospective Comment

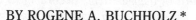

## BY ROGENE A. BUCHHOLZ *

The development of a professional creed for management grew out of the managerial revolution so aptly described by Sheldon in the closing chapter of his book on the philosophy of management. He states that the managerial function is a constant factor in any industrial organization no matter what external forces exist or the nature of the economic system in which the organization operates. The function of management remains much the same under any set of external conditions and is that element charged with guiding the organization through periods of change. Many of these themes related to the development of a managerial function that cuts across political and economic systems were later echoed by James Burnham in a book appropriately entitled *The Managerial Revolution*.

The problem that the development of a managerial function poses for capitalist economies is one of legitimacy. What gives managers the right to exercise their function of control over large-scale, complex organizations and direct the activities of modern industrial giants? This issue was raised a few years after Sheldon wrote his book by Adolf A. Berle and Gardiner C. Means who developed a thesis related to the separation of ownership and control in the modern corporation—that stockownership was so diffuse that control over these organizations had passed into the hands of professional managers. But the legitimacy of the managerial function did not stem from ownership of private property, the traditional legitimizing device for free enterprise economies. Thus the legitimacy of the management function became a problem that still exists in modern management literature under the rubric of corporate governance.

One way to deal with this problem is to develop a managerial creed, to devise a philosophy of management or a code of principles, as Sheldon states, that is "scientifically determined and generally accepted," which will act as a guide for the daily practice of the profession. Without such a creed, there can be "no guarantee of efficiency, no hope of concerted effort, and no assurance of stability." Such a creed, in other words, can help to establish the legitimacy of the managerial function and assure its continuity.

Sheldon's creed links the managerial function to the well-being of the community of which it is a part, and encourages management to take the initiative in raising the general ethical standards and conception of social justice that exists in the community. The goods and services produced by a company "must be furnished at the lowest prices compatible with an adequate standard of quality, and distributed in such a way as directly or indirectly to promote the highest ends of the community." Such a statement calls for management to be responsible and ethical in relation to broader community interests. Management is encouraged to look beyond the bottom-line and the interests of stockholders and be concerned about what could be called the public interest. The creed recognizes that management serves at the discretion of society and derives its legitimacy from being a useful social function, a theme found in modern social responsibility literature.

But what are the interests of the community, at least as Sheldon sees them? A close reading of the creed shows that it is based on the ethic of economizing, that the primary concern of management, according to Sheldon, is to promote the efficient use of resources, both personal or human resources, and capital or material resources. The primary focus of the creed is on economic utilization of the factors of production which can be determined by the scientific method. Thus the community is presumably interested in an efficient use of resources in order to increase its standard of living. Management thus derives its legitimacy from applying scientific principles in running corporate organizations to accomplish this objective.

There is no mention in the creed about what is now called the social responsibilities of management. While Sheldon recognizes the importance of certain aspects of the external environment, such as government, public attitudes, foreign trade, etc., social issues are not mentioned. Perhaps it is not fair to criticize Sheldon for this omission, as his creed only reflects the times in which he wrote. Problems such as pollution, equal opportunity, occupational safety and health, and other social issues were not generally recognized as serious problems that needed attention in those years. Yet these problems were in large part created by the drive for efficiency that Sheldon advocates. A creed that doesn't include these social aspects of corporate activities, and encourages management to pay attention to the social impact of corporate operations, provides no means or rationale for management to internalize the social costs of production and leaves this task to government regulation, a social control mechanism that is generally unacceptable to management.

But perhaps an even more fundamental contradiction exists in the method Sheldon advocates to make the creed specific and develop a set of standards to guide managerial practice. These standards, according to Sheldon, can be determined by the analytical and synthetical methods of science. The aim of those who are practicing the management profession should be to develop a "Science of Industrial Management" which is distinct from the science it employs and the technique of any particular industry. Yet, if management is truly a science, and the practice of management can be circumscribed by a set of scientific principles, what need is there for a philosophy of management or a professional creed for management? If management is a science, it becomes nothing more than the application of scientific principles to concrete situations. It involves no consideration of responsibilities to the larger community or any ethical reflection that is a part of a true professional activity.

While Sheldon wants to see management in a broader social and ethical context, he ends up being a victim of his own scientific outlook. Science is descriptive in nature, and cannot prescribe for management or society the objectives that are worth pursuing. While the scientific method is crucially important to management, it is not sufficient in and of itself to provide a basis for the problem of legitimacy Sheldon attempts to address. Such legitimacy will not come solely from the notion of economizing, but must be found in the broader purposes of the community and its welfare, an ethical vision that Sheldon so eloquently states in one part of his chapter, but then fails to develop.

---

* Professor of Business and Public Policy, The University of Texas at Dallas.

# Part 2
# THE SECOND
# GENERATION

◆

We chose the title of "The Second Generation" for this section because the three writers represented here—Mayo, Barnard, and Maslow—made their major contributions in the period between 1920 and 1950. Moreover, each of them approached management and organizational behavior with something more of a *behavioral* perspective than most of their predecessors had. Taylor and Fayol were engineers by training. Mayo and Maslow were psychologists and Barnard, despite his lack of formal training, demonstrated himself to be a social theorist of the first rank.

One other distinction separates the second generation writers from the earlier contributors. Each of our second generation developed a major challenge to basic assumptions which permeated management theory up to their time. Mayo, particularly in the famous Hawthorne studies (1927–1933), demolished the accepted notion that workers were motivated only by economic needs and that they responded to management's incentive plans as independent individuals operating according to economically rational criteria (Taylor's work is particularly vulnerable on this count). The Hawthorne studies produced ample data to show that social and group membership concerns frequently took precedence in the motivation of the workers.

Maslow, a clinical psychologist, published his paper outlining his new theory of motivation in 1943. More than a theory of motivation, the paper represents a theory of human nature. Contrary to the then prevailing modes of psychological thought (generally either Freudian or behavioristic), Maslow presented a highly optimistic view of human personality—an entity that had a built-in tendency to seek self-actualization and perfection of its own capacities. Maslow's self-actualizing person did not need to be coerced or seduced to work; self-actualizing persons will naturally seek out opportunities for constructive self-expression if they are provided a work environment that does not unnaturally impede these inherent tendencies. Argyris and McGregor (See the selections in the next section) were the two major organizational theorists to explore the implications of Maslow's concepts for management and organization.

As you read the Maslow piece, you might do well to wonder that such a totally humanistic and optimistic view of human nature could spring from the pen of a psychologist writing in the middle of World War II—and a Jewish psychologist at that!

Barnard's major book, *The Functions of the Executive,* appeared in 1938. The book is difficult and demanding reading—but well worth the effort. Barnard tends to describe organizations as systems of cooperative effort (rather than as simple hierarchies of specialized tasks). His view allows him to emphasize the informal as well as the formal aspects of organization. Because he views authority as being based in the consent of the governed, his discussion of authority is as much a treatise on leadership and other forms of influence as it is a treatment of the more legalistic notion of authority which had preoccupied earlier writers such as Weber and Fayol. As we see in the selection which follows, Barnard's view allows him to ask and explore questions like:

> "What is it about a particular communication in an organization that will cause organization members to regard it as an authoritative order and react accordingly?"

To ask the question in this way shows us that Barnard understood well the relationships between concepts such as authority, leadership, and motivation.

Iconoclast that he was, Barnard's contribution is recognized as seminal by one managerial historian. "Chester Barnard has probably had a more profound impact on the thinking about the complex subject matter of human organization than any other contributor to the continuum of management thought." (George, 1968, p. 132).

# REFERENCES

George, C. S., Jr., *The History of Management Thought.* Englewood Cliffs, N.J.: Prentice-Hall, 1968.

# 6

# *Hawthorne and the Western Electric Company*

## ELTON MAYO

## *About the Author*

---

**Elton Mayo** (1880–1949), was born in Australia and once taught philosophy at Queensland University. Later, while studying medicine in Edinburgh, Scotland, he began his study of psychopathology. He moved to the United States and joined the faculty of the Wharton School of the University of Pennsylvania. In 1926, he became associated professor of industrial research at Harvard.

Mayo is frequently identified as the "father of human relations" because of his leadership in the conduct of the Hawthorne studies and other early investigations of people at work. The analysis of his data led Mayo and his co-workers to emphasize the need to recognize the importance of non-economic (especially social) motivations of workers.

---

From Elton Mayo, *The Social Problems of an Industrial Civilization.* (Boston: Division of Research, Harvard Business School, 1945) pp. 69–84. Used with permission. Photograph courtesy of the Baker Library, Harvard University.

# PREVIEW

A. The three persistent problems faced by management in a modern large-scale industry are:
   1. The application of science and technical skill to some material good or product.
   2. The systematic ordering of operations.
   3. The organization of teamwork.
B. While the first two operate to make an industry effective, the third operates to make it efficient.
C. The failure of the illumination experiment by Western Electric engineers made them alert to the need for maintaining careful records of everything that happened in the room where the experiment was conducted.
D. The First Phase—The Test Room—began its inquiry by securing the active collaboration of the workers, and by changing the conditions of work, so that there was no actual return to original conditions.
   1. This resulted in six individuals working wholeheartedly as a team, without coercion from above or limitation from below.
E. The Second Phase—The Interview Program—was initiated by the officers of the company, who felt that there was something quite important that was overlooked, something to which the experiment should have flashed a warning signal.
F. The passage from an established to an adaptive social order has brought with it new and unanticipated problems for management and for the individual worker.
   1. Since the scientific method has a dual approach, representative of the clinic and the laboratory, the interview program initiated at Hawthorne represented for its research staff a return from the laboratory to clinical study.
   2. The workers had needs for "emotional release" and the first observation emerging from these interviews was confined to personal rather than company matters.
   3. Whatever the problem, it was partly and sometimes fully determined by the attitude of the individual worker as a consequence of his/her past and/or present experience.
   4. "Emotional release" and "personal situation" became convenient titles for the first phases of observation and seemed to resume for the interviewers the effective work that they were carrying out.
   5. There was a gradual change of attitude in the research group, as the close study of individuals continued, but in combination with an equally close study of groups.
   6. From this the researchers were redirected to the fact that the working group as a whole actually determined the output of the individual workers, and this represented the group conception of a fair day's work.

7. The influence of communication in the interview was not limited to the individual but extended to the group.
8. An important fact brought to the attention of the research division was the mistaken notion that management-worker relationship existed between the management and individuals rather than management and working groups.
9. The insight gained by the interviewing group implies a need for competent study of complaints and the grievances that provoke them, a need for knowledge of the actual facts rather than acceptance of an outdated theory.
10. In recent years, the Hawthorne interview program has acknowledged the fact that the relation of working groups to management is one of the fundamental problems of large-scale industry.

---

A highly competent group of Western Electric engineers refused to accept defeat when experiments to demonstrate the effect of illumination on work seemed to lead nowhere. The conditions of scientific experiment had apparently been fulfilled—experimental room, control room; changes introduced one at a time; all other conditions held steady. And the results were perplexing: Roethlisberger gives two instances—lighting improved in the experimental room, production went up; but it rose also in the control room. The opposite of this: lighting diminished from 10 to 3 foot-candles in the experimental room and production again went up; simultaneously in the control room, with illumination constant, production also rose.[1] Many other experiments, and all inconclusive; yet it had seemed so easy to determine the effect of illumination on work.

In matters of mechanics or chemistry the modern engineer knows how to set about the improvement of process or the redress of error. But the determination of optimum working conditions for the human being is left largely to dogma and tradition, guess, or quasi-philosophical argument. In modern large-scale industry the three persistent problems of management are:

1. The application of science and technical skill to some material good or product.
2. The systematic ordering of operations.
3. The organization of teamwork—that is, of sustained cooperation.

The last must take account of the need for continual reorganization of teamwork as operating conditions are changed in an *adaptive* society.

The first of these holds enormous prestige and interest and is the subject of continuous experiment. The second is well developed in practice. The third, by comparison with the other two, is almost wholly neglected. Yet it remains true that if these three are out of balance, the organization as a whole will not be successful. The first two operate to make an industry *effective,* in Chester Barnard's phrase,[2] the third, to make it *efficient.* For the larger and more complex the institution, the more dependent is it upon the wholehearted cooperation of every member of the group.

This was not altogether the attitude of Mr. G. A. Pennock and his colleagues when they set up the experimental "test room." But the illumination fiasco had made them alert to the need that every careful records should be kept of everything that happened in the room in addition to the obvious engineering and industrial devices.[3] Their observations therefore included not only records of industrial and engineering changes but also records of physiological or medical changes, and, in a sense, of social and anthropological. This last took the form of a "log" that gave us full an account as possible of the actual events of every day, a record that proved most useful to Whitehead when he was re-measuring the recording tapes and recalculating the changes in productive output. He was able to relate eccentricities of the output curve to the actual situation at a given time—that is to say, to the events of a specific day or week.

## First Phase—The Test Room

The facts are by now well known. Briefly restated, the test room began its inquiry by, first, attempting to secure the active collaboration of the workers. This took some time but was gradually successful, especially after the retirement of the original first and second workers and after the new worker at the second bench had assumed informal leadership of the group. From this point on, the evidence presented by Whitehead or Roethlisberger and Dickson seems to show that the individual workers became a team, wholeheartedly committed to the project. Second, the conditions of work were changed one at a time: rest periods of different numbers and length, shorter working day, shorter working week, food with soup or coffee in the morning break. And the results seemed satisfactory: slowly at first, but later with increasing certainty, the output record (used as an index of well-being) mounted. Simultaneously the girls claimed that they felt less fatigued, felt that they were not making any special effort. Whether these claims were accurate or no, they at least indicated increased contentment with the general situation in the test room by comparison with the department outside. At every point in the program, the workers had been consulted with respect to proposed changes; they had arrived at the point of free expression of ideas and feelings to management. And it had been arranged thus that the twelfth experimental change should be a return to the original conditions of work—no rest periods, no midmorning lunch, no shortened day or week. It had also been arranged that, after 12 weeks of this, the group should return to the conditions of Period 7, a 15-minute midmorning break with lunch and a 10-minute midafternoon rest. The story is now well known: in Period 12 the daily and weekly output rose to a point higher than at any other time (the hourly rate adjusted itself downward by a small fraction), and in the whole 12 weeks "there was no downward trend." In the following period, the return to the conditions of work as in the seventh experimental change, the output curve soared to even greater heights: this thirteenth period lasted for 31 weeks.

These periods, 12 and 13, made it evident that increments of production could not be related point for point to the experimental changes introduced. Some major change was taking place that was chiefly responsible for the index of improved conditions—the steadily increasing output. Period 12—but for minor qualifications, such as "personal time out"—ignored the nominal return to original conditions of work and the output curve continued its upward passage. Put in other words, there was no actual return to original conditions. This served to bring another fact to the attention of the observers. Periods 7, 10, and 13 had nominally the same working conditions, as above described—15-minute rest and lunch in midmorning, 10-minute rest in the afternoon. But the average weekly output for each girl was:

Period 7—2,500 units
Period 10—2,800 units
Period 13—3,000 units

Periods 3 and 12 resembled each other also in that both required a full day's work without rest periods. But here also the difference of average weekly output for each girl was:

Period 3—less than 2,500 units
Period 12—more than 2,900 units

Here then was a situation comparable perhaps with the illumination experiment, certainly suggestive of the Philadelphia experience where improved conditions for one team of mule spinners were reflected in improved morale not only in the experimental team but in the two other teams who had received no such benefit.

This interesting, and indeed amusing, result has been so often discussed that I need make no mystery of it now. I have often heard my colleague Roethlisberger declare that the major experimental change was introduced when those in charge sought to hold the situation humanly steady (in the interest of critical changes to be introduced) by getting the cooperation of the workers. What actually happened was that six individuals became a team and the team gave itself wholeheartedly and spontaneously to cooperation in the experiment. The consequence was that they felt themselves to be participating freely and without afterthought, and were happy in the knowledge that they were working without coercion from above or limitation from below. They were themselves astonished at the consequence, for they felt they were working under less pressure than ever before: and in this, their feelings and performance echoed that of the mule spinners.

Here then are two topics which deserve the closest attention of all those engaged in administrative work—the organization of working teams and the free participation of such teams in the task and purpose of the organization as it directly affects them in their daily round.

## Second Phase—The Interview Program

But such conclusions were not possible at the time: the major change, the question as to the exact difference between conditions of work in the test room and in the plant departments, remained something of a mystery. Officers of the company determined to "take another look" at departments outside the test room—this, with the idea that something quite important was there to be observed, something to which the experiment should have made them alert. So the interview program was introduced.

It was speedily discovered that the question-and-answer type of interview was useless in situation. Workers wished to talk, and to talk freely under the seal of professional confidence (which was never abused) to someone who seemed representative of the company or who seemed, by his very attitude, to carry authority. The experience itself was unusual; there are few people in this world who have had the experience of finding someone intelligent, attentive, and eager to listen without interruption to all that he or she has to say. But to arrive at this point it became necessary to train interviewers how to listen, how to avoid interruption or the giving of advice, how generally to avoid anything that might put an end to free expression in an individual instance. Some approximate rules to guide the interviewer in his work were therefore set down. These were, more or less, as follows: [4]

1. Give your whole attention to the person interviewed, and make it evident that you are doing so.
2. Listen—don't talk.
3. Never argue; never give advice.
4. Listen to:
   (a) What he wants to say.
   (b) What he does not want to say.
   (c) What he cannot say without help.
5. As you listen, plot out tentatively and for subsequent correction the pattern (personal) that is being set before you. To test this, from time to time summarize what has been said and present for comment (e.g., "Is this what you are telling me?"). Always do this with the greatest caution, that is, clarify but do not add or twist.
6. Remember that everything said must be considered a personal confidence and not divulged to anyone. (This does not prevent discussion of a situation between professional colleagues. Nor does it prevent some form of public report when due precaution has been taken.)

It must not be thought that this type of interviewing is easily learned. It is true that some persons, men and women alike, have a natural flair for the work, but, even with them, there tends to be an early period of discouragement, a feeling of futility, through which the experience and coaching of a senior interviewer must carry them. The important rules in the interview (important, that is, for the development of high skill) are two. First, Rule 4 that indicates the need to help the individual interviewed to articulate expression of an idea or attitude that he has not before expressed; and, second, Rule 5 which indicates the need from time to time to summarize what has been said and to present it for comment. Once equipped to do this effectively, interviewers develop very considerable skill. But, let me say again, this skill is not easily acquired. It demands of the interviewer a real capacity to follow the contours of another person's thinking, to understand the meaning for him of what he says.

I do not believe that any member of the research group or its associates had anticipated the immediate response that would be forthcoming to the introduction of such an interview program. Such comments as "This is the best thing the Company has ever done," or "The Company should have done this long ago," were frequently heard. It was as if workers had been awaiting an opportunity for expressing freely and without afterthought their feelings on a great variety of modern situations, not by any means limited to the various departments of the plant. To find an intelligent person who was not only eager to listen but also anxious to help to express ideas and feelings but dimly understood—this, for many thousand persons, was an experience without precedent in the modern world.

In a former statement I named two questions that inevitably presented themselves to the interviewing group in these early stages of the study:

(1) Is some experience which might be described as an experience of personal futility a common incident of industrial organization for work?
(2) Does life in a modern industrial city, in some unrealized way, predispose workers to obsessive response? [5]

And I said that these two questions "in some form" continued to preoccupy those in charge of the research until the conclusion of the study.[6]

After twelve years of further study (not yet concluded), there are certain developments that demand attention. For example, I had not fully realized in 1932, when the above was written, how profoundly the social structure of civilization has been shaken by scientific, engineering, and industrial development. This radical change—the passage from an established to an adaptive social order— has brought into being a host of new and unanticipated problems for management and for the individual worker. The management problem appears at its acutest in the work of the supervisor. No longer does the supervisor work with a team of persons that he has known for many years or perhaps a lifetime; he is leader of a group of individuals that forms and disappears almost as he watches it. Now it is difficult, if not impossible, to relate oneself to a working group one by one; it is relatively easy to do so if they are already a fully constituted team. A communication from the supervisor, for example, in the latter instance has to be made to one person only with the appropriate instructions; the individual will pass it on and work it out with the team. In the former instance, it has to be repeated to every individual and may often be misunderstood.

But for the individual worker the problem is really much more serious. He has suffered a profound loss of security and certainty in his actual living and in the background of his thinking. For all of us the feeling of security and certainty derives always from assured membership of a group. If this is lost, no monetary gain, no job guarantee, can be sufficient compensation. Where groups change ceaselessly as jobs and mechanical processes change, the individual inevitably experiences a sense of void, of emptiness, where his fathers knew the joy of comradeship and security. And in such situation, his anxieties—many, no doubt, irrational or ill-founded—increase and he becomes more difficult both to fellow workers and to supervisor. The extreme of this is perhaps rarely encountered as yet, but increasingly we move in this direction as the tempo of industrial change is speeded by scientific and technical discovery.

In the first chapter of this book I have claimed that scientific method has a dual approach—represented in medicine by the clinic and the laboratory. In the clinic one studies the whole situation with two ends in view: first, to develop intimate knowledge of and skill in handling the facts, and, second, on the basis of such a skill to separate those aspects of the situation that skill has shown to be closely related for detailed laboratory study. When a study based upon laboratory method fails, or partially fails, because some essential factor has been unknowingly and arbitrarily excluded, the investigator, if he is wise, returns to clinical study of the entire situation to get some hint as to the nature of the excluded determinant. The members of the research division at Hawthorne, after the twelfth experimental period in the test room, were faced by just such a situation and knew it. The so-called interview program represented for them a return from the laboratory to clinical study. And, as in all clinical study, there was no immediate and welcome revelation of a single discarded determinant: there was rather a slow progress from one observation to another, all of them important—but only gradually building up into a single complex finding. This slow development has been elsewhere described, in *Management and the Worker;* one can however attempt a succinct résumé of the various observations, more or less as they occurred.

Officers of the company had prepared a short statement, a few sentences, to be repeated to the individual interviewed before the conversation began. This statement was designed to assure the worker that nothing he said would be repeated to his supervisors or to any company official outside the interviewing group. In many instances, the worker waved this aside and began to talk freely and at once. What doubts there were seemed to be resident in the interviewers rather than in those interviewed. Many workers, I cannot say the majority for we have no statistics, seemed to have something "on their minds," in ordinary phrase, about which they wished to talk freely to a competent listener. And these topics were by no means confined to matters affecting the company. This was, I think, the first observation that emerged from the mass of interviews reported daily. The research group began to talk about the need for *"emotional release"* and the great advantage that accrued to the individual when he had "talked off" his problem. The topics varied greatly. One worker two years before had been sharply reprimanded by his supervisor for not working as usual: in interview he wished to explain that on the night preceding the day of the incident his wife and child had both died, apparently unexpectedly. At the time he was unable to explain; afterwards he had no opportunity to do so. He told the story dramatically and in great detail; there was no doubt whatever that telling it thus benefited him greatly. But this story naturally was exceptional; more often a worker would speak of his family and domestic situation, of his church, of his relations with other members of the working group—quite usually the topic of which he spoke presented itself to him as a problem difficult for him to resolve. This led to the next successive illumination for the inquiry. It became manifest that, whatever the problem, it was partly, and sometimes wholly, determined by the attitude of the individual worker. And this defect or distortion of attitude was consequent on his past experience or his present situation, or, more usually, on both at once. One woman worker, for example, discovered for herself during an interview that her dislike of a certain supervisor was based upon a fancied resemblance to a detested stepfather. Small wonder that the same supervisor had warned the interviewer that she was "difficult to handle." But the discovery by the worker that her dislike was wholly irrational eased the situation considerably.[7] This type of case led the interviewing group to study carefully each worker's *personal situation* and attitude. These two phrases "emotional release" and "personal situation" became convenient titles for the first phases of observation and seemed to resume for the interviewers the effective work that they were doing. It was at this point that a change began to show itself in the study and in the conception of the study.

The original interviewers, in these days, after sixteen years of industrial experience, are emphatic on the point that the first cases singled out for report were special cases—individuals—and not representative either of the working group or of the interviews generally. It is estimated that such cases did not number more than an approximate two per cent of the twenty thousand persons originally interviewed. Probably this error of emphasis was inevitable and for two reasons: first, the dramatic changes that occur in such instances seemed good evidence of the efficacy of the method, and, second, this type of interviewing had to be insisted upon as *necessary to the training of a skilled interviewer*. This last still holds good; a skilled interviewer must have passed through the stage of careful and observant listening to what an individual says and to all that he says. This stage of an interviewing program closely resembles the therapeutic method and its triumphs are apt to be therapeutic. And I do not believe that the study would have been equipped to advance further if it had failed to observe the great benefit of emotional release and the extent to which every individual's problems are conditioned by his personal history and situation. Indeed, even when one has advanced beyond the merely psychotherapeutic study of individuals to study of industrial groups, one has to beware of distortions similar in kind to those named; one has to know how to deal with such problems. The first phase of the interview program cannot therefore be discarded; it still retains its origianl importance. But industrial studies must nevertheless move beyond the individual in need of therapy. And this is the more true when the change from established routines to adaptive changes of routine seems generally to carry a consequence of loss of security for many persons.

A change of attitude in the research group came gradually. The close study of individuals continued, but in combination with an equally close study of groups. An early incident did much to set the new pattern for inquiry. One of the earliest questions proposed before the original test room experiment began was a question as to the fatigue involved in this or that type of work. Later a foreman of high reputation, no doubt with this in mind, came to the research group, now for the most part engaged in interviewing, and asserted that the girls in his department worked hard all day at their machines and must be considerably fatigued by the evening; he wanted an inquiry. Now the interviewers had discovered that this working group claimed a habit of doing most of their work in the morning period and "taking things easy" during the afternoon. The foreman obviously realized nothing of this, and it was therefore fortunate that the two possibilities could be directly tested. The officer in charge of the research made a quiet arrangement with the engineers to measure during a period the amount of electric current used by the group to operate its machines; this quantity indicated the over-all amount of work being done. The results of this test wholly supported the statements made by the girls in interview; far more current was used in the morning period than during the afternoon. And the attention of the research group was, by this and other incidents, thus redirected to a fact already known to them, namely, that the working group as a whole actually determined the output of individual workers by reference to a standard, predetermined but never clearly stated, that represented the group conception of a fair day's work. This standard was rarely, if ever, in accord with the standards of the efficiency engineers.

The final experiment, reported under the title of the Bank Wiring Observation Room, was set up to extend and confirm these observations.[8] Simultaneously it was realized that these facts did not in any way imply low working morale as suggested by such phrases as "restriction of output." On the contrary, the failure of free communication between management and workers in modern large-scale industry leads inevitably to the exercise of caution by the working group until such time as it knows clearly the range and meaning of changes imposed from above. The enthusiasm of the efficiency engineer for the organization of operations is excellent; his attempt to resume problems of cooperation under this heading is not. At the moment, he attempts to solve the many human difficulties involved in wholehearted cooperation by organizing the organization of organization without any reference whatever to workers themselves. This procedure inevitably blocks communication and defeats his own admirable purpose.[9]

This observation, important as it is, was not however the leading point for the interviewers. The existence and influence of the group—those in active daily relationship with one another—became the important fact. The industrial interviewer must learn to distinguish and specify, as he listens to what a worker says, references to "personal" or group situations. More often than not, the special case, the individual who talks himself out of a gross distortion, is a solitary—one who has not "made the team." The usual interview, on the other hand, though not by any means free from distortion, is speaking as much for the working group as for the person. The influence of the communication in the interview, therefore, is not limited to the individual but extends to the group.

Two girl workers in a large industry were recently offered "upgrading"; to accept would mean leaving their group and taking a job in another department: they refused. Then representatives of the union put some pressure on them, claiming that, if they continued to refuse, the union organizers "might just as well give up" their efforts. With reluctance the girls reversed their decision and accepted the upgrading. Both girls at once needed the attention of an interviewer: they had liked the former group in which they had earned informal membership. Both felt adjustment to a new group and a novel situation as involving effort and private discontent. From both much was learned of the intimate organization and common practices of their groups, and their adjustments to their new groups were eased, thereby effectively helping reconstitute the teamwork in those groups.

In another recent interview a girl of eighteen protested to an interviewer that her mother was continually urging her to ask Mr. X, her supervisor, for a "raise." She had refused, but her loyalty to her mother and the pressure the latter exerted were affecting her work and her relations at work. She talked her situation out with an interviewer, and it became clear that to her a "raise" would mean departure from her daily companions and associates. Although not immediately relevant, it is interesting to note that, after explaining the situation at length to the interviewer, she was able to present her case dispassionately to her mother—without exaggeration or potest. The mother immediately understood and abandoned pressure for advancement, and the girl returned to effective work. This last instance illustrates one way in which the interview clears lines of communication of emotional blockage—within as without the plant. But this is not my immediate topic; my point is rather that the age-old human desire for persistence of human association will seriously complicate the development of an adaptive society if we cannot devise systematic methods of easing individuals from one group of associates into another.

But such an observation was not possible in the earliest inquiry. The important fact brought to the attention of the research division was that the ordinary conception of management-worker relation as existing between company officials, on the one hand, and an unspecified number of individuals, on the other, is utterly mistaken. Management, in any continuously successful plant, is not related to single workers but always to working groups. In every department that continues to operate, the workers have—whether aware of it or not—formed themselves into a group with appropriate customs, duties, routines, even rituals; and management succeeds (or fails) in proportion as it is accepted without reservation by the group as authority and leader. This, for example, occurred in the relay assembly test room at Hawthorne. Management, by consultation with the girl workers, by clear explanation of the proposed experiments and the reasons for them, by accepting the workers' verdict in special instances, unwittingly scored a success in two most important human matters—the girls became a self-governing team, and a team that cooperated wholeheartedly with management. The test room was responsible for many important findings—rest periods, hours of work, food, and the like: but the most important finding of all was unquestionably in the general area of teamwork and cooperation.

It was at this time that the research division published, for private circulation within the company, a monograph entitled "Complaints and Grievances." Careful description of many varied situations within the interviewers' experience showed that an articulate complaint only rarely, if ever, gave any logical clue to the grievance in which it had origin; this applied at least as strongly to groups as to individuals. Whereas economists and industry generally *tend to concentrate upon the complaint and upon logical inferences from its articulate statement* as an appropriate procedure, the interviewing group had learned almost to ignore, except as symptom, the—sometimes noisy—manifestation of discomfort and to study the situation anew to gain knowledge of its source. Diagnosis rather than argument became the proper method of procedure.

It is possible to quote an illustration from a recently published book, *China Enters the Machine Age.*[10] When industries had to be moved, during this war, from Shanghai and the Chinese coast to Kunming in the interior of China, the actual operation of industry still depended for the most part on skilled workers who were refugees from Shanghai and elsewhere. These skilled workers knew their importance to the work and gained considerable prestige from it; nevertheless discontent was rife among them. Evidence of this was manifested by the continual, deliberate breaking of crockery in the company mess hall and complaints about the quality of the food provided. Yet this food was much better than could have been obtained outside the plant—especially at the prices charged. And in interview the individual workers admitted freely that the food was good and could not rightly be made the subject of complaint. But the relationship between the skilled workers as a group and the *Chih Yuan*—the executive and supervisory officers— was exceedingly unsatisfactory.

Many of these officers—the *Chih Yuan*—have been trained in the United States—enough at least to set a pattern for the whole group. Now in America we have learned in actual practice to accept the rabble hypothesis with reservations. But the logical Chinese student of engineering or economics, knowing nothing of these practical reservations, returns to his own country convinced that the workman who is not wholly responsive to the "financial incentive" is a troublemaker and a nuisance. And the Chinese worker lives up to this conviction by breaking plates.[11] Acceptance of the complaint about the food and collective bargaining of a logical type conducted at that level would surely have been useless.

Yet this is what industry, not only in China, does every day, with the high sanction of State authority and the alleged aid of lawyers and economists. In their behavior and their statements, economists indicate that they accept the rabble hypothesis and its dismal corollary of financial incentive as the only effective human motive. They substitute a logical hypothesis of small practical value for the actual facts.

The insight gained by the interviewing group, on the other hand, cannot be described as substituting irrational for rational motive, emotion for logic. On the contrary, it implies a need for competent study of complaints and the grievances that provoke them, a need for knowledge of the actual facts rather than acceptance of an outdated theory. It is amusing that certain industrialists, rigidly disciplined in economic theory, attempt to shrug off the Hawthorne studies as "theoretic." Actually the shoe is on the other foot; Hawthorne has restudied the facts without prejudice, whereas the critics have unquestioningly accepted that theory of man which had its vogue in the nineteenth century and has already outlived its usefulness.

The Hawthorne interview program has moved far since its beginning in 1929. Originally designed to study the comfort of workers in their work as a mass of individuals, it has come to clear specification of the relation of working groups to management as one of the fundamental problems of large-scale industry. It was indeed this study that first enabled us to assert that the third major preoccupation of management must be that of organizing teamwork, that is to say, of developing and sustaining cooperation.

## FOOTNOTES

1. Roethlisberger, F. J., *Management and Morale*. Cambridge: Harvard University Press, n.d. Pp. 9–10.
2. Barnard, C. I., *The Functions of the Executive*. Cambridge: Harvard University Press, 1938. P. 56.
3. For a full account of the experimental setup, see F. J. Roethlisberger and William J. Dickson, *Management and the Worker*. Cambridge: Harvard University Press, 1949 and T. North Whitehead, *The Industrial Worker* (Vol. 1). Cambridge, Mass.: Harvard University Press, 1938.
4. For a full discussion of this type of interview, see F. J. Roethlisberger and William J. Dickson, op. cit., Chap. XIII. For a more summary and perhaps less technical discussion, see George C. Homans, *Fatigue of Workers*. New York: Reinhold, 1941.
5. Mayo, E. *The Human Problems of an Industrial Civilization*. New York: MacMillan, 1933. Reprinted by Division of Research, Harvard Business School, 1946. P. 114.
6. *Ibid.*
7. F. J. Roethlisberger and William J. Dickson, *op. cit.*, pp. 307–310.
8. *Ibid.*, Part IV, pp. 379 ff.
9. For further evidence on this point, see Stanley B. Mathewson, *Restriction of Output Among Unorganized Workers*. New York: Viking, 1931 and E. Mayo, *op. cit.*, pp. 119–121.
10. Kuo-Heng, Shih, *China Enters the Machine Age*. Cambridge: Harvard University Press, 1944.
11. *Ibid.*, Chap VIII, pp. 111–127; also Chap. X, pp. 151–153.

---

## *Learning Review*

*Questions:*

1. The conditions of the scientific experiment that had been fulfilled to demonstrate the effect of _____ were: an _____ room; a _____ room; changes introduced _____ at a time; all other conditions held steady.

2. The first two problems faced by management in a modern large-scale industry operate to make an industry _____, while the third to make it _____.

3. All the persons engaged in administrative work need to pay close attention to the _____ of _____ teams and the _____ of such teams in the task and purpose of the organization as it directly affects them.

4. One rule in the _____ that is important for the development of high _____, indicates the need from time to time to _____ what has been said and to present it for _____.

5. Each worker's _____ _____ and _____ _____, constituted the first phases of observation made by the interviewers.

*Answers:*

5. emotional release, personal situation

1. illumination, experimental, control, one 2. effective, efficient 3. organization, working, free participation 4. interview, skill, summarize, comment

---

# Retrospective Comment

## BY GEORGE F. F. LOMBARD *

The excerpt from Elton Mayo's *The Social Problems of an Industrial Civilization* illustrates two of his important contributions to the social and behavioral sciences and their practice. The first of these is in respect to interviewing methods and the second in respect to the importance of group or social patterns in understanding behavior.

Mayo believed that the interviewing method was the most important tool for research and practice which he brought with him when he came to this country from Australia in the early 1920s and that it was the most important contribution that he left when he returned to England in 1948. Though Roethlisberger and Dickson made a more formal statement of the method, in Chapter XIII of *Management and the Worker,* (Harvard University Press, Cambridge, Mass. 1939), Mayo liked his six rules, the practice of which is a much more complex matter than their statement. In this excerpt he calls special attention to rules 4 and 5, which other discussions of the method in their frequent emphasis on rules 1 and 2 tend to overlook.

Mayo developed his views about interviewing in his work in Australia with shell-shocked veterans from World War I, as he recounts all too briefly in his *Some Notes on the Psychology of Pierre Janet* (Harvard University Press, Cambridge, Mass. 1948). The importance of his method was that it kept the interviewer's attention focused on the situation of the person whom he was interviewing, not on the interviewer's assumptions about the other person. Therefore, if the interviewer's views about the other person needed correcting, the method would help provide information that would lead to the correction. As he comments, Mayo believed that much of the conventional wisdom of the social sciences of his day—not just in interviewing—needed this kind of correction before the development of knowledge could proceed rapidly through experimental and laboratory methods analogous to those used in the physical sciences.

Both Mayo and Roethlisberger recognized the contributions to the theory and practice of interviewing that Carl Rogers and his students made. Indeed, Rogers' statement so clearly went beyond Mayo's and Roethlisberger's, particularly in respect to therapeutic settings, that little reference is made to the latters' today, much as they offer to an interviewer who is working in research, administrative and organizational settings.

Mayo's views on the importance of group or social patterns in understanding behavior have been the source of many misunderstandings. (For a useful summary of the controversies, see Landsberger, Henry H., *Hawthorne Revisited,* Cornell University, Ithaca, N.Y., 1958). In this excerpt Mayo points to the evidence of the Hawthorne experiments as a referent for a more general discussion in the earlier chapters of *The Social Problems.* His concern was that science and technology were being used in ways that eroded the social patterns of living that are necessary to support the capacity of people to work together. The result could only be an increase in the conditions of loneliness, rootlessness, alienation, anomie, and isolation among individuals and the growth of special interests. He believed that industrial administrators held positions of responsibility in society such that their actions as leaders of organizations could make a difference in respect to these matters.

These views are much more familiar today than they were when Mayo first expressed them, but they are still the subject of much controversy, debate, and misunderstanding. Much as they have contributed to the training of supervisors and managers, they have not been practiced consistently on a wide scale at high levels of organizations.

Were Mayo alive today, I doubt that he would have changed his views about the importance of the interviewing method or of social patterns of behavior. But Mayo, I think, did not envision the elaboration of organizational behavior as a special field of knowledge and practice as we know it today. His roots were in the older disciplines of medicine, psychology, psychopathology, sociology, and anthropology. He studied all of them intensively, though he did not have a formal degree in any of them. He was not himself a builder of the kind of systematic knowledge that is represented by many of the excerpts selected for this book. His contributions to the development of the field were clinical insights and a capacity to inspire and train other students. He would have been both appalled and amused at the controversies and debates that have characterized the field and admiring of and generous to those whose work has gone beyond his own.

---

* Louis E. Kirstein Professor of Human Relations Emeritus, Harvard University Graduate School of Business Administration.

# 7

## *The Theory of Authority*

### CHESTER I. BARNARD

### *About the Author*

After attending Harvard (from which he failed to graduate because he refused to take a lab section of a laboratory science course), **Chester I. Barnard** (1886–1961) joined American Telephone and Telegraph as a statistical clerk. In 1927, he became president of New Jersey Bell where he served until his retirement. He also served as President of the Rockefeller Foundation (1948–52) and the USO (1942–5).

Barnard was a close associate and intellectual colleague of Lowell, Henderson, Whitehead, Donham and other Harvard faculty who pioneered the study of management in universities.

Barnard's most famous work, *The Functions of the Executive,* from which the present excerpt comes, is a difficult but challenging book which questions much of the conventional wisdom about management in Barnard's day—and today as well.

Reprinted by permission of the publishers from *The Functions of the Executive* by Chester I. Barnard, Cambridge, Mass.: Harvard University Press, Copyright 1938, copyright by the President and Fellows of Harvard College; copyright 1966 by Grace N. Barnard. Barnard photo courtesy of Historical Pictures Service, Chicago.

# PREVIEW

A. The nature of authority existing in a simple organization unit is also inherent in all complex organizations.
  1. All complex organizations consist of aggregations of unit organizations.
  2. The essentials of authority in elementary and simple organizations should be the same for larger organizations.
B. The definition of authority involves two aspects—a subjective aspect and an objective aspect.
C. The subjective aspect of authority is the personal aspect, the acceptance of a communication as authoritative.
  1. A person will accept an order as authoritative only when four conditions are met.
    a. The communication is understood.
    b. At the time of the decision, the receiver believes that it is consistent with the purpose of the organization.
    c. At the time of the decision, the receiver believes that it is compatible with his or her personal interests.
    d. The receiver is both mentally and physically able to comply with the order.
  2. There exists a *zone of indifference* in each individual within which orders are acceptable without conscious questioning of their authority.
D. The objective characteristic of a communication of authority is that aspect which induces acceptance.
  1. The character of authority in organizational communications lies in the potentiality of assent of those to whom they are sent.
  2. The system of communication is a primary continuing problem of a formal organization.
  3. There are controlling factors in the character of the communication system as a system of objective authority.

## The Source of Authority

If it is true that all complex organizations consist of aggregations of unit organizations and have grown only from unit organizations, we may reasonably postulate that, whatever the nature of authority, it is inherent in the simple organization unit; and that a correct theory of authority must be consistent with what is essentially true of these unit organizations. We shall, therefore, regard the observations which we can make of the actual conditions as at first a source for discovering what is essential in elementary and simple organizations.

I

Now a most significant fact of general observation relative to authority is the extent to which it is ineffective in specific instances. It is so ineffective that the violation of authority is accepted as a matter of course and its implications are not considered. It is true that we are sometimes appalled at the extent of major criminal activities; but we pass over very lightly the universal violations, particularly of sumptuary laws, which are as "valid" as any others. Even clauses of constitutions and statutes carrying them "into effect," such as the Eighteenth Amendment, are violated in wholesale degrees.

Violation of law is not, however, peculiar to our own country. I observed recently in a totalitarian state under a dictator, where personal liberty is supposed to be at a minimum and arbitrary authority at a maximum, many violations of positive law or edict, some of them open and on a wide scale; and I was reliably informed of others.

Nor is this condition peculiar to the authority of the state. It is likewise true of the authority of churches. The Ten Commandments and the prescriptions and prohibitions of religious authority are repeatedly violated by those who profess to acknowledge their formal authority.

\*    \*    \*

It may be thought that ineffectiveness of authority in specific cases is chiefly exemplified in matters of state and church, but not in those of smaller organizations which are more closely knit or more concretely managed. But this is not true. It is surprising how much that in theory is authoritative, in the best of organizations in practice lacks authority—or, in plain language, how generally orders are disobeyed. For many years the writer has been interested to observe this fact, not only in organizations with which he was directly connected, but in many others. In all of them, armies, navies, universities, penal institutions, hospitals, relief organizations, corporations, the same conditions prevail—dead laws, regulations, rules, which no one dares bury but which are not obeyed; obvious disobedience carefully disregarded; vital practices and major institutions for which there is no authority, like the Democratic and Republican parties, not known to the Constitution.

II

We may leave the secondary stages of this analysis for later consideration. What we derive from it is an approximate definition of authority for our purpose: Authority is the character of a communication (order) in a formal organization by virtue of which it is accepted by a contributor to or "member" of the organization as governing the action he contributes; that is, as governing or determining what he does or is not to do so far as the organization is concerned. According to this definition, authority involves two aspects: first, the subjective, the personal, the *accepting* of a communication as authoritative, the aspects which I shall present in this section; and, second, the objective aspect—the character in the communication by virtue of which it is accepted—which I present in the second section, "The System of Coördination."

If a directive communication is accepted by one to whom it is addressed, its authority for him is confirmed or established. It is admitted as the basis of action. Disobedience of such a communication is a denial of its authority for him. Therefore, under this definition the decision as to whether an order has authority or not lies with the persons to whom it is addressed, and does not reside in "persons of authority" or those who issue these orders.

\* \* \*

Our definition of authority . . . no doubt will appear to many whose eyes are fixed only on enduring organizations to be a platform of chaos. And so it is—exactly so in the preponderance of attempted organizations. They fail because they can maintain no authority, that is, they cannot secure sufficient contributions of personal efforts to be effective or cannot induce them on terms that are efficient. In the last analysis the authority fails because the individuals in sufficient numbers regard the burden involved in accepting necessary orders as changing the balance of advantage against their interest, and they withdraw or withhold the indispensable contributions.

## III

. . . The necessity of the assent of the individual to establish authority *for him* is inescapable. A person can and will accept a communication as authoritative only when four conditions simultaneously obtain: (*a*) he can and does understand the communication; (*b*) *at the time of his decision* he believes that it is not inconsistent with the purpose of the organization; (*c*) *at the time of his decision,* he believes it to be compatible with his personal interest as a whole; and (*d*) he is able mentally and physically to comply with it.

(*a*) A communication that cannot be understood *can* have no authority. An order issued, for example, in a language not intelligible to the recipient is no order at all—no one would so regard it. Now, many orders are exceedingly difficult to understand. They are often necessarily stated in general terms, and the persons who issued them could not themselves apply them under many conditions. Until interpreted they have no meaning. The recipient either must disregard them or merely do anything in the hope that that is compliance.

Hence, a considerable part of administrative work consists in the interpretation and reinterpretation of orders in their application to concrete circumstances that were not or could not be taken into account initially.

(*b*) A communication believed by the recipient to be incompatible with the purpose of the organization, as he understands it, could not be accepted. Action would be frustrated by cross purposes. The most common practical example is that involved in conflicts of orders. They are not rare. An intelligent person will deny the authority of that one which contradicts the purpose of the effort as *he* understands it. In extreme cases many individuals would be virtually paralyzed by conflicting orders. They would be literally unable to comply—for example, an employee of a water system ordered to blow up an essential pump, or soldiers ordered to shoot their own comrades. I suppose all experienced executives know that when it is necessary to issue orders that will appear to the recipients to be contrary to the main purpose, especially as exemplified in prior habitual practice, it is usually necessary and always advisable, if practicable, to explain or demonstrate why the appearance of conflict is an illusion. Otherwise the orders are likely not to be executed, or to be executed inadequately.

(*c*) If a communication is believed to involve a burden that destroys the net advantage of connection with the organization, there no longer would remain a net inducement to the individual to contribute to it. The existence of a net inducement is the only reason for accepting *any* order as having authority. Hence, if such an order is received it must be disobeyed (evaded in the more usual cases) as utterly inconsistent with personal motives that are the basis of accepting any orders at all. Cases of voluntary resignation from all sorts of organizations are common for this sole reason. Malingering and intentional lack of dependability are the more usual methods.

(*d*) If a person is unable to comply with an order, obviously it must be disobeyed, or, better, disregarded. To order a man who cannot swim to swim a river is a sufficient case. Such extreme cases are not frequent; but they occur. The more usual case is to order a man to do things only a little beyond his capacity; but a little impossible is still impossible.

### IV

Naturally the reader will ask: How is it possible to secure such important and enduring coöperation as we observe if in principle and in fact the determination of authority lies with the subordinate individual? It is possible because the decisions of individuals occur under the following conditions: (*a*) orders that are deliberately issued in enduring organizations usually comply with the four conditions mentioned above; (*b*) there exists a "zone of indifference" in each individual within which orders are acceptable without conscious questioning of their authority; (*c*) the interests of the persons who contribute to an organization as a group result in the exercise of an influence on the subject, or on the attitude of the individual, that maintains a certain stability of this zone of indifference.

(*a*) There is no principle of executive conduct better established in good organizations than that orders will not be issued that cannot or will not be obeyed. Executives and most persons of experience who have thought about it know that to do so destroys authority, discipline, and morale.[1] For reasons to be stated shortly, this principle cannot ordinarily be formally admitted, or at least cannot be professed. When it appears necessary to issue orders which are initially or apparently unacceptable, either careful preliminary education, or persuasive efforts, or the prior offering of effective inducements will be made, so that the issue will not be raised, the denial of authority will not occur, and orders will be obeyed. It is generally recognized that those who least understand this fact— newly appointed minor or "first line" executives—are often guilty of "disorganiz- ing" their groups for this reason, as do experienced executives who lose self-control or become unbalanced by a delusion of power or for some other reason. Inexperienced persons take literally the current notions of authority and are then said "not to know how to use authority" or "to abuse authority." Their superiors often profess the same beliefs about authority in the abstract, but their successful practice is easily observed to be inconsistent with their professions.

(*b*) The phrase "zone of indifference" may be explained as follows: If all the orders for actions reasonably practicable be arranged in the order of their acceptability to the person affected, it may be conceived that there are a number which are clearly unacceptable, that is, which certainly will not be obeyed; there is another group somewhat more or less on the neutral line, that is, either barely acceptable or barely unacceptable; and a third group unquestionably acceptable. This last group lies within the "zone of indifference." The person affected will accept orders lying within the zone and is relatively indifferent as to what the order is so far as the question of authority is concerned. Such an order lies within the range that in a general way was anticipated at time of undertaking the connection with the organization. For example, if a soldier enlists, whether voluntarily or not, in an army in which the men are ordinarily moved about within a certain broad region, it is a matter of indifference whether the order be to go to A or B, C or D, and so on; and goings to A, B, C, D, etc., are in the zone of indifference.

The zone of indifference will be wider or narrower depending upon the degree to which the inducements exceed the burdens and sacrifices which determine the individual's adhesion to the organization. It follows that the range of orders that will be accepted will be very limited among those who are barely induced to contribute to the system.

(*c*) Since the efficiency of organization is affected by the degree to which individuals assent to orders, denying the authority of an organization communication is a threat to the interests of all individuals who derive a net advantage from their connection with the organization, unless the orders are unacceptable to them also. Accordingly, at any given time there is among most of the contributors an active personal interest in the maintenance of the authority of all orders which to them are within the zone of indifference. The maintenance of this interest is largely a function of informal organization. Its expression goes under the names of "public opinion," "organization opinion," "feeling in the ranks," "group attitude," etc. Thus the common sense of the community informally arrived at affects the attitude of individuals, and makes them, as individuals, loath to question authority that is within or near the zone of indifference. The formal statement of this common sense is the fiction that authority comes down from above, from the general to the particular. This fiction merely establishes a presumption among individuals in favor of the acceptability of orders from superiors, enabling them to avoid making issues of such orders without incurring a sense of personal subserviency or a loss of personal or individual status with their fellows.

Thus the contributors are willing to maintain the authority of communications because, where care is taken to see that only acceptable communications in general are issued, most of them fall within the zone of personal indifference;

and because communal sense influences the motives of most contributors most of the time. The practical instrument of this sense is the fiction of superior authority, which makes it possible normally to treat a personal question impersonally.

The fiction [2] of superior authority is necessary for two main reasons:

(1) It is the process by which the individual delegates upward, or to the organization, responsibility for what is an organization decision—an action which is depersonalized by the fact of its coördinate character. This means that if an instruction is disregarded, an executive's risk of being wrong must be accepted, a risk that the individual cannot and usually will not take unless in fact his position is at least as good as that of another with respect to correct appraisal of the relevant situation. Most persons are disposed to grant authority because they dislike the personal responsibility which they otherwise accept, especially when they are not in a good position to accept it. The practical difficulties in the operation of organization seldom lie in the excessive desire of individuals to assume responsibility for the organization action of themselves or others, but rather lie in the reluctance to take responsibility for their own actions in organization.

(2) The fiction gives impersonal notice that what is at stake is the good of the organization. If objective authority is flouted for arbitrary or merely temperamental reasons, if, in other words, there is deliberate attempt to twist an organization requirement to personal advantage, rather than properly to safeguard a substantial personal interest, then there is a deliberate attack on the organization itself. To remain outside an organization is not necessarily to be more than not friendly or not interested. To fail in an obligation intentionally is an act of hostility. This no organization can permit; and it must respond with punitive action if it can, even to the point of incarcerating or executing the culprit. This is rather generally the case where a person has agreed in advance in general what he will do. Leaving an organization in the lurch is not often tolerable.

The correctness of what has been said above will perhaps appear most probably from a consideration of the difference between executive action in emergency and that under "normal" conditions. In times of war the disciplinary atmosphere of an army is intensified—it is rather obvious to all that its success and the safety of its members are dependent upon it. In other organizations, abruptness of command is not only tolerated in times of emergency, but expected, and the lack of it often would actually be demoralizing. It is the sense of the justification which lies in the obvious situation which regulates the exercise of the veto by the final authority which lies at the bottom. This is a commonplace of executive experience, though it is not a commonplace of conversation about it.

## The System of Coordination

Up to this point we have devoted our attention to the subjective aspect of authority. The executive, however, is predominantly occupied not with this subjective aspect, which is fundamental, but with the objective character of a communication which induces acceptance.

## I

Authority has been defined in part as a "character of a communication in a formal organization." A "superior" is not in our view an authority nor does he have authority strictly speaking; nor is a communication authoritative except when it is an effort or action of organization. This is what we mean when we say that individuals are able to exercise authority only when they are acting "officially," a principle well established in law, and generally in secular and religious practice. Hence the importance ascribed to time, place, dress, ceremony, and authentication of a communication to establish its official character. These practices confirm the statement that authority relates to a communication "in a formal organization." There often occur occasions of complusive power of individuals and of hostile groups; but authority is always concerned with something *within* a definitely organized system. Current usage conforms to the definition in this respect. The word "authority" is seldom employed except where formal organization connection is stated or implied (unless, of course, the reference is obviously figurative).

These circumstances arise from the fact that the character of authority in organization communications lies in the *potentiality of assent* of those to whom they are sent. Hence, they are only sent to contributors or "members" of the organization. Since all authoritative communications are official and relate only to organization action, they have no meaning to those whose actions are not included within the coöperative system. This is clearly in accord with the common understanding. The laws of one country have no authority for citizens of another, except under special circumstances. Employers do not issue directions to employees of other organizations. Officials would appear incompetent who issued orders to those outside their jurisdiction.

A communication has the presumption of authority when it originates at sources of organization information—a communications center—better than individual sources. It loses this presumption, however, if not within the scope or field of this center. The presumption is also lost if the communication shows an absence of adjustment to the actual situation which confronts the recipient of it.

Thus men impute authority to communications from superior positions, provided they are reasonably consistent with advantages of scope and perspective that are credited to those positions. This authority is to a considerable extent independent of the personal ability of the incumbent of the position. It is often recognized that though the incumbent may be of limited personal ability his advice may be superior solely by reason of the advantage of position. This is the *authority of position.*

But it is obvious that some men have superior ability. Their knowledge and understanding regardless of position command respect. Men impute authority to what they say in an organization for this reason only. This is the *authority of leadership.* When the authority of leadership is combined with the authority of position, men who have an established connection with an organization generally will grant authority, accepting orders far outside the zone of indifference. The confidence engendered may even make compliance an inducement in itself.

Nevertheless, the determination of authority remains with the individual. Let these "positions" of authority in fact show ineptness, ignorance of conditions, failure to communicate what ought to be said, or let leadership fail (chiefly by its concrete action) to recognize implicitly its dependence upon the essential character of the relationship of the individual to the organization, and the authority if tested disappears.

This objective authority is only maintained if the positions or leaders continue to be adequately informed. In very rare cases persons possessing great knowledge, insight, or skill have this adequate information without occupying executive position. What they say ought to be done or ought not to be done will be accepted. But this is usually personal advice at the risk of the taker. Such persons have influence rather than authority. In most cases genuine leaders who give advice concerning organized efforts are required to accept positions of responsibility; for knowledge of the applicability of their special knowledge or judgment to concrete *organization* action, not to abstract problems, is essential to the worth of what they say as a basis of organization authority. In other words, they have an organization personality, as distinguished from their individual personality, commensurate with the influence of their leadership. The common way to state this is that there cannot be authority without corresponding responsibility. A more exact expression would be that objective authority cannot be imputed to persons in organization positions unless subjectively they are dominated by the organization as respects their decisions.

It may be said, then, that the maintenance of objective authority adequate to support the fiction of superior authority and able to make the zone of indifference an actuality depends upon the operation of the system of communication in the organization. The function of this system is to supply adequate information to the positions of authority and adequate facilities for the issuance of orders. To do so it requires commensurate capacities in those able to be leaders. High positions that are not so supported have weak authority, as do strong men in minor positions.

Thus authority depends upon a coöperative personal attitude of individuals on the one hand; and the system of communication in the organization on the other. Without the latter, the former cannot be maintained. The most devoted adherents of an organization will quit it, if its system results in inadequate, contradictory, inept orders, so that they cannot know who is who, what is what, or have the sense of effective coördination.

This system of communication, or its maintenance, is a primary or essential continuing problem of a formal organization. Every other practical question of effectiveness or efficiency—that is, of the factors of survival—depends upon it. In technical language the system of communication of which we are now speaking is often known as the "lines of authority."

## II

. . . We may now consider the controlling factors in the character of the communication system as a system of objective authority.

(*a*) The first is that *channels of communication should be definitely known.* The language in which this principle is ordinarily stated is, "The lines of authority must be definitely established." The method of doing so is by making official appointments known; by assigning each individual to his position; by general announcements; by organization charts; by educational effort, and most of all by habituation, that is, by securing as much permanence of system as is practicable. Emphasis is laid either upon the position, or upon the persons; but usually the fixing of authority is made both to positions and, less emphatically, to persons.

(*b*) Next, we may say that *objective authority requires a definite formal channel of communication to every member of an organization.* In ordinary language this means "everyone must report to someone" (communication in one direction) and "everyone must be subordinate to someone" (communication in the other direction). In other words, in formal organizations everyone must have definite formal relationship to the organization.

(*c*) Another factor is that *the line of communication must be as direct or short as possible.* This may be explained as follows: Substantially all formal communication is verbal (written or oral). Language as a vehicle of communication is limited and susceptible of misunderstanding. Much communication is necessarily without preparation. Even communications that are carefully prepared require interpretation. Moreover, communications are likely to be in more general terms the more general—that is, the higher—the position. It follows that something may be lost or added by transmission at each stage of the process, especially when communication is oral, or when at each stage there is combination of several communications. Moreover, when communications go from high positions down they often must be made more specific as they proceed; and when in the reverse direction, usually more general. In addition, the speed of communicaton, other things equal, will be less the greater the number of centers through which it passes. Accordingly, the shorter the line the greater the speed and the less the error.

How important this factor is may be indicated by the remarkable fact that in great complex organizations the number of levels of communication is not much larger than in smaller organizations. In most organizations consisting of the services of one or two hundred men the levels of communication will be from three to five. In the Army the levels are: President, (Secretary of War), General, Major-General, Brigadier-General, Colonel, Major, Captain, Lieutenant, Sergeant, men—that is, nine or ten. In the Bell Telephone System, with over 300,000 working members, the number is eight to ten. A similar shortness of the line of communication is noteworthy in the Catholic Church viewed from the administrative standpoint.

Many organization practices or inventions are used to accomplish this end, depending upon the purpose and technical conditions. Briefly, these methods are: The use of expanded executive organizations at each stage; the use of the staff department (technical, expert, advisory); the division of executive work into functional bureaus; and processes of delegating responsibility with automatic coördination through regular conference procedures, committees for special temporary functions, etc.

(*d*) Another factor is that, in principle, *the complete line of communication should usually be used.* By this is meant that a communication from the head of an organization to the bottom should pass through every stage of the line of authority. This is due to the necessity of avoiding conflicting communications (in either direction) which might (and would) occur if there were any "jumping of the line" of organization. It is also necessary because of the need of interpretation, and to maintain responsibility.[3]

(*e*) Again, the *competence of the persons serving as communication centers, that is, officers, supervisory heads, must be adequate.* The competence required is that of more and more *general* ability with reference to the work of the entire organization the more central the office of communication and the larger the organization. For the function of the center of communication in an organization is to translate incoming communications concerning external conditions, the progress of activity, successes, failures, difficulties, dangers, into outgoing communications in terms of new activities, preparatory steps, etc., all shaped according to the ultimate as well as the immediate purposes to be served. There is accordingly required more or less mastery of the technologies involved, of the capabilities of the personnel, of the informal organization situation, of the character and status of the subsidiary organizations, of the principles of action relative to purpose, of the interpretation of environmental factors, and a power of discrimination between communications that can possess authority because they are recognizably compatible with *all* the pertinent conditions and those which will not possess authority because they will not or cannot be accepted.

It is a fact, I think, that we hardly nowadays expect individual personal ability adequate to positional requirements of communication in modern large-scale organization. The limitations of individuals as respects time and energy alone preclude such personal ability, and the complexity of the technologies or other special knowledge involved make it impossible. For these reasons each major center of communication is itself organized, sometimes quite elaborately. The immediate staff of the executive (commanding officer), consisting of deputies, or chief clerks, or adjutants, or auxiliaries with their assistants, constitute an executive unit organization only one member of which is perhaps an "executive," that is, occupies the *position* of authority; and the technical matters are assigned to staff departments or organizations of experts. Such staff departments often are partly "field" departments in the sense that they directly investigate or secure information on facts or conditions external to the organizations; but in major part in most cases they digest and translate information from the field, and prepare the plans, orders, etc., for transmission. In this capacity they are advisory or adjutant to the executives. In practice, however, these assistants have the function of semi-formal advice under regulated conditions to the organizations as a whole. In this way, both the formal channels and the informal organization are supplemented by intermediate processes.

In some cases the executive (either chief or some subordinate executive) may be not a person but a board, a legislature, a committee. I know of no important organizations, except some churches and some absolute governments in which the highest objective authority is not lodged in an *organized* executive group, that is, a "highest" unit of organization.

(*f*) Again, *the line of communications should not be interrupted during the time when the organization is to function.* Many organizations (factories, stores) function intermittently, being closed or substantially so during the night, Sundays, etc. Others, such as army, police, railroad systems, telephone systems, never cease to operate. During the times when organizations are at work, in principle the line of authority must never be broken; and practically this is almost, if not quite, literally true in many cases. This is one of the reasons which may be given for the great importance attached to hereditary succession in states, and for the elaborate provision that is made in most organizations (except possibly small "personal" organizations) for the temporary filling of offices automatically during incapacity or absence of incumbents. These provisions emphasize the non-personal and communication character of organization authority, as does the persistent emphasis upon the *office* rather than the *man* that is a matter of indoctrination of many organizations, especially those in which "discipline" is an important feature.

The necessity for this is not merely that specific communications cannot otherwise be attended to. It is at least equally that the *informal* organization disintegrates very quickly if the formal "line of authority" is broken. In organization parlance, "politics" runs riot. Thus, if an office were vacant, but the fact were not known, an organization might function for a considerable time without serious disturbance, except in emergency. But if known, it would quickly become disorganized.

(*g*) The final factor I shall mention is that *every communication should be authenticated.* This means that the person communicating must be known actually to occupy the "position of authority" concerned; that the position includes the type of communication concerned—that is, it is "within its authority"; and that it actually is an authorized communication from this office. The process of authentication in all three respects varies in different organizations under different conditions and for different positions. The practice is undergoing rapid changes in the modern technique, but the principles remain the same. Ceremonials of investiture, inaugurations, swearing-in, general orders of appointment, induction, and introduction, are all essentially appropriate methods of making known who actually fills a position and what the position includes as authority. In order that these *positions* may function it is often necessary that the filling of them should be dramatized, an essential process to the creation of authority *at the bottom,* where only it can be fundamentally—that is, it is essential to inculcate the "sense of organization." This is merely stating that it is essential to "organization loyalty and solidarity" as it may be otherwise expressed. Dignifying the superior position is an important method of dignifying *all* connection with organization, a fact which has been well learned in both religious and political organizations where great attention to the subjective aspects of the "membership" is the rule.

This statement of the principles of communication systems of organizations from the viewpoint of the maintenance of objective authority has necessarily been in terms of complex organizations, since in a simple unit organization the concrete applications of these principles are fused. The principles are with difficulty isolated under simple conditions. Thus, as a matter of course, in unit organizations the channels of communication are known, indeed usually obvious; they are definite; they are the shortest possible; the only lines of authority are complete lines; there is little question of authentication. The doubtful points in unit organization are the competence of the leader, never to be taken for granted even in simple organizations; and whether he is functioning when the organization is in operation. Yet as a whole the adequately balanced maintenance of these aspects of simple leadership is the basis of objective authority in the unit organization, as the maintenance of the more formal and observable manifestations of the same aspects is the basis of authority in the complex organizations.

## FOOTNOTES

1.   Barring relatively few individual cases, when the attitude of the individual indicates in advance likelihood of disobedience (either before or after connection with the organization), the connection is terminated or refused before the formal question arises.

2.   The word "fiction" is used because from the standpoint of logical construction it merely explains overt acts. Either as a superior officer or as a subordinate, however, I know nothing that I actually regard as more "real" than "authority."

3.   These by no means exhaust the considerations. The necessity of maintaining personal prestige of executives as an *inducement to them* to function is on the whole an important additional reason.

---

## *Learning Review*

*Questions:*

1.   Authority involves two aspects: the _____ aspect and the _____ aspect.

2.   Circumstances arise from the fact that the character of authority in organization communications in the _____ _____ _____ of those to whom they are sent.

3.   The line of communication in organizations must be as _____ as possible. The _____ the line, the _____ the speed and the _____ the error.

4.   The objective character of a communication induces _____.

5.   The fiction of _____ _____ makes it possible to treat a personal question impersonally.

*Answers:*

1. subjective, objective;   2. potentiality of assent;   3. short, shorter, greater, less;   4. acceptance;   5. superior authority

## *Retrospective Comment*

### BY WILLIAM B. WOLF*

Chester I. Barnard's theory of authority is a seminal piece. Soon after Barnard's book was written, it became a focal point for a polemic as to whether authority is a managerial right to command or is based upon the acceptance of those in subordinate positions. Unfortunately, Barnard never responded to his critics and the debate that followed contributed little to our understanding of management. However, in a personal interview two months before he died, Barnard did comment relative to this treatment of "authority": He felt that he had put too much emphasis on "authority" and not enough on "responsibility".

If one follows the Barnardian approach to authority to its logical conclusions, the whole concept of authority melts into issues of communication, (i.e., how individuals receive messages and decode them), and moral responsibility, (i.e., the individual's acceptance of communications as orders).

In summary, if Barnard had a chance to rework his chapter on authority, he would probably have dealt more with the question of responsibility and its delegation. Authority is the subordinate subject. It is a secondary and derivitive aspect of responsibility.[1]

---

* Prior to his recent retirement, Professor Wolf was Professor and Chairman, Department of Personnel and Human Resource Management, New York School of Industrial and Labor Relations, Cornell University.

### FOOTNOTES

1. Wolf, William B. *The Basic Barnard*. Ithaca, N.Y.: ILR Paperback, 1974, P. 85.

# 8

# *A Theory of Human Motivation*

## A. H. MASLOW

### *About the Author*

**Abraham H. Maslow** (1908–1970) earned his Ph.D. in psychology at the University of Wisconsin in 1934. He taught five years at Wisconsin and then moved to New York where he served on the faculties of Columbia and Brooklyn College. In 1951, he accepted a post as Professor and Chairman of the Department of Psychology at Brandeis University. Although Maslow was a prolific writer and published several books, his second—*Motivation and Personality*—is the most renowned.

# PREVIEW

A. Physiological needs rank first in the hierarchy of human needs.
  1. When these needs are not met, they become the major motivating force.
  2. In the developed nations of the world most persons have satisfied (or have the capacity to quickly satisfy) their physiological needs.

Abridged from "A Theory of Human Motivation," *Psychological Review*, 1943, *50*, 370–396. Photo courtesy of The Bettmann Archive.

    3. When these needs are continuously met they cease to exist as active determiners of behavior.

B. Safety needs come into play as physiological needs are met.

C. Love needs are the third category on the needs hierarchy.

    1. The thwarting of love and belongingness needs is the most commonly found core of maladjustment.

    2. The love need is not synonymous with sex.

D. Esteem or self-respect represents the fourth need in Maslow's hierarchy. This need has two subsidiary sets.

    1. The first is a need for achievement and adequacy.

    2. The second is a need for reputation or prestige.

E. The need for self-actualization is the fifth need in the hierarchy.

    1. Self-actualization is the need to become everything one is capable of becoming.

    2. Not much is known about these needs since their emergence depends on satisfaction of the other four categories of needs.

F. Certain conditions exist which are immediate prerequisites for the basic need satisfactions.

    1. Since these conditions are related to the basic needs, they must be defended.

    2. These conditions include freedom of action and freedom to defend one's self.

---

In a previous paper (10) various propositions were presented which would have to be included in any theory of human motivation that could lay claim to being definitive. These conclusions may be briefly summarized as follows:

1. The integrated wholeness of the organism must be one of the foundation stones of motivation theory.

2. The hunger drive (or any other physiological drive) was rejected as a centering point or model for a definitive theory of motivation. Any drive that is somatically based and localizable was shown to be atypical rather than typical in human motivation.

3. Such a theory should stress and center itself upon ultimate or basic goals rather than partial or superficial ones, upon ends rather than means to these ends. Such a stress would imply a more central place for unconscious than for conscious motivations.

4. There are usually available various cultural paths to the same goal. Therefore conscious, specific, local-cultural desires are not as fundamental in motivation theory as the more basic, unconscious goals.

5. Any motivated behavior, either preparatory or consummatory, must be understood to be a channel through which many basic needs may be simultaneously expressed or satisfied. Typically an act has *more* than one motivation.

6. Practically all organismic states are to be understood as motivated and as motivating.

7. Human needs arrange themselves in hierarchies of prepotency. That is to say, the appearance of one need usually rests on the prior satisfaction of another, more pre-potent need. Man is a perpetually wanting animal. Also no need or drive can be treated as if it were isolated or discrete; every drive is related to the state of satisfaction or dissatisfaction of other drives.

8. *Lists* of drives will get us nowhere for various theoretical and practical reasons. Furthermore any classification of motivations must deal with the problem of levels of specificity or generalization of the motives to be classified.

9. Classifications of motivations must be based upon goals rather than upon instigating drives or motivated behavior.

10. Motivation theory should be human-centered rather than animal-centered.

11. The situation or the field in which the organism reacts must be taken into account but the field alone can rarely serve as an exclusive explanation for behavior. Furthermore the field itself must be interpreted in terms of the organism. Field theory cannot be a substitute for motivation theory.

12. Not only the integration of the organism must be taken into account, but also the possibility of isolated, specific, partial or segmental reactions. It has become necessary to add to these another affirmation.

13. Motivation theory is not synonymous with behavior theory. The motivations are only one class of determinants of behavior. While behavior is almost always motivated, it is also almost always biologically, culturally and situationally determined as well.

The present paper is an attempt to formulate a positive theory of motivation which will satisfy these theoretical demands and at the same time conform to the known facts, clinical and observational as well as experimental. It derives most directly, however, from clinical experience. This theory is, I think, in the functionalist tradition of James and Dewey, and is fused with the holism of Wertheimer (14), Goldstein (4), and Gestalt Psychology, and with the dynamicism of Freud (2) and Adler (1). This fusion or synthesis may arbitrarily be called a 'general-dynamic' theory.

It is far easier to perceive and to criticize the aspects in motivation theory than to remedy them. Mostly this is because of the very serious lack of sound data in this area. I conceive this lack of sound facts to be due primarily to the absence of a valid theory of motivation. The present theory then must be considered to be a suggested program or framework for future research and must stand or fall, not so much on facts available or evidence presented, as upon researches yet to be done, researches suggested perhaps, by the questions raised in this paper.

## The Basic Needs

**The 'physiological' needs.**   The needs that are usually taken as the starting point for motivation theory are the so-called physiological drives. Two recent lines of research make it necessary to revise our customary notions about these needs, first, the development of the concept of homeostasis, and second, the finding that appetites (preferential choices among foods) are a fairly efficient indication of actual needs or lacks in the body.

Homeostasis refers to the body's automatic efforts to maintain a constant, normal state of the blood stream. Cannon (2) has described this process for (1) the water content of the blood, (2) salt content, (3) sugar content, (4) protein content, (5) fat content, (6) calcium content, (7) oxygen content, (8) constant hydrogen-ion level (acid-base balance) and (9) constant temperature of the blood. Obviously this list can be extended to include other minerals, the hormones, vitamins, etc.

Young (15) has summarized the work on appetite in its relation to body needs. If the body lacks some chemical, the individual will tend to develop a specific appetite or partial hunger for that food element.

Thus it seems impossible as well as useless to make any list of fundamental physiological needs for they can come to almost any number one might wish, depending on the degree of specificity of description. We can not identify all physiological needs as homeostatic. That sexual desire, sleepiness, sheer activity and maternal behavior in animals, are homeostatic, has not yet been demonstrated. Furthermore, this list would not include the various sensory pleasures (tastes, smells, tickling, stroking) which are probably physiological and which may become the goals of motivated behavior.

In a previous paper (10) it has been pointed out that these physiological drives or needs are to be considered unusual rather than typical because they are isolable, and because they are localizable somatically. That is to say, they are relatively independent of each other, of other motivations and of the organism as a whole, and secondly, in many cases, it is possible to demonstrate a localized, underlying somatic base for the drive. This is true less generally than has been thought (exceptions are fatigue, sleepiness, maternal responses) but it is still true in the classic instances of hunger, sex, and thirst.

It should be pointed out again that any of the physiological needs and the consummatory behavior involved with them serve as channels for all sorts of other needs as well. That is to say, the person who thinks he is hungry may actually be seeking more for comfort, or dependence, than for vitamins or proteins. Conversely, it is possible to satisfy the hunger need in part by other activities such as drinking water or smoking cigarettes. In other words, relatively isolable as these physiological needs are, they are not completely so.

Undoubtedly these physiological needs are the most prepotent of all needs. What this means specifically is, that in the human being who is missing everything in life in an extreme fashion, it is most likely that the major motivation would be the physiological needs rather than any others. A person who is lacking food, safety, love, and esteem would most probably hunger for food more strongly than for anything else.

If all the needs are unsatisfied, and the organism is then dominated by the physiological needs, all other needs may become simply nonexistent or be pushed into the background. It is then fair to characterize the whole organism by saying simply that it is hungry, for consciousness is almost completely preempted by hunger. All capacities are put into the service of hunger-satisfaction, and the organization of these capacities is almost entirely determined by the one purpose of satisfying hunger. The receptors and effectors, the intelligence, memory, habits, all may now be defined simply as hunger-gratifying tools. Capacities that are not useful for this purpose lie dormant, or are pushed into the background. The urge to write poetry, the desire to acquire an automobile, the interest in American history, the desire for a new pair of shoes are, in the extreme case, forgotten or become of secondary importance. For the man who is extremely and dangerously hungry, no other interests exist but food. He dreams food, he remembers food, he thinks about food, he emotes only about food, he perceives only food and he wants only food. The more subtle determinants that ordinarily fuse with the physiological drives in organizing even feeding, drinking or sexual behavior, may now be so completely overwhelmed as to allow us to speak at this time but *only* at this time) of pure hunger drive and behavior, with the one unqualified aim of relief.

Another peculiar characteristic of the human organism when it is dominated by a certain need is that the whole philosophy of the future tends also to change. For our chronically and extremely hungry man, Utopia can be defined very simply as a place where there is plenty of food. He tends to think that, if only he is guaranteed food for the rest of his life, he will be perfectly happy and will never want anything more. Life itself tends to be defined in terms of eating. Anything else will be defined as unimportant. Freedom, love, community feeling, respect, philosophy, may all be waved aside as fripperies which are useless since they fail to fill the stomach. Such a man may fairly be said to live by bread alone.

It cannot possibly be denied that such things are true but their *generality* can be denied. Emergency conditions are, almost by definition, rare in the normally functioning peaceful society. That this truism can be forgotten is due mainly to two reasons. First, rats have few motivations other than physiological ones, and since so much of the research upon motivation has been made with these animals, it is easy to carry the rat-picture over to the human being. Secondly, it is too often not realized that culture itself is an adaptive tool, one of whose main functions is to make the physiological emergencies come less and less often. In most of the known societies, chronic extreme hunger of the emergency type is rare, rather than common. In any case, this is still true in the United States. The average American citizen is experiencing appetite rather than hunger when he says "I am hungry." He is apt to experience sheer life-and-death hunger only by accident and then only a few times through his entire life.

Obviously a good way to obscure the 'higher' motivations, and to get a lopsided view of human capacities and human nature, is to make the organism extremely and chronically hungry or thirsty. Anyone who attempts to make an emergency picture into a typical one, and who will measure all of man's goals and desires by his behavior during extreme physiological deprivation is certainly being blind to many things. It is quite true that man lives by bread alone—when there is no bread. But what happens to man's desires when there *is* plenty of bread and when his belly is chronically filled?

*At once other* (*and 'higher'*) *needs emerge* and these, rather than physiological hungers, dominate the organism. And when these in turn are satisfied, again new (and still 'higher') needs emerge and so on. This is what we mean by saying that the basic human needs are organized into a hierarchy of relative prepotency.

One main implication of this phrasing is that gratification becomes as important a concept as deprivation in motivation theory, for it releases the organism from the domination of a relatively more physiological need, permitting thereby the emergence of other more social goals. The physiological needs, along with their partial goals, when chronically gratified cease to exist as active determinants or organizers of behavior. They now exist only in a potential fashion in the sense that they may emerge again to dominate the organism if they are thwarted. But a want that is satisfied is no longer a want. The organism is dominated and its behavior organized only by unsatisfied needs. If hunger is satisfied, it becomes unimportant in the current dynamics of the individual.

This statement is somewhat qualified by a hypothesis to be discussed more fully later, namely that it is precisely those individuals in whom a certain need has always been satisfied who are best equipped to tolerate deprivation of that need in the future, and that furthermore, those who have been deprived in the past will react differently to current satisfactions than the one who has never been deprived.

**The Safety Needs.**  If the physiological needs are relatively well gratified, there then emerges a new set of needs, which we may categorize roughly as the safety needs. All that has been said of the physiological needs is equally true, although in lesser degree, of these desires. The organism may equally well be wholly dominated by them. They may serve as the almost exclusive organizers of behavior, recruiting all the capacities of the organism in their service, and we may then fairly describe the whole organism as a safety-seeking mechanism. Again we may say of the receptors, the effectors, of the intellect and the other capacities that they are primarily safety-seeking tools. Again, as in the hungry man, we find that the dominating goal is a strong determinant not only of his current world-outlook and philosophy but also of his philosophy of the future. Practically everything looks less important than safety, (even sometimes the physiological needs which being satisfied, are now underestimated). A man, in this state, if it is extreme enough and chronic enough, may be characterized as living almost for safety alone.

Although in this paper we are interested primarily in the needs of the adult, we can approach an understanding of his safety needs perhaps more efficiently by observation of infants and children, in whom these needs are much more simple and obvious. One reason for the clearer appearance of the threat or danger reaction in infants is that they do not inhibit this reaction at all, whereas adults in our society have been taught to inhibit it at all costs. Thus even when adults do feel their safety to be threatened we may not be able to see this on the surface. Infants will react in a total fashion and as if they were endangered, if they are disturbed or dropped suddenly, startled by loud noises, flashing light, or other unusual sensory stimulation, by rough handling, by general loss of support in the mother's arms, or by inadequate support.[1]

In infants we can also see a much more direct reaction to bodily illnesses of various kinds. Sometimes these illnesses seem to be immediately and *per se* threatening and seem to make the child feel unsafe. For instance, vomiting, colic or other sharp pains seem to make the child look at the whole world in a different way. At such a moment of pain, it may be postulated that, for the child, the appearance of the whole world suddenly changes from sunniness to darkness, so to speak, and becomes a place in which anything at all might happen, in which previously stable things have suddenly become unstable. Thus a child who because of some bad food is taken ill may, for a day or two, develop fear, nightmares, and a need for protection and reassurance never seen in him before his illness.

Another indication of the child's need for safety is his preference for some kind of undisrupted routine or rhythm. He seems to want a predictable, orderly world. For instance, injustice, unfairness, or inconsistency in the parents seems to make a child feel anxious and unsafe. This attitude may be not so much because of the injustice *per se* or any particular pains involved, but rather because this treatment threatens to make the world look unreliable, or unsafe, or unpredictable. Young children seem to thrive better under a system which has at least a skeletal outline of rigidity, in which there is a schedule of a kind, some sort of routine, something that can be counted upon, not only for the present but also far into the future. Perhaps one could express this more accurately by saying that the child needs an organized world rather than an unorganized or unstructured one.

The central role of the parents and the normal family setup are indisputable. Quarreling, physical assault, separation, divorce or death within the family may be particularly terrifying. Also parental outbursts of rage or threats of punishment directed to the child, calling him names, speaking to him harshly, shaking him, handling him roughly, or actual physical punishment sometimes elicit such total panic and terror in the child that we must assume more is involved than the physical pain alone. While it is true that in some children this terror may represent also a fear of loss of parental love, it can also occur in completely rejected children, who seem to cling to the hating parents more for sheer safety and protection than because of hope of love.

Confronting the average child with new, unfamiliar, strange, unmanageable stimuli or situations will too frequently elicit the danger or terror reaction, as for example, getting lost or even being separated from the parents for a short time, being confronted with new faces, new situations or new tasks, the sight of strange, unfamiliar or uncontrollable objects, illness or death. Particularly at such times, the child's frantic clinging to his parents is eloquent testimony to their role as protectors (quite apart from their roles as food-givers and love-givers).

From these and similar observations, we may generalize and say that the average child in our society generally prefers a safe, orderly, predictable, organized world, which he can count on, and in which unexpected, unmanageable or other dangerous things do not happen, and in which, in any case, he has all-powerful parents who protect and shield him from harm.

That these reactions may so easily be observed in children is in a way a proof of the fact that children in our society feel too unsafe (or, in a word, are badly brought up). Children who are reared in an unthreatening, loving family do *not* ordinarily react as we have described above (13). In such children the danger reactions are apt to come mostly to objects or situations that adults too would consider dangerous.[2]

The healthy, normal, fortunate adult in our culture is largely satisfied in his safety needs. The peaceful, smoothly running, 'good' society ordinarily makes its members feel safe enough from wild animals, extremes of temperature, criminals, assault and murder, tyranny, etc. Therefore, in a very real sense, he no longer has any safety needs as active motivators. Just as a sated man no longer feels hungry, a safe man no longer feels endangered. If we wish to see these needs directly and clearly we must turn to neurotic or near-neurotic individuals, and to the economic and social underdogs. In between these extremes, we can perceive the expressions of safety needs only in such phenomena as, for instance, the common preference for a job with tenure and protection, the desire for a savings account, and for insurance of various kinds (medical, dental, unemployment, disability, old age).

Other broader aspects of the attempt to seek safety and stability in the world are seen in the very common preference for familiar rather than unfamiliar things, or for the known rather than the unknown. The tendency to have some religion or world-philosophy that organizes the universe and the men in it into some sort of satisfactorily coherent, meaningful whole is also in part motivated by safety-seeking. Here too we may list science and philosophy in general as partially motivated by the safety needs (we shall see later that there are also other motivations to scientific, philosophical or religious endeavor).

Otherwise the need for safety is seen as an active and dominant mobilizer of the organism's resources only in emergencies, *e.g.*, war, disease, natural catastrophes, crime waves, societal disorganization, neurosis, brain injury, chronically bad situation.

Some neurotic adults in our society are, in many ways, like the unsafe child in their desire for safety, although in the former it takes on a somewhat special appearance. Their reaction is often to unknown, psychological dangers in a world that is perceived to be hostile, overwhelming and threatening. Such a person behaves as if a great catastrophe were almost always impending, *i.e.*, he is usually responding as if to an emergency. His safety needs often find specific expression in a search for a protector, or a stronger person on whom he may depend, or perhaps, a Fuehrer.

The neurotic individual may be described in a slightly different way with some usefulness as a grown-up person who retains his childish attitudes toward the world. That is to say, a neurotic adult may be said to behave 'as if' he were actually afraid of a spanking, or of his mother's disapproval, or of being abandoned by his parents, or having his food taken away from him. It is as if his childish attitudes of fear and threat reaction to a dangerous world had gone underground, and untouched by the growing up and learning processes, were now ready to be called out by any stimulus that would make a child feel endangered and threatened.[3]

The neurosis in which the search for safety takes its clearest form is in the compulsive-obsessive neurosis. Compulsive-obsessives try frantically to order and stabilize the world so that no unmanageable, unexpected or unfamiliar dangers will ever appear (11). They hedge themselves about with all sorts of ceremonials, rules and formulas so that every possible contingency may be provided for and so that no new contingencies may appear. They are much like the brain injured cases, described by Goldstein (4), who manage to maintain their equilibrium by avoiding everything unfamiliar and strange and by ordering their restricted world in such a neat, disciplined, orderly fashion that everything in the world can be counted upon. They try to arrange the world so that anything unexpected (dangers) cannot possibly occur. If, through no fault of their own, something unexpected does occur, they go into a panic reaction as if this unexpected occurrence constituted a grave danger. What we can see only as a none-too-strong preference in the healthy person, *e.g.,* preference for the familiar, becomes a life-and-death necessity in abnormal cases.

**The Love Needs.**   If both the physiological and the safety needs are fairly well gratified, then there will emerge the love and affection and belongingness needs, and the whole cycle already described will repeat itself with this new center. Now the person will feel keenly, as never before, the absence of friends, or a sweetheart, or a wife, or children. He will hunger for affectionate relations with people in general, namely, for a place in his group, and he will strive with great intensity to achieve this goal. He will want to attain such a place more than anything else in the world and may even forget that once, when he was hungry, he sneered at love.

In our society the thwarting of these needs is the most commonly found core in cases of maladjustment and more severe psychopathology. Love and affection, as well as their possible expression in sexuality, are generally looked upon with ambivalence and are customarily hedged about with many restrictions and inhibitions. Practically all theorists of psychopathology have stressed thwarting of the love needs as basic in the picture of maladjustment. Many clinical studies have therefore been made of this need and we know more about it perhaps than any of the other needs except the physiological ones (11).

One thing that must be stressed at this point is that love is not synonymous with sex. Sex may be studied as a purely physiological need. Ordinarily sexual behavior is multi-determined, that is to say, determined not only by sexual but also by other needs, chief among which are the love and affection needs. Also not to be overlooked is the fact that the love needs involve both giving *and* receiving love.[4]

**The Esteem Needs.**   All people in our society (with a few pathological exceptions) have a need or desire for a stable, firmly based, (usually) high evaluation of themselves, for self-respect, or self-esteem, and for the esteem of others. By firmly based self-esteem, we mean that which is soundly based upon real capacity, achievement and respect from others. These needs may be classified into two subsidiary sets. These are, first, the desire for strength, for achievement, for adequacy, for confidence in the face of the world, and for independence and freedom.[5] Secondly, we have what we may call the desire for reputation or prestige (defining it as respect or esteem from other people), recognition, attention, importance or appreciation.[6] These needs have been relatively stressed by Alfred Adler and his followers, and have been relatively neglected by Freud and the psychoanalysts. More and more today however there is appearing widespread appreciation of their central importance.

Satisfaction of the self-esteem need leads to feelings of self-confidence, worth, strength, capability and adequacy of being useful and necessary in the world. But thwarting of these needs produces feelings of inferiority, of weakness and of helplessness. These feelings in turn give rise to either basic discouragement or else compensatory or neurotic trends. An appreciation of the necessity of basic self-confidence and an understanding of how helpless people are without it, can be easily gained from a study of severe traumatic neurosis (5).[7]

**The Need for Self-Actualization.**     Even if all these needs are satisfied, we may still often (if not always) expect that a new discontent and restlessness will soon develop, unless the individual is doing what he is fitted for. A musician must make music, an artist must paint, a poet must write, if he is to be ultimately happy. What a man *can* be, he *must* be. This need we may call self-actualization.

This term, first coined by Kurt Goldstein, is being used in this paper in a much more specific and limited fashion. It refers to the desire for self-fulfillment, namely, to the tendency for him to become actualized in what he is potentially. This tendency might be phrased as the desire to become more and more what one is, to become everything that one is capable of becoming.

The specific form that these needs will take will of course vary greatly from person to person. In one individual it may take the form of the desire to be an ideal mother, in another it may be expressed athletically, and in still another it may be expressed in painting pictures or in inventions. It is not necessarily a creative urge although in people who have any capacities for creation it will take this form.

The clear emergence of these needs rests upon prior satisfaction of the physiological, safety, love and esteem needs. We shall call people who are satisfied in these needs, basically satisfied people, and it is from these that we may expect the fullest (and healthiest) creativeness.[8] Since, in our society, basically satisfied people are the exception, we do not know much about self-actualization, either experimentally or clinically. It remains a challenging problem for research.

**The Preconditions for the Basic Need Satisfactions.**     There are certain conditions which are immediate prerequisites for the basic need satisfactions. Danger to these is reacted to almost as if it were a direct danger to the basic needs themselves. Such conditions as freedom to speak, freedom to do what one wishes so long as no harm is done to others, freedom to express one's self, freedom to investigate and seek for information, freedom to defend one's self, justice, fairness, honesty, orderliness in the group are examples of such preconditions for basic need satisfactions. Thwarting in these freedoms will be reacted to with a threat or emergency response. These conditions are not ends in themselves but they are *almost* so since they are so closely related to the basic needs, which are apparently the only ends in themselves. These conditions are defended because without them the basic satisfactions are quite impossible, or at least, very severely endangered.

*   *   *

## Further Characteristics of the Basic Needs

**The Degree of Fixity of the Hierarchy of Basic Needs.**   We have spoken so far as if this hierarchy were a fixed order but actually it is not nearly as rigid as we may have implied. It is true that most of the people with whom we have worked have seemed to have these basic needs in about the order that has been indicated. However, there have been a number of exceptions.

(1) There are some people in whom, for instance, self-esteem seems to be more important than love. This most common reversal in the hierarchy is usually due to the development of the notion that the person who is most likely to be loved is a strong or powerful person, one who inspires respect or fear, and who is self confident or aggressive. Therefore such people who lack love and seek it, may try hard to put on a front of aggressive, confident behavior. But essentially they seek high self-esteem and its behavior expressions more as a means-to-an-end than for its own sake; they seek self-assertion for the sake of love rather than for self-esteem itself.

(2) There are other, apparently innately creative people in whom the drive to creativeness seems to be more important than any other counter-determinant. Their creativeness might appear not as self-actualization released by basic satisfaction, but in spite of lack of basic satisfaction.

(3) In certain people the level of aspiration may be permanently deadened or lowered. That is to say, the less prepotent goals may simply be lost, and may disappear forever, so that the person who has experienced life at a very low level, *i.e.*, chronic unemployment, may continue to be satisfied for the rest of his life if only he can get enough food.

(4) The so-called 'psychopathic personality' is another example of permanent loss of the love needs. These are people who, according to the best data available (6), have been starved for love in the earliest months of their lives and have simply lost forever the desire and the ability to give and to receive affection (as animals lose sucking or pecking reflexes that are not exercised soon enough after birth).

(5) Another cause of reversal of the hierarchy is that when a need has been satisfied for a long time, this need may be underevaluated. People who have never experienced chronic hunger are apt to underestimate its effects and to look upon food as a rather unimportant thing . . .

(6) Another partial explanation of *apparent* reversals is seen in the fact that we have been talking about the hierarchy of prepotency in terms of consciously

felt wants or desires rather than of behavior. Looking at behavior itself may give us the wrong impression. What we have claimed is that the person will *want* the more basic of two needs when deprived in both. There is no necessary implication here that he will act upon his desires. Let us say again that there are many determinants of behavior other than the needs and desires.

(7) Perhaps more important than all these exceptions are the ones that involve ideals, high social standards, high values and the like. With such values people become martyrs; they will give up everything for the sake of a particular ideal, or value. These people may be understood, at least in part, by reference to one basic concept (or hypothesis) which may be called 'increased frustration-tolerance through early gratification.' People who have been satisfied in their basic needs throughout their lives, particularly in their earlier years, seem to develop exceptional power to withstand present or future thwarting of these needs simply because they have strong, healthy character structure as a result of basic satisfaction. They are the 'strong' people who can easily weather disagreement or opposition, who can swim against the stream of public opinion and who can stand up for the truth at great personal cost. It is just the ones who have loved and been well loved, and who have had many deep friendships who can hold out against hatred, rejection or persecution . . .

*  *  *

**Degrees of Relative Satisfaction.**   So far, our theoretical discussion may have given the impression that these five sets of needs are somehow in a step-wise, all-or-none relationships to each other. We have spoken in such terms as the following: "If one need is satisfied, then another emerges." This statement might give the false impression that a need must be satisfied 100 percent before the next need emerges. In actual fact, most members of our society who are normal, are partially satisfied in all their basic needs and partially unsatisfied in all their basic needs at the same time. A more realistic description of the hierarchy would be in terms of decreasing percentages of satisfaction as we go up the hierarchy of prepotency. For instance, if I may assign arbitrary figures for the sake of illustration, it is as if the average citizen is satisfied perhaps 85 percent in his physiological needs, 70 percent in his safety needs, 50 percent in his love needs, 40 percent in his self-esteem needs, and 10 percent in his self-actualization needs . . .

*  *  *

**Cultural Specificity and Generality of Needs.**   This classification of basic needs makes some attempt to take account of the relative unity behind the superficial differences in specific desires from one culture to another. Certainly in any particular culture an individual's conscious motivational content will usually be extremely different from the conscious motivational content of an individual in another society. However, it is the common experience of anthropologists that people, even in different societies, are much more alike than we would think from our first contact with them, and that as we know them better we seem to find more and more of this commonness. We then recognize the most startling differences to be superficial rather than basic, *e.g.*, differences in style of hairdress, clothes, tastes in food, etc. Our classification of basic needs is in part an attempt to account for this unity behind the apparent diversity from culture to culture. No claim is made that it is ultimate or universal for all cultures. The claim is made only that it is relatively *more* ultimate, more universal, more basic, than the superficial conscious desires from culture to culture, and makes a somewhat closer approach to common-human characteristics. Basic needs are *more* common-human than superficial desires or behaviors . . .

\* \* \*

**Animal- and Human-Centering.**   This theory starts with the human being rather than any lower and presumably 'simpler' animal. Too many of the findings that have been made in animals have been proven to be true for animals but not for the human being. There is no reason whatsoever why we should start with animals in order to study human motivation . . .

\* \* \*

**Motivation and the Theory of Psychopathogenesis.**   The conscious motivational content of everyday life has, according to the foregoing, been conceived to be relatively important or unimportant accordingly as it is more or less closely related to the basic goals. A desire for an ice cream cone might actually be an indirect expression of a desire for love. If it is, then this desire for the ice cream cone becomes extremely important motivation. If however the ice cream is simply something to cool the mouth with, or a casual appetitive reaction, then the desire is relatively unimportant. Everyday conscious desires are to be regarded as symptoms, as *surface indicators of more basic needs.* If we were to take these superficial desires at their face value we would find ourselves in a state of complete confusion which could never be resolved, since we would be dealing seriously with symptoms rather than with what lay behind the symptoms.

Thwarting of unimportant desires produces no psychopathological results; thwarting of a basically important need does produce such results. Any theory of psychopathogenesis must then be based on a sound theory of motivation. A conflict or a frustration is not necessarily pathogenic. It becomes so only when it threatens or thwarts the basic needs, or partial needs that are closely related to the basic needs (7) . . .

\* \* \*

. . . [A] man who is thwarted in any of his basic needs may fairly be envisaged simply as a sick man. This is a fair parallel to our designation as 'sick' of the man who lacks vitamins or minerals. Who is to say that a lack of love is less important than a lack of vitamins?

\* \* \*

## Summary

(1) There are at least five sets of goals, which we may call basic needs. These are briefly physiological, safety, love, esteem, and self-actualization. In addition, we are motivated by the desire to achieve or maintain the various conditions upon which these basic satisfactions rest and by certain more intellectual desires.

(2) These basic goals are related to each other, being arranged in a hierarchy of prepotency. This means that the most prepotent goal will monopolize consciousness and will tend of itself to organize the recruitment of the various capacities of the organism. The less prepotent needs are minimized, even forgotten or denied. But when a need is fairly well satisfied, the next prepotent ('higher') need emerges, in turn to dominate the conscious life and to serve as the center of organization of behavior, since gratified needs are not active motivators.

Thus man is a perpetually wanting animal. Ordinarily the satisfaction of these wants is not altogether mutually exclusive, but only tends to be. The average member of our society is most often partially satisfied and partially unsatisfied in all of his wants. The hierarchy principle is usually empirically observed in terms of increasing percentages of nonsatisfaction as we go up the hierarchy. Reversals of the average order of the hierarchy are sometimes observed. Also it has been observed that an individual may permanently lose the higher wants in the hierarchy under special conditions. There are not only ordinarily multiple motivations for usual behavior, but in addition many determinants other than motives.

(3) Any thwarting or possibility of thwarting of these basic human goals, or danger to the defenses which protect them, or to the conditions upon which they rest, is considered to be a psychological threat. With a few exceptions, all psychopathology may be partially traced to such threats. A basically thwarted man may actually be defined as a 'sick' man, if we wish.

(4) It is such basic threats which bring about the general emergency reactions.

(5) Certain other basic problems have not been dealt with because of limitations of space. . . .

## FOOTNOTES

1. As the child grows up, sheer knowledge and familiarity as well as better motor development make these 'dangers' less and less dangerous and more and more manageable. Throughout life it may be said that one of the main conative functions of education is this neutralizing of apparent dangers through knowledge, *e.g.*, I am not afraid of thunder because I know something about it.

2. A 'test battery' for safety might be confronting the child with a small exploding firecracker, or with a bewhiskered face, having the mother leave the room, putting him upon a high ladder, a hypodermic infection, having a mouse crawl up to him, etc. Of course I cannot seriously recommend the deliberate use of such 'tests' for they might very well harm the child being tested. But these and similar situations come up by the score in the child's ordinary day-to-day living and may be observed. There is no reason why these stimuli should not be used with, for example, young chimpanzees.

3.  Not all neurotic individuals feel unsafe. Neurosis may have at its core a thwarting of the affection and esteem needs in a person who is generally safe.

4.  For further details see (9) and (12, Chap. 5).

5.  Whether or not this particular desire is universal we do not know. The crucial question, especially important today, is "Will men who are enslaved and dominated, inevitably feel dissatisfied and rebellious?" We may assume on the basis of commonly known clinical data that a man who has known true freedom (not paid for by giving up safety and security but rather built on the basis of adequate safety and security) will not willingly or easily allow his freedom to be taken away from him. But we do not know that this is true for the person born into slavery. The events of the next decade should give us our answer. See discussion of this problem in (3).

6.  Perhaps the desire for prestige and respect from others is subsidiary to the desire for self-esteem or confidence in oneself. Observation of children seems to indicate that this is so, but clinical data give no clear support for such a conclusion.

7.  For more extensive discussion of normal self-esteem, as well as for reports of various researches, see (8).

8.  Clearly creative behavior, like painting, is like any other behavior in having multiple determinants. It may be seen in 'innately creative' people whether they are satisfied or not, happy or unhappy, hungry or sated. Also it is clear that creative activity may be compensatory, ameliorative or purely economic. It is my impression (as yet unconfirmed) that it is possible to distinguish the artistic and intellectual products of basically satisfied people from those of basically unsatisfied people by inspection alone. In any case, here too we must distinguish, in a dynamic fashion, the overt behavior itself from its various motivations or purposes.

# REFERENCES

1.  Adler, A. *Social interest.* London: Faber & Faber, 1938.

2.  Freud, S. *New introductory lectures on psychoanalysis.* New York: Norton, 1933.

3.  Fromm, E. *Escape from freedom.* New York: Farrar and Rinehart, 1941.

4.  Goldstein, K. *The organism.* New York: American Book Co., 1939.

5.  Kardiner, A. *The traumatic neuroses of war.* New York: Hoeber, 1941.

6.  Levy, D. M. Primary affect hunger. *Amer. J. Psychiat.,* 1937, *94,* 643–652.

7.  Maslow, A. H. Conflict, frustration, and the theory of threat. *J. abnorm. (soc.) Psychol.,* 1943, *38,* 81–86.

8.  _____ . Dominance, personality and social behavior in women. *J. soc. Psychol.,* 1939, *10,* 3–39.

9.  _____ . The dynamics of psychological security-insecurity. *Character & Pers.,* 1942, *10,* 331–344.

10. _____ . A preface to motivation theory. *Psychosomatic Med.,* 1943, *5,* 85–92.

11. _____ , & Mittelmann, B. *Principles of abnormal psychology.* New York: Harper & Bros., 1941.

12. Plant, J. *Personality and the cultural pattern.* New York: Commonwealth Fund, 1937.

13. Shirley, M. Children's adjustments to a strange situation. *J. abnorm. (soc.) Psychol.,* 1942, *37,* 201–217.

14. Wertheimer, M. Unpublished lectures at the New School for Social Research.

15. Young, P. T. The experimental analysis of appetite. *Psychol. Bull.,* 1941, *38,* 129–164.

## Learning Review

Questions:

1.  The basic human needs are organized in a _____.

2.  The five categories in Maslow's needs hierarchy are _____, _____, _____, _____, and _____.

3.  Maslow points out that a _____ _____ is no longer a motivator.

Answers:

1. hierarchy 2. physiological, safety, love (belongingness), esteem, self-actualization 3. satisfied need

# *Retrospective Comment*

♦

## BY DONALD D. BOWEN *

Perhaps the single most influential theory of motivation during the 1950's and 1960's was Maslow's concept of the need hierarchy originally formulated in the article reprinted here. Maslow influenced not only behavioral scientists studying organizations (e.g., see McGregor's formulation of "Theory X" and "Theory Y" also reprinted in this volume), but also the practitioners of management. Both academics and managers were attracted by Maslow's argument because of the humanistic and optimistic view of human nature it suggested.

The solid research evidence for the hierarchical arrangement of needs has always been extremely slim. Hall and Nougaim[1] failed to confirm the theory in a study of managers at AT&T. Lawler and Suttle[2] found some evidence for a two-step hierarchy (security needs must be satisfied before others become active), and Alderfer[3] has propounded an intriguing revision of Maslow's theory (ERG theory, for *E*xistence, *R*elatedness, and *G*rowth) for which he provides impressive data.

Maslow's approach to research was always clinical rather than experimental and statistical. Criticized frequently for his aversion to more traditional research approaches, Maslow said, shortly before his death, that if his critics did not feel that his approach was adequately "scientific", then he was content to call his work "pre-science" to indicate that he was more interested in developing new ideas than in carefully verifying them.

Maslow's work continues to be influential, particularly among managers who may be less aware of the shaky empirical backing for need hierarchy theory. More recent theories of human nature[4] seem to take a more balanced view of human nature, seeing us as being both capable of good and altruistic behavior in some instances and also of selfish, mean and shortsighted actions under other conditions. Contingency theories of leadership (see Fiedler's article) and organization structure (see Lorsch's piece) assume that human needs and behavior vary from situation to situation, and thus are more consistent with the newer theories than with Maslow's view.

---

\* Professor of Management, University of Tulsa.

# REFERENCES

1.  Hall, D. T., & Nougaim, K. E., An examination of Maslow's need hierarchy in an organizational setting. *Organizational Behavior and Human Performance,* 1968, *3,* 12–35.
2.  Lawler, E. E., & Suttle, J. L., A causal correlation test of the need hierarchy concept. *Organizational Behavior and Human Performance,* 1972, *7,* 265–287.
3.  Alderfer, C. P., *Existence, relatedness, and growth: Human needs in organizational settings.* New York: Free Press, 1972.
4.  Schein, E. H., *Organizational psychology* (2nd ed.) Englewood Cliffs, N.J.: Prentice-Hall, 1970.

# Part 3
# THE PARADIGM
# CREATORS

◆

The second half of the decade of the 1950's saw the appearance of a series of books and articles that were to determine the fundamental direction of the study of organizations and management for many years to come. At no time before or since have both managers and academicians both been so thoroughly influenced by a handful of theorists.

Peter Drucker, an economist and one-time journalist, was first on the scene with his *The Practice of Management* (Drucker, 1954). Drucker's lively style as well as his provocative iconoclasm gained a widespread audience. He raised numerous issues about the goal-setting and planning processes of the organization (see the selection which follows), and about accepted practices in organizing work according to the principles of "scientific management." He also introduced the concept of "Management by Objectives."

Shortly after the appearance of Drucker's book, Douglas McGregor developed two of the most widely-known concepts in the entire literature—his famous "Theory X" and "Theory Y". First articulated in 1957, McGregor based his approach in Maslow's theory of motivation. McGregor argues that a theory of management and organization must reflect and be consistent with basic assumptions about human nature. If an optimistic view of humanity is more realistic, a more humanistic managerial strategy such as Theory Y must follow.

At almost the same time, a young psychologist at Yale University, Chris Argyris, developed a careful review of the psychological literature on the developmental trends in human personality. Argyris showed (as in the brief piece which is reprinted here), that if standard management principles of the day were followed as prescribed by management writers, there would be a fundamental incompatibility between the natural self-actualizing propensities of the adult personality and the constraints of organization imposed by management.

Other investigators also pressed home the attack on previously accepted views of management—the concepts which McGregor had labeled Theory X. Herzberg and his collaborators (1959) argued that extrinsic rewards (e.g., pay, promotion, working conditions, etc.) could never create real work motivation. Their initial study (and many follow-ups) sparked a debate among motivation theorists which rages from time-to-time, even today. Even those who question the validity of Herzberg's findings, however, recognize that his theory led him to develop a major management innovation, the concept of "job enrichment."

While Herzberg questioned the motivational capacity of most rewards organizations offer for productivity, Rensis Likert (1961) published an extensive review of years of investigation of job satisfaction and productivity at the University of Michigan. Likert felt that a "new pattern" was apparent in the findings—a pattern of supervision which was more people-oriented and humane, and which emphasized democracy, participation and supportiveness in its leadership style. Likert concluded that such a style would create *both* higher productivity and higher job satisfaction.

James G. March and Herbert A. Simon, both at Carnegie Institute of Technology at the time, developed a somewhat different (but also highly influential) analysis in their book *Organizations* (1958). An extensive review of the organizational literature in psychology, sociology, economics and political science, *Organizations* focuses on decision-making processes in organizations. March and Simon develop an impressive case for a more realistic view of both people and organizations as decision-makers than was available in the classic description of how managers decide. Both the psychological characteristics of human beings and the political realities of groups and organizations must be considered in our theories of decision-making, they argue.

Toward the end of the decade of the 1950's, one further important development emerged. McGregor, Argyris, Likert, and other early contributors are often interpreted as advocating a single, employee-centered, participative style of management for all organizations and under all conditions. Such an interpretation is a drastic over-simplification of the views of these authors. It is true, however, that situational variations in the requirements of management and organization were not the central focus of their prescriptions. In 1958, Tannenbaum and Schmidt wrote their famous piece for the *Harvard Business Review* on "How to Choose a Leadership Pattern". The basic thrust of the article is that a manager has choices to make in deciding how to influence a subordinate, and the best choice depends on the personality of the subordinate and the situation that the manager faces. With the appearance of this article the perspective of *contingency theory,* the dominant theme in management and organizational theory for the next twenty years, was introduced.

Contingency theory basically argues that there is no one right way to manage. The manager must develop a reward system, a leadership style, or an organizational structure to be appropriate for the unique combination of such factors as the nature of the subordinates, the technology of the business and the tasks that result, the rate of change in the organization, the degree of integration of functions required, the amount of time that the manager has to accomplish an assignment, the quality of the manager's relationship with subordinates, and so forth. Tannenbaum and Schmidt introduced this idea as it applies to leadership in the article reproduced in this section. Burns and Stalker developed a contingency view of organization which appeared in their 1961 book, *Management of Innovation.* They argue that the type of impersonal, authoritarian, hierarchical organization advocated by Weber, Taylor, and other early management writers may be appropriate for relatively stable types of organizations where there is little need for change—"mechanistic systems", in their words. For organizations that must change and adapt rather quickly, "organic systems" are more appropriate.

In a series of books and articles beginning in 1967, Paul Lawrence and Jay Lorsch of Harvard (here represented by an overview of their basic ideas authored by Lorsch) developed, extended, and popularized the ideas that began in Burns and Stalker.

By 1960, the fledgling disciplines of organizational behavior, organizational theory, management theory and their many subdisciplines were all the subjects of considerable study and research. As publications of new findings and perspectives began to mount, it became increasingly difficult to keep one's place and make sense out of the "bloomin', buzzin' confusion" of findings, viewpoints, and positions. Responding to the exploding literature of the late 1950's the late Professor Harold Koontz made one attempt at imposing order on the field in his "The Management Theory Jungle" (1961). Professor Koontz had been a pioneer of the managerial functions or process school of thought which developed most directly from the work of Fayol and a number of subsequent writers. Twenty years later, shortly before his death, Koontz took a second shot at the task. In an article prepared specifically for the first edition of this book he observed that an overview of the field indicated a continuing trend toward proliferation of schools of thought, rather than a tendency to focus on integration of knowledge. Both versions are included for your enjoyment.

# REFERENCES

Burns, T. & Stalker, G. M. *The Management of Innovation.* London: Tavistock Publications, 1961.

Drucker, P. F. *The Practice of Management.* New York: Harper, 1954.

Herzberg, F. Mausner, B. & Snyderman, B. *The Motivation to Work.* (2nd ed.). New York: Wiley, 1959.

Lawrence, P. R. & Lorsch, J. W. *Organization and Environment.* Boston: Graduate School of Business Administration, Harvard University, 1967.

Likert, R. *New Patterns of Management.* New York: McGraw Hill, 1961.

March, J. G. & Simon, H. A. *Organizations.* New York: Wiley, 1958.

# 9

# *The Human Side of Enterprise*

## DOUGLAS M. McGREGOR

### *About the Author*

**DOUGLAS M. McGREGOR** rose from service station attendant in 1928 to president of Antioch College in 1948. His A.B. was from Wayne University and his Ph.D. was awarded by Harvard University in 1935. McGregor's teaching spanned the disciplines of psychology and industrial management. He taught at Harvard, MIT, and Antioch. His concepts of Theory X and Theory Y and his contributions to the new field of organization development (OD) made him the best known among managers of all behavioral theorists until his untimely death in 1964.

# PREVIEW

A. Theory X is a set of propositions of the conventional view of management's task in harnessing human energy to organizational requirements.

    1. It is management's responsibility to organize the elements of productive enterprise—money, materials, equipment, people—in the interest of economic ends.

Reprinted by permission of the publisher from *Management Review,* November 1957 © 1957 by the American Management Association, Inc. All rights reserved. Photo courtesy of The MIT Museum.

2. To fit the needs of the organization, the behavior of people must be directed, motivated, controlled and modified or else they would be passive.
3. Additional beliefs behind this conventional view show the worker to be indolent by nature, lacking ambition, inherently self-centered, resistant to changes, and gullible.
4. To accomplish its task, management uses these assumptions as guidelines and ranges its possibilities between "hard" or "strong" and "soft" or "weak" approaches.
5. Since difficulties exist between the hard and soft approach, the current view is "firm but fair."

B. Although social scientists do not deny that the worker's behavior is similar to what the management perceives, they feel that this behavior is not a consequence of the worker's inherent nature, but rather the result of the nature of industrial organizations, of management philosophy, policy, and practice.

C. The subject of motivation is supposedly the best way of indicating the inadequacy of the conventional concepts of management.
1. At the lowest level in the hierarchy of individual needs are the *physiological needs.*
2. The next higher level of needs are called *safety needs.*
3. When the worker's physiological needs and safety needs are satisfied, his other behavior is motivated by *social needs.*
4. Above the social needs are two kinds of *egoistic needs;* (a) those that relate one's *self-esteem,* and (b) those that relate to one's *reputation.* Unlike the lower needs, these are rarely satisfied.
5. Finally, there are needs for *self-fulfillment.*

D. Just as deprivation of physiological needs has behavioral consequences, the same is true for higher level needs.

E. In the carrot-and-stick approach, management can provide or withhold the means for satisfying the worker's physiological and safety needs.
1. But today the philosophy of management by direction and control is inadequate to motivate, because the human needs under the carrot-and-stick approach are important motivators of behavior.

F. Theory Y is based on more adequate assumptions about human nature and human motivation and therefore has broader dimensions.
1. Responsibility lies with management for organizing the elements of productive enterprise in the interest of economic ends.
2. People have become passive or resistant to organizational needs because of their experience in organizations.
3. Management should enable people to recognize and develop motivational characteristics.
4. By arranging organizational conditions and methods of operation, management's task is to allow people to achieve their own goals by directing their own best efforts towards organizational objectives.
5. Peter Drucker calls this process "management by objectives" in contrast to management by control.

G. The major difference associated with these theories is that Theory X places exclusive reliance upon external control of human behavior, while Theory Y relies heavily on self-control and self-direction.
H. The ideas associated with Theory Y are being applied slowly but with success.
   1. Sears, Roebuck and Company is an example where decentralization in the organization and delegation of duties is consistent with what the theory proposes.
   2. IBM and Detroit Edison are pioneers in job enlargement.
   3. The Scanlon Plan illustrates the ideas of participative and consultative management.
   4. Most conventional programs of performance appraisal within management ranks reveal consistency with Theory X, although a few companies are taking steps in the direction of Theory Y.
I. Until full implementation of Theory Y is successful, only management that has confidence in human capacities and is itself directed towards organizational objectives rather than towards the preservation of personal power can grasp its implications.

---

It has become trite to say that industry has the fundamental know-how to utilize physical science and technology for the material benefit of mankind, and that we must now learn how to utilize the social sciences to make our human organizations truly effective.

To a degree, the social sciences today are in a position like that of the physical sciences with respect to atomic energy in the thirties. We know that past conceptions of the nature of man are inadequate and, in many ways, incorrect. We are becoming quite certain that under proper conditions, unimagined resources of creative human energy could become available within the organizational setting.

We cannot tell industrial management how to apply this new knowledge in simple, economic ways. We know it will require years of exploration, much costly development research, and a substantial amount of creative imagination on the part of management to discover how to apply this growing knowledge to the organization of human effort in industry.

## Management's Task: The Conventional View

The conventional conception of management's task in harnessing human energy to organizational requirements can be stated broadly in terms of three propositions. In order to avoid the complications introduced by a label, let us call this set of propositions "Theory X":

1. Management is responsible for organizing the elements of productive enterprise—money, materials, equipment, people—in the interest of economic ends.
2. With respect to people, this is a process of directing their efforts, motivating

them, controlling their actions, modifying their behavior to fit the needs of the organization.

3. Without this active intervention by management, people would be passive—even resistant—to organizational needs. They must therefore be persuaded, rewarded, punished, controlled—their activities must be directed. This is management's task. We often sum it up by saying that management consists of getting things done through other people.

Behind this conventional theory there are several additional beliefs—less explicit, but widespread:

4. The average man is by nature indolent—he works as little as possible.

5. He lacks ambition, dislikes responsibility, prefers to be led.

6. He is inherently self-centered, indifferent to organizational needs.

7. He is by nature resistant to change.

8. He is gullible, not very bright, the ready dupe of the charlatan and the demagogue.

The human side of economic enterprise today is fashioned from propositions and beliefs such as these. Conventional organization structures and managerial policies, practices, and programs reflect these assumptions.

In accomplishing its task—with these assumptions as guides—management has conceived of a range of possibilities.

At one extreme, management can be "hard" or "strong." The methods for directing behavior involve coercion and threat (usually disguised), close supervision, tight controls over behavior. At the other extreme, management can be "soft" or "weak." The methods for directing behavior involve being permissive, satisfying people's demands, achieving harmony. Then they will be tractable, accept direction.

This range has been fairly completely explored during the past half century, and management has learned some things from the exploration. There are difficulties in the "hard" approach. Force breeds counter-forces: restriction of output, antagonism, militant unionism, subtle but effective sabotage of management objectives. This "hard" approach is especially difficult during times of full employment.

There are also difficulties in the "soft" approach. It leads frequently to the abdication of management—to harmony, perhaps, but to indifferent performance. People take advantage of the soft approach. They continually expect more, but they give less and less.

Currently, the popular theme is "firm but fair." This is an attempt to gain the advantages of both the hard and the soft approaches. It is reminiscent of Teddy Roosevelt's "speak softly and carry a big stick."

## Is the Conventional View Correct?

The findings which are beginning to emerge from the social sciences challenge this whole set of beliefs about man and human nature and about the task of management. The evidence is far from conclusive, certainly, but it is suggestive.

It comes from the laboratory, the clinic, the schoolroom, the home, and even to a limited extent from industry itself.

The social scientist does not deny that human behavior in industrial organization today is approximately what management perceives it to be. He has, in fact, observed it and studied it fairly extensively. But he is pretty sure that this behavior is *not* a consequence of man's inherent nature. It is a consequence rather of the nature of industrial organizations, of management philosophy, policy, and practice. The conventional approach of Theory X is based on mistaken notions of what is cause and what is effect.

Perhaps the best way to indicate why the conventional approach of management is inadequate is to consider the subject of motivation.

## Physiological Needs

Man is a wanting animal—as soon as one of his needs is satisfied, another appears in its place. This process is unending. It continues from birth to death.

Man's needs are organized in a series of levels—a hierarchy of importance. At the lowest level, but pre-eminent in importance when they are thwarted, are his *physiological needs*. Man lives for bread alone, when there is no bread. Unless the circumstances are unusual, his needs for love, for status, for recognition are inoperative when his stomach has been empty for a while. But when he eats regularly and adequately, hunger ceases to be an important motivation. The same is true of the other physiological needs of man—for rest, exercise, shelter, protection from the elements.

*A satisfied need is not a motivator of behavior!* This is a fact of profound significance that is regularly ignored in the conventional approach to the management of people. Consider your own need for air: Except as you are deprived of it, it has no appreciable motivating effect upon your behavior.

## Safety Needs

When the physiological needs are reasonably satisfied, needs at the next higher level begin to dominate man's behavior—to motivate him. These are called *safety needs*. They are needs for protection against danger, threat, deprivation. Some people mistakenly refer to these as needs for security. However, unless man is in a dependent relationship where he fears arbitrary deprivation, he does not demand security. The need is for the "fairest possible break." When he is confident of this, he is more than willing to take risks. But when he feels threatened or dependent, his greatest need is for guarantees, for protection, for security.

The fact needs little emphasis that, since every industrial employee is in a dependent relationship, safety needs may assume considerable importance. Arbitrary management actions, behavior which arouses uncertainty with respect to continued employment or which reflects favoritism or discrimination, unpredictable administration of policy—these can be powerful motivators of the safety needs in the employment relationship *at every level,* from worker to vice president.

## Social Needs

When man's physiological needs are satisfied and he is no longer fearful about his physical welfare, his *social needs* become important motivators of his behavior— needs for belonging, for association, for acceptance by his fellows, for giving and receiving friendship and love.

Management knows today of the existence of these needs, but it often assumes quite wrongly that they represent a threat to the organization. Many studies have demonstrated that the tightly knit, cohesive work group may, under proper conditions, be far more effective than an equal number of separate individuals in achieving organizational goals.

Yet management, fearing group hostility to its own objectives, often goes to considerable lengths to control and direct human efforts in ways that are inimical to the natural "groupiness" of human beings. When man's social needs—and perhaps his safety needs, too—are thus thwarted, he behaves in ways which tend to defeat organizational objectives. He becomes resistant, antagonistic, uncooperative. But this behavior is a consequence, not a cause.

## Ego Needs

Above the social needs—in the sense that they do not become motivators until lower needs are reasonably satisfied—are the needs of greatest significance to management and to man himself. They are the *egoistic needs,* and they are of two kinds:

1. Those needs that relate to one's self-esteem—needs for self-confidence, for independence, for achievement, for competence, for knowledge.
2. Those needs that relate to one's reputation—needs for status, for recognition, for appreciation, for the deserved respect of one's fellows.

Unlike the lower needs, these are rarely satisfied; man seeks indefinitely for more satisfaction of these needs once they have become important to him. But they do not appear in any significant way until physiological, safety, and social needs are all reasonably satisfied.

The typical industrial organization offers few opportunities for the satisfaction of these egoistic needs to people at lower levels in the hierarchy. The conventional methods of organizing work, particularly in mass-production industries, give little heed to these aspects of human motivation. If the practices of scientific management were deliberately calculated to thwart these needs, they could hardly accomplish this purpose better than they do.

## Self-Fulfillment Needs

Finally—a capstone, as it were, on the hierarchy of man's needs—there are what we may call the *needs for self-fulfillment.* These are the needs for realizing one's own potentialities, for continued self-development, for being creative in the broadest sense of that term.

It is clear that the conditions of modern life give only limited opportunity for these relatively weak needs to obtain expression. The deprivation most people experience with respect to other lower-level needs diverts their energies into the struggle to satisfy *those* needs, and the needs for self-fulfillment remain dormant.

## Management and Motivation

We recognize readily enough that a man suffering from a severe dietary deficiency is sick. The deprivation of physiological needs has behavioral consequences. The same is true—although less well recognized—of deprivation of higher-level needs. The man whose needs for safety, association, independence, or status are thwarted is sick just as surely as the man who has rickets. And his sickness will have behavioral consequences. We will be mistaken if we attribute his resultant passivity, his hostility, his refusal to accept responsibility to his inherent "human nature." These forms of behavior are *symptoms* of illness—of deprivation of his social and egoistic needs.

The man whose lower-level needs are satisfied is not motivated to satisfy those needs any longer. For practical purposes they exist no longer. Management often asks, "Why aren't people more productive? We pay good wages, provide good working conditions, have excellent fringe benefits and steady employment. Yet people do not seem to be willing to put forth more than minimum effort."

The fact that management has provided for these physiological and safety needs has shifted the motivational emphasis to the social and perhaps to the egoistic needs. Unless there are opportunities *at work* to satisfy these higher-level needs, people will be deprived; and their behavior will reflect this deprivation. Under such conditions, if management continues to focus its attention on physiological needs, its efforts are bound to be ineffective.

People *will* make insistent demands for more money under these conditions. It becomes more important than ever to buy the material goods and services which can provide limited satisfaction of the thwarted needs. Although money has only limited value in satisfying many higher-level needs, it can become the focus of interest if it is the *only* means available.

## The Carrot-and-Stick Approach

The carrot-and-stick theory of motivation (like Newtonian physical theory) works reasonably well under certain circumstances. The *means* for satisfying man's physiological and (within limits) his safety needs can be provided or withheld by management. Employment itself is such a means, and so are wages, working conditions, and benefits. By these means the individual can be controlled so long as he is struggling for subsistence.

But the carrot-and-stick theory does not work at all once man has reached an adequate subsistence level and is motivated primarily by higher needs. Management cannot provide a man with self-respect, or with the respect of his fellows, or with the satisfaction of needs for self-fulfillment. It can create such conditions that he is encouraged and enabled to seek such satisfactions for *himself,* or it can thwart him by failing to create those conditions.

But this creation of conditions is not "control." It is not a good device for directing behavior. And so management finds itself in an odd position. The high standard of living created by our modern technological know-how provides quite adequately for the satisfaction of physiological and safety needs. The only significant exception is where management practices have not created confidence in a "fair break"—and thus where safety needs are thwarted. But by making possible the satisfaction of low-level needs, management has deprived itself of the ability to use as motivators the devices on which conventional theory has taught it to rely—rewards, promises, incentives, or threats and other coercive devices.

The philosophy of management by direction and control—*regardless of whether it is hard or soft*—is inadequate to motivate because the human needs on which this approach relies are today unimportant motivators of behavior. Direction and control are essentially useless in motivating people whose important needs are social and egoistic. Both the hard and the soft approach fail today because they are simply irrelevant to the situation.

People, deprived of opportunities to satisfy at work the needs which are now important to them, behave exactly as we might predict—with indolence, passivity, resistance to change, lack of responsibility, willingness to follow the demagogue, unreasonable demands for economic benefits. It would seem that we are caught in a web of our own weaving.

## A New Theory of Management

For these and many other reasons, we require a different theory of the task of managing people based on more adequate assumptions about human nature and human motivation. I am going to be so bold as to suggest the broad dimensions of such a theory. Call it "Theory Y," if you will.

1. Management is responsible for organizing the elements of productive enterprise—money, materials, equipment, people—in the interest of economic ends.

2. People are *not* by nature passive or resistant to organizational needs. They have become so as a result of experience in organizations.

3. The motivation, the potential for development, the capacity for assuming responsibility, the readiness to direct behavior toward organizational goals are all present in people. Management does not put them there. It is a responsibility of management to make it possible for people to recognize and develop these human characteristics for themselves.

4. The essential task of management is to arrange organizational conditions and methods of operation so that people can achieve their own goals *best* by directing *their own* efforts toward organizational objectives.

This is a process primarily of creating opportunities, releasing potential, removing obstacles, encouraging growth, providing guidance. It is what Peter Drucker has called "management by objectives" in contrast to "management by control." It does *not* involve the abdication of management, the absence of leadership, the lowering of standards, or the other characteristics usually associated with the "soft" approach under Theory X.

## Some Difficulties

It is no more possible to create an organization today which will be a full, effective application of this theory than it was to build an atomic power plant in 1945. There are many formidable obstacles to overcome.

The conditions imposed by conventional organization theory and by the approach of scientific management for the past half century have tied men to limited jobs which do not utilize their capabilities, have discouraged the acceptance of responsibility, have encouraged passivity, have eliminated meaning from work. Man's habits, attitudes, expectations—his whole conception of membership in an industrial organization—have been conditioned by his experience under these circumstances.

People today are accustomed to being directed, manipulated, controlled in industrial organizations and to finding satisfaction for their social, egoistic, and self-fulfillment needs away from the job. This is true of much of management as well as of workers. Genuine "industrial citizenship"—to borrow again a term from Drucker—is a remote and unrealistic idea, the meaning of which has not even been considered by most members of industrial organizations.

Another way of saying this is that Theory X places exclusive reliance upon external control of human behavior, while Theory Y relies heavily on self-control and self-direction. It is worth noting that this difference is the difference between treating people as children and treating them as mature adults. After generations of the former, we cannot expect to shift to the latter overnight.

## Steps in the Right Direction

Before we are overwhelmed by the obstacles, let us remember that the application of theory is always slow. Progress is usually achieved in small steps. Some innovative ideas which are entirely consistent with Theory Y are today being applied with some success.

### Decentralization and Delegation
These are ways of freeing people from the too-close control of conventional organization, giving them a degree of freedom to direct their own activities, to assume responsibility, and, importantly, to satisfy their egoistic needs. In this connection, the flat organization of Sears, Roebuck and Company provides an interesting example. It forces "management by objectives," since it enlarges

the number of people reporting to a manager until he cannot direct and control them in the conventional manner.

### Job Enlargement

This concept, pioneered by I.B.M. and Detroit Edison, is quite consistent with Theory Y. It encourages the acceptance of responsibility at the bottom of the organization; it provides opportunities for satisfying social and egoistic needs. In fact, the reorganization of work at the factory level offers one of the more challenging opportunities for innovation consistent with Theory Y.

### Participation and Consultative Management

Under proper conditions, participation and consultative management provide encouragement to people to direct their creative energies toward organizational objectives, give them some voice in decisions that affect them, provide significant opportunities for the satisfaction of social and egoistic needs. The Scanlon Plan is the outstanding embodiment of these ideas in practice.

### Performance Appraisal

Even a cursory examination of conventional programs of performance appraisal within the ranks of management will reveal how completely consistent they are with Theory X. In fact, most such programs tend to treat the individual as though he were a product under inspection on the assembly line.

A few companies—among them General Mills, Ansul Chemical, and General Electric—have been experimenting with approaches which involve the individual in setting "targets" or objectives *for himself* and in a *self*-evaluation of performance semiannually or annually. Of course, the superior plays an important leadership role in this process—one, in fact, which demands substantially more competence than the conventional approach. The role is, however, considerably more congenial to many managers than the role of "judge" or "inspector" which is usually forced upon them. Above all, the individual is encouraged to take a greater responsibility for planning and appraising his own contribution to organizational objectives; and the accompanying effects on egoistic and self-fulfillment needs are substantial.

## Applying the Ideas

The not infrequent failure of such ideas as these to work as well as expected is often attributable to the fact that a management has "bought the idea" but applied it within the framework of Theory X and its assumptions.

Delegation is not an effective way of exercising management by control. Participation becomes a farce when it is applied as a sales gimmick or a device for kidding people into thinking they are important. Only the management that has confidence in human capacities and is itself directed toward organizational objectives rather than toward the preservation of personal power can grasp the implications of this emerging theory. Such management will find and apply successfully other innovative ideas as we move slowly toward the full implementation of a theory like Y.

## The Human Side of Enterprise

It is quite possible for us to realize substantial improvements in the effectiveness of industrial organizations during the next decade or two. The social sciences can contribute much to such developments; we are only beginning to grasp the implications of the growing body of knowledge in these fields. But if this conviction is to become a reality instead of a pious hope, we will need to view the process much as we view the process of releasing the energy of the atom for constructive human ends—as a slow, costly, sometimes discouraging approach toward a goal which would seem to many to be quite unrealistic.

The ingenuity and the perseverance of industrial management in the pursuit of economic ends have changed many scientific and technological dreams into commonplace realities. It is now becoming clear that the application of these same talents to the human side of enterprise will not only enhance substantially these materialistic achievements, but will bring us one step closer to "the good society."

---

### *Learning Review*

*Questions:*

1. The conventional approach of Theory _____ proposes that management is responsible for organizing the elements _____, _____, _____, _____ in the interest of economic ends.

2. Individual needs according to Maslow's hierarchy of importance include _____, _____, _____, _____ and _____ _____needs.

3. Although the _____ for satisfying physiological and safety needs of workers can be provided or withheld by management, once the employee has reached an adequate subsistence level, this _____ and _____ theory of motivation does not work.

4. Theory _____ based on more adequate assumptions about human _____and human _____ is what Peter Drucker called management by _____ in contrast to management by _____.

5. While theory _____ places _____ reliance on self-control and self-direction of human behavior, theory _____ places _____ reliance upon _____ control of human behavior.

*Answers:*

jectives, control 5. Y, heavy, X, exclusive, external. ·qo ‘uoᴉʇɐʌᴉʇoɯ ‘ǝɹnʇɐu ‘⅄ ·ㄣ ·ʞɔᴉʇs ‘ʇoɹɹɐɔ ‘suɐǝɯ ·Ɛ ʇuǝɯllᴉɟlnɟ-ɟlǝs ‘ɔᴉʇsᴉoƃǝ ‘lɐᴉɔos ‘⅄ʇǝɟɐs ‘lɐɔᴉƃoloᴉs⅄ɥd ·ᄅ ǝldoǝd ‘ʇuǝɯdᴉnbǝ ‘slɐᴉɹǝʇɐɯ ‘⅄ǝuoɯ ‘X ·⇂

---

# Retrospective Comment

### BY RAYMOND E. MILES *

It is my guess that the late Douglas McGregor would make few if any changes today in the basic thrust of his classic article "The Human Side of Enterprise." He would be troubled that we have made so little progress toward improving the world of work. On the other hand, I suspect that he would be pleased that because of his writings and the work of those he inspired, we are at least more aware of the gap between what is and what might be. McGregor was, of course, aware that "years of exploration . . ." would be required to implement our increasing awareness of human potential and alternative approaches to channeling it into productive work arrangements.

I do feel that McGregor would today add to his essay a few pages of explanation and examples of Theory Y in practice, under varying organizational conditions. He began such an effort in his last writings (see particularly, "The Professional Manager," 1967, p. 79), and by now he would be able to incorporate both the advances which have been made in common managerial practice and the changes in expectations of organization members generated in the turbulent 1960's. He would take pains to emphasize points made in his earliest writings—that clearly not all people are alike and no single set of managerial behaviors will draw out the full potential of all organization members.

At the same time, McGregor would, I believe, be critical of the current use of the concept of "contingency" in leadership writings. McGregor would argue, I believe, that managers do not—in fact, cannot—rapidly adjust their basic assumptions about people and their potential for self-direction and self-control. He would argue that managers should vary their behavior with subordinates *around* a basic thrust aimed at allowing each organization member maximum possible opportunity for growth and the exercise of mature responsibility. McGregor was totally aware that managers on an assembly line do not have the same opportunity to afford members growth opportunities that they may have in a research laboratory. He would, however, expect the manager to go as far as possible in the direction of enhancing self-respect (and self-management) as the circumstances (and the particular individual's capacities) might permit.

In addition, I believe that McGregor would expand his too brief statements that managers, under Theory Y, give up neither their right nor obligation to manage. He would emphasize that participative management is not a device for pushing responsibility for tough decisions off on subordinates. He would instead demand that managers grow and learn along with subordinates, utilizing their own capacities fully in seeking jointly acceptable approaches to organizational objectives which may or may not be amenable to group influence.

Finally, I think that McGregor today would, understandably, make major changes in his section describing then (1950's) current "Theory Y" practices (*Steps in the Right Direction*). He would, of course, be forced to acknowledge that Sears, Roebuck has essentially abandoned its "flat" structure emphasizing store and departmental management discretion, but he might also wryly observe that Sears' current performance plight followed rather than preceded the demise of decentralized control. Similarly, he would expand his treatment of "job enlargement" to include recent examples of total systems redesign (see, for example, Walton, R. E., "How to Counter Alienation in the Plant," *Harvard Business Review,* Nov.-Dec. 1972, pp. 70–81) but his penchant for honest appraisal would force him to point out that many of these experiments were apparently undertaken under circumstances where "management has 'bought the idea' but applied it within the framework of Theory X and its assumptions" and are thus currently in danger of disappearing.

In sum, McGregor would change little in his article because, in my view, little needs to be changed.

---

* Professor of Business Administration, University of California, Berkeley.

# 10

# The Individual and Organization: Some Problems of Mutual Adjustment

CHRIS ARGYRIS

## *About the Author*

**CHRIS ARGYRIS** is James B. Conant Professor of Education and Organizational Behavior, Graduate School of Education, Harvard University, and member of the Faculty of Business Administration, Harvard Business School. Prior to teaching at Harvard, he was on the faculty at Yale. He earned degrees at Clark University, Kansas, and Cornell and was the recipient of honorary doctorate degrees from McGill, Louven, and the Stockholm School of Economics. He has served as consultant to the major firms of the United States—IBM, General Foods, DuPont, Shell Oil, Standard of New Jersey, Lever Brothers—and to the governments of France, England, Norway, Holland, Italy, Greece, and Germany on problems of executive development and productivity. Argyris has published twenty-five books and over 200 articles. His most recent book is *Strategy, Change, and Defensive Routines* (Boston: Ballinger, 1985).

Reprinted by permission of the author and publisher from *Administrative Science Quarterly,* Vol. 2 (June 1957), pp. 1–24.

# PREVIEW

A. It is difficult to find agreement regarding the basic properties of human personality.
   1. Human personality tends to develop along many and specific trends which are operationally definable and empirically observable.
   2. At a given moment in time every individual could conceivably have his or her degree of development plotted by analyzing a basic multidimensional development process.
   3. After reviewing the dimensions of personality development, one might conclude that an independent person is one whose behavior is not caused by the influence of others.
   4. However, no individual is completely independent; all have healthy dependence.
B. The most basic property of formal organization is its logical foundation or its essential rationality.
   1. No organizational structure will be ideal; none will exemplify the maximum expression of the principles of formal organization.
   2. A satisfactory aspiration for organizations is to modify the ideal structure to take into account the individual and environmental factors.
   3. Task specialization inhibits self-actualization and provides expression for superficial abilities that do not provide the "endless challenge" desired by the healthy personality.
   4. With organizational chain of command, workers must be motivated to accept direction, control and coordination of their behavior, but this inhibits four of the growth trends of the personality.
   5. Unity of direction for individuals in an organization violates a basic characteristic of personality.
   6. The principle of span of control tends to create a work situation which requires immature, rather than mature, workers.
C. There exists some basic inconsistencies between the growth trends of a healthy personality and the requirements of formal organizations.
   1. The needs of healthy individuals are often incongruent with the requirements of the formal organization.
   2. The results of these inconsistencies are frustration, failure, short-time perspective, and conflict.
   3. The nature of organizations tends to cause the worker to experience competition, rivalry, intersubordinate hostility, and to develop a focus toward the parts rather than the whole.
D. There are many ways in which both workers and organizations react to this problem.

It is a fact that most industrial organizations have some sort of formal structure within which individuals must work to achieve the organization's objectives.[1] Each of these basic components of organization (the formal structure and the individuals) has been and continues to be the subject of much research, discussion, and writing. An extensive search of the literature leads us to conclude, however, that most of these inquiries are conducted by persons typically interested in one or the other of the basic components. Few focus on both the individual and the organization.

Since in real life the formal structure and the individuals are continuously interacting and transacting, it seems useful to consider a study of their simultaneous impact upon each other. It is the purpose of this paper to outline the beginnings of a systematic framework by which to analyze the nature of the relationship between formal organization and individuals and from which to derive specific hypotheses regarding their mutual impact. Although a much more detailed definition of formal organization will be given later, it is important to emphasize that this analysis is limited to those organizations whose original formal structure is defined by such traditional principles of organization as "chain of command," "task specialization," "span of control," and so forth. Another limitation is that since the nature of individuals varies from culture to culture, the conclusions of this paper are also limited to those cultures wherein the proposed model of personality applies (primarily American and some Western European cultures).

The method used is a simple one designed to take advantage of the existing research on each component. The first objective is to ascertain the basic properties of each component. Exactly what is known and agreed upon by the experts about each of the components? Once this information has been collected, the second objective follows logically. When the basic properties of each of these components are known, what predictions can be made regarding their impact upon one another once they are brought together?

## Some Properties of Human Personality

The research on the human personality is so great and voluminous that it is indeed difficult to find agreement regarding its basic properties.[2] It is even more difficult to summarize the agreements once they are inferred from the existing literature. Because of space limitations it is only possible to discuss in detail one of several agreements which seems to the writer to be the most relevant to the problem at hand. The others may be summarized briefly as follows. Personality is conceptualized as (1) being an organization of parts where the parts maintain the whole and the whole maintains the parts; (2) seeking internal balance (usually called adjustment) and external balance (usually called adaptation); (3) being propelled by psychological (as well as physical) energy; (4) located in the need systems; and (5) expressed through the abilities. (6) The personality organization may be called "the self" which (7) acts to color all the individual's experiences, thereby causing him to live in "private worlds," and which (8) is capable of defending (maintaining) itself against threats of all types.

The self, in this culture, tends to develop along specific trends which are operationally definable and empirically observable. The basic developmental trends may be described as follows. The human being, in our culture:

1. tends to develop from a state of being passive as an infant to a state of increasing activity as an adult. (This is what E. H. Erikson has called self-initiative and Urie Bronfenbrenner has called self-determination.[3])

2. tends to develop from a state of dependence upon others as an infant to a state of relative independence as an adult. Relative independence is the ability to "stand on one's own two feet" and simultaneously to acknowledge healthy dependencies.[4] It is characterized by the individual's freeing himself from his childhood determiners of behavior (e.g., the family) and developing his own set of behavioral determiners. The individual does not tend to react to others (e.g., the boss) in terms of patterns learned during childhood.[5]

3. tends to develop from being capable of behaving in only a few ways as an infant to being capable of behaving in many different ways as an adult.[6]

4. tends to develop from having erratic, casual, shallow, quickly dropped interests as an infant to possessing a deepening of interests as an adult. The mature state is characterized by an endless series of challenges where the reward comes from doing something for its own sake. The tendency is to analyze and study phenomena in their full-blown wholeness, complexity, and depth.[7]

5. tends to develop from having a short-time perspective (i.e., the present largely determines behavior) as an infant to having a much longer time perspective as an adult (i.e., the individual's behavior is more affected by the past and the future).[8]

6. tends to develop from being in a subordinate position in the family and society as an infant to aspiring to occupy at least an equal and/or superordinate position relative to his peers.

7. tends to develop from having a lack of awareness of the self as an infant to having an awareness of and control over the self as an adult. The adult who experiences adequate and successful control over his own behavior develops a sense of integrity (Erikson) and feelings of self-worth (Carl R. Rogers).[9]

These characteristics are postulated as being descriptive of a basic multidimensional developmental process along which the growth of individuals in our culture may be measured. Presumably every individual, at any given moment in time, could have his degree of development plotted along these dimensions. The exact location on each dimension will probably vary with each individual and even with the same individual at different times. Self-actualization may now be defined more precisely as the individual's plotted scores (or profile) along the above dimensions.[10]

A few words of explanation may be given concerning these dimensions of personality development:

1. They are only one aspect of the total personality. All the properties of personality mentioned above must be used in trying to understand the

behavior of a particular individual. For example, much depends upon the individual's self-concept, his degree of adaptation and adjustment, and the way he perceives his private world.

2. The dimensions are continua, where the growth to be measured is assumed to be continuously changing in degree. An individual is presumed to develop continuously in degree from infancy to adulthood.

3. The only characteristic assumed to hold for all individuals is that, barring unhealthy personality development, they will move from the infant toward the adult end of each continuum. This description is a model outlining the basic growth trends. As such, it does not make any predictions about any specific individual. It does, however, presume to supply the researcher with basic developmental continua along which the growth of any individual in our culture may be described and measured.

4. It is postulated that no individual will ever obtain maximum expression of all these developmental trends. Clearly all individuals cannot be maximally independent, active, and so forth all the time and still maintain an organized society. It is the function of culture (e.g. norms, mores, and so forth) to inhibit maximum expression and to help an individual adjust and adapt by finding his optimum expression.

   A second factor that prevents maximum expression and fosters optimum expression are the limits set by the individual's own personality. For example, some people fear the same amount of independence and activity that others desire, and some people do not have the necessary abilities to perform certain tasks. No given individual is known to have developed all known abilities to their full maturity.

5. The dimensions described above are constructed in terms of latent or geno-typical characteristics. If one states that an individual needs to be dependent, this need may be ascertained by clinical inference, because it is one that individuals are not usually aware of. Thus one may observe an employee acting as if he were independent, but it is possible that if one goes below the behavioral surface the individual may be quite dependent. The obvious example is the employee who always seems to behave in a manner contrary to that desired by management. Although this behavior may look as if he is independent, his contrariness may be due to his great need to be dependent upon management which he dislikes to admit to himself and to others.

One might say that an independent person is one whose behavior is not caused by the influence others have over him. Of course, no individual is completely independent. All of us have our healthy dependencies (i.e., those which help us to be creative and to develop). One operational criterion to ascertain whether an individual's desire to be, let us say, independent and active is truly a mature manifestation is to ascertain the extent to which he permits others to express the same needs. Thus an autocratic leader may say that he needs to be active and independent; he may also say that he wants subordinates who are the same. There is ample research to suggest, however, that his leadership pattern only makes him and his subordinates more dependence-ridden.

## Some Basic Properties of Formal Organization

The next step is to focus the analytic spotlight on the formal organization. What are its properties? What are its basic "givens"? What probable impact will they have upon the human personality? How will the human personality tend to react to this impact? What sorts of chain reactions are probable when these two basic components are brought together?

**Formal Organizations as Rational Organizations.** Probably the most basic property of formal organization is its logical foundation or, as it has been called by students of administration, its essential rationality. It is the planners' conception of how the intended consequences of the organization may best be achieved. The underlying assumption, made by the creators of formal organization is that within respectable tolerances man will behave rationally, that is, as the formal plan requires him to behave. Organizations are formed with particular objectives in mind, and their structures mirror these objectives. Although man may not follow the prescribed paths, and consequently the objectives may never be achieved, Herbert A. Simon suggests that by and large man does follow these prescribed paths:

> Organizations are formed with the intention and design of accomplishing goals; and the people who work in organizations believe, at least part of the time, that they are striving toward these same goals. We must not lose sight of the fact that however far organizations may depart from the traditional description . . . nevertheless most behavior in organizations is intendedly rational behavior. By "intended rationality" I mean the kind of adjustment of behavior to goals of which humans are capable—a very incomplete and imperfect adjustment, to be sure, but one which nevertheless does accomplish purposes and does carry out programs.[11]

In an illuminating book, L. Urwick eloquently describes this underlying characteristic.[12] He insists that the creation of a formal organization requires a logical "drawing-office" approach. Although he admits that "nine times out of ten it is impossible to start with a clean sheet," the organizer should sit down and in a "cold-blooded, detached spirit . . . draw an ideal structure." The section from which I quote begins with Urwick's description of how the formal structure should be planned. He then continues:

> Manifestly that is a drawing-office job. It is a designing process. And it may be objected with a great deal of experience to support the contention that organization is never done that way . . . human organization. Nine times out of ten it is impossible to start with a clean sheet. The organizer has to make the best possible use of the human material that is already available. And in 89 out of those 90 per cent of cases he has to adjust jobs around to fit the man; he can't change the man to fit the job. He can't sit down in a cold-blooded, detached spirit and draw an ideal structure, an optimum distribution of duties and responsibilities and relationships, and then expect the infinite variety of human nature to fit into it.
> To which the reply is that he can and he should. If he has not got a

clean sheet, that is no earthly reason why he should not make the slight
effort of imagination required to assume that he has a clean sheet. It is
not impossible to forget provisionally the personal facts—that old Brown
is admirably methodical but wanting in initiative, that young Smith got into
a mess with Robinson's wife and that the two men must be kept at opposite
ends of the building, that Jones is one of those creatures who can think
like a Wrangler about other people's duties but is given to periodic amnesia
about certain aspects of his own.[13]

The task of the organizer, therefore, is to create a logically ordered world where,
as Fayol suggests, there is a "proper order" and in which there is a "place for
everything (everyone)."[14]

The possibility that the formal organization can be altered by personalities,
as found by Conrad M. Arensberg and Douglas McGregor[15] and Ralph M. Stogdill
and Katheleen Koehler,[16] is not denied by formal organizational experts. Urwick,
for example, states in the passage below that the planner must take into account
the human element. But it is interesting to note that he perceives these adjustments as "temporary deviations from the pattern in order to deal with idiosyncrasy
of personality." If possible, these deviations should be minimized by careful
preplanning.

> He [the planner] should never for a moment pretend that these (human)
> difficulties don't exist. They do exist; they are realities. Nor, when he has
> drawn up an ideal plan of organization, is it likely that he will be able to fit
> in all the existing human material perfectly. There will be small adjustments
> of the job to the man in all kinds of directions. But those adjustments are
> deliberate and temporary deviations from the pattern in order to deal with
> idiosyncrasy. There is a world of difference between such modification and
> drifting into an unworkable organization because Green has a fancy for
> combining bits of two incompatible functions, or White is "empire-building"
> . . . or Black has always looked after the canteen, so when he is promoted
> to Sales Manager, he might as well continue to sell buns internally, though
> the main product of the business happens to be battleships.
> What is suggested is that problems of organization should be handled *in
> the right order*. Personal adjustments must be made, insofar as they are
> necessary. But fewer of them will be necessary and they will present fewer
> deviations from what is logical and simple, if the organizer first makes a
> plan, a design—to which he would work if he had the ideal human material.
> He should expect to be driven from it here and there. But he will be
> driven from it far less and his machine will work much more smoothly if
> he *starts* with a plan. If he starts with a motley collection of human oddities
> and tries to organize to fit them all in, thinking first of their various shapes
> and sizes and colors, he may have a patchwork quilt; he will not have an
> organization.[17]

The majority of experts on formal organization agree with Urwick. Most of
them emphasize that no organizational structure will be ideal. None will exemplify
the maximum expression of the principles of formal organization. A satisfactory
aspiration is for optimum expression, which means modifying the ideal structure
to take into account the individual and any (environmental) conditions. Moreover,
they urge that the people must be loyal to the formal structure if it is to work

effectively. Thus Taylor emphasizes that scientific management would never succeed without a "mental revolution." [18] Fayol has the same problem in mind when he emphasizes the importance of *esprit de corps*.

It is also true, however, that these experts have provided little insight into *why* they believe that people should undergo a "mental revolution," or why an *esprit de corps* is necessary if the principles are to succeed. The only hints found in the literature are that resistance to scientific management occurs because human beings "are what they are" or "because it's human nature." But *why* does "human nature" resist formal organizational principles? Perhaps there is something inherent in the principles which cause human resistance. Unfortunately too little research specifically assesses the impact of formal organizational principles upon human beings.

Another argument for planning offered by the formal organizational experts is that the organization created by logical, rational design, in the long run, is more human than one created haphazardly. They argue that it is illogical, cruel, wasteful, and inefficient not to have a logical design. It is illogical because design must come first. It does not make sense to pay a large salary to an individual without clearly defining his position and its relationship to the whole. It is cruel because, in the long run, the participants suffer when no clear organizational structure exists. It is wasteful because, unless jobs are clearly predefined, it is impossible to plan logical training, promotion, resigning, and retiring policies. It is inefficient because the organization becomes dependent upon personalities. The personal touch leads to playing politics, which Mary Follett has described as a "deplorable form of coercion." [19]

Unfortunately, the validity of these arguments tends to be obscured in the eyes of the behavioral scientist because they imply that the only choice left, if the formal, rational, predesigned structure is not accepted, is to have no organizational structure at all, with the organizational structure left to the whims, pushes, and pulls of human beings. Some human-relations researchers, on the other hand, have unfortunately given the impression that formal structures are "bad" and that the needs of the individual participants should be paramount in creating and administering an organization. A recent analysis of the existing research, however, points up quite clearly that the importance of the organization is being recognized by those who in the past have focused largely upon the individual. [20]

In the past, and for the most part in the present, the traditional organizational experts based their "human architectural creation" upon certain basic principles or assumptions about the nature of organization. These principles have been described by such people as Urwick,[21] Mooney, Holden *et al.*, Fayol, Dennison, Brown, Gulick, White, Gaus, Stene, Hopf, and Taylor. Although these principles have been attacked by behavioral scientists, the assumption is made in this paper that to date no one has defined a more useful set of formal organization principles. Therefore the principles are accepted as givens. This frees us to inquire about their probable impact upon people, *if they are used as defined*.

**Task (Work) Specialization.**     As James J. Gillespie suggests, the roots of these principles of organization may be traced back to certain principles of industrial economics, the most important of which is the basic economic assumption held by builders of the industrial revolution that "the concentration of effort on a limited field of endeavor increases quality and quantity of output." [22] It follows from the above that the necessity for specialization should increase as the quantity of similar things to be done increases.

If concentrating effort on a limited field of endeavor increases the quality and quantity of output, it follows that organizational and administrative efficiency is increased by the specialization of tasks assigned to the participants of the organization.[23] Inherent in this assumption are three others. The first is that the human personality will behave more efficiently as the task that it is to perform becomes specialized. Second is the assumption that there can be found a one best way to define the job so that it is performed at greater speed.[24] Third is the assumption that any individual differences in the human personality may be ignored by transferring more skill and thought to machines.[25]

A number of difficulties arise concerning these assumptions when the properties of the human personality are recalled. First, the human personality we have seen is always attempting to actualize its unique organization of parts resulting from a continuous, emotionally laden, ego-involving process of growth. It is difficult, if not impossible, to assume that this process can be choked off and the resultant unique differences of individuals ignored. This is tantamount to saying that self-actualization can be ignored. The second difficulty is that task specialization requires the individual to use only a few of his abilities. Moreover, as specialization increases, the less complex motor abilities are used more frequently. These, research suggests, tend to be of lesser psychological importance to the individual. Thus the principle violates two basic givens of the healthy adult human personality. It inhibits self-actualization and provides expression for a few, shallow, superficial abilities that do not provide the "endless challenge" desired by the healthy personality.

Harold L. Wilensky and Charles N. Lebeaux correctly point out that task specialization causes what little skill is left in a job to become very important.[26] Now small differences in ability may make enormous differences in output. Thus two machine-shovel operators or two drill-press operators of different degrees of skill can produce dramatically different outputs. Ironically, the increasing importance of this type of skill for the healthy, mature worker means that he should feel he is performing self-satisfying work while using a small number of psychologically unchallenging abilities, when in actuality he may be predisposed to feel otherwise. Task specialization, therefore, requires a healthy adult to behave in a less mature manner, but it also requires that he feel good about it!

Not only is the individual affected, but the social structure as well is modified as a result of the situation described above. Wilensky and Lebeaux, in the same analysis, point out that placing a great emphasis on ability makes "Who you are" become less important than "What you can do." Thus the culture begins to reward relatively superficial, materialistic characteristics.

**Chain of Command.**  The principle of task specialization creates an aggregate of parts, each performing a highly specialized task. An aggregate of parts, each busily performing its particular objective, does not form an organization, however. A pattern of parts must be formed so that the interrelationships among the parts create the organization. Following the logic of specialization, the planners create a new function (leadership) the primary responsibility of which is to control, direct, and coordinate the interrelationships of the parts and to make certain that each part performs its objective adequately. Thus the planner makes the assumption that administrative and organizational efficiency is increased by arranging the parts in a determinate hierarchy of authority in which the part on top can direct and control the part on the bottom.

If the parts being considered are individuals, then they must be motivated to accept direction, control, and coordination of their behavior. The leader, therefore, is assigned formal power to hire, discharge, reward, and penalize the individuals in order to mold their behavior in the pattern of the organization's objectives.

The impact of such a state of affairs is to make the individuals dependent upon, passive, and subordinate to the leader. As a result, the individuals have little control over their working environment. At the same time their time perspective is shortened because they do not control the information necessary to predict their futures. These requirements of formal organization act to inhibit four of the growth trends of the personality, because to be passive, subordinate, and to have little control and a short time perspective exemplify in adults the dimensions of immaturity, not adulthood.

The planners of formal organization suggest three basic ways to minimize this admittedly difficult position. First, ample rewards should be given to those who perform well and who do not permit their dependence, subordination, passivity, and so forth to influence them in a negative manner. The rewards should be material and psychological. Because of the specialized nature of the worker's job, however, few psychological rewards are possible. It becomes important, therefore, that adequate material rewards are made available to the productive employee. This practice can lead to new difficulties, since the solution is, by its nature, not to do anything about the on-the-job situation (which is what is causing the difficulties) but to pay the individual for the dissatisfactions he experiences. The result is that the employee is paid for his dissatisfaction while at work and his wages are given to him to gain satisfactions outside his work environment.

Thus the management helps to create a psychological set which leads the employees to feel that basic causes of dissatisfaction are built into industrial life, that the rewards they receive are wages for dissatisfaction and that if satisfaction is to be gained the employee must seek it outside the organization.

To make matters more difficult, there are three assumptions inherent in the above solution that also violate the basic givens of human personality. First, the solution assumes that a whole human being can split his personality so that he will feel satisfied in knowing that the wages for his dissatisfaction will buy him satisfaction outside the plant. Second, it assumes that the employee is primarily interested in maximizing his economic gains. Third, it assumes that the employee is best rewarded as an individual producer. The work group in which he belongs is not viewed as a relevant factor. If he produces well, he should be rewarded. If he does not, he should be penalized even though he may be restricting production because of informal group sanctions.

The second solution suggested by the planners of formal organization is to have technically competent, objective, rational, loyal leaders. The assumption is made that if the leaders are technically competent presumably they cannot have "the wool pulled over their eyes" and that therefore the employees will have a high respect for them. The leaders should be objective and rational and personify the rationality inherent in the formal structure. Being rational means that they must avoid becoming emotionally involved. As one executive states, "We try to keep our personality out of the job." The leader must also be impartial; he must not permit his feelings to operate when he is evaluating others. Finally, the leader must be loyal to the organization so that he can inculcate the loyalty in the employees that Taylor, Fayol, and others believe is so important.

Admirable as this solution may be, it also violates several of the basic properties of personality. If the employees are to respect an individual for what he does rather than for who he is, the sense of integrity based upon evaluation of the total self which is developed in people is lost. Moreover, to ask the leader to keep his personality out of his job is to ask him to stop actualizing himself. This is not possible as long as he is alive. Of course, the executive may want to feel that he is not involved, but it is a basic given that the human personality is an organism always actualizing itself. The same problem arises with impartiality. No one can be completely impartial. As has been shown, the self concept always operates when we are making judgments. In fact, as Rollo May has pointed out, the best way to be impartial is to be as partial as one's needs predispose one to be but to be aware of this partiality in order to correct for it at the moment of decision.[27] Finally, if a leader can be loyal to an organization under these conditions, there may be adequate grounds for questioning the health of his personality make-up.

The third solution suggested by many adherents to formal organizational principles is to motivate the subordinates to have more initiative and to be more creative by placing them in competition with one another for the positions of power that lie above them in the organizational ladder. This solution is traditionally called "the rabble hypothesis." Acting under the assumption that employees will be motivated to advance upward, the adherents of formal organizations further assume that competition for the increasingly (as one goes up the ladder) scarcer positions will increase the effectiveness of the participants. D. C. S. Williams, conducting some controlled experiments, shows that the latter assumption is not necessarily valid. People placed in competitive situations are not necessarily better learners than those placed in noncompetitive situations.[28] M. Deutsch, as a result of extensive controlled experimental research, supports Williams' result and goes much further to suggest that competitive situations tend to lead to an increase in tension and conflict and decrease in human effectiveness.[29]

**Unity of Direction.** If the tasks of everyone in a unit are specialized, then it follows that the objective or purpose of the unit must be specialized. The principle of unity of direction states that organizational efficiency increases if each unit has a single activity (or homogeneous set of activities) that are planned and directed by the leader.[30]

This means that the goal toward which the employees are working, the path toward the goal, and the strength of the barriers they must overcome to achieve the goal are defined and controlled by the leader. Assuming that the work goals do not involve the egos of the employees, (i.e., they are related to peripheral, superficial needs), then ideal conditions for psychological failure have been created. The reader may recall that a basic given of a healthy personality is the aspiration for psychological success. Psychological success is achieved when each individual is able to define his own goals, in relation to his inner needs and the strength of the barriers to be overcome in order to reach these goals. Repetitive as it may sound, it is nevertheless true that the principle of unity of direction also violates a basic given of personality.

**Span of Control.**   The principle of span of control [31] states that administrative efficiency is increased by limiting the span of control of a leader to no more than five or six subordinates whose work interlocks. [32]

It is interesting to note that Ernest Dale, in an extensive study of organizational principles and practices in one hundred large organizations, concludes that the actual limits of the executive span of control are more often violated than not, [33] while in a recent study James H. Healey arrives at the opposite conclusion. [34] James C. Worthy reports that it is formal policy in his organization to extend the span of control of the top management much further than is theoretically suggested. [35] Finally, W. W. Suojanen, in a review of the current literature on the concept of span of control, concludes that it is no longer valid, particularly as applied to the larger government agencies and business corporations. [36]

In a recent article, however, Urwick criticizes the critics of the span-of-control principle. [37] For example, he notes that in the case described by Worthy, the superior has a large span of control over subordinates whose jobs do not interlock. The buyers in Worthy's organization purchase a clearly defined range of articles; therefore they find no reason to interlock with others.

Simon criticizes the span-of-control principle on the grounds that it increases the "administrative distance" between individuals. An increase in administrative distance violates, in turn, another formal organizational principle that administrative efficiency is enhanced by keeping at a minimum the number of organizational levels through which a matter must pass before it is acted on. [38] Span of control, continues Simon, inevitably increases red tape, since each contact between agents must be carried upward until a common superior is found. Needless waste of time and energy result. Also, since the solution of the problem depends upon the superior, the subordinate is in a position of having less control over his own work situation. This places the subordinate in a work situation in which he is less mature.

Although the distance between individuals in different units increases (because they have to find a common superior), the administrative distance between superior and subordinate within a given unit decreases. As Whyte correctly points out, the principle of span of control, by keeping the number of subordinates at a minimum, places great emphasis on close supervision. [39] Close supervision leads the subordinates to become dependent upon, passive toward, and subordinate to, the leader. Close supervision also tends to place the control in the superior.

Thus we must conclude that span of control, if used correctly, will tend to increase the subordinate's feelings of dependence, submissiveness, passivity, and so on. In short, it will tend to create a work situation which requires immature, rather than mature, participants.

## An Incongruency Between the Needs of a Mature Personality and of Formal Organization

Bringing together the evidence regarding the impact of formal organizational principles upon the individual, we must conclude that there are some basic incongruencies between the growth trends of a healthy personality in our culture and the requirements of formal organization. If the principles of formal organization are used as ideally defined, then the employees will tend to work in an environment where (1) they are provided minimal control over their work-a-day world, (2) they are expected to be passive, dependent, subordinate, (3) they are expected to have a short-time perspective, (4) they are induced to perfect and value the frequent use of a few superficial abilities, and (5) they are expected to produce under conditions leading to psychological failure.

All of these characteristics are incongruent to the ones healthy human beings are postulated to desire. They are much more congruent with the needs of infants in our culture. In effect, therefore, formal organizations are willing to pay high wages and provide adequate seniority if mature adults will, for eight hours a day, behave in a less mature manner. If this analysis is correct, this inevitable incongruency increases (1) as the employees are of increasing maturity, (2) as the formal structure (based upon the above principles) is made more clear-cut and logically tight for maximum formal organizational effectiveness, (3) as one goes down the line of command, and (4) as the jobs become more and more mechanized (i.e., take on assembly-line characteristics).

As in the case of the personality developmental trends, this picture of formal organization is also a model. Clearly, no company actually uses the formal principles of organization exactly as stated by their creators. There is ample evidence to suggest that they are being modified constantly in actual situations. Those who expound these principles, however, probably would be willing to defend their position that this is the reason that human-relations problems exist; the principles are not followed as they should be.

In the model of the personality and the formal organization, we are assuming the extreme of each in order that the analysis and its results can be highlighted. Speaking in terms of extremes helps us to make the position sharper. In doing this, we make no assumption that all situations in real life are extreme (i.e., that the individuals will always want to be more mature and that the formal organization will always tend to make people more dependent, passive, and so forth, all the time).[40] The model ought to be useful, however, to plot the degree to which each component tends toward extremes and then to predict the problems that will tend to arise.

Returning to the analysis, it is not difficult to see why some students of organization suggest that immature and even mentally retarded individuals probably would make excellent employees in certain jobs. There is very little documented experience to support such a hypothesis. One reason for this lack of information is probably the delicacy of the subject. Examples of what might be obtained if a systematic study were made may be found in a recent work by Mal Brennan.[41] He cites the Utica Knitting Mill, which made arrangements during 1917 with the Rome Institution for Mentally Defective Girls to employ twenty-four girls whose mental age ranged from six to ten years of age. The girls were such excellent workers that they were employed after the war emergency ended. In fact, the company added forty more in another of their plants. It is interesting to note that the managers praised the subnormal girls highly. According to Brennan, in several important reports they said that

> when business conditions required a reduction of the working staff, the hostel girls were never "laid off" in disproportion to the normal girls; that they were more punctual, more regular in their habits, and did not indulge in as much "gossip and levity." They received the same rate of pay, and they had been employed successfully at almost every process carried out in the workshops.

In another experiment reported by Brennan, the Works Manager of the Radio Corporation, Ltd., reported that of five young morons employed, "three girls compared very favorably with the normal class of employee in that age group. The boy employed in the store performed his work with satisfaction. . . . Although there was some doubt about the fifth child, it was felt that getting the most out of him was just a matter of right placement." In each of the five cases, the morons were reported to be quiet, respectful, well behaved, and very obedient. The Works Manager was specially impressed by their truthfulness. A year later the same Works Manager was still able to advise that "in every case, the girls proved to be exceptionally well-behaved, particularly obedient, and strictly honest and trustworthy. They carried out work required of them, to such a degree of efficiency that *we were surprised they were classed as subnormals for their age.*" [42]

## Summary of Findings

If one were to put these basic findings in terms of propositions, one could state:

PROPOSITION I. *There Is a Lack of Congruency between the Needs of Healthy Individuals and the Demands of the Formal Organization.*

If one uses the traditional formal principles of organization (i.e., chain of command, task specialization, and so on) to create a social organization, and

if one uses as an input agents who tend toward mature psychological development (i.e., who are predisposed toward relative independence, activeness, use of important abilities, and so on),

then one creates a disturbance, because the needs of healthy individuals listed above are not congruent with the requirements of formal organization, which tends to require the agents to work in situations where they are dependent, passive, use few and unimportant abilities, and so forth.

Corollary 1. The disturbance will vary in proportion to the degree of incongruency between the needs of the individuals and the requirements of the formal organization.[43]

An administrator, therefore, is always faced with a tendency toward continual disturbance inherent in the work situation of the individuals over whom he is in charge.

Drawing on the existing knowledge of the human personality, a second proposition can be stated.

PROPOSITION II. *The Results of this Disturbance Are Frustration, Failure, Short-Time Perspective, and Conflict.*[44]

If the agents are predisposed to a healthy, mature self-actualization, the following results will occur:

1. They will tend to experience frustration because their self-actualization will be blocked.
2. They will tend to experience failure because they will not be permitted to define their own goals in relation to their central needs, the paths to these goals, and so on.
3. They will tend to experience short-time perspective, because they have no control over the clarity and stability of their future.
4. They will tend to experience conflict, because, as healthy agents, they will dislike the frustration, failure, and short-time perspective which is characteristic of their present jobs. If they leave, however, they may not find new jobs easily, and even if new jobs are found, they may not be much different.[45]

Based upon the analysis of the nature of normal organization, one may state a third proposition.

PROPOSITION III. *The Nature of the Formal Principles of Organization Cause the Subordinate, at Any Given Level, to Experience Competition, Rivalry, Intersubordinate Hostility, and to Develop a Focus toward the Parts Rather than the Whole.*

1. Because of the degree of dependence, subordination, and so on of the subordinates upon the leader, and because the number of positions above any given level always tends to decrease, the subordinates aspiring to perform effectively and to advance will tend to find themselves in competition with, and receiving hostility from, each other.[46]
2. Because, according to the formal principles, the subordinate is directed toward and rewarded for performing his own task well, the subordinate tends to develop an orientation toward his own particular part rather than toward the whole.

3. This part-orientation increases the need for the leader to coordinate the activity among the parts in order to maintain the whole. This need for the leader, in turn, increases the subordinates' degree of dependence, subordination, and so forth. This is a circular process whose impact is to maintain and/or increase the degree of dependence, subordination, and so on, as well as to stimulate rivalry and competition for the leader's favor.

## A Bird's Eye, Cursory Picture of Some Other Related Findings

It is impossible in the short space available to present all of the results obtained from the analysis of the literature. For example, it can be shown that employees tend to adapt to the frustration, failure, short-time perspective, and conflict involved in their work situations by any one or a combination of the following acts:

1. Leaving the organization.
2. Climbing the organizational ladder.
3. Manifesting defense reactions such as daydreaming, aggression, ambivalence, regression, projection, and so forth.
4. Becoming apathetic and disinterested toward the organization, its make-up, and its goals. This leads to such phenomena as: (a) employees reducing the number and potency of the needs they expect to fulfill while at work; (b) employees goldbricking, setting rates, restricting quotas, making errors, cheating, slowing down and so on.
5. Creating informal groups to sanction the defense reactions and the apathy, disinterest, and lack of self-involvement.
6. Formalizing the informal group.
7. Evolving group norms that perpetuate the behavior outlined in 3, 4, 5, and 6 above.
8. Evolving a psychological set in which human or nonmaterial factors become increasingly unimportant while material factors become increasingly important.
9. Acculturating youth to accept the norms outlined in 7 and 8.

Furthermore, it can also be shown that many managements tend to respond to the employee's behavior by:

1. Increasing the degree of their pressure-oriented leadership.
2. Increasing the degree of their use of management controls.
3. Increasing the number of "pseudo"-participation and communication programs.

These three reactions by management actually compound the dependence, subordination, and so on that the employee's experience, which in turn cause the employees to increase their adaptive behavior, the very behavior management desired to curtail in the first place.

Is there a way out of this circular process? The basic problem is the reduction in the degree of dependency, subordination, submissiveness, and so on experienced by the employee in his work situation. It can be shown that job enlargement and employee-centered (or democratic or participative) leadership are elements which, if used correctly, can go a long way toward ameliorating the situation. These are limited, however, because their success depends upon having employees who are ego-involved and highly interested in the organization. This dilemma between individual needs and organization demands is a basic, continual problem posing an eternal challenge to the leader. How is it possible to create an organization in which the individuals may obtain optimum expression and, simultaneously, in which the organization itself may obtain optimum satisfaction of its demands? Here lies a fertile field for future research in organizational behavior.

---

### Learning Review

*Questions:*

1. The personality of the organization acts to color all of the individual's experiences, thereby causing him or her to live in "_____ _____."

2. All of us have our _____ dependencies (i.e., those which help us to be creative and to develop).

3. The most basic property of formal organization is its _____ _____ or its _____ _____.

4. The principle of _____ _____ _____ states that organizational efficiency increases if each unit has a single activity that is planned and directed by the leader.

5. The characteristics of formal organization are much more congruent with the needs of _____ than of mature _____.

*Answers:*

1. "private worlds"; 2. healthy; 3. logical foundations, essential rationality; 4. unity of direction; 5. infants (children), individuals or adults

---

## FOOTNOTES

1. Temporarily, "formal structure" is defined as that which may be found on the organization charts and in the standard operating procedures of an organization.

2. The relevant literature in clinical, abnormal, child, and social psychology, and in personality theory, sociology, and anthropology was investigated. The basic agreements inferred regarding the properties of personality are assumed to be valid for most contemporary points of view. Allport's "trait theory," Cattell's factor analytic approach, and Kretsch-

mer's somatotype framework are not included. For lay description see the author's *Personality Fundamentals for Administrators,* rev. ed. (New Haven, 1954).

3.   E. H. Erikson, *Childhood and Society* (New York, 1950); Urie Bronfenbrenner, "Toward an Integrated Theory of Personality," in Robert R. Blake and Glenn V. Ramsey, *Perception* (New York, 1951), pp. 206–257. See also R. Kotinsky, *Personality in the Making* (New York, 1952), pp. 8–25.

4.   This is similar to Erikson's sense of autonomy and Bronfenbrenner's state of creative interdependence.

5.   Robert W. White, *Lives in Progress* (New York, 1952), pp. 339 ff.

6.   Lewin and Kounin believe that as the individual develops needs and abilities the boundaries between them become more rigid. This explains why an adult is better able than a child to be frustrated in one activity and behave constructively in another. See Kurt Lewin, *A Dynamic Theory of Personality* (New York, 1935) and Jacob S. Kounin, "Intellectual Development and Rigidity," in R. Barker, J. Kounin, and H. R. Wright, eds., *Child Behavior and Development* (New York, 1943), pp. 179–198.

7.   Robert White, *op. cit.,* pp. 347 ff.

8.   Lewin reminds those who may believe that a long-time perspective is not characteristic of the majority of individuals of the billions of dollars that are invested in insurance policies. Kurt Lewin, *Resolving Social Conflicts* (New York, 1948), p. 105.

9.   Carl R. Rogers, *Client-Centered Therapy* (New York, 1951).

10.   Another related but discrete set of developmental dimensions may be constructed to measure the protective (defense) mechanisms individuals tend to create as they develop from infancy to adulthood. Exactly how these would be related to the above model is not clear.

11.   Herbert A. Simon, *Research Frontiers in Politics and Government* (Washington, D.C., 1955), ch. ii, p. 30.

12.   L. Urwick, *The Elements of Administration* (New York, 1944).

13.   *Ibid.,* pp. 36–39; quoted by permission of Harper & Brothers.

14.   Cited in Harold Koontz and Cyril O'Donnell, *Principles of Management* (New York, 1955), p. 24.

15.   Conrad M. Arensberg and Douglas McGregor, "Determination of Morale in an Industrial Company," *Applied Anthropology,* 1 (Jan.-March 1942), 12–34.

16.   Ralph M. Stogdill and Katheleen Koehler, *Measures of Leadership Structure and Organization Change* (Columbus, O., 1952).

17.   *Ibid.,* pp. 36–39; quoted by permission of Harper & Brothers.

18.   For a provocative discussion of Taylor's Philosophy, see Reinhard Bendix, *Work and Authority in Industry* (New York, 1956), pp. 274–319.

19.   Quoted in *ibid.,* pp. 36–39.

20.   Chris Argyris, *The Present State of Research in Human Relations* (New Haven, 1954), ch. i.

21.   Urwick, *op. cit.*

22.   James J. Gillespie, *Free Expression in Industry* (London, 1948), pp. 34–37.

23.   Herbert A. Simon, *Administrative Behavior* (New York, 1947), pp. 80–81.

24.   For an interesting discussion see Georges Friedman, *Industrial Society* (Glencoe, Ill., 1955), pp. 54 ff.

25.   *Ibid.,* p. 20. Friedman reports that 79 per cent of Ford employees had jobs for which they could be trained in one week.

26.   Harold L. Wilensky and Charles N. Lebeaux, *Industrialization and Social Welfare* (New York, 1955), p. 43.

27.   Rollo May, "Historical and Philosophical Presuppositions for Understanding Therapy," in O. H. Mowrer, *Psychotherapy Theory and Research* (New York, 1953), pp. 38–39.

28.   D. C. S. Williams, Effects of Competition between Groups in a Training Situation, *Occupational Psychology,* 30 (April 1956), 85–93.

29.   M. Deutsch, An Experimental Study of the Effects of Cooperation and Competition upon Group Process, *Human Relations,* 2 (1949), 199–231.

30.   The sacredness of these principles is questioned by a recent study. Gunnar Heckscher concludes that the principles of unity of command and unity of direction are formally violated in Sweden: "A fundamental principle of public administration in Sweden is the duty of all public agencies to cooperate directly without necessarily passing through a common superior. This principle is even embodied in the constitution itself, and in actual fact it is being employed daily. It is traditionally one of the most important characteristics of Swedish administration that especially central agencies, but also central and local agencies of different levels, cooperate freely and that this is being regarded as a perfectly normal procedure" (*Swedish Public Administration at Work* (Stockholm, 1955), p. 12).

31.   First defined by V. A. Graicunas in an article entitled "Relationship in Organization," in L. Gulick and L. Urwick, eds., *Papers on the Science of Administration,* 2d ed. (New York, 1947), pp. 183–187.

32.   L. Urwick, *Scientific Principles and Organization* (New York, 1938), p. 8.

33.   Ernest Dale, *Planning and Developing the Company Organization Structure* (New York, 1952), ch. xx.

34.   James H. Healey, Coordination and Control of Executive Functions, *Personnel,* 33 (Sept. 1956), 106–117.

35.   James C. Worthy, Organizational Structure and Employee Morale, *American Sociological Review,* 15 (April 1950), 169–179.

36.   W. W. Suojanen, The Span of Control-Fact or Fable? *Advanced Management,* 20 (1955), 5–13.

37.   L. Urwick, The Manager's Span of Control, *Harvard Business Review,* 34 (May-June 1956), 39–47.

38.   Simon, *op. cit.,* pp. 26–28.

39.   William Whyte, "On the Evolution of Industrial Sociology" (mimeographed paper presented at the 1956 meeting of the American Sociological Society).

40.   In fact, much evidence is presented in the book from which this article is drawn to support contrary tendencies.

41.   Mal Brennan, *The Making of a Moron* (New York, 1953), pp. 13–18.

42.   Mr. Brennan's emphasis.

43.   This proposition does not hold under certain conditions.   *

44.   In the full analysis, specific conditions are derived under which the basic incongruency increases or decreases.

45.   These points are taken, in order, from: Roger G. Barker, T. Dembo, and K. Lewin, "Frustration and Regression: An Experiment with Young Children," *Studies in Child Welfare,* vol. XVIII, No. 2 (Iowa City, Ia., 1941); John Dollard *et al., Frustration and Aggression* (New Haven, 1939); Kurt Lewin *et al.,* "Level of Aspiration," in J. McV. Hunt, ed., *Personality and the Behavior Disorders* (New York, 1944), pp. 333–378; Ronald Lippitt and Leland Bradford, Employee Success in Work Groups, *Personnel Administration,* 8 (Dec. 1945), 6–10; Kurt Lewin, "Time Perspective and Morale," in Gertrud Weiss Lewin, ed., *Resolving Social Conflicts* (New York, 1948), pp. 103–124; and Theodore M. Newcomb, *Social Psychology* (New York, 1950), pp. 361–373.

46.   These problems may not arise for the subordinate who becomes apathetic, disinterested, and so on.

# Retrospective Comment

◆

## BY CHRIS ARGYRIS

Many years ago I was asked by the Social Science Research Council to review the empirical literature in our field. The final report contained four hundred pages of concepts and generalizations about behavior within organizations. I was not satisfied with the report. I wanted to find a theory that might organize the knowledge in such a way that it explained the results to-date and perhaps make predictions about the future.

The strategy that I used was to assume that the bloomin' buzzing complex world that I was experiencing began with, at least, two factors interacting; namely, people and organizations. I decided to bring together and organize what was known about human personality and about formal organizations. I could then inquire into what would happen if these two unities were required to interact with each other in order to accomplish the goals of formal organization. The result was *Personality and Organization,* from which this article was taken.

As I see it now, my analysis accurately describes only one part of the dilemma of individual-organizational actualization. What it misses is that the problem is more than a dilemma; it is a paradox. I now know that an additional reason why formal organizations may have the "negative" or "inhuman" consequences upon individuals is that they are attending to a set of human characteristics that I did not consider in my original analysis. I refer to the information processing and information handling capacities of human beings. The formal organization may be "inhumane" along one set of dimensions because it must pay attention to another set of human qualities (Argyris, 1977, 1978).

The new analysis does not disconfirm the old. The consequences that I described in 1957 have not been disconfirmed in several published re-examinations of the literature. The new analysis points out the paradox and describes the managerial problem more accurately: how to manage systems whose designs are intended to reduce error, actually reduce and increase error (Argyris and Schön, 1978). The challenge for management and organizational theory is to dig beneath the surface and highlight this and other important inner contradictions that so far have been ignored.

# REFERENCES

Argyris, Chris, "Is capitalism the culprit," *Organizational Dynamics,* Spring 1978, pp. 21–37.

———, "Organizational learning and management information systems," *Accounting, Organizations and Society,* Vol. 2, No. 2, 1977, pp. 113–123.

Argyris, Chris and Donald Schön, *Organizational Learning,* Addison-Wesley, 1978.

# 11

## *Administrative Decision Making*

### JAMES G. MARCH        HERBERT A. SIMON

## *About the Authors*

**James G. March** is Professor of Management at Stanford University where he also holds joint appointments in political science, sociology, and education. He is also a fellow of the Hoover Institution.

Upon receipt of his Ph.D. from Yale in 1953, he joined the faculty of Carnegie Institute of Technology. In 1964 he became the first dean of the School of Social Sciences at University of California, Irvine. In 1970, he joined the faculty at Stanford.

Dr. March is best known for his work in organization theory (where he has authored or co-authored five books), but he has also published two books on quantitative methods in the social sciences and four books of poetry.

**Herbert A. Simon,** recipient of the Nobel Prize in Economics in 1978 and the National Medal of Science in 1986, is truly a unique individual. He is recognized as a major contributor to the fields of management, organizational behavior, economics, psychology, political science, sociology, and computer science. The ideas which won him the Nobel Prize were originally developed in his *Administrative Behavior* (New York: Macmillan, 1947) and expanded upon in *Organizations,* from which the following excerpt is taken.

Professor Simon received his Ph.D. from the University of Chicago in 1943. He has taught at Illinois Institute of Technology (1942–1949) and at Carnegie Mellon University (1949–present).

# PREVIEW

A. The "economic man" of orthodox economic theory makes "optimal" choices in a highly specified and clearly defined environment.
   1. All alternatives are identified.
   2. Each alternative has a set of consequences attached (certainty, risk, and uncertainty).
   3. The decision maker has a utility function.
   4. The decision maker selects the alternative leading to the preferred set of circumstances.
B. The rationality of the "administrative man" is different from the economists' description.
   1. The "administrative man" is a reaction to the unrealistic assumptions of the economists
      a. that all the alternatives of choice are "given".
      b. that the consequences attached to each alternative are known.
      c. that a rational decision maker has a complete utility-ordering for all possible sets of consequences.
C. Decision making of the "administrative man" may be labeled either routinized or problem-solving responses.
   1. A stimulus evokes a response—sometimes very elaborate—that has been developed and learned at some previous time as an appropriate response for a stimulus of this class (a *routinized* response that calls for a performance program).
   2. *Problem-solving* responses can generally be identified by the extent to which they involve search—search aimed at discovering alternatives or consequences of action.
D. Most human decision making, whether individual or organizational, is concerned with the discovery and selection of *satisfactory* alternatives.
   1. Only in exceptional cases is it concerned with the discovery and selection of optimal alternatives.

## The Concept of Rationality

How does the rationality of "administrative man" compare with that of classical "economic man" or with the rational man of modern statistical decision theory? The rational man of economics and statistical decision theory makes "optimal" choices in a highly specified and clearly defined environment:

1. When we first encounter him in the decision-making situation, he already has laid out before him the whole set of alternatives from which he will choose his action. This set of alternatives is simply "given"; the theory does not tell how it is obtained.

2. To each alternative is attached a set of consequences—the events that will ensue if that particular alternative is chosen. Here the existing theories fall into three categories: (*a*) *Certainty:* theories that assume the decision maker has complete and accurate knowledge of the consequences that will follow on each alternative. (*b*) *Risk:* theories that assume accurate knowledge of a probability distribution of the consequences of each alternative. (*c*) *Uncertainty:* theories that assume that the consequences of each alternative belong to some subset of all possible consequences, but that the decision maker cannot assign definite probabilities to the occurrence of particular consequences.

3. At the outset, the decision maker has a "utility function" or a "preference-ordering" that ranks all sets of consequences from the most preferred to the least preferred.

4. The decision maker selects the alternative leading to the preferred set of consequences. In the case of *certainty*, the choice is unambiguous. In the case of *risk*, rationality is usually defined as the choice of that alternative for which the expected utility is greatest. Expected utility is defined here as the average, weighted by the probabilities of occurrence, of the utilities attached to all possible consequences. In the case of *uncertainty*, the definition of rationality becomes problematic. One proposal that has had wide currency is the rule of "minimax risk": consider the worst set of consequences that may follow from each alternative, then select the alternative whose "worst set of consequences" is preferred to the worst sets attached to other alternatives. There are other proposals (e.g., the rule of "minimax regret"), but we shall not discuss them here.

**Some Difficulties in the Classical Theory.** There are difficulties with this model of rational man. In the first place, only in the case of certainty does it agree well with common-sense notions of rationality. In the case of uncertainty, especially, there is little agreement, even among exponents of statistical decision theory, as to the "correct" definition, or whether, indeed, the term "correct" has any meaning here (Marschak, 1950).

A second difficulty with existing models of rational man is that it makes three exceedingly important demands upon the choice-making mechanism. It assumes (1) that all the alternatives of choice are "given"; (2) that all the consequences attached to each alternative are known (in one of the three senses corresponding to certainty, risk, and uncertainty respectively); (3) that the rational man has a complete utility-ordering (or cardinal function) for all possible sets of consequences.

One can hardly take exception to these requirements in a normative model— a model that tells people how they *ought* to choose. For if the rational man lacked information, he might have chosen differently "if only he had known." At best, he is "subjectively" rational, not "objectively" rational. But the notion of objective rationality assumes there is some objective reality in which the "real" alternatives, the "real" consequences, and the "real" utilities exist. If this is so, it is not even clear why the cases of choice under risk and under uncertainty are admitted as rational. If it is not so, it is not clear why only limitations upon knowledge of consequences are considered, and why limitations upon knowledge of alternatives and utilities are ignored in the model of rationality.

From a phenomenological viewpoint we can only speak of rationality relative to a frame of reference; and this frame of reference will be determined by the limitations on the rational man's knowledge. We can, of course, introduce the notion of a person observing the choices of a subject, and can speak of the rationality of the subject relative to the frame of reference of the observer. If the subject is a rat and the observer is a man (especially if he is the man who designed the experimental situation), we may regard the man's perception of the situation as objective and the rat's as subjective. (We leave out of account the specific difficulty that the rat presumably knows his own utility function better than the man does.) If, however, both subject and observer are men—and particularly if the situation is a natural one not constructed for experimental purposes by the observer—then it becomes difficult to specify the objective situation. It will be safest, in such situations, to speak of rationality only relative to some specified frame of reference.

The classical organization theory described in Chapter 2, like classical economic theory, failed to make explicit this subjective and relative character of rationality, and in so doing, failed to examine some of its own crucial premises. The organizational and social environment in which the decision maker finds himself determines what consequences he will anticipate, what ones he will not; what alternatives he will consider, what ones he will ignore. In a theory of organization these variables cannot be treated as unexplained independent factors, but must themselves be determined and predicted by the theory.

**Routinized and Problem-Solving Responses.**   The theory of rational choice put forth here incorporates two fundamental characteristics: (1) Choice is always exercised with respect to a limited, approximate, simplified "model" of the real situation [A-6.1].[1] We call the chooser's model his "definition of the situation." (2) The elements of the definition of the situation are not "given"—that is, we do not take these as data of our theory—but are themselves the outcome of psychological and sociological processes, including the chooser's own activities and the activities of others in his environment [A-6.2] (Simon, 1947, 1955; March, 1955; Cyert and March, 1955, 1956; Newell, Shaw, and Simon, 1958).

Activity (individual or organizational) can usually be traced back to an environmental stimulus of some sort, e.g., a customer order or a fire gong. The responses to stimuli are of various kinds. At one extreme, a stimulus evokes a response—sometimes very elaborate—that has been developed and learned at some previous time as an appropriate response for a stimulus of this class. This is the "routinized" end of the continuum, where a stimulus calls forth a performance program almost instantaneously.

At the other extreme, a stimulus evokes a larger or smaller amount of problem-solving activity directed toward finding performance activities with which to complete the response. Such activity is distinguished by the fact that it can be dispensed with once the performance program has been learned. Problem-solving activities can generally be identified by the extent to which they involve *search*: search aimed at discovering alternatives of action or consequences of action. "Discovering" alternatives may involve inventing and elaborating whole performance programs where these are not already available in the problem solver's repertory (Katona, 1951).

When a stimulus is of a kind that has been experienced repeatedly in the past, the response will ordinarily be highly routinized [A-6.3]. The stimulus will evoke, with a minimum of problem-solving or other computational activity, a well-structured definition of the situation that will include a repertory of response programs, and programs for selecting an appropriate specific response from the repertory. When a stimulus is relatively novel, it will evoke problem-solving activity aimed initially at constructing a definition of the situation and then at developing one or more appropriate performance programs [A-6.4].

Psychologists (e.g., Wertheimer, Duncker, de Groot, Maier) and observant laymen (e.g., Poincaré, Hadamard) who have studied creative thinking and problem-solving have been unanimous in ascribing a large role in these phenomena to search processes. Search is partly random, but in effective problem-solving it is not blind. The design of the search process is itself often an object of rational decision. Thus, we may distinguish substantive planning—developing new performance programs—from procedural planning—developing programs for the problem-solving process itself. The response to a particular stimulus may involve more than performance—the stimulus may evoke a spate of problem-solving activity—but the problem-solving activity may itself be routinized to a greater or lesser degree. For example, search processes may be systematized by the use of check lists.

**Satisfactory Versus Optimal Standards.** What kinds of search and other problem-solving activity are needed to discover an adequate range of alternatives and consequences for choice depends on the criterion applied to the choice. In particular, finding the optimal alternative is a radically different problem from finding a satisfactory alternative. An alternative is *optimal* if: (1) there exists a set of criteria that permits all alternatives to be compared, and (2) the alternative in question is preferred, by these criteria, to all other alternatives. An alternative is *satisfactory* if: (1) there exists a set of criteria that describes minimally satisfactory alternatives, and (2) the alternative in question meets or exceeds all these criteria.

*Most human decision-making, whether individual or organizational, is concerned with the discovery and selection of satisfactory alternatives; only in exceptional cases is it concerned with the discovery and selection of optimal alternatives* [A-6.5]. To optimize requires processes several orders of magnitude more complex than those required to satisfice. An example is the difference between searching a haystack to find the *sharpest* needle in it and searching the haystack to find a needle sharp enough to sew with.

In making choices that meet satisfactory standards, the standards themselves are part of the definition of the situation. Hence, we need not regard these as given—any more than the other elements of the definition of the situation—but may include in the theory the processes through which these standards are set and modified. The standard-setting process may itself meet standards of rationality: for example, an "optimizing" rule would be to set the standard at the level where the marginal improvement in alternatives obtainable by raising it would be just balanced by the marginal cost of searching for alternatives meeting the higher standard. Of course, in practice the "marginal improvement" and the "marginal cost" are seldom measured in comparable units, or with much accuracy. Nevertheless, a similar result would be automatically attained if the standards were raised whenever alternatives proved easy to discover, and lowered whenever they were difficult to discover. Under these circumstances, the alternatives chosen would not be far from the optima, if the cost of search were taken into consideration. Since human standards tend to have this characteristic under many conditions, some theorists have sought to maintain the optimizing model by introducing cost-of-search considerations. Although we doubt whether this will be a fruitful alternative to the model we are proposing in very many situations, neither model has been used for predictive purposes often enough to allow a final judgment.

**Performance Programs.**   We have seen that under certain circumstances, the search and choice processes are very much abridged. At the limit, an environmental stimulus may evoke immediately from the organization a highly complex and organized set of responses. Such a set of responses we call a *performance program,* or simply a *program.* For example, the sounding of the alarm gong in a fire station initiates such a program. So does the appearance of a relief applicant at a social worker's desk. So does the appearance of an automobile chassis in front of the work station of a worker on the assembly line.

Situations in which a relatively simple stimulus sets off an elaborate program of activity without any apparent interval of search, problem-solving, or choice are not rare. They account for a very large part of the behavior of all persons, and for almost all of the behavior of persons in relatively routine positions. Most behavior, and particularly most behavior in organizations, is governed by performance programs.

The term "program" is not intended to connote complete rigidity. The content of the program may be adaptive to a large number of characteristics of the stimulus that initiates it. Even in the simple case of the fire gong, the response depends on the location of the alarm, as indicated by the number of strokes. The program may also be conditional on data that are independent of the initiating stimuli. It is then more properly called a *performance strategy.* For example, when inventory records show that the quantity on hand of a commodity has decreased to the point where it should be reordered, the decision rule that governs the behavior of the purchasing agent may call upon him to determine the amount to be ordered on the basis of a formula into which he inserts the quantity that has been sold over the past 12 months. In this case, search has been eliminated from the problem, but choice—of a very routinized kind, to be sure—remains.

We will regard a set of activities as routinized, then, to the degree that choice has been simplified by the development of a fixed response to defined stimuli. If search has been eliminated, but a choice remains in the form of a clearly defined and systematic computing routine, we will still say that the activities are routinized. We will regard activities as unroutinized to the extent that they have to be preceded by program-developing activities of a problem-solving kind.

## FOOTNOTES

1. Numbers in brackets refer to a list of propositions which appear at the end of the original work. The propositions are not repeated in this abridgement. —Eds.

## REFERENCES

Katona, G. *Psychological Analysis of Economic Behavior.* New York: McGraw-Hill, 1951.

March, J. G. An introduction to the Theory and Measurement of influence. *American Political Science Review,* 1955, *49,* 431–451.

Marschak, J. The role of liquidity under complete and incomplete information. *Econometrica,* 1949, *17,* 180–182.

Newell, A., Shaw, J. C., & Simon, H. A. Elements of a theory of human problem solving. *Psychological Review,* 1958, *65,* 151–166.

Simon, H. A. *Administrative Behavior.* New York: Macmillan, 1947.

---

### *Learning Review*

*Questions:*

1. There are a set of consequences attached to alternatives, the existing theories of the events that will ensue if a particular alternative is chosen: _____, _____, and _____.

2. The decision maker has a _____ _____ that ranks all sets of consequences from the most preferred to least preferred.

3. Simon discusses and provides examples of two types of responses that may be utilized in the decision making process. They are _____ and _____-_____.

4. "_____" alternatives may involve inventing and elaborating whole performance programs where these are not already available in the problem solver's repertory.

5. Most behavior—and particularly most behavior in organizations—is governed by _____ programs.

*Answers:*

1. certainty, risk, uncertainty; 2. utility function; 3. routinized, problem-solving; 4. Discovering; 5. performance

## Retrospective Comment

### BY JOHN R. SCHERMERHORN, JR.*

Any student of organizations should recognize that humans are limited in their cognitive capacities. Furthermore, the presence of these limitations is one reason why organizations are so important as social phenomena. A well designed and managed organization helps its members to collectively overcome their cognitive limitations and to subsequently achieve things which they would otherwise be incapable of accomplishing as individuals.

Even in organizations, however, cognitive limits influence individual behavior. This point is the most fundamental of several insights offered by March and Simon in the preceding passage from their book *Organizations*. The passage views this influence as being manifested in a tendency for people to make "satisficing" as opposed to "optimizing" decisions. The practicing manager is wise to carefully consider the differences between these two approaches to decision-making in organizations.

The "satisficing" model of decision-making is a useful way of describing how people actually make many decisions in the course of their day-to-day activities. Choose a sample decision from your experience, or choose one from the observed experiences of others. You will probably find that only a limited number of possible alternatives were considered, and that the first alternative to prove satisfactory was the one chosen for action. This is true *satisficing* behavior. By contrast, a person who would have "optimized" in the sample decision situation would have initially identified *all* possible alternatives, and then gone on to choose for action the one alternative that *best* met the criteria of evaluation. March and Simon essentially argue that cognitive limitations make it difficult for individuals to actually behave in accord with the latter example.

It is true that the satisficing model is capable of describing decision-making behavior in organizations. Describing such behavior is one thing; however, *prescribing* how such behavior should be accomplished is quite another. March and Simon's readers should not let this key point become obscured. An all-encompassing endorsement of the satisficing decision model as a guideline for managerial behavior would be unfortunate from the perspectives of both theory and practice.

The informed manager will recognize that both the satisficing and optimizing decision models are integral components of her or his decision-making repertoiré. Because of its efficiency, the satisficing model is bound to be important and useful on many occasions. But, there are certainly other circumstances in which the alternative optimizing model is more appropriate. Thus, the manager's challenge emerges twofold: 1) To learn *how* to use *each* of the decision-making models, and, 2) to learn *when* to use each to its maximum advantage.

Throughout your study of management and organizations you will find that scholars are increasingly concerned with contingency theories; i.e., theories which try to match behavior with situations rather than trying to specify one best way to handle all situations. This same concept of contingency is pertinent to the present discussion. Just because the satisficing decision model is a powerful way of describing behavior in organizations, managers should not be too quick to legitimate this model as the correct way to make all decisions. In fact, a satisficing approach will prove advantageous in some circumstances and disadvantageous in others. Given the impetus provided by March and Simon, you can now begin to identify the contingencies that should govern your future choices to make decisions via satisficing or optimizing methods.

---

\* Professor, College of Business Administration, Southern Illinois University at Carbondale.

# 12

# *One More Time: How Do You Motivate Employees?*

## FREDERICK HERZBERG

### *About the Author*

**Frederick Herzberg** is University Distinguished Professor of Management at the University of Utah. A student of motivation in the United States and abroad, Herzberg received his B.S. from CCNY and his Ph.D. from the University of Pittsburgh. His best-known books are *The Motivation to Work* (with Bernard Mausner and Barbara Snyderman), *Work and the Nature of Man,* and *The Managerial Choice: To Be Efficient and to Be Human.* He is also the author of over 100 articles and a widely-employed consultant and management educator in the U.S. and in over 30 foreign nations. His renown stems from both his motivator-hygiene theory (see below) and his pioneering work in job enrichment.

Reprinted by permission of the *Harvard Business Review.* "One More Time: How Do You Motivate Employees?" by Frederick Herzberg (January/February 1968). Copyright © 1968 by the President and Fellows of Harvard College; all rights reserved.

*Author's note:* I should like to acknowledge the contributions that Robert Ford of the American Telephone and Telegraph Company has made to the ideas expressed in this paper, and in particular to the successful application of these ideas in improving work performance and the job satisfaction of employees.

# PREVIEW

A. Motivating employees with KITA (kick in the pants).
   1. Negative physical KITA results in employee performance through a negative physical action taken by management.
   2. Negative psychological KITA results in employee performance through forcing their moves. This is accomplished by using the system to do the dirty work.
   3. Positive KITA is designed to motivate employees through the use of positive reinforcements as motivators.
   4. The use of KITA as motivators has diminished due to its poor track record.
B. Myths of past theories of motivation.
   1. Early positive KITA personnel practices focused on monetary and recreational rewards as motivators.
   2. Later theories of motivation took a more humanistic approach.
   3. While theories of motivation progressed, they still tended to focus on short-term, rather than lasting motivation.
C. The development of *hygiene* and *motivator* factors.
   1. This approach suggests that the factors involved in producing job satisfaction are distinct and separate from those factors that lead to job dissatisfaction.
   2. Hygiene factors relate only to job dissatisfaction.
   3. Motivator factors are utilized in promoting job satisfaction.
D. Use of job loading in job enrichment.
   1. Empirical evidence shows that performance and attitudes can be improved through the use of vertical job loading.
   2. Horizontal job loading is ineffective in motivating workers.
E. Development of job enrichment.
   1. Job enlargement represented an early development in this area of motivation.
   2. Job enrichment combines the positive points of job enlargement with the opportunity for the employee's psychological growth.
F. Steps involved in implementing job enrichment as a motivating tool.

How many articles, books, speeches, and workshops have pleaded plaintively, "How do I get an employee to do what I want him to do?"

The psychology of motivation is tremendously complex, and what has been unraveled with any degree of assurance is small indeed. But the dismal ratio of knowledge to speculation has not dampened the enthusiasm for new forms of snake oil that are constantly coming on the market, many of them with academic testimonials. Doubtless this article will have no depressing impact on the market for snake oil, but since the ideas expressed in it have been tested in many corporations and other organizations, it will help—I hope—to redress the imbalance in the aforementioned ratio.

## 'Motivating' with KITA

In lectures to industry on the problem, I have found that the audiences are anxious for quick and practical answers, so I will begin with a straightforward, practical formula for moving people.

What is the simplest, surest, and most direct way of getting someone to do something? Ask him? But if he responds that he does not want to do it, then that calls for a psychological consultation to determine the reason for his obstinacy. Tell him? His response shows that he does not understand you, and now an expert in communication methods has to be brought in to show you how to get through to him. Give him a monetary incentive? I do not need to remind the reader of the complexity and difficulty involved in setting up and administering an incentive system. Show him? This means a costly training program. We need a simple way.

Every audience contains the "direct action" manager who shouts, "Kick him!" And this type of manager is right. The surest and least circumlocuted way of getting someone to do something is to kick him in the pants—give him what might be called the KITA.

There are various forms of KITA, and here are some of them:

□ *Negative physical KITA.* This is a literal application of the term and was frequently used in the past. It has, however, three major drawbacks: (1) it is inelegant; (2) it contradicts the precious image of benevolence that most organizations cherish; and (3) since it is a physical attack, it directly stimulates the autonomic nervous system, and this often results in negative feedback—the employee may just kick you in return. These factors give rise to certain taboos against negative physical KITA.

The psychologist has come to the rescue of those who are no longer permitted to use negative physical KITA. He has uncovered infinite sources of psychological vulnerabilities and the appropriate methods to play tunes on them. "He took my rug away"; "I wonder what he meant by that"; "The boss is always going around me"—these symptomatic expressions of ego sores that have been rubbed raw are the result of application of:

□ *Negative Psychological KITA.* This has several advantages over negative physical KITA. First, the cruelty is not visible; the bleeding is internal and comes much later. Second, since it affects the higher cortical centers of the brain with its inhibitory powers, it reduces the possibility of physical backlash. Third, since the number of psychological pains that a person can feel is almost infinite, the direction and site possibilities of the KITA are increased many times. Fourth, the person administering the kick can manage to be above it all and let the system accomplish the dirty work. Fifth, those who practice it receive some ego satisfaction (oneupmanship), whereas they would find drawing blood abhorrent. Finally, if the employee does complain, he can always be accused of being paranoid, since there is no tangible evidence of an actual attack.

Now, what does negative KITA accomplish? If I kick you in the rear (physically or psychologically), who is motivated? *I* am motivated; *you* move! Negative KITA does not lead to motivation, but to movement. So:

□ *Positive KITA.* Let us consider motivation. If I say to you, "Do this for me or the company, and in return I will give you a reward, an incentive, more status, a promotion, all the quid pro quos that exist in the industrial organization," am I motivating you? The overwhelming opinion I receive from management people is, "Yes, this is motivation."

I have a year-old Schnauzer. When it was a small puppy and I wanted it to move, I kicked it in the rear and it moved. Now that I have finished its obedience training, I hold up a dog biscuit when I want the Schnauzer to move. In this instance, who is motivated—I or the dog? The dog wants the biscuit, but it is I who want it to move. Again, I am the one who is motivated, and the dog is the one who moves. In this instance all I did was apply KITA frontally; I exerted a pull instead of a push. When industry wishes to use such positive KITAs, it has available an incredible number and variety of dog biscuits (jelly beans for humans) to wave in front of the employee to get him to jump.

Why is it that managerial audiences are quick to see that negative KITA is *not* motivation, while they are almost unanimous in their judgment that positive KITA *is* motivation? It is because negative KITA is rape, and positive KITA is seduction. But it is infinitely worse to be seduced than to be raped; the latter is an unfortunate occurrence, while the former signifies that you were a party to your own downfall. This is why positive KITA is so popular: it is a tradition; it is in the American way. The organization does not have to kick you; you kick yourself.

## Myths About Motivation

Why is KITA not motivation? If I kick my dog (from the front or the back), he will move. And when I want him to move again, what must I do? I must kick him again. Similarly, I can charge a man's battery, and then recharge it, and recharge it again. But it is only when he has his own generator that we can talk about motivation. He then needs no outside stimulation. He *wants* to do it.

With this in mind, we can review some positive KITA personnel practices that were developed as attempts to instill "motivation":

1. *Reducing time spent at work*—This represents a marvelous way of motivating people to work—getting them off the job! We have reduced (formally and infor-

mally) the time spent on the job over the last 50 or 60 years until we are finally on the way to the "6½-day weekend." An interesting variant of this approach is the development of off-hour recreation programs. The philosophy here seems to be that those who play together, work together. The fact is that motivated people seek more hours of work, not fewer.

2. *Spiraling wages*—Have these motivated people? Yes, to seek the next wage increase. Some medievalists still can be heard to say that a good depression will get employees moving. They feel that if rising wages don't or won't do the job, perhaps reducing them will.

3. *Fringe benefits*—Industry has outdone the most welfare-minded of welfare states in dispensing cradle-to-the-grave succor. One company I know of had an informal "fringe benefit of the month club" going for a while. The cost of fringe benefits in this country has reached approximately 25% of the wage dollar, and we still cry for motivation.

People spend less time working for more money and more security than ever before, and the trend cannot be reversed. These benefits are no longer rewards; they are rights. A 6-day week is inhuman, a 10-hour day is exploitation, extended medical coverage is a basic decency, and stock options are the salvation of American initiative. Unless the ante is continuously raised, the psychological reaction of employees is that the company is turning back the clock.

When industry began to realize that both the economic nerve and the lazy nerve of their employees had insatiable appetites, it started to listen to the behavioral scientists who, more out of a humanist tradition than from scientific study, criticized management for not knowing how to deal with people. The next KITA easily followed.

4. *Human relations training*—Over 30 years of teaching and, in many instances, of practicing psychological approaches to handling people have resulted in costly human relations programs and, in the end, the same question: How do you motivate workers? Here, too, escalations have taken place. Thirty years ago it was necessary to request, "Please don't spit on the floor." Today the same admonition requires three "pleases" before the employee feels that his superior has demonstrated the psychologically proper attitudes toward him.

The failure of human relations training to produce motivation led to the conclusion that the supervisor or manager himself was not psychologically true to himself in his practice of interpersonal decency. So an advanced form of human relations KITA, sensitivity training, was unfolded.

5. *Sensitivity training*—Do you really, really understand yourself? Do you really, really, really trust the other man? Do you really, really, really, really cooperate? The failure of sensitivity training is now being explained, by those who have become opportunistic exploiters of the technique, as a failure to really (five times) conduct proper sensitivity training courses.

With the realization that there are only temporary gains from comfort and economic and interpersonal KITA, personnel managers concluded that the fault lay not in what they were doing, but in the employee's failure to appreciate what they were doing. This opened up the field of communications, a whole new area of "scientifically" sanctioned KITA.

6. *Communications*—The professor of communications was invited to join the faculty of management training programs and help in making employees understand what management was doing for them. House organs, briefing sessions, supervisory instruction on the importance of communication, and all sorts of propaganda have proliferated until today there is even an International Council of Industrial Editors. But no motivation resulted, and the obvious thought occurred that perhaps management was not hearing what the employees were saying. That led to the next KITA.

7. *Two-way communication*—Management ordered morale surveys, suggestion plans, and group participation programs. Then both employees and management were communicating and listening to each other more than ever, but without much improvement in motivation.

The behavioral scientists began to take another look at their conceptions and their data, and they took human relations one step further. A glimmer of truth was beginning to show through in the writings of the so-called higher-order-need psychologists. People, so they said, want to actualize themselves. Unfortunately, the "actualizing" psychologists got mixed up with the human relations psychologists, and a new KITA emerged.

8. *Job participation*—Though it may not have been the theoretical intention, job participation often became a "give them the big picture" approach. For example, if a man is tightening 10,000 nuts a day on an assembly line with a torque wrench, tell him he is building a Chevrolet. Another approach had the goal of giving the employee a *feeling* that he is determining, in some measure, what he does on his job. The goal was to provide a *sense* of achievement rather than a substantive achievement in his task. Real achievement, of course, requires a task that makes it possible.

But still there was no motivation. This led to the inevitable conclusion that the employees must be sick, and therefore to the next KITA.

9. *Employee counseling*—The initial use of this form of KITA in a systematic fashion can be credited to the Hawthorne experiment of the Western Electric Company during the early 1930's. At that time, it was found that the employees harbored irrational feelings that were interfering with the rational operation of the factory. Counseling in this instance was a means of letting the employees unburden themselves by talking to someone about their problems. Although the counseling techniques were primitive, the program was large indeed.

The counseling approach suffered as a result of experiences during World War II, when the programs themselves were found to be interfering with the operation of the organizations; the counselors had forgotten their role of benevolent listeners and were attempting to do something about the problems that they heard about. Psychological counseling, however, has managed to survive the negative impact of World War II experiences and today is beginning to flourish with renewed sophistication. But, alas, many of these programs, like all the others, do not seem to have lessened the pressure of demands to find out how to motivate workers.

Since KITA results only in short-term movement, it is safe to predict that the cost of these programs will increase steadily and new varieties will be developed as old positive KITAs reach their satiation points.

## Hygiene vs. Motivators

Let me rephrase the perennial question this way: How do you install a generator in an employee? A brief review of my motivation-hygiene theory of job attitudes is required before theoretical and practical suggestions can be offered. The theory was first drawn from an examination of events in the lives of engineers and accountants. At least 16 other investigations, using a wide variety of populations (including some in the Communist countries), have since been completed, making the original research one of the most replicated studies in the field of job attitudes.

The findings of these studies, along with corroboration from many other investigations using different procedures, suggest that the factors involved in producing job satisfaction (and motivation) are separate and distinct from the factors that lead to job dissatisfaction. Since separate factors need to be considered, depending on whether job satisfaction or job dissatisfaction is being examined, it follows that these two feelings are not opposites of each other. The opposite of job satisfaction is not job dissatisfaction but, rather, *no* job satisfaction; and, similarly, the opposite of job dissatisfaction is not job satisfaction, but *no* job dissatisfaction.

Stating the concept presents a problem in semantics, for we normally think of satisfaction and dissatisfaction as opposites—i.e., what is not satisfying must be dissatisfying, and vice versa. But when it comes to understanding the behavior of people in their jobs, more than a play on words is involved.

Two different needs of man are involved here. One set of needs can be thought of as stemming from his animal nature—the built-in drive to avoid pain from the environment, plus all the learned drives which become conditioned to the basic biological needs. For example, hunger, a basic biological drive, makes it necessary to earn money, and then money becomes a specific drive. The other set of needs relates to that unique human characteristic, the ability to achieve and, through achievement, to experience psychological growth. The stimuli for the growth needs are tasks that induce growth; in the industrial setting, they are the *job content*. Contrariwise, the stimuli inducing pain-avoidance behavior are found in the *job environment*.

The growth or *motivator* factors that are intrinsic to the job are: achievement, recognition for achievement, the work itself, responsibility, and growth or advancement. The dissatisfaction-avoidance or *hygiene* (KITA) factors that are extrinsic to the job include: company policy and administration, supervision, interpersonal relationships, working conditions, salary, status, and security.

A composite of the factors that are involved in causing job satisfaction and job dissatisfaction, drawn from samples of 1,685 employees, is shown in *Exhibit I*. The results indicate that motivators were the primary cause of satisfaction, and hygiene factors the primary cause of unhappiness on the job. The employees, studied in 12 different investigations, included lower-level supervisors, profes-

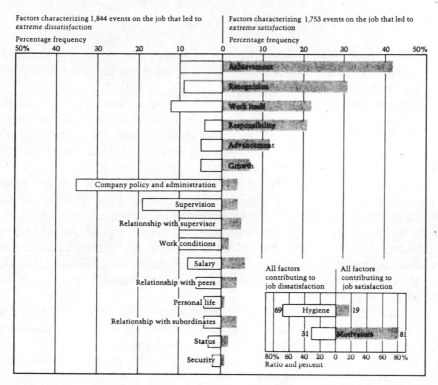

*Exhibit I.* Factors affecting job attitudes, as reported in 12 investigations

sional women, agricultural administrators, men about to retire from management positions, hospital maintenance personnel, manufacturing supervisors, nurses, food handlers, military officers, engineers, scientists, housekeepers, teachers, technicians, female assemblers, accountants, Finnish foremen, and Hungarian engineers.

They were asked what job events had occurred in their work that had led to extreme satisfaction or extreme dissatisfaction on their part. Their responses are broken down in the exhibit into percentages of total "positive" job events and of total "negative" job events. (The figures total more than 100% on both the "hygiene" and "motivators" sides because often at least two factors can be attributed to a single event; advancement, for instance, often accompanies assumption of responsibility.)

To illustrate, a typical response involving achievement that had a negative effect for the employee was, "I was unhappy because I didn't do the job successfully." A typical response in the small number of positive job events in the Company Policy and Administration grouping was, "I was happy because the company reorganized the section so that I didn't report any longer to the guy I didn't get along with."

As the lower right-hand part of the exhibit shows, of all the factors contributing to job satisfaction, 81% were motivators. And of all the factors contributing to the employees' dissatisfaction over their work, 69% involved hygiene elements.

## Eternal Triangle

There are three general philosophies of personnel management. The first is based on organizational theory, the second on industrial engineering, and the third on behavioral science.

The organizational theorist believes that human needs are either so irrational or so varied and adjustable to specific situations that the major function of personnel management is to be as pragmatic as the occasion demands. If jobs are organized in a proper manner, he reasons, the result will be the most efficient job structure, and the most favorable job attitudes will follow as a matter of course.

The industrial engineer holds that man is mechanistically oriented and economically motivated and his needs are best met by attuning the individual to the most efficient work process. The goal of personnel management therefore should be to concoct the most appropriate incentive system and to design the specific working conditions in a way that facilitates the most efficient use of the human machine. By structuring jobs in a manner that leads to the most efficient operation, the engineer believes that he can obtain the optimal organization of work and the proper work attitudes.

The behavioral scientist focuses on group sentiments, attitudes of individual employees, and the organization's social and psychological climate. According to his persuasion, he emphasizes one or more of the various hygiene and motivator needs. His approach to personnel management generally emphasizes some form of human relations education, in the hope of instilling healthy employee attitudes and an organizational climate which he considers to be felicitous to human values. He believes that proper attitudes will lead to efficient job and organizational structure.

There is always a lively debate as to the overall effectiveness of the approaches of the organizational theorist and the industrial engineer. Manifestly they have achieved much. But the nagging question for the behavioral scientist has been: What is the cost in human problems that eventually cause more expense to the organization—for instance, turnover, absenteeism, errors, violation of safety rules, strikes, restriction of output, higher wages, and greater fringe benefits? On the other hand, the behavioral scientist is hard put to document much manifest improvement in personnel management, using his approach.

The three philosophies can be depicted as a triangle, as is done in *Exhibit II,* with each persuasion claiming the apex angle. The motivation-hygiene theory claims the same angle as industrial engineering, but for opposite goals. Rather than rationalizing the work to increase efficiency, the theory suggests that work be *enriched* to bring about effective utilization of personnel. Such a systematic attempt to motivate employees by manipulating the motivator factors is just beginning.

The term *job enrichment* describes this embryonic movement. An older term, job enlargement, should be avoided because it is associated with past failures stemming from a misunderstanding of the problem. Job enrichment provides the opportunity for the employee's psychological growth, while job enlargement merely makes a job structurally bigger. Since scientific job enrichment is very

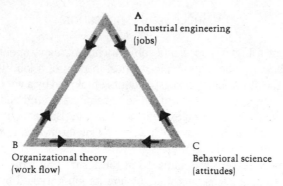

**A**
Industrial engineering
(jobs)

**B**
Organizational theory
(work flow)

**C**
Behavioral science
(attitudes)

*Exhibit II.* 'Triangle' of philosophies of personnel management

new, this article only suggests the principles and practical steps that have recently emerged from several successful experiments in industry.

## Job Loading

In attempting to enrich an employee's job, management often succeeds in reducing the man's personal contribution, rather than giving him an opportunity for growth in his accustomed job. Such an endeavor, which I shall call horizontal job loading (as opposed to vertical loading, or providing motivator factors), has been the problem of earlier job enlargement programs. This activity merely enlarges the meaninglessness of the job. Some examples of this approach, and their effect, are:

☐ Challenging the employee by increasing the amount of production expected of him. If he tightens 10,000 bolts a day, see if he can tighten 20,000 bolts a day. The arithmetic involved shows that multiplying zero by zero still equals zero.

☐ Adding another meaningless task to the existing one, usually some routine clerical activity. The arithmetic here is adding zero to zero.

☐ Rotating the assignments of a number of jobs that need to be enriched. This means washing dishes for a while, then washing silverware. The arithmetic is substituting one zero for another zero.

☐ Removing the most difficult parts of the assignment in order to free the worker to accomplish more of the less challenging assignments. This traditional industrial engineering approach amounts to subtraction in the hope of accomplishing addition.

These are common forms of horizontal loading that frequently come up in preliminary brainstorming sessions on job enrichment. The principles of vertical loading have not all been worked out as yet, and they remain rather general, but I have furnished seven useful starting points for consideration in *Exhibit III*.

## A Successful Application

An example from a highly successful job enrichment experiment can illustrate the distinction between horizontal and vertical loading of a job. The subjects of this study were the stockholder correspondents employed by a very large corporation. Seemingly, the task required of these carefully selected and highly trained correspondents was quite complex and challenging. But almost all indexes of performance and job attitudes were low, and exit interviewing confirmed that the challenge of the job existed merely as words.

A job enrichment project was initiated in the form of an experiment with one group, designated as an achieving unit, having its job enriched by the principles described in *Exhibit III*. A control group continued to do its job in the traditional way. (There were also two "uncommitted" groups of correspondents formed to measure the so-called Hawthorne Effect—that is, to gauge whether productivity and attitudes toward the job changed artificially merely because employees sensed that the company was paying more attention to them in doing something different or novel. The results for these groups were substantially the same as for the control group, and for the sake of simplicity I do not deal with them in this summary.) No changes in hygiene were introduced for either group other than those that would have been made anyway, such as normal pay increases.

The changes for the achieving unit were introduced in the first two months, averaging one per week of the seven motivators listed in *Exhibit III*. At the end of six months the members of the achieving unit were found to be outperforming their counterparts in the control group, and in addition indicated a marked

| Principle | Motivators Involved |
|---|---|
| A. Removing some controls while retaining accountability | Responsibility and personal achievement |
| B. Increasing the accountability of individuals for own work | Responsibility and recognition |
| C. Giving a person a complete natural unit of work (module, division, area, and so on) | Responsibility, achievement, and recognition |
| D. Granting additional authority to an employee in his activity; job freedom | Responsibility, achievement, and recognition |
| E. Making periodic reports directly available to the worker himself rather than to the supervisor | Internal recognition |
| F. Introducing new and more difficult tasks not previously handled | Growth and learning |
| G. Assigning individuals specific or specialized tasks, enabling them to become experts | Responsibility, growth, and advancement |

*Exhibit III.*   Principles of vertical job loading

increase in their liking for their jobs. Other results showed that the achieving group had lower absenteeism and, subsequently, a much higher rate of promotion.

*Exhibit IV* illustrates the changes in performance, measured in February and March, before the study period began, and at the end of each month of the study period. The shareholder service index represents quality of letters, including accuracy of information, and speed of response to stockholders' letters of inquiry. The index of a current month was averaged into the average of the two prior months, which means that improvement was harder to obtain if the indexes of the previous months were low. The "achievers" were performing less well before the six-month period started, and their performance service index continued to decline after the introduction of the motivators, evidently because of uncertainty over their newly granted responsibilities. In the third month, however, performance improved, and soon the members of this group had reached a high level of accomplishment.

*Exhibit V* shows the two groups' attitudes toward their job, measured at the end of March, just before the first motivator was introduced, and again at the

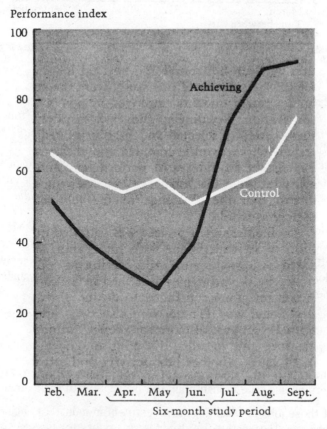

Exhibit IV.   Shareholder service index in company experiment (*Three-month cumulative average*)

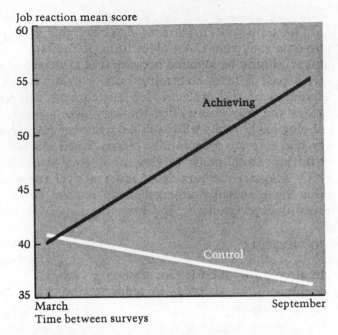

Job reaction mean score

*Exhibit V.* Changes in attitudes toward tasks in company experiment (*Changes in mean scores over six-month period*)

end of September. The correspondents were asked 16 questions, all involving motivation. A typical one was, "As you see it, how many opportunities do you feel that you have in your job for making worthwhile contributions?" The answers were scaled from 1 to 5, with 80 as the maximum possible score. The achievers became much more positive about their job, while the attitude of the control unit remained about the same (the drop is not statistically significant).

How was the job of these correspondents restructured? *Exhibit VI* lists the suggestions made that were deemed to be horizontal loading, and the actual vertical loading changes that were incorporated in the job of the achieving unit. The capital letters under "Principle" after "Vertical loading" refer to the corresponding letters in *Exhibit III.* The reader will note that the rejected forms of horizontal loading correspond closely to the list of common manifestations of the phenomenon on page 172.

## Steps to Job Enrichment

Now that the motivator idea has been described in practice, here are the steps that managers should take in instituting the principle with their employees:

1. Select those jobs in which (a) the investment in industrial engineering does not make changes too costly, (b) attitudes are poor, (c) hygiene is becoming very costly, and (d) motivation will make a difference in performance.

| Horizontal Loading Suggestions (Rejected) | Vertical Loading Suggestions (Adopted) | Principle |
|---|---|---|
| Firm quotas could be set for letters to be answered each day, using a rate which would be hard to reach. | Subject matter experts were appointed within each unit for other members of the unit to consult with before seeking supervisory help. (The supervisor had been answering all specialized and difficult questions.) | G |
| The women could type the letters themselves, as well as compose them, or take on any other clerical functions. | Correspondents signed their own names on letters. (The supervisor had been signing all letters.) | B |
| All difficult or complex inquiries could be channeled to a few women so that the remainder could achieve high rates of output. These jobs could be exchanged from time to time. | The work of the more experienced correspondents was proofread less frequently by supervisors and was done at the correspondents' desks, dropping verification from 100% to 10%. (Previously, all correspondents' letters had been checked by the supervisor.) | A |
| The women could be rotated through units handling different customers, and then sent back to their own units. | Production was discussed, but only in terms such as "a full day's work is expected." As time went on, this was no longer mentioned. (Before, the group had been constantly reminded of the number of letters that needed to be answered.) | D |
| | Outgoing mail went directly to the mailroom without going over supervisors' desks. (The letters had always been routed through the supervisors. | A |
| | Correspondents were encouraged to answer letters in a more personalized way. (Reliance on the form-letter approach had been standard practice.) | C |
| | Each correspondent was held personally responsible for the quality and accuracy of letters. (This responsibility had been the province of the supervisor and the verifier.) | B, E |

*Exhibit VI.* Enlargement vs. enrichment of correspondents' tasks in company experiment

2. Approach these jobs with the conviction that they can be changed. Years of tradition have led managers to believe that the content of the jobs is sacrosanct and the only scope of action that they have is in ways of stimulating people.

3. Brainstorm a list of changes that may enrich the jobs, without concern for their practicality.

4. Screen the list to eliminate suggestions that involve hygiene, rather than actual motivation.

5. Screen the list for generalities, such as "give them more responsibility," that are rarely followed in practice. This might seem obvious, but the motivator words have never left industry; the substance has just been rationalized and organized out. Words like "responsibility," "growth," "achievement," and "challenge," for example, have been elevated to the lyrics of the patriotic anthem for all organizations. It is the old problem typified by the pledge of allegiance to the flag being more important than contributions to the country—of following the form, rather than the substance.

6. Screen the list to eliminate any *horizontal* loading suggestions.

7. Avoid direct participation by the employees whose jobs are to be enriched. Ideas they have expressed previously certainly constitute a valuable source for recommended changes, but their direct involvement contaminates the process with human relations *hygiene* and, more specifically, gives them only a *sense* of making a contribution. The job is to be changed, and it is the content that will produce the motivation, not attitudes about being involved or the challenge inherent in setting up a job. That process will be over shortly, and it is what the employees will be doing from then on that will determine their motivation. A sense of participation will result only in short-term movement.

8. In the initial attempts at job enrichment, set up a controlled experiment. At least two equivalent groups should be chosen, one an experimental unit in which the motivators are systematically introduced over a period of time, and the other one a control group in which no changes are made. For both groups, hygiene should be allowed to follow its natural course for the duration of the experiment. Pre- and post-installation tests of performance and job attitudes are necessary to evaluate the effectiveness of the job enrichment program. The attitude test must be limited to motivator items in order to divorce the employee's view of the job he is given from all the surrounding hygiene feelings that he might have.

9. Be prepared for a drop in performance in the experimental group the first few weeks. The changeover to a new job may lead to a temporary reduction in efficiency.

10. Expect your first-line supervisors to experience some anxiety and hostility over the changes you are making. The anxiety comes from their fear that the changes will result in poorer performance for their unit. Hostility will arise when the employees start assuming what the supervisors regard as their own responsibility for performance. The supervisor without checking duties to perform may then be left with little to do.

After a successful experiment, however, the supervisor usually discovers the supervisory and managerial functions he has neglected, or which were never his because all his time was given over to checking the work of his subordinates. For example, in the R&D division of one large chemical company I know of, the supervisors of the laboratory assistants were theoretically responsible for their training and evaluation. These functions, however, had come to be performed in a routine, unsubstantial fashion. After the job enrichment program, during which the supervisors were not merely passive observers of the assistants' performance, the supervisors actually were devoting their time to reviewing performance and administering thorough training.

What has been called an employee-centered style of supervision will come about not through education of supervisors, but by changing the jobs that they do.

## Concluding Note

Job enrichment will not be a one-time proposition, but a continuous management function. The initial changes, however, should last for a very long period of time. There are a number of reasons for this:

□ The changes should bring the job up to the level of challenge commensurate with the skill that was hired.

□ Those who have still more ability eventually will be able to demonstrate it better and win promotion to higher-level jobs.

□ The very nature of motivators, as opposed to hygiene factors, is that they have a much longer-term effect on employees' attitudes. Perhaps the job will have to be enriched again, but this will not occur as frequently as the need for hygiene.

Not all jobs can be enriched, nor do all jobs need to be enriched. If only a small percentage of the time and money that is now devoted to hygiene, however, were given to job enrichment efforts, the return in human satisfaction and economic gain would be one of the largest dividends that industry and society have ever reaped through their efforts at better personnel management.

The argument for job enrichment can be summed up quite simply: If you have someone on a job, use him. If you can't use him on the job, get rid of him, either via automation or by selecting someone with lesser ability. If you can't use him and you can't get rid of him, you will have a motivation problem.

---

### *Learning Review*

*Questions:*

1. Factors that relate to job satisfaction are called ＿＿＿＿＿ factors, while ＿＿＿＿＿factors relate to job dissatisfaction.

2. The author identifies three KITAs: ＿＿＿＿＿ ＿＿＿＿＿ KITA, ＿＿＿＿＿ ＿＿＿＿＿KITA, and ＿＿＿＿＿ KITA.

3. Some of the motivator factors that are intrinsic to the job include _____, _____, _____, _____, and _____.

4. Three general philosophies of personnel management are _____ _____, _____ _____, and _____ _____.

*Answers:*

1. motivator, hygiene; 2. negative physical, negative psychological, positive; 3. achievement, recognition, responsibility, growth, advancement; 4. organizational theory, industrial engineering, behavioral science

---

# Retrospective Comment

## BY FREDERICK HERZBERG

It has been more than eighteen years since I wrote the "One More Time: How Do You Motivate Employees" article. Having it become the all-time most popular article in the *Harvard Business Review* and remain so each year since it was published has given me great Hygiene satisfaction.[1] That it continues to be an accurate analysis of work motivation and the problems that we now call the quality of work life gives me Motivator satisfaction as well.

I consider the most important point in the article to have been the distinction between Movement and Motivation. While business leaders unanimously agree that it costs them more and more to produce less and less, they still try to *move* their employees and to pour their resources into the job context features while mostly paying lip service to the design of the job itself. In spite of the success of the article and particularly the concept of job enrichment first described and illustrated in the article, the majority of business firms still depend on KITA to move their employees.

During the two decades since the article was published, contributions of the Organizational Behavior specialists appear to have reached a zenith. Yet, I see no evidence that productivity has improved one iota through their procedures. I can't resist the urge to say "I told you so!" But, at the same time, in retrospect, I may have been a little too harsh in referring to the behavioral science community as purveyors of "snake oil."

If I were to write "One More Time" today, I would emphasize that Organizational Behavior has a more positive and important role to play than the tone of the article at that time reflected. Certainly, we all can learn to get along better on the job. Reduction in tension through more congenial interpersonal relations is a necessary ingredient of a pleasant work environment. This is a worthwhile goal and one which the behavioral science community can help most businesses to achieve.

. The point, of course, and one which my article makes over and over again, is that improvements in the job context will NOT have a lasting impact on productivity. Only through changes to job content that give the worker more meaningful tasks to accomplish will you find the answer to the question, "How do you motivate employees?" Of course, I would also add the insights of experience, particularly in job enrichment, gained in these past two decades, some of which I have shared in numerous publications that have followed since 1968, including my latest book, *The Managerial Choice: To Be Efficient and To Be Human.*[2]

# REFERENCES

1. *Harvard Business Review,* 1977, *55* (6).
2. Herzberg, Frederick, *The Managerial Choice: To Be Efficient and To Be Human.* (2nd ed.) Salt Lake City, UT: Olympus Publishing, Inc., 1982.

# 13

# Business Objectives and Survival Needs: Notes on a Discipline of Business Enterprise

## PETER F. DRUCKER

### About the Author

**Peter F. Drucker** is an internationally recognized management consultant and best-selling author. His book, *The Practice of Management,* has sold over 200,000 copies since it was published in 1954 and continues to sell 20,000 copies a year. Most of his twenty-six books are on political and economic topics, but he has also written a book on oriental art and a book of fiction.

Drucker, a native of Vienna, received his doctorate in public and international law from Frankfort University. From 1950 to 1972, he was Professor of Management at New York University, where he continues to serve as Distinguished University Lecturer. Since 1971, he has been Clarke Professor of Social Science and Management at Claremont Graduate School in California. From 1979 to 1985, he was also Professorial Lecturer in Oriental Art at Pomona College.

Drucker has received fifteen honorary doctorates from universities in the United States, Belgium, England, Japan, and Switzerland.

Reprinted by permission of the author from the *Journal of Business,* Vol. 31 (April 1958), pp. 81–90. Photo courtesy of Alfred Eisenstaedt.

# PREVIEW

A. At present there is an absence of an adequate theory of business enterprise.
   1. This absence underlies four problems central to business.
      a. the inability of the layman to understand modern business enterprise and its behavior.
      b. the lack of a bridge of understanding between the macroeconomics of an economy and the microeconomics of the business enterprise.
      c. problems involved with the internal integration of the organization.
      d. the general negative attitudes of most businesspersons toward "theory".
B. Development of survival needs and objectives of the business enterprise.
   1. Central question is "What does business have to be, to do, to achieve— to exist at all?"
   2. For each survival need there should be a corresponding objective for the business.
   3. Every business should have similar survival objectives.
   4. The concept of survival objectives fulfills the first requirement of a genuine theory: that it be both formal and practical.
C. Illustration of survival functions and their relevance to business enterprise.
   1. Five survival functions exist and together define the areas in which each business must achieve a standard of performance and produce results above a minimum level if it is to survive.
   2. Management must be aware of each survival function, since a malfunction in any of the five endangers the entire business.
D. Essential tasks in developing a discipline of business enterprise.
   1. Development of clear concepts and usable measurements to set objectives and measure performance.
   2. Acceptance of the fact that business objectives are multidimensional.
   3. A rational and systematic approach to selection and balancing of objectives in order to ensure the survival and growth of the enterprise.

The literature of business management, confined to a few "how to do" books only fifty years ago, has grown beyond any one man's capacity even to catalogue it. Professional education for business has become the largest and most rapidly growing field of professional education in this country and is growing rapidly in all other countries in the free world. It also has created in the advanced postgraduate education for experienced, mature, and successful executives—perhaps first undertaken in systematic form at the University of Chicago—the only really new educational concept in a hundred and fifty years.

Yet so far we have little in the way of a "discipline" of business enterprise, little in the way of an organized, systematic body of knowledge, with its own theory, its own concepts, and its own methodology of hypothesis, analysis, and verification.

## The Need for a Theory of Business Behavior

The absence of an adequate theory of business enterprise is not just an "academic" concern; on the contrary, it underlies four major problems central to business as well as to a free-enterprise society.

1. One is the obvious inability of the layman to understand modern business enterprise and its behavior. What goes on, and why, "at the top" or "on the fourteenth floor" of the large corporation—the central economic and one of the central social institutions of modern industrial society—is as much of a mystery to the "outsider" as the magician's slight of hand is to the small boy in the audience. And the "outsiders" include not only those truly outside business enterprise. They include workers and shareholders; they include many professionally trained men in the business—the engineers or chemists, for instance—indeed, they include a good many management people themselves: supervisors, junior executives, functional managers. They may accept what "top management" does, but they accept on faith rather than by reason of knowledge and understanding. (Yet such understanding is needed for the success of the individual business as well as for the survival of industrial society and of the free-enterprise system.)

One of the real threats is the all-but-universal resistance to profit in such a system, the all-but-universal (but totally fallacious) belief that socialism—or any other ism—can operate an industrial economy without the "rake-off" of profit, and the all-but-universal concern lest profit be too high. That the danger in a dynamic, industrial economy is that profit may be too low to permit the risks of innovation, growth, and expansion—that, indeed, there may be no such thing as "profit" but only provision for the costs of the future—very few people understand.

This ignorance has resisted all attempt at education; this resistance to profits has proved impervious to all propaganda or appeals, even to the attempts at "profit-sharing."

The only thing capable of creating understanding of the essential and necessary function of profit in an expanding, risk-taking, industrial economy is an understanding of business enterprise. And that for all without personal, immediate experience in the general management of a business can come only through a general "model" of business enterprise, that is, through the general theory of a systematic discipline.

2. The second problem is the lack of any bridge of understanding between the "macro-economics" of an economy and the "micro-economics" of the most important actor in this economy, the business enterprise. The only "micro-economic" concept to be found in economic theory today is that of "profit maximization." To make it fit the actual, observable behavior of business enterprise, however, economists have had to bend, stretch, and qualify it until it has lost

all meaning and all usefulness. It has become as complicated as the "epicycles" with which pre-Copernican astronomers tried to save the geocentric view of the universe: "profit maximization" may mean short-run, immediate revenue or long-range basic profitability of wealth-producing resources; it may have to be qualified by a host of unpredictables such as managerial power drives, union pressures, technology, etc.; and it completely fails even then to account for business behavior in a growing economy. It does not enable the economist to predict business reaction to public policy any more; to the governmental policy-maker business reaction is as "irrational" as government policy, by and large, seems to the businessman.

But in modern industrial society we must be able to "translate" easily from public policy to business behavior and back again. The policymaker must be able to assess the impact of public policy on business behavior; and the business-man—especially in the large enterprise—must be able to assess the impact of his decisions and actions on the "macro-economy." "Profit-maximization" does not enable us to do either, as this paper intends to show, primarily because it fails to understand the role and function of profit.

3. The third area in which the absence of a genuine theory of business enterprise creates very real problems is that of the internal integration of the organization. The management literature is full of discussions of the "problem of the specialist" who sees only his own functional area or of the "problem of the scientist in business" who resents the demand that he subordinate his knowledge to business ends. Yet we will be getting ever more specialized; we will, of necessity, employ more and more highly trained "professionals." Each of those must be dedicated to his specialty; yet each must share a common vision and common goals and must voluntarily engage in a common effort. To bring this about is already the most time- and energy-consuming job of management, certainly in our big businesses, and no one I know claims to be able to do it successfully.

Twenty years ago it was still possible to see a business as a mechanical assemblage of "functions." Today we know that, when we talk of a "business," the "functions" simply do not exist. There is only business profit, business risk, business product, business investment, and business customer. The functions are irrelevant to any one of them. And yet it is equally obvious, if we look at the business, that the work has to be done by people who specialize, because nobody can know enough even to know all there is to be known about one of the major functions today—they are growing too fast. It is already asking a great deal of a good man to be a good functional man, and, in some areas, it is rapidly becoming almost too much to ask of a man. How, then, do we transmute functional knowledge and functional contribution into general direction and general results? The ability of big business—but even of many small ones—to survive depends on our ability to solve this problem.

4. The final problem—also a symptom both of the lack of discipline and of the need for it—is of course the businessman's own attitude toward "theory." When he says, "This is theoretical," he by and large still means: "This is irrele-vant." Whether managing a business enterprise could or should be a "science" (and one's answer to this question depends primarily on how one defines the

word "science"), we need to be able to consider theory the foundation for good practice. We would have no modern doctors, unless medicine (without itself being a "science" in any strict sense of the word) considered the life-sciences and their theories the foundation of good practice. Without such a foundation in a discipline of business enterprise we cannot make valid general statements, cannot therefore predict the outcome of actions or decisions; and can judge them only by hindsight and by their results—when it is too late to do anything. All we can have at the time of decision would be "hunches," "hopes," and "opinions," and, considering the dependence of modern society on business enterprise and the impact of managerial decisions, this is not good enough.

Without such a discipline we could also neither teach nor learn, let alone work systematically on the improvement of our knowledge and of our performance as managers of a business. Yet the need both for managers and for constant improvement of their knowledge and performance is so tremendous, quantitatively as well as qualitatively, that we simply cannot depend on the "natural selection" of a handful of "geniuses."

The need for a systematic discipline of business enterprise is particularly pressing in the underdeveloped growth countries of the world. Their ability to develop themselves will depend, above all, on their ability rapidly to develop men capable of managing business enterprise, that is, on the availability of a discipline that can be taught and can be learned. If all that is available to them is development through experience, they will almost inevitably be pushed toward some form of collectivism. For, however wasteful all collectivism is of economic resources, however destructive it is of freedom, dignity, and happiness, it economizes the managerial resource through its concentration of entrepreneurial and managerial decisions in the hands of a few "planners" at the top.

## What Are the Survival Needs Of Business Enterprise?

We are still a long way from a genuine "discipline" of business enterprise. But there is emerging today a foundation of knowledge and understanding. It is being created in some of our large companies and in some of our universities. In some places the starting point is economics, in some marketing, in some the administrative process, in others such new methodologies as operations research and synthesis or long-range planning. But what all these approaches, regardless of starting point or terminology, have in common is that they start out with the question: What are the survival needs of business enterprise? What, in other words, does it have to be, to do, to achieve—to exist at all? For each of these "needs" there has, then, to be an "objective."

It may be said that this approach goes back to the pioneering work on business objectives that was done at the Bell Telephone System under the presidency of Theodore Vail a full forty years ago. Certainly, that was the first time the management of a large business enterprise refused to accept the old, glib statement, "The objective of a business is to make a profit," and asked instead, "On what will our survival as a privately owned business depend?" The practical effectiveness of the seemingly so obvious and simple approach is proved by the survival, unique in developed countries, of privately owned telecommunications in the United States and Canada. A main reason for this was certainly the "survival objective" Vail set for the Bell System: "Public satisfaction with our service." Yet, though proved in practice, this remained, until recently, an isolated example. And it probably had to remain such until, within the last generation, the biologists developed the approach to understanding of "systems" by means of defining "essential survival functions."

"Survival objectives" are general; they must be the same in general for each and every business. Yet they are also specific; different performance and different results would be needed in each objective area for any particular business. And every individual business will also need its own specific balance between them at any given time.

The concept of survival objectives thus fulfils the first requirement of a genuine "theory"—that it be both formal and yet concretely applicable, that is, "practical." Survival objectives are also "objective" both as to their nature and as to the specific requirements in a given situation. They do not depend on "opinion" or "hunch." Yet—and that is essential—they do not "determine" entrepreneurial or managerial decisions; they are not (as is so much of traditional economics or of contemporary behavioral science) an attempt to substitute formulas for risk-taking decision or responsible judgment. They attempt rather to establish the foundation for decision and judgment, to make what is the specific task of entrepreneur and manager possible, effective, and rational, and to make it understandable and understood.

We have reached the stage where we know the "functions" of a business enterprise, with "function" being used the way the biologist talks about "procreation" as a "function" essential for the perpetuation of a living species.

There are *five such "survival functions"* of business enterprise. Together they define the areas in which each business, to survive, has to reach a standard of performance and produce results above a minimum level. They are also the areas affected by every business decision and, in turn, affecting every business result. Together these five areas of "survival objectives" describe therefore (operationally) the "nature of business enterprise."

1. The enterprise needs, first, a *human organization designed for joint performance* and capable of perpetuating itself.

It is an assemblage not of brick and mortar but of people. These people must work as individuals; they cannot work any other way. Yet they must voluntarily work for a common result and must therefore be organized for joint performance. The first requirement of business is therefore that there be an effective human organization.

But business must also be capable of perpetuating itself as a human organization if only because all the things we decide every day—if, indeed, we are managers— take for their operation more time than the good Lord has allotted us. We are not making a single decision the end of which we are likely to see while still working. How many managerial decisions will be liquidated within twenty years, will have disappeared, unless they are totally foolish decisions? Most of the decisions we make take five years before they even begin to have an impact; this is the short range of a decision. And then they take ten or fifteen years before (at the very earliest) they are liquidated, have ceased to be effective, and, therefore, have ceased to have to be reasonably right.

This means that the enterprise as a human organization has to be able to perpetuate itself. It has to be able to survive the life-span of any one man.

2. The second survival objective arises from the fact that the enterprise exists in *society and economy*. In business schools and business thinking we often tend to assume that the business enterprise exists by itself in a vacuum. We look at it from the inside. But the business enterprise is a creature of society and economy. If there is one thing we do know, it is that society and/or economy can put any business out of existence overnight—nothing is simpler. The enterprise exists on sufferance and exists only as long as society and economy believe that it does a job and a necessary, a useful, and a productive one.

I am not talking here of "public relations"; they are only one means. I am not talking of something that concerns only the giants. And I am not talking of "socialism." Even if the free-enterprise system survives, individual businesses and industries within it may be—and of course often have been—restricted, penalized, or even put out of business very fast by social or political action such as taxes or zoning laws, municipal ordinances or federal regulation, and so forth. Anticipation of social climate and economic policy, on the one hand, and organized behavior to create what business needs to survive in respect to both are therefore genuine survival needs of each business at all times. They have to be "factored" into every business decision.

Equally, the business is a creature of the economy and at the mercy of changes in it—in population and income, ways of life and spending patterns, expectations and values. Again here is need for objectives which anticipate so as to enable the business to adapt and which at the same time aim at creating the most favorable conditions.

3. Then, of course, there is the area of the specific purpose of business, of its contribution. The purpose is certainly to *supply an economic good and service.* This is the only reason why business exists. We would not suffer this complicated, difficult, and controversial institution except for the fact that we have not found any better way of supplying economic goods and services productively, economically, and efficiently. So, as far as we know, no better way exists. But that is its only justification, its only purpose.

4. There is another purpose characteristic which I would, so to speak, call the nature of the beast; namely, that this all happens in a *changing* economy and a *changing* technology. Indeed, in the business enterprise we have the first institution which is designed to produce change. All human institutions since the dawn of prehistory or earlier had always been designed to prevent change—all of them: family, government, church, army. Change has always been a catastrophic threat to human security. But in the business enterprise we have an institution that is designed to create change. This is a very novel thing. Incidentally,

it is one of the basic reasons for the complexity and difficulty of the institution.

This means not only that business must be able to adapt to change—that would be nothing very new. It means that every business, to survive, must strive to *innovate*. And innovation, that is, purposeful, organized action to bring about the new, is as important in the social field—the ways, methods, and organization of business, its marketing and market, its financial and personnel management, and so on—as it is in the technological areas of product and process.

In this country industrial research expenditures have risen from a scant one-tenth of 1 per cent of national income to 1½ or 2 per cent in less than thirty years. The bulk of this increase has come in the last ten years; this means that the impact in the form of major technological changes is still ahead of us. The speed of change in non-technological innovation, for instance, in distribution channels, has been equally great. Yet many businesses are still not even geared to adaptation to change; and only a mere handful are geared to innovation—and then primarily in the technological areas. Here lies therefore a great need for a valid theory of business enterprise but also a great opportunity for contribution.

5. Finally, there is an absolute requirement of survival, namely, that of *profitability*, for the very simple reason that everything I have said so far spells out *risk*. Everything I have said so far says that it is the purpose, the nature, and the necessity of this institution to take risks, to create risks. *And risks are genuine costs.* They are as genuine a cost as any the accountant can put his finger on. The only difference is that, until the future has become past, we do not know how big a cost; but they *are* costs. Unless we provide for costs, we are going to destroy capital. Unless we provide for loss, which is another way of saying for future cost, we are going to destroy wealth. Unless we provide for risk, we are going to destroy capacity to produce. And, therefore, a minimum profitability, adequate to the risks which we, by necessity, assume and create, is an absolute condition of survival not only for the enterprise but for society.

This says three things. First, the need for profitability is objective. It is of the nature of business enterprise and as such is independent of the motives of the businessman or of the structure of the "system." If we had archangels running businesses (who, by definition, are deeply disinterested in the profit motive), they would have to make a profit and would have to watch profitability just as eagerly, just as assiduously, just as faithfully, just as responsibly, as the most greedy wheeler-dealer or as the most convincedly Marxist commissar in Russia.

Second, profit is not the "entrepreneur's share" and the "reward" to one "factor of production." It does not rank on a par with the other "shares," such as that of "labor," for instance, but above them. It is not a claim *against* the enterprise but the claim *of* the enterprise—without which it cannot survive. How the profits are distributed and to whom is of great political importance; but for the understanding of the needs and behavior of a business it is largely irrelevant.

Finally, "profit maximization" is the wrong concept, whether it be interpreted to mean short-range or long-range profits or a balance of the two. The relevant question is, "What minimum does the business need?" not "What maximum can it make?" This "survival minimum" will, incidentally, be found to exceed present "maxima" in many cases. This, at least, has been my experience in most companies where a conscious attempt to think through the risks of the business has been attempted.

Here are five dimensions; and each of these five is a genuine view of the whole business enterprise. It is a human organization, and we can look upon it only in that aspect, as does our human relations literature. We can look at it from its existence in society and economy, which is what the economist does. This is a perfectly valid, but a one-sided view.

We can, similarly, look at the enterprise only from the point of view of its goods and services. Innovation and change are yet another dimension, and profitability is yet another. These are all genuine, true aspects of the same being. But only if we have all five of them in front of us do we have a theory of business enterprise on which practice can be built.

*For managing a business enterprise means making decisions, every one of which both depends on needs and opportunities in each of these five areas and, in turn, affects performance and results in each.*

## The Work to Be Done

The first conclusion from this is that every business needs objectives—explicit or not—in each of these five areas, for malfunction in any one of these endangers the entire business. And failure in any one area destroys the entire business— no matter how well it does in the other four areas. Yet these are not interdependent but autonomous areas.

1. *Here, then, is the first task of a discipline of business enterprise:* to develop clear concepts and usable measurements to set objectives and to measure performance in each of these five areas.

The job is certainly a big one—and a long one. There is no area as yet where we can really define the objectives, let alone measure results. Even in respect to profitability we have, despite great recent advances in managerial economics, figures for the past rather than measurements that relate current or expected profitability to the specific future risks and needs. In the other areas we do not even have that, by and large. And in some—the effectiveness of the human organization, the public standing in economy and society, or the area of innovation—we may, for a long time to come, perhaps forever, have to be content with qualitative appraisal making possible judgment. Even this would be tremendous progress.

2. A second conclusion is hardly less important: *no one simple objective is "the" objective of a business; no one single yardstick "the" measure of performances, prospects, and results of a business; no one single area "the" most important area.*

Indeed, the most dangerous oversimplification of business enterprise may well be that of the "one yardstick," whether "return on investment," "market standing," "product leadership," or what have you. At their best these measure performance in one genuine survival area. But malfunction or failure in any one area is not counterbalanced by performance in any other area, just as a sturdy respiratory or circulatory system will not save an animal if its digestive or nervous system collapses. Success, like failure, in business enterprise is *multidimensional*.

3. This, however, brings out another important need: a rational and systematic approach to the *selection and balance among objectives* so as best to provide for survival and growth of the enterprise. These can be called the "ethics" of business enterprise, insofar as ethics is the discipline that deals with rational value choices among means to ends. It can also be the "strategy" of entrepreneurship. Neither "ethics" nor "strategy" is capable of being absolutely determined, yet neither can be absolutely arbitrary. We need a discipline here that encompasses both the "typical" decision which adapts to circumstances and "plays" the averages of statistical probability, and the innovating, "unique event" of entrepreneurial vision and courage breaking with precedent and trends and creating new ones— and there are already some first beginnings of such a discipline of entrepreneurship. But such a discipline can never be more than theory of composition is to the musical composer or theory of strategy to the military leader: a safeguard against oversight, an appraisal of risks, and, above all, a stimulant to independence and innovation.

Almost by definition the demands of different survival objectives pull in different directions, at least for any one time period. And it is axiomatic that the resources even of the wealthiest business, or even of the richest country, never cover in full all demands in all areas; there is never so much that there has to be no allocation. Higher profitability can thus be achieved only by taking a risk in market standing, in product leadership, or in tomorrow's human organization, and vice versa. Which of these risks the enterprise can take, which it cannot take, and what it cannot afford not to take—these risk-taking, value-decisions between goals in one area versus goals in others, and between goals in one area today versus goals in others tomorrow, is a specific job of the entrepreneur. This decision itself will remain a "judgment," that is, a matter of human values, appraisal of the situation, weighing of alternatives, and balancing of risks. But an understanding of survival objectives and their requirements can supply both the rational foundation for the decision itself and the rational criteria for the analysis and appraisal of entrepreneurial performance.

## An Operational View of the Budgeting Process

The final conclusion is that we need a new approach to the process in which we make our value decisions between different objective areas—the budgeting process. And in particular do we need a real understanding of that part of the budget that deals with the expenses that express these decisions, that is, the "managed" and "capital" expenditures.

Commonly today, budgeting is conceived as a "financial" process. But it is only the notation that is financial; the decisions are entrepreneurial. Commonly today, "managed" expenditures and "capital" expenditures are considered quite separate. But the distinction is an accounting (and tax) fiction and misleading; both commit scarce resources to an uncertain future; both are, economically speaking, "capital" expenditures. And they, too, have to express the same basic decisions on survival objectives to be viable. Finally, today, most of our attention in the "operating budget" is given, as a rule, to other than the "managed" expenses, especially to the "variable" expenses, for that is where, historically, most money was spent. But, no matter how large or small the sums, it is in our decisions on the "managed" expenses that we decide on the future of the enterprise.

Indeed, we have little control over what the accountant calls "variable" expenses—the expenses which relate directly to units of production and are fixed by a certain way of doing things. We can change them, but not fast. We can change a relationship between units of production and labor costs (which we, with a certain irony, still consider "variable expenses" despite the fringe benefits). But within any time period these expenses can only be kept at a norm and cannot be changed. This is of course even more true for the expenses in respect to the decisions of the past, our "fixed" expenses. We cannot make them undone at all, whether these are capital expenses or taxes or what-have-you. They are beyond our control.

In the middle, however, are the expenses for the future which express our risk-taking value choices: the "capital expenses" and the "managed expenses." Here are the expenses on facilities and equipment, on research and merchandising, on product development and people development, on management and organization. This managed expense budget is the area in which we really make our decisions on our objectives. (That, incidentally, is why I dislike accounting ratios in that area so very much, because they try to substitute the history of the dead past for the making of the prosperous future.)

We make decisions in this process in two respects. First, what do we allocate people for? For the money in the budget is really people. What do we allocate people, and energy, and efforts to? To what objectives? We have to make choices, as we cannot do everything.

And, second, what is the time scale? How do we, in other words, *balance* expenditures for long-term permanent efforts against any decision with immediate impact? The one shows results only in the remote future, if at all. The development of people (a fifteen-year job), the effectiveness of which is untested and unmeasurable, is, for instance, a decision on faith over the long range. The other may show results immediately. To slight the one, however, might, in the long range, debilitate the business and weaken it. And, yet, there are certain real short-term needs that have to be met in the business—in the present as well as in the future.

Until we develop a clear understanding of basic survival objectives and some yardsticks for the decisions and choices in each area, budgeting will not become a rational exercise of responsible judgment; it will retain some of the "hunch" character that it now has. But our experience has shown that the concept of survival objectives alone can greatly improve both the quality and effectiveness of the process and the understanding of what is being decided. Indeed, it gives us, we are learning, an effective tool for the integration of functional work and specialized efforts and especially for creating a common understanding throughout the organization and common measurements of contribution and performance.

The approach to a discipline of business enterprise through an analysis of survival objectives is still a very new and a very crude one. Yet it is already proving itself a unifying concept, simply because it is the first *general* theory of the business enterprise we have had so far. It is not yet a very refined, a very elegant, let alone a very *precise,* theory. Any physicist or mathematician would say: This is not a theory; this is still only rhetoric. But at least, while maybe only in rhetoric, we are talking about something real. For the first time we are no longer in the situation in which theory is irrelevant, if not an impediment, and in which practice has to be untheoretical, which means cannot be taught, cannot be learned, and cannot be conveyed, as one can only convey the general.

This should thus be one of the "breakthrough" areas; and twenty years hence this might well have become the *central* concept around which we can organize the mixture of knowledge, ignorance, and experience, of prejudices, insights, and skills, which we call "management" today.

---

### *Learning Review*

**Questions:**

1. One problem encountered by business enterprises is a lack of any bridge of understanding between the _____-economics of the economy and the _____-economics of a business.

2. The concept of survival objectives fulfills the first requirement of a genuine "_____": that it be both _____ and yet _____.

3. Drucker argues that managers must accept the fact that business objectives are _____.

**Answers:**

1. macro, micro; 2. theory, formal, practical; 3. multidimensional

---

## *Retrospective Comment*

✦

### BY M. M. HARGROVE *

When a clarion call comes from Peter Drucker for the business and educational leaders to focus on the urgent need for developing a theory of management, both industrial and scholastic leaders pay attention.

Peter Drucker has established a far-ranging reputation as a consultant who espouses a no-nonsense, practical, and realistic approach to the solution of situations and problems confronting industrial, governmental, and non-profit organizations. His practical approach has earned for him a great following of practitioners. As *Fortune* has so accurately reported, Peter Drucker is Mr. Management to thousands of living managers.

His ideas, findings, and conclusions have had such widespread acceptance among the practitioners that they have become established in the accepted wisdom of management. For example, his early insistence that planning emphasis should be directed toward results expected and away from the task found wide acceptance. This is reflected in management practice today.

Peter Drucker has not permitted himself to be relegated into any particular school of management thought. His eclectic approach draws upon the verifiable wisdom of all the schools of management thought. Because of the breadth of his interests, he is known, read, and respected among the academicians of the free world. And, because of this eclectic approach, the inception, blooming, and fading of management fads have had, and will have, little to do with Drucker's place in the contemporary history of management.

With one foot planted solidly in the real world of the daily practice of the managers of business, government, and non-profit human organizations; and with the other foot planted solidly in the field of learning and research in the management education world, Peter Drucker is uniquely qualified to redirect the energies of both groups from practice to the development of the desperately needed theory of management.

A hindrance to the development of management theory has been the distrust of conceptual thinking and theory by pragmatic businessmen. A rather dramatic change in our business world which has been taking place since World War II is producing a milieu much more conclusive to development of theory. The collegiate study of business has greatly expanded and has produced hundreds of thousands of graduates. Substantial numbers of these graduates have pursued graduate studies, receiving MBA and Ph.D. degrees. These graduates have found a ready market, especially in the larger corporations and organizations. College trained managers are now by far the greatest sector of the executives in *Fortune's* 500 largest corporations. These managers know the importance of theory in fields such as mathematics, physics, chemistry, the life sciences, and economics. Peter Drucker's plea for the development of concepts and theories now falls on more receptive ears.

The growth in the size and complexity of businesses is another factor which reveals the great need for theory. Theories give sense and understanding to complex, confusing, and intricate relationships. Confused administrators reach out for the assistance flowing from scientific methodology.

The world of business has joined with the world of education to make pinnacles of progress in our times. The atomic bomb was conceived, produced, tested, and used. The man-on-the-moon project was similarly successful. Such showcases of results are indicative of the kind of progress possible when science, theory, and practice join forces.

Other creative thinkers in business and in education are calling for the development of integrating theories which can add to the understanding and success of our economics undertakings. The enormity of the problems requires a multifaceted approach by many innovative leaders before improved operational results can be achieved. These additional thinkers are at work in business and in education, using differing approaches. The various approaches include the functional, mathematical, psychological, sociological, behavioral, etc.

The insufficiency of the maximization of profits theory is apparent. A new base for thinking is required. Peter Drucker believes that the new theory must be directed at five survival objectives of business. These are (1) effective human organizations, (2) business exists at the sufferance of society, (3) the prime function is to produce goods and services, (4) minimum profits are an absolute requisite, and (5) the nature of business is to effect change.

No better evaluation has been advanced for the construction of a theory of management. An evaluation of the need for better understanding, the present state of the arts, the qualifications of the thinkers and the practitioners, the impetus of grand national achievements when energies and abilities were committed, etc., reveal the timeliness of Drucker's writings.

Since the writing of "Business Objectives and Survival Needs: Notes on a Discipline of Business Enterprise," others have made contributions. Knowledge builds on knowledge; research stimulates research. The resulting findings have ever added to the advancement of civilization. It is reasonable to state that Drucker has made a major contribution to understanding. The involvement of more innovators and practitioners will add to the successes and rewards in the future.

---

* The late Professor Hargrove was Trustees' Emeritus Professor of Management, University of Tulsa.

# 14

# *Introduction to the Structural Design of Organizations*

## JAY W. LORSCH

## *About the Author*

**Jay W. Lorsch** is the Louis Kirstein Professor at the Harvard Business School as well as Senior Associate Dean and Director of Research. He is the author of over a dozen books, the most recent of which is *Decision Making at the Top: The Shaping of Strategic Direction* (with Gordon Donaldson). Having taught in all of the School's educational programs, he has been Chairman of the Advanced Management Program for the past five years. Prior to that he was Chairman of the Organizational Behavior Area. He has consulted with such diverse firms as Citicorp, Chubb and Sons, Digital Equipment, First Bank Systems, General Electric, Morgan Stanley, and Shaw's Supermarkets. He is also a Faculty Principal of Management Analysis Center and a Director of Brunswick Corporation and Sweetlife, Inc.

# PREVIEW

A. The structure of an organization is a set of complex variables.
1. Managers can exercise considerable choice on the structure.
2. *Basic* structure is the central base of organizational structure, while *operating mechanisms* implement and reinforce the basic structure.
B. A number of different approaches are utilized in structural design.
1. The widely used classical approach has severe limitations.
2. Organizational theorists suggest that jobs be divided to give the individual meaningful work over which he or she can have some feeling of control and influence.
C. A systemic approach is proposed which provides a conceptual framework for analyzing and solving structural design problems.
1. *Differentiation* and *integration* are two central concepts in this framework.
2. Empirical evidence from three different industries is used to illustrate the framework and its uses.

Our purpose is to introduce you to a useful way of thinking about the structural design of organizations, and to make you aware that the structure of an organization is not an immutable given, but rather a set of complex variables about which managers can exercise considerable choice.

## Definition of Structural Design

It is useful to make a distinction between the basic structure and the operating mechanisms which implement and reinforce this basic structure.[1] Design of the *basic structure* involves such central issues as how the work of the organization will be divided and assigned among positions, groups, departments, divisions, etc., and how the coordination necessary to accomplish total organizational objectives will be achieved. Choices made about these issues are usually publicized in organization charts and job descriptions. If we recognize that behavior in an organization is influenced by a system of variables (technical, individual, social and organizational inputs), it is obvious that such formal documents are only one method of signaling to individuals what behavior is expected of them. Nevertheless, this method is important because it is so widely used by managers to define and communicate their expectations of other organization members.

Managers also can reinforce the intent of their basic structural design through what we call *operating mechanisms.* Operating mechanisms include such factors as control procedures, information systems, reward and appraisal systems, standardized rules and procedures, and even spatial arrangements. These structural variables can be used to more clearly signal to organizational members what is expected of them, to motivate them toward their assigned part of the organization's goal, and, as necessary, to encourage them to undertake collaborative activity. While our central focus is on the basic structure, we shall have more to say about these operating mechanisms later.

## Conventional Approaches to Structural Design

In the past, the most widely used ideas about structural design were those developed by a group of organization theorists who have been labeled the *classicists*.[2] Fayol, Gulick, Urwick, Mooney and their colleagues and successors drew heavily on their own experience in early twentieth century organizations and on the industrial engineering ideas of Frederick W. Taylor. While a detailed review of these ideas is beyond our scope, we can briefly summarize the central features of their "principles of organization."

With regard to the division of work, most of the authors recommended dividing up the work by function (i.e., sales, manufacturing, engineering, etc.) The one exception was Gulick, who suggested that the work of an organization could be divided on several bases: by function; by product; by territory; by time. In any case these writers emphasized economic and technical efficiency. The only human variable given major attention was the limited intellectual capacity of the individual. To cope with this limitation, division of labor was advocated. Each individual would have a narrow task which, given his limited capacity, he could accomplish in the most technically efficient manner. While these ideas are based on the simplistic assumption that man is motivated only by money and will do as he is directed, they still persist and are widely used as a basis for making decisions about organization structure.

According to these writers, coordination was not a major problem. Work was to be divided so that the subgoals of various units would add up to the overall organizational goals. Any remaining coordinating issues would be handled through the management hierarchy. Since people followed the direction of their superiors, the management hierarchy was the only coordinating device necessary.

While this approach has been widely used, it has severe limitations. First, it provides little help in designing a task with intrinsic motivation. Second, it is of limited value in dealing with the multiple levels of division of work in most large organizations. Third, managers have become more aware that the management hierarchy is not sufficient as a mechanism to achieve the coordination required in an organization. The goals of individuals and units do not automatically add up to the total goals of the organization.

Because of these shortcomings, other organizational theorists, most of whom were psychologists or social psychologists, began conducting research into these issues and have more recently come up with a second set of prescriptions which, while less widely applied, are sufficiently used to be worthy of mention. Perhaps the most concise statement of these ideas is offered by Likert.[3] This approach considers the motivational and collaborative issues left unattended by the classical theorists. While these behavioral scientists do not deal explicitly with the issue of division of labor, they do implicitly suggest that jobs should be divided to give the individual meaningful work over which he can have some feeling of control and influence. According to this view, the individual is motivated by self-actualization, and it follows that he will seek more complicated and engaging jobs. This must be taken into account in the division of work. The individual is also motivated by social needs and it is therefore important, according to Likert, to structure the organization so that each individual belongs to a cohesive work group in which participation in decision making is the accepted norm.

While this approach offers no explicit recommendation about how to divide up the work of an organization to provide self-actualizing work and group membership, it is very explicit about how to achieve collaboration or coordinated effort. This is done by linking work groups together by members who hold overlapping membership in two or more groups. This "linking pin" individual is a key figure in the organization, since it is through him that information about group objectives and decisions is transmitted and conflicting viewpoints are resolved.

One shortcoming of this approach is the implicit assumption that all individuals are motivated by similar needs. No attention is focused on the important differences in individual needs. A second problem is, because of either the needs of organization members or the nature of the task, linking pin and participative decision-making practices are often impractical. For example, some managers find it difficult because of their own predispositions to involve subordinates in all decisions. Similarly, some tasks require decisions for which the information is not available to all the members of the work group.

Both of these approaches described above are subject to a more general criticism. While each offers a particular prescription about how to design the basic structure of an organization, both approaches are offered as the one best way to organize. To the readers who have already been exposed to a systemic conceptual framework, it should be obvious that any blanket prescription is an oversimplification. As the recent title of a book on organization theory states, "It all depends." [4] Furthermore, recent research which utilizes the systemic approach suggests that the choices made in designing a basic structure depend on the task and human inputs involved.

## A Systemic Approach to the Design of Organization Structure

Two recent studies point to the validity of this conclusion. Burns and Stalker, in their pioneering study of firms in both a dynamic, changing industry and a more established, stable industry, report that there were important structural differences between the successful firms in each industry. [5] In the stable industry, successful organizations tended to be what the authors called "mechanistic." There was more reliance on formal rules and procedures. Decisions were made at the higher levels of the organization. The spans of supervisory control were narrow. In the more dynamic industry, the authors characterized the effective organizations as "organic." Spans of supervisory control were wider; less attention was paid to formal procedures; and more decisions were reached at the lower levels of the organization. The second study was conducted by Joan Woodward.[6] She found that economically successful organizations in industries with different production technologies were characterized by different organization structures. For example, successful firms in industries with a unit or job-shop technology had wider spans of supervisory control and fewer hierarchical levels than did successful firms with continuous process technologies.

While both of these studies consider the structure of an organization as one variable in a system affecting behavior in organizations, they do not provide a conceptual framework which is sufficiently comprehensive for analyzing and solving structural design problems. A more recent study by Lawrence and Lorsch builds on the basic idea of Woodward, Burns and Stalker, and others, and provides a more comprehensive analytic framework for working on structural design problems.[7]

## Differentiation and Integration

Before describing the analytic framework which Lawrence and Lorsch have developed, it is important to emphasize three points.[8] First, this conceptual scheme is based on an empirical study of ten organizations with varying levels of economic performance in three different industrial environments (plastics, consumer foods, standardized containers) and these findings have been corroborated by research in several additional settings. Second, this conceptual model does not provide a prescription for the one best way to organize. Instead, it provides a framework for thinking about structural design issues based on the demands of the organization's particular market and technological environment. Third, this set of concepts can be used to analyze the structural design which seems to best fit an organization's environment. These concepts can also be used to understand the organization's current strengths and weaknesses and to help determine what design changes will move a particular organization toward a better fit with the demands of its specific environment.

As we begin this discussion, we must first define two of the central concepts in this framework. First, *differentiation* is defined as *the differences in cognitive and emotional orientations among managers in different functional departments, and the differences in formal structure among these departments.* Rather than thinking of division of work as only affecting the economies and efficiencies of task performance, as did the classicists, Lawrence and Lorsch recognized that each unit was itself a subsystem in which members would develop particular orientations and structural patterns, depending on their task and their predispositions. Since different units were working with different parts of the organization's environment [e.g., market, scientific techno-economic (manufacturing) variables], these units would develop differentiation to some degree or other, depending upon the specific environment.

The second concept which we want to define is *integration—the quality of the state of collaboration that exists among departments that are required to achieve unity of effort by the environment.*

As we have already indicated, different environments require varying degrees of differentiation among organizational units. Basically, the extent of organizational differentiation depends upon the *certainty or uncertainty of the environment* and its *diversity or homogeneity*. Rather than being concerned with the environment as a single entity, the authors recognized that complex organizations—those with more than one unit—actually segment their environments into parts. The authors then identified the relative certainty of the parts of any environment. For example, each of the ten organizations was dealing with a market subenvironment (the task of the sales organization), a techno-economic subenvironment (the task of the manufacturing unit) and a scientific subenvironment (the task of the research or design unit). Each of these subenvironments within any one industry had a different degree of certainty of information about what needed to be done. How similar or different these parts of any environment were on the certainty-uncertainty continuum determined whether that environment was relatively homogeneous or diverse. For example, in one of the environments studied, the container industry, all parts of the environment were relatively certain and the environment was characterized as homogeneous. On the other hand, in a second environment, the plastics industry, the parts of the environment ranged from a highly certain techno-economic sector to a very uncertain scientific subenvironment and the total environment was characterized as more diverse. As suggested above, the degree of differentiation in an effective organization was found to be related to the diversity of the environment. Thus, in the economically effective container industry there was less differentiation than in an effective plastic organization. The less effective organizations in these industries did not meet the environmental demand for differentiation so well.

We can now summarize the general relationship the authors found between the certainty of the subenvironment a unit is dealing with and three of the unit characteristics along which differentiation was measured (Figure 1).

The fourth characteristic of units along which differentiation was measured—goal orientation—was not related to the certainty of the environment, but instead to the goals inherent in each part of the environment—e.g., the market (customer service, competitive action, etc.); techno-economic (costs, quality, efficient schedules, etc.); science (discovery of new knowledge; utilization of technical talent, etc.).

*Figure 1*

| | | | |
|---|---|---|---|
| Uncertainty of environmental sector . . . . . . . . . . . . . . . . . | High | Moderate | Low |
| Extent of formalized unit structure . . . . . . . . . . . . . . . . . | Low | Medium | High |
| Interpersonal orientation* . . . . . . . . . . . . . . . . . . . . . . . | Task | Social | Task |
| Time orientation . . . . . . . . . . . . . . . . . . . . . . . . . . . . . | Long | Medium | Short |

* This curvilinear relation between the members' interpersonal orientation in a task-oriented/ social-oriented continuum is consistent with the work of Fred E. Fiedler, *Technical Report No. 10* (Urbana, Ill.: Group Effectiveness Research Laboratory, Department of Psychology, University of Illinois, May 1962).

We can quote from the original study for a more detailed picture of how the varying degrees of differentiation manifest themselves in the high-performing organizations in two of the three industries studied.[9]

To illustrate the varying states of differentiation among these three organizations, we can use hypothetical encounters among managers in both the plastics and the container high-performing organizations. In the plastics organization we might find a sales manager discussing a potential new product with a fundamental research scientist and an integrator. In this discussion the sales manager is concerned with the needs of the customer. What performance characteristics must a new product have to perform in the customer's machinery? How much can the customer afford to pay? How long can the material be stored without deteriorating? Further, our sales manager, while talking about these matters, may be thinking about more pressing current problems. Should he lower the price on an existing product? Did the material shipped to another customer meet his specifications? Is he going to meet this quarter's sales targets?

In contrast, our fundamental scientist is concerned about a different order of problems. Will this new project provide a scientific challenge? To get the desired result, could he change the molecular structure of a known material without affecting its stability? What difficulties will he encounter in solving these problems? Will this be a more interesting project to work on than another he heard about last week? Will he receive some professional recognition if he is successful in solving the problem? Thus our sales manager and our fundamental scientist not only have quite different goal orientations, but they are thinking about different time dimensions—the sales manager about what's going on today and in the next few months; the scientist, how he will spend the next few years.

But these are not the only ways in which these two specialists are different. The sales manager may be outgoing and concerned with maintaining a warm, friendly relationship with the scientist. He may be put off because the scientist seems withdrawn and disinclined to talk about anything other than the problems in which he is interested. He may also be annoyed that the scientist seems to have such freedom in choosing what he will work on. Furthermore, the scientist is probably often late for appointments, which, from the salesman's point of view, is no way to run a business. Our scientist, for his part, may feel uncomfortable because the salesman seems to be pressing for immediate answers to technical questions that will take a long time to investigate. All these discomforts are concrete manifestations of the relatively wide differences between these two men in respect to their working and thinking styles and the departmental structures to which each is accustomed.

Between these different points of view stands our integrator. If he is effective, he will understand, and to some extent share, the viewpoints of both specialists and will be working to help them communicate with each other. We do not want to dwell on his role at this point, but the mere fact that he is present is a result of the great differences among specialists in his organization.

In the high-performing container organization we might find a research scientist meeting with a plant manager to determine how to solve a quality problem. The plant manager talks about getting the problem solved as quickly as possible, in order to reduce the spoilage rate. He is probably thinking about how this problem will affect his ability to meet the current production schedule and to operate within cost constraints. The researcher is also seeking an immediate answer to the problem. He is concerned not with its theoretical niceties, but with how he can find an immediate applied solution. (Research in this industry tended to focus on short-term process development.) What adjustments in materials or machine procedures can he suggest to get the desired effect? In fact, these specialists may share a concern with finding the most feasible solution. They also operate in a similar, short-term time dimension. The differences in their interpersonal styles are also not too large. Both are primarily concerned with getting the job done, and neither finds the other's style of behavior strange. They are also accustomed to quite similar organizational practices. Both see that they are rewarded for quite specific short-run accomplishments, and both might be feeling similar pressures from their superiors to get the job done. In essence, these two specialists, while somewhat different in their thinking and behavior patterns, would not find it uncomfortable or difficult to work together in seeking a joint solution to a problem. Thus they would need no integrator.

The authors summarize this approach as follows: "These two hypothetical examples show clearly that the differentiation in the [effective] plastics organization is much greater than in the equally effective container concern. The high-performing food organization fell between the extremes of differentiation represented by the other two organizations." [10]

But the environment of an organization imposes requirements other than differentiation upon the organization. One of these is the *dominant competitive issue*. In the plastics and food environment, this was the issue of innovating new products and processes; for the container industry the dominant issue was the scheduling and allocation of production facilities to meet market demands.

The dominant competitive issue was also related to the final environmental characteristic of interest to the authors—the pattern and degree of integration required among units. In all three environments the tightness of integration required was found to be identical. However, there was an important difference in the pattern around which this integration was occurring. In plastics and foods, where innovative issues are dominant, the tight integration was required between sales and research and production and research.

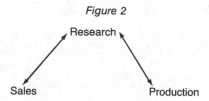

Figure 2

In the container industry, the tight integration was required between production and sales and between production and research.

*Figure 3*

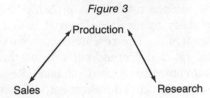

The authors report that in each industry the high-performing organizations achieved more effective integration around these critical interdependencies than their less effective competitor. Thus, the effective organization more satisfactorily met the demands of its environment for both differentiation and integration than did the less effective organization(s) in the same environment.

This finding is particularly interesting, because the authors found a strong inverse relationship between differentiation and integration within any one organization. When highly interdependent units are highly differentiated, it is more difficult to achieve integration among them than when members of the units have similar ways of thinking and behaving. This antagonistic relationship is illustrated by Figure 4, taken from the original study.[11]

Thus, we are presented with an interesting paradox: effective organizations in a given environment achieve more differentiation *and* more integration, but these two states are basically antagonistic. How does an organization get both? The authors found that two related factors made this possible.

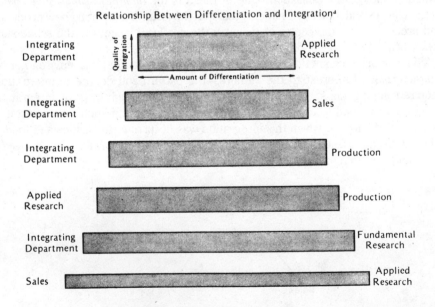

a. This is a schematic representation of the relationship among departments in one organization. The longer the bar, the more differentiation; the wider the bar, the better the integration. This relationship held between pairs of units in all six organizations.

*Figure 4*   Relationship between differentiation and integration

First, when an organization is both highly differentiated and well integrated, it is necessary for the organization to develop more complicated mechanisms for achieving integration. Of course the basic organizational device for achieving integration is the management hierarchy. In an organization such as the effective container firm, with relatively low differentiation, the authors found that the hierarchy, along with formal plans and controls, was sufficient to achieve the required integration. However, the effective plastics and food organizations, faced with a requirement for both high differentiation and close integration, developed other supplemental integrating devices. These included individual coordinators (integrators), cross-unit teams, and even whole departments of integrators—individuals whose basic contribution is achieving integration among units. The integrative devices present in the high-performing organization in each environment are summarized in Figure 5 on page 210.

The authors point out that while the effective organization always had integrative devices which were sufficient to handle both the differentiation and integration required, often the less effective firm also had appropriate integrative devices. Thus, the integrative devices alone do not explain why the more effective firms were able to achieve the required states of differentiation and integration while the less effective firms did not.

A second set of factors seems to account for this difference. This is the behavior pattern used within the organization to manage intergroup conflict. As individuals with different points of view attempt to attain unity of effort, conflicts inevitably arise. How well the organization does in achieving integration in the face of differentiation is very dependent upon how the individuals involved resolve their conflicts. Lawrence and Lorsch's findings indicate that the behavior which leads to effective conflict resolution in certain respects varies with environmental demands, but in other respects shows no such variations.

Those conflict management factors which vary with environmental influence include the pattern of power or influence among groups and at various levels of the management hierarchy of each group. In the high-performing organizations where conflict was managed effectively, influence was concentrated at the level within each group where the information relevant to the decision was also present. The exact level in any unit depended upon the certainty of information in its part of the particular environment. For example, in the research units of the effective plastics organization, because of the uncertainty of knowledge, influence was concentrated at the lowest management level. In the production unit of this same plastics organization, where environmental information was more certain, influence was concentrated at a higher level of the management hierarchy. Because of the diversity of this environment, the hierarchical influence in this organization was distributed differently among different levels in each function. The same was true of the effective food organization for similar reasons. However, in the container organization, dealing with more certain and more homogeneous environment, the information could be efficiently gathered by upper levels of management in all functions. Thus, hierarchical influence in this organization was concentrated at the top in all units.

The required pattern of influence among units also varied with environmental

| Industry | Environment Diversity | Actual Differentiation | Actual Integration | Integrative Devices | | Conflict Management Variables | |
|---|---|---|---|---|---|---|---|
| | | | | Type of Integrative Devices | Special Integration Personnel as % of Total Management | Hierarchical Influence | Unit Having High Influence |
| Plastics........ | High | High | High | Teams, roles, departments, hierarchy, plans and procedures | 22%* | Evenly distributed | Integrating unit |
| Foods......... | Moderate | Moderate | High | Roles, plans, hierarchy, procedures | 17%* | Evenly distributed | Sales and research |
| Container ....... | Low | Low | High | Hierarchy, plans and procedures | 0%* | Top high, bottom low | Sales |

* This proportion was constant for the high and low performer within these industries.

Figure 5. Introduction to the Structural Design of Organizations (environmental factors and organizational characteristics of effective organizations)

requirements. In the effective organization the unit(s) which had the central knowledge about environmental conditions related to the dominant strategic variable was the one with the most influence. For instance, in the effective plastics organization, where a separate integrating unit had been established, this group had the highest influence because it was in a position to have information about the various parts of the environment, all of which were important in achieving innovation. In the food organization, where the dominant issue was also innovation, the situation was slightly different. Here no integrating department had been established, because the differentiation required was not as high as in the plastics environment. Also, because of the consumer products involved, the dominant knowledge was in the market and scientific sectors of the environment. Therefore, the sales and research units had similar high levels of power in relation to the production unit. In the container industry the dominant issue of customer service meant that the sales unit must call the tune, and this unit did have the highest influence.

The two factors which led to effective resolution under all environmental conditions were the mode of conflict resolution, and the basis from which high influence was derived. In high-performing organizations in all environments, it was found that conflict was managed by involved individuals who dealt openly with the conflict and worked a problem until a resolution was reached which best met total organizational goals. In the effective organizations, there was more of a tendency to *confront* conflict instead of using raw power to *force* one party's compliance or instead of *smoothing* over the conflict by agreeing to disagree.

In all the high-performing organizations, the authors also found that the individuals primarily involved in resolving conflict, whether they were a common superior in the hierarchy or persons in special integrating positions, had influence based to a large extent on their perceived competence and knowledge. This was in contrast to the less effective organizations where such persons usually drew their power solely from their position or from their control over scarce resources. The persons centrally involved in achieving integration in the high-performing organizations were followed not only because they had formal positional authority, but also because they were seen as knowledgeable about the issues which had to be resolved.

In those organizations where special integrators existed, Lawrence and Lorsch found one additional conflict management factor which seemed important. In the effective organizations, such integrators had orientations which were balanced between those of the groups whose efforts they were integrating. This made it possible for them to understand and communicate with each of the groups concerned. In the less effective organizations, these integrators tended to have one-sided orientations. They thought and acted like sales personnel or like researchers and this made it difficult for them to work with other groups.

All of these conflict management variables taken together suggest why the effective organizations in each environment were able to achieve the differentiation and integration required by the particular environment when less effective firms were not able to do so. These conflict management practices were the glue which held the differentiated units together as they worked toward integrated goals.

To summarize, then, the Lawrence and Lorsch study provides a set of research findings and concepts which enable us to understand what characteristics an organization must have to be effective in a particular set of environmental circumstances. This study directs our attention to the environmental demands placed on the organization in terms of the degree of differentiation, the pattern and degree of integration, integrative mechanisms, and conflict management behaviors. Those factors in the study which varied among high-performing organizations in the three environments studied are summarized in Figure 5.

With this summary of the findings of this study, we now want to examine briefly how these ideas can be put to use to work on the issues of structural design.

## Applying Differentiation and Integration Concepts To Structural Design

As we consider these concepts as they apply to structural design decisions, we will also suggest the sequence of structural subproblems. While these subproblems are stated as discrete issues, the reader should be aware that in practice it is necessary to move back and forth among them as one thinks about the whole problem of structural design in a given organization. We will look first at the design of the basic structure and then at the necessary operating mechanisms.

*Grouping activities into units* is the logical first step in designing a basic structure. The differentiation and integration concepts focus our attention on two criteria for making decisions about grouping activity. First, units which will have similar orientations and tasks should be grouped together, both because they can reinforce each other's common concerns to achieve the needed differentiation and because this will simplify the coordinating task of the common boss. Second, units which are required to integrate their activities closely should be grouped together, because the common superior can then work to achieve the required integration through the management hierarchy. Therefore units which have a requirement for both low differentiation and tight integration, should be grouped together. However, when some units are low in differentiation but are not highly interdependent, or conversely, high in differentiation but also highly interdependent, the choice about grouping becomes more complex. In these cases, we must use our judgment to determine which criterion—low differentiation or high integration—we want to optimize in grouping activities.

*Designing integrative devices* is the second step in determining the basic structure. As we suggested above, the grouping of activities itself has an effect upon the design of integrative devices. A primary integrative device in any organization is the management hierarchy. In grouping activities, we are essentially making choices about which units we want to integrate through the hierarchy. However, as the Lawrence and Lorsch findings suggest, even after the units are grouped and decisions have been made about where the hierarchy can be used to achieve integration, we are still left with the question of what other integrating devices are desirable and necessary. Their findings suggest that as the environment requires more differentiation and tighter integration it is necessary to build supplemental integrating mechanisms such as integrating departments or crossfunctional teams into the organization. This study also suggests that these special devices should be built into the organization in such a way that they facilitate the interaction of integrators with functional specialists who have the relevant knowledge to contribute to joint decisions. Alternatively, they may also need to facilitate the direct interaction among functional specialists who have the necessary knowledge to contribute to these joint decisions.

*Structuring the individual units* is a third step in the design process. Here the emphasis is on operating mechanisms, which will be consistent with the unit task and the needs of its members. Issues of individual motivation are particularly relevant here.[12] In addition, the Lawrence and Lorsch findings underline the importance of designing measurement and reward procedures to encourage orientations which are appropriate to the unit task. Similarly, reliance on formal rules and standardized procedures should be consistent with the task. Finally, the unit hierarchy and spans of control should be designed not only to provide the intra-unit coordination required by the task, but also to encourage involvement in decision making at the level where the relevant information is available.

## Other Operating Mechanisms

In addition to the operating mechanisms within each unit, it is necessary to consider operating mechanisms which are applied across the whole organization. Do rewards and measurements encourage collaboration around the critical integrative issues? Do they demand consistency and conformity among units where more differentiation is required? Again, issues of individual rewards and motivation should be helpful here, but we must also realize that some operating mechanisms must be built to encourage differentiation, while others are necessary to encourage integration. We must understand the environmental demands on the organization so that reward and measurement systems can be designed to encourage both the differentiated and integrated behavior required.

## Factors Affecting Conflict Management

Finally, we should consider the effect of the basic structure and the operating mechanisms on conflict resolution. The basic structure should assign responsibility for cross-functional liaison to individuals who have the relevant knowledge. If individuals who have such knowledge are formally assigned the responsibility for joint decision making, there is the highest probability they will develop the power necessary to resolve conflict effectively. A second issue is related to operating mechanisms. Do they induce unnecessary conflict? Do they cause organization members to see conflicts as win-lose rather than integrative? If so, can they be altered to encourage more integrative problem solving?

Finally, there is the issue of training and its impact on conflict-resolving behavior.

While this topic could lead into a long discussion of organizational change, it is useful to mention here that some forms of laboratory training and education may be helpful to encourage the confrontation of conflict.[13] The ideas we have been discussing may be helpful in identifying which organization members are so involved in conflict management that such training might be useful.

## Summary

In this introduction we have explored the approaches available to solving structural design problems. In concluding, we offer a word of caution. Our understanding of organizations as systems is new and it is growing rapidly. The ideas which are presented here will certainly be modified and improved. But as crude as they are, they represent better tools than the principles which have been relied on in the past. These ideas clearly move us in a new and promising direction— that of tailoring the organization to its environment and to the complex needs of its members.

## FOOTNOTES

1.  I am indebted to my colleague, Larry E. Greiner, for suggesting this conceptual distinction.

2.  Henri Fayol, *Industrial and General Administration,* Part II, Chapter I, "General Principles of Organization"; Chapter II, "Elements of Administration." (Paris: Dunod, 1925); Luther Gulick, "Notes on the Theory of Organization," in Luther Gulick and Lyndall F. Urwick, (eds.), *Papers on the Science of Administration* (New York: Institute of Public Administration, Columbia University, 1937); Lyndall F. Urwick, "Organization as a Technical Problem," *ibid.;* James D. Mooney, "The Principles of Organization," *ibid.*

3.  Rensis Likert, *The Human Organization* (New York: McGraw-Hill, 1968). See also Douglas McGregor, *The Human Side of Enterprise* (New York: McGraw-Hill, 1960).

4.  Harvey Sherman, *It All Depends: A Pragmatic Approach to Organization* (Tuscaloosa: University of Alabama Press, 1966).

5.  T. Burns and G. M. Stalker, *The Management of Innovation* (London: Tavistock Publications, 1961).

6.  Joan Woodward, *Industrial Organization: Theory and Practice* (Oxford: Oxford University Press, 1965).

7.  P. R. Lawrence and J. W. Lorsch, *Organization and Environment: Managing Differentiation and Integration* (Boston: Division of Research, Harvard Graduate School of Business Administration, 1967).

8.  A more complete statement of their findings can be found in *Organization and Environment.*

9.  *Ibid.,* pp. 134–136.

10.  *Ibid.,* p. 137.

11.  *Ibid.,* Figure II-2, p. 48.

12.  See G. W. Dalton and P. R. Lawrence, *Organizational Motivation and Control* (Homewood, Illinois: Irwin, 1970).

13.  See G. W. Dalton and P. R. Lawrence, *Organizational Change and Development* (Homewood, Illinois: Irwin, 1970).

### Learning Review

*Questions:*

1. _____ _____ include such factors as control procedures, information systems, and reward systems.

2. The study referred to in the reading analyzed three industries: _____, _____, and _____.

3. The two central concepts of the proposed framework are _____ and _____.

*Answers:*

1. Operating mechanisms;   2. plastics, container, food;   3. differentiation, integration

## *Retrospective Comment*

### BY ROBERT DUNCAN *

The contingency perspective of Lawrence and Lorsch has been one of the most important developments in organizational theory in the past 15 years. The essence of this work is that it indicated that there was no one best way for organizations to structure themselves. Also, even the same organization may be structured differently from department to department. The Lawrence and Lorsch perspective has thus led to a framework for organizational design that indicates that an organization's structure must fit the demands of *both* its technology and its external environment.

Another important contribution of this work is that when the organizations organize around their environments, organizational units such as marketing and production may become differentiated from one another. This differentiation then leads to the need to coordinate and integrate the diverse units in the organization. This focus on integration has alerted organizational designers to be concerned with how they are going to make the structure work and that there are communication and coordination processes required for managers to "manage" the design function.

Lawrence and Lorsch's work thus provides managers with a practical theory for how to organize and then make the organization's structure work.

\* Professor, Graduate School of Management, Northwestern University.

# 15

# *An Integrating Principle and An Overview*

## RENSIS LIKERT

### *About the Author*

**RENSIS LIKERT** (1903–1981) received his A.B. degree from the University of Michigan and his Ph.D. from Columbia. He was well-known for his research and ideas on leadership, motivation, and organization theory which appeared in *New Patterns of Management* (1962), *The Human Organization: Its Management and Value* (1967) and *New Ways of Managing Conflict (1976—co-authored* with Jane Gibson Likert).

Until his retirement in 1970, Likert served as Director of the Survey Research Center, and, since 1946, as Director of the Institute for Social Research at the University of Michigan. In these positions he organized a highly productive group of researchers who conducted much of the most important research on organizations, leadership, organization development, and motivation during the 1950's and 1960's. From 1979 until his death, he was chairman of the board of Rensis Likert Associates, Inc., a management consulting firm based in Ann Arbor, Michigan.

# PREVIEW

A. The general pattern of operations of high-producing managers tends to differ from those of mediocre and low-producing managers.
   1. Favorable attitudes toward all aspects of the job are predominant with workers for high-producing managers.
   2. High-producing organizations consist of effectively functioning social systems.
   3. Measurements of organizational performance are used primarily for self-guidance in high-producing units.
   4. The highest producing managers use all the technical resources of the classical theories of management.
B. The general pattern of highly motivated, cooperative members appears to be a central characteristic of the newer management systems developed by the highest-producing managers.
   1. High producing managers more often think of employees as "human beings" instead of just inputs designed to accomplish work goals.
   2. This attitude toward subordinates is perceived favorably by subordinates of the high producing manager.
   3. Behavior of the high producing manager in directing the work is characterized by fair and equitable treatment of subordinates.
C. High-producing managers appear to be employing the *principle of supportive relationships*.
   1. This principle emphasizes the importance of all members of the organization understanding the mission of the organization.
   2. The subordinate should see his or her job experience contributing to or maintaining his or her own sense of personal worth and importance.
   3. Managers who employ this principle need direct evidence of what subordinates think and should attempt to see things through the eyes of subordinates.
D. The use of work groups in organizations is essential if managers are to make full use of the capacities of their subordinates.
   1. Organizations function best when their personnel view themselves as individual members of highly effective work groups with high performance goals.
   2. Linking these work groups to the overall organization is accomplished through people who hold overlapping group memberships.
   3. Organizations employing this group system eliminate many problems of the person-to-person organization.
E. Effective group decision-making is an offshoot of the group system of operations.
   1. Responsibility and situational requirements limit the effectiveness of group decision-making.
   2. Suboptimization is reduced when group decision-making is utilized.

The managers whose performance is impressive appear to be fashioning a better system of management. At the end of Chapter 4 two generalizations were stated based on the available research findings:

- The supervisors and managers in American industry and government who are achieving the highest productivity, lowest costs, least turnover and absence, and the highest levels of employee motivation and satisfaction display, on the average, a different pattern of leadership from those managers who are achieving less impressive results. The principles and practices of these high-producing managers are deviating in important ways from those called for by present-day management theories.
- The high-producing managers whose deviations from existing theory and practice are creating improved procedures have not yet integrated their deviant principles into a theory of management. Individually, they are often clearly aware of how a particular practice of theirs differs from generally accepted methods, but the magnitude, importance, and systematic nature of the differences when the total pattern is examined do not appear to be recognized.

Based upon the principles and practices of the managers who are achieving the best results, a newer theory of organization and management can be stated. An attempt will be made in this chapter to present briefly some of the over-all characteristics of such a theory and to formulate a general integrating principle which can be useful in attempts to apply it.

There is no doubt that further research and experimental testing of the theory in pilot operations will yield evidence pointing to modifications of many aspects of the newer theory suggested in this volume. Consequently, in reading this and subsequent chapters it will be well not to quarrel with the specific aspects of the newer theory as presented. These specifics are intended as stimulants for discussion and as encouragement for experimental field tests of the theory. It will be more profitable to seek to understand the newer theory's general basic character and, whenever a specific aspect or derivation appears to be in error, to formulate more valid derivations and propositions.

Research findings indicate that the general pattern of operations of the highest-producing managers tends to differ from that of the managers of mediocre and low-producing units by more often showing the following characteristics:

- A preponderance of favorable attitudes on the part of each member of the organization toward all the other members, toward superiors, toward the work, toward the organization—toward all aspects of the job. These favorable attitudes toward others reflect a high level of mutual confidence and trust throughout the organization. The favorable attitudes toward the organization and the work are not those of easy complacency, but are the attitudes of identification with the organization and its objectives and a high sense of involvement in achieving them. As a consequence, the performance goals are high and dissatisfaction may occur whenever achievement falls short of the goals set.
- This highly motivated, cooperative orientation toward the organization and its objectives is achieved by harnessing effectively all the major motivational forces

which can exercise significant influence in an organizational setting and which, potentially, can be accompanied by cooperative and favorable attitudes. Reliance is not placed solely or fundamentally on the economic motive of buying a man's time and using control and authority as the organizing and coordinating principle of the organization. On the contrary, the following motives are all used fully and in such a way that they function in a cumulative and reinforcing manner and yield favorable attitudes:

- The ego motives. These are referred to throughout this volume as the desire to achieve and maintain a sense of personal worth and importance. This desire manifests itself in many forms, depending upon the norms and values of the persons and groups involved. Thus, it is responsible for such motivational forces as the desire for growth and significant achievement in terms of one's own values and goals, i.e., self-fulfillment, as well as the desire for status, recognition, approval, acceptance, and power and the desire to undertake significant and important tasks.
- The security motives.
- Curiosity, creativity, and the desire for new experiences.
- The economic motives.

By tapping all the motives which yield favorable and cooperative attitudes, maximum motivation oriented toward realizing the organization's goals as well as the needs of each member of the organization is achieved. The substantial decrements in motivational forces which occur when powerful motives are pulling in opposite directions are thereby avoided. These conflicting forces exist, of course, when hostile and resentful attitudes are present.

- The organization consists of a tightly knit, effectively functioning social system. This social system is made up of interlocking work groups with a high degree of group loyalty among the members and favorable attitudes and trust between superiors and subordinates. Sensitivity to others and relatively high levels of skill in personal interaction and the functioning of groups are also present. These skills permit effective participation in decisions on common problems. Participation is used, for example, to establish organizational objectives which are a satisfactory integration of the needs and desires of all members of the organization and of persons functionally related to it. High levels of reciprocal influence occur, and high levels of total coordinated influence are achieved in the organization. Communication is efficient and effective. There is a flow from one part of the organization to another of all the relevant information important for each decision and action. The leadership in the organization has developed what might well be called a highly effective social system for interaction and mutual influence.
- Measurements of organizational performance are used primarily for self-guidance rather than for superimposed control. To tap the motives which bring cooperative and favorable rather than hostile attitudes, participation and involvement in decisions is a habitual part of the leadership processes. This kind of decision-making, of course, calls for the full sharing of available measurements and information. Moreover, as it becomes evident in the decision-making process

that additional information or measurements are needed, steps are taken to obtain them.

In achieving operations which are more often characterized by the above pattern of highly cooperative, well-coordinated activity, the highest producing managers use all the technical resources of the classical theories of management, such as time-and-motion study, budgeting, and financial controls. They use these resources at least as completely as do the low-producing managers, but in quite different ways. This difference in use arises from the differences in the motives which the high-producing, in contrast to the low-producing, managers believe are important in influencing human behavior.

The low-producing managers, in keeping with traditional practice, feel that the way to motivate and direct behavior is to exercise control through authority. Jobs are organized, methods are prescribed, standards are set, performance goals and budgets are established. Compliance with them is sought through the use of hierarchical and economic pressures.

The highest-producing managers feel, generally, that this manner of functioning does not produce the best results, that the resentment created by direct exercise of authority tends to limit its effectiveness. They have learned that better results can be achieved when a different motivational process is employed. As suggested above, they strive to use all those major motives which have the potentiality of yielding favorable and cooperative attitudes in such a way that favorable attitudes are, in fact, elicited and the motivational forces are mutually reinforcing. Motivational forces stemming from the economic motive are not then blunted by such other motivations as group goals which restrict the quantity or quality of output. The full strength of all economic, ego, and other motives is generated and put to use.

Widespread use of participation is one of the more important approaches employed by the high-producing managers in their efforts to get full benefit from the technical resources of the classical theories of management coupled with high levels of reinforcing motivation. This use of participation applies to all aspects of the job and work, as, for example, in setting work goals and budgets, controlling costs, organizing the work, etc.

In these and comparable ways, the high-producing managers make full use of the technical resources of the classical theories of management. They use these resources in such a manner, however, that favorable and cooperative attitudes are created and all members of the organization endeavor to pull concertedly toward commonly accepted goals which they have helped to establish.

This brief description of the pattern of management which is more often characteristic of the high-producing than of the low-producing managers points to what appears to be a critical difference. The high-producing managers have developed their organizations into highly coordinated, highly motivated, cooperative social systems. Under their leadership, the different motivational forces in each member of the organization have coalesced into a strong force aimed at accomplishing the mutually established objectives of the organization. This general pattern of highly motivated, cooperative members seems to be a central characteristic of the newer management system being developed by the highest-producing managers.

How do these high-producing managers build organizations which display this central characteristic? Is there any general approach or underlying principle which they rely upon in building highly motivated organizations? There seems to be, and clues as to the nature of the principle can be obtained by reexamining some of the materials in [earlier chapters] . . . The research findings show, for example, that those supervisors and managers whose pattern of leadership yields consistently favorable attitudes more often think of employees as "human beings rather than just as persons to get the work done." Consistently, in study after study, the data show that treating people as "human beings" rather than as "cogs in a machine" is a variable highly related to the attitudes and motivation of the subordinate at every level in the organization . . .

The superiors who have the most favorable and cooperative attitudes in their work groups display the following characteristics:

- The attitude and behavior of the superior toward the subordinate as a person, *as perceived by the subordinate,* is as follows:
  - He is supportive, friendly, and helpful rather than hostile. He is kind but firm, never threatening, genuinely interested in the well-being of subordinates and endeavors to treat people in a sensitive, considerate way. He is just, if not generous. He endeavors to serve the best interests of his employees as well as of the company.
  - He shows confidence in the integrity, ability, and motivations of subordinates rather than suspicion and distrust.
  - His confidence in subordinates leads him to have high expectations as to their level of performance. With confidence that he will not be disappointed, he expects much, not little. (This, again, is fundamentally a supportive rather than a critical or hostile relationship.)
  - He sees that each subordinate is well trained for his particular job. He endeavors also to help subordinates be promoted by training them for jobs at the next level. This involves giving them relevant experience and coaching whenever the opportunity offers.
  - He coaches and assists employees whose performance is below standard. In the case of a subordinate who is clearly misplaced and unable to do his job satisfactorily, he endeavors to find a position well suited to that employee's abilities and arranges to have the employee transferred to it.
- The behavior of the superior in directing the work is characterized by such activity as:
  - Planning and scheduling the work to be done, training subordinates, supplying them with material and tools, initiating work activity, etc.
  - Providing adequate technical competence, particularly in those situations where the work has not been highly standardized.
- The leader develops his subordinates into a working team with high group loyalty by using participation and the other kinds of group-leadership practices summarized in [an earlier chapter].

## The Integrating Principle

These results and similar data from other studies (Argyris, 1957c; March & Simon, 1958; Viteles, 1953) show that subordinates react favorably to experiences which they feel are supportive and contribute to their sense of importance and personal worth. Similarly, persons react unfavorably to experiences which are threatening and decrease or minimize their sense of dignity and personal worth. These findings are supported also by substantial research on personality development (Argyris, 1957c; Rogers, 1942; Rogers, 1951) and group behavior (Cartwright & Zander, 1960). Each of us wants appreciation, recognition, influence, a feeling of accomplishment, and a feeling that people who are important to us believe in us and respect us. We want to feel that we have a place in the world.

This pattern of reaction appears to be universal and seems to be the basis for the general principle used by the high-producing managers in developing their highly motivated, cooperative organizations. These managers have discovered that the motivational forces acting in each member of an organization are most likely to be cumulative and reinforcing when the interactions between each individual and the others in the organization are of such a character that they convey to the individual a feeling of support and recognition for his importance and worth as a person. These managers, therefore, strive to have the interactions between the members of their organization of such a character that each member of the organization feels confident in his potentialities and believes that his abilities are being well used.

A second factor, however, is also important. As we have seen in Chapter 7, an individual's reaction to any situation is always a function not of the absolute character of the interaction, but of his perception of it. It is how he sees things that counts, not objective reality. Consequently, an individual member of an organization will always interpret an interaction between himself and the organization in terms of his background and culture, his experience and expectations. The pattern of supervision and the language used that might be effective with a railroad's maintenance-of-way crew, for example, would not be suitable in an office full of young women. A subordinate tends also to expect his superior to behave in ways consistent with the personality of the superior. All this means that each of us, as a subordinate or as a peer or as a superior, reacts in terms of his own particular background, experience, and expectations. In order, therefore, to have an interaction viewed as supportive, it is essential that it be of such a character that the individual himself, in the light of his experience and expectations, sees it as supportive. This provides the basis for stating the general principle which the high-producing managers seem to be using and which will be referred to as the *principle of supportive relationships*. This principle, which provides an invaluable guide in any attempt to apply the newer theory of management in a specific plant or organization, can be briefly stated: *The leadership and other processes of the organization must be such as to ensure a maximum probability that in all interactions and all relationships with the organization each member will, in the light of his background, values, and expectations, view the experience as supportive and one which builds and maintains his sense of personal worth and importance.*

## The Principle of Supportive Relationships as an Organizing Concept

This general principle provides a fundamental formula for obtaining the full potential of every major motive which can be constructively harnessed in a working situation. There is impressive evidence, for example, that economic motivations will be tapped more effectively when the conditions specified by the principle of supportive relationships are met (Katz & Kahn, 1951; Krulee, 1955). In addition, as motives are used in the ways called for by this general principle, the attitudes accompanying the motives will be favorable and the different motivational forces will be cumulative and reinforcing. Under these circumstances, the full power from each of the available motives will be added to that from the others to yield a maximum of coordinated, enthusiastic effort.

The principle of supportive relationships points to a dimension essential for the success of every organization, namely, that the mission of the organization be seen by its members as genuinely important. To be highly motivated, each member of the organization must feel that the organization's objectives are of significance and that his own particular task contributes in an indispensable manner to the organization's achievement of its objectives. He should see his role as difficult, important, and meaningful. This is necessary if the individual is to achieve and maintain a sense of personal worth and importance. When jobs do not meet this specification they should be reorganized so that they do. This is likely to require the participation of those involved in the work in a manner suggested in subsequent chapters.

The term "supportive" is used frequently in subsequent chapters and also is a key word in the principle of supportive relationships. Experiences, relationships, etc., are considered to be supportive when the individual involved sees the experience (in terms of his values, goals, expectations, and aspirations) as contributing to or maintaining his sense of personal worth and importance.

The principle of supportive relationships contains within it an important clue to its effective use. To apply this general principle, a superior must take into consideration the experience and expectations of each of his subordinates. In determining what these expectations are, he cannot rely solely on his observations and impressions. It helps the superior to try to put himself in his subordinate's shoes and endeavor to see things as the subordinate sees them, but this is not enough. Too often, the superior's estimates are wrong. He needs direct evidence if he is to know how the subordinate views things and to estimate the kinds of behavior and interaction which will be seen by the subordinate as supportive. The superior needs accurate information as to how his behavior is actually seen by the subordinate. Does the subordinate, in fact, perceive the superior's behavior as supportive?

There are two major ways to obtain this evidence. In a complex organization

it can be found by the use of measurements of the intervening variables . . .
It can also be obtained by the development of work-group relationships, which
not only facilitate but actually require, as part of the group building and maintenance
functions, candid expressions by group members of their perceptions and reactions
to the behavior of others . . .

## The Central Role of the Work Group

An important theoretical derivation can be made from the principle of supportive
relationships. This derivation is based directly on the desire to achieve and
maintain a sense of personal worth, which is a central concept of the principle.
The most important source of satisfaction for this desire is the response we
get from the people we are close to, in whom we are interested, and whose
approval and support we are eager to have. The face-to-face groups with whom
we spend the bulk of our time are, consequently, the most important to us.
Our work group is one in which we spend much of our time and one in which
we are particularly eager to achieve and maintain a sense of personal worth.
As a consequence, most persons are highly motivated to behave in ways consistent
with the goals and values of their work group in order to obtain recognition,
support, security, and favorable reactions from this group. It can be concluded,
therefore, that *management will make full use of the potential capacities of its
human resources only when each person in an organization is a member of one
or more effectively functioning work groups that have a high degree of group loyalty,
effective skills of interaction, and high performance goals.*

The full significance of this derivation becomes more evident when we examine
the research findings that show how groups function when they are well knit
and have effective interaction skills. Research shows, for example, that the greater
the attraction and loyalty to the group, the more the individual is motivated (1)
to accept the goals and decisions of the group; (2) to seek to influence the
goals and decisions of the group so that they are consistent with his own experience
and his own goals; (3) to communicate fully to the members of the group; (4)
to welcome communication and influence attempts from the other members;
(5) to behave so as to help implement the goals and decisions that are seen as
most important to the group; and (6) to behave in ways calculated to receive
support and favorable recognition from members of the group and especially
from those who the individual feels are the more powerful and higher-status
members (Cartwright & Zander, 1960). Groups which display a high level of
member attraction to the group and high levels of the above characteristics will
be referred to in this volume as *highly effective groups.* These groups are described
more fully [elsewhere].

As our theoretical derivation has indicated, an organization will function best
when its personnel function not as individuals but as members of highly effective
work groups with high performance goals. Consequently, management should
deliberately endeavor to build these effective groups, linking them into an overall organization by means of people who hold overlapping group membership

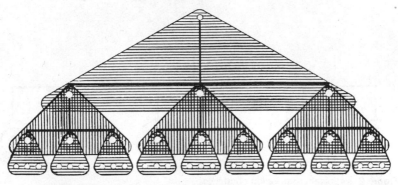

Figure 1.   The overlapping group form of organization. Work groups vary in size as circumstances require although shown here as consisting of four persons.

(Figure 1). The superior in one group is a subordinate in the next group, and so on through the organization. If the work groups at each hierarchical level are well knit and effective, the linking process will be accomplished well. Staff as well as line should be characterized by this pattern of operation.

The dark lines in Figure 1 are intended to show that interaction occurs between individuals as well as in groups. The dark lines are omitted at the lowest level in the chart in order to avoid complexity. Interaction between individuals occurs there, of course, just as it does at higher levels in the organization.

In most organizations, there are also various continuing and *ad hoc* committees, committees related to staff functions, etc., which should also become highly effective groups and thereby help further to tie the many parts of the organization together. These links are in addition to the linking provided by the overlapping members in the line organization. Throughout the organization, the supervisory process should develop and strengthen group functioning. This theoretically ideal organizational structure provides the framework for the management system called for by the newer theory.

## The Traditional Company Organization

Let us examine the way an organization would function were it to apply this one derivation and establish highly effective groups with high performance goals, instead of adhering to the traditional man-to-man pattern. First, let us look briefly at how the traditional man-to-man pattern usually functions. Figure 2 shows the top of an ordinary organization chart. Such an organization ordinarily functions on a man-to-man basis as shown in Figure 3a. In Figure 3a, the president, vice presidents, and others reporting to the president are represented by 0's. The solid lines in Figure 3a indicate the boundaries of well-defined areas of responsibility.

The president of such a man-to-man organization has said to us, "I have been made president of this company by the board of directors because they

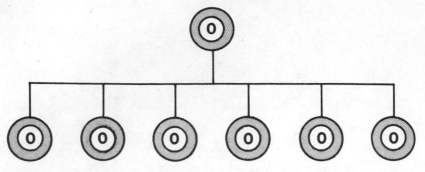

*Figure 2.* Typical organization chart.

believe I am more intelligent or better trained or have more relevant experience than my fellow managers. Therefore, it is my responsibility to make the top-level decisions." He regularly holds meetings of the people who report to him for purposes of sharing information, but *not* for decision-making.

What happens? The vice president in charge of manufacturing, for example, may go to the president with a problem and a recommendation. Because it

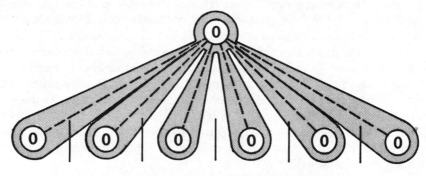

(a) Man-to-man pattern of organization.

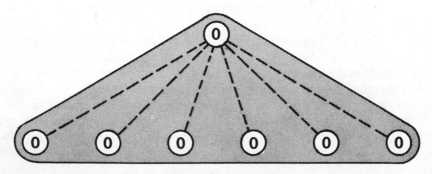

(b) Group pattern of organization.

*Figure 3.* Man-to-man and group patterns of organization.

involves a model change, the vice president in charge of sales is called in. On the basis of the discussion with the two vice presidents and the recommendations they make, the president arrives at a decision. However, in any organization larger than a few hundred employees, that decision usually will affect other vice presidents and subordinates whose interests were not represented in it. Under the circumstances, they are not likely to accept this decision wholeheartedly nor strive hard to implement it. Instead, they usually begin to plan how they can get decisions from the president which are going to be beneficial to them but not necessarily to sales and manufacturing.

And what happens to the communication process? This president, it will be recalled, holds meetings for the primary purpose of sharing information. But if the manufacturing vice president, for example, has some important facts bearing on an action which he wants the president to approve, does he reveal them at these meetings? No, he does not. He waits until he is alone with the president and can use the information to obtain the decision he seeks. Each vice president is careful to share in these communication meetings only trivial information. The motivational pressures are against sharing anything of importance.

The man-to-man pattern of operation enables a vice president or manager to benefit by keeping as much information as possible to himself. Not only can he obtain decisions from his superior beneficial to himself, but he can use his knowledge secretly to connive with peers or subordinates or to pit one peer or subordinate against the other. In these ways, he often is able to increase his own power and influence. He does this, however, at the expense of the total organization. The distrust and fear created by his behavior adversely affect the amount of influence which the organization can exert in coordinating the activities of its members. Measures of the amount of influence an organization can exert on its members show that distrust of superiors, colleagues, and subordinates adversely affects the amount of influence that can be exercised.

Another serious weakness of the communication process in the man-to-man method of operating is that communications upward are highly filtered and correspondingly inaccurate. Orders and instructions flow down through the organization, at times with some distortion. But when management asks for information on the execution of orders and on difficulties encountered, incomplete and partially inaccurate information is often forthcoming. With these items and with other kinds of communication as well, those below the boss study him carefully to discover what he is interested in, what he approves and disapproves of, and what he wants to hear and does not want to hear. They then tend to feed him the material he wants. It is difficult and often hazardous for an individual subordinate in man-to-man discussion to tell the boss something which he needs to know but which runs counter to the boss's desires, convictions, or prejudices. A subordinate's future in an organization often is influenced appreciably by how well he senses and communicates to his boss material which fits the latter's orientation.

Another characteristic of the man-to-man pattern concerns the point of view from which problems are solved. When a problem is brought to the president, each vice president usually states and discusses the problem from a departmental orientation, despite efforts by the president to deal with it from a companywide point of view. This operates to the disadvantage of the entire organization. Problems tend to be solved in terms of what is best for a department, not what is best for the company as a whole.

## Effect of Competition between Functions

In the man-to-man situation it is clear that sharply defined lines of responsibility are necessary (Figure 3a) because of the nature of the promotion process and because the men involved are able people who want promotion.

Now, what are the chances of having one's competence so visible that one moves up in such an organization or receives offers elsewhere? Two factors are important: the magnitude of one's responsibility and the definition of one's functions so as to assure successful performance. For example, if you are head of sales and can get the president to order the manufacturing department to make a product or to price it in such a way that it is highly competitive, that will be to your advantage, even though it imposes excessive difficulties and cost problems on the manufacturing operation.

Each man, in short, is trying to enlarge his area of responsibility, thereby encroaching on the other's territory. He is also trying to get decisions from the president which set easily attained goals for him and enable him to achieve excellent performance. Thus, the sales vice president may get prices set which make his job easy but which put undue pressure on the manufacturing vice president to cut production costs.

One consequence of this struggle for power is that each department or operation has to be staffed for peak loads, and job responsibilities and boundaries have to be precisely defined. No one dares let anybody else take over any part of his activity temporarily for fear that the line of responsibility will be moved over permanently.

The tighter the hierarchical control in an organization, in the sense that decisions are made at the top and orders flow down, the greater tends to be the hostility among subordinates. In autocratic organizations, subordinates bow down to superiors and fight among themselves for power and status. Consequently, the greater the extent to which the president makes the decisions, the greater is the probability that competition, hostility, and conflict will exist between his vice presidents and staff members.

## The Group System of Operation

Figure 3b represents a company patterned on the group system of organization. One of the presidents we interviewed follows this pattern. He will not permit an organization chart to be drawn because he does not want people to think in terms of man-to-man hierarchy. He wants to build working groups. He holds meetings of his top staff regularly to solve problems and make decisions. Any member of his staff can propose problems for consideration, but each problem is viewed from a company-wide point of view. It is virtually impossible for one department to force a decision beneficial to it but detrimental to other departments if the group, as a whole, makes the decisions.

An effectively functioning group pressing for solutions in the best interest of *all* the members and refusing to accept solutions which unduly favor a particular member or segment of the group is an important characteristic of the group pattern of organization. It also provides the president, or the superior at any level in an organization, with a powerful managerial tool for dealing with special requests or favors from subordinates. Often the subordinate may feel that the request is legitimate even though it may not be in the best interest of the organization. In the man-to-man operation (Figure 3*a*), the chief sometimes finds it difficult to turn down such requests. With the group pattern of operation, however, the superior can suggest that the subordinate submit his proposal to the group at their next staff meeting. If the request is legitimate and in the best interest of the organization, the group will grant the request. If the request is unreasonable, an effectively functioning group can skillfully turn it down by analyzing it in relation to what is best for the entire organization. Subordinates in this situation soon find they cannot get special favors or preferred treatment from the chief. This leads to a tradition that one does not ask for any treatment or decision which is recognized as unfair to one's colleagues.

The capacity of effective groups to press for decisions and action in the best interest of all members can be applied in other ways. An example is provided by the president of a subsidiary of a large corporation. He was younger (age forty-two) than most of his staff and much younger than two of his vice presidents (ages sixty-one and sixty-two). The subsidiary had done quite well under its previous president, but the young president was eager to have it do still better. In his first two years as president, his company showed substantial improvement. He found, however, that the two older vice presidents were not effectively handling their responsibilities. Better results were needed from them if the company was to achieve the record performance which the president and the other vice presidents sought.

The president met the situation by using his regular staff meetings to analyze the company's present position, evaluate its potential, and decide on goals and on the action required to reach them. The president had no need to put pressure on his coasting vice presidents. The other vice presidents did it for him. One vice president, in particular, slightly younger but with more years of experience than the two who were dragging their feet, gently but effectively pushed them to commit themselves to higher performance goals. In the regular staff meetings, progress toward objectives was watched and new short-term goals were set as needed. Using this group process, steady progress was made. The two oldest vice presidents became as much involved and worked as enthusiastically as did the rest of the staff.

## Group Decision-making

With the model of organization shown in Figure 3*b*, persons reporting to the president, such as vice presidents for sales, research, and manufacturing, contribute their technical knowledge in the decision-making process. They also make other contributions. One member of the group, for example, may be an imaginative person who comes up rapidly with many stimulating and original ideas. Others, such as the general counsel or the head of research, may make the group do a rigorous job of sifting ideas. In this way, the different contributions required for a competent job of thinking and decision-making are introduced.

In addition, these people become experienced in effective group functioning. They know what leadership involves. If the president grows absorbed in some detail and fails to keep the group focused on the topic for discussion, the members will help by performing appropriate leadership functions, such as asking, "Where are we? What have we decided so far? Why don't we summarize?" (These functions are discussed [elsewhere].)

There are other advantages to this sort of group action. The motivation is high to communicate accurately all relevant and important information. If any one of these men holds back important facts affecting the company so that he can take it to the president later, the president is likely to ask him why he withheld the information and request him to report it to the group at the next session. The group also is apt to be hard on any member who withholds important information from them. Moreover, the group can get ideas across to the boss that no subordinate dares tell him. As a consequence, there is better communication, which brings a better awareness of problems, and better decision-making than with the man-to-man system.

Another important advantage of effective group action is the high degree of motivation on the part of each member to do his best to implement decisions and to achieve the group goals. Since the goals of the group are arrived at through group decisions, each individual group member tends to have a high level of ego identification with the goals because of his involvement in the decisions.

Finally, there are indications that an organization operating in this way can be staffed for less than peak loads at each point. When one man is overburdened, some of his colleagues can pick up part of the load temporarily. This is possible with group methods of supervision because the struggle for power and status is less. Everybody recognizes his broad area of responsibility and is not alarmed by occasional shifts in one direction or the other. Moreover, he knows that his chances for promotion depend not upon the width of his responsibility, but upon his total performance, of which his work in the group is an important part. The group, including the president, comes to know the strengths and weaknesses of each member well as a result of working closely with him.

A few years ago a department of fifteen people in a medium-sized company shifted from a man-to-man pattern of supervision to the group pattern. Each operation under the man-to-man system was staffed to carry adequately the peak loads encountered, but these peaks virtually never occurred for all jobs at the same time. In shifting to group supervision, the department studied how the work was being done. They concluded that seven persons instead of fifteen could carry the load except in emergencies. Gradually, over several months, the persons not needed transferred to other departments and the income of those doing the work was increased 50 per cent. The work is being done well, peak loads are handled, those doing it have more favorable attitudes, and there is less absence and turnover than under the man-to-man system.

## Responsibility and Situational Requirements

In every organization there are many basic facts of life which cannot be ignored if the organization is to achieve its objectives. For example, there are often deadlines or minimum financial conditions as to earnings and reserves to be met. These hard, objective realities are the *situational requirements* which impose limitations on the decision-making processes.

The supervisor of every work group must be fully aware of the situational requirements which apply to the operation of his group. In making decisions, he and his group should never lose sight of them. If the group is so divided in opinion that there is not time to reach decisions by consensus which adequately meet these requirements, the superior has the responsibility of making a decision which does meet them. In this event, the superior may be wise to accept the solution preferred by the individuals in the group who will have the major responsibility for implementing the decision, provided, of course, the superior himself feels that the solution is reasonably sound.

Sometimes the differences of opinion exist not between members of the work group, but between the superior and his subordinates. In this event, the superior should participate fully in the discussion and present clearly the evidence which makes him hold another point of view. If after further discussion, the group still prefers a course of action different from that which the chief favors, the superior faces a tough decision. He can overrule the group and take the action he favors. This is likely to affect adversely group loyalties and the capacity of his work group to function well as a group. Or he can go along with the group and accept the decision they prefer. If he overrules the group, the superior usually reduces the amount of work-group loyalty which he has "in the bank." If the costs of a mistake are not too great, he may prefer to accept the group's decision in order to strengthen the group as a group and to provide an opportunity for his group to learn from its mistakes. If the costs of a mistake are likely to be excessive, the superior may feel that he has no choice but to do what his own experience indicates is best. But whatever course of action is taken, *he is responsible and must accept full responsibility for what occurs.*

## The "Linking Pin" Function

Figure 3 and the preceding discussion have been concerned with the group pattern of organization at the very top of a company. Our theoretical derivation indicates, however, that this pattern is equally applicable at all levels of an organization. If an organization is to apply this system effectively at all organizational levels, an important linking function must be performed.

The concept of the "linking pin" is shown by the arrows in Figure 4. The

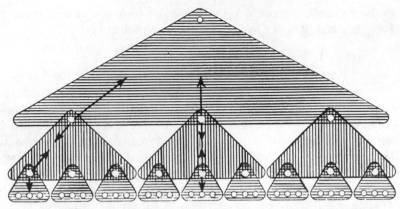

(The arrows indicate the linking pin function.)

*Figure 4.* The linking pin.

research pointing to the importance of upward influence in an organization has already been described [elsewhere]. The study by Pelz (1951; 1952) showed that there was only a slight relationship between some fifty different measures of supervisory practices and points of view, as reported by the supervisors, and the attitudes and morale of the subordinates. Pelz found that an important variable was responsible for the absence of more marked relationships. This variable proved to be the amount of influence which a supervisor felt he had with his own superior. To function effectively, a supervisor must have sufficient influence with his own superior to be able to affect the superior's decisions. Subordinates expect their supervisors to be able to exercise an influence upward in dealing with problems on the job and in handling problems which affect them and their well-being. As Pelz's analysis shows, when a supervisor cannot exert sufficient influence upward in the hierarchy to handle these problems constructively, an unfavorable reaction to the supervisor and to the organization is likely to occur.

Other research confirms the importance of Pelz's findings and also indicates that the ability to exert an influence upward affects not only morale and motivation but also productivity and performance variables (Katz et al., 1950; Likert & Willits, 1940). Ronken and Lawrence (1952) summarize their findings on this matter as follows:

> "An additional complication for the foreman was the necessity of learning how to work with new supervisors and a new group of subordinates. When the foreman experienced difficulty in communicating with his superior, he was not able to understand his subordinates' programs or to gain their spontaneous cooperation, and the work suffered. When he felt more confident of his relations upward, he administered his own group with greater skill. During such periods his operators showed considerable initiative in their work, contributed more useful suggestions, and raced with themselves and each other to increase output."

These results demonstrate that *the capacity to exert influence upward is essential if a supervisor (or manager) is to perform his supervisory functions successfully.* To be effective in leading his own work group, a superior must be able to influence his own boss; that is, he needs to be skilled both as a supervisor and as a subordinate. In terms of group functioning, he must be skilled in both leadership and membership functions and roles.

Effective groups with high group loyalty are characterized by efficient and full communication and by the fact that their members respect each other, welcome attempts by the other members to influence them, and are influenced in their thinking and behavior when they believe that the evidence submitted by the other members warrants it. The linking pin function, consequently, will be performed well in an organization when each work group at all the different hierarchical levels above the nonsupervisory level is functioning effectively as a group and when every member of each group is performing his functions and roles well. Whenever an individual member of one of these groups fails in his leadership and membership roles . . ., the group or groups under him will not be linked into the organization effectively and will fail in the performance of their tasks. When an entire work group ceases to function effectively as a group, the activities and performance of all the work groups below such a group will be correspondingly adversely affected.

The linking pin function requires effective group processes and points to the following:

- An organization will not derive the full benefit from its highly effective groups unless they are linked to the total organization by means of equally effective overlapping groups such as those illustrated in Figures 1 and 4. The use of highly effective groups in only one part or in scattered portions of an organization will fail, therefore, to achieve the full potential value of such groups.
- The potential power of the overlapping group form of organization will not be approached until all the groups in the organization are functioning reasonably well. The failure of any group will adversely affect the performance of the total organization.
- The higher an ineffective group is in the hierarchy, the greater is the adverse effect of its failure on the performance of the organization. The linking process is more important at high levels in an organization than at low because the policies and problems dealt with are more important to the total organization and affect more people.
- To help maintain an effective organization, it is desirable for superiors not only to hold group meetings of their own subordinates, but also to have occasional meetings over two hierarchical levels. This enables the superior to observe any breakdown in the linking pin process as performed by the subordinates reporting to him. If in such meetings the subordinates under one of his subordinates are reluctant to talk, never question any procedure or policy, or give other evidence of fear, the superior can conclude that he has a coaching job to do with his own subordinate, who is failing both as a leader and in his performance of the linking pin function. This subordinate needs help in learning

how to build his own subordinates into a work group with high group loyalty and with confidence and trust in their supervisor . . .

• An organization takes a serious risk when it relies on a single linking pin or single linking process to tie the organization together. As will be discussed further in subsequent chapters, an organization is strengthened by having staff groups and *ad hoc* committees provide multiple overlapping groups through which linking functions are performed and the organization bound together.

## Organizational Objectives and Goals of Units

The ability of a superior to behave in a supportive manner is circumscribed by the degree of compatibility between the objectives of the organization and the needs of the individuals comprising it. If the objectives of the organization are in basic conflict with the needs and desires of the individual members, it is virtually impossible for the superior to be supportive to subordinates and at the same time serve the objectives of the organization. The principle of supportive relationships, consequently, points to the necessity for an adequate degree of harmony between organizational objectives and the needs and desires of its individual members.

This conclusion is applicable to every kind of organization: industrial, governmental, or voluntary. A business organization, if it is to function well, needs to have objectives which represent a satisfactory integration of the needs and desires of all the major segments involved: its shareowners, its suppliers, its consumers, its employees (including all levels of supervisory and nonsupervisory personnel), and its union(s). If governmental agencies are to function effectively, their objectives similarly must be a satisfactory integration of the needs and desires of all the different segments involved in their activities: employees, citizens, and legislators.

Neither the needs and desires of individuals nor the objectives of organizations are stable and unchanging. The desires of individuals grow and change as people interact with other people. Similarly, the objectives of organizations must change continuously to meet the requirements of changed technologies, changed conditions, and the changes in needs and desires of those involved in the organization or served by it. The interaction process of the organization must be capable of dealing effectively with these requirements for continuous change.

In every healthy organization there is, consequently, an unending process of examining and modifying individual goals and organizational objectives as well as consideration of the methods for achieving them. The newer theory specifies that:

• The objectives of the entire organization and of its component parts must be in satisfactory harmony with the relevant needs and desires of the great majority, if not all, of the members of the organization and of the persons served by it.
• The goals and assignments of each member of the organization must be established in such a way that he is highly motivated to achieve them.

- The methods and procedures used by the organization and its subunits to achieve the agreed-upon objectives must be developed and adopted in such a way that the members are highly motivated to use these methods to their maximum potentiality.
- The members of the organization and the persons related to it must feel that the reward system of the organization—salaries, wages, bonuses, dividends, interest payments—yields them equitable compensation for their efforts and contributions.

The overlapping group form of organization offers a structure which, in conjunction with a high level of group interactional skills, is particularly effective in performing the processes necessary to meet these requirements.

## Constructive Use of Conflict

An organization operating under the newer theory is not free from conflict. Conflict and differences of opinion always exist in a healthy, virile organization, for it is usually from such differences that new and better objectives and methods emerge. Differences are essential to progress, but bitter, unresolved differences can immobilize an organization. The central problem, consequently, becomes not how to reduce or eliminate conflict, but how to deal constructively with it. Effective organizations have extraordinary capacity to handle conflict. Their success is due to three very important characteristics:

1. They possess the machinery to deal constructively with conflict. They have an organizational structure which facilitates constructive interaction between individuals and between work groups.

2. The personnel of the organization is skilled in the processes of effective interaction and mutual influence. (Skills in group leadership and membership roles and in group building and maintenance functions are discussed [elsewhere].)

3. There is high confidence and trust among the members of the organization in each other, high loyalty to the work group and to the organization, and high motivation to achieve the organization's objectives. Confidence, loyalty, and cooperative motivation produce earnest, sincere, and determined efforts to find solutions to conflict. There is greater motivation to find a constructive solution than to maintain an irreconcilable conflict. The solutions reached are often highly creative and represent a far better solution than any initially proposed by the conflicting interests (Metcalf & Urwick, 1940).

The discussion in this chapter has deliberately focused on and emphasized the group aspects of organization and management. This has been done to make clear some of the major differences between the classical and the newer theories of management. It should also sharpen the awareness of the kind of changes needed to start applying the newer theory.

Any organization which bases its operation on this theory will necessarily make use of individual counseling and coaching by superiors of subordinates.

There is need in every situation for a balanced use of both procedures, individual and group. Here, as with other aspects of supervision, the balance which will be most appropriate and work best will depend upon the experience, expectations, and skills of the people involved.

## Tests of the Newer Theory

The validity of the newer theory of management and of its derivations can be tested in two ways. Tests can be applied experimentally in pilot plants to see whether the newer system significantly improves all aspects of performance: productivity, quality, costs, employee satisfaction, etc. Although it will take several years to know the results, this kind of test is now under way.

The second kind of test is an examination of the extent to which the methods and procedures called for by the theory, or by the derivations based on the theory, are associated with above-average performance in the current operations of companies. The results of this kind of test do not require waiting for the outcome of an experimental application of the theory, but can be examined now. Several tests of this latter kind have recently been made. These were based on data which have been collected during the past few years. The results indicate, as we shall see in [a later chapter], that the newer theory, skillfully used, will produce an organization with impressive performance characteristics.

# REFERENCES

Argyris, C. *Personality and organization.* New York: Harper, 1957.

Cartwright, D., & Zander, A. (Eds.) *Group dynamics: research and theory* (2d ed.) Evanston, Ill.: Row, Peterson, 1960.

Katz, D., & Kahn, R. L. Human organization and worker motivation. In L. Reed Tripp (Ed.), *Industrial productivity.* Madison, Wis.: Industrial Relations Research Association, 1951. Pp. 146–171.

Katz, D., Maccoby, N., & Morse, Nancy. *Productivity, supervision and morale in an office situation.* Ann Arbor, Mich.: Institute for Social Research, 1950.

Krulee, G. K. The Scanlon plan: co-operation through participation. *J. Business, Univer. of Chicago,* 1955, *28*(2), 100–113.

Likert, R., & Willits, J. M. *Morale and agency management.* Hartford, Conn.: Life Insurance Agency Management Asso., 1940. 4 vols.

March, J. G., & Simon, H. A. *Organizations.* New York: Wiley, 1958.

Metcalf, H. C., & Urwick, L. (Eds.) *Dynamic administration: the collected works of Mary Parker Follett.* New York: Harper, 1940.

Pelz, D. C. The influence of the supervisor within his department as a conditioner of the way supervisory practices affect employee attitudes. Unpublished doctoral dissertation, Univer. of Michigan, 1951.

Pelz, D. C. Influence: a key to effective leadership in the first-line supervisor. *Personnel,* November, 1952, 3–11.

Rogers, C. R. *Counseling and psychotherapy.* Boston: Houghton Mifflin, 1942.

Rogers, C. R. *Client-centered therapy*. Boston: Houghton Mifflin, 1951.

Ronken, H. O., & Lawrence, P. R. *Administering changes*. Boston: Harvard Graduate Sch. of Business Administration, 1952.

Viteles, M. S. *Motivation and morale in industry*. New York: Norton, 1953.

---

## Learning Review

*Questions*

1. _____-producing managers see employees as "human beings rather than just as cogs in a machine."

2. The_____ motives are the desire to achieve and maintain a sense of personal worth and importance.

3. Most high-producing organizations tend to follow the_____pattern of organization.

4. _____and_____ requirements limit the effectiveness of group decision-making.

*Answers:*

1. High; 2. ego; 3. group; 4. Responsibility, situational

---

## Retrospective Comment

### BY RENSIS LIKERT

This chapter was written approximately twenty years ago. The "newer theory of management" which it describes has been labeled, subsequently, System 4 (Likert, 1967).

The sizable volume of research on System 4 done since this chapter was written has amplified and clarified this initial discussion of the newer theory of management. This subsequent work, however, has not altered in any important way the concepts and principles presented in this chapter.

Several hundred studies done during the past twenty years have found quite consistently that organizations (or organizational units) using System 4, or a management system close to it (Likert, 1977):

—achieve 10 percent to more than 40 percent greater productivity (earnings, etc.) than that achieved by organizational units under average or poor managers.

(The average manager in United States business is about System 2 ½ in the management system being used.[1])

—have much higher levels of employee satisfaction and much better employee health, both physical and mental.

—have much better labor relations.

—have less absence and less turnover.

—obtain better product quality and less scrap loss.

—have better customer satisfaction as a result of better products and services.

When managers move closer to System 4 in their management system, their organizational units show improvements in performance of the same magnitude as those described above.

System 4 is being found to be as effective in other kinds of organizations as in business in yielding superior performance. Studies show this to be true in the following kinds of organizations: governmental (Federal, State, and local), military, hospitals, nursing, outpatient, schools and school systems, colleges and universities, libraries, correctional, religious and voluntary.

Studies in many parts of the world show the same pattern: organizations whose management systems are closer to System 4 achieve better performance than those whose management system is closer to System 1.

The "newer theory of management" described in the above chapter (System 4) was discovered as a result of many millions of dollars of social science research. This research has vastly accelerated the recognition of how the management behavior of the highest producing managers differs from that of the average manager. These differences in time would have been recognized without this research but it would probably have taken one or more decades.

System 4 is a more socially-evolved and sophisticated system of managing an organization's human resources. To use System 4 successfully most managers require training and coaching to help them understand its basic concepts and to use its principles skillfully.


# FOOTNOTES

1.   System 1 is punitive authoritarian; System 2 is benevolent authoritarian; System 3 is consultative; System 4 is a participative group model.


# REFERENCES

Likert, R. *The Human Organization: Its Management and Value.* New York: McGraw-Hill, 1967.
Likert, R. *Past and Future Perspectives on System 4 and Appendices A and B.* Ann Arbor: Rensis Likert Associates, Inc., 1977.

# 16
## *The Management Theory Jungle*
### HAROLD KOONTZ

### *About the Author*

**Harold Koontz,** at the time of his death in 1985, was Emeritus Mead Johnson Professor of Management at the Graduate School of Management, University of California, Los Angeles. A former President of the Academy of Management, Koontz authored twenty books and over 85 articles. His books were translated into thirteen languages, including Swedish, Czech, Chinese, Portuguese, Polish, Indonesian, Turkish, and Arabic. Koontz received his doctorate from Yale. He gave lectures on management throughout the world and served as consultant to major firms in the United States, the Netherlands, and Japan.

## PREVIEW

A. Until recent years there has been a noteworthy absence of academic writing and research in management theory.

B. Today people who see great potential from improved management are proposing so many approaches to management theory that this has led to a kind of confused and destructive jungle warfare.

Reprinted by permission of the author and the *Journal of the Academy of Management,* Vol. 4, (December 1961), pp. 174–188.

C. The major schools of management theory can be classified into six main groups.

    I. The *Management Process School,* founded by Henri Fayol and often referred to as the "traditional" or "universalist" school, views management as a process of getting things done through and with people operating in organized groups.

        1. The basic approach of this school is to look first to the functions of managers and then classify the analysis around the nature, purpose, structure and process of the function.

    II. The *Empirical School* approach states that, by studying the experiences of successful managers, or the mistakes made in management, or by attempting to solve management problems, we will somehow understand and learn to apply the most effective kinds of management techniques.

        1. This approach tends to move in the same direction as the Management Process School approach, so far as drawing generalizations from research is concerned.

    III. The *Human Behavior School* concentrates on the "people" part of management, and is based on the principle that people should understand people when working together as groups to accomplish objectives.

        1. In this school, there are scholars who are heavily oriented to psychology and social psychology.

        2. There are those who emphasize human relations as an art that the manager should understand.

        3. Then there are others who focus attention on the manager as a leader and sometimes equate management to leadership.

        4. Finally there are those who view studying group dynamics and interpersonal relationships as simply a study of socio-psychological relationships.

    IV. The *Social System School* is one that identifies the nature of the cultural relationships of various social groups and attempts to show these as a related and usually an integrated system.

        1. This school is closely related and often confused with the Human Behavior School.

        2. It was founded by Chester Barnard while searching for an answer to fundamental explanations underlying the managing process.

        3. This School's noteworthy contributions to management are:

            (a) recognition of organized enterprise as a social organism, subject to all pressures and conflicts of the cultural environment,

            (b) awareness of the institutional foundations of organizational authority,

            (c) the influence of informal organization.

    V. The approach of *Decision Theory School* is to deal with the decision itself, or with the persons or organizational group making the decision, or an analysis of the decision process.

        1. This School, which is an apparent outgrowth of the theory of consumers' choice, has members who are mostly economic theorists.

2. The content of this School is heavily oriented to model construction and mathematics.

VI. The *Mathematical School* views management as a system of mathematical models and processes.

　　1. It includes operations researchers or operations analysts, who believe that if management, or organization, or planning or decision making is a logical process, it can be expressed by mathematical symbols and relationships.

　　2. In spite of all the meaningful contributions mathematics has made to society, the author views it as a tool for solving or simplifying complex phenomena rather than a school of management theory.

D. Although the various schools of management theory have arrived at similar conclusions from the physical and cultural environment surrounding us, many differences still exist.

E. The major sources of the mental entanglement in the management theory jungle are the following:

　　1. The semantics problem is particularly severe when it comes to defining words such as management, organization, decision making, leadership, communications and human relations.

　　2. The greatest single semantics confusion lies in the word "organization".

　　3. While most members of the Management Process School use "organization" to define the activity-authority structure of an enterprise, a large number of "organization" theorists conceive it to be the sum total of human relationships in any group activity and still others use it to mean "enterprise".

　　4. Since so many differences exist in the definition of management (as a body of knowledge) how can one expect management theory to be regarded as very useful or scientific to the practitioner?

　　5. Confusion has also increased because outsiders who enter the field for the first time have put aside significant observations and analyses of the past, on the basis that they are a *a priori* in nature.

　　6. Some researchers generalize from their studies of management the same fundamental truths (in different words) that certain criticized "universalists" have discovered.

　　7. Others have the tendency to prove the wrong things through either misstatement or misapplication of principles.

　　8. The author believes that much of the management theory jungle is the result of unwillingness rather than the inability of the management theorists to understand each other.

F. The following steps should aid in disentangling the management theory jungle:

　　1. Define the body of knowledge to give it fairly specific content and at the same time distinguish it from its tools.

　　2. Regard management as a specific discipline and integrate it with other disciplines.

　　3. Adopt the semantics of the intelligent practitioners by establishing a

commission representing relevant academic societies and associations of practicing managers.
4. Test the maturity and usefulness of the science for sharpness and validity of the underlying principles.

---

Although students of management would readily agree that there have been problems of management since the dawn of organized life, most would also agree that systematic examination of management, with few exceptions, is the product of the present century and more especially of the past two decades. Moreover, until recent years almost all of those who have attempted to analyze the management process and look for some theoretical underpinnings to help improve research, teaching, and practice were alert and perceptive practitioners of the art who reflected on many years of experience. Thus, at least in looking at *general* management as an intellectually based art, the earliest meaningful writing came from such experienced practitioners as Fayol, Mooney, Alvin Brown, Sheldon, Barnard, and Urwick. Certainly not even the most academic worshipper of empirical research can overlook the empiricism involved in distilling fundamentals from decades of experience by such discerning practitioners as these. Admittedly done without questionnaires, controlled interviews, or mathematics, observations by such men can hardly be accurately regarded as a priori or "armchair."

The noteworthy absence of academic writing and research in the formative years of modern management theory is now more than atoned for by a deluge of research and writing from the academic halls. What is interesting and perhaps nothing more than a sign of the unsophisticated adolescence of management theory is how the current flood has brought with it a wave of great differences and apparent confusion. From the orderly analysis of management at the shoproom level by Frederick Taylor and the reflective distillation of experience from the general management point of view by Henri Fayol, we now see these and other early beginnings overgrown and entangled by a jungle of approaches and approachers to management theory.

There are the behavioralists, born of the Hawthorne experiments and the awakened interest in human relations during the 1930s and 1940s, who see management as a complex of interpersonal relationships and the basis of management theory the tentative tenets of the new and undeveloped science of psychology. There are also those who see management theory as simply a manifestation of the institutional and cultural aspects of sociology. Still others, observing that the central core of management is decision making, branch in all directions from this core to encompass everything in organization life. Then, there are mathematicians who think of management primarily as an exercise in logical relationships expressed in symbols and the omnipresent and ever revered model. But the entanglement of growth reaches its ultimate when the study of management is regarded as a study of one of a number of systems and subsystems, with an understandable tendency for the researcher to be dissatisfied until he has encompassed the entire physical and cultural universe as a management system.

With the recent discovery of an ages old problem area by social, physical, and biological scientists, and with the supersonic increase in interest by all types of enterprise managers, the apparent impenetrability of the present thicket which we call management theory is not difficult to comprehend. One can hardly be surprised that psychologists, sociologists, anthropologists, sociometricists, economists, mathematicians, physicists, biologists, political scientists, business administration scholars, and even practicing managers, should hop on this interesting, challenging, and profitable band wagon.

This welling of interest from every academic and practicing corner should not upset anyone concerned with seeing the frontiers of knowledge pushed back and the intellectual base of practice broadened. But what is rather upsetting to the practitioner and the observer, who sees great social potential from improved management, is that the variety of approaches to management theory has led to a kind of confused and destructive jungle warfare. Particularly among academic disciplines and their disciples, the primary interests of many would-be cult leaders seem to be to carve out a distinct (and hence "original") approach to management. And to defend this originality, and thereby gain a place in posterity (or at least to gain a publication which will justify academic status or promotion), it seems to have become too much the current style to downgrade, and sometimes misrepresent, what anyone else has said, or thought, or done.

In order to cut through this jungle and bring to light some of the issues and problems involved in the present management theory area so that the tremendous interest, intelligence, and research results may become more meaningful, it is my purpose here to classify the various "schools" of management theory, to identify briefly what I believe to be the major source of differences, and to offer some suggestions for disentangling the jungle. It is hoped that a movement for clarification can be started so at least we in the field will not be a group of blind men identifying the same elephant with our widely varying and sometimes viciously argumentative theses.

## The Major "Schools" of Management Theory

In attempting to classify the major schools of management theory into six main groups, I am aware that I may overlook certain approaches and cannot deal with all the nuances of each approach. But it does seem that most of the approaches to management theory can be classified in one of these so-called schools.

### The Management Process School

This approach to management theory perceives management as a process of getting things done through and with people operating in organized groups. It aims to analyze the process, to establish a conceptual framework for it, to identify principles underlying it, and to build up a theory of management from them. It regards management as a universal process, regardless of the type of enterprise, or the level in a given enterprise, although recognizing, obviously, that the environment of management differs widely between enterprises and levels. It looks upon management theory as a way of organizing experiences so that practice can be improved through research, empirical testing of principles, and teaching of fundamentals involved in the management process. [1]

Often referred to, especially by its critics, as the "traditional" or "universalist" school, this school can be said to have been fathered by Henri Fayol, although many of his offspring did not know of their parent, since Fayol's work was eclipsed by the bright light of his contemporary, Frederick Taylor, and clouded by the lack of a widely available English translation until 1949. Other than Fayol, most of the early contributors to this school dealt only with the organization portion of the management process, largely because of their greater experience with this facet of management and the simple fact that planning and control, as well as the function of staffing, were given little attention by managers before 1940.

This school bases its approach to management theory on several fundamental beliefs:

(1) that managing is a process and can best be dissected intellectually by analyzing the functions of the manager;

(2) that long experience with management in a variety of enterprise situations can be grounds for distillation of certain fundamental truths or generalizations—usually referred to as principles—which have a clarifying and predictive value in the understanding and improvement of managing;

(3) that these fundamental truths can become focal points for useful research both to ascertain their validity and to improve their meaning and applicability in practice;

(4) that such truths can furnish elements, at least until disproved, and certainly until sharpened, of a useful theory of management;

(5) that managing is an art, but one like medicine or engineering, which can be improved by reliance on the light and understanding of principles;

(6) that principles in management, like principles in the biological and physical sciences, are nonetheless true even if a prescribed treatment or design by a practitioner in a given case situation chooses to ignore a principle and the costs involved, or attempts to do something else to offset the costs incurred (this is, of course, not new in medicine, engineering, or any other art, for art is the creative task of compromising fundamentals to attain a desired result); and

(7) that, while the totality of culture and of the physical and biological universe has varying effects on the manager's environment and subjects, as indeed they do in every other field of science and art, the theory of management does not need to encompass the field of all knowledge in order for it to serve as a scientific or theoretical foundation.

The basic approach of this school, then, is to look, first, to the functions of managers. As a second step in this approach, many of us have taken the functions of managers and further dissected them by distilling what we see as fundamental truths in the understandably complicated practice of management. I have found it useful to classify my analysis of these functions around the essentials involved in the following questions:

(1) What is the nature of the function?
(2) What is the purpose of the function?
(3) What explains the structure of the function?
(4) What explains the process of the function?

Perhaps there are other more useful approaches, but I have found that I can place everything pertaining to management (even some of the rather remote research and concepts) in this framework.

Also, purely to make the area of management theory intellectually manageable, those who subscribe to this school do not usually attempt to include in the theory the entire areas of sociology, economics, biology, psychology, physics, chemistry, or others. This is done not because these other areas of knowledge are unimportant and have no bearing on management, but merely because no real progress has ever been made in science or art without significant partitioning of knowledge. Yet, anyone would be foolish not to realize that a function which deals with people in their various activities of producing and marketing anything from money to religion and education is completely independent of the physical, biological, and cultural universe in which we live. And, are there not such relationships in other "compartments" of knowledge and theory?

## The Empirical School

A second approach to management I refer to as the "empirical" school. In this, I include those scholars who identify management as a study of experience, sometimes with intent to draw generalizations but usually merely as a means of teaching experience and transferring it to the practitioner or student. Typical of this school are those who see management or "policy" as the study and analysis of cases and those with such approaches as Ernest Dale's "comparative approach." [2]

This approach seems to be based upon the premise that, if we study the experience of successful managers, or the mistakes made in management, or if we attempt to solve management problems, we will somehow understand and learn to apply the most effective kinds of management techniques. This approach, as often applied, assumes that, by finding out what worked or did not work in individual circumstances, the student or the practitioner will be able to do the same in comparable situations.

No one can deny the importance of studying experience through such study, or of analyzing the "how-it-was-done" of management. But management, unlike law, is not a science based on precedent, and situations in the future exactly comparable to the past are exceedingly unlikely to occur. Indeed, there is a positive danger of relying too much on past experience and on undistilled history of managerial problem solving for the simple reason that a technique or approach found "right" in the past may not fit a situation of the future.

Those advocating the empirical approach are likely to say that what they really do in analyzing cases or history is to draw from certain generalizations which can be applied as useful guides to thought or action in future case situations. As a matter of fact, Ernest Dale, after claiming to find "so little practical value" from the principles enunciated by the "universalists," curiously drew certain "generalizations" or "criteria" from his valuable study of a number of great practitioners of management. [3] There is some question as to whether Dale's "comparative" approach is not really the same as the "universalist" approach he decries, except with a different distiller of basic truths.

By the emphasis of the empirical school on study of experience, it does appear that the research and thought so engendered may assist in hastening the day for verification of principles. It is also possible that the proponents of this school may come up with a more useful framework of principles than that of the management process school. But, to the extent that the empirical school draws generalizations from its research, and it would seem to be a necessity to do so unless its members are satisfied to exchange meaningless and structureless experience, this approach tends to be and do the same as the management process school.

## The Human Behavior School

This approach to the analysis of management is based on the central thesis that, since managing involves getting things done with and through people, the study of management must be centered on interpersonal relations. Variously called the "human relations," "leadership," or "behavioral sciences" approach, this school brings to bear "existing and newly developed theories, methods, and techniques of the relevant social sciences upon the study of inter- and intrapersonal phenomena, ranging fully from the personality dynamics of individuals at one extreme to the relations of cultures at the other." [4] In other words, this school concentrates on the "people" part of management and rests on the principle that, where people work together as groups in order to accomplish objectives, "people should understand people."

The scholars in this school have a heavy orientation to psychology and social psychology. Their primary focus is the individual as a socio-psychological being and what motivates him. The members of this school vary from those who see it as a portion of the manager's job, a tool to help him understand and get the best from people by meeting their needs and responding to their motivations, to those who see the psychological behavior of individuals and groups as the total of management.

In this school are those who emphasize human relations as an art that the manager should advantageously understand and practice. There are those who focus attention on the manager as a leader and sometimes equate management to leadership, thus, in effect, tending to treat all group activities as "managed" situations. There are those who see the study of group dynamics and interpersonal relationships as simply a study of socio-psychological relationships and seem, therefore, merely to be attaching the term "management" to the field of social psychology.

That management must deal with human behavior can hardly be denied. That the study of human interactions, whether in the environment of management or in unmanaged situations, is important and useful one could not dispute. And it would be a serious mistake to regard good leadership as unimportant to good managership. But whether the field of human behavior is the equivalent of the field of management is quite another thing. Perhaps it is like calling the study of the human body the field of cardiology.

## The Social System School

Closely related to the human behavior school and often confused or intertwined with it is one which might be labeled the social system school. This includes those researchers who look upon management as a social system, that is, a system of cultural interrelationships. Sometimes, as in the case of March and Simon,[5] the system is limited to formal organizations, using the term "organization" as equivalent to enterprise, rather than the authority-activity concept used most often in management. In other cases, the approach is not to distinguish the formal organization, but rather to encompass any kind of system of human relationships.

Heavily sociological in flavor, this approach to management does essentially what any study of sociology does. It identifies the nature of the cultural relationships of various social groups and attempts to show these as a related, and usually an integrated, system.

Perhaps the spiritual father of this ardent and vocal school of management theorists is Chester Barnard.[6] In searching for an answer to fundamental explanations underlying the managing process, this thoughtful business executive developed a theory of cooperation grounded in the needs of the individual to solve, through cooperation, the biological, physical, and social limitations of himself and his environment. Barnard then carved from the total of cooperative systems so engendered one set of interrelationships which he defines as "formal organization." His formal organization concept, quite unlike that usually held by management practitioners, is any cooperative system in which there are persons able to communicate with each other and who are willing to contribute action toward a conscious common purpose.

The Barnard concept of cooperative systems pervades the work of many contributors to the social system school of management. For example, Herbert Simon at one time defined the subject of organization theory and the nature of human organizations as "systems of interdependent activity, encompassing at least several primary groups and usually characterized, at the level of consciousness of participants, by a high degree of rational direction of behavior toward ends that are objects of common knowledge." [7] Simon and others have subsequently seemed to have expanded this concept of social systems to include any cooperative and purposeful group interrelationship or behavior.

This school has made many noteworthy contributions to management. The recognition of organized enterprise as a social organism, subject to all the pressures and conflicts of the cultural environment, has been helpful to the management theorist and the practitioner alike. Among some of the more helpful aspects are the awareness of the institutional foundations of organization authority, the influence of informal organization, and such social factors as those Wight Bakke has called the "bonds of organization." [8] Likewise, many of Barnard's helpful insights, such as his economy of incentives and his theory of opportunism, have brought the power of sociological understanding into the realm of management practice.

Basic sociology, analysis of concepts of social behavior, and the study of group behavior in the framework of social systems do have great value in the field of management. But one may well ask the question whether this *is* management.

Is the field of management coterminous with the field of sociology? Or is sociology an important underpinning like language, psychology, physiology, mathematics, and other fields of knowledge? Must management be defined in terms of the universe of knowledge?

## *The Decision Theory School*

Another approach to management theory, undertaken by a growing and scholarly group, might be referred to as the decision theory school. This group concentrates on rational approach to decision—the selection from among possible alternatives of a course of action or of an idea. The approach of this school may be to deal with the decision itself, or with the persons or organizational group making the decision, or with an analysis of the decision process. Some limit themselves fairly much to the economic rationale of the decision, while others regard anything which happens in an enterprise the subject of their analysis, and still others expand decision theory to cover the psychological and sociological aspect and environment of decisions and decision makers.

The decision making school is apparently an outgrowth of the theory of consumer's choice with which economists have been concerned since the days of Jeremy Bentham early in the nineteenth century. It has arisen out of such economic problems and analyses as utility maximization, indifference curves, marginal utility, and economic behavior under risks and uncertainties. It is, therefore, no surprise that one finds most of the members of this school to be economic theorists. It is likewise no surprise to find the content of this school to be heavily oriented to model construction and mathematics.

The decision theory school has tended to expand its horizon considerably beyond the process of evaluating alternatives. That point has become for many only a springboard for examination of the entire sphere of human activity, including the nature of the organization structure, psychological and social reactions of individuals and groups, the development of basic information for decisions, an analysis of values and particularly value considerations with respect to goals, communications networks, and incentives. As one would expect, when the decision theorists study the small, but central, area of decision *making*, they are led by this keyhole look at management to consider the entire field of enterprise operation and its environment. The result is that decision theory becomes no longer a neat and narrow concentration on decision, but rather a broad view of the enterprise as a social system.

There are those who believe that, since management is characterized by its concentration on decisions, the future development of management theory will tend to use the decision as its central focus and the rest of management theory will be hung on this structural center. This may occur and certainly the study of the decision, the decision process, and the decision maker can be extended to cover the entire field of management as anyone might conceive it. Nevertheless, one wonders whether this focus cannot also be used to build around it the entire area of human knowledge. For, as most decision theorists recognize, the problem of choice is individual, as well as organizational, and most of what has been said that is pure decision theory can be applied to the existence and thinking of a Robinson Crusoe.

## The Mathematical School

Although mathematical methods can be used by any school of management theory, and have been, I have chosen to group under a school those theorists who see management as a system of mathematical models and processes. Perhaps the most widely known group I arbitrarily so lump are the operations researchers or operations analysts, who have sometimes anointed themselves with the rather pretentious name of "management scientists." The abiding belief of this group is that, if management, or organization, or planning, or decision making is a logical process, it can be expressed in terms of mathematical symbols and relationships. The central approach of this school is the model, for it is through these devices that the problem is expressed in its basic relationships and in terms of selected goals or objectives.

There can be no doubt of the great usefulness of mathematical approaches to any field of inquiry. It forces upon the researcher the definition of a problem or problem area, it conveniently allows the insertion of symbols for unknown data, and its logical methodology, developed by years of scientific application and abstraction, furnishes a powerful tool for solving or simplifying complex phenomena.

But it is hard to see mathematics as a truly separate school of management theory, any more than it is a separate "school" in physics, chemistry, engineering, or medicine. I only deal with it here as such because there has appeared to have developed a kind of cult around mathematical analysts who have subsumed to themselves the area of management.

In pointing out that mathematics is a tool, rather than a school, it is not my intention to underestimate the impact of mathematics on the science and practice of management. By bringing to this immensely important and complex field the tools and techniques of the physical sciences, the mathematicians have already made an immense contribution to orderly thinking. They have forced on people in management the means and desirability of seeing many problems more clearly, they have pressed on scholars and practitioners the need for establishing goals and measures of effectiveness, they have been extremely helpful in getting the management area seen as a logical system of relationships, and they have caused people in management to review and occasionally reorganize information sources and systems so that mathematics can be given sensible quantitative meaning. But with all this meaningful contribution and the greater sharpness and sophistication of planning which is resulting, I cannot see that mathematics is management theory any more than it is astronomy.

# The Major Sources
# of Mental Entanglement in the Jungle

In outlining the various schools, or approaches, of management theory, it becomes clear that these intellectual cults are not drawing greatly different inferences from the physical and cultural environment surrounding us. Why, then, have there been so many differences between them and why such a struggle, particularly among our academic brethren, to obtain a place in the sun by denying the approaches of others? Like the widely differing and often contentious denominations of the Christian religion, all have essentially the same goals and deal with essentially the same world.

While there are many sources of the mental entanglement in the management theory jungle, the major ones are the following:

## The Semantics Jungle
As is so often true when intelligent men argue about basic problems, some of the trouble lies in the meaning of key words. The semantics problem is particularly severe in the field of management. There is even a difference in the meaning of the word "management." Most people would agree that it means getting things done through and with people, but is it people in formal organizations, or in all group activities? Is it governing, leading, or teaching?

Perhaps the greatest single semantics confusion lies in the word "organization." Most members of the management process school use it to define the activity-authority structure of an enterprise and certainly most practitioners believe that they are "organizing" when they establish a framework of activity groupings and authority relationships. In this case, organization represents the formal framework within an enterprise that furnishes the environment in which people perform. Yet a large number of "organization" theorists conceive of organization as the sum total of human relationships in any group activity; they thus seem to make it equivalent to *social* structure. And some use "organization" to mean "enterprise."

If the meaning of organization cannot be clarified and a standard use of the term adopted by management theorists, understanding and criticism should not be based on this difference. It hardly seems to me to be accurate for March and Simon, for example, to criticize the organization theories of the management process, or "universalist," school for not considering the management planning function as part of organizing, when they have chosen to treat it separately. Nor should those who choose to treat the training, selecting, guiding or leading of people under staffing and direction be criticized for a tendency to "view the employee as an inert instrument" or a "given rather than a variable." [9] Such accusations, proceeding from false premises, are clearly erroneous.

Other semantic entanglements might be mentioned. By some, decision making is regarded as a process of choosing from among alternatives; by others, the total managerial task and environment. Leadership is often made synonymous with managership and is analytically separated by others. Communications may mean everything from a written or oral report to a vast network of formal and informal relationships. Human relations to some implies a psychiatric manipulation of people, but to others the study and art of understanding people and interpersonal relationships.

## Differences in Definition of Management as a Body of Knowledge
As was indicated in the discussion of semantics, "management" has far from a standard meaning, although most agree that it at least involves getting things done through and with people. But, does it mean the dealing with all human

relationships? Is a street peddler a manager? Is a parent a manager? Is a leader of a disorganized mob a manager? Does the field of management equal the fields of sociology and social psychology combined? Is it the equivalent of the entire system of social relationships?

While I recognize that sharp lines cannot be drawn in management any more than they are in medicine or engineering, there surely can be a sharper distinction drawn than at present. With the plethora of management writing and experts, calling almost everything under the sun management, can one expect management theory to be regarded as very useful or scientific to the practitioner?

## The A Priori Assumption

Confusion in management theory has also been heightened by the tendency for many newcomers in the field to cast aside significant observations and analyses of the past on the grounds that they are a priori in nature. This is an often-met accusation made by those who wish to cast aside the work of Fayol, Mooney, Brown, Urwick, Gulick, and others who are branded as "universalists." To make the assumption that the distilled experiences of men such as these represent a priori reasoning is to forget that experience in and with managing *is* empirical. While the conclusions that perceptive and experienced practitioners of the art of management draw are not infallible, they represent an experience which is certainly real and not "armchair." No one could deny, I feel sure, that the ultimate test of accuracy of management theory must be practice and management theory and science must be developed from reality.

## The Misunderstanding of Principles

Those who feel that they gain caste or a clean slate for advancing a particular notion or approach often delight in casting away anything which smacks of management principles. Some have referred to them as platitudes, forgetting that a platitude is still a truism and a truth does not become worthless because it is familiar. (As Robert Frost has written, "Most of the changes we think we see in life are merely truths going in or out of favor.") Others cast away principles of Fayol and other practitioners, only to draw apparently different generalizations from their study of management; but many of the generalizations so discovered are often the same fundamental truths in different words that certain criticized "universalists" have discovered.

One of the favorite tricks of the managerial theory trade is to disprove a whole framework of principles by reference to one principle which the observer sees disregarded in practice. Thus, many critics of the universalists point to the well-known cases of dual subordination in organized enterprise, coming to the erroneous conclusion that there is no substance to the principle of unity of command. But this does not prove that there is no cost to the enterprise by designing around, or disregarding, the principle of unity of command; nor does it prove that there were not other advantages which offset the costs, as there often are in cases of establishing functional authorities in organization.

Perhaps the almost hackneyed standby for those who would disprove the validity of all principles by referring to a single one is the misunderstanding around the principle of span of management (or span of control). The usual source of authority quoted by those who criticize is Sir Ian Hamilton, who never intended to state a universal principle, but rather to make a personal observation in a book of reflections on his Army experience, and who did say, offhand, that he found it wise to limit his span to 3 to 6 subordinates. No modern universalist relies on this single observation, and, indeed, few can or will state an absolute or universal numerical ceiling. Since Sir Ian was not a management theorist and did not intend to be, let us hope that the ghost of his innocent remark may be laid to deserved rest!

What concerns those who feel that a recognition of fundamental truths, or generalizations, may help in the diagnosis and study of management, and who know from managerial experience that such truths or principles do serve an extremely valuable use, is the tendency for some researchers to prove the wrong things through either misstatement or misapplication of principles. A classic case of such misunderstanding and misapplication is in Chris Argyris' interesting book on *Personality and Organization.*[10] This author, who in this book and his other works has made many noteworthy contributions to management, concludes that "formal organization principles make demands on relatively healthy individuals that are incongruent with their needs," and that "frustration, conflict, failure, and short-time perspective are predicted as results of this basic incongruency."[11] This startling conclusion—the exact opposite of what "good" formal organization based on "sound" organization principles should cause, is explained when one notes that, of four "principles" Argyris quotes, one is not an organization principle at all but the economic principle of specialization and three other "principles" are quoted incorrectly.[12] With such a postulate, and with no attempt to recognize, correctly or incorrectly, any other organization and management principles, Argyris has simply proved that wrong principles badly applied will lead to frustration; and every management practitioner knows this to be true!

### The Inability or Unwillingness of Management Theorists to Understand Each Other

What has been said above leads one to the conclusion that much of the management theory jungle is caused by the unwillingness or inability of the management theorists to understand each other. Doubting that it is inability, because one must assume that a person interested in management theory is able to comprehend, at least in concept and framework, the approaches of the various "schools," I can only come to the conclusion that the roadblock to understanding is unwillingness.

Perhaps this unwillingness comes from the professional "walls" developed by learned disciplines. Perhaps the unwillingness stems from a fear that someone or some new discovery will encroach on professional and academic status. Perhaps it is fear of professional or intellectual obsolescence. But whatever the cause, it seems that these walls will not be torn down until it is realized that they exist, until all cultists are willing to look at the approach and content of other schools, and until, through exchange and understanding of ideas some order may be brought from the present chaos.

## Disentangling the Management Theory Jungle

It is important that steps be taken to disentangle the management theory jungle. Perhaps, it is too soon and we must expect more years of wandering through a thicket of approaches, semantics, thrusts, and counter thrusts. But in any field as important to society where the many blunders of an unscientifically based managerial art can be so costly, I hope that this will not be long.

There do appear to be some things that can be done. Clearly, meeting what I see to be the major sources of the entanglement should remove much of it. The following considerations are important:

*1.* **The Need for Definition of a Body of Knowledge.** Certainly, if a field of knowledge is not to get bogged down in a quagmire of misunderstandings, the first need is for definition of the field. Not that it need be defined in sharp, detailed, and inflexible lines, but rather along lines which will give it fairly specific content. Because management is reality, life, practice, my suggestion would be that it be defined in the light of the able and discerning practitioner's frame of reference. A science unrelated to the art for which it is to serve is not likely to be a very productive one.

Although the study of managements in various enterprises, in various countries, and at various levels made by many persons, including myself, may neither be representative nor adequate, I have come to the conclusion that management is the art of getting things done through and with people in *formally organized groups,* the art of creating an environment in such an organized group where people can perform as individuals and yet cooperate toward attainment of group goals, the art of removing blocks to such performance, the art of optimizing efficiency in effectively reaching goals. If this kind of definition of the field is unsatisfactory, I suggest at least an agreement that the area should be defined to reflect the field of the practitioner and that further research and study of practice be done to this end.

In defining the field, too, it seems to me imperative to draw some limits for purposes of analysis and research. If we are to call the entire cultural, biological, and physical universe the field of management, we can no more make progress than could have been done if chemistry or geology had not carved out a fairly specific area and had, instead, studied all knowledge.

In defining the body of knowledge, too, care must be taken to distinguish between tools and content. Thus mathematics, operations research, accounting, economic theory, sociometry, and psychology, to mention a few, are significant *tools* of management but are not, in themselves, a part of the *content* of the field. This is not to mean that they are unimportant or that the practicing manager should not have them available to him, nor does it mean that they may not be the means of pushing back the frontiers of knowledge of management. But they should not be confused with the basic content of the field.

This is not to say that fruitful study should not continue on the underlying disciplines affecting management. Certainly knowledge of sociology, social systems, psychology, economics, political science, mathematics, and other areas, pointed toward contributing to the field of management, should be continued and encouraged. And significant findings in these and other fields of knowledge might well cast important light on, or change concepts in, the field of management. This has certainly happened in other sciences and in every other art based upon significant science.

2.   **Integration of Management and Other Disciplines.** If recognition of the proper content of the field were made, I believe that the present crossfire of misunderstanding might tend to disappear. Management would be regarded as a specific discipline and other disciplines would be looked upon as important bases of the field. Under these circumstances, the allied and underlying disciplines would be welcomed by the business and public administration schools, as well as by practitioners, as loyal and helpful associates. Integration of management and other disciplines would then not be difficult.

3.   **The Clarification of Management Semantics.** While I would expect the need for clarification and uniformity of management semantics would largely be satisfied by definition of the field as a body of knowledge, semantics problems might require more special attention. There are not too many places where semantics are important enough to cause difficulty. Here again, I would suggest the adoption of the semantics of the intelligent practitioners, unless words are used by them so inexactly as to require special clarification. At least, we should not complicate an already complex field by developing a scientific or academic jargon which would build a language barrier between the theorist and the practitioner.

Perhaps the most expeditious way out of this problem is to establish a commission representing academic societies immediately concerned and associations of practicing managers. This would not seem to be difficult to do. And even if it were, the results would be worth the efforts.

4.   **Willingness to Distill and Test Fundamentals.** Certainly, the test of maturity and usefulness of a science is the sharpness and validity of the principles underlying it. No science, now regarded as mature, started out with a complete statement of incontrovertibly valid principles. Even the oldest sciences, such as physics, keep revising their underlying laws and discovering new principles. Yet any science has proceeded, and more than that has been useful, for centuries on the basis of generalizations, some laws, some principles, and some hypotheses.

One of the understandable sources of inferiority of the social sciences is the recognition that they are inexact sciences. On the other hand, even the so-called exact sciences are subject to a great deal of inexactness, have principles which are not completely proved, and use art in the design of practical systems and components. The often-encountered defeatist attitude of the social sciences, of which management is one, overlooks the fact that management may be explained, practice may be improved, and the goals of research may be more meaningful if we encourage attempts at perceptive distillation of experience by stating principles (or generalizations) and placing them in a logical framework. As two scientists recently said on this subject:

> The reason for this defeatist point of view regarding the social sciences
> may be traceable to a basic misunderstanding of the nature of scientific

endeavor. What matters is not whether or to what extent inexactitudes in procedures and predictive capability can eventually be removed . . . rather it is *objectivity*, i.e., the intersubjectivity of findings independent of any one person's intuitive judgment, which distinguishes science from intuitive guesswork however brilliant. . . . But once a new fact or a new idea has been conjectured, no matter how intuitive a foundation, it must be capable of objective test and confirmation by anyone. And it is this crucial standard of scientific objectivity rather than any purported criterion of exactitude to which the social sciences must conform.[13]

In approaching the clarification of management theory, then, we should not forget a few criteria:

1. The theory should deal with an area of knowledge and inquiry that is "manageable"; no great advances in knowledge were made so long as man contemplated the whole universe;
2. The theory should be *useful* in improving practice and the task and person of the practitioner should not be overlooked;
3. The theory should not be lost in semantics, especially useless jargon not understandable to the practitioner;
4. The theory should give direction and efficiency to research and teaching; and
5. The theory must recognize that it is a part of a larger universe of knowledge and theory.

# FOOTNOTES

1. It is interesting that one of the scholars strongly oriented to human relations and behavioral approaches to management has recently noted that "theory can be viewed as a way of organizing experience" and that "once initial sense is made out of experienced environment, the way is cleared for an even more adequate organization of this experience." See Robert Dubin in "Psyche, Sensitivity, and Social Structure," critical comment in Robert Tannenbaum, I. R. Weschler, and Fred Massarik, *Leadership and Organization: A Behavioral Science Approach* (New York: McGraw-Hill Book Co., 1961), p. 401.
2. *The Great Organizers* (New York: McGraw-Hill Book Co., 1960), pp. 11–28.
3. *Ibid.*, pp. 11, 26–28, 62–68.
4. R. Tannenbaum, I. R. Weschler, and F. Massarik, *Leadership and Organization* (New York: McGraw-Hill Book Co., 1961), p. 9.
5. *Organizations* (New York: John Wiley & Sons, Inc., 1958).
6. *The Functions of the Executive* (Cambridge: Harvard University Press, 1938).
7. "Comments on the Theory of Organizations," *American Political Science Review,* Vol. 46, No. 4 (December, 1952), p. 1130.
8. *Bonds of Organization* (New York: Harper & Brothers, 1950). These "bonds" or "devices" of organization are identified by Bakke as (1) the functional specifications system (a system of teamwork arising from job specifications and arrangements for association); (2) the status system (a vertical hierarchy of authority); (3) the communications system; (4) the reward and penalty system; and (5) the organization charter (ideas and means which give character and individuality to the organization, or enterprise).
9. J. G. March and H. A. Simon, *Organizations* (New York: John Wiley & Sons, Inc., 1958), pp. 29–33.
10. New York: Harper & Brothers, 1957.
11. *Ibid.*, p. 74.

12. *Ibid.*, pp. 58–66.

13. O. Helmer and N. Rescher, "On the Epistemology of the Inexact Sciences" (Santa Monica, California: The Rand Corporation, P-1513, 1958), pp. 4–5.

---

## Learning Review

**Questions:**

1. The six major schools of management theory include the _____ _____School, the _____ School, the _____ _____ School, the _____ _____ School, the _____ _____ School, and the _____ School.

2. The basic approach of the _____ _____ School, founded by Fayol, is to look first to the _____ of managers.

3. The approach of the _____ _____ School of management is based on the central thesis that since managing involves getting things done with and through _____, the study of management must be centered on _____relations.

4. Although the _____ problem is particularly severe when it comes to defining _____, the greatest single _____ confusion lies in the word _____.

5. One of the steps that should be taken to disentangle the management theory involves _____ the _____ of knowledge and at the same time distinguishing between _____ and _____.

**Answers:**

5. defining, body, tools, content.
ior, people, interpersonal 4. semantics, words, semantics, organization
Theory, Mathematical 2. Management Process, functions 3. Human Behav-
1. Management Process, Empirical, Human Behavior, Social System, Decision

---

# *Retrospective Comment*

## BY HAROLD KOONTZ

As it may be recalled, I wrote my article on "The Management Theory Jungle" [1] as a means of satisfying a need for finding the key to the differing analyses and recommendations made by various scholars in the field of management. I had expected differing opinions among academic researchers and teachers but, when these differences tended to confuse perceptive and intelligent practicing managers, I felt that there must be a reason.

I found that reason in the various approaches or "schools" specialists took in analyzing management. These differences were caused by (1) the different perceptions of specialists including even differences in defining management as a body of thought; (2) the semantics jungle of specialists; (3) the tendency of many newcomers to cast aside intelligent analyses of practitioners as being "a priori" or "armchair" in nature; (4) the misunderstanding of the nature of principles; and (5) the unwillingness or inability of specialists to understand each other.

Since writing this article, I have had hundreds of inquiries as to whether the "jungle" still exists. The fact is that it does still exist. It is perhaps more dense and impenetrable in 1978 than it was in 1961. I now find nearly twice the number of "schools" or approaches to management theory that I found in 1961. Yet, with all the confusion this implies, I see some hopeful signs for convergence of these varying theories.

## The Approaches in 1978

The approaches (and I now prefer to call them this rather than "schools") I now find are the following:

1. *The Empirical or Case Approach*—the same as in 1961 but with more emphasis in 1978 on distilling fundamentals from case experience.
2. *The Interpersonal Behavior Approach*—the study of management centered on interpersonal relations and heavily oriented to individual psychology.
3. *The Group Behavior Approach*—closely related to the interpersonal behavior approach but concerned primarily with behavior of people in groups. It varies all the way from the study of small groups to characteristics of large groups. It is often called "organization behavior."
4. *The Cooperative Social System Approach*—focuses on the study of management as one of human relationships in cooperative social systems. Its emphasis is on system.
5. *The Sociotechnical Systems Approach*—the study of management as a combination of social systems and technical systems (machines and methods), particularly with an emphasis on how the technical system influences the social system.
6. *The Decision Theory Approach*—as in 1961, this approach expresses the belief that, since managers make decisions, the study of management must be a study of decision making.
7. *The Systems Approach*—having seen scientists and practitioners utilize systems thinking and analyses in other fields, an increasing number of scholars and writers in management have attempted to exercise the systems approach to this field.
8. *The Mathematics or "Management Science" Approach*—essentially the same as the mathematical "school" identified in 1961. But it has become increas-

ingly apparent that the use of mathematical techniques represents a tool and is no more management than it is physics, biology, or geology.

9. *The Contingency, or Situational, Approach*—this approach has tended to take academicians by storm in recent years. Actually, it is not a new approach to management thinking. Essentially, this approach emphasizes the fact that what managers do in practice depends upon a given set of circumstances, or the "situation." All this is, of course, nothing more than a realization—long held by practitioners in all fields from mechanics to baseball—that practice demands the application of knowledge (science) to realities.

10. *The Management Roles Approach*—sparked by the research and writing of Professor Henry Mintzberg, this approach is to observe what managers actually do and study management as a number of roles (for example, interpersonal, informational, and decisional) which managers act in practice.

11. *The Operational Approach*—originally referred to in 1961 as The Management Process School, this approach, as it has developed from the idea

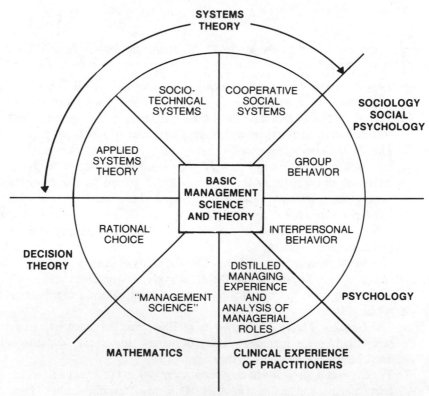

Operational management science and theory is that part of the diagram enclosed in the circle. It shows how operational management science and theory has a core of basic science and theory and draws from other fields of knowledge pertaining to management. It is thus, in part, an eclectic science and theory.

*Figure 1.*   The scope of operation science and theory

of management process, attempts to draw together the pertinent knowledge of management by classifying it according to the function of managers. Like other operational sciences, it endeavors to put together for the field of management the concepts, principles, theory, and techniques which underpin the actual practice of managing. The nature of the operational approach can perhaps best be appreciated by reference to Figure 1. As this diagram shows, the operational approach includes a central core of science and theory unique to managing plus knowledge eclectically drawn from various other schools and approaches. As the circle is intended to show, this approach is interested only in that knowledge in the various fields that is pertinent to management.

## Some Hopeful Tendencies Toward Convergence

While the management theory jungle does tend to flourish, there are some hopeful signs of convergence of the various approaches. They are:

1. *Greater Emphasis on Distillation of Basics Within the Empirical Approach—* a tendency in case teaching and research to go beyond what happened in the case to an analysis of the basic causes and reasons for what happened.
2. *Recognizing that Systems Theory is Not a Separate Approach to Management Any more than it is to Physics or Chemistry.*
3. *Recognizing that Situational and Contingency Approaches Are Not New or Separate Approaches to the Organization of Management Knowledge.* It has become increasingly clear that the concepts of situational or contingency management are merely a way of distinguishing between science and art— knowledge and practice—and not a new approach to management knowledge.
4. *Finding that Organization Theory is Too Broad an Approach.* While many scholars attempted to make this field equal to management theory, it is now fairly well agreed that managing is a narrower activity and that management theory is only that related to managing.
5. *The New Understanding of Motivation.* The more recent researches into motivation have tended to emphasize the importance of organizational climate and to fit the new operational school definition of the task of the manager as one of designing and maintaining an environment, or climate, for performance.
6. *The Melding of Motivation and Leadership Theory.* Recent research and analysis has tended to mold motivation and leadership theory and to recognize the importance of organizational climate in both motivation and leadership.
7. *The New Managerially Oriented Organization Development.* Many of the scientists and practitioners in the field of Organization Development or Organizational Behavior are now beginning to see that basic operational management theory and techniques will now fit their programs of behavioral intervention.
8. *Defection Among "Management Scientists."* There are clear signs among the so-called "management scientists" that there are defectors who realize

that their interests go far beyond the use of mathematics, models, and the computer. For example, one of the leading pioneers in management science, Professor C. West Churchman (in conversation with the author) has been highly critical of the excessive absorption with models and mathematics in operations research and has even resigned from the Operations Research Society.

\* \* \*

Despite some hopeful signs, the fact is that the "management theory jungle" is still with us. Although some slight progress appears to be occurring, in the interest of a far better society through improved managerial practice, it is hoped that some means can be found to accelerate this progress. Perhaps the most effective way is for intelligent, successful, perceptive practicing managers to press on our colleges and universities the compelling need for management theory and research to be based on the needs of real life practice.

## FOOTNOTE

1. Under that title in the *Journal of the Academy of Management* (now the *Academy of Management Journal*) Vol. 4, no. 3., pp. 174–188 (December 1961) and in another version under the title of "Making Sense of Management Theory" in the *Harvard Business Review,* vol. 40, no. 4, pp. 24 ff. (July-August 1962).

# 17

# *How to Choose a Leadership Pattern*

ROBERT TANNENBAUM                    WARREN H. SCHMIDT

## *About the Authors*

**Robert Tannenbaum** is Emeritus Professor of the Development of Human Systems, Graduate School of Management, University of California, Los Angeles and a consulting faculty member at Saybrook Institute in San Francisco. A University of Chicago Ph.D., he is well-known for his pioneering contributions to the areas of leadership, sensitivity training, and organization development. He has consulted widely with American firms and has served as director of an organization renewal project for Israeli kibbutzim. He has written numerous articles, and his most recent book is *Human Systems Development* (Jossey-Bass, 1985).

**Warren H. Schmidt** is Professor of Public Administration and Director of the Institute for Public-Private Partnership at the University of Southern California. He is also President of Chrysalis, Inc., a management training and consulting firm. Dr. Schmidt was a member of the faculty at UCLA from 1955 to 1977. Prior to that, he taught at the University of Washington, Missouri, Springfield College, and Union College. His most recent book is *Organization Frontiers and Human Values* (Wadsworth, 1970). He is an active consultant and has screen credits for more than 50 management and education films, one of which was the recipient of an Academy Award in 1971.

# PREVIEW

A. In recent years there has been an increasing problem of how the manager can be democratic in relations with subordinates and at the same time maintain authority and control in the organization for which he or she is responsible.

B. The concept of "group dynamics" emerged from the social sciences and focused on the group rather than a single leader.

   1. Training laboratories that sprang up across the country gave people a first-hand experience in full participation and decision making.

   2. Group members were responsible for setting their own goals and methods.

   3. This contrast in leadership behavior was categorized as "democratic" vs. "authoritarian".

C. The modern manager is at times confused between exerting "strong" leadership and "permissive" leadership.

D. The continuum or range of a manager's behavior varies from one where a high degree of control is exercised, to one where a high degree of control is released. The points of behavior occurring along this continuum are:

   1. The manager makes the decision and announces it.

   2. The manager "sells" his or her decision.

   3. The manager presents his or her ideas, and invites questions.

   4. The manager presents a tentative decision subject to change.

   5. The manager presents the problem, gets suggestions, and then makes his or her decision.

   6. The manager defines the limits and requests the group to make a decision.

   7. The manager permits the group to make decisions within the prescribed limits.

E. The authors' answers to the type of questions that may arise when business leadership is viewed in this manner are:

   1. Q. Can a boss's responsibility be relinquished by delegation to someone else?

      A. The manager must expect to be held responsible by his or her superior for the quality of decisions made by the group.

   2. Q. Should the manager participate with subordinates after delegating responsibility to them?

      A. Because the manager can contribute useful ideas, he or she should function as an additional group member rather than an authoritative person.

   3. Q. What is the importance of the manager's leadership behavior to the group?

      A. It is very important for the manager to be honest and clear in describing his or her authority as well as the role of subordinates to avoid occurrence of any confusion and resentment later on.

   4. Q. Is it possible to judge how "democratic" a manager is by the number of decisions his or her subordinates make?

    A. It is the significance of the decisions which the boss entrusts subordinates with, rather than the sheer number of decisions, that indicate the amount of freedom that a subordinate group enjoys.

F. The factors or forces that a manager should consider in deciding how to manage should be both practical and desirable.

    I. Forces in the Manager—those that operate within the manager's own personality.

        1. Value system—the importance he or she attaches to organizational efficiency, personal growth of subordinates and company profits.

        2. Confidence in subordinates—who is best qualified to deal with a particular problem?

        3. Leadership inclinations—to function independently or in a team role.

        4. Feelings of security in an uncertain situation—tolerance of ambiguity in dealing with problems.

    II. Forces in the Subordinate—those that affect subordinates' behavior.

        1. Their needs for independence.

        2. Their readiness to assume responsibility.

        3. Their tolerance for ambiguity.

        4. Their interest in the problem and its importance.

        5. Their knowledge and experience in dealing with the problem.

        6. Their learning to expect to share in decision making.

    III. Forces in the Situation—the more critical environmental pressures that surround the manager are those which stem from:

        1. Type of organization—what are its values and traditions, the numerous ways of communicating these values and traditions, and the amount of employee participation?

        2. Group effectiveness—how effectively and with what degree of confidence will a group of members work together as a unit?

        3. The problem itself—after hearing everyone's contribution towards solving the problem, deciding upon the person/s best equipped in terms of knowledge and experience.

        4. The pressure of time—the most obvious pressure on the manager when immediate decisions need to be made especially in organizations that are in a constant state of "crisis" and "crash programming".

G. In conclusion, the successful manager can be primarily characterized neither as a strong leader nor as a permissive one. Rather he or she is one who can determine what the most appropriate behavior at any given time should be and actually behave accordingly.

"I put most problems into my group's hands and leave it to them to carry the ball from there. I serve merely as a catalyst, mirroring back the people's thoughts and feelings so that they can better understand them."

"It's foolish to make decisions oneself on matters that affect people. I always talk things over with my subordinates, but I make it clear to them that I'm the one who has to have the final say."

"Once I have decided on a course of action, I do my best to sell my ideas to my employees."

"I'm being paid to lead. If I let a lot of other people make the decisions I should be making, then I'm not worth my salt."

"I believe in getting things done. I can't waste time calling meetings. Someone has to call the shots around here, and I think it should be me."

Each of these statements represents a point of view about "good leadership." Considerable experience, factual data, and theoretical principles could be cited to support each statement; even though they seem to be inconsistent when placed together. Such contradictions point up the dilemma in which the modern manager frequently finds himself.

## New Problem

The problem of how the modern manager can be "democratic" in his relations with subordinates and at the same time maintain the necessary authority and control in the organization for which he is responsible has come into focus increasingly in recent years.

Earlier in the century this problem was not so acutely felt. The successful executive was generally pictured as possessing intelligence, imagination, initiative, the capacity to make rapid (and generally wise) decisions, and the ability to inspire subordinates. People tended to think of the world as being divided into "leaders" and "followers."

*New focus:* Gradually, however, from the social sciences emerged the concept of "group dynamics" with its focus on *members* of the group rather than solely on the leader. Research efforts of social scientists underscored the importance of employee involvement and participation in decision making. Evidence began to challenge the efficiency of highly directive leadership, and increasing attention was paid to problems of motivation and human relations.

Through training laboratories in group development that sprang up across the country, many of the newer notions of leadership began to exert an impact. These training laboratories were carefully designed to give people a firsthand experience in full participation and decision making. The designated "leaders" deliberately attempted to reduce their own power and to make group members as responsible as possible for setting their own goals and methods within the laboratory experience.

It was perhaps inevitable that some of the people who attended the training laboratories regarded this kind of leadership as being truly "democratic" and went home with the determination to build fully participative decision making into their own organizations. Whenever their bosses made a decision without convening a staff meeting, they tended to perceive this as authoritarian behavior. The true symbol of democratic leadership to some was the meeting—and the less directed from the top, the more democratic it was.

Some of the more enthusiastic alumni of these training laboratories began to get the habit of categorizing leader behavior as "democratic" *or* "authoritarian." The boss who made too many decisions himself was thought of as an authoritarian, and his directive behavior was often attributed solely to his personality.

*New need:* The net result of the research findings and of the human relations training based upon them has been to call into question the stereotype of an effective leader. Consequently, the modern manager often finds himself in an uncomfortable state of mind.

Often he is not quite sure how to behave; there are times when he is torn between exerting "strong" leadership and "permissive" leadership. Sometimes new knowledge pushes him in one direction ("I should really get the group to help make this decision"), but at the same time his experience pushes him in another direction ("I really understand the problem better than the group and therefore I should make the decision"). He is not sure when a group decision is really appropriate or when holding a staff meeting serves merely as a device for avoiding his own decision-making responsibility.

The purpose of our article is to suggest a framework which managers may find useful in grappling with this dilemma. First, we shall look at the different patterns of leadership behavior that the manager can choose from in relating himself to his subordinates. Then, we shall turn to some of the questions suggested by this range of patterns. For instance, how important is it for a manager's subordinates to know what type of leadership he is using in a situation? What factors should he consider in deciding on a leadership pattern? What difference do his long-run objectives make as compared to his immediate objectives?

## Range of Behavior

*Exhibit I* presents the continuum or range of possible leadership behavior available to a manager. Each type of action is related to the degree of authority used by the boss and to the amount of freedom available to his subordinates in reaching decisions. The actions seen on the extreme left characterize the manager who maintains a high degree of control while those seen on the extreme right characterize the manager who releases a high degree of control. Neither extreme is absolute; authority and freedom are never without their limitations.

Now let us look more closely at each of the behavior points occurring along this continuum.

### The Manager Makes the Decision
### and Announces It
In this case the boss identifies a problem, considers alternative solutions, chooses one of them, and then reports this decision to his subordinates for implementation.

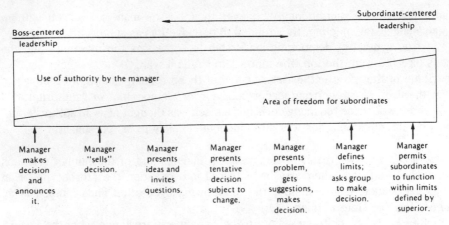

*Exhibit I.* Continuum of leadership behavior

He may or may not give consideration to what he believes his subordinates will think or feel about his decision; in any case, he provides no opportunity for them to participate directly in the decision-making process. Coercion may or may not be used or implied.

### The Manager "Sells" His Decision

Here the manager, as before, takes responsibility for identifying the problem and arriving at a decision. However, rather than simply announcing it, he takes the additional step of persuading his subordinates to accept it. In doing so, he recognizes the possibility of some resistance among those who will be faced with the decision, and seeks to reduce this resistance by indicating, for example, what the employees have to gain from his decision.

### The Manager Presents His Ideas, Invites Questions

Here the boss who has arrived at a decision and who seeks acceptance of his ideas provides an opportunity for his subordinates to get a fuller explanation of his thinking and his intentions. After presenting the ideas, he invites questions so that his associates can better understand what he is trying to accomplish. This "give and take" also enables the manager and the subordinates to explore more fully the implications of the decision.

### The Manager Presents a Tentative Decision Subject to Change

This kind of behavior permits the subordinates to exert some influence on the decision. The initiative for identifying and diagnosing the problem remains with the boss. Before meeting with his staff, he has thought the problem through and arrived at a decision—but only a tentative one. Before finalizing it, he presents his proposed solution for the reaction of those who will be affected by it. He says in effect, "I'd like to hear what you have to say about this plan that I have developed. I'll appreciate your frank reactions, but will reserve for myself the final decision."

### The Manager Presents the Problem,
### Gets Suggestions, and Then Makes His Decision

Up to this point the boss has come before the group with a solution of his own. Not so in this case. The subordinates now get the first chance to suggest solutions. The manager's initial role involves identifying the problem. He might, for example, say something of this sort: "We are faced with a number of complaints from newspapers and the general public on our service policy. What is wrong here? What ideas do you have for coming to grips with this problem?"

The function of the group becomes one of increasing the manager's repertory of possible solutions to the problem. The purpose is to capitalize on the knowledge and experience of those who are on the "firing line." From the expanded list of alternatives developed by the manager and his subordinates, the manager then selects the solution that he regards as most promising.[1]

### The Manager Defines the Limits and
### Requests The Group to Make a Decision

At this point the manager passes to the group (possibly including himself as a member) the right to make decisions. Before doing so, however, he defines the problem to be solved and the boundaries within which the decision must be made.

An example might be the handling of a parking problem at a plant. The boss decides that this is something that should be worked on by the people involved, so he calls them together and points up the existence of the problem. Then he tells them:

"There is the open field just north of the main plant which has been designated for additional employee parking. We can build underground or surface multilevel facilities as long as the cost does not exceed $100,000. Within these limits we are free to work out whatever solution makes sense to us. After we decide on a specific plan, the company will spend the available money in whatever way we indicate."

### The Manager Permits the Group to Make Decisions
### within Prescribed Limits

This represents an extreme degree of group freedom only occasionally encountered in formal organizations, as, for instance, in many research groups. Here the team of managers or engineers undertakes the identification and diagnosis of the problem, develops alternative procedures for solving it, and decides on one or more of these alternative solutions. The only limits directly imposed on the group by the organization are those specified by the superior of the team's boss. If the boss participates in the decision-making process, he attempts to do so with no more authority than any other member of the group. He commits himself in advance to assist in implementing whatever decision the group makes.

# Key Questions

As the continuum in *Exhibit I* demonstrates, there are a number of alternative ways in which a manager can relate himself to the group or individuals he is supervising. At the extreme left of the range, the emphasis is on the manager— on what *he* is interested in, how *he* sees things, how *he* feels about them. As we move toward the subordinate-centered end of the continuum, however, the focus is increasingly on the subordinates—on what *they* are interested in, how *they* look at things, how *they* feel about them.

When business leadership is regarded in this way, a number of questions arise. Let us take four of especial importance:

## Can a Boss Ever Relinquish His Responsibility by Delegating it to Someone Else?

Our view is that the manager must expect to be held responsible by his superior for the quality of the decisions made, even though operationally these decisions may have been made on a group basis. He should, therefore, be ready to accept whatever risk is involved whenever he delegates decision-making power to his subordinates. Delegation is not a way of "passing the buck." Also, it should be emphasized that the amount of freedom the boss gives to his subordinates cannot be greater than the freedom which he himself has been given by his own superior.

## Should the Manager Participate with His Subordinates Once He Has Delegated Responsibility to Them?

The manager should carefully think over this question and decide on his role prior to involving the subordinate group. He should ask if his presence will inhibit or facilitate the problem-solving process. There may be some instances when he should leave the group to let it solve the problem for itself. Typically, however, the boss has useful ideas to contribute, and should function as an additional member of the group. In the latter instance, it is important that he indicate clearly to the group that he sees himself in a *member* role rather than in an authority role.

## How Important Is It for the Group to Recognize What Kind of Leadership Behavior the Boss Is Using?

It makes a great deal of difference. Many relationship problems between boss and subordinate occur because the boss fails to make clear how he plans to use his authority. If, for example, he actually intends to make a certain decision himself, but the subordinate group gets the impression that he has delegated this authority, considerable confusion and resentment are likely to follow. Problems may also occur when the boss uses a "democratic" façade to conceal the fact that he has already made a decision which he hopes the group will accept as its own. The attempt to "make them think it was their idea in the first place" is a risky one. We believe that it is highly important for the manager to be honest and clear in describing what authority he is keeping and what role he is asking his subordinates to assume in solving a particular problem.

## Can You Tell How "Democratic" a Manager Is By the Number of Decisions His Subordinates Make?

The sheer *number* of decisions is not an accurate index of the amount of freedom that a subordinate group enjoys. More important is the *significance* of the decisions which the boss entrusts to his subordinates. Obviously a decision on how to arrange desks is of an entirely different order from a decision involving the introduction of new electronic data-processing equipment. Even though the widest possible limits are given in dealing with the first issue, the group will sense no particular degree of responsibility. For a boss to permit the group to decide equipment policy, even within rather narrow limits, would reflect a greater degree of confidence in them on his part.

## Deciding How to Lead

Now let us turn from the types of leadership which are possible in a company situation to the question of what types are *practical* and *desirable*. What factors or forces should a manager consider in deciding how to manage? Three are of particular importance:

Forces in the manager.

Forces in the subordinates.

Forces in the situation.

We should like briefly to describe these elements and indicate how they might influence a manager's action in a decision-making situation.[2] The strength of each of them will, of course, vary from instance to instance, but the manager who is sensitive to them can better assess the problems which face him and determine which mode of leadership behavior is most appropriate for him.

**Forces in the Manager:** The manager's behavior in any given instance will be influenced greatly by the many forces operating within his own personality. He will, of course, perceive his leadership problems in a unique way on the basis of his background, knowledge, and experience. Among the important internal forces affecting him will be the following:

1. *His value system.* How strongly does he feel that individuals should have a share in making the decisions which affect them? Or, how convinced is he that the official who is paid to assume responsibility should personally carry the burden of decision making? The strength of his convictions on questions like these will tend to move the manager to one end or the other of the continuum shown in *Exhibit I*. His behavior will also be influenced by the relative importance that he attaches to organizational efficiency, personal growth of subordinates, and company profits.[3]

2. *His confidence in his subordinates.* Managers differ greatly in the amount of trust they have in other people generally, and this carries over to the particular employees they supervise at a given time. In viewing his particular group of subordinates, the manager is likely to consider their knowledge and competence with respect to the problem. A central question he might ask himself is: "Who

is best qualified to deal with this problem?" Often he may, justifiably or not, have more confidence in his own capabilities than in those of his subordinates.

3. *His own leadership inclinations.* There are some managers who seem to function more comfortably and naturally as highly directive leaders. Resolving problems and issuing orders come easily to them. Other managers seem to operate more comfortably in a team role, where they are continually sharing many of their functions with their subordinates.

4. *His feelings of security in an uncertain situation.* The manager who releases control over the decision-making process thereby reduces the predictability of the outcome. Some managers have a greater need than others for predictability and stability in their environment. This "tolerance for ambiguity" is being viewed increasingly by psychologists as a key variable in a person's manner of dealing with problems.

The manager brings these and other highly personal variables to each situation he faces. If he can see them as forces which consciously or unconsciously, influence his behavior, he can better understand what makes him prefer to act in a given way. And understanding this, he can often make himself more effective.

**Forces in the Subordinate:** Before deciding how to lead a certain group, the manager will also want to consider a number of forces affecting his subordinates' behavior. He will want to remember that each employee, like himself, is influenced by many personality variables. In addition, each subordinate has a set of expectations about how the boss should act in relation to him (the phrase "expected behavior" is one we hear more and more often these days at discussions of leadership and teaching). The better the manager understands these factors, the more accurately he can determine what kind of behavior on his part will enable his subordinates to act most effectively.

Generally speaking, the manager can permit his subordinates greater freedom if the following essential conditions exist:

If the subordinates have relatively high needs for independence. (As we all know, people differ greatly in the amount of direction that they desire.)

If the subordinates have a readiness to assume responsibility for decision making. (Some see additional responsibility as a tribute to their ability; others see it as "passing the buck.")

If they have a relatively high tolerance for ambiguity. (Some employees prefer to have clear-cut directive given to them; other prefer a wider area of freedom.)

If they are interested in the problem and feel that it is important.

If they understand and identify with the goals of the organization.

If they have the necessary knowledge and experience to deal with the problem.

If they have learned to expect to share in decision making. (Persons who have come to expect strong leadership and are then suddenly confronted with the request to share more fully in decision making are often upset by this new experience. On the other hand, persons who have enjoyed a considerable amount of freedom resent the boss who begins to make all the decisions himself.)

The manager will probably tend to make fuller use of his own authority if the above conditions do *not* exist; at times there may be no realistic alternative to running a "one-man show."

The restrictive effect of many of the forces will, of course, be greatly modified by the general feeling of confidence which subordinates have in the boss. Where they have learned to respect and trust him, he is free to vary his behavior. He will feel certain that he will not be perceived as an authoritarian boss on those occasions when he makes decisions by himself. Similarly, he will not be seen as using staff meetings to avoid his decision-making responsibility. In a climate of mutual confidence and respect, people tend to feel less threatened by deviations from normal practice, which in turn makes possible a higher degree of flexibility in the whole relationship.

**Forces in the Situation:** In addition to the forces which exist in the manager himself and in his subordinates, certain characteristics of the general situation will also affect the manager's behavior. Among the more critical environmental pressures that surround him are those which stem from the organization, the work group, the nature of the problem, and the pressures of time. Let us look briefly at each of these:

*Type of organization*—Like individuals, organizations have values and traditions which inevitably influence the behavior of the people who work in them. The manager who is a newcomer to a company quickly discovers that certain kinds of behavior are approved while others are not. He also discovers that to deviate radically from what is generally accepted is likely to create problems for him.

These values and traditions are communicated in numerous ways—through job descriptions, policy pronouncements, and public statements by top executives. Some organizations, for example, hold to the notion that the desirable executive is one who is dynamic, imaginative, decisive, and persuasive. Other organizations put more emphasis upon the importance of the executive's ability to work effectively with people—his human relations skills. The fact that his superiors have a defined concept of what the good executive should be will very likely push the manager toward one end or the other of the behavioral range.

In addition to the above, the amount of employee participation is influenced by such variables as the size of the working units, their geographical distribution, and the degree of inter- and intra-organizational security required to attain company goals. For example, the wide geographical dispersion of an organization may preclude a practical system of participative decision making, even though this would otherwise be desirable. Similarly, the size of the working units or the need for keeping plans confidential may make it necessary for the boss to exercise more control than would otherwise be the case. Factors like these may limit considerably the manager's ability to function flexibly on the continuum.

*Group effectiveness*—Before turning decision-making responsibility over to a subordinate group, the boss should consider how effectively its members work together as a unit.

One of the relevant factors here is the experience the group has had in working together. It can generally be expected that a group which has functioned for some time will have developed habits of cooperation and thus be able to tackle a problem more effectively than a new group. It can also be expected that a group of people with similar backgrounds and interests will work more quickly and easily than people with dissimilar backgrounds, because the communication problems are likely to be less complex.

The degree of confidence that the members have in their ability to solve problems as a group is also a key consideration. Finally, such group variables as cohesiveness, permissiveness, mutual acceptance, and commonality of purpose will exert subtle but powerful influence on the group's functioning.

*The problem itself*—The nature of the problem may determine what degree of authority should be delegated by the manager to his subordinates. Obviously he will ask himself whether they have the kind of knowledge which is needed. It is possible to do them a real disservice by assigning a problem that their experience does not equip them to handle.

Since the problems faced in large or growing industries increasingly require knowledge of specialists from many different fields, it might be inferred that the more complex a problem, the more anxious a manager will be to get some assistance in solving it. However, this is not always the case. There will be times when the very complexity of the problem calls for one person to work it out. For example, if the manager has most of the background and factual data relevant to a given issue, it may be easier for him to think it through himself than to take the time to fill in his staff on all the pertinent background information.

The key question to ask, of course, is: "Have I heard the ideas of everyone who has the necessary knowledge to make a significant contribution to the solution of this problem?"

*The pressure of time*—This is perhaps the most clearly felt pressure on the manager (in spite of the fact that it may sometimes be imagined). The more that he feels the need for an immediate decision, the more difficult is it to involve other people. In organizations which are in a constant state of "crisis" and "crash programming" one is likely to find managers personally using a high degree of authority with relatively little delegation to subordinates. When the time pressure is less intense, however, it becomes much more possible to bring subordinates in on the decision-making process.

These, then, are the principal forces that impinge on the manager in any given instance and that tend to determine his tactical behavior in relation to his subordinates. In each case his behavior ideally will be that which makes possible the most effective attainment of his immediate goal within the limits facing him.

## Long-Run Strategy

As the manager works with his organization on the problems that come up day by day, his choice of a leadership pattern is usually limited. He must take account of the forces just described and, within the restrictions they impose on him, do the best that he can. But as he looks ahead months or even years, he can shift his thinking from tactics to large-scale strategy. No longer need he be fettered by all of the forces mentioned, for he can view many of them as variables over which he has some control. He can, for example, gain new insights or skills for himself, supply training for individual subordinates, and provide participative experiences for his employee group.

In trying to bring about a change in these variables, however, he is faced with a challenging question: At which point along the continuum *should* he act?

**Attaining Objectives:**   The answer depends largely on what he wants to accomplish. Let us suppose that he is interested in the same objectives that most modern managers seek to attain when they can shift their attention from the pressure of immediate assignments:

1. To raise the level of employee motivation.
2. To increase the readiness of subordinates to accept change.
3. To improve the quality of all managerial decisions.
4. To develop teamwork and morale.
5. To further the individual development of employees.

In recent years the manager has been deluged with a flow of advice on how best to achieve these longer-run objectives. It is little wonder that he is often both bewildered and annoyed. However, there are some guidelines which he can usefully follow in making a decision.

Most research and much of the experience of recent years give a strong factual basis to the theory that a fairly high degree of subordinate-centered behavior is associated with the accomplishment of the five purposes mentioned.[4] This does not mean that a manager should always leave all decisions to his assistants. To provide the individual or the group with greater freedom than they are ready for at any given time may very well tend to generate anxieties and therefore inhibit rather than facilitate the attainment of desired objectives. But this should not keep the manager from making a continuing effort to confront his subordinates with the challenge of freedom.

## Conclusion

In summary, there are two implications in the basic thesis that we have been developing. The first is that the successful leader is one who is keenly aware of those forces which are most relevant to his behavior at any given time. He accurately understands himself, the individuals and group he is dealing with, and the company and broader social environment in which he operates. And certainly he is able to assess the present readiness for growth of his subordinates.

But this sensitivity or understanding is not enough, which brings us to the second implication. The successful leader is one who is able to behave appropriately in the light of these perceptions. If direction is in order, he is able to direct; if considerable participative freedom is called for, he is able to provide such freedom.

Thus, the successful manager of men can be primarily characterized neither as a strong leader nor as a permissive one. Rather, he is one who maintains a high batting average in accurately assessing the forces that determine what his most appropriate behavior at any given time should be and in actually being able to behave accordingly. Being both insightful and flexible, he is less likely to see the problems of leadership as a dilemma.

## FOOTNOTES

1. For a fuller explanation of this approach, see Leo Moore, "Too Much Management, Too Little Change," *Harvard Business Review,* January-February 1956, p. 41.

2. See also Robert Tannenbaum and Fred Massarik, "Participation by Subordinates in the Managerial Decision-Making Process," *Canadian Journal of Economics and Political Science,* August 1950, p. 413.

3. See Chris Argyris, "Top Management Dilemma: Company Needs vs. Individual Development," *Personnel,* September, 1955, pp. 123–134.

4. For example, see Warren H. Schmidt and Paul C. Buchanan, *Techniques that Produce Teamwork* (New London: Arthur C. Croft Publications, 1954); and Morris S. Viteles, *Motivation and Morale in Industry* (New York: W. W. Norton and Co., Inc., 1953).

---

## *Learning Review*

### *Questions:*

1. Today there is an increasing problem of how the modern manager can be _____ in relations with subordinates and at the same time be responsible for exercising _____ and _____ in the organization.

2. The continuum or range of leadership behavior varies from _____ a high degree of control on the one extreme, to _____ a high degree of control on the other extreme.

3. The three important forces or factors that a manager should consider in deciding how to manage are forces in the _____, the _____, and the _____.

4. Certain characteristics of the general situation which affect the manager's behavior stem from the _____, the work _____, the nature of the _____, and the _____ of _____.

### *Answers:*

1. democratic, authority, control  2. maintaining, releasing  3. manager, subordinates, situation  4. organization, group, problem, pressure, time

## Retrospective Comment

BY ROBERT TANNENBAUM AND WARREN H. SCHMIDT

Since this HBR classic was first published in 1958, there have been many changes in organizations and in the world that have affected leadership patterns. While the article's continued popularity attests to its essential validity, we believe it can be reconsidered and updated to reflect subsequent societal changes and new management concepts.

The reasons for the article's continued relevance can be summarized briefly:

The article contains insights and perspectives which mesh well with, and help clarify, the experiences of managers, other leaders, and students of leadership. Thus it is useful to individuals in a wide variety of organizations—industrial, governmental, educational, religious, and community.

The concept of leadership the article defines is reflected in a continuum of leadership behavior (see *Exhibit I* in original article). Rather than offering a choice between two styles of leadership, democratic or authoritarian, it sanctions a range of behavior.

The concept does not dictate to managers but helps them to analyze their own behavior. The continuum permits them to review their behavior within a context of other alternatives, without any style being labeled right or wrong.

(We have sometimes wondered if we have, perhaps, made it too easy for anyone to justify his or her style of leadership. It may be a small step between being nonjudgmental and giving the impression that all behavior is equally valid and useful. The latter was not our intention. Indeed, the thrust of our endorsement was for the manager who is insightful in assessing relevant forces within himself, others, and the situation, and who can be flexible in responding to these forces.)

In recognizing that our article can be updated, we are acknowledging that organizations do not exist in a vacuum but are affected by changes that occur in society. Consider, for example, the implications for organizations of these recent social developments:

The youth revolution that expresses distrust and even contempt for organizations identified with the establishment.

The civil rights movement that demands all minority groups be given a greater opportunity for participation and influence in the organizational processes.

The ecology and consumer movements that challenge the right of managers to make decisions without considering the interest of people outside the organization.

The increasing national concern with the quality of working life and its relationship to worker productivity, participation, and satisfaction.

These and other societal changes make effective leadership in this decade a more challenging task, requiring even greater sensitivity and flexibility than was needed in the 1950's. Today's manager is more likely to deal with employees who resent being treated as subordinates, who may be highly critical of any organizational system, who expect to be consulted and to exert influence, and who often stand on the edge of alienation from the institution that needs their loyalty and commitment. In addition, he is frequently confronted by a highly turbulent, unpredictable environment.

In response to these social pressures, new concepts of management have emerged in organizations. Open-system theory, with its emphasis on subsystems' interdependency *and* on the interaction of an organization with its environment, has made a powerful impact on managers' approach to problems. Organization development has emerged as a new behavioral science approach to the improvement of individual, group, organizational, and interorganizational performance. New research has added to our understanding of motivation in the work situation. More and more executives have become concerned with social responsibility and have explored the feasibility of social audits. And a growing number of organizations, in Europe and in the United States, have conducted experiments in industrial democracy.

In light of these developments, we submit the following thoughts on how we would rewrite certain points in our original article.

The article described forces in the manager, subordinates, and the situation as givens, with the leadership pattern a resultant of these forces. We would now give more attention to the *interdependency* of these forces. For example, such interdependency occurs in: (a) the interplay between the manager's confidence in his subordinates, their readiness to assume responsibility, and the level of group effectiveness; and (b) the impact of the behavior of the manager on that of his subordinates, and vice versa.

In discussing the forces in the situation, we primarily identified organizational phenomena. We would now include forces lying outside the organization, and would explore the relevant interdependencies between the organization and its environment.

In the original article, we presented the size of the rectangle in *Exhibit I* as a given, with its boundaries already determined by external forces—in effect, a closed system. We would now recognize the possibility of the manager and/or his subordinates taking the initiative to change those boundaries through interaction with relevant external forces—both within their own organization and in the larger society.

The article portrayed the manager as the principal and almost unilateral actor. He initiated and determined group functions, assumed responsibility, and exercised control. Subordinates made inputs and assumed power only at the will of the manager. Although the manager might have taken into account forces outside himself, it was *he* who decided where to operate on the continuum—that is, whether to announce a decision instead of trying to sell his idea to his subordinates, whether to invite questions, to let subordinates decide an issue, and so on. While the manager has retained this clear prerogative in many organizations, it has been challenged in others. Even in situations where he has retained it, however, the balance in the relationship between manager and subordinates at any given time is arrived at by interaction—direct or indirect—between the two parties.

Although power and its use by the manager played a role in our article, we now realize that our concern with cooperation and collaboration, common goals, commitment, trust, and mutual caring limited our vision with respect to the realities of power. We did not attempt to deal with unions, other forms of joint worker action, or with individual workers' expressions of resistance. Today, we would recognize much more clearly the power available to *all* parties, and the factors that underlie the interrelated decisions on whether to use it.

In the original article, we used the terms "manager" and "subordinate." We are now uncomfortable with "subordinate" because of its demeaning, dependency-laden connotations and prefer "nonmanager." The titles "manager" and "nonmanager" make the terminological difference functional rather than hierarchical.

We assumed fairly traditional organizational structures in our original article. Now we would alter our formulation to reflect newer organizational modes which are slowly emerging, such as industrial democracy, intentional communities, and "phenomenarchy." [1] These new modes are based on observations such as the following:

Both manager and nonmanagers may be governing forces in their group's environment, contributing to the definition of the total area of freedom.

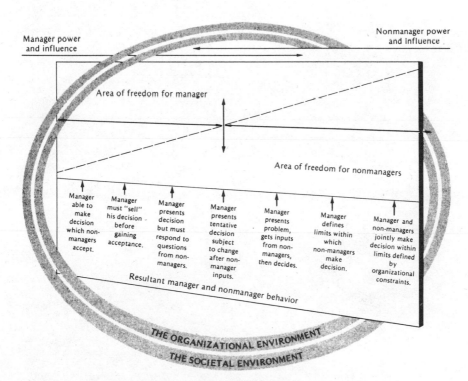

*Exhibit II.*   Continuum of manager-nonmanager behavior

A group can function without a manager, with managerial functions being shared by group members.

A group, as a unit, can be delegated authority and can assume responsibility within a larger organizational context.

Our thoughts on the question of leadership have prompted us to design a new behavior continuum (see *Exhibit II*) in which the total area of freedom shared by manager and nonmanagers is constantly redefined by interactions between them and the forces in the environment.

The arrows in the exhibit indicate the continual flow of interdependent influence among systems and people. The points on the continuum designate the types of manager and nonmanager behavior that become possible with any given amount of freedom available to each. The new continuum is both more complex and more dynamic than the 1958 version, reflecting the organizational and societal realities of 1973.

## FOOTNOTE

1. For a description of phenomenarchy, see Will McWhinney, "Phenomenarchy: A Suggestion for Social Redesign," *Journal of Applied Behavioral Science,* May 1973.

# Part 4
# MAJOR CURRENT CONTRIBUTIONS

♦

In this last section, we will sample some of the major threads of research and theory being pursued today. The authors represented here, in our judgment, are likely to continue to be major influences in the organizational sciences for years to come.

It is difficult to categorize the topics represented in this section, largely because many of the articles are relevant to more than one issue. For example, Hackman, Oldham, Janson and Purdy's "A New Strategy for Job Enrichment" is just that— but also, in applying ideas from expectancy theory (see Lawler and Porter) and Maslow's theory, it is clearly an article on applied *motivation* theory as well. Moreover, job design is a component of the *structure* of the organization. Finally, there are many implications for the behavior of *leaders* in the piece, so one might legitimately consider it a contribution to our knowledge of leadership.

Perhaps Hackman, *et al.* represent an emerging trend among major current contributors in their ability to integrate ideas and findings from past years into creative applications of great practical potential.

Henry Mintzberg's description of what managers do, the lead-off article in this section, has generated many insights for researchers in the field. Before Mintzberg, the dominant research approaches were the *functional* approach of classical management theory (Fayol and Koontz are the primary examples in this volume) and research into the *activities* of managers (where the primary finding has been that managers spend 60 to 80 percent of their time interacting and communicating with other people).

Mintzberg's contribution, breaking the managerial job into *roles* the manager plays (sometimes more than one simultaneously), helps us to think about the manager's job and the problems she or he faces more precisely than before. Mintzberg's observations about the manager's preferences for certain types of information and certain forms of interaction are another valuable insight into managerial behavior. For years, management theorists have entreated managers to be more systematic and strategic planners—to take time to think before acting. If Mintzberg's conclusions are correct, management seems to attract a kind of person who may find such a contemplative role very uncomfortable.

Several of the articles in this section represent *contingency theory* perspectives on leadership—extending the views of Tannenbaum and Schmidt included in the previous section. Fred Fiedler describes task and organizational variables his research identifies as determinants of the leadership style which is likely to be most productive in a given situation. House and Mitchell draw upon an expectancy theory perspective to prescribe the critical factors as they see them. Finally, Vroom provides a decision tree framework to help managers select between unilateral or participative strategies in arriving at decisions. All three articles agree on one point: There is no one right way to be an effective leader. Leadership effectiveness requires different behaviors in different situations.

Four modern themes in motivation are represented in this section. Lawler and Porter demonstrate an important insight from *expectancy theory*—namely that job satisfaction may be the result of, not the cause of, job performance. Latham and Locke describe the research indicating that *goal-setting* is a powerful stimulant to higher productivity. Steve Kerr's humorous but insightful description of how organizational reward systems often encourage the very behavior that they seek to avoid is an example of the application of *reinforcement theory* to organizational phenomena. All three of these perspectives may be classed as *process theories* of motivation—they say relatively little about what needs motivate people. They concentrate on *how* motivation works; what the process is that causes behavior to be energized and directed.

David McClelland's work on achievement motivation (and subsequent research on other needs, particularly power), contrasts with the process approaches in that it represents a contemporary *content theory* of motivation. Since motivation is such an essential topic for the manager (whose primary responsibility is to get others to be productive), the effective manager must be aware of both the content and process aspects of motivation. In the vernacular, the manager must understand both "what turns people on" and how it works (or doesn't work).

The final (and most recent) article in this section is Ed Schein's discussion of *organizational culture*. Theorists and practicing managers alike have long recognized that there is more to an organization than its structure, its policies and plans, its personnel, its tasks, and its resources. Mix all of these elements together and the result is greater than and different from the simple sum of its components. A synergistic entity emerges which is unique to each organization, and which becomes a powerful determinant of how members of the organization behave and, hence, of how effective the organization will be. Schein discusses this emergent entity of culture in terms of the basic assumptions that members of the organization come to share and apply to solving the problems the organization faces. Culture is affected by, but is not entirely a reflection of the needs of the members of the organization. Culture is what the leader must change in order to make the organization more adaptive or productive. Culture includes, but again is not limited to, the structure, the tasks, the technology, the policies, the rules, the rituals and ceremonies, and the typical ways that an organization responds to a particular situation. Culture would seem to be a truly global and encompassing perspective on organizations—one that brings together and integrates many of the variables discussed by the contributors to this volume. For that reason, perhaps it is a most appropriate final selection for *The Great Writings in Management and Organizational Behavior.*

# 18

# *Managerial Work: Analysis From Observation*

## HENRY MINTZBERG

### *About the Author*

**Henry Mintzberg** is Bronfman Professor of Management at McGill University in Montreal, where he also earned his Bachelors degree in Engineering. His Masters and Ph.D. are from Massachusetts Institute of Technology. Author of four books and numerous articles in professional journals, Professor Mintzberg has lectured widely on management in North and South America and Europe. He has served as a visiting professor at Universite d'Aix-Marseille, Carnegie Mellon University, and Ecole des Hautes Etudes Commercial de Montreal. He is a fellow of the Royal Society of Canada and is President-elect of the Strategic Management Society.

His current research focuses on patterns of strategy formation and the theory of management policy formation.

Reprinted by permission of Henry Mintzberg and *Management Science*. Henry Mintzberg, "Managerial Work: Analysis From Observation," *Management Science*, Vol. 18, No. 2, October 1971, pp. B97–110. Copyright © 1971, The Institute of Management Sciences.

# PREVIEW

A. The traditional concept of managerial work is that it consists of planning, organizing, coordination, and controlling. Empirical studies of managerial activities reveal that managers do not actually fit this model.
   1. Rather than being reflective and systematic planners, managers work at activities characterized by brevity, variety, and discontinuity; they are more oriented toward activity than reflection.
   2. Rather than spending most of their time in planning and delegating, managers perform a number of regular duties as an integral part of their job.
   3. Rather than using the aggregated information provided by a formal management information system, managers strongly favor the immediacy of verbal media.
   4. Most management procedures exist solely within the minds of managers, and thus are not prescribable by scientific analysis.
B. The actual work of managers can be divided into roles in three categories.
   1. Interpersonal roles consist of the figurehead for ceremonial functions; the leader responsible for directing and influencing work; and the liaison for contacts outside the vertical chain of command.
   2. Informational roles consist of the monitor, who screens the environment for information; the disseminator, who passes information to subordinates; and the spokesperson, who passes information out of the unit.
   3. Decisional roles consist of the entrepreneur, for improving the unit by using new ideas; the disturbance handler, who responds to pressures; the resource allocator; and the negotiator.
   4. All of these roles must be played by the manager, but managers of different functional areas or at different organizational levels may concentrate more upon different roles.
C. Managerial effectiveness is influenced by their insight into their work. Managers can be challenged to improve their effectiveness in three ways:
   1. Devising systematic methods of sharing privileged information with subordinates to provide them with access to it.
   2. Dealing with the problem of superficiality by devoting serious attention to issues that require it, stepping back from bits of information in order to view the entire situation, and making use of analytical inputs.
   3. Gaining control of time by turning obligations into advantages and turning desired activities into obligations.

What do managers do? Ask this question and you will likely be told that managers plan, organize, coordinate, and control. Since Henri Fayol [9] first proposed these words in 1916, they have dominated the vocabulary of management. (See, for example, [8], [12], [17].) How valuable are they in describing managerial work? Consider one morning's work of the president of a large organization:

> As he enters his office at 8:23, the manager's secretary motions for him to pick up the telephone. "Jerry, there was a bad fire in the plant last night, about $30,000 damage. We should be back in operation by Wednesday. Thought you should know."
> At 8:45, a Mr. Jamison is ushered into the manager's office. They discuss Mr. Jamison's retirement plans and his cottage in New Hampshire. Then the manager presents a plaque to him commemorating his thirty-two years with the organization.
> Mail processing follows: An innocent-looking letter, signed by a Detroit lawyer, reads: "A group of us in Detroit has decided not to buy any of your products because you used that anti-flag, anti-American pinko, Bill Lindell, upon your Thursday night TV show." The manager dictates a restrained reply.
> The 10:00 meeting is scheduled by a professional staffer. He claims that his superior, a high-ranking vice-president of the organization, mistreats his staff, and that if the man is not fired, they will all walk out. As soon as the meeting ends, the manager rearranges his schedule to investigate the claim and to react to this crisis.

Which of these activities may be called planning, and which may be called organizing, coordinating, and controlling? Indeed, what do words such as "coordinating" and "planning" mean in the context of real activity? In fact, these four words do not describe the actual work of managers at all; they describe certain vague objectives of managerial work. ". . . they are just ways of indicating what we need to explain." [1, p. 537]

Other approaches to the study of managerial work have developed, one dealing with managerial decision-making and policy-making processes, another with the manager's interpersonal activities. (See, for example, [2] and [10].) And some empirical researchers, using the "diary" method, have studied what might be called managerial "media"—by what means, with whom, how long, and where managers spend their time.[1] But in no part of this literature is the actual content of managerial work systematically and meaningfully described.[2] Thus, the question posed at the start—what do managers do?—remains essentially unanswered in the literature of management.

This is indeed an odd situation. We claim to teach management in schools of both business and public administration; we undertake major research programs in management; we find a growing segment of the management science community concerned with the problems of senior management. Most of these people— the planners, information and control theorists, systems analysts, etc.—are attempting to analyze and change working habits that they themselves do not understand. Thus, at a conference called at M.I.T. to assess the impact of the computer on the manager, and attended by a number of America's foremost management scientists, a participant found it necessary to comment after lengthy discussion [20, p. 198]:

I'd like to return to an earlier point. It seems to me that until we get into the question of what the top manager does or what the functions are that define the top management job, we're not going to get out of the kind of difficulty that keeps cropping up. What I'm really doing is leading up to my earlier question which no one really answered. And that is: Is it possible to arrive at a specification of what constitutes the job of a top manager?

His question was not answered.

## Research Study on Managerial Work

In late 1966, I began research on this question, seeking to replace Fayol's words by a set that would more accurately describe what managers do. In essence, I sought to develop by the process of induction a statement of managerial work that would have empirical validity. Using a method called "structured observation," I observed for one-week periods the chief executives of five medium to large organizations (a consulting firm, a school system, a technology firm, a consumer goods manufacturer, and a hospital).

Structured as well as unstructured (i.e., anecdotal) data were collected in three "records." In the *chronology record,* activity patterns throughout the working day were recorded. In the *mail record,* for each of 890 pieces of mail processed during the five weeks, were recorded its purpose, format and sender, the attention it received and the action it elicited. And, recorded in the *contact record,* for each of 368 verbal interactions, were the purpose, the medium (telephone call, scheduled or unscheduled meeting, tour), the participants, the form of initiation, and the location. It should be noted that all categorizing was done during and after observation so as to ensure that the categories reflected only the work under observation. [19] contains a fuller description of this methodology and a tabulation of the results of the study.

Two sets of conclusions are presented below. The first deals with certain characteristics of managerial work, as they appeared from analysis of the numerical data (e.g., How much time is spent with peers? What is the average duration of meetings? What proportion of contacts are initiated by the manager himself?). The second describes the basic content of managerial work in terms of ten roles. This description derives from an analysis of the data on the recorded *purpose* of each contact and piece of mail.

The liberty is taken of referring to these findings as descriptive of managerial, as opposed to chief executive, work. This is done because many of the findings are supported by studies of other types of managers. Specifically, most of the conclusions on work characteristics are to be found in the combined results of a group of studies of foremen [11], [13], middle managers [4], [5], [15], [25], and chief executives [6]. And although there is little useful material on managerial roles, three studies do provide some evidence of the applicability of the role set. Most important, Sayles' empirical study of production managers [24] suggests that at least five of the ten roles are performed at the lower end of the managerial hierarchy. And some further evidence is provided by comments in Whyte's study of leadership in a street gang [26] and Neustadt's study of three U.S. presidents

[21]. (Reference is made to these findings where appropriate.) Thus, although most of the illustrations are drawn from my study of chief executives, there is some justification in asking the reader to consider when he sees the terms "manager" and his "organization" not only "presidents" and their "companies," but also "foremen" and their "shops," "directors" and their "branches," "vice-presidents" and their "divisions." The term *manager* shall be used with reference to all those people in charge of formal organizations or their subunits.

## Some Characteristics of Managerial Work

Six sets of characteristics of managerial work derive from analysis of the data of this study. Each has a significant bearing on the manager's ability to administer a complex organization.

### Characteristic 1. The Manager Performs a Great Quantity of Work at an Unrelenting Pace

Despite a semblance of normal working hours, in truth managerial work appears to be very taxing. The five men in this study processed an average of thirty-six pieces of mail each day, participated in eight meetings (half of which were scheduled), engaged in five telephone calls, and took one tour. In his study of foremen, Guest [11] found that the number of activities per day averaged 583, with no real break in the pace.

Free time appears to be very rare. If by chance a manager has caught up with the mail, satisfied the callers, dealt with all the disturbances, and avoided scheduled meetings, a subordinate will likely show up to usurp the available time. It seems that the manager cannot expect to have much time for leisurely reflection during office hours. During "off" hours, our chief executives spent much time on work-related reading. High-level managers appear to be able to escape neither from an environment which recognizes the power and status of their positions nor from their own minds which have been trained to search continually for new information.

### Characteristic 2. Managerial Activity is Characterized by Variety, Fragmentation, and Brevity

There seems to be no pattern to managerial activity. Rather, variety and fragmentation appear to be characteristic, as successive activities deal with issues that differ greatly both in type and in content. In effect the manager must be prepared to shift moods quickly and frequently.

A typical chief executive day may begin with a telephone call from a director who asks a favor (a "status request"); then a subordinate calls to tell of a strike at one of the facilities (fast movement of information, termed "instant communication"); this is followed by a relaxed scheduled event at which the manager speaks to a group of visiting dignitaries (ceremony); the manager returns to find a message from a major customer who is demanding the renegotiation of a contract (pressure); and so on. Throughout the day, the managers of our study encountered this great variety of activity. Most surprisingly, the significant activities were interspersed with the trivial in no particular pattern.

Furthermore, these managerial activities were characterized by their brevity. Half of all the activities studied lasted less than nine minutes and only ten percent exceeded one hour's duration. Guest's foremen averaged 48 seconds per activity, and Carlson [6] stressed that his chief executives were unable to work without frequent interruption.

In my own study of chief executives, I felt that the managers demonstrated a preference for tasks of short duration and encouraged interruption. Perhaps the manager becomes accustomed to variety, or perhaps the flow of "instant communication" cannot be delayed. A more plausible explanation might be that the manager becomes conditioned by his workload. He develops a sensitive appreciation for the opportunity cost of his own time. Also, he is aware of the ever present assortment of obligations associated with his job—accumulations of mail that cannot be delayed, the callers that must be attended to, the meetings that require his participation. In other words, no matter what he is doing, the manager is plagued by what he must do and what he might do. Thus, the manager is forced to treat issues in an abrupt and superficial way.

### Characteristic 3. Managers Prefer Issues That Are Current, Specific, and Ad Hoc

Ad hoc operating reports received more attention than did routine ones; current, uncertain information—gossip, speculation, hearsay—which flows quickly was preferred to historical, certain information; "instant communication" received first consideration; few contacts were held on a routine or "clocked" basis; almost all contacts concerned well-defined issues. The managerial environment is clearly one of stimulus-response. It breeds, not reflective planners, but adaptable information manipulators who prefer the live, concrete situation, men who demonstrate a marked action-orientation.

### Characteristic 4. The Manager Sits Between His Organization and a Network of Contacts

In virtually every empirical study of managerial time allocation, it was reported that managers spent a surprisingly large amount of time in horizontal or lateral (nonline) communication. It is clear from this study and from that of Sayles [24] that the manager is surrounded by a diverse and complex web of contacts which serves as his self-designed external information system. Included in this web can be clients, associates and suppliers, outside staff experts, peers (managers of related or similar organizations), trade organizations, government officials, independents (those with no relevant organizational affiliation), and directors or superiors. (Among these, directors in this study and superiors in other studies did *not* stand out as particularly active individuals.)

The managers in this study received far more information than they emitted, much of it coming from contacts, and more from subordinates who acted as filters. Figuratively, the manager appears as the neck of an hourglass, sifting information into his own organization from its environment.

## Characteristic 5. The Manager Demonstrates a Strong Preference for the Verbal Media

The manager has five media at his command—mail (documented), telephone (purely verbal), unscheduled meeting (informal face-to-face), scheduled meeting (formal face-to-face), and tour (observational). Along with all the other empirical studies of work characteristics, I found a strong predominance of verbal forms of communication.

**Mail.**  By all indications, managers dislike the documented form of communication. In this study, they gave cursory attention to such items as operating reports and periodicals. It was estimated that only thirteen percent of the input mail was of specific and immediate use to the managers. Much of the rest dealt with formalities and provided general reference data. The managers studied initiated very little mail, only twenty-five pieces in the five weeks. The rest of the outgoing mail was sent in reaction to mail received—a reply to a request, an acknowledgment, some information forwarded to a part of the organization. The managers appeared to dislike this form of communication, perhaps because the mail is a relatively slow and tedious medium to use.

**Telephone and Unscheduled Meetings.**  The less formal means of verbal communication—the telephone, a purely verbal form, and the unscheduled meeting, a face-to-face form—were used frequently (two-thirds of the contacts in the study) but for brief encounters (average duration of six and twelve minutes respectively). They were used primarily to deliver requests and to transmit pressing information to those outsiders and subordinates who had informal relationships with the manager.

**Scheduled Meetings.**  These tended to be of long duration, averaging sixty-eight minutes in this study, and absorbing over half the managers' time. Such meetings provided the managers with their main opportunities to interact with large groups and to leave the confines of their own offices. Scheduled meetings were used when the participants were unfamiliar to the manager (e.g., students who request that he speak at a university), when a large quantity of information had to be transmitted (e.g., presentation of a report), when ceremony had to take place, and when complex strategy-making or negotiation had to be undertaken. An important feature of the scheduled meeting was the incidental, but by no means irrelevant, information that flowed at the start and end of such meetings.

**Tours.**  Although the walking tour would appear to be a powerful tool for gaining information in an informal way, in this study tours accounted for only three percent of the managers' time.

In general, it can be concluded that the manager uses each medium for particular purposes. Nevertheless, where possible, he appears to gravitate to verbal media since these provide greater flexibility, require less effort, and bring faster response. It should be noted here that the manager does not leave the telephone or the meeting to get back to work. Rather, communication is his work, and these media are his tools. The operating work of the organization—producing a product, doing research, purchasing a part—appears to be undertaken infrequently by the senior manager. The manager's productive output must be measured in terms of information, a great part of which is transmitted verbally.

*Characteristic 6. Despite the Preponderance of Obligations,*
*the Manager Appears to Be Able to Control His Own Affairs*
Carlson suggested in his study of Swedish chief executives that these men were puppets, with little control over their own affairs. A cursory examination of our data indicates that this is true. Our managers were responsible for the initiation of only thirty-two percent of their verbal contacts and a smaller proportion of their mail. Activities were also classified as to the nature of the managers' participation, and the active ones were outnumbered by the passive ones (e.g., making requests vs. receiving requests). On the surface, the manager is indeed a puppet, answering requests in the mail, returning telephone calls, attending meetings initiated by others, yielding to subordinates' requests for time, reacting to crises.

However, such a view is misleading. There is evidence that the senior manager can exert control over his own affairs in two significant ways: (1) It is he who defines many of his own long-term commitments, by developing appropriate information channels which later feed him information, by initiating projects which later demand his time, by joining committees or outside boards which provide contacts in return for his services, and so on. (2) The manager can exploit situations that appear as obligations. He can lobby at ceremonial speeches; he can impose his values on his organization when his authorization is requested; he can motivate his subordinates whenever he interacts with them; he can use the crisis situation as an opportunity to innovate.

Perhaps these are two points that help distinguish successful and unsuccessful managers. All managers appear to be puppets. Some decide who will pull the strings and how, and they then take advantage of each move that they are forced to make. Others, unable to exploit this high-tension environment, are swallowed up by this most demanding of jobs.


# The Manager's Work Roles

In describing the essential content of managerial work, one should aim to model managerial activity, that is, to describe it as a set of programs. But an undertaking as complex as this must be preceded by the development of a useful typological description of managerial work. In other words, we must first understand the distinct components of managerial work. At the present time we do not.

In this study, 890 pieces of mail and 368 verbal contacts were categorized as to purpose. The incoming mail was found to carry acknowledgements, requests and solicitations of various kinds, reference data, news, analytical reports, reports on events and on operations, advice on various situations, and statements of problems, pressures, and ideas. In reacting to mail, the managers acknowledged some, replied to the requests (e.g., by sending information), and forwarded much to subordinates (usually for their information). Verbal contacts involved a variety of purposes. In 15% of them activities were scheduled, in 6% ceremonial events took place, and a few involved external board work. About 34% involved requests of various kinds, some insignificant, some for information, some for authorization of proposed actions. Another 36% essentially involved the flow of information to and from the manager, while the remainder dealt specifically with issues of strategy and with negotiations. (For details, see [19].)

In this study, each piece of mail and verbal contact categorized in this way was subjected to one question: Why did the manager do this? The answers were collected and grouped and regrouped in various ways (over the course of three years) until a typology emerged that was felt to be satisfactory. While an example, presented below, will partially explain this process to the reader, it must be remembered that (in the words of Bronowski [3, p. 62]): "Every induction is a speculation and it guesses at a unity which the facts present but do not strictly imply."

Consider the following sequence of two episodes: A chief executive attends a meeting of an external board on which he sits. Upon his return to his organization, he immediately goes to the office of a subordinate, tells of a conversation he had with a fellow board member, and concludes with the statement: "It looks like we shall get the contract."

The purposes of these two contacts are clear—to attend an external board meeting, and to give current information (instant communication) to a subordinate. But why did the manager attend the meeting? Indeed, why does he belong to the board? And why did he give this particular information to his subordinate?

Basing analysis on this incident, one can argue as follows: The manager belongs to the board in part so that he can be exposed to special information which is of use to his organization. The subordinate needs the information but has not the status which would give him access to it. The chief executive does. Board memberships bring chief executives in contact with one another for the purpose of trading information.

Two aspects of managerial work emerge from this brief analysis. The manager serves in a "liaison" capacity because of the status of his office, and what he learns here enables him to act as "disseminator" of information into his organization. We refer to these as *roles*—organized sets of behaviors belonging to identifiable offices or positions [23]. Ten roles were chosen to capture all the activities observed during this study.

All activities were found to involve one or more of three basic behaviors— interpersonal contact, the processing of information, and the making of decisions. As a result, our ten roles are divided into three corresponding groups. Three roles—labelled *figurehead, liaison,* and *leader*—deal with behavior that is essentially interpersonal in nature. Three others—*nerve center, disseminator,* and *spokesman*—deal with information-processing activities performed by the manager. And the remaining four—*entrepreneur, disturbance handler, resource allocator,* and *negotiator*—cover the decision-making activities of the manager. We describe each of these roles in turn, asking the reader to note that they form a *gestalt,* a unified whole whose parts cannot be considered in isolation.

## The Interpersonal Roles

Three roles relate to the manager's behavior that focuses on interpersonal contact. These roles derive directly from the authority and status associated with holding managerial office.

**Figurehead.**  As legal authority in his organization, the manager is a symbol, obliged to perform a number of duties. He must preside at ceremonial events, sign legal documents, receive visitors, make himself available to many of those who feel, in the words of one of the men studied, "that the only way to get something done is to get to the top." There is evidence that this role applies at other levels as well. Davis [7, pp. 43–44] cites the case of the field sales manager who must deal with those customers who believe that their accounts deserve his attention.

**Leader.**  Leadership is the most widely recognized of managerial roles. It describes the manager's relationship with his subordinates—his attempts to motivate them and his development of the milieu in which they work. Leadership actions pervade all activity—in contrast to most roles, it is possible to designate only a few activities as dealing exclusively with leadership (these mostly related to staffing duties). Each time a manager encourages a subordinate, or meddles in his affairs, or replies to one of his requests, he is playing the *leader* role. Subordinates seek out and react to these leadership clues, and, as a result, they impart significant power to the manager.

**Liaison.**  As noted earlier, the empirical studies have emphasized the importance of lateral or horizontal communication in the work of managers at all levels. It is clear from our study that this is explained largely in terms of the *liaison* role. The manager establishes his network of contacts essentially to bring information and favors to his organization. As Sayles notes in his study of production supervisors [24, p. 258], "The one enduring objective [of the manager] is the effort to build and maintain a predictable, reciprocating system of relationships. . . ."

Making use of his status, the manager interacts with a variety of peers and other people outside his organization. He provides time, information, and favors in return for the same from others. Foremen deal with staff groups and other foremen; chief executives join boards of directors, and maintain extensive networks of individual relationships. Neustadt notes this behavior in analyzing the work of President Roosevelt [21, p. 150]:

> His personal sources were the product of a sociability and curiosity that reached back to the other Roosevelt's time. He had an enormous acquaintance in various phases of national life and at various levels of government; he also had his wife and her variety of contacts. He extended his acquaintanceships abroad; in the war years Winston Churchill, among others, became a "personal source." Roosevelt quite deliberately exploited these relationships and mixed them up to widen his own range of information. He changed his sources as his interests changed, but no one who had ever interested him was quite forgotten or immune to sudden use.

## The Informational Roles

A second set of managerial activities relates primarily to the processing of information. Together they suggest three significant managerial roles, one describing the manager as a focal point for a certain kind of organizational information, the other two describing relatively simple transmission of this information.

**Nerve Center.**   There is indication, both from this study and from those by Neustadt and Whyte, that the manager serves as the focal point in his organization for the movement of nonroutine information. Homans, who analyzed Whyte's study, draws the following conclusions [26, p. 187]:

> Since interaction flowed toward [the leaders], they were better informed about the problems and desires of group members than were any of the followers and therefore better able to decide on an appropriate course of action. Since they were in close touch with other gang leaders, they were also better informed than their followers about conditions in Cornerville at large. Moreover, in their positions at the focus of the chains of interaction, they were better able than any follower to pass on to the group decisions that had been reached.

The term *nerve center* is chosen to encompass those many activities in which the manager receives information.

Within his own organization, the manager has legal authority that formally connects him—and only him—to *every* member. Hence, the manager emerges as *nerve center* of internal information. He may not know as much about any one function as the subordinate who specializes in it, but he comes to know more about his total organization than any other member. He is the information generalist. Furthermore, because of the manager's status and its manifestation in the *liaison* role, the manager gains unique access to a variety of knowledgeable outsiders including peers who are themselves *nerve centers* of their own organizations. Hence, the manager emerges as his organization's *nerve center* of external information as well.

As noted earlier, the manager's nerve center information is of a special kind. He appears to find it most important to get his information quickly and informally. As a result, he will not hesitate to bypass formal information channels to get it, and he is prepared to deal with a large amount of gossip, hearsay, and opinion which has not yet become substantiated fact.

**Disseminator.**   Much of the manager's information must be transmitted to subordinates. Some of this is of a *factual* nature, received from outside the organization or from other subordinates. And some is of a *value* nature. Here, the manager acts as the mechanism by which organizational influencers (owners, governments, employee groups, the general public, etc., or simply the "boss") make their preferences known to the organization. It is the manager's duty to integrate these value positions, and to express general organizational preferences as a guide to decisions made by subordinates. One of the men studied commented: "One of the principal functions of this position is to integrate the hospital interests with the public interests." Papandreou describes his duty in a paper published in 1952, referring to management as the "peak coordinator" [22].

**Spokesman.**  In his *spokesman* role, the manager is obliged to transmit his information to outsiders. He informs influencers and other interested parties about his organization's performance, its policies, and its plans. Furthermore, he is expected to serve outside his organization as an expert in its industry. Hospital administrators are expected to spend some time serving outside as public experts on health, and corporation presidents, perhaps as chamber of commerce executives.

## The Decisional Roles

The manager's legal authority requires that he assume responsibility for all of his organization's important actions. The *nerve center* role suggests that only he can fully understand complex decisions, particularly those involving difficult value tradeoffs. As a result, the manager emerges as the key figure in the making and interrelating of all significant decisions in his organization, a process that can be referred to as *strategy-making*. Four roles describe the manager's control over the strategy-making system in his organization.

**Entrepreneur.**  The *entrepreneur* role describes the manager as initiator and designer of much of the controlled change in his organization. The manager looks for opportunities and potential problems which may cause him to initiate action. Action takes the form of *improvement projects*—the marketing of a new product, the strengthening of a weak department, the purchasing of new equipment, the reorganization of formal structure, and so on.

The manager can involve himself in each improvement project in one of three ways: (1) He may *delegate* all responsibility for its design and approval, implicitly retaining the right to replace that subordinate who takes charge of it. (2) He may delegate the design work to a subordinate, but retain the right to *approve* it before implementation. (3) He may actively *supervise* the design work himself.

Improvement projects exhibit a number of interesting characteristics. They appear to involve a number of subdecisions, consciously sequenced over long periods of time and separated by delays of various kinds. Furthermore, the manager appears to supervise a great many of these at any one time—perhaps fifty to one hundred in the case of chief executives. In fact, in his handling of improvement projects, the manager may be likened to a juggler. At any one point, he maintains a number of balls in the air. Periodically, one comes down, receives a short burst of energy, and goes up again. Meanwhile, an inventory of new balls waits on the sidelines and, at random intervals, old balls are discarded and new ones added. Both Lindblom [2] and Marples [18] touch on these aspects of strategy-making, the former stressing the disjointed and incremental nature of the decisions, and the latter depicting the sequential episodes in terms of a stranded rope made up of fibres of different lengths each of which surfaces periodically.

**Disturbance Handler.**   While the *entrepreneur* role focuses on voluntary change, the *disturbance handler* role deals with corrections which the manager is forced to make. We may describe this role as follows: The organization consists basically of specialist operating programs. From time to time, it experiences a stimulus that cannot be handled routinely, either because an operating program has broken down or because the stimulus is new and it is not clear which operating program should handle it. These situations constitute disturbances. As generalist, the manager is obliged to assume responsibility for dealing with the stimulus. Thus, the handling of disturbances is an essential duty of the manager.

There is clear evidence for this role both in our study of chief executives and in Sayles' study of production supervisors [24, p. 162]:

> The achievement of this stability, which is the manager's objective, is a never-to-be-attained ideal. He is like a symphony orchestra conductor, endeavoring to maintain a melodious performance in which contributions of the various instruments are coordinated and sequenced, patterned and paced, while the orchestra members are having various personal difficulties, stage hands are moving music stands, alternating excessive heat and cold are creating audience and instrument problems, and the sponsor of the concert is insisting on irrational changes in the program.

Sayles goes further to point out the very important balance that the manager must maintain between change and stability. To Sayles, the manager seeks "a dynamic type of stability" (p. 162). Most disturbances elicit short-term adjustments which bring back equilibrium; persistent ones require the introduction of long-term structural change.

**Resource Allocator.**   The manager maintains ultimate authority over his organization's strategy-making system by controlling the allocation of its resources. By deciding who will get what (and who will do what), the manager directs the course of his organization. He does this in three ways:

(1) *In scheduling his own time,* the manager allocates his most precious resource and thereby determines organizational priorities. Issues that receive low priority do not reach the *nerve center* of the organization and are blocked for want of resources.

(2) In designing the organizational structure and in carrying out many improvement projects, the manager *programs the work of his subordinates.* In other words, he allocates their time by deciding what will be done and who will do it.

(3) Most significantly, the manager maintains control over resource allocation by the requirement that he *authorize all significant decisions* before they are implemented. By retaining this power, the manager ensures that different decisions are interrelated—that conflicts are avoided, that resource constraints are respected, and that decisions complement one another.

Decisions appear to be authorized in one of two ways. Where the costs and benefits of a proposal can be quantified, where it is competing for specified resources with other known proposals, and where it can wait for a certain time of year, approval for a proposal is sought in the context of a formal *budgeting* procedure. But these conditions are most often not met—timing may be crucial, nonmonetary costs may predominate, and so on. In these cases, approval is sought in terms of an *ad hoc request for authorization*. Subordinate and manager meet (perhaps informally) to discuss one proposal alone.

Authorization choices are enormously complex ones for the manager. A myriad of factors must be considered (resource constraints, influencer preferences, consistency with other decisions, feasibility, payoff, timing, subordinate feelings, etc.). But the fact that the manager is authorizing the decision rather than supervising its design suggests that he has little time to give to it. To alleviate this difficulty, it appears that managers use special kinds of *models* and *plans* in their decision-making. These exist only in their minds and are loose, but they serve to guide behavior. Models may answer questions such as, "Does this proposal make sense in terms of the trends that I see in tariff legislation?" or "Will the EDP department be able to get along with marketing on this?" Plans exist in the sense that, on questioning, managers reveal images (in terms of proposed improvement projects) of where they would like their organizations to go: "Well, once I get these foreign operations fully developed, I would like to begin to look into a reorganization," said one subject of this study.

**Negotiator.** The final role describes the manager as participant in negotiation activity. To some students of the management process [8, p. 343], this is not truly part of the job of managing. But such distinctions are arbitrary. Negotiation is an integral part of managerial work, as this study notes for chief executives and as that of Sayles made very clear for production supervisors [24, p. 131]: "Sophisticated managers place great stress on negotiations as a way of life. They negotiate with groups who are setting standards for their work, who are performing support activity for them, and to whom they wish to 'sell' their services."

The manager must participate in important negotiation sessions because he is his organization's legal authority, its *spokesman* and its *resource allocator*. Negotiation is resource trading in real time. If the resource commitments are to be large, the legal authority must be present.

These ten roles suggest that the manager of an organization bears a great burden of responsibility. He must oversee his organization's status system; he must serve as a crucial informational link between it and its environment; he must interpret and reflect its basic values; he must maintain the stability of its operations; and he must adapt it in a controlled and balanced way to a changing environment.

## Management as a Profession and as a Science

Is management a profession? To the extent that different managers perform one set of basic roles, management satisfies one criterion for becoming a profession. But a profession must require, in the words of the *Random House Dictionary,* "knowledge of some department of learning or science." Which of the ten roles now requires specialized learning? Indeed, what school of business or public administration teaches its students how to disseminate information, allocate resources, perform as figurehead, make contacts, or handle disturbances? We simply know very little about teaching these things. The reason is that we have never tried to document and describe in a meaningful way the procedures (or programs) that managers use.

The evidence of this research suggests that there is as yet no science in managerial work—that managers do not work according to procedures that have been prescribed by scientific analysis. Indeed, except for his use of the telephone, the airplane, and the dictating machine, it would appear that the manager of today is indistinguishable from his predecessors. He may seek different information, but he gets much of it in the same way—from word-of-mouth. He may make decisions dealing with modern technology but he uses the same intuitive (that is, nonexplicit) procedures in making them. Even the computer, which has had such a great impact on other kinds of organizational work, has apparently done little to alter the working methods of the general manager.

How do we develop a scientific base to understand the work of the manager? The description of roles is a first and necessary step. But tighter forms of research are necessary. Specifically, we must attempt to model managerial work— to describe it as a system of programs. First, it will be necessary to decide what programs managers actually use. Among a great number of programs in the manager's repertoire, we might expect to find a time-scheduling program, an information-disseminating program, and a disturbance-handling program. Then, researchers will have to devote a considerable amount of effort to studying and accurately describing the content of each of these programs—the information and heuristics used. Finally, it will be necessary to describe the interrelationships among all of these programs so that they may be combined into an integrated descriptive model of managerial work.

When the management scientist begins to understand the programs that managers use, he can begin to design meaningful systems and provide help for the manager. He may ask: Which managerial activities can be fully reprogrammed (i.e., automated)? Which cannot be reprogrammed because they require human responses? Which can be partially reprogrammed to operate in a man-machine system? Perhaps scheduling, information collecting, and resource-allocating activities lend themselves to varying degrees of reprogramming. Management will emerge as a science to the extent that such efforts are successful.

## Improving the Manager's Effectiveness

Fayol's fifty-year-old description of managerial work is no longer of use to us. And we shall not disentangle the complexity of managerial work if we insist on viewing the manager simply as a decision-maker or simply as a motivator of subordinates. In fact, we are unlikely to overestimate the complexity of the manager's work, and we shall make little headway if we take overly simple or narrow points of view in our research.

A major problem faces today's manager. Despite the growing size of modern organizations and the growing complexity of their problems (particularly those in the public sector), the manager can expect little help. He must design his own information system, and he must take full charge of his organization's strategy-making system. Furthermore, the manager faces what might be called the *dilemma of delegation*. He has unique access to much important information but he lacks a formal means of disseminating it. As much of it is verbal, he cannot spread it around in an efficient manner. How can he delegate a task with confidence when he has neither the time nor the means to send the necessary information along with it?

Thus, the manager is usually forced to carry a great burden of responsibility in his organization. As organizations become increasingly large and complex, this burden increases. Unfortunately, the man cannot significantly increase his available time or significantly improve his abilities to manage. Hence, in the large, complex bureaucracy, the top manager's time assumes an enormous opportunity cost and he faces the real danger of becoming a major obstruction in the flow of decisions and information.

Because of this, as we have seen, managerial work assumes a number of distinctive characteristics. The quantity of work is great; the pace is unrelenting; there is great variety, fragmentation, and brevity in the work activities; the manager must concentrate on issues that are current, specific, and ad hoc, and to do so, he finds that he must rely on verbal forms of communications. Yet it is on this man that the burden lies for designing and operating strategy-making and information-processing systems that are to solve his organization's (and society's) problems.

The manager can do something to alleviate these problems. He can learn more about his own roles in his organization, and he can use this information to schedule his time in a more efficient manner. He can recognize that only he has much of the information needed by his organization. Then, he can seek to find better means of disseminating it into the organization. Finally, he can turn to the skills of his management scientists to help reduce his workload and to improve his ability to make decisions.

The management scientist can learn to help the manager to the extent he can develop an understanding of the manager's work and the manager's information. To date, strategic planners, operations researchers, and information system designers have provided little help for the senior manager. They simply have had no framework available by which to understand the work of the men who employed them, and they have had poor access to the information which has never been documented. It is folly to believe that a man with poor access to the organization's true *nerve center* can design a formal management information system. Similarly, how can the long-range planner, a man usually uninformed about many of the *current* events that take place in and around his organization, design meaningful strategic plans? For good reason, the literature documents many manager complaints of naïve planning and many planner complaints of disinterested managers. In my view, our lack of understanding of managerial work has been the greatest block to the progress of management science.

The ultimate solution to the problem—to the overburdened manager seeking meaningful help—must derive from research. We must observe, describe, and understand the real work of managing; then and only then shall we significantly improve it.

## FOOTNOTES

1.　Carlson [6] carried out the classic study just after World War II. He asked nine Swedish managing directors to record on diary pads details of each activity in which they engaged. His method was used by a group of other researchers, many of them working in the U.K. (See [4], [5], [15], [25].)

2.　One major project, involving numerous publications, took place at Ohio State University and spanned three decades. Some of the vocabulary used followed Fayol. The results have generated little interest in this area. (See, for example, [13].)

## REFERENCES

1.　Braybrooke, David. "The Mystery of Executive Success Re-examined," *Administrative Science Quarterly*, Vol. 8 (1964), pp. 533–60.

2.　_____ and Lindblom, Charles E. *A Strategy of Decision*, Free Press, New York, 1963.

3.　Bronowski, J. "The Creative Process," *Scientific American*, Vol. 199 (September 1958), pp. 59–65.

4.　Burns, Tom. "The Directions of Activity and Communications in a Departmental Executive Group," *Human Relations*, Vol. 7 (1954), pp. 73–97.

5.　_____ . "Management in Action," *Operational Research Quarterly*, Vol. 8 (1957), pp. 45–60.

6.　Carlson, Sune. *Executive Behavior*, Strömbergs, Stockholm, 1951.

7.　Davis, Robert T. *Performance and Development of Field Sales Managers*, Division of Research, Graduate School of Business Administration, Harvard University, Boston, 1957.

8.　Drucker, Peter F. *The Practice of Management*, Harper and Row, New York, 1954.

9.　Fayol, Henri. *Administration industrielle et générale*, Dunods, Paris, 1950 (first published 1916).

10.　Gibb, Cecil A. "Leadership," Chapter 31 in Gardner Lindzey and Elliot A. Aronson (editors), *The Handbook of Social Psychology*, Vol. 4, Second edition, Addison-Wesley, Reading, Mass., 1969.

11.　Guest, Robert H. "Of Time and the Foreman," *Personnel*, Vol. 32 (1955–56), pp. 478–86.

12.　Gulick, Luther H. "Notes on the Theory of Organization," in Luther Gulick and Lyndall Urwick (editors), *Papers on the Science of Administration*, Columbia University Press, New York, 1937.

13.　Hemphill, John K. *Dimensions of Executive Positions*, Bureau of Business Research Monograph Number 98, The Ohio State University, Columbus, 1960.

14.　Homans, George C. *The Human Group*, Harcourt, Brace, New York, 1950.

15. Horne, J. H. and Lupton, Tom. "The Work Activities of Middle Managers— An Exploratory Study," *The Journal of Management Studies,* Vol. 2 (February 1965), pp. 14–33.

16. Kelly, Joe. "The Study of Executive Behavior by Activity Sampling," *Human Relations,* Vol. 17 (August 1964), pp. 277–87.

17. Mackenzie, R. Alex. "The Management Process in 3D," *Harvard Business Review* (November–December 1969), pp. 80–87.

18. Marples, D. L. "Studies of Managers—A Fresh Start?," *The Journal of Management Studies,* Vol. 4 (October 1967), pp. 282–99.

19. Mintzberg, Henry. "Structured Observation as a Method to Study Managerial Work," *The Journal of Management Studies,* Vol. 7 (February 1970), pp. 87– 104.

20. Myers, Charles A. (Ed.). *The Impact of Computers on Management,* The M.I.T. Press, Cambridge, Mass., 1967.

21. Neustadt, Richard E. *Presidential Power: The Politics of Leadership,* The New American Library, New York, 1964.

22. Papandreou, Andreas G. "Some Basic Problems in the Theory of the Firm," in Bernard F. Haley (ed.), *A Survey of Contemporary Economics,* Vol. II, Irwin, Homewood, Illinois, 1952, pp. 183–219.

23. Sarbin, T. R. and Allen, V. L. "Role Theory," in Gardner Lindzey and Elliot A. Aronson (eds.), *The Handbook of Social Psychology,* Vol. I, Second edition, Addison-Wesley, Reading, Mass., 1968, pp. 488–567.

24. Sayles, Leonard R. *Managerial Behavior: Administration in Complex Enterprises,* McGraw-Hill, New York, 1964.

25. Stewart, Rosemary. *Managers and Their Jobs,* Macmillan, London, 1967.

---

## Learning Review

*Questions:*

1. The traditional view of the manager's job is that it consists of _____, _____, _____, and _____.

2. Regular duties of managers include _____, _____ and _____ _____.

3. Managers prefer _____ information to _____ information.

4. Impersonal roles consist of _____, _____, and _____ roles.

5. Information roles consist of the _____, _____, and _____ roles.

6. Decisional roles consist of the _____, _____, _____, and _____ roles.

7. One reason for the difficulty experienced by managers in delegating tasks is that _____ _____ _____ _____ _____ _____ _____ _____ _____.

---

# *Retrospective Comment*

## HENRY MINTZBERG

In looking over this article some 15 years after it was first published, I must admit that I remain pleased with most of what I wrote way back then, particularly the body of the article that describes the characteristics and content of managerial work. If there are any sections I would change, they are at the end of the article—two in particular.

First, I have less faith now in the notion of programming the manager's job—even describing parts of it precisely in terms of programs, let alone using these for prescriptive purposes. I believe that looser kinds of description, as in the body of the article itself, may make more sense in our efforts to understand and improve managerial work. Second, I imply in this article (although I discussed the issue more directly in some other, related ones) that the manager's job breeds a certain superficiality; to perform effectively, mangers must become proficient at their superficiality. More and more, I am coming to believe that superficiality *is* the problem, that the main problem of our large organizations is that their senior managers can hardly escape the pressures to be superficial (or perhaps I should say, only the very exceptional managers can), with devastating consequences.

In any event, I feel that I tripped over some important issues back then, even though I was not fully aware of them. Everything I have done since—on strategy and structure and social issues in and about organizations—really finds its roots in this, my initial piece of research.

# 19

# *Engineer the Job to Fit the Manager*

## FRED E. FIEDLER

## *About the Author*

**Fred E. Fiedler** is Professor of Psychology and Management at the University of Washington. He is a University of Chicago Ph.D. where he also taught before moving to the University of Illinois in 1951. At Illinois he was Professor of Psychology and Director of the Group Effectiveness Research Laboratory until 1969 when he moved to Washington. He has also been a visiting faculty member at the Universities of Amsterdam and Louvain.

Professor Fiedler is the author of more than 180 articles and five books. In 1979, he was recognized as one of the 100 psychologists most frequently cited in the scientific literature. He has consulted with numerous governmental and private agencies and business concerns in the U.S., Europe, and Australia.

# PREVIEW

A. Success or failure of an organization depends upon the quality of its management.
B. Leadership styles are determined in most instances by the different situations.
   1. Three major dimensions affect leadership styles.
   2. These dimensions may be used to develop a model for classifying groups by the most appropriate leadership style.
C. Empirical evidence verifies the appropriateness of the eight-step model.
D. Changing the group to match the executive's leadership style is investigated.
   1. Preliminary results indicate that the new approach should be successful and less costly.
   2. It is easier to place managers in a situation that is compatible with their natural leadership style than to force them to adapt to the demands of the job.

What kind of leadership style does business need? Should company executives be decisive, directive, willing to give orders, and eager to assume responsibility? Should they be human relations-oriented, nondirective, willing to share leadership with the men in their group? Or should we perhaps start paying attention to the more important problem of defining under what conditions each of these leadership styles works best and what to do about it?

The success or failure of an organization depends on the quality of its management. How to get the best possible management is a question of vital importance; but it is perhaps even more important to ask how we can make better use of the management talent which *we already have.*

To get good business executives we have relied primarily on recruitment, selection, and training. It is time for businessmen to ask whether this is the only way or the best way for getting the best possible management. Fitting the man to the leadership job by selection and training has not been spectacularly successful. It is surely easier to change almost anything in the job situation than a man's personality and his leadership style. Why not try, then, to fit the leadership job to the man?

Executive jobs are surprisingly pliable, and the executive manpower pool is becoming increasingly small. The luxury of picking a "natural leader" from among a number of equally promising or equally qualified specialists is rapidly fading into the past. Business must learn how to utilize the available executive talent as effectively as it now utilizes physical plant and machine tools. Your financial expert, your top research scientist, or your production genius may be practically irreplaceable. Their jobs call for positions of leadership and responsibility. Replacements for these men can be neither recruited nor trained overnight, and they may not be willing to play second fiddle in their departments. If their leadership style does not fit the job, *we must learn how to engineer the job to fit their leadership style.*

In this article I shall describe some studies that illuminate this task of job engineering and adaptation. It will be seen that there are situations where the authoritarian, highly directive leader works best, and other situations where the egalitarian, more permissive, human relations-oriented leader works best; but almost always there are possibilities for changing the situation around somewhat to match the needs of the particular managers who happen to be available. The executive who appreciates these differences and possibilities has knowledge that can be valuable to him in running his organization.

To understand the problems that a new approach would involve, let us look first at some of the basic issues in organizational and group leadership.

## Styles of Leadership

Leadership is a personal relationship in which one person directs, coordinates, and supervises others in the performance of a common task. This is especially so in "interacting groups," where men must work together cooperatively in achieving organizational goals.

In oversimplified terms, it can be said that the leader manages the group in either of two ways. He can:

- Tell people what to do and how to do it.
- Or share his leadership responsibilities with his group members and involve them in the planning and execution of the task.

There are, of course, all shades of leadership styles in between these two polar positions, but the basic issue is this: the work of motivating and coordinating group members has to be done either by brandishing the proverbial stick or by dangling the equally proverbial carrot. The former is the more orthodox job-centered, autocratic style. The latter is the more nondirective, group-centered procedure.

Research evidence exists to support both approaches to leadership. Which, then, should be judged more appropriate? On the face of it, the first style of leadership is best under some conditions, while the second works better under others. Accepting this proposition immediately opens two avenues of approach. Management can:

- Determine the specific situation in which the directive or the nondirective leadership style works best, and then select or train men so that their leadership style fits the particular job.
- Or determine the type of leadership style which is most natural for the man in the executive position, and then change the job to fit the man.

The first alternative has been discussed many times before; the second has not. We have never seriously considered whether it would be easier to fit the executive's job to the man.

## Needed Style?

How might this be done? Some answers have been suggested by a research program on leadership effectiveness that I have directed under Office of Naval Research auspices since 1951.[1] This program has dealt with a wide variety of different groups, including basketball teams, surveying parties, various military combat crews, and men in open-hearth steel shops, as well as members of management and boards of directors. When possible, performance was measured in terms of objective criteria—for instance, percentage of games won by high school basketball teams; tap-to-tap time of open-hearth shops (roughly equivalent to the tonnage of steel output per unit of time); and company net income over a three-year period. Our measure of leadership style was based on a simple scale indicating the degree to which a man described, favorably or unfavorably, his least-preferred co-worker (LPC). This co-worker did not need to be someone he actually worked with at the time, but could be someone the respondent had known in the past. Whenever possible, the score was obtained before the leader was assigned to his group.

The study indicates that a person who describes his least-preferred co-worker in a relatively favorable manner tends to be permissive, human relations-oriented, and considerate of the feelings of his men. But a person who describes his least-preferred co-worker in an unfavorable manner—who has what we have come to call a low LPC rating—tends to be managing, task-controlling, and less concerned with the human relations aspects of the job. It also appears that the directive, managing, and controlling leaders tend to perform best in basketball and surveying teams, in open-hearth shops, and (provided the leader is accepted by his group) in military combat crews and company managements. On the other hand, the nondirective, permissive, and human relations-oriented leaders tend to perform best in decision- and policy-making teams and in groups that have a creative task—provided that the group likes the leader or the leader feels that the group is pleasant and free of tension.

### Critical Dimensions

But in order to tell which style fits which situation, we need to categorize groups. Our research has shown that "it all depends" on the situation. After reviewing the results of all our work and the findings of other investigators, we have been able to isolate three major dimensions that seem to determine, to a large part, the kind of leadership style called for by different situations.

It is obviously a mistake to think that groups and teams are all alike and that each requires the same kind of leadership. We need some way of categorizing the group-task situation, or the job environment within which the leader has to operate. If leadership is indeed a process of influencing other people to work together effectively in a common task, then it surely matters how easy or difficult it is for the leader to exert his influence in a particular situation.

**Leader-Member Relations.**   The factor that would seem most important in determining a man's leadership influence is the degree to which his group members trust and like him, and are willing to follow his guidance. The trusted and well-liked leader obviously does not require special rank or power in order to get things done. We can measure the leader-member relationship by the so-called sociometric nomination techniques that ask group members to name in their group the most influential person, or the man they would most like to have as a leader. It can also be measured by a group-atmosphere scale indicating the degree to which the leader feels accepted and comfortable in the group.

**The Task Structure.** The second important factor is the "task structure." By this term I mean the degree to which the task (a) is spelled out step by step for the group and, if so, the extent to which it can be done "by the numbers" or according to a detailed set of standard operating instructions, or (b) must be left nebulous and undefined. Vague and ambiguous or unstructured tasks make it difficult to exert leadership influence, because neither the leader nor his members know exactly what has to be done or how it is to be accomplished.

Why single out this aspect of the task rather than the innumerable other possible ways of describing it? Task groups are almost invariably components of a larger organization that assigns the task and has, therefore, a big stake in seeing it performed properly. However, the organization can control the quality of a group's performance only if the task is clearly spelled out and programmed or structured. When the task can be programmed or performed "by the numbers," the organization is able to back up the authority of the leader to the fullest; the man who fails to perform each step can be disciplined or fired. But in the case of ill-defined, vague, or unstructured tasks, the organization and the leader have very little control and direct power. By close supervision one can ensure, let us say, that a man will correctly operate a machine, but one cannot ensure that he will be creative.

It is therefore easier to be a leader in a structured task situation in which the work is spelled out than in an unstructured one which presents the leader and his group with a nebulous, poorly defined problem.

**Position Power.** Thirdly, there is the power of the leadership position, as distinct from any personal power the leader might have. Can he hire or fire and promote or demote? Is his appointment for life, or will it terminate at the pleasure of his group? It is obviously easier to be a leader when the position power is strong than when it is weak.

## Model for Analysis
When we now classify groups on the basis of these three dimensions, we get a classification system that can be represented as a cube; see Exhibit I. As each group is high or low in each of the three dimensions, it will fall into one of the eight cells.

From examination of the cube, it seems clear that exerting leadership influence will be easier in a group in which the members like a powerful leader with a clearly defined job and where the job to be done is clearly laid out (Cell 1); it

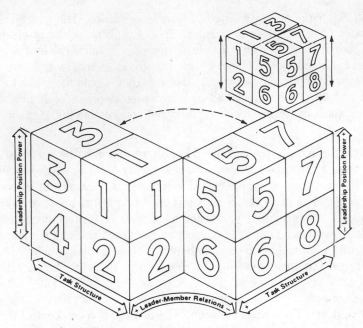

*Exhibit 1.*   A model for classifying group-task situations

will be difficult in a group where a leader is disliked, has little power, and has a highly ambiguous job (Cell 8).

In other words, it is easier to be the well-esteemed foreman of a construction crew working from a blueprint than it is to be the disliked chairman of a volunteer committee preparing a new policy.

I consider the leader-member relations the most important dimension, and the position-power dimension the least important, of the three. It is, for instance, quite possible for a man of low rank to lead a group of higher-ranking men in a structured task—as is done when enlisted men or junior officers conduct some standardized parts of the training programs for medical officers who enter the Army. But it is not so easy for a disrespected manager to lead a creative, policy-formulating session well, even if he is the senior executive present.

### Varying Requirements
By first sorting the eight cells according to leader-member relations, then task structure, and finally leader position power, we can now arrange them in order according to the favorableness of the environment for the leader. This sorting leads to an eight-step scale, as in Exhibit II. This exhibit portrays the results of a series of studies of groups performing well but (a) in different situations and conditions, and (b) with leaders using different leadership styles. In explanation:

The *horizontal* axis shows the range of situations that the groups worked in, as described by the classification scheme used in Exhibit I.

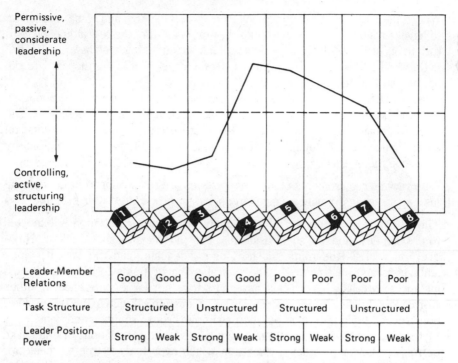

Permissive,
passive,
considerate
leadership

Controlling,
active,
structuring
leadership

| Leader-Member Relations | Good | Good | Good | Good | Poor | Poor | Poor | Poor | |
|---|---|---|---|---|---|---|---|---|---|
| Task Structure | Structured | | Unstructured | | Structured | | Unstructured | | |
| Leader Position Power | Strong | Weak | Strong | Weak | Strong | Weak | Strong | Weak | |

*Exhibit II.* How the style of effective leadership varies with the situation

The *vertical* axis indicates the leadership style which was best in a certain situation, as shown by the correlation coefficient between the leader's LPC and his group's performance.

A positive correlation (falling above the midline) shows that the permissive, nondirective, and human relations-oriented leaders performed best; a negative correlation (below the midline) shows that the task-controlling, managing leader performed best. For instance, leaders of effective groups in situation categories 1 and 2 had LPC-group performance correlations of −.40 to −.80, with the average between −.50 and −.60; whereas leaders of effective groups in situation categories 4 and 5 had LPC-group performance correlations of .20 to .80, with the average between .40 and .50.

Exhibit II shows that both the directive, managing, task-oriented leaders and the nondirective, human relations-oriented leaders are successful under some conditions. Which leadership style is the best depends on the favorableness of the particular situation for the leader. In very favorable or in very unfavorable situations for getting a task accomplished by group effort, the autocratic, task-controlling, managing leadership works best. In situations intermediate in difficulty, the nondirective, permissive leader is more successful.

This corresponds well with our everyday experience. For instance:

- Where the situation is very favorable, the group expects and wants the leader to give directions. We neither expect nor want the trusted airline pilot to turn to his crew and ask, "What do you think we ought to check before takeoff?"
- If the disliked chairman of a volunteer committee asks his group what to do, he may be told that everybody ought to go home.
- The well-liked chairman of a planning group or research team must be nondirective and permissive in order to get full participation from his members. The directive, managing leader will tend to be more critical and to cut discussion short; hence he will not get the full benefit of the potential contributions by his group members.

The varying requirements of leadership styles are readily apparent in organizations experiencing dramatic changes in operating procedures. For example:

- The manager or supervisor of a routinely operating organization is expected to provide direction and supervision that the subordinates should follow. However, in a crisis the routine is no longer adequate, and the task becomes ambiguous and unstructured. The typical manager tends to respond in such instances by calling his principal assistants together for a conference. In other words, the effective leader changes his behavior from a directive to a permissive, nondirective style until the operation again reverts to routine conditions.
- In the case of a research planning group, the human relations-oriented and permissive leader provides a climate in which everybody is free to speak up, to suggest, and to criticize. Osborn's brainstorming method [2] in fact institutionalizes these procedures. However, after the research plan has been completed, the situation becomes highly structured. The director now prescribes the task in detail, and he specifies the means of accomplishing it. Woe betide the assistant who decides to be creative by changing the research instructions!

## Practical Tests

Remember that the ideas I have been describing emanate from studies of real-life situations; accordingly, as might be expected, they can be validated by organizational experience. Take, for instance, the dimension of leader-member relations described earlier. We have made three studies of situations in which the leader's position power was strong and the task relatively structured with clear-cut goals and standard operating procedures. In such groups as these the situation will be very favorable for the leader if he is accepted; it will be progressively unfavorable in proportion to how much a leader is disliked. What leadership styles succeed in these varying conditions? The studies confirm what our theory would lead us to expect:

- The first set of data come from a study of B-29 bomber crews in which the criterion was the accuracy of radar bombing. Six degrees of leader-member relations were identified, ranging from those in which the aircraft commander was the first choice of crew members and highly endorsed his radar observer and navigator (the key men in radar bombing), to those in which he was chosen by his crew but did not endorse his key men, and finally to crews in which the commander was rejected by his crew and rejected his key crew members. What leadership styles were effective? The results are plotted in Exhibit III.

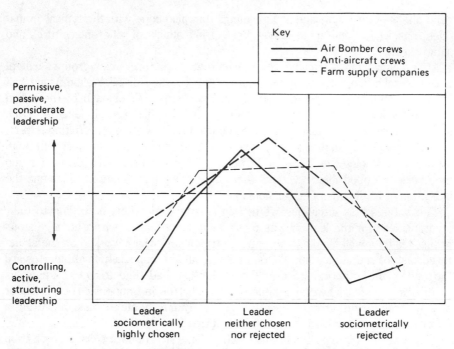

Permissive,
passive,
considerate
leadership

Controlling,
active,
structuring
leadership

Key
———————— Air Bomber crews
– – – – – Anti-aircraft crews
– – – – – Farm supply companies

Leader
sociometrically
highly chosen

Leader
neither chosen
nor rejected

Leader
sociometrically
rejected

*Exhibit III.*    How effective leadership styles vary depending on group acceptance

- A study of anti-aircraft crews compares the 10 most chosen crew commanders, the 10 most rejected ones, and 10 of intermediate popularity. The criterion is the identification and "acquisition" of unidentified aircraft by the crew. The results shown in Exhibit III are similar to those for bomber crew commanders.
- Exhibit III also summarizes data for 32 small-farm supply companies. These were member companies of the same distribution system, each with its own board of directors and its own management. The performance of these highly comparable companies was measured in terms of percentage of company net income over a three-year period. The first quarter of the line (going from left to right) depicts endorsement of the general manager by his board of directors and his staff of assistant managers; the second quarter, endorsement by his board but not his staff; the third quarter, endorsement by his staff but not his board; the fourth quarter, endorsement by neither.

As can be seen from the results of all three studies, the highly accepted and strongly rejected leaders perform best if they are controlling and managing, while the leaders in the intermediate acceptance range, who are neither rejected nor accepted, perform best if they are permissive and nondirective.

Now let us look at some research on organizations in another country:

Recently in Belgium a study was made of groups of mixed language and cultural composition. Such teams, which are becoming increasingly frequent as international business and governmental activities multiply, obviously present a difficult situation for the leader. He must not only deal with men who do not fully comprehend one another's language and meanings, but also cope with the typical antipathies, suspicions, and antagonisms dividing individuals of different cultures and nationalities.

At a Belgian naval training center we tested 96 three-man groups, half of which were homogeneous in composition (all Flemish or all Walloon) and half heterogeneous (the leader differing from his men). Half of each of these had powerful leader positions (petty officers), and half had recruit leaders. Each group performed three tasks: one unstructured task (writing a recruiting letter); and two parallel structured tasks (finding the shortest route for ships through 10 ports, and doing the same for 12 ports). After each task, leaders and group members described their reactions—including group-atmosphere ratings and the indication of leader-member relations.

The various task situations were then arranged in order, according to their favorableness for the leader. The most favorable situation was a homogeneous group, led by a well-liked and accepted petty officer, which worked on the structured task of routing a ship. The situation would be especially favorable toward the end of the experiment, after the leader had had time to get to know his members. The least favorable situation was that of an unpopular recruit leader of a heterogeneous group where the relatively unstructured task of writing a letter came up as soon as the group was formed.

There were six groups that fell into each of these situations or cells. A correlation was then computed for each set of six groups to determine which type of leadership style led to best team performance. The results, indicated in Exhibit IV, support the conclusions earlier described.

Of particular interest is the fact that the difficult heterogeneous groups generally required controlling, task-oriented leadership for good performance. This fits

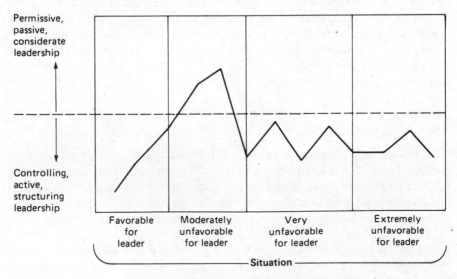

*Exhibit IV.* Effective leadership styles at Belgian Naval training center

the descriptions of successful leader behavior obtained from executives who have worked in international business organizations.

# Conclusion

Provided our findings continue to be supported in the future, what do these results and the theory mean for executive selection and training? What implications do they have for the management of large organizations?

## Selection & Training

Business and industry are now trying to attract an increasingly large share of exceptionally intelligent and technically well-trained men. Many of these are specialists whose talents are in critically short supply. Can industry really afford to select only those men who have a certain style of leadership in addition to their technical qualifications? The answer is likely to be negative, at least in the near future.

This being the case, can we then train the men selected in one leadership style or the other? This approach is always offered as a solution, and it does have merit. But we must recognize that training people is at best difficult, costly, and time-consuming. It is certainly easier to place people in a situation compatible with their natural leadership style than to force them to adapt to the demands of the job.

As another alternative, should executives learn to recognize or diagnose group-task situations so that they can place their subordinates, managers, and department heads in the jobs best suited to their leadership styles? Even this procedure has serious disadvantages. The organization may not always happen to have the place that fits the bright young man. The experienced executive may not want to be moved, or it may not be possible to transfer him.

Should the organization try to "engineer" the job to fit the man? This alternative is potentially the most feasible for management. As has been shown already, the type of leadership called for depends on the favorableness of the situation. The favorableness, in turn, is a product of several factors. These include leader-member relations, the homogeneity of the group, and the position power and degree to which the task is structured, as well as other, more obvious factors such as the leader's knowledge of his group, his familiarity with the task, and so forth.

It is clear that management can change the characteristic favorableness of the leadership situation; it can do so in most cases more easily than it can transfer the subordinate leader from one job to another or train him in a different style of interacting with his members.

## Possibilities of Change

Although this type of organizational engineering has not been done systematically up to now, we can choose from several good possibilities for getting the job done:

1. *We can change the leader's position power.* We can either give him subordinates of equal or nearly equal rank or we can give him men who are two or three ranks below him. We can either give him sole authority for the job or require that he consult with this group, or even obtain unanimous consent for all decisions. We can either punctiliously observe the channels of the organization to increase the leader's prestige or communicate directly with the men of his group as well as with him in person.

2. *We can change the task structure.* The tasks given to one leader may have to be clarified in detail, and he may have to be given precise operating instructions; another leader may have to be given more general problems that are only vaguely elucidated.

3. *We can change the leader-member relations.* The Belgian study, referred to earlier, demonstrates that changing the group composition changes the leader's relations with his men. We can increase or decrease the group's heterogeneity by introducing men with similar attitudes, beliefs, and backgrounds, or by bringing in men different in training, culture, and language.

The foregoing are, of course, only examples of what could be done. The important point is that we now have a model and a set of principles that permit predictions of leadership effectiveness in interacting groups and allow us to take a look at the factors affecting team performance. This approach goes beyond the traditional notions of selection and training. It focuses on the more fruitful possibility of organizational engineering as a means of using leadership potentials in the management ranks.

## FOOTNOTES

1.  Conducted under Office of Naval Research contracts 170–106, N6-ori-07135 and NR 177–142, Nonr-1834 (36).

2.  See Alex F. Osborn, *Applied Imagination* (New York, Charles Scribner's Sons, 1953).

---

## *Learning Review*

*Questions:*

1.  Leadership is a personal relationship in which one person _____, _____, and _____ others in the performance of a common task.

2.  The measure used by Fiedler to measure leadership style is called the _____ scale.

3.  The three major dimensions that appear to determine the appropriate leadership style in different situations are _____-_____, _____, and _____.

*Answers:*

3. leader-member relations, task structure, position power
1. directs, coordinates, supervises; 2. LPC (least preferred co-worker);

## Retrospective Comment

◆

*[Editors' note: When Professor Fiedler was requested to write a retrospective comment on his article, he replied that he had recently written an entire article [1] covering the points he would like to make. The following is an abstract of the article.]*

Briefly, Fiedler reviews the research evidence over the past 15 years and concludes that:

1. The reliability and validity of the LPC ("Least Preferred Co-worker") score are adequately documented in several studies. While there has been some disagreement as to what the LPC measures, Fiedler feels that it is now relatively clear that a high LPC person is oriented toward relationships with others, and a low LPC person is primarily concerned with task accomplishment.

2. The formula for weighting and combining elements of situational control is justified by several studies. The formulation is:

$$4 \begin{pmatrix} \text{Leader-} \\ \text{member} \\ \text{relations} \end{pmatrix} + 2 \begin{pmatrix} \text{Task} \\ \text{Structure} \end{pmatrix} + \text{Leader Power} = \begin{matrix} \text{Situational} \\ \text{Control Score} \end{matrix}$$

In other words, the leader's power is only half as important as the task structure, which, in turn, is just half as important as the leader-member relationships in determining the degree of favorableness of the situation for the leader's influence.

3. Reviewing studies of the validity of the contingency model, Fiedler observes: "Most competent studies have supported the theory" (p. 215). Fiedler presents 47 correlations between leadership style and group performance—covering seven of the octants in the model. (Octant six is not counted because no predictions are made here). Thirty-eight of the correlations found are in the direction predicted by the model (only four are significant).

4. Fiedler describes six studies where leaders trained to diagnose leadership situations performed more effectively than control groups of untrained leaders.

*[More recently, Professor Fiedler [2] reports that reviews of the extensive research conducted with his LPC scale [3] indicate impressive levels of reliability and validity for the scale.]*

\* \* \*

Clearly, Fiedler's "contingency theory" approach to leadership has sparked a great deal of interest among both researchers and practitioners. Fiedler feels strongly that the many studies which have resulted provide convincing support for his theory.

# REFERENCES

1. Fiedler, F. E., Recent developments in research on the contingency model. In L. Berkowitz (Ed.) *Group Processes: Papers from Advances in Experimental Social Psychology.* New York: Academic Press, 1978. Pp. 209–225.
2. Personal communication to the editors, June 8, 1986.
3. Peters, L. H., Hartke, D. D., & Pohlman, J. T., Fiedler's contingency theory of leadership: An application of the meta-analysis of Schmidt and Hunter, *Psychological Bulletin,* in press; Rice, R. W., Psychometric properties of the least preferred coworker (LPC) scale, *Academy of Management Review,* 1978, 106–118; Strube, M. J. & Garcia, J. E., A meta-analytical investigation of Fiedler's contingency model of leadership effectiveness, *Psychological Bulletin,* 1981, 307–321.

# 20

# *A New Strategy For Job Enrichment*

### J. RICHARD HACKMAN

### GREG OLDHAM

### ROBERT JANSON

### KENNETH PURDY

## *About the Authors*

**J. Richard Hackman,** Professor of Social and Organizational Psychology at Harvard University, received his undergraduate degree in mathematics from MacMurray College in 1962 and his Ph.D. in social psychology from the University of Illinois in 1966. He taught at Yale until moving to Harvard in 1986.

Professor Hackman, author of five books and over 50 articles, was winner of the Sixth Annual AIR Creative Talent Award in the field of "Measurement and Evaluation: Individual and Group Behavior" and co-winner of the 1972 Cattell Award of the American Psychological Association. His research centers on topics such as work team performance, social influences on individual behavior, and design and leadership of self-managing units in organizations. He serves on the editorial boards of several journals and consults widely on work and organizational design issues.

**Greg R. Oldham** is Professor of Organizational Behavior in the Department of Business Administration and in the Institute of Labor and Industrial Relations,

University of Illinois at Urbana-Champaign. He earned his undergraduate degree in sociology at the University of California, Irvine in 1969 and his doctorate in Organizational Behavior from Yale University in 1974, after which he joined the University of Illinois. His research is in the areas of work and workspace design.

**Robert Janson,** Certified Management Consultant, is President of Roy M. Walters & Associates, Inc., a management consulting firm in Mahwah, New Jersey. A specialist in helping CEO's achieve large-scale changes, Mr. Janson's projects have included productivity improvement, organization diagnosis, quality improvement, organization structure analysis, integration of technology, and motivational work design. He is a graduate of Manhattan College, and author of several articles for managers.

**Kenneth L. Purdy,** Certified Management Consultant, is Vice President and Director of Consulting Services for Roy W. Walters, Inc. Before joining Walters and Associates, he was an executive and internal consultant for the Bell System for seven years and served in naval intelligence in the U.S. Navy. He is a graduate of Amherst College. He is a joint author of *Job Enrichment for Results,* and writes frequently on the application of behavioral science to management problems.

---

# PREVIEW

A. A new strategy for job enrichment can be based upon the findings of both management practice and psychological theory. It contains four major elements:
   1. The strategy is grounded in basic theory of what motivates people in their work.
   2. It emphasizes that planning for job change should be based on job-related data collected with a set of diagnostic tools.
   3. It provides a set of specific implementation concepts to guide the actual job changes, as well as a set of theory-based rules to select those steps most likely to be most successful in a given situation.
   4. Research findings demonstrate the validity of the theory, practicality and informative nature of the diagnostic procedures, and the fact that implementation procedures lead to beneficial changes.
B. Three psychological states, critical in motivating workers, can be achieved through the dimensions of a job.
   1. The worker must view the work as meaningful. This is achieved through the job dimensions of skill variety, task identity, and task significance.
   2. Workers must experience responsibility for the outcome of their efforts. This can be achieved by task autonomy.
   3. Workers require knowledge of results provided in the form of feedback.
   4. All three states must be present for the worker to be motivated.
   5. These three states will result in high internal motivation for workers with high growth-need strength, but may cause those with lower growth-needs to feel "pushed."

C.  Job diagnosis is necessary to implement a job enrichment strategy. Instruments are used to measure characteristics of the job, current motivation levels, and levels of employee growth-need strength. The diagnosis typically involves a four-step sequence of questions:
1.  Are motivation and satisfaction central to the problem?
2.  Is the job low in motivating potential?
3.  What specific aspects of the job are causing the difficulty?
4.  How ready are the employees for change?
D.  The process of job enrichment involves five implementation concepts. Each concept enhances one or more core dimensions of the job.
1.  Forming natural work units improves task identity and significance.
2.  Combining tasks to form larger work modules results in improved task identity and skill variety.
3.  Establishing relationships between workers and clients leads to increased feedback, skill variety, and autonomy.
4.  Vertical loading increases autonomy.
5.  Opening feedback channels leads to improved feedback.
E.  Empirical evidence exists to support the effectiveness of this strategy.
1.  The job enrichment theory is supported by studies linking higher motivational factors with improved job satisfaction and performance.
2.  Actual implementation of the strategy has resulted in improvements in both productivity and job satisfaction.

---

Practitioners of job enrichment have been living through a time of excitement, even euphoria. Their craft has moved from the psychology and management journals to the front page and the Sunday supplement. Job enrichment, which began with the pioneering work of Herzberg and his associates, originally was intended as a means to increase the motivation and satisfaction of people at work—and to improve productivity in the bargain.[1-5] Now it is being acclaimed in the popular press as a cure for problems ranging from inflation to drug abuse.

Much current writing about job enrichment is enthusiastic, sometimes even messianic, about what it can accomplish. But the hard questions of exactly what should be done to improve jobs, and how, tend to be glossed over. Lately, because the harder questions have not been dealt with adequately, critical winds have begun to blow. Job enrichment has been described as yet another "management fad," as "nothing new," even as a fraud. And reports of job-enrichment failures are beginning to appear in management and psychology journals.

This article attempts to redress the excesses that have characterized some of the recent writings about job enrichment. As the technique increases in popularity as a management tool, top managers inevitably will find themselves making decisions about its use. The intent of this paper is to help both managers and behavioral scientists become better able to make those decisions on a solid basis of fact and data.

Succinctly stated, we present here a new strategy for going about the redesign of work. The strategy is based on three years of collaborative work and cross-fertilization among the authors—two of whom are academic researchers and two of whom are active practitioners in job enrichment. Our approach is new, but it has been tested in many organizations. It draws on the contributions of both management practice and psychological theory, but it is firmly in the middle ground between them. It builds on and complements previous work by Herzberg and others, but provides for the first time a set of tools for *diagnosing* existing jobs—and a map for translating the diagnostic results into specific action steps for change.

What we have, then, is the following:

1. A theory that specifies when people will get personally "turned on" to their work. The theory shows what kinds of jobs are most likely to generate excitement and commitment about work, and what kinds of employees it works best for.
2. A set of action steps for job enrichment based on the theory, which prescribe in concrete terms what to do to make jobs more motivating for the people who do them.
3. Evidence that the theory holds water and that it can be used to bring about measurable—and sometimes dramatic—improvements in employee work behavior, in job satisfaction, and in the financial performance of the organizational unit involved.

## The Theory Behind the Strategy

**What makes people get turned on to their work?**    For workers who are really prospering in their jobs, work is likely to be a lot like play. Consider, for example, a golfer at a driving range, practicing to get rid of a hook. His activity is *meaningful* to him; he has chosen to do it because he gets a "kick" from testing his skills by playing the game. He knows that he alone is *responsible* for what happens when he hits the ball. And he has *knowledge of the results* within a few seconds.

Behavioral scientists have found that the three "psychological states" experienced by the golfer in the above example also are critical in determining a person's motivation and satisfaction on the job.

- *Experienced meaningfulness:* The individual must perceive his work as worthwhile or important by some system of values he accepts.
- *Experienced responsibility:* He must believe that he personally is accountable for the outcomes of his efforts.
- *Knowledge of results:* He must be able to determine, on some fairly regular basis, whether or not the outcomes of his work are satisfactory.

When these three conditions are present, a person tends to feel very good about himself when he performs well. And those good feelings will prompt him to try to continue to do well—so he can continue to earn the positive feelings in the future. That is what is meant by "internal motivation"—being turned on to one's work because of the positive internal feelings that are generated by doing well, rather than being dependent on external factors (such as incentive pay or compliments from the boss) for the motivation to work effectively.

What if one of the three psychological states is missing? Motivation drops markedly. Suppose, for example, that our golfer has settled in at the driving range to practice for a couple of hours. Suddenly a fog drifts in over the range. He can no longer see if the ball starts to tail off to the left a hundred yards out. The satisfaction he got from hitting straight down the middle—and the motivation to try to correct something whenever he didn't—are both gone. If the fog stays, it's likely that he soon will be packing up his clubs.

The relationship between the three psychological states and on-the-job outcomes is illustrated in Figure 1. When all three are high, then internal work motivation, job satisfaction, and work quality are high, and absenteeism and turn-over are low.

**What job characteristics make it happen?**     Recent research has identified five "core" characteristics of jobs that elicit the psychological states described above.[6-8] These five core job dimensions provide the key to objectively measuring jobs and to changing them so that they have high potential for motivating people who do them.

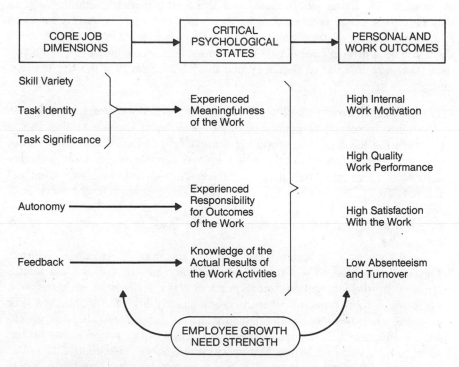

*Figure 1.* Relationships among core job dimensions, critical psychological states, and on-the-job outcomes.

- Toward meaningful work. Three of the five core dimensions contribute to a job's meaningfulness for the worker:

1. Skill Variety—the degree to which a job requires the worker to perform activities that challenge his skills and abilities. When even a single skill is involved, there is at least a seed of potential meaningfulness. When several are involved, the job has the potential of appealing to more of the whole person, and also of avoiding the monotony of performing the same task repeatedly, no matter how much skill it may require.

2. Task Identity—the degree to which the job requires completion of a "whole" and identifiable piece of work—doing a job from beginning to end with a visible outcome. For example, it is clearly more meaningful to an employee to build complete toasters than to attach electrical cord after electrical cord, especially if he never sees a completed toaster. (Note that the whole job, in this example, probably would involve greater skill variety as well as task identity.)

3. Task Significance—the degree to which the job has a substantial and perceivable impact on the lives of other people, whether in the immediate organization or the world at large. The worker who tightens nuts on aircraft brake assemblies is more likely to perceive his work as significant than the worker who fills small boxes with paper clips—even though the skill levels involved may be comparable.

Each of these three job dimensions represents an important route to experienced meaningfulness. If the job is high in all three, the worker is quite likely to experience his job as very meaningful. It is not necessary, however, for a job to be very high in all three dimensions. If the job is low in any one of them, there will be a drop in overall experienced meaningfulness. But even when two dimensions are low the worker may find the job meaningful if the third is high enough.

- Toward personal responsibility. A fourth core dimension leads a worker to experience increased responsibility in his job. This is *autonomy,* the degree to which the job gives the worker freedom, independence, and discretion in scheduling work and determining how he will carry it out. People in highly autonomous jobs know that they are personally responsible for successes and failures. To the extent that their autonomy is high, then, how the work goes will be felt to depend more on the individual's own efforts and initiatives—rather than on detailed instructions from the boss or from a manual of job procedures.
- Toward knowledge of results. The fifth and last core dimension is *feedback.* This is the degree to which a worker, in carrying out the work activities required by the job, gets information about the effectiveness of his efforts. Feedback is most powerful when it comes directly from the work itself—for example, when a worker has the responsibility for gauging and otherwise checking a component he has just finished, and learns in the process that he has lowered his reject rate by meeting specifications more consistently.
- The overall "motivating potential" of a job. Figure 1 shows how the five core dimensions combine to affect the psychological states that are critical in determining whether or not an employee will be internally motivated to work effectively.

Indeed, when using an instrument to be described later, it is possible to compute a "motivating potential score" (MPS) for any job. The MPS provides a single summary index of the degree to which the objective characteristics of the job will prompt high internal work motivation. Following the theory outlined above, a job high in motivating potential must be high in at least one (and hopefully more) of the three dimensions that lead to experienced meaningfulness and high in both autonomy and feedback as well. The MPS provides a quantitative index of the degree to which this is in fact the case (see Appendix for detailed formula). As will be seen later, the MPS can be very useful in diagnosing jobs and in assessing the effectiveness of job-enrichment activities.

**Does the theory work for everybody?** Unfortunately not. Not everyone is able to become internally motivated in his work, even when the motivating potential of a job is very high indeed.

Research has shown that the *psychological needs* of people are very important in determining who can (and who cannot) become internally motivated at work. Some people have strong needs for personal accomplishment, for learning and developing themselves beyond where they are now, for being stimulated and challenged, and so on. These people are high in "growth-need strength."

Figure 2 shows diagrammatically the proposition that individual growth needs have the power to moderate the relationship between the characteristics of jobs and work outcomes. Many workers with high growth needs will turn on eagerly when they have jobs that are high in the core dimensions. Workers whose growth needs are not so strong may respond less eagerly—or, at first, even balk at being "pushed" or "stretched" too far.

Psychologists who emphasize human potential argue that everyone has within him at least a spark of the need to grow and develop personally. Steadily accumulating evidence shows, however, that unless that spark is pretty strong, chances are it will get snuffed out by one's experiences in typical organizations. So, a person who has worked for twenty years in stultifying jobs may find it difficult or impossible to become internally motivated overnight when given the opportunity.

We should be cautious, however, about creating rigid categories of people based on their measured growth-need strength at any particular time. It is true that we can predict from these measures who is likely to become internally

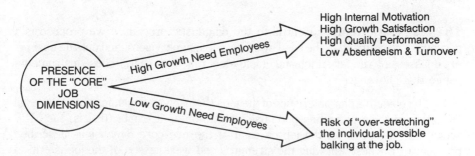

*Figure 2.* The moderating effect of employee growth-need strength.

motivated on a job and who will be less willing or able to do so. But what we do not know yet is whether or not the growth-need "spark" can be rekindled for those individuals who have had their growth needs dampened by years of growth-depressing experience in their organizations.

Since it is often the organization that is responsible for currently low levels of growth desires, we believe that the organization also should provide the individual with the chance to reverse that trend whenever possible, even if that means putting a person in a job where he may be "stretched" more than he wants to be. He can always move back later to the old job—and in the meantime the embers of his growth needs just might burst back into flame, to his surprise and pleasure, and for the good of the organization.

## From Theory to Practice: A Technology for Job Enrichment

When job enrichment fails, it often fails because of inadequate *diagnosis* of the target job and employees' reactions to it. Often, for example, job enrichment is assumed by management to be a solution to "people problems" on the job and is implemented even though there has been no diagnostic activity to indicate that the root of the problem is in fact how the work is designed. At other times, some diagnosis is made—but it provides no concrete guidance about what specific aspects of the job require change. In either case, the success of job enrichment may wind up depending more on the quality of the intuition of the change agent—or his luck—than on a solid base of data about the people and the work.

In the paragraphs to follow, we outline a new technology for use in job enrichment which explicitly addresses the diagnostic as well as the action components of the change process. The technology has two parts: (1) a set of diagnostic tools that are useful in evaluating jobs and people's reactions to them prior to change—and in pinpointing exactly what aspects of specific jobs are most critical to a successful change attempt; and (2) a set of "implementing concepts" that provide concrete guidance for action steps in job enrichment. The implementing concepts are tied directly to the diagnostic tools; the output of the diagnostic activity specifies which action steps are likely to have the most impact in a particular situation.

**The diagnostic tools.** Central to the diagnostic procedure we propose is a package of instruments to be used by employees, supervisors, and outside observers in assessing the target job and employees' reactions to it.[9] These instruments gauge the following:

1. The objective characteristics of the jobs themselves, including both an overall indication of the "motivating potential" of the job as it exists (that is, the MPS score) and the score of the job on each of the five core dimensions described previously. Because knowing the strengths and weaknesses of the job is critical

to any work-redesign effort, assessments of the job are made by supervisors and outside observers as well as the employees themselves—and the final assessment of a job uses data from all three sources.

2. The current levels of motivation, satisfaction, and work performance of employees on the job. In addition to satisfaction with the work itself, measures are taken of how people feel about other aspects of the work setting, such as pay, supervision, and relationships with co-workers.

3. The level of growth-need strength of the employees. As indicated earlier, employees who have strong growth needs are more likely to be more responsive to job enrichment than employees with weak growth needs. Therefore, it is important to know at the outset just what kinds of satisfactions the people who do the job are (and are not) motivated to obtain from their work. This will make it possible to identify which persons are best to start changes with, and which may need help in adapting to the newly enriched job.

What, then, might be the actual steps one would take in carrying out a job diagnosis using these tools? Although the approach to any particular diagnosis depends upon the specifics of the particular work situation involved, the sequence of questions listed below is fairly typical.

- *Step 1. Are motivation and satisfaction central to the problem?* Sometimes organizations undertake job enrichment to improve the work motivation and satisfaction of employees when in fact the real problem with work performance lies elsewhere—for example, in a poorly designed production system, in an error-prone computer, and so on. The first step is to examine the scores of employees on the motivation and satisfaction portions of the diagnostic instrument. (The questionnaire taken by employees is called the Job Diagnostic Survey and will be referred to hereafter as the JDS.) If motivation and satisfaction are problematic, the change agent would continue to Step 2; if not, he would look to other aspects of the work situation to identify the real problem.
- *Step 2. Is the job low in motivating potential?* To answer this question, one would examine the motivating potential score of the target job and compare it to the MPS's of other jobs to determine whether or not *the job itself* is a probable cause of the motivational problems documented in Step 1. If the job turns out to be low on the MPS, one would continue to Step 3; if it scores high, attention should be given to other possible reasons for the motivational difficulties (such as the pay system, the nature of supervision, and so on).
- *Step 3. What specific aspects of the job are causing the difficulty?* This step involves examining the job on each of the five core dimensions to pinpoint the specific strengths and weaknesses of the job as it is currently structured. It is useful at this stage to construct a "profile" of the target job, to make visually apparent where improvements need to be made. An illustrative profile for two jobs (one "good" job and one job needing improvement) is shown in Figure 3.

Job A is an engineering maintenance job and is high on all of the core dimensions; the MPS of this job is a very high 260. (MPS scores can range from 1 to about 350; an "average" score would be about 125.) Job enrichment would

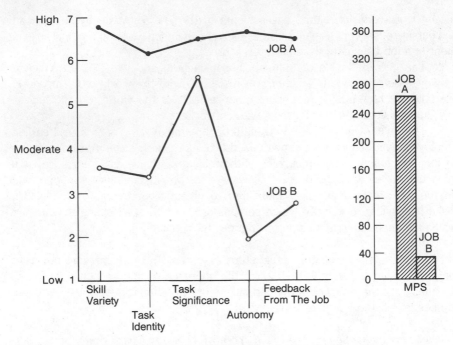

*Figure 3.*    The JDS diagnostic profile for a "good" and a "bad" job.

not be recommended for this job; if employees working on the job were unproductive and unhappy, the reasons are likely to have little to do with the nature or design of the work itself.

Job B, on the other hand, has many problems. This job involves the routine and repetitive processing of checks in the "back room" of a bank. The MPS is 30, which is quite low—and indeed, would be even lower if it were not for the moderately high task significance of the job. (Task significance is moderately high because the people are handling large amounts of other people's money, and therefore the quality of their efforts potentially has important consequences for their unseen clients.) The job provides the individuals with very little direct feedback about how effectively they are doing it; the employees have little autonomy in how they go about doing the job; and the job is moderately low in both skill variety and task identity.

For Job B, then, there is plenty of room for improvement—and many avenues to examine in planning job changes. For still other jobs, the avenues for change often turn out to be considerably more specific: for example, feedback and autonomy may be reasonably high, but one or more of the core dimensions that contribute to the experienced meaningfulness of the job (skill variety, task identity, and task significance) may be low. In such a case, attention would turn to ways to increase the standing of the job on these latter three dimensions.

• *Step 4. How "ready" are the employees for change?* Once it has been documented that there is need for improvement in the job—and the particularly troublesome aspects of the job have been identified—then it is time to begin to think about the specific action steps which will be taken to enrich the job. An important factor in such planning is the level of growth needs of the employees, since employees high on growth needs usually respond more readily to job enrichment than do employees with little need for growth. The JDS provides a direct measure of the growth-need strength of the employees. This measure can be very helpful in planning how to introduce the changes to the people (for instance, cautiously versus dramatically), and in deciding who should be among the first group of employees to have their jobs changed.

In actual use of the diagnostic package, additional information is generated which supplements and expands the basic diagnostic questions outlined above. The point of the above discussion is merely to indicate the kinds of questions which we believe to be most important in diagnosing a job prior to changing it. We now turn to how the diagnostic conclusions are translated into specific job changes.

**The implementing concepts.** Five "implementing concepts" for job enrichment are identified and discussed below.[10] Each one is a specific action step aimed at improving both the quality of the working experience for the individual and his work productivity. They are: (1) forming natural work units; (2) combining tasks; (3) establishing client relationships; (4) vertical loading; (5) opening feedback channels.

The links between the implementing concepts and the core dimensions are shown in Figure 4—which illustrates our theory of job enrichment, ranging from the concrete action steps through the core dimensions and the psychological states to the actual personal and work outcomes.

After completing the diagnosis of a job, a change agent would know which of the core dimensions were most in need of remedial attention. He could then turn to Figure 4 and select those implementing concepts that specifically deal with the most troublesome parts of the existing job. How this would take place in practice will be seen below.

Forming natural work units. The notion of distributing work in some logical way may seem to be an obvious part of the design of any job. In many cases, however, the logic is one imposed by just about any consideration except jobholder satisfaction and motivation. Such considerations include technological dictates, level of worker training or experience, "efficiency" as defined by industrial engineering, and current workload. In many cases the cluster of tasks a worker faces during a typical day or week is natural to anyone *but* the worker.

For example, suppose that a typing pool (consisting of one supervisor and ten typists) handles all work for one division of a company. Jobs are delivered in rough draft or dictated form to the supervisor, who distributes them as evenly as possible among the typists. In such circumstances the individual letters, reports, and other tasks performed by a given typist in one day or week are randomly assigned. There is no basis for identifying with the work or the person or department for whom it is performed, or for placing any personal value upon it.

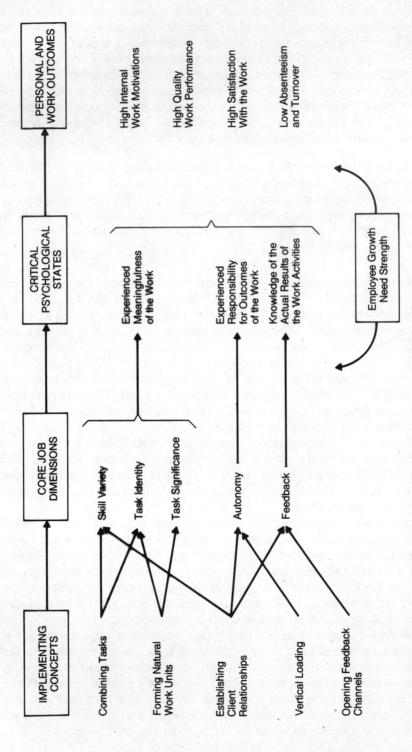

*Figure 4.* The full model: how use of the implementing concepts can lead to positive outcomes.

The principle underlying natural units of work, by contrast, is "ownership"—a worker's sense of continuing responsibility for an identifiable body of work. Two steps are involved in creating natural work units. The first is to identify the basic work items. In the typing pool, for example, the items might be "pages to be typed." The second step is to group the items in natural categories. For example, each typist might be assigned continuing responsibility for all jobs requested by one or several specific departments. The assignments should be made, of course, in such a way that workloads are about equal in the long run. (For example, one typist might end up with all the work from one busy department, while another handles jobs from several smaller units.)

At this point we can begin to see specifically how the job-design principles relate to the core dimensions (cf. Figure 4). The ownership fostered by natural units of work can make the difference between a feeling that work is meaningful and rewarding and the feeling that it is irrelevant and boring. As the diagram shows, natural units of work are directly related to two of the core dimensions: task identity and task significance.

A typist whose work is assigned naturally rather than randomly—say, by departments—has a much greater chance of performing a whole job to completion. Instead of typing one section of a large report, the individual is likely to type the whole thing, with knowledge of exactly what the product of the work is (task identity). Furthermore, over time the typist will develop a growing sense of how the work affects coworkers in the department serviced (task significance).

Combining tasks. The very existence of a pool made up entirely of persons whose sole function is typing reflects a fractionalization of jobs that has been a basic precept of "scientific management." Most obvious in assembly-line work, fractionalization has been applied to nonmanufacturing jobs as well. It is typically justified by efficiency, which is usually defined in terms of either low costs or some time-and-motion type of criteria.

It is hard to find fault with measuring efficiency ultimately in terms of cost-effectiveness. In doing so, however, a manager should be sure to consider *all* the costs involved. It is possible, for example, for highly fractionalized jobs to meet all the time-and-motion criteria of efficiency, but if the resulting job is so unrewarding that performing it day after day leads to high turn-over, absenteeism, drugs and alcohol, and strikes, then productivity is really lower (and costs higher) than data on efficiency might indicate.

The principle of combining tasks, then, suggests that whenever possible existing and fractionalized tasks should be put together to form new and larger modules of work. At the Medfield, Massachusetts plant of Corning Glass Works the assembly of a laboratory hot plate has been redesigned along the lines suggested here. Each hot plate now is assembled from start to finish by one operator, instead of going through several separate operations that are performed by different people.

Some tasks, if combined into a meaningfully large module of work, would be more than an individual could do by himself. In such cases, it is often useful to consider assigning the new, larger task to a small *team* of workers—who are given great autonomy for its completion. At the Racine, Wisconsin plant of Emerson Electric, the assembly process for trash disposal appliances was restructured this way. Instead of a sequence of moving the appliance from station to station, the assembly now is done from start to finish by one team. Such teams include both men and women to permit switching off the heavier and more delicate aspects of the work. The team responsible is identified on the appliance. In case of customer complaints, the team often drafts the reply.

As a job-design principle, task combination, like natural units of work, expands the task identity of the job. For example, the hot-plate assembler can see and identify with a finished product ready for shipment, rather than a nearly invisible junction of solder. Moreover, the more tasks that are combined into a single worker's job, the greater the variety of skills he must call on in performing the job. So task combination also leads directly to greater skill variety—the third core dimension that contributes to the overall experienced meaningfulness of the work.

Establishing client relationships. One consequence of fractionalization is that the typical worker has little or no contact with (or even awareness of) the ultimate user of his product or service. By encouraging and enabling employees to establish direct relationships with the clients of their work, improvements often can be realized simultaneously on three of the core dimensions. Feedback increases, because of additional opportunities for the individual to receive praise or criticism of his work outputs directly. Skill variety often increases, because of the necessity to develop and exercise one's interpersonal skills in maintaining the client relationship. And autonomy can increase because the individual often is given personal responsibility for deciding how to manage his relationships with the clients of his work.

Creating client relationships is a three-step process. First, the client must be identified. Second, the most direct contact possible between the worker and the client must be established. Third, criteria must be set up by which the client can judge the quality of the product or service he receives. And whenever possible, the client should have a means of relaying his judgments directly back to the worker.

The contact between worker and client should be as great as possible and as frequent as necessary. Face-to-face contact is highly desirable, at least occasionally. Where that is impossible or impractical, telephone and mail can suffice. In any case, it is important that the performance criteria by which the worker will be rated by the client must be mutually understood and agreed upon.

Vertical loading. Typically the split between the "doing" of a job and the "planning" and "controlling" of the work has evolved along with horizontal fractionalization. Its rationale, once again, has been "efficiency through specialization." And once again, the excess of specialization that has emerged has resulted in unexpected but significant costs in motivation, morale, and work quality. In vertical loading, the intent is to partially close the gap between the doing and the controlling parts of the job—and thereby reap some important motivational advantages.

Of all the job-design principles, vertical loading may be the single most crucial one. In some cases, where it has been impossible to implement any other changes, vertical loading alone has had significant motivational effects.

When a job is vertically loaded, responsibilities and controls that formerly were reserved for higher levels of management are added to the job. There are many ways to accomplish this:

- Return to the job holder greater discretion in setting schedules, deciding on work methods, checking on quality, and advising or helping to train less experienced workers.
- Grant additional authority. The objective should be to advance workers from a position of no authority or highly restricted authority to positions of reviewed, and eventually, near-total authority for his own work.
- Time management. The job holder should have the greatest possible freedom to decide when to start and stop work, when to break, and how to assign priorities.
- Troubleshooting and crisis decisions. Workers should be encouraged to seek problem solutions on their own, rather than calling immediately for the supervisor.
- Financial controls. Some degree of knowledge and control over budgets and other financial aspects of a job can often be highly motivating. However, access to this information frequently tends to be restricted. Workers can benefit from knowing something about the costs of their jobs, the potential effect upon profit, and various financial and budgetary alternatives.

When a job is vertically loaded it will inevitably increase in *autonomy*. And as shown in Figure 4, this increase in objective personal control over the work will also lead to an increased feeling of personal responsibility for the work, and ultimately to higher internal work motivation.

Opening feedback channels. In virtually all jobs there are ways to open channels of feedback to individuals or teams to help them learn whether their performance is improving, deteriorating, or remaining at a constant level. While there are numerous channels through which information about performance can be provided, it generally is better for a worker to learn about his performance *directly as he does his job*—rather than from management on an occasional basis.

Job-provided feedback usually is more immediate and private than supervisor-supplied feedback, and it increases the worker's feelings of personal control over his work in the bargain. Moreover, it avoids many of the potentially disruptive interpersonal problems that can develop when the only way a worker has to find out how he is doing is through direct messages or subtle cues from the boss.

Exactly what should be done to open channels for job-provided feedback will vary from job to job and organization to organization. Yet in many cases the changes involve simply removing existing blocks that isolate the worker from naturally occurring data about performance—rather than generating entirely new feedback mechanisms. For example:

- Establishing direct client relationships often removes blocks between the worker and natural external sources of data about his work.
- Quality-control efforts in many organizations often eliminate a natural source

*job enrichment perspective*

of feedback. The quality check on a product or service is done by persons other than those responsible for the work. Feedback to the workers—if there is any—is belated and diluted. It often fosters a tendency to think of quality as "someone else's concern." By placing quality control close to the worker (perhaps even in his own hands), the quantity and quality of data about performance available to him can dramatically increase.

- Tradition and established procedure in many organizations dictate that records about performance be kept by a supervisor and transmitted up (not down) in the organizational hierarchy. Sometimes supervisors even check the work and correct any errors themselves. The worker who made the error never knows it occurred—and is denied the very information that could enhance both his internal work motivation and the technical adequacy of his performance. In many cases it is possible to provide standard summaries of performance records directly to the worker (as well as to his superior), thereby giving him personally and regularly the data he needs to improve his performance.

- Computers and other automated operations sometimes can be used to provide the individual with data now blocked from him. Many clerical operations, for example, are now performed on computer consoles. These consoles often can be programmed to provide the clerk with immediate feedback in the form of a CRT display or a printout indicating that an error has been made. Some systems even have been programmed to provide the operator with a positive feedback message when a period of error-free performance has been sustained.

Many organizations simply have not recognized the importance of feedback as a motivator. Data on quality and other aspects of performance are viewed as being of interest only to management. Worse still, the *standards* for acceptable performance often are kept from workers as well. As a result, workers who would be interested in following the daily or weekly ups and downs of their performance, and in trying accordingly to improve, are deprived of the very guidelines they need to do so. They are like the golfer we mentioned earlier, whose efforts to correct his hook are stopped dead by fog over the driving range.

## The Strategy in Action: How Well Does It Work?

So far we have examined a basic theory of how people get turned on to their work; a set of core dimensions of jobs that create the conditions for such internal work motivation to develop on the job; and a set of five implementing concepts that are the action steps recommended to boost a job on the core dimensions and thereby increase employee motivation, satisfaction, and productivity.

The remaining question is straightforward and important: *Does it work?* In reality, that question is twofold. First, does the theory itself hold water, or are we barking up the wrong conceptual tree? And second, does the change strategy really lead to measurable differences when it is applied in an actual organizational setting?

This section summarizes the findings we have generated to date on these questions.

**Is the job-enrichment theory correct?** In general, the answer seems to be yes. The JDS instrument has been taken by more than 1,000 employees working on about 100 diverse jobs in more than a dozen organizations over the last two years. These data have been analyzed to test the basic motivational theory—and especially the impact of the core job dimensions on worker motivation, satisfaction, and behavior on the job. An illustrative overview of some of the findings is given below.

1. People who work on jobs high on the core dimensions are more motivated and satisfied than are people who work on jobs that score low on the dimensions. Employees with jobs high on the core dimensions (MPS scores greater than 240) were compared to those who held unmotivating jobs (MPS scores less than 40). As shown in Figure 5, employees with high MPS jobs were higher on (a) the three psychological states, (b) internal work motivation, (c) general satisfaction, and (d) "growth" satisfaction.

2. Figure 6 shows that the same is true for measures of actual behavior at work—absenteeism and performance effectiveness—although less strongly so for the performance measure.

3. Responses to jobs high in motivating potential are more positive for people who have strong growth needs than for people with weak needs for growth. In Figure 7 the linear relationship between the motivating potential of a job and employees' level of internal work motivation is shown, separately for people with high versus low growth needs as measured by the JDS. While both groups of employees show increases in internal motivation as MPS increases, the *rate*

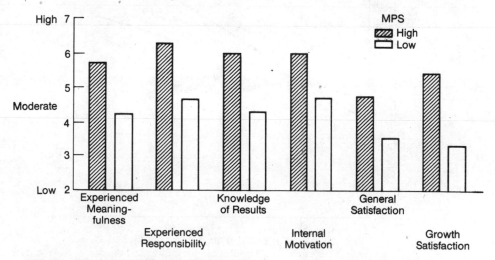

*Figure 5.* Employee reactions to jobs high and low in motivating potential for two banks and a steel firm.

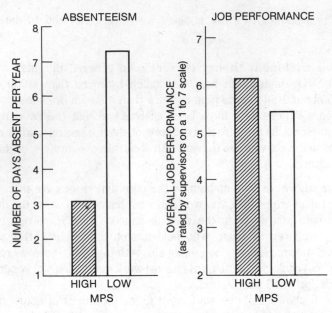

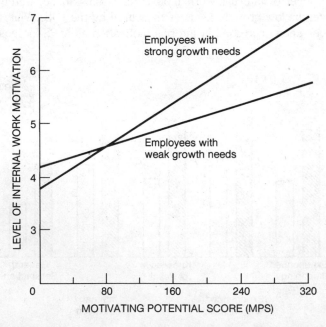

Figure 6.    Absenteeism and job performance for employees with jobs high and low in motivating potential.

Figure 7.    Relationship between the motivating potential of a job and the internal work motivation of employees. (Shown separately for employees with strong versus weak growth-need strength.)

of increase is significantly greater for the group of employees who have strong needs for growth.

**How does the change strategy work in practice?**   The results summarized above suggest that both the theory and the diagnostic instrument work when used with real people in a real organizations. In this section, we summarize a job-enrichment project conducted at The Travelers Insurance Companies, which illustrates how the change procedures themselves work in practice.

The Travelers project was designed with two purposes in mind. One was to achieve improvements in morale, productivity, and other indicators of employee well-being. The other was to test the general effectiveness of the strategy for job enrichment we have summarized in this article.

The work group chosen was a keypunching operation. The group's function was to transfer information from printed or written documents onto punched cards for computer input. The work group consisted of ninety-eight keypunch operators and verifiers (both in the same job classification), plus seven assignment clerks. All reported to a supervisor who, in turn, reported to the assistant manager and manager of the data-input division.

The size of individual punching orders varied considerably, from a few cards to as many as 2,500. Some work came to the work group with a specified delivery date, while other orders were to be given routine service on a predetermined schedule.

Assignment clerks received the jobs from the user departments. After reviewing the work for obvious errors, omissions, and legibility problems, the assignment clerk parceled out the work in batches expected to take about one hour. If the clerk found the work not suitable for punching it went to the supervisor, who either returned the work to the user department or cleared up problems by phone. When work went to operators for punching, it was with the instruction, "Punch only what you see. Don't correct errors, no matter how obvious they look."

Because of the high cost of computer time, keypunched work was 100 percent verified—a task that consumed nearly as many man-hours as the punching itself. Then the cards went to the supervisor, who screened the jobs for due dates before sending them to the computer. Errors detected in verification were assigned to various operators at random to be corrected.

The computer output from the cards was sent to the originating department, accompanied by a printout of errors. Eventually the printout went back to the supervisor for final correction.

A great many phenomena indicated that the problems being experienced in the work group might be the result of poor motivation. As the only person performing supervisory functions of any kind, the supervisor spent most of his time responding to crisis situations, which recurred continually. He also had to deal almost daily with employees' salary grievances or other complaints. Employees frequently showed apathy or outright hostility toward their jobs.

Rates of work output, by accepted work-measurement standards, were inadequate. Error rates were high. Due dates and schedules frequently were missed.

Absenteeism was higher than average, especially before and after weekends and holidays.

The single, rather unusual exception was turnover. It was lower than the companywide average for similar jobs. The company has attributed this fact to a poor job market in the base period just before the project began, and to an older, relatively more settled work force—made up, incidentally, entirely of women.

**The diagnosis.**   Using some of the tools and techniques we have outlined, a consulting team from the Management Services Department and from Roy W. Walters & Associates concluded that the keypunch-operator's job exhibited the following serious weaknesses in terms of the core dimensions.

- Skill variety: there was none. Only a single skill was involved—the ability to punch adequately the data on the batch of documents.
- Task identity: virtually nonexistent. Batches were assembled to provide an even workload, but not whole identifiable jobs.
- Task significance: not apparent. The keypunching operation was a necessary step in providing service to the company's customers. The individual operator was isolated by an assignment clerk and a supervisor from any knowledge of what the operation meant to the using department, let alone its meaning to the ultimate customer.
- Autonomy: none. The operators had no freedom to arrange their daily tasks to meet schedules, to resolve problems with the using department, or even to correct, in punching, information that was obviously wrong.
- Feedback: none. Once a batch was out of the operator's hands, she had no assured chance of seeing evidence of its quality or inadequacy.

**Design of the experimental trial.**   Since the diagnosis indicated that the motivating potential of the job was extremely low, it was decided to attempt to improve the motivation and productivity of the work group through job enrichment. Moreover, it was possible to design an experimental test of the effects of the changes to be introduced: the results of changes made in the target work group were to be compared with trends in a control work group of similar size and demographic make-up. Since the control group was located more than a mile away, there appeared to be little risk of communication between members of the two groups.

A base period was defined before the start of the experimental trial period, and appropriate data were gathered on the productivity, absenteeism, and work attitudes of members of both groups. Data also were available on turnover; but since turnover was already below average in the target group, prospective changes in this measure were deemed insignificant.

An educational session was conducted with supervisors, at which they were given the theory and implementing concepts and actually helped to design the job changes themselves. Out of this session came an active plan consisting of about twenty-five change items that would significantly affect the design of the target jobs.

**The implementing concepts and the changes.** Because the job as it existed was rather uniformly low on the core job dimensions, all five of the implementing concepts were used in enriching it.

- Natural units of work. The random batch assignment of work was replaced by assigning to each operator continuing responsibility for certain accounts— either particular departments or particular recurring jobs. Any work for those accounts now always goes to the same operator.
- Task combination. Some planning and controlling functions were combined with the central task of keypunching. In this case, however, these additions can be more suitably discussed under the remaining three implementing concepts.
- Client relationships. Each operator was given several channels of direct contact with clients. The operators, not their assignment clerks, now inspect their documents for correctness and legibility. When problems arise, the operator, not the supervisor, takes them up with the client.
- Feedback. In addition to feedback from client contact, the operators were provided with a number of additional sources of data about their performance. The computer department now returns incorrect cards to the operators who punched them, and operators correct their own errors. Each operator also keeps her own file of copies of her errors. These can be reviewed to determine trends in error frequency and types of errors. Each operator receives weekly a computer printout of her errors and productivity, which is sent to her directly, rather than given to her by the supervisor.
- Vertical loading. Besides consulting directly with clients about work questions, operators now have the authority to correct obvious coding errors on their own. Operators may set their own schedules and plan their daily work, as long as they meet schedules. Some competent operators have been given the option of not verifying their work and making their own program changes.

**Results of the trial.** The results were dramatic. The number of operators declined from ninety-eight to sixty. This occurred partly through attrition and partly through transfer to other departments. Some of the operators were promoted to higher-paying jobs in departments whose cards they had been handling— something that had never occurred before. Some details of the results are given below.

- Quantity of work. The control group, with no job changes made, showed an increase in productivity of 8.1 percent during the trial period. The experimental group showed an increase of 39.6 percent.
- Error rates. To assess work quality, error rates were recorded for about forty operators in the experimental group. All were experienced, and all had been in their jobs before the job-enrichment program began. For two months before the study, these operators had a collective error rate of 1.53 percent. For two months toward the end of the study, the collective error rate was 0.99 percent. By the end of the study the number of operators with poor performance had dropped from 11.1 percent to 5.5 percent.
- Absenteeism. The experimental group registered a 24.1 percent decline in absences. The control group, by contrast, showed a 29 percent *increase*.

- Attitudes toward the job. An attitude survey given at the start of the project showed that the two groups scored about average, and nearly identically, in nine different areas of work satisfaction. At the end of the project the survey was repeated. The control group showed an insignificant 0.5 percent improvement, while the experimental group's overall satisfaction score rose 16.5 percent.
- Selective elimination of controls. Demonstrated improvements in operator proficiency permitted them to work with fewer controls. Travelers estimates that the reduction of controls had the same effect as adding seven operators—a saving even beyond the effects of improved productivity and lowered absenteeism.
- Role of the supervisor. One of the most significant findings in the Travelers experiment was the effect of the changes on the supervisor's job, and thus on the rest of the organization. The operators took on many responsibilities that had been reserved at least to the unit leaders and sometimes to the supervisor. The unit leaders, in turn, assumed some of the day-to-day supervisory functions that had plagued the supervisor. Instead of spending his days supervising the behavior of subordinates and dealing with crises, he was able to devote time to developing feedback systems, setting up work modules and spearheading the enrichment effort—in other words, managing. It should be noted, however, that helping supervisors change their own work activities when their subordinates' jobs have been enriched is itself a challenging task. And if appropriate attention and help are not given to supervisors in such cases, they rapidly can become disaffected—and a job-enrichment "backlash" can result.[11]

**Summary.**   By applying work-measurement standards to the changes wrought by job enrichment—attitude and quality, absenteeism, and selective administration of controls—Travelers was able to estimate the total dollar impact of the project. Actual savings in salaries and machine rental charges during the first year totaled $64,305. Potential savings by further application of the changes were put at $91,937 annually. Thus, by almost any measure used—from the work attitudes of individual employees to dollar savings for the company as a whole—The Travelers test of the job-enrichment strategy proved a success.

## Conclusions

In this article we have presented a new strategy for the redesign of work in general and for job enrichment in particular. The approach has four main characteristics:

1. It is grounded in a basic psychological theory of what motivates people in their work.
2. It emphasizes that planning for job changes should be done on the basis of *data* about the jobs and the people who do them—and a set of diagnostic instruments is provided to collect such data.

3. It provides a set of specific implementing concepts to guide actual job changes, as well as a set of theory-based rules for selecting *which* action steps are likely to be most beneficial in a given situation.
4. The strategy is buttressed by a set of findings showing that the theory holds water, that the diagnostic procedures are practical and informative, and that the implementing concepts can lead to changes that are beneficial both to organizations and to the people who work in them.

We believe that job enrichment is moving beyond the stage where it can be considered "yet another management fad." Instead, it represents a potentially powerful strategy for change that can help organizations achieve their goals for higher quality work—and at the same time further the equally legitimate needs of contemporary employees for a more meaningful work experience. Yet there are pressing questions about job enrichment and its use that remain to be answered.

Prominent among these is the question of employee participation in planning and implementing work redesign. The diagnostic tools and implementing concepts we have presented are neither designed nor intended for use only by management. Rather, our belief is that the effectiveness of job enrichment is likely to be enhanced when the tasks of diagnosing and changing jobs are undertaken *collaboratively* by management and by the employees whose work will be affected.

Moreover, the effects of work redesign on the broader organization remain generally uncharted. Evidence now is accumulating that when jobs are changed, turbulence can appear in the surrounding organization—for example, in supervisory-subordinate relationships, in pay and benefit plans, and so on. Such turbulence can be viewed by management either as a problem with job enrichment, or as an opportunity for further and broader organizational development by teams of managers and employees. To the degree that management takes the latter view, we believe, the oft-espoused goal of achieving basic organizational change through the redesign of work may come increasingly within reach.

The diagnostic tools and implementing concepts we have presented are useful in deciding on and designing basic changes in the jobs themselves. They do not address the broader issues of who plans the changes, how they are carried out, and how they are followed up. The way these broader questions are dealt with, we believe, may determine whether job enrichment will grow up—or whether it will die an early and unfortunate death, like so many other fledgling behavioral-science approaches to organizational change.

**Appendix:**
For the algebraically inclined, the Motivating Potential Score is computed as follows

$$\text{MPS} = \left[ \frac{\text{Skill Variety} + \text{Task Identify} + \text{Task Significance}}{3} \right] \times \frac{\text{Auto-}}{\text{nomy}} \times \frac{\text{Feed-}}{\text{back}}$$

It should be noted that in some cases the MPS score can be *too* high for positive job satisfaction and effective performance—in effect overstimulating the person who holds the job. This paper focuses on jobs which are toward the low end of the scale—and which potentially can be improved through job enrichment.

*Acknowledgments: The authors acknowledge with great appreciation the editorial assistance of John Hickey in the preparation of this paper, and the help of Kenneth Brousseau, Daniel Feldman, and Linda Frank in collecting the data that are summarized here. The research activities reported were supported in part by the Organizational Effectiveness Research Program of the Office of Naval Research, and the Manpower Administration of the U.S. Department of Labor, both through contracts to Yale University.*

## FOOTNOTES

1.  F. Herzberg, B. Mausner and B. Snyderman, *The Motivation to Work* (New York: John Wiley & Sons, 1959).

2.  F. Herzberg, *Work and the Nature of Man* (Cleveland: World, 1966).

3.  F. Herzberg, "One More Time: How Do You Motivate Employees?" *Harvard Business Review* (1968), pp. 53–62.

4.  W. J. Paul, Jr.; K. B. Robertson and F. Herzberg, "Job Enrichment Pays Off," *Harvard Business Review* (1969), pp. 61–78.

5.  R. N. Ford, *Motivation Through the Work Itself* (New York: American Management Association, 1969).

6.  A. N. Turner and P. R. Lawrence, *Industrial Jobs and the Worker* (Cambridge, Mass.: Harvard Graduate School of Business Administration, 1965).

7.  J. R. Hackman and E. E. Lawler, "Employee Reactions to Job Characteristics," *Journal of Applied Psychology Monograph* (1971), pp. 259–286.

8.  J. R. Hackman and G. R. Oldham, *Motivation Through the Design of Work: Test of a Theory,* Technical Report No. 6, Department of Administrative Sciences, Yale University, 1974.

9.  J. R. Hackman and G. R. Oldham, "Development of the Job Diagnostic Survey," *Journal of Applied Psychology* (1975), pp. 159–170.

10.  R. W. Walters and Associates, *Job Enrichment for Results* (Cambridge, Mass.: Addison-Wesley, 1975).

11.  E. E. Lawler III; J. R. Hackman, and S. Kaufman, "Effects of Job Redesign: A Field Experiment," *Journal of Applied Social Psychology* (1973), pp. 49–62.

---

## *Learning Review*

*Questions:*

1.  The three states which are critical in determining internal motivation are: _____, _____, and _____.

2.  Core dimensions of jobs include _____, _____, _____, _____, and _____.

3. The extent to which individual workers are motivated by job enrichment depends upon their _____-_____ needs.

4. Successful job enrichment involves _____ and implementation of _____.

5. Autonomy can be increased by _____ and _____.

6. Task identity can be increased by _____ and _____.

7. Task significance can be increased by _____.

8. Skill variety can be increased by _____ and _____.

**Answers:**

1. experienced meaningfulness, experienced responsibility, knowledge of results; 2. skill variety, task identity, task significance, autonomy, feedback; 3. growth-strength; 4. job diagnosis, motivating factors; 5. establishing client relations, vertical loading; 6. forming natural work units, combining tasks; 7. forming natural work units; 8. combining tasks, establishing client relationships.

---

# Retrospective Comment

♦

## BY J. RICHARD HACKMAN

It was great fun writing the article reprinted here. This was the first time that Oldham and I had written something collaboratively with people who spend their time out in the world making a living by fostering constructive organizational change. And although Janson and Purdy had previously published some of their ideas, this was the first time they had collaborated with academics in writing an article. The excitement was high, and the disagreements were vigorous. As I look back on the product, I wish both we and they had been just a little more adventuresome in moving away from the ways of thinking with which we were most familiar and comfortable.

In retrospect, I think Oldham and I let ourselves be too constrained by the trappings of science, particularly cause-effect theorizing. We wanted to specify the exact causal relations between job characteristics and psychological states, and between implementing concepts and job characteristics. I now have less confidence in the usefulness of such tightly linked causal models for understanding and changing social systems, preferring instead nondeterministic models that address the multiple *conditions* that increase the likelihood that people will choose some behaviors over others. Moreover, the notions of redundant causation and overdetermination of outcomes, not addressed in our paper, now strike me as key to understanding behavior in social systems (see, for example, Hackman, 1985).

On the other side of the collaboration, Janson and Purdy may have been a bit too committed to step-by-step strategies for organizational change, in which change agents proceed sequentially from problem definition through diagnosis to action planning, implementation, and evaluation. In retrospect, change processes involving work redesign turn out to be more opportunistic and political than is suggested in our article. The Job Diagnostic Survey, for example, can be quite useful as one tool for assessing the state of a work system, but it is only one of many ways to assess the motivational properties of jobs—and it is not always the best way. (Particularly painful to me are reports I occasionally hear of people using the JDS—or some home-brew adaptation of it—as their *only* means of assessing a work system prior to change, something that none of the authors of the article would ever have advocated. The JDS is an aid to thought, not a substitute for it.)

Were I writing this article today, I would make some changes along the lines outlined above. But I would not change the main message. Research and experience since 1975 have affirmed that how work is set up powerfully influences what happens in organizations, and that work redesign is one viable "handle" for initiating constructive organizational change. Things really do turn out better for people, and for the organizations where they work, when the work is meaningful to the people who do it, when they have lots of autonomy to decide how to carry it out, and when they receive regular, trustworthy data about how well they are performing.

# REFERENCE

Hackman, J. R. "Doing research that makes a difference." In E. E. Lawler, A. M. Mohrman, S. A. Mohrman, G. E. Ledford & T. G. Cummings (Eds.), *Doing research that is useful for theory and practice.* San Francisco: Jossey-Bass, 1985.

# 21

## *Path-Goal Theory of Leadership*

### ROBERT J. HOUSE

### TERENCE R. MITCHELL

## *About the Authors*

**Robert J. House** is the Shell Professor of Organization Behavior at the University of Toronto. He received his Ph.D. from Ohio State University in 1960. Dr. House holds a B.S. and MBA from the University of Detroit and has previously taught at Bernard M. Baruch College, the University of Michigan, and at Ohio State University. He also served as Executive Director of the McKinsey Foundation for Management Research from 1965 to 1968, and has worked as a management development specialist in industry.

Dr. House has published approximately fifty articles in business and academic journals and is author or co-author of five books including (with Allen Filley and Steven Kerr) the widely used text, *Managerial Process and Organizational Behavior* (Scott, Foresman, 1976). He is a Fellow of the Academy of Management and the American Psychological Association and a member of the editorial review boards of the Academy of Management Review, *Canadian Journal of Behavioural Science,* and *Exchange: The Organizational Behavior Teaching Journal.*

**Terence R. Mitchell** is Edward E. Carlson Professor of Business Administration and Professor of Psychology at the University of Washington. He earned an Advanced Diploma in Public Administration at the University of Exeter, and his M.A. and Ph.D. in Social Psychology at the University of Illinois. He is the author of numerous articles and has recently co-authored two books: *People*

From Robert J. House and Terence R. Mitchell, "Path-Goal Theory of Leadership", *Journal of Contemporary Business,* Autumn 1974, pp. 81–97. Reprinted by permission of the authors and publisher.

341

*in Organizations* (McGraw-Hill, 1987, with J. Larson) and *Organization Theory: A Structural and Behavioral Analysis* (Irwin-Dorsey, 1987, with Birnbaum and Scott). He is currently studying leadership and subordinate motivation in several organizational settings.

# PREVIEW

A. Historical foundations of the path-goal theory.
   1. Path-goal theory has its roots in the expectancy theory of motivation.
   2. Early studies focused on leadership and its effect on the paths and goals of subordinates.
   3. Later studies attempted to explain the effects of specific kinds of leader behavior on various subordinate expectations.
   4. Studies show that different leadership styles may be utilized by the same leader in various situations.
B. Path-goal theory of motivation.
   1. Theory is based on three general propositions.
   2. Two classes of situational variables are asserted to be contingency factors: subordinate characteristics and environmental factors.
   3. The contingency factors possess certain characteristics which will influence the preferred leadership style.
C. Empirical support for the path-goal theory.
   1. Leader directiveness has a positive effect on subordinates' satisfaction when they are involved in ambiguous tasks and a negative effect when clear tasks are involved.
   2. The achievement-oriented leader is more effective when ambiguous, non-repetitive tasks are involved.
   3. Supportive leadership is most effective for subordinates who work on stressful, frustrating, or dissatisfying tasks.

An integrated body of conjecture by students of leadership, referred to as the "Path-Goal Theory of Leadership," is currently emerging. According to this theory, leaders are effective because of their impact on subordinates' motivation, ability to perform effectively and satisfactions. The theory is called Path-Goal because its major concern is how the leader influences the subordinates' perceptions of their work goals, personal goals and paths to goal attainment. The theory suggests that a leader's behavior is motivating or satisfying to the degree that the behavior increases subordinate goal attainment and clarifies the paths to these goals.

## Historical Foundations

The path-goal approach has its roots in a more general motivational theory called expectancy theory.[1] Briefly, expectancy theory states that an individual's attitudes (e.g., satisfaction with supervision or job satisfaction) or behavior (e.g., leader behavior or job effort) can be predicted from: (1) the degree to which the job, or behavior, is seen as leading to various outcomes (expectancy) and (2) the evaluation of these outcomes (valences). Thus, people are satisfied with their job if they think it leads to things that are highly valued, and they work hard if they believe that effort leads to things that are highly valued. This type of theoretical rationale can be used to predict a variety of phenomena related to leadership, such as why leaders behave the way they do, or how leader behavior influences subordinate motivation.[2]

This latter approach is the primary concern of this article. The implication for leadership is that subordinates are motivated by leader behavior to the extent that this behavior influences expectancies, e.g., goal paths and valences, e.g., goal attractiveness.

Several writers have advanced specific hypotheses concerning how the leader affects the paths and the goals of subordinates.[3] These writers focused on two issues: (1) how the leader affects subordinates' expectations that effort will lead to effective performance and valued rewards, and (2) how this expectation affects motivation to work hard and perform well.

While the state of theorizing about leadership in terms of subordinates' paths and goals is in its infancy, we believe it is promising for two reasons. First, it suggest effects of leader behavior that have not yet been investigated but which appear to be fruitful areas of inquiry. And, second, it suggests with some precision the situational factors on which the effects of leader behavior are contingent.

The initial theoretical work by Evans asserts that leaders will be effective by making rewards available to subordinates and by making these rewards contingent on the subordinate's accomplishment of specific goals.[4] Evans argued that one of the strategic functions of the leader is to clarify for subordinates the kind of behavior that leads to goal accomplishment and valued rewards. This function might be referred to as path clarification. Evans also argued that the leader increases the rewards available to subordinates by being supportive toward subordinates, i.e., by being concerned about their status, welfare and comfort. Leader supportiveness is in itself a reward that the leader has at his or her disposal, and the judicious use of this reward increases the motivation of subordinates.

Evans studied the relationship between the behavior of leaders and the subordinates' expectations that effort leads to rewards and also studied the resulting impact on ratings of the subordinates' performance. He found that when subordinates viewed leaders as being supportive (considerate of their needs) and when these superiors provided directions and guidance to the subordinates, there was a positive relationship between leader behavior and subordinates' performance ratings.

However, leader behavior was only related to subordinates' performance when the leader's behavior also was related to the subordinates' expectations that their effort would result in desired rewards. Thus, Evans' findings suggest that the major impact of a leader on the performance of subordinates is clarifying the path to desired rewards and making such rewards contingent on effective performance.

Stimulated by this line of reasoning, House, and House and Dessler advanced a more complex theory of the effects of leader behavior on the motivation of subordinates.[5] The theory intends to explain the effects of four specific kinds of leader behavior on the following three subordinate attitudes or expectations: (1) the satisfaction of subordinates, (2) the subordinates' acceptance of the leader and (3) the expectations of subordinates that effort will result in effective performance and that effective performance is the path to rewards. The four kinds of leader behavior included in the theory are: (1) directive leadership, (2) supportive leadership, (3) participative leadership and (4) achievement-oriented leadership. Directive leadership is characterized by a leader who lets subordinates know what is expected of them, gives specific guidance as to what should be done and how it should be done, makes his or her part in the group understood, schedules work to be done, maintains definite standards of performance and asks that group members follow standard rules and regulations. Supportive leadership is characterized by a friendly and approachable leader who shows concern for the status, well-being and needs of subordinates. Such a leader does little things to make the work more pleasant, treats members as equals and is friendly and approachable. Participative leadership is characterized by a leader who consults with subordinates, solicits their suggestions and takes these suggestions seriously into consideration before making a decision. An achievement-oriented leader sets challenging goals, expects subordinates to perform at their highest level, continuously seeks improvement in performance *and* shows a high degree of confidence that the subordinates will assume responsibility, put forth effort and accomplish challenging goals. This kind of leader constantly emphasizes excellence in performance and simultaneously displays confidence that subordinates will meet high standards of excellence.

A number of studies suggest that these different leadership styles can be shown by the same leader in various situations.[6] For example, a leader may show directiveness toward subordinates in some instances and be participative or supportive in other instances.[7] Thus, the traditional method of characterizing a leader as either highly participative and supportive *or* highly directive is invalid; rather, it can be concluded that leaders vary in the particular fashion employed for supervising their subordinates. Also, the theory, in its present stage, is a tentative explanation of the effects of leader behavior—it is incomplete because it does not explain other kinds of leader behavior and does not explain the effects of the leader on factors other than subordinate acceptance, satisfaction and expectations. However, the theory is stated so that additional variables may be included in it as new knowledge is made available.

## Path-Goal Theory

### General Propositions

The first proposition of path-goal theory is that leader behavior is acceptable and satisfying to subordinates to the extent that the subordinates see such behavior as either an immediate source of satisfaction or as instrumental to future satisfaction.

The second proposition of this theory is that the leader's behavior will be motivational, i.e., increase effort, to the extent that (1) such behavior makes satisfaction of subordinate's needs contingent on effective performance and (2) such behavior complements the environment of subordinates by providing the coaching, guidance, support and rewards necessary for effective performance.

These two propositions suggest that the leader's strategic functions are to enhance subordinates' motivation to perform, satisfaction with the job and acceptance of the leader. From previous research on expectancy theory of motivation, it can be inferred that the strategic functions of the leader consist of: (1) recognizing and/or arousing subordinates' needs for outcomes over which the leader has some control, (2) increasing personal payoffs to subordinates for work-goal attainment, (3) making the path to those payoffs easier to travel by coaching and direction, (4) helping subordinates clarify expectancies, (5) reducing frustrating barriers and (6) increasing the opportunities for personal satisfaction contingent on effective performance.

Stated less formally, the motivational functions of the leader consist of increasing the number and kinds of personal payoffs to subordinates for work-goal attainment and making paths to these payoffs easier to travel by clarifying the paths, reducing road blocks and pitfalls and increasing the opportunities for personal satisfaction en route.

## Contingency Factors

Two classes of situational variables are asserted to be contingency factors. A contingency factor is a variable which moderates the relationship between two other variables such as leader behavior and subordinate satisfaction. For example, we might suggest that the degree of structure in the task moderates the relationship between leaders' directive behavior and subordinates' job satisfaction. Figure I shows how such a relationship might look. Thus, subordinates are satisfied with directive behavior in an unstructured task and are satisfied with nondirective behavior in a structured task. Therefore, we say that the relationship between leader directiveness and subordinate satisfaction is contingent upon the structure of the task.

The two contingency variables are (a) personal characteristics of the subordinates and (b) the environmental pressures and demands with which subordinates must cope in order to accomplish the work goals and to satisfy their needs. While other situational factors also may operate to determine the effects of leader behavior, they are not presently known.

With respect to the first class of contingency factors, the characteristics of subordinates, path-goal theory asserts that leader behavior will be acceptable to subordinates to the extent that the subordinates see such behavior as either an immediate source of satisfaction or as instrumental to future satisfaction. Subordinates' characteristics are hypothesized to partially determine this perception. For example, Runyon[8] and Mitchell[9] show that the subordinate's score on a measure called Locus of Control moderates the relationship between participative leadership style and subordinate satisfaction. The Locus-of-Control measure reflects the degree to which an individual sees the environment as systematically

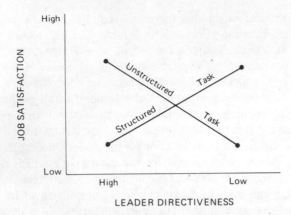

*Figure 1*  Hypothetical relationship between directive leadership and subordinate satisfaction with task structure as a contingency factor.

responding to his or her behavior. People who believe that what happens to them occurs because of their behavior are called internals; people who believe that what happens to them occurs because of luck or chance are called externals. Mitchell's findings suggest that internals are more satisfied with a participative leadership style and externals are more satisfied with a directive style.

A second characteristic of subordinates on which the effects of leader behavior are contingent is subordinates' perception of their own ability with respect to their assigned tasks. The higher the degree of perceived ability relative to task demands, the less the subordinate will view leader directiveness and coaching behavior as acceptable. Where the subordinate's perceived ability is high, such behavior is likely to have little positive effect on the motivation of the subordinate and to be perceived as excessively close control. Thus, the acceptability of the leader's behavior is determined in part by the characteristics of the subordinates.

The second aspect of the situation, the environment of the subordinate, consists of those factors that are not within the control of the subordinate but which are important to need satisfaction or to ability to perform effectively. The theory asserts that effects of the leader's behavior on the psychological states of subordinates are contingent on other parts of the subordinates' environment that are relevant to subordinate motivation. Three broad classifications of contingency factors in the environment are:

• The subordinates' tasks
• The formal authority system of the organization
• The primary work group.

Assessment of the environmental conditions makes it possible to predict the kind and amount of influence that specific leader behaviors will have on the motivation of subordinates. Any of the three environmental factors could act upon the subordinate in any of three ways: first, to serve as stimuli that motivate and direct the subordinate to perform necessary task operations; second, to constrain variability in behavior. Constraints may help the subordinate by clarifying expectancies that effort leads to rewards or by preventing the subordinate from experiencing conflict and confusion. Constraints also may be counter-productive to the extent that they restrict initiative or prevent increases in effort from being associated positively with rewards. Third, environmental factors may serve as rewards for achieving desired performance, e.g., it is possible for the subordinate to receive the necessary cues to do the job and the needed rewards for satisfaction from sources other than the leader, e.g., coworkers in the primary work group. Thus, the effect of the leader on subordinates' motivation will be a function of how deficient the environment is with respect to motivational stimuli, constraints or rewards.

With respect to the environment, path-goal theory asserts that when goals and paths to desired goals are apparent because of the routine nature of the task, clear group norms or objective controls of the formal authority systems, attempts by the leader to clarify paths and goals will be both redundant and seen by subordinates as imposing unnecessary, close control. Although such control may increase performance by preventing soldiering or malingering, it also will result in decreased satisfaction (see Figure I). Also with respect to the work environment, the theory asserts that the more dissatisfying the task, the more the subordinates will resent leader behavior directed at increasing productivity or enforcing compliance to organizational rules and procedures.

Finally, with respect to environmental variables the theory states that leader behavior will be motivational to the extent that it helps subordinates cope with environmental uncertainties, threats from others or sources of frustration. Such leader behavior is predicted to increase subordinates' satisfaction with the job context and to be motivational to the extent that it increases the subordinates' expectations that their effort will lead to valued rewards.

These propositions and specification of situational contingencies provide a heuristic framework on which to base future research. Hopefully, this will lead to a more fully developed, explicitly formal theory of leadership.

Figure II presents a summary of the theory. It is hoped that these propositions, while admittedly tentative, will provide managers with some insights concerning the effects of their own leader behavior and that of others.

| Leader behavior | and | Contingency factors | | Cause | Subordinate attitudes and behavior |
|---|---|---|---|---|---|
| 1 Directive | | 1 Subordinate characteristics | | Personal perceptions | 1 Job satisfaction Job → Rewards |
| 2 Supportive | | Authoritarianism Locus of control | *influence* | | |
| 3 Achievement-oriented | | Ability | | | 2 Acceptance of leader Leader → Rewards |
| 4 Participative | | 2 Environmental factors The task Formal authority system Primary work group | *influence* | Motivational stimuli Constraints Rewards | 3 Motivational behavior Effort → Performance Performance → Rewards |

*Figure II*    Summary of Path-Goal Relationships

## Empirical Support

The theory has been tested in a limited number of studies which have generated considerable empirical support for our ideas and also suggest areas in which the theory requires revision. A brief review of these studies follows.

### Leader Directiveness

Leader directiveness has a positive correlation with satisfaction and expectancies of subordinates who are engaged in ambiguous tasks and has a negative correlation with satisfaction and expectancies of subordinates engaged in clear tasks. These findings were predicted by the theory and have been replicated in seven organizations. They suggest that when task demands are ambiguous or when the organization procedures, rules and policies are not clear, a leader behaving in a directive manner complements the tasks and the organization by providing the necessary guidance and psychological structure for subordinates.[10] However, when task demands are clear to subordinates, leader directiveness is seen more as a hindrance.

However, other studies have failed to confirm these findings.[11] A study by Dessler [12] suggests a resolution to these conflicting findings—he found that for subordinates at the lower organizational levels of a manufacturing firm who were doing routine, repetitive, unambiguous tasks, directive leadership was preferred by closed-minded, dogmatic, authoritarian subordinates and nondirective leadership was preferred by nonauthoritarian, open-minded subordinates. However, for subordinates at higher organizational levels doing nonroutine, ambiguous tasks, directive leadership was preferred for both authoritarian and nonauthoritarian subordinates. Thus, Dessler found that two contingency factors appear to operate simultaneously: subordinate task ambiguity and degree of subordinate authoritarianism. When measured in combination, the findings are as predicted by the theory; however, when the subordinate's personality is not taken into account, task ambiguity does not always operate as a contingency variable as predicted by the theory. House, Burill and Dessler recently found a similar interaction between subordinate authoritarianism and task ambiguity in a second manufacturing firm, thus adding confidence in Dessler's original findings.[13]

### Supportive Leadership

The theory hypothesizes that supportive leadership will have its most positive effect on subordinate satisfaction for subordinates who work on stressful, frustrating or dissatisfying tasks. This hypothesis has been tested in 10 samples of employees,[14] and in only one of these studies was the hypothesis disconfirmed.[15] Despite some inconsistency in research on supportive leadership, the evidence is sufficiently positive to suggest that managers should be alert to the critical need for supportive leadership under conditions where tasks are dissatisfying, frustrating or stressful to subordinates.

### Achievement-Oriented Leadership

The theory hypothesizes that achievement-oriented leadership will cause subordinates to strive for higher standards of performance and to have more confidence in the ability to meet challenging goals. A recent study by House, Valency and Van der Krabben provides a partial test of this hypothesis among white collar employees in service organizations.[16] For subordinates performing ambiguous, nonrepetitive tasks, they found a positive relationship between the amount of achievement orientation of the leader and subordinates' expectancy that their effort would result in effective performance. Stated less technically, for subordinates performing ambiguous, nonrepetitive tasks, the higher the achievement orientation of the leader, the more the subordinates were confident that their efforts would pay off in effective performance. For subordinates performing moderately unambiguous, repetitive tasks, there was no significant relationship between achievement-oriented leadership and subordinate expectancies that their effort would lead to effective performance. This finding held in four separate organizations.

Two plausible interpretations may be used to explain these data. First, people who select ambiguous, nonrepetitive tasks may be different in personality from those who select a repetitive job and may, therefore, be more responsive to an achievement-oriented leader. A second explanation is that achievement orientation only affects expectancies in ambiguous situations because there is more flexibility and autonomy in such tasks. Therefore, subordinates in such tasks are more likely to be able to change in response to such leadership style. Neither of the above interpretations have been tested to date; however, additional research is currently under way to investigate these relationships.

## Participative Leadership

In theorizing about the effects of participative leadership it is necessary to ask about the specific characteristics of both the subordinates and their situation that would cause participative leadership to be viewed as satisfying and instrumental to effective performance.

Mitchell recently described at least four ways in which a participative leadership style would impact on subordinate attitudes and behavior as predicted by expectancy theory.[17] First, a participative climate should increase the clarity of organizational contingencies. Through participation in decision making, subordinates should learn what leads to what. From a path-goal viewpoint participation would lead to greater clarity of the paths to various goals. A second impact of participation would be that subordinates, hopefully, should select goals they highly value. If one participates in decisions about various goals, it makes sense that this individual would select goals he or she wants. Thus, participation would increase the correspondence between organization and subordinate goals. Third, we can see how participation would increase the control the individual has over what happens on the job. If our motivation is higher (based on the preceding two points), then having greater autonomy and ability to carry out our intentions should lead to increased effort and performance. Finally, under a participative system, pressure towards high performance should come from sources other than the leader or the organization. More specifically, when people participate in the decision process they become more ego-involved; the decisions made are in some part their own. Also, their peers know what is expected and the social pressure has a greater impact. Thus, motivation to perform well stems from internal and social factors as well as formal external ones.

A number of investigations prior to the above formulation supported the idea that participation appears to be helpful,[18] and Mitchell presents a number of recent studies that support the above four points.[19] However, it is also true that we would expect the relationship between a participative style and subordinate behavior to be moderated by both the personality characteristics of the subordinate and the situational demands. Studies by Tannenbaum and Allport and Vroom have shown that subordinates who prefer autonomy and self-control respond more positively to participative leadership in terms of both satisfaction and performance than subordinates who do not have such preferences.[20] Also, the studies mentioned by Runyon [21] and Mitchell [22] showed that subordinates who were external in orientation were less satisfied with a participative style of leadership than were internal subordinates.

House also has reviewed these studies in an attempt to explain the ways in which the situation or environment moderates the relationship between participation and subordinate attitudes and behavior.[23] His analysis suggests that where participative leadership is positively related to satisfaction, regardless of the predispositions of subordinates, the tasks of the subjects appear to be ambiguous and ego-involving. In the studies in which the subjects' personalities or predispositions moderate the effect of participative leadership, the tasks of the subjects are inferred to be highly routine and/or nonego-involving.

House reasoned from this analysis that the task may have an overriding effect on the relationship between leader participation and subordinate responses, and that individual predispositions or personality characteristics of subordinates may have an effect only under some tasks. It was assumed that when task demands are ambiguous, subordinates will have a need to reduce the ambiguity. Further, it was assumed that when task demands are ambiguous, participative problem solving between the leader and the subordinate will result in more effective decisions than when the task demands are unambiguous. Finally, it was assumed that when the subordinates are ego-involved in their tasks they are more likely to want to have a say in the decisions that affect them. Given these assumptions, the following hypotheses were formulated to account for the conflicting findings reviewed above:

- When subjects are highly ego-involved in a decision or a task and the decision or task demands are ambiguous, participative leadership will have a positive effect on the satisfaction and motivation of the subordinate, *regardless* of the subordinate's predisposition toward self-control, authoritarianism or need for independence.
- When subordinates are not ego-involved in their tasks and when task demands are clear, subordinates who are not authoritarian and who have high needs for independence and self-control will respond favorably to leader participation and their opposite personality types will respond less favorably.

These hypotheses were derived on the basis of path-goal theorizing; i.e., the rationale guiding the analysis of prior studies was that both task characteristics and characteristics of subordinates interact to determine the effect of a specific kind of leader behavior on the satisfaction, expectancies and performance of subordinates. To date, one major investigation has supported some of these predictions [24] in which personality variables, amount of participative leadership, task ambiguity and job satisfaction were assessed for 324 employees of an industrial manufacturing organization. As expected, in nonrepetitive, ego-involving tasks, employees (regardless of their personality) were more satisfied under a participative style than a nonparticipative style. However, in repetitive tasks which were less ego-involving the amount of authoritarianism of subordinates moderated the relationship between leadership style and satisfaction. Specifically, low authoritarian subordinates were *more satisfied* under a participative style. These findings are exactly as the theory would predict, thus, it has promise in reconciling a set of confusing and contradictory findings with respect to participative leadership.

## Summary and Conclusions

We have attempted to describe what we believe is a useful theoretical framework for understanding the effect of leadership behavior on subordinate satisfaction and motivation. Most theorists today have moved away from the simplistic notions that all effective leaders have a certain set of personality traits or that the situation completely determines performance. Some researchers have presented rather complex attempts at matching certain types of leaders with certain types of situations, e.g., the articles written by Vroom and Fiedler in this issue. But, we believe that a path-goal approach goes one step further. It not only suggests what type of style may be most effective in a given situation—it also attempts to explain *why* it is most effective.

We are optimistic about the future outlook of leadership research. With the guidance of path-goal theorizing, future research is expected to unravel many confusing puzzles about the reasons for and effects of leader behavior that have, heretofore, not been solved. However, we add a word of caution: the theory, and the research on it, are relatively new to the literature of organizational behavior. Consequently, path-goal theory is offered more as a tool for directing research and stimulating insight than as a proven guide for managerial action.

## FOOTNOTES

* This article is also to be reprinted in *Readings in Organizational and Industrial Psychology* by G. A. Yukl and K. N. Wexley, 2nd edition (1975). The research by House and his associates was partially supported by a grant from the Shell Oil Company of Canada. The research by Mitchell and his associates was partially supported by the Office of Naval Research Contract NR 170–761, N00014–67–A–0103–0032 (Terence R. Mitchell, Principal Investigator).

1. T. R. Mitchell, "Expectancy Model of Job Satisfaction, Occupational Preference and Effort: A Theoretical, Methodological and Empirical Appraisal," *Psychological Bulletin* (1974, in press).

2. D. M. Nebeker and T. R. Mitchell, "Leader Behavior: An Expectancy Theory Approach," *Organization Behavior and Human Performance,* 11(1974), pp. 355–367.

3. M. G. Evans, "The Effects of Supervisory Behavior on the Path-Goal Relationship," *Organization Behavior and Human Performance,* 55(1970), pp. 277–298; T. H. Hammer and H. T. Dachler, "The Process of Supervision in the Context of Motivation Theory," Research Report No. 3 (University of Maryland, 1973); F. Dansereau, Jr., J. Cashman and G. Graen, "Instrumentality Theory and Equity Theory As Complementary Approaches in Predicting the Relationship of Leadership and Turnover Among Managers," *Organization Behavior and Human Performance,* 10(1973), pp. 184–200; R. J. House, "A Path-Goal Theory of Leader Effectiveness, *Administrative Science Quarterly,* 16, 3(September 1971), pp. 321–338; T. R. Mitchell, "Motivation and Participation: An Integration," *Academy of Management Journal,* 16, 4(1973), pp. 160–179; G. Graen, F. Dansereau, Jr. and T. Minami, "Dysfunctional Leadership Styles," *Organization Behavior and Human Performance,* 7(1972), pp. 216–236; _____, "An Empirical Test of the Man-in-the-Middle Hypothesis Among Executives in a Hierarchical Organization Employing a Unit Analysis," *Organization Behavior and Human Performance,* 8(1972), pp. 262–285; R. J. House and G. Dessler, "The Path-Goal Theory of Leadership: Some Post Hoc and A Priori Tests," to appear in J. G. Hunt, ed., *Contingency Approaches to Leadership* (Carbondale, Ill.: Southern Illinois University Press, 1974).

4. M. G. Evans, "Effects of Supervisory Behavior"; _____, "Extensions of a Path-Goal Theory of Motivation," *Journal of Applied Psychology,* 59 (1974), pp. 172–178.

5. R. J. House, "A Path-Goal Theory"; R. J. House and G. Dessler, "Path-Goal Theory of Leadership."

6. R. J. House and G. Dessler, "Path-Goal Theory of Leadership"; R. M. Stogdill, *Managers, Employees, Organization* (Ohio State University, Bureau of Business Research, 1965); R. J. House, A. Valency and R. Van der Krabben, "Some Tests and Extensions of the Path-Goal Theory of Leadership," (in preparation).

7. W. A. Hill and D. Hughes, "Variations in Leader Behavior As a Function of Task Type," *Organization Behavior and Human Performance* (1974, in press).

8. K. E. Runyon, "Some Interactions Between Personality Variables and Management Styles," *Journal of Applied Psychology,* 57, 3(1973), pp. 288–294; T. R. Mitchell, C. R. Smyser and S. E. Weed, "Locus of Control: Supervision and Work Satisfaction," *Academy of Management Journal* (in press).

9. T. R. Mitchell, "Locus of Control."

10. R. J. House, "A Path-Goal Theory"; _____ and G. Dessler, "Path-Goal Theory of Leadership"; A. D. Szalagyi and H. P. Sims, "An Exploration of the Path-Goal Theory of Leadership in a Health Care Environment," *Academy of Management Journal* (in press); J. D. Dermer, "Supervisory Behavior and Budget Motivation" (Cambridge, Mass.: unpublished, MIT, Sloan School of Management, 1974); R. W. Smetana, "The Relationship Between Managerial Behavior and Subordinate Attitudes and Motivation: A Contribution to a Behavioral Theory of Leadership" (Ph.D. diss, Wayne State University, 1974).

11. S. E. Weed, T. R. Mitchell and C. R. Smyser, "A Test of House's Path-Goal Theory of Leadership in an Organizational Setting" (paper presented at Western Psychological Assoc., 1974); J. D. Dermer and J. P. Siegel, "A Test of Path-Goal Theory: Disconfirming Evidence and a Critique" (unpublished, University of Toronto, Faculty of Management Studies, 1973); R. S. Schuler, "A Path-Goal Theory of Leadership: An Empirical Investigation" (Ph.D. diss, Michigan State University, 1973); H. K. Downey, J. E. Sheridan and J. W. Slocum, Jr., "Analysis of Relationships Among Leader Behavior, Subordinate Job Performance and Satisfaction: A Path-Goal Approach" (unpublished mimeograph, 1974); J. E. Stinson and T. W. Johnson, "The Path-Goal Theory of Leadership: A Partial Test and Suggested Refinement," *Proceedings* (Kent, Ohio: 7th Annual Conference of the Midwest Academy of Management, April 1974), pp. 18–36.

12. G. Dessler, "An Investigation of the Path-Goal Theory of Leadership" (Ph.D. diss, City University of New York, Bernard M. Baruch College, 1973).

13. R. J. House, D. Burrill and G. Dessler, "Tests and Extensions of Path-Goal Theory of Leadership, I" (unpublished, in process).

14. R. J. House, "A Path-Goal Theory"; _____ and G. Dessler, "Path-Goal Theory of Leadership"; A. D. Szalagyi and H. P. Sims, "Exploration of Path-Goal"; J. E. Stinson and T. W. Johnson, _Proceedings;_ R. S. Schuler, "Path-Goal: Investigation"; H. K. Downey, J. E. Sheridan and J. W. Slocum, Jr., "Analysis of Relationships"; S. E. Weed, T. R. Mitchell and C. R. Smyser, "Test of House's Path-Goal."

15. A. D. Szalagyi and H. P. Sims, "Exploration of Path-Goal."

16. R. J. House, A. Valency and R. Van der Krabben, "Tests and Extensions of Path-Goal Theory of Leadership, II" (unpublished, in process).

17. T. R. Mitchell, "Motivation and Participation."

18. H. Tosi, "A Reexamination of Personality As a Determinant of the Effects of Participation," _Personnel Psychology,_ 23(1970), pp. 91–99; J. Sadler "Leadership Style, Confidence in Management and Job Satisfaction," _Journal of Applied Behavioral Sciences,_ 6(1970), pp. 3–19; K. N. Wexley, J. P. Singh and G. A. Yukl, "Subordinate Personality As a Moderator of the Effects of Participation in Three Types of Appraisal Interviews," _Journal of Applied Psychology,_ 83, 1(1973), pp. 54–59.

19. T. R. Mitchell, "Motivation and Participation."

20. A. S. Tannenbaum and F. H. Allport, "Personality Structure and Group Structure: An Interpretive Study of Their Relationship Through an Event-Structure Hypothesis," _Journal of Abnormal and Social Psychology,_ 53(1956), pp. 272–280; V. H. Vroom, "Some Personality Determinants of the Effects of Participation," _Journal of Abnormal and Social Psychology,_ 59(1959), pp. 322–327.

21. K. E. Runyon, "Some Interactions Between Personality Variables and Management Styles," _Journal of Applied Psychology,_ 57,3(1973), pp. 288–294.

22. T. R. Mitchell, C. R. Smyser and S. E. Weed, "Locus of Control."

23. R. J. House, "Notes on the Path-Goal Theory of Leadership" (University of Toronto, Faculty of Management Studies, May 1974).

24. R. S. Schuler, "Leader Participation, Task Structure and Subordinate Authoritarianism (unpublished mimeograph, Cleveland State University, 1974).

## Learning Review

### Questions:

1. The four leadership styles discussed in the reading are _____, _____, _____, _____-_____, and _____.

2. The two contingency factors of the path-goal theory include _____ _____and _____ _____.

3. _____leader directiveness should be used in situations where subordinates are engaged in unstructured tasks.

### Answers:

1. directive, supportive, achievement-oriented, participative; 2. subordinate characteristics, environmental factors; 3. High

# *Retrospective Comment* [1]

## BY ROBERT J. HOUSE

I am honoured that the paper by Terry Mitchell and myself is included in this book and also by the editors' invitation to provide a commentary on the Path Goal Theory of Leadership. My commentary is necessarily guided by my philosophy of science with respect to the nature of theory. It is my belief that the role of theory is to integrate and summarize existing knowledge about a phenomena, to attempt to explain how the phenomena occurs and to suggest meaningful directions for future research by identifying important variables to be studied, new questions to be asked and hypotheses to be tested.

Two quotes that I am fond of citing express my attitude toward the development and testing of any theory. These quotes are:

> "A theory which cannot be mortally endangered cannot be alive" (cited in Platt (1964) from personal communication by W. A. H. Ruston).

> "A good theory is one that holds together long enough to get you to a better theory." (Hebb, 1962, p. 21).

These quotes serve to illustrate my belief that since theories are the products of man's cognitions they are subject to the human frailties of the theorists. Thus, as Kenneth Mackenzie and I have stated, ". . . all theories, no matter how good at explaining a set of phenomena, are ultimately incorrect and consequently, will undergo modification over time (see Kuhn, 1972, for evidence of this assumption)." Further, ". . . the fate of the better theories is to become explanations that hold for some phenomena in some limited conditions" (Mackenzie and House, 1978).

Having stated my beliefs concerning the purposes and ultimate destiny of any theory I will next describe the historical development of the Path Goal Theory. Following the historical description I will review, in a very general manner, the research relevant to the validity of the Path Goal Theory. Finally, I will advance some speculations on the current status of the theory and my expectations for its future development.

## Historical Perspective

As with many theories, the Path Goal Theory of Leadership was stimulated by a set of inconsistent empiric findings that required reconciliation. Specifically, in a study of engineering and scientific personnel in three organizations Alan Filley, Steve Kerr and I (House, Filley and Kerr, 1971) found generally positive relationships between: a) leader initiating structure and leader consideration and

b) subordinate satisfaction in two of the three companies, and generally lower but positive relationships between these variables in the third company. The first two companies were engaged in oil refining and business machine manufacturing whereas the third company was engaged in government contracted air frame manufacturing.

These findings presented a puzzle in that prior research had shown leader initiating structure to be almost always negatively related to subordinate satisfaction whereas leader consideration was consistently positively related to subordinate satisfaction. We speculated that the positive relationships between leader initiating structure and subordinate satisfaction in the first two organizations (the refining and business machine companies) was possibly due to the fact that our subjects, who were technicians, engineers and scientists, worked under ambiguous job conditions and did more intrinsically satisfying work. Thus we speculated that these subjects would be less likely to have highly programmed, routine, repetitive tasks than the subjects studied in prior studies who were almost all semi-skilled or skilled laborers. Further, we speculated that the subjects studied in prior studies would be more likely to resent leader initiating structure because when doing work that is less satisfying or even dissatisfying leader structuring behavior would be viewed as an imposition of deadlines and controls and thus would be distasteful to subordinates.

We also speculated that the low relationships between leader behaviors and subordinate satisfaction in the third company (an air frame company working exclusively under government contracts) was likely due to the fact that it was a defense contractor. As such, task assignments and satisfactions associated with work could be more determined by specific contractual arrangements than by the behavior of immediate superiors.

Thus we saw the formalization of relationships specified by the government contract as a limit to the supervisor's ability to make demands on the subordinate that were not consistent with task requirements. Such constraints would thus negate the effects of varying amounts of consideration by preventing inconsiderate superiors from exercising arbitrary authority. Further, formalization resulting from the government contract could have served to structure the environment of the respondents, thus causing leader initiating structure to be viewed as redundant with the existing formalization resulting from the contract, or merely as unnecessary to clarify the requirements that subordinates were expected to meet.

Shortly after arriving at these findings a paper was published by Martin G. Evans entitled "The Effects of Supervisory Behavior on Path-Goal Relationships" (1970). Evans conceived of leadership as a determinant of subordinates' motivation, within the context of valence-expectancy theory of motivation. Evans hypothesized that leader consideration affects the abundance of potential outcomes available to subordinates but does not affect the expectation that a particular action on the part of subordinates will lead to these outcomes. He further hypothesized that leader initiating structure would affect the subordinates' expectations that their actions would be rewarded but would not affect the abundance of the available rewards. Evans presented findings that the impact of supervisory behavior on performance and satisfaction is indirect—through subordinate expectations—which he viewed as intervening variables leading to performance and satisfaction.

This research by Evans suggested to me that there are likely to be situations in which subordinates' expectations are clarified by organizational formalization, peer group norms or task technology. Under such conditions it seemed reasonable to expect that leader behavior would have a weaker effect on subordinates' expectations than when there were no alternative sources available to the subordinates which would serve as cues for the clarification of their expectations. Reconsideration of our prior research findings in terms of the effects of leader behavior on subordinate expectations, under varying conditions of organizational formalization, task specificity or clarity of peer group norms in turn led to the conceptualization of the Path Goal Theory of Leadership.

The theory was originally presented at the First Southern Illinois University Symposium on Leadership in 1971 and subsequently published in the proceedings of that symposium (Fleishman & Hunt, 1973) and in the *Administrative Science Quarterly* (House, 1971). Evans, who was a discussant of the Path Goal Theory which was presented at that symposium characterized the theory as ". . . a compensatory model in which the highest levels of satisfaction and performance occur when environmental, organizational, task, and leadership variables complement each other. A lack of one is made up for in strength of another" (Fleishman & Hunt, p. 174). Further, Evans hypothesized that desires of subordinates for certain kinds of tasks or for certain leader behaviors might determine the appropriateness of the leader behaviors. That is, if organizations employ a variety of people, some of whom have high growth needs and others who have low growth needs then a compensatory model might be most appropriate since the organization has to accomodate diversity of demands of its members. Evans also argued that the particular scales originally used by House (1971) (that is the Leader Behavior Description Questionnaire) might be too limited for an adequate test of the implicit constructs of the Path Goal Theory of Leadership. Subsequently, House & Dessler (1974) developed a preliminary set of scales to more closely approximate the leader behaviors specified in the theory. Using these scales House and Dessler found additional support for the differential predictions of the effects of leader behaviors on subordinates' expectations, under varying levels of task clarity. Thus, this study provided a more direct test of the theory and stronger support for its validity.

Since the publication of the House and Dessler findings the theory was reformulated by House and Mitchell and is presented in its most recent version in their paper in this text. The House and Mitchell reformulation of the theory takes into consideration Evans' suggestion that individual differences among subordinates be considered in making differential predictions of the effects of leader behavior on subordinate motivation. This reformulation also takes into consideration Evans' concern about the use of leader initiating structure and leader consideration as being too limited to adequately test the implicit constructs of the theory.

Having reviewed the history of the theory's formulation we now turn to a brief review of its usefulness in accomodating prior research evidence and reconciling disparate and conflicting findings.

## Integrative Power of the Theory

The Path Goal Theory of Leadership is a situational theory which is deliberately so phrased that additional variables (such as personality variables) can be added as the effects of these new variables become known. The theory is presented in the preceding article by House and Mitchell. A more concise summary of the theory follows: Briefly, the theory consists of two propositions. The first proposition is that leader behavior is acceptable and satisfying to subordinates to the extent that they see it as either an immediate source of satisfaction or as instrumental to future satisfaction. The second proposition of the theory is that leader behavior will be motivational to the extent that (1) it makes satisfaction of subordinate needs contingent on effective performance, and (2) it complements the environment of subordinates by providing the coaching, guidance, support, and rewards which are necessary for effective performance and which may otherwise be lacking in subordinates or in their environment (p. 254).[2]

Two classes of contingency variables are specified by the theory. These are: a) personal characteristics of subordinates (locus of control, perceptions of one's own ability with respect to assigned tasks, authoritarianism, and possibly others that remain to be identified) and b) environmental variables (the subordinate's task demands, formal authority system and the primary work group).

The manner in which these contingency variables moderate the relationship between leader behavior and the dependent variables of the theory, (that is subordinates' acceptance of the leader, expectancies, valences, and satisfaction) is specified in the prior paper by House and Mitchell.

The theory and the research it has generated has helped reconcile previous findings regarding relationships between leader behavior and subordinate responses. For example, House and Baetz (1979) have shown how Path Goal Theory can accomodate and reconcile contradictory findings resulting from prior leadership literature concerning participative leadership. Further, the original statement of the theory purports to accomodate findings concerning leader initiating structure, consideration, closeness of supervision, hierarchical influence and authoritarianism (House, 1971).

In an extensive review of the literature concerned with leader consideration and initiating structure Kerr, Schriesheim, Murphy and Stogdill (1974) inductively arrived at a set of ten propositions concerning specific moderators of the relationship between leader initiating structure and consideration and subordinate satisfaction, motivation and performance. They concluded that the prior research evidence is consistent with five of the original hypotheses of the Path Goal Theory (House, 1971). Further, they summarize their review with two postulates that synthesize their findings. These two postulates are:

1. The more that subordinates are dependent upon the leader for provision of valued or needed services, the higher the positive relationship will be between leader behavior measures and subordinate satisfaction and performance.

2. The more the leader is able to provide subordinates with valued, needed or expected services, the higher the positive relationship will be between

leader behavior measures and subordinate satisfaction and performance (p. 75).

As can be seen, and as pointed out by Kerr *et al.,* these postulates are consistent with and supported by the Path Goal Theory of Leadership. In fact, there is a rather striking similarity between these two propositions and the two basic propositions of the theory.

Path Goal theory also offers an explanation as to why low LPC leaders are effective in conditions of either very high or very low situation favorability, as predicted by the Contingency Theory, then we would expect such leaders to exhibit considerate relations-oriented behavior under favorable conditions and controlling, assertive, directive behavior under unfavorable conditions. According to Contingency Theory, under favorable conditions the jobs of subordinates are highly structured and low LPC leaders are most effective. According to Path Goal Theory, task-oriented, directive, path-clarifying leader behavior is unnecessary under these conditions and would be viewed as redundant with the situation by subordinates. Further, if highly structured jobs are assumed to be more routine and thus less satisfying, supportive, relations-oriented leader behavior would be required to offset the boredom and frustration resulting from such jobs. Under such conditions, influence attempts by supportive leaders are more likely to be accepted by subordinates. Assuming the leaders are competent, if their influence attempts are accepted the groups are likely to be more effective. Thus, the effectiveness of low LPC leaders who are asserted by Contingency Theory to be nondirective and supportive under favorable conditions is explained by Path Goal Theory.

Under unfavorable conditions the tasks of subordinates are unstructured. Under such conditions, according to Contingency Theory, low LPC leaders will be directive and task-oriented. According to Path Goal Theory, task-oriented leader behavior that clarifies task requirements and paths to goals is likely to be more effective. Thus, under this condition, task-oriented leadership would be seen as instrumental to subordinate goal achievement. Assuming that the leader is competent and the leader's goals are congruent with organizational goals, such task-oriented leader behavior is likely to be more readily accepted and the group is thus likely to be more effective. Thus Path Goal Theory also explains why low LPC leaders are most effective under unfavorable conditions.

## Tests of the Theory

**Tests of the Moderating Effect of Task Characteristics:** Since 1975 approximately twenty-five studies have tested hypotheses concerning the moderating effects of task characteristics specified in the theory. The findings have been quite mixed. These mixed findings raise several questions about the theory and research to date. Firstly, the task characteristics that have been measured vary somewhat from study to study. Future research is likely to identify the specific task characteristics which have the greatest and most consistent moderating effects. Progress is presently being made on this front (Schriesheim and DeNisi, 1978). Secondly, it appears that task characteristics interact with the degree to which subordinates are authoritarian. Dessler's (1973) and Schuler's (1976) studies, which are described in the House and Mitchell paper support this position and indicate the need to consider subordinate personal characteristics as well as task characteristics when testing hypotheses about the moderating effect of the task.

**Personal Characteristics of Subordinates:**   Additional research, such as that reported by Mitchell, Smyser and Weed (also reviewed in the preceding House and Mitchell paper) is clearly indicated as promising in that such research is likely to identify additional personality characteristics of subordinates that are relevant to their perceptions and reactions to leaders.

Additional research is also needed to determine the degree to which subordinates' perceptions of their own abilities and the degree to which their actual abilities moderate the relationship between leader behaviors and subordinate responses. To date, the moderating effect of these variables remains to be tested.

**The Moderating Effects of the Formal Authority System:**   The theory also asserts that the formal authority system will moderate the relationship between leader behavior and subordinate responses. Specifically, the more clear and bureaucratic the formal authority relationships within the organization the more negative should be the relationship between initiating structure and dependent variables and the more positive should be the relationship between consideration and dependent variables.

Miles and Petty (1977) conducted a study relevant to this hypothesis. They reviewed the evidence on the relationship between organization size and degree of bureaucratization and concluded that there is a strong positive relationship between these two variables. That is formalization, routinization, standardization and specialization were concluded to be higher in large organizations. From this conclusion they reasoned that social service professionals in large organizations would view leader initiating structure as redundant with the high degree of formalization found in such organizations. They reasoned that leader consideration would be an alternative source of satisfaction or relief from the presumed dissatisfaction that occurs as a result of bureaucratization in large agencies. As predicted, these authors found the correlations between (a) leader initiating structure and (b) employee work satisfaction, satisfaction with coworkers and motivation were significantly higher in small agencies than in large agencies. In the smaller agencies the correlations were all positive whereas in the larger agencies they were either nonsignificant or negative. Further, they found the correlations between consideration and employee satisfaction tended to be higher in large agencies than in small agencies. However, these differences were not statistically significant.

**The Moderating Effect of the Primary Work Group:**   The theory also makes predictions concerning the moderating effect of the primary work group.

Katz (in press) recently has incorporated intragroup conflict among the primary work group into the theory.

Katz distinguished affective intragroup conflict from substantive intragroup conflict and argued that as the different kinds of conflict vary in strength and importance the leader behavior required would also change. Specifically he hypothesized that increasing affective conflict will precipitate the desire by group members for more considerate and less structuring leader behavior in order to satisfy the needs of group members. Similarly increasing substantive conflict was hypothesized to evoke a desire by group members for more structuring and less considerate leader behavior.

Finally Katz argued that either kind of conflict will generate tension and stress, as well as hinder subordinates' perceived path goal relationships. Thus, he hypothesized that overall effectiveness will be more positively related to leader initiating structure and less positively related to leader consideration under conditions of either high affective or substantive conflict.

Katz tested his hypothesis in a field study, using correlational methods and in two laboratory studies using confederate leaders, questionnaires and objective measures of performance. His major findings were: (a) the need for or desire for structuring leader behavior is significantly positively related to the degree of substantive or affective conflict, and (b) the relationship between leader structuring and group performance was significantly higher under high conflict conditions. Only slight evidence was in favor of a similar conclusion for leader consideration. Thus Katz's hypotheses with respect to initiating structure were strongly supported. However he did not find support for the hypothesis that affective conflict will be positively related to the desire for increased leader consideration. To explain his failure to confirm the hypothesized relationship between affective conflict and desired leader consideration Katz speculates that preferences for leader consideration may be invariably positive. Katz states that an alternative explanation may lie in the Path Goal Theory in that leader consideration is simply not as relevant or as meaningful a dimension as initiating structure for individuals who have jobs with considerable intrinsic satisfaction. Clearly this hypothesis warrants testing.

**Future Research Directions:**   Path Goal Theory is rich with opportunities for refinement and extension. There are many variables which have been the subject of other leadership research which are not yet included in the Path Goal model. For example, substantial research has shown that leader task competence is an important variable in predicting leader effectiveness (c.f. House & Baetz, pp. 378–9 for a review of this evidence). The theory in its present form assumes the leader to have the task competence when she/he engages in clarifying behaviors. Leader competence thus constitutes a boundary variable of the theory. It is hypothesized here that the predictions of the theory concerning leader path clarifying behaviors will not hold under conditions where the leader does not have the competence to clarify subordinates' task demands, or where the leader's intelligence is either below or too far above the intelligence of subordinates. Further, the theory assumes that the leader's goals are congruent with organizational goals. Where this assumption does *not hold,* the leader may induce subordinates to behave in a manner that is ineffective in terms of organizational performance.

Other leader personality variables might be incorporated into the theory. For example, the traits of dominance and self-confidence are likely predictive of leaders who will initiate path clarifying behaviors. The traits of sociability, interpersonal skills and social participation were found by Stogdill (1948, 1974) to be related to criteria of leader effectiveness in a large number of studies. These traits may be used as surrogates for measures of supportive leader behavior.

Subordinate personality variables which might be investigated in addition to authoritarianism and locus of control, include subordinate need for achievement, need for affiliation, and tolerance for ambiguity.

A recent study by Graen and Ginzberg (1977) suggests another variable that might be incorporated into the theory. These authors found that when subordinates perceive their job as relevant to their future career objectives, leader supportiveness was unrelated to their subsequent tendency to resign. However, when the subordinates perceived their jobs as not relevant to career objectives leader supportiveness had a strong negative relationship to subsequent tendency to resign. This perception of the employee, which Graen and Ginzberg (1977) refer to as Role Orientation, thus interacts with leader supportiveness according to Path Goal Theory. It thus appears that subordinate role orientation may be a better moderator of the relationships between leader behavior and the dependent variables of the theory than the task characteristics originally specified in the theory. Research to test the relative importance of Role Orientation and task characteristics is called for.

Recently the methodologies used to test the theory have been questioned. Sheridan, Downey & Slocum (1975) and Dessler & Valenzi (1977) have argued that path analysis should be used to test the Path Goal Theory when relying on correlation data. Dessler & Valenzi argue that. ". . . the use of the path analysis procedures may help explain (the conflicting findings regarding the moderating effect of task structure on the relationship between initiating structure and satisfaction) by focusing directly on the underlying expectancy motivation linkage specified in the Path Goal theory" (p. 252).

Using path analysis Sheridan *et al.* (1975) did not find support for the direct causal relationships hypothesized in Path Goal theory. Green (1975) attributed the disconfirming findings of Sheridan *et al.* (1975) to methodological deficiencies of their research design. Dessler & Valenzi (1977) did not find support for the hypotheses that occupational level moderates the relationship between initiation of structure and intrinsic job satisfaction. However, Dessler & Valenzi did find support for the hypothesized linkages between leader behavior and subordinates' expectancies. This contradiction in findings will need to be resolved through future research.

Finally, the appropriateness of the conceptualization and measurement of leader behavior currently in use needs to be addressed. To date, most tests of the theory are based on the Ohio State leadership scales which measure leader initiating structure and consideration. These scales are at best rough approximations of instrumental and supportive leader behavior. Schriesheim (1979) has recently developed and validated a set of leader behavior scales that measure the constructs of the theory much better than measures used in prior tests. Evans and I (reported in Evans, 1979) have attempted to conceptualize more clearly the kinds of leader behaviors relevant to each of the five components of the motivation theory posited in my 1971 paper. Others, Oldham (1976) and Yukl and Nemeroff (1978) and Klimoski & Hayes (unpublished manuscript), have also recently conceptualized leader behavior variables relevant to subordinate motivation. Thus, there appears to be a convergence of thought concerning the kinds of leader behaviors that need to be measured to better understand the effects of leader behavior on the motivation of subordinates. Future development and validation of these variables, together with the scales developed by Schriesheim (1979) might well enrich the theory and make tests of the theory more powerful.

## Conclusion

The review of the theory presented above shows how the theory is capable of integrating and reconciling many of the discrepant findings in the leadership literature. Further, several of the studies cited above show how the theory can be operationalized to test hypotheses concerning the moderating effects of task characteristics, formal authority systems, and primary work group characteristics on relationships between leader behaviors and subordinate responses. As mentioned, the theory is deliberately phrased such that additional variables can be added as the effects of new variables become known. Further, the philosophy of science stated above implies that the theory will and should change over time. Invalid propositions and poorly conceptualized variables are expected to be deleted and/or replaced by more appropriate ones.

The theory has stimulated a substantial amount of research and a number of questions that imply new directions for future leadership research. While it is hoped that a knowledge of the theory will assist managers in engaging in more effective leader behavior, the theory is offered primarily as a tool for directing research and stimulating insight than as a proven guide for managerial action.

## FOOTNOTES

1.  The review of prior research presented here is largely drawn from a recent paper by House and Baetz (1979) which reviews the same and additional research in more technical detail.

2.  It is implicit in the theory that when leader behavior is accepted by subordinates and when subordinates are highly motivated to expend effort they will comply with the leader's expectations of them and thus be more effective. This implicit assumption rests on a further assumption that the leader is competent to set expectations for subordinates and that these expectations are congruent with organizational goals. When these assumptions do not hold satisfying and motivational leader behavior will likely result in dysfunctional consequences for the organization.

# REFERENCES

Dessler, G. An Investigation of the Path Goal Theory of Leadership. Ph.D. Dissertation, Baruch College, The City University of New York, 1973.

Dessler, G., and Valenzi, E. R. Initiation of structure and subordinate satisfaction: A path analysis test of Path-Goal theory. *Academy of Management Journal,* 1977, *20*, 251–259.

Evans, M. G. Leadership. In S. Kerr, *Organizational Behavior,* Columbus, Ohio: Grid Publishing Co., 1979.

Fiedler, F. E. *A Theory of Leadership Effectiveness.* New York: McGraw-Hill, 1967.

Fleishman, E. A., and Hunt, J. G. *Current Developments in the Study of Leadership.* Carbondale, Ill.: Southern Illinois University Press, 1973.

Filley, A. C., House, R. J., and Kerr, S. *Managerial Process and Organizational Behavior.* Glenview, Ill.: Scott Foresman & Co., 1976.

Greene, C. N. Limitations of cross-lagged correlational designs and an alternative approach. In J. G. Hunt and L. L. Larson (Eds.), *Leadership Frontiers,* Kent, Ohio: Kent State University Press, 1975, pp. 121–126.

Hebb, D. O. Hebb on hocus-pocus: A conversation with Elizabeth Hall, *Psychology Today,* 1969, *6.*

House, R. J. A path goal theory of leader effectiveness. *Administrative Science Quarterly,* 1971, *16,* 321–338.

House, R. J. and Baetz, M. L. Leadership: Some empirical generalizations and new research directions. In B. M. Staw (Ed.), *Research in Organizational Behavior: An Annual Series of Analytical Essays and Critical Review,* Greenwich, Conn.: JAI Press Inc., 1979.

House, R. J. and Dessler, G. The Path-Goal Theory of Leadership: Some post hoc and a priori tests. In J. G. Hunt and L. L. Larson (Eds.), *Contingency Approaches to Leadership,* Carbondale, Ill.: Southern Illinois University Press, 1974.

House, R. J., Filley, A. C., and Kerr, S. Relation of leader consideration and initiating structure to R&D subordinates' satisfaction, *Administrative Science Quarterly,* 1971, *16,* 19–30.

Katz, R. The influence of group conflict on leadership effectiveness. *Organization Behavior and Human Performance,* (in press).

Kerr, S., Schriesheim, C. A., Murphy, C. J., & Stogdill, R. M. Toward a contingency theory of leadership based upon the consideration and initiating structure literature, *Organization Behavior and Human Performance,* 1974, *12,* 62–82.

Klimoski, R. J. and Hayes, N. J. Leader Behavior and Subordinate Motivation. Unpublished manuscript, Department of Psychology, The Ohio State University, 1978.

Kuhn, T. S. *The Structure of Scientific Revolutions,* Chicago, Ill.: University of Chicago Press, 1964.

Mackenzie, K. D. and House, R. J. Paradigm development in the social sciences: A proposed research strategy. *Academy of Management Review,* 1978, *3,* 7–24.

Miles, R. H., and Petty, M. M. Leader effectiveness in small bureaucracies. *Academy of Management Journal,* 1977, *20,* 238–250.

Oldham, G. The motivational strategies used by supervisors: Relationships to effectiveness indicators. *Organizational Behavior and Human Performance,* 1976, *15,* 66–86.

Platt, J. R. Strong inference, *Science,* 1964, 347–353.

Schuler, R. S. Participation with supervisor and subordinate authoritarianism: A Path-Goal Theory reconciliation. *Administrative Science Quarterly,* 1976, *21,* 320–325.

Sheridan, J. E., Downey, H. K., and Slocum, J. W., Jr. Testing causal relationships of House's Path-Goal Theory of Leadership effectiveness. In J. G. Hunt and L. L. Larson (Eds.), *Leadership Frontiers,* Kent, Ohio: Kent State University Press, 1975.

Schriesheim, C. A. The Development and Validation of Measures of Leader Behavior to Test the Path Goal Theory of Leadership. Ph.D. Dissertation, The Ohio State University.

Schriesheim, C. A. The moderating effects of three task dimensions on the relationship between instrumental leadership and subordinate satisfaction: A two-sample replicated test of path-goal leadership theory. Unpublished manuscript, University of Southern California, Graduate School of Business Administration, 1979.

Yukl, G. A. and Nemeroff, W. F. Identification and measurement of specific categories of leadership behavior: A progress report. To appear in J. G. Hunt, and L. L. Larson (Eds.), *Crosscurrents in Leadership,* Carbondale, Ill.: Southern Illinois University Press, 1979.

# 22

# *A New Look at Managerial Decision Making*

VICTOR H. VROOM

## *About the Author*

**Victor H. Vroom** received his bachelor's and master's degrees from McGill University and his Ph.D. from the University of Michigan. He has taught at the University of Pennsylvania, Carnegie-Mellon, and is presently at Yale as John G. Searle Professor of Administrative Sciences and Professor of Psychology.

Professor Vroom is noted for his research in the field of motivation where he has been a pioneer in expectancy theory. He has authored fifty articles and six books including the landmark volumes, *Work and Motivation* (Wiley, 1964) and *Leadership and Decision Making* (University of Pittsburgh Press, 1973, co-authored with Phillip Yetton). He is currently at work on a new book on leadership to be published by Prentice-Hall in 1987. He is also an active consultant to several major firms.

Reprinted by permission of the author and publisher from *Organizational Dynamics*, 1973, *2* (1), 66–80. Copyright © 1973 by AMACOM, a division of American Management Associations. All rights reserved.

# PREVIEW

A. Managerial decision making may be viewed in either a normative or a descriptive perspective or some combination of the two.
B. Vroom and Yetton have developed a normative model of decision making.
   1. A set of ground rules has been developed for matching a manager's leadership behavior to the demands of the situation.
   2. Three classes of outcomes that bear on the ultimate effectiveness of decisions are identified.
   3. A seven-question decision tree is utilized to diagnose a given situation and recommend an appropriate managerial style.
   4. Case studies provide empirical evidence of the workability of the model.
C. Two different research methods were employed in an attempt to develop a descriptive model of leader behavior.
   1. The methods used consisted of a general recall test of 500 managers and a standardized test for managers.
D. A combination of these two models can help to make decision making a social process.

All managers are decision makers. Furthermore, their effectiveness as managers is largely reflected in their "track record" in making the "right decisions." These "right decisions" in turn largely depend on whether or not the manager has utilized the right person or persons in the right ways in helping him solve the problem.

Our concern in this article is with decision making as a social process. We view the manager's task as determining how the problem is to be solved, not the solution to be adopted. Within that overall framework, we have attempted to answer two broad sets of questions: What decision-making processes should managers use to deal effectively with the problems they encounter in their jobs? What decision-making processes do they use in dealing with these problems and what considerations affect their decisions about how much to share their decision-making power with subordinates?

· The reader will recognize the former as a normative or prescriptive question. A rational and analytic answer to it would constitute a normative model of decision making as a social process. The second question is descriptive, since it concerns how managers do, rather than should, behave.

## Toward a Normative Model

About four years ago, Philip Yetton, then a graduate student at Carnegie-Mellon University, and I began a major research program in an attempt to answer these normative and descriptive questions.

AI    You solve the problem or make the decision yourself, using information available to you at that time.

AII    You obtain the necessary information from your subordinate(s), then decide on the solution to the problem yourself. You may or may not tell your subordinates what the problem is in getting the information from them. The role played by your subordinates in making the decision is clearly one of providing the necessary information to you, rather than generating or evaluating alternative solutions.

CI    You share the problem with relevant subordinates individually, getting their ideas and suggestions without bringing them together as a group. Then *you* make the decision that may or may not reflect your subordinates' influence.

CII    You share the problem with your subordinates as a group, collectively obtaining their ideas and suggestions. Then *you* make the decision that may or may not reflect your subordinates' influence.

GII    You share a problem with your subordinates as a group. Together you generate and evaluate alternatives and attempt to reach agreement (consensus) on a solution. Your role is much like that of chairman. You do not try to influence the group to adopt "your" solution and you are willing to accept and implement any solution that has the support of the entire group.

(GI is omitted because it applies only to more comprehensive models outside the scope of the article.)

*Table 1.* Types of management decision styles

We began with the normative question. What would be a rational way of deciding on the form and amount of participation in decision making that should be used in different situations? We were tired of debates over the relative merits of Theory X and Theory Y and of the truism that leadership depends upon the situation. We felt that it was time for the behavioral sciences to move beyond such generalities and to attempt to come to grips with the complexities of the phenomena with which they intended to deal.

Our aim was ambitious—to develop a set of ground rules for matching a manager's leadership behavior to the demands of the situation. It was critical that these ground rules be consistent with research evidence concerning the consequences of participation and that the model based on the rules be operational, so that any manager could see it to determine how he should act in any decision-making situation.

Table I shows a set of alternative decision processes that we have employed in our research. Each process is represented by a symbol (e.g., AI, CI, GII) that will be used as a convenient method of referring to each process. The first letter in this symbol signifies the basic properties of the process (A stands for autocratic; C for consultative; and G for group). The Roman numerals that follow the first letter constitute variants on that process. Thus, AI represents the first variant on an autocratic process, and AII the second variant.

## Conceptual and Empirical Basis of the Model

A model designed to regulate, in some rational way, choices among the decisions processes shown in Table 1 should be based on sound empirical evidence concerning the likely consequences of the styles. The more complete the empirical base of knowledge, the greater the certainty with which we can develop the model and the greater will be its usefulness. To aid in understanding the conceptual basis of the model, it is important to distinguish among three classes of outcomes that bear on the ultimate effectiveness of decisions. These are:

1. The quality or rationality of the decision.
2. The acceptance or commitment on the part of subordinates to execute the decision effectively.
3. The amount of time required to make the decision.

The effects of participation on each of these outcomes or consequences were summed up by the author in *The Handbook of Social Psychology* as follows:

> The results suggest that allocating problem solving and decision-making tasks to entire groups requires a greater investment of man hours but produces higher acceptance of decisions and a higher probability that the decision will be executed efficiently. Differences between these two methods in quality of decisions and in elapsed time are inconclusive and probably highly variable . . . It would be naive to think that group decision making is always more "effective" than autocratic decision making, or vice versa; the relative effectiveness of these two extreme methods depends both on the weights attached to quality, acceptance and time variables and on differences in amounts of these outcomes resulting from these methods, neither of which is invariant from one situation to another. The critics and proponents of participative management would do well to direct their efforts toward identifying the properties of situations in which different decision-making approaches are effective rather than wholesale condemnation or deification of one approach.

We have gone on from there to identify the properties of the situation or problem that will be the basic elements in the model. These problem attributes are of two types: 1) Those that specify the importance for a particular problem of quality and acceptance, and 2) those that, on the basis of available evidence, have a high probability of moderating the effects of participation on each of these outcomes. Table II shows the problem attributes used in the present form of the model. For each attribute a question is provided that might be used by a leader in diagnosing a particular problem prior to choosing his leadership style.

In phrasing the questions, we have held technical language to a minimum. Furthermore, we have phrased the questions in Yes-No form, translating the continuous variables defined above into dichotomous variables. For example, instead of attempting to determine how important the decision quality is to the effectiveness of the decision (attribute A), the leader is asked in the first question to judge whether there is any quality component to the problem. Similarly, the difficult task of specifying exactly how much information the leader possesses that is relevant to the decision (attribute B) is reduced to a simple judgment by the leader concerning whether or not he has sufficient information to make a high quality decision.

We have found that managers can diagnose a situation quickly and accurately by answering this set of seven questions concerning it. But how can such responses

| Problem Attributes | Diagnostic Questions |
| --- | --- |
| A. The importance of the quality of the decision. | Is there a quality requirement such that one solution is likely to be more rational than another? |
| B. The extent to which the leader possesses sufficient information/expertise to make a high-quality decision by himself. | Do I have sufficient information to make a high-quality decision? |
| C. The extent to which the problem is structured. | Is the problem structured? |
| D. The extent to which acceptance or commitment on the part of subordinates is critical to the effective implementation of the decision. | Is acceptance of decision by subordinates critical to effective implementation? |
| E. The prior probability that the leader's autocratic decision will receive acceptance by subordinates. | If you were to make the decision by yourself, is it reasonably certain that it would be accepted by your subordinates? |
| F. The extent to which subordinates are motivated to attain the organizational goals as represented in the objectives explicit in the statement of the problem. | Do subordinates share the organizational goals to be obtained in solving this problem? |
| G. The extent to which subordinates are likely to be in conflict over preferred solutions. | Is conflict among subordinates likely in preferred solutions? |

*Table 2.*   Problem attributes used in the model

generate a prescription concerning the most effective leadership style or decision process? What kind of normative model of participation in decision making can be built from this set of problem attributes?

Figure 1 shows one such model expressed in the form of a decision tree. It is the seventh version of such a model that we have developed over the last three years. The problem attributes, expressed in question form, are arranged along the top of the figure. To use the model for a particular decision-making situation, one starts at the left-hand side and works toward the right asking oneself the question immediately above any box that is encountered. When a terminal node is reached, a number will be found designating the problem type and one of the decision-making processes appearing in Table I. AI is prescribed for four problem types (1, 2, 4, and 5); AII is prescribed for two problem types (9 and 10); CI is prescribed for only one problem type (8); CII is prescribed for four problem types (7, 11, 13, and 14); GII is prescribed for three problem types (3, 6, and 12). The relative frequency with which each of the five decision processes would be prescribed for any manager would, of course, depend on the distribution of problem types encountered in his decision making.

**Rationale Underlying the Model:**   The decision processes specified for each problem type are not arbitrary. The model's behavior is governed by a set of principles intended to be consistent with existing evidence concerning the consequences of participation in decision making on organizational effectiveness.

There are two mechanisms underlying the behavior of the model. The first is a set of seven rules that serve to protect the quality and the acceptance of

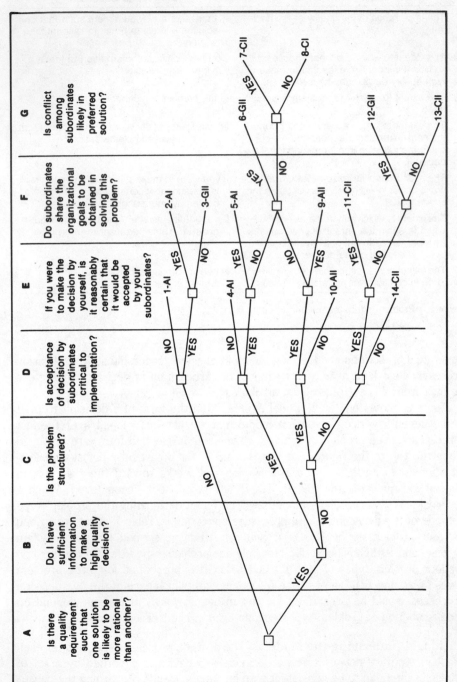

Figure 1. Decision model

the decision by eliminating alternatives that risk one or the other of these decision outcomes. Once the rules have been applied, a feasible set of decision processes is generated. The second mechanism is a principle for choosing among alternatives in the feasible set where more than one exists.

Let us examine the rules first, because they do much of the work of the model. As previously indicated, the rules are intended to protect both the quality and acceptance of the decision. In the form of the model shown, there are three rules that protect decision quality and four that protect acceptance.

1. *The Information Rule.* If the quality of the decision is important and if the leader does not possess enough information or expertise to solve the problem by himself, AI is eliminated from the feasible set. (Its use risks a low-quality decision.)

2. *The Goal Congruence Rule.* If the quality of the decision is important and if the subordinates do not share the organizational goals to be obtained in solving the problem, GII is eliminated from the feasible set. (Alternatives that eliminate the leader's final control over the decision reached may jeopardize the quality of the decision.)

3. *The Unstructured Problem Rule.* In decisions in which the quality of the decision is important, if the leader lacks the necessary information or expertise to solve the problem by himself, and if the problem is unstructured, i.e., he does not know exactly what information is needed and where it is located, the method used must provide not only for him to collect the information but to do so in an efficient and effective manner. Methods that involve interaction among all subordinates with full knowledge of the problem are likely to be both more efficient and more likely to generate a high-quality solution to the problem. Under these conditions, AI, AII, and CI are eliminated from the feasible set. (AI does not provide for him to collect the necessary information, and AII and CI represent more cumbersome, less effective, and less efficient means of bringing the necessary information to bear on the solution of the problem than methods that do permit those with the necessary information to interact.)

4. *The Acceptance Rule.* If the acceptance of the decision by subordinates is critical to effective implementation, and if it is not certain that an autocratic decision made by the leader would receive that acceptance, AI and AII are eliminated from the feasible set. (Neither provides an opportunity for subordinates to participate in the decision and both risk the necessary acceptance.)

5. *The Conflict Rule.* If the acceptance of the decision is critical, and an autocratic decision is not certain to be accepted, and subordinates are likely to be in conflict or disagreement over the appropriate solution, AI, AII, and CI are eliminated from the feasible set. (The method used in solving the problem should enable those in disagreement to resolve their differences with full knowledge of the problem. Accordingly, under these conditions, AI, AII, and CI, which involve no interaction or only "one-on-one" relationships and therefore provide no opportunity for those in conflict to resolve their differences, are eliminated from the feasible set. Their use runs the risk of leaving some of the subordinates with less than the necessary commitment to the final decision.)

6. *The Fairness Rule.* If the quality of decision is unimportant and if acceptance is critical and not certain to result from an autocratic decision, AI, AII, CI, and CII are eliminated from the feasible set. (The method used should maximize the probability of acceptance as this is the only relevant consideration in determining the effectiveness of the decision. Under these circumstances, AI, AII, CI, and CII, which create less acceptance or commitment than GII, are eliminated from the feasible set. To use them is to run the risk of getting less than the needed acceptance of the decision.)

7. *The Acceptance Priority Rule.* If acceptance is critical, not assured by an autocratic decision, and if subordinates can be trusted, AI, AII, CI, and CII are eliminated from the feasible set. (Methods that provide equal partnership in the decision-making process can provide greater acceptance without risking decision quality. Use of any method other than GII results in an unnecessary risk that the decision will not be fully accepted or receive the necessary commitment on the part of subordinates.)

Once all seven rules have been applied to a given problem, we emerge with a feasible set of decision processes. The feasible set for each of the fourteen problem types is shown in Table III. It can be seen that there are some problem types for which only one method remains in the feasible set, others for which two methods remain feasible, and still others for which five methods remain feasible.

When more than one method remains in the feasible set, there are a number of ways in which one might choose among them. The mechanism we have selected and the principle underlying the choices of the model in Figure 1 utilizes the number of man-hours used in solving the problem as the basis for choice. Given

| Problem Type | Acceptable Methods |
|:---:|:---|
| 1. | AI, AII, CI, CII, GII |
| 2. | AI, AII, CI, CII, GII |
| 3. | GII |
| 4. | AI, AII, CI, CII, GII * |
| 5. | AI, AII, CI, CII, GII * |
| 6. | GII |
| 7. | CII |
| 8. | CI, CII |
| 9. | AII, CI, CII, GII * |
| 10. | AII, CI, CII, GII * |
| 11. | CII, GII * |
| 12. | GII |
| 13. | CII |
| 14. | CII, GII * |

\* Within the feasible set only when the answer to question F is Yes.

*Table 3.* Problem types and the feasible set of decision processes

a set of methods with equal likelihood of meeting both quality and acceptance requirements for the decision, it chooses that method that requires the least investment in man-hours. On the basis of the empirical evidence summarized earlier, this is deemed to be the method furthest to the left within the feasible set. For example, since AI, AII, CI, CII, and GII are all feasible as in Problem Types 1 and 2, AI would be the method chosen.

To illustrate application of the model in actual administrative situations, we will analyze four cases with the help of the model. While we attempt to describe these cases as completely as is necessary to permit the reader to make the judgments required by the model, there may remain some room for subjectivity. The reader may wish after reading the case to analyze it himself using the model and then to compare his analysis with that of the author.

CASE I. You are a manufacturing manager in a large electronics plant. The company's management has recently installed new machines and put in a new simplified work system, but to the surprise of everyone, yourself included, the expected increase in productivity was not realized. In fact, production has begun to drop, quality has fallen off, and the number of employee separations has risen.

You do not believe that there is anything wrong with the machines. You have had reports from other companies that are using them and they confirm this opinion. You have also had representatives from the firm that built the machines go over them and they report that they are operating at peak efficiency.

You suspect that some parts of the new work system may be responsible for the change, but this view is not widely shared among your immediate subordinates who are four first-line supervisors, each in charge of a section, and your supply manager. The drop in production has been variously attributed to poor training of the operators, lack of an adequate system of financial incentives, and poor morale. Clearly, this is an issue about which there is considerable depth of feeling within individuals and potential disagreement among your subordinates.

This morning you received a phone call from your division manager. He had just received your production figures for the last six months and was calling to express his concern. He indicated that the problem was yours to solve in any way that you think best, but that he would like to know within a week what steps you plan to take.

You share your division manager's concern with the falling productivity and know that your men are also concerned. The problem is to decide what steps to take to rectify the situation.

### Analysis
Questions—
   A (Quality?) = Yes
   B (Manager's Information?) = No
   C (Structured?) = No
   D (Acceptance?) = Yes

E (Prior Probability of Acceptance?) = No
F (Goal Congruence?) = Yes
G (Conflict?) = Yes
Problem Type—12
Feasible Set—GII
Minimum Man-Hours Solution (from Figure 1)—GII
Rule Violations—
   AI violates rules 1, 3, 4, 5, 7
   AII violates rules 3, 4, 5, 7
   CI violates rules 3, 5, 7
   CII violates rule 7

CASE II. You are general foreman in charge of a large gang laying an oil pipeline and have to estimate your expected rate of progress in order to schedule material deliveries to the next field site.

You know the nature of the terrain you will be traveling and have the historical data needed to compute the mean and variance in the rate of speed over that type of terrain. Given these two variables, it is a simple matter to calculate the earliest and latest times at which materials and support facilities will be needed at the next site. It is important that your estimate be reasonably accurate. Underestimates result in idle foremen and workers, and an overestimate results in tying up materials for a period of time before they are to be used.

Progress has been good and your five foremen and other members of the gang stand to receive substantial bonuses if the project is completed ahead of schedule.

### Analysis
Questions—
   A (Quality?) = Yes
   B (Manager's Information?) = Yes
   D (Acceptance?) = No
Problem Type—4
Feasible Set—AI, AII, CI, CII, GII
Minimum Man-Hours Solution (from Figure 1)—AI
Rule Violations—None

CASE III. You are supervising the work of 12 engineers. Their formal training and work experience are very similar, permitting you to use them interchangeably on projects. Yesterday, your manager informed you that a request had been received from an overseas affiliate for four engineers to go abroad on extended loan for a period of six to eight months. For a number of reasons, he argued and you agreed that this request should be met from your group.

All your engineers are capable of handling this assignment and, from the stand-point of present and future projects, there is no particular reason why anyone should be retained over any other. The problem is somewhat complicated by the fact that the overseas assignment is in what is generally regarded as an undesirable location.

### Analysis
Questions—
  A (Quality?) = No
  D (Acceptance?) = Yes
  E (Prior Probability of Acceptance?) = No
  G (Conflict?) = Yes
Problem Type—3
Feasible Set—GII
Minimum Man-Hours Solution (from Figure 1)—GII
Rule Violations—
  AI and VII violate rules 4, 5, and 6
  CI violates rules 5 and 6
  CII violates rule 6

CASE IV. You are on the division manager's staff and work on a wide variety of problems of both an administrative and technical nature. You have been given the assignment of developing a standard method to be used in each of the five plants in the division for manually reading equipment registers, recording the readings, and transmitting the scorings to a centralized information system.

Until now there has been a high error rate in the reading and/or transmittal of the data. Some locations have considerably higher error rates than others, and the methods used to record and transmit the data vary among plants. It is probable, therefore, that part of the error variance is a function of specific local conditions rather than anything else, and this will complicate the establishment of any system common to all plants. You have the information on error rates but no information on the local practices that generate these errors or on the local conditions that necessitate the different practices.

Everyone would benefit from an improvement in the quality of the data; it is used in a number of important decisions. Your contacts with the plants are through the quality-control supervisors who are responsible for collecting the data. They are a conscientious group committed to doing their jobs well, but are highly sensitive to interference on the part of higher management in their own operations. Any solution that does not receive the active support of the various plant supervisors is unlikely to reduce the error rate significantly.

### Analysis
Questions—
  A (Quality?) = Yes
  B (Manager's Information?) = No
  C (Structured?) = No
  D (Acceptance?) = Yes
  E (Prior Probability of Acceptance?) = No
  F (Goal Congruence?) = Yes

Problem Type—12
Feasible Set—GII
Minimum Man-Hours Solution (from Figure 1)—GII
Rule Violations—
   AI violates rules 1, 3, 4, and 7
   AII violates rules 3, 4, and 7
   CI violates rules 3 and 7
   CII violates rule 7

## Short Versus Long-Term Models

The model described above seeks to protect the quality of the decision and to expend the least number of man-hours in the process. Because it focuses on conditions surrounding the making and implementation of a particular decision rather than any long-term considerations, we can term it a short-term model.

It seems likely, however, that the leadership methods that may be optimal for short-term results may be different from those that would be optimal over a longer period of time. Consider a leader, for example, who has been uniformly pursuing an autocratic style (AI or AII) and, perhaps as a consequence, has subordinates who might be termed "yes men" (attribute E) but who also cannot be trusted to pursue organizational goals (attribute F), largely because the leader has never bothered to explain them.

It appears likely, however, that the manager who used more participative methods would, in time, change the status of these problem attributes so as to develop ultimately a more effective problem-solving system. A promising approach to the development of a long-term model is one that places less weight on man-hours as the basis for choice of method within the feasible set. Given a long-term orientation, one would be interested in the possibility of a trade-off between man-hours in problem solving and team development, both of which increase with participation. Viewed in these terms, the time-minimizing model places maximum relative weight on man-hours and no weight on development, and hence chooses the style farthest to the left within the feasible set. A model that places less weight on man-hours and more weight on development would, if these assumptions are correct, choose a style further to the right within the feasible set.

We recognize, of course, that the minimum man-hours solution suggested by the model is not always the best solution to every problem. A manager faced, for example, with the problem of handling any one of the four cases previously examined might well choose more time-consuming alternatives on the grounds that the greater time invested would be justified in developing his subordinates. Similar considerations exist in other decision-making situations. For this reason we have come to emphasize the feasible set of decision methods in our work with managers. Faced with considerations not included in the model, the manager should consider any alternative within the feasible set, not opt automatically for the minimum man-hours solution.

As I am writing this, I have in front of me a "black box" that constitutes an electronic version of the normative model discussed on the preceding pages. (The author is indebted to Peter Fuss of Bell Telephone Laboratories for his interest in the model and his skill in developing the "black box".) The box, which is small enough to fit into the palm of one hand, has a set of seven switches, each appropriately labeled with the questions (A through G) used in Figure 1. A manager faced with a concrete problem or decision can "diagnose" that problem by setting each switch in either its "yes" or "no" position. Once the problem has been described, the manager depresses a button that illuminates at least one or as many as five lights, each of which denotes one of the decision processes (AI, AII, etc.). The lights that are illuminated constitute the feasible set of decision processes for the problem as shown in Table III. The lights not illuminated correspond to alternatives that violate one or more of the seven rules previously stated.

In this prototype version of the box, the lights are illuminated in decreasing order of brightness from left to right within the feasible set. The brightest light corresponds to the alternative shown in Figure 1. Thus, if both CII and GII were feasible alternatives, CII would be brighter than GII, since it requires fewer man-hours. However, a manager who was not under any undue time pressure and who wished to invest time in the development of his subordinates might select an alternative corresponding to one of the dimmer lights.

## Toward a Descriptive Model of Leader Behavior

So far we have been concerned with the normative questions defined at the outset. But how do managers really behave? What considerations affect their decisions about how much to share their decision-making power with their subordinates? In what respects is their behavior different from or similar to that of the model? These questions are but a few of those that we attempted to answer in a large-scale research program aimed at gaining a greater understanding of the factors that influence managers in their choice of decision processes to fit the demands of the situation. This research program was financially supported by the McKinsey Foundation, General Electric Foundation, Smith Richardson Foundation, and the Office of Naval Research.

Two different research methods have been utilized in studying these factors. The first investigation utilized a method that we have come to term "recalled problems." Over 500 managers from 11 different countries representing a variety of firms were asked to provide a written description of a problem that they had recently had to solve. These varied in length from one paragraph to several pages and covered virtually every facet of managerial decision making. For each case, the manager was asked to indicate which of the decision processes shown in Table I they used to solve the problem. Finally, each manager was asked to answer the questions shown in Table II corresponding to the problem attributes used in the normative model.

The wealth of data, both qualitative and quantitative, served two purposes.

Since each manager had diagnosed a situation that he had encountered in terms that are used in the normative model and had indicated the methods that he had used in dealing with it, it is possible to determine what differences, if any, there were between the model's behavior and his own behavior. Second, the written cases provided the basis for the construction of a standard set of cases used in later research to determine the factors that influence managers to share or retain their decision-making power. Each case depicted a manager faced with a problem to solve or decision to make. The cases spanned a wide range of managerial problems including production scheduling, quality control, portfolio management, personnel allocation, and research and development. In each case, a person could readily assume the role of the manager described and could indicate which of the decision processes he would use if he actually were faced with that situation.

In most of our research, a set of thirty cases has been used and the subjects have been several thousand managers who were participants in management development programs in the United States and abroad. Cases were selected systemically. We desired cases that could not only be coded unambiguously in the terms used in the normative model but that would also permit the assessment of the affects of each of the problem attributes used in the model on the person's behavior. The solution was to select cases in accordance with an experimental design so that they varied in terms of the seven attributes used in the model and variation in each attribute was independent of each other attribute. Several such standardized sets of cases have been developed, and over a thousand managers have now been studied using this approach.

To summarize everything we learned in the course of this research is well beyond the scope of this paper, but it is possible to discuss some of the highlights. Since the results obtained from the two research methods—recalled and standardized problems—are consistent, we can present the major results independent of the method used.

Perhaps the most striking finding is the weakening of the widespread view that participativeness is a general trait that individual managers exhibit in different amounts. To be sure, there were differences *among* managers in their general tendencies to utilize participative methods as opposed to autocratic ones. On the standardized problems, these differences accounted for about 10 percent of the total variance in the decision processes observed. These differences in behavior between managers, however, were small in comparison with differences *within* managers. On the standardized problems, no manager has indicated that he would use the same decision process on all problems or decisions, and most use all five methods under some circumstances.

Some of this variance in behavior within managers can be attributed to widely shared tendencies to respond to some situations by sharing power and others by retaining it. It makes more sense to talk about participative and autocratic situations than it does to talk about participative and autocratic managers. In fact, on the standardized problems, the variance in behavior across problems or cases is about three times as large as the variance across managers!

What are the characteristics of an autocratic as opposed to a participative situation? An answer to this question would constitute a partial descriptive model of this aspect of the decision-making process and has been our goal in much of the research that we have conducted. From our observations of behavior on both recalled problems and on standardized problems, it is clear that the decision-making process employed by a typical manager is influenced by a large number of factors, many of which also show up in the normative model. Following are several conclusions substantiated by the results on both recalled and standardized problems: Managers use decision processes providing less opportunity for participation (1) when they possess all the necessary information than when they lack some of the needed information, (2) when the problem that they face is well-structured rather than unstructured, (3) when their subordinates' acceptance of the decision is not critical for the effective implementation of the decision or when the prior probability of acceptance of an autocratic decision is high, and (4) when the personal goals of their subordinates are *not* congruent with the goals of the organization as manifested in the problem.

So far we have been talking about relatively common or widely shared ways of dealing with organizational problems. Our results strongly suggest that there are ways of "tailoring" one's approach to the situation that distinguish managers from one another. Theoretically, these can be thought of as differences among managers in decision rules that they employ about when to encourage participation. Statistically, they are represented as interactions between situational variables and personal characteristics.

Consider, for example, two managers who have identical distributions of the use of the five decision processes shown in Table I on a set of thirty cases. In a sense, they are equally participative (or autocratic). However, the situations in which they permit or encourage participation in decision making on the part of their subordinates may be very different. One may restrict the participation of his subordinates to decisions without a quality requirement, whereas the other may restrict their participation to problems with a quality requirement. The former would be more inclined to use participative decision processes (like GII) on such decisions as what color the walls should be painted or when the company picnic should be held. The latter would be more likely to encourage participation in decision making on decisions that have a clear and demonstrable impact on the organization's success in achieving its external goals.

Use of the standardized problem set permits the assessment of such differences in decision rules that govern choices among decision-making processes. Since the cases are selected in accordance with an experimental design, they can indicate differences in the behavior of managers attributable not only to the existence of a quality requirement in the problem but also in the effects of acceptance requirements, conflict, information requirements, and the like.

The research using both recalled and standardized problems has also enabled us to examine similarities and differences between the behavior of the normative model and the behavior of a typical manager. Such an analysis reveals, at the very least, what behavioral changes could be expected if managers began using the normative model as the basis for choosing their decision-making processes.

A typical manager says he would (or did) use exactly the same decision process as that shown in Figure 1 in 40 percent of the situations. In two thirds of the situations, his behavior is consistent with the feasible set of methods proposed in the model. In other words, in about one third of the situations his behavior violates at least one of the seven rules underlying the model.

The four rules designed to protect the acceptance or commitment of the decision have substantially higher probabilities of being violated than do the three rules designed to protect the quality or rationality of the decision. One of the acceptance rules, the Fairness Rule (Rule 6) is violated about three quarters of the time that it could have been violated. On the other hand, one of the quality rules, the Information Rule, (Rule 1) is violated in only about 3 percent of occasions in which it is applicable. If we assume for the moment that these two sets of rules have equal validity, these findings strongly suggest that the decisions made by typical managers are more likely to prove ineffective due to deficiencies of acceptance by subordinates than due to deficiencies in decision quality.

Another striking difference between the behavior of the model and of the typical manager lies in the fact that the former shows far greater variance with the situation. If a typical manager voluntarily used the model as the basis for choosing his methods of making decisions, he would become both more autocratic and more participative. He would employ autocratic methods more frequently in situations in which his subordinates were unaffected by the decision and participative methods more frequently when his subordinates' cooperation and support were critical and/or their information and expertise were required.

It should be noted that the typical manager to whom we have been referring is merely a statistical average of the several thousand who have been studied over the last three or four years. There is a great deal of variance around that average. As evidenced by their behavior on standardized problems, some managers are already behaving in a manner that is highly consistent with the model, while others' behavior is clearly at variance with it.

## A New Technology for Leadership Development

The investigations that have been summarized here were conducted for research purposes to shed some light on the causes and consequences of participation in decision making. In the course of the research, we came to realize, partly because of the value attached to it by the managers themselves, that the data collection procedures, with appropriate additions and modifications, might also serve as a valuable guide to leadership development. From this realization evolved an important by-product of the research activities—a new approach to leadership development based on the concepts in the normative model and the empirical methods of the descriptive research.

This approach is based on the assumption stated previously that one of the critical skills required of all leaders is the ability to adapt their behavior to the demands of the situation and that one component of this skill involves the ability to select the appropriate decision-making process for each problem or decision he confronts.

Managers can derive value from the model by comparing their past or intended behavior in concrete decisions with that prescribed by the model and by seeing what rules, if any, they violate. Used in this way, the model can provide a mechanism for a manager to analyze both the circumstances that he faces and what decisions are feasible under these circumstances.

While use of the model without training is possible, we believe that the manager can derive the maximum value from a systematic examination of his leadership style, and its similarities to and dissimilarities from the model, as part of a formal leadership development program.

During the past two years we have developed such a program. It is not intended to "train" participants in the use of the model, but rather to encourage them to examine their own leadership style and to ask themselves whether the methods they are using are most effective for their own organization. A critical part of the program involves the use of a set of standardized cases, each depicting a leader faced with an administrative problem to solve. Each participant then specifies the decision-making process that he would use if faced with each situation. His responses are processed by computer, which generates a highly detailed analysis of his leadership style. The responses for all participants in the course are typically processed simultaneously, permitting the economical representation of differences between the person and other participants in the same program.

In its present form, a single computer printout for a person consists of three 15" x 11" pages, each filled with graphs and tables highlighting different features of his behavior. Understanding the results requires a detailed knowledge of the concepts underlying the model, something already developed in one of the previous phases of the training program. The printout is accompanied by a manual that aids in explaining results and provides suggested steps to be followed in extracting full meaning from the printout.

Following are a few of the questions that the printout answers:

1. How autocratic or participative am I in my dealings with subordinates in comparison with other participants in the program?

2. What decision processes do I use more or less frequently than the average?

3. How close does my behavior come to that of the model? How frequently does my behavior agree with the feasible set? What evidence is there that my leadership style reflects the pressure of time as opposed to a concern with the development of my subordinates? How do I compare in these respects with other participants in the class?

4. What rules do I violate most frequently and least frequently? How does this compare with other participants? On what cases did I violate these rules? Does my leadership style reflect more concern with getting decisions that are high in quality or with getting decisions that are accepted?

5. What circumstances cause me to behave in an autocratic fashion; what circumstances cause me to behave participatively? In what respects is the way in which I attempt to vary my behavior with the demands of the situation similar to that of the model?

When a typical manager receives his printout, he immediately goes to work trying to understand what it tells him about himself. After most of the major results have been understood, he goes back to the set of cases to re-read those on which he has violated rules. Typically, managers show an interest in discussing and comparing their results with others in the program. Gatherings of four to six people comparing their results and their interpretation of them, often for several hours at a stretch, were such a common feature that they have recently been institutionalized as part of the procedure.

We should emphasize that the method of providing feedback to managers on their leadership style is just one part of the total training experience, but it is an important part. The program is sufficiently new so that, to date, no long-term evaluative studies have been undertaken. The short-term results, however, appear quite promising.

## Conclusion

The efforts reported in this article rest on the conviction that social scientists can be of greater value in solving problems of organizational behavior if their prescriptive statements deal with the complexities involved in the phenomena with which they study. The normative model described in this paper is one step in that direction. Some might argue that it is premature for social scientists to be prescriptive. Our knowledge is too limited and the issues too complex to warrant prescriptions for action, even those that are based on a diagnosis of situational demands. However, organizational problems persist, and managers cannot wait for the behavioral sciences to perfect their disciplines before attempting to cope with them. Is it likely that models that encourage them to deal analytically with the forces impinging upon them would produce less rational choices than those that they now make? We think the reverse is more probable—reflecting on the models will result in decisions that are more rational and more effective. The criterion for social utility is not perfection but improvement over present practice.

## Selected Bibliography

The interested reader may wish to consult *Leadership and Decision-Making* by Vroom and Yetton, which presents a more complete explication of the model, other models dealing with related aspects of the decision-making process, and their use in leadership development. This book will be published in June 1973 by the University of Pittsburgh Press. For another perspective on the normative questions with which this article deals, the leader should consult "How to Choose a Leadership Pattern" by Robert Tannenbaum and Warren Schmidt (*Harvard Business Review*, September 1958). The descriptive questions are explored by Frank Heller in his new book *Managerial Decision-Making* (Tavistock, 1971).

Finally, *Problem-Solving Discussions and Conferences* (McGraw-Hill, 1963) by Norman R. F. Maier represents the most useful account of the conference leadership techniques and skills required to implement participative approaches to management.

The reader interested in exploring the approach to managerial training discussed in this article should contact Kepner-Tregoe and Associates, Research Road, P.O. Box 704, Princeton, New Jersey 08540.

## Learning Review

*Questions:*

1. Managerial decision making may be viewed in either a _____ or a _____ fashion.

2. The Vroom-Yetton model identifies _____ types of management decision styles.

3. The two research methods employed in an attempt to develop a descriptive model of leader behavior included _____ and _____ problems.

4. The aim of the normative model is to develop a set of ground rules for matching a manager's _____ _____ to the demands of the situation.

5. The aim of the descriptive model is to gain greater understanding of the factors that influence managers in their choice of _____ _____ to fit the demands of the situation.

*Answers:*

1. Normative, descriptive; 2. six; 3. recalled, standardized; 4. leadership behavior; 5. decision processes.

---

## Retrospective Comment

### BY VICTOR H. VROOM

This article was the first in what has proven to be a large-scale continuing research program on leadership styles. As I read over the article, I am made aware of the intellectual debts to Tannenbaum and Schmidt, who contributed to my thinking concerning the taxonomy of styles, and to Norman Maier, who helped to distinguish decision quality from decision acceptance. While there is little that I find wrong in what I wrote at that time, I am impressed by how much we have learned since this article was written, particularly about the descriptive aspects of the problem. There have also been important developments along normative lines. Arthur Jago, of the University of Houston, and I have been working on a substantially revised model which is both more complex and more valid than the model described here. In this new model there are twelve problem attributes, most of which can assume 5 levels. The complexity of the model lends itself to representation as a computer program which can easily run on a personal computer.

# 23

## *That Urge to Achieve*

### DAVID C. McCLELLAND

### *About the Author*

**David C. McClelland** is Chairman of the Board of Directors of McBer and Company and Professor of Psychology at Harvard University. Before Harvard, he taught at Wesleyan University, Connecticut College for Women, and at Bryn Mawr College.

McClelland received his B.A. from Wesleyan, his M.S. from Harvard, and his Ph.D. from Yale. He has received honorary degrees from Harvard, Wesleyan, MacMurray, Albion, and Johannes Gutenberg Universitat. He is the author of fourteen books and over 90 articles. He has lectured in Europe and Asia and has served as a consultant to government agencies in the U.S. and abroad.

## PREVIEW

A. Most people can be divided psychologically into two broad groups.
   1. A minority of persons who are challenged by opportunity and are willing to work hard to achieve something.
   2. The majority—those who are not greatly challenged to achieve results.

a. A study of high achievement persons was conducted by psychologists among laid off workers during a plant shutdown in Erie, Pennsylvania.

b. A small minority of workers who were laid off were motivated by a personality characteristic labeled *Motive A*.

c. Characteristics of Motive A include:

(i) Persons who set challenges for themselves.

(ii) Persons who do not take chances, preferring to work at a problem rather than leave the outcome to chance or to others.

(iii) Persons with a strong preference for work situations in which they receive concrete feedback on how well they are doing.

B. People who behave in this manner spend their time thinking about doing things better.

1. Psychologists can determine an individual's *nAch* Score ("need for Achievement") by the frequency with which the person mentions doing things better.

2. Some people think in this manner, not because they are born that way but because of special training they get at home from their parents.

3. Much public and business policy is based on the simple-minded notion that people work harder, "if they have to." This is only a half-truth.

C. A study of human motives shows that each may lead a person to behave in different ways.

1. People with a higher nAch tend to choose experts over their friends when given a choice of selecting a working partner, while people with more nAff ("need to affiliate with others") would choose friends over experts.

2. A distinction between the need for power and the need for achievement lies in the fact that persons with high n Power are not as concerned with improving their work performance daily as those with high nAch.

D. A method of developing nAch in individuals or nations, began with the introduction of "total push" training courses for business persons designed to increase their nAch.

1. The broad outline for the courses had four main goals.

a. To teach the participants how to think, talk and act like a person with high nAch.

b. To stimulate the participants to set higher but carefully planned and realistic work goals for themselves over the next two years.

c. To utilize techniques for giving the participants knowledge about themselves.

d. The courses also usually created a group *esprit de corps* from learning about each other's hopes and fears, successes and failures, and from going through an emotional experience together, away from everyday life, in a retreat setting.

2. Applications of this method of developing achievement motivation are (a) in helping underdeveloped countries, (b) in helping businesses that need to take a more enterprising approach toward their growth and development, and (c) in developing more nAch among lower-income groups.

E. These training techniques are still in their infancy, but society should be willing to invest heavily in them in view of their tremendous potential for contributing to human betterment.

Most people in this world, psychologically, can be divided into two broad groups. There is that minority which is challenged by opportunity and willing to work hard to achieve something, and the majority which really does not care all that much.

For nearly twenty years now, psychologists have tried to penetrate the mystery of this curious dichotomy. Is the need to achieve (or the absence of it) an accident, is it hereditary, or is it the result of environment? Is it a single, isolatable human motive, or a combination of motives—the desire to accumulate wealth, power, fame? Most important of all, is there some technique that could give this will to achieve to people, even whole societies, who do not now have it?

While we do not yet have complete answers for any of these questions, years of work have given us partial answers to most of them and insights into all of them. There is a distinct human motive, distinguishable from others. It can be found, in fact tested for, in any group.

Let me give you one example. Several years ago, a careful study was made of 450 workers who had been thrown out of work by a plant shutdown in Erie, Pennsylvania. Most of the unemployed workers stayed home for a while and then checked back with the United States Employment Service to see if their old jobs or similar ones were available. But a small minority among them behaved differently: the day they were laid off, they started job-hunting.

They checked both the United States and the Pennsylvania Employment Office; they studied the "Help Wanted" sections of the papers; they checked through their union, their church, and various fraternal organizations; they looked into training courses to learn a new skill; they even left town to look for work, while the majority when questioned said they would not under any circumstances move away from Erie to obtain a job. Obviously the members of that active minority were differently motivated. All the men were more or less in the same situation objectively: they needed work, money, food, shelter, job security. Yet only a minority showed initiative and enterprise in finding what they needed. Why? Psychologists, after years of research, now believe they can answer that question. They have demonstrated that these men possessed in greater degree a specific type of human motivation. For the moment let us refer to this personality characteristic as "Motive A" and review some of the other characteristics of the men who have more of the motive than other men.

Suppose they are confronted by a work situation in which they can set their own goals as to how difficult a task they will undertake. In the psychological laboratory, such a situation is very simply created by asking them to throw rings over a peg from any distance they may choose. Most men throw more or less randomly, standing now close, now far away, but those with Motive A seem to calculate carefully where they are most likely to get a sense of mastery.

They stand nearly always at moderate distances, not so close as to make the task ridiculously easy, nor so far away as to make it impossible. They set moderately difficult, but potentially achievable goals for themselves, where they objectively have only about a 1-in-3 chance of succeeding. In other words, they are always setting challenges for themselves, tasks to make them stretch themselves a little.

But they behave like this only if *they* can influence the outcome by performing the work themselves. They prefer not to gamble at all. Say they are given a choice between rolling dice with one in three chances of winning and working on a problem with a one-in-three chance of solving in the time allotted, they choose to work on the problem even though rolling the dice is obviously less work and the odds of winning are the same. They prefer to work at a problem rather than leave the outcome to chance or to others.

Obviously they are concerned with personal achievement rather than with the rewards of success *per se,* since they stand just as much chance of getting those rewards by throwing the dice. This leads to another characteristic the Motive A men show—namely, a strong preference for work situations in which they get concrete feedback on how well they are doing, as one does, say in playing golf, or in being a salesman, but as one does not in teaching, or in personnel counseling. A golfer always knows his score and can compare how well he is doing with par or with his own performance yesterday or last week. A teacher has no such concrete feedback on how well he is doing in "getting across" to his students.

## The *n* Ach Men

But why do certain men behave like this? At one level the reply is simple: because they habitually spend their time thinking about doing things better. In fact, psychologists typically measure the strength of Motive A by taking samples of a man's spontaneous thoughts (such as making up a story about a picture they have been shown) and counting the frequency with which he mentions doing things better. The count is objective and can even be made these days with the help of a computer program for content analysis. It yields what is referred to technically as an individual's *n* Ach score (for "need for Achievement"). It is not difficult to understand why people who think constantly about "doing better" are more apt to do better at job-hunting, to set moderate, achievable goals for themselves, to dislike gambling (because they get no achievement satisfaction from success), and to prefer work situations where they can tell easily whether they are improving or not. But why some people and not others come to think this way is another question. The evidence suggests it is not because they are born that way, but because of special training they get in the home from parents who set moderately high achievement goals but who are warm, encouraging and nonauthoritarian in helping their children reach these goals.

Such detailed knowledge about one motive helps correct a lot of common sense ideas about human motivation. For example, much public policy (and much business policy) is based on the simpleminded notion that people will work harder "if they have to." As a first approximation, the idea isn't totally wrong, but it is only a half-truth. The majority of unemployed workers in Erie "had to" find work as much as those with higher $n$ Ach, but they certainly didn't work as hard at it. Or again, it is frequently assumed that *any* strong motive will lead to doing things better. Wouldn't it be fair to say that most of the Erie workers were just "unmotivated"? But our detailed knowledge of various human motives shows that each one leads a person to behave in *different* ways. The contrast is not between being "motivated" or "unmotivated" but between being motivated toward A or toward B or C, etc.

A simple experiment makes the point nicely: subjects were told that they could choose as a working partner either a close friend or a stranger who was known to be an expert on the problem to be solved. Those with higher $n$ Ach (more "need to achieve") chose the experts over their friends, whereas those with more $n$ Aff (the "need to affiliate with others") chose friends over experts. The latter were not "unmotivated"; their desire to be with someone they liked was simply a stronger motive than their desire to excel at the task. Other such needs have been studied by psychologists. For instance, the need for Power is often confused with the need for Achievement because both may lead to "outstanding" activities. There is a distinct difference. People with a strong need for Power want to command attention, get recognition, and control others. They are more active in political life and tend to busy themselves primarily with controlling the channels of communication both up to the top and down to the people so that they are more "in charge." Those with high $n$ Power are not as concerned with improving their work performance daily as those with high $n$ Ach.

It follows, from what we have been able to learn, that not all "great achievers" score high in $n$ Ach. Many generals, outstanding politicians, great research scientists do not, for instance, because their work requires other personality characteristics, other motives. A general or a politician must be more concerned with power relationships, a research scientist must be able to go for long periods without the immediate feedback the person with high $n$ Ach requires, etc. On the other hand, business executives, particularly if they are in positions of real responsibility or if they are salesmen, tend to score high in $n$ Ach. This is true even in a Communist country like Poland: apparently there, as well as in a private enterprise economy, a manager succeeds if he is concerned about improving all the time, setting moderate goals, keeping track of his or the company's performance, etc.

## Motivation and Half-truths

Since careful study has shown that common sense notions about motivation are at best half-truths, it also follows that you cannot trust what people tell you about their motives. After all, they often get their ideas about their own motives from common sense. Thus a general may say he is interested in achievement (because he has obviously achieved), or a businessman that he is interested only in making money (because he has made money), or one of the majority of unemployed in Erie that he desperately wants a job (because he knows he needs one); but a careful check of what each one thinks about and how he spends his time may show that each is concerned about quite different things. It requires special measurement techniques to identify the presence of *n* Ach and other such motives. Thus what people say and believe is not very closely related to these "hidden" motives which seem to affect a person's "style of life" more than his political, religious or social attitudes. Thus *n* Ach produces enterprising men among labor leaders or managers, Republicans or Democrats, Catholics or Protestants, capitalists or Communists.

Wherever people begin to think often in *n* Ach terms, things begin to move. Men with higher *n* Ach get more raises and are promoted more rapidly, because they keep actively seeking ways to do a better job. Companies with many such men grow faster. In one comparison of two firms in Mexico, it was discovered that all but one of the top executives of a fast growing firm had higher *n* Ach scores than the highest scoring executive in an equally large but slow-growing firm. Countries with many such rapidly growing firms tend to show above-average rates of economic growth. This appears to be the reason why correlations have regularly been found between the *n* Ach content in popular literature (such as popular songs or stories in children's textbooks) and subsequent rates of national economic growth. A nation which is thinking about doing better all the time (as shown in its popular literature) actually does do better economically speaking. Careful quantitative studies have shown this to be true in Ancient Greece, in Spain in the Middle Ages, in England from 1400–1800, as well as among contemporary nations, whether capitalist or Communist, developed or underdeveloped.

Contrast these two stories for example. Which one contains more *n* Ach? Which one reflects a state of mind which ought to lead to harder striving to improve the way things are?

*Excerpt from story A* (4th grade reader): "Don't Ever Owe a Man—The world is an illusion. Wife, children, horses and cows are all just ties of fate. They are ephemeral. Each after fulfilling his part in life disappears. So we should not clamour after riches which are not permanent. As long as we live it is wise not to have any attachments and just think of God. We have to spend our lives without trouble, for is it not time that there is an end to grievances? So it is better to live knowing the real state of affairs. Don't get entangled in the meshes of family life."

*Excerpt from story B* (4th grade reader): "How I Do Like to Learn—I was sent to an accelerated technical high school. I was so happy I cried. Learning is not very easy. In the beginning I couldn't understand what the teacher taught us. I always got a red cross mark on my papers. The boy sitting next to me was very enthusiastic and also an outstanding student. When he found I couldn't do the problems he offered to show me how he had done them. I could not copy his work. I must learn through my own reasoning. I gave his paper back and explained I had to do it myself. Sometimes I worked on a problem until midnight. If I couldn't finish, I started early in the morning. The red cross marks on my work were getting less common. I conquered my difficulties. My marks rose. I graduated and went on to college."

Most readers would agree, without any special knowledge of the *n* Ach coding system, that the second story shows more concern with improvement than the first, which comes from a contemporary reader used in Indian public schools. In fact the latter has a certain Horatio Alger quality that is reminiscent of our own McGuffey readers of several generations ago. It appears today in the text-books of Communist China. It should not, therefore, come as a surprise if a nation like Communist China, obsessed as it is with improvement, tended in the long run to outproduce a nation like India, which appears to be more fatalistic.

The *n* Ach level is obviously important for statesmen to watch and in many instances to try to do something about, particularly if a nation's economy is lagging. Take Britain, for example. A generation ago (around 1925) it ranked fifth among 25 countries where children's readers were scored for *n* Ach—and its economy was doing well. By 1950 the *n* Ach level had dropped to 27th out of 39 countries—well below the world average—and today, its leaders are feeling the severe economic effects of this loss in the spirit of enterprise.

## Economics and *n* Ach

If psychologists can detect *n* Ach levels in individuals or nations, particularly before their effects are widespread, can't the knowledge somehow be put to use to foster economic development? Obviously detection or diagnosis is not enough. What good is it to tell Britain (or India for that matter) that it needs more *n* Ach, a greater spirit of enterprise? In most such cases, informed observers of the local scene know very well that such a need exists, though they may be slower to discover it than the psychologist hovering over *n* Ach scores. What is needed is some method of developing *n* Ach in individuals or nations.

Since about 1960, psychologists in my research group at Harvard have been experimenting with techniques designed to accomplish this goal, chiefly among business executives whose work requires the action characteristics of people with high *n* Ach. Initially, we had real doubts as to whether we could succeed, partly because like most American psychologists we had been strongly influenced by the psychoanalytic view that basic motives are laid down in childhood and cannot really be changed later, and partly because many studies of intensive psychotherapy and counseling have shown minor if any long-term personality effects. On the other hand we were encouraged by the nonprofessionals: those enthusiasts like Dale Carnegie, the Communist ideologue or the Church mission-ary, who felt they could change adults and in fact seemed to be doing so. At any rate we ran some brief (7 to 10 days) "total push" training courses for businessmen, designed to increase their *n* Ach.

## Four Main Goals

In broad outline the courses had four main goals: (1) They were designed to teach the participants how to think, talk and act like a person with high *n* Ach, based on our knowledge of such people gained through 17 years of research. For instance, men learned how to make up stories that would code high in *n* Ach (i.e., how to think in *n* Ach terms), how to set moderate goals for themselves in the ring toss game (and in life). (2) The courses stimulated the participants to set higher but carefully planned and realistic work goals for themselves over the next two years. Then we checked back with them every six months to see how well they were doing in terms of their own objectives. (3) The courses also utilized techniques for giving the participants knowledge about themselves. For instance, in playing the ring toss game, they could observe that they behaved differently from others—perhaps in refusing to adjust a goal downward after failure. This would then become a matter for group discussion and the man would have to explain what he had in mind in setting such unrealistic goals. Discussion could then lead on to what a man's ultimate goals in life were, how much he cared about actually improving performance v. making a good impression or having many friends. In this way the participants would be freer to realize their achievement goals without being blocked by old habits and attitudes. (4) The courses also usually created a group *esprit de corps* from learning about each other's hopes and fears, successes and failures, and from going through an emotional experience together, away from everyday life, in a retreat setting. This membership in a new group helps a man achieve his goals, partly because he knows he has their sympathy and support and partly because he knows they will be watching to see how well he does. The same effect has been noted in other therapy groups like Alcoholics Anonymous. We are not sure which of these course "inputs" is really absolutely essential—that remains a research question—but we were taking no chances at the outset in view of the general pessimism about such efforts, and we wanted to include any and all techniques that were thought to change people.

The courses have been given to executives in a large American firm, and in several Mexican firms; to underachieving high school boys; and to businessmen in India from Bombay and from a small city—Kakinada in the state of Andhra Pradesh. In every instance save one (the Mexican case), it was possible to demonstrate statistically, some two years later, that the men who took the course had done better (made more money, got promoted faster, expanded their businesses faster) than comparable men who did not take the course or who took some other management course.

Consider the Kakinada results, for example. In the two years preceding the course 9 men, 18 percent of the 52 participants, had shown "unusual" enterprise in their businesses. In the 18 months following the course 25 of the men, in other words nearly 50 percent, were unusually active. And this was not due to a general upturn of business in India. Data from a control city, some forty-five miles away, show the same base rate of "unusually active" men as in Kakinada before the course—namely, about 20 percent. Something clearly happened in Kakinada: the owner of a small radio shop started a chemical plant; a banker was so successful in making commercial loans in an enterprising way that he was promoted to a much larger branch of his bank in Calcutta; the local political leader accomplished his goal (it was set in the course) to get the federal government to deepen the harbor and make it into an all-weather port; plans are far along for establishing a steel rolling mill, etc. All this took place without any substantial capital input from the outside. In fact, the only costs were for four 10-day courses plus some brief follow-up visits every six months. The men are raising their own capital and using their own resources for getting business and industry moving in a city that had been considered stagnant and unenterprising.

The promise of such a method of developing achievement motivation seems very great. It has obvious applications in helping underdeveloped countries, or "pockets of poverty" in the United States, to move faster economically. It has great potential for businesses that need to "turn around" and take a more enterprising approach toward their growth and development. It may even be helpful in developing more $n$ Ach among low-income groups. For instance, data show that lower-class Negro Americans have a very low level of $n$ Ach. This is not surprising. Society has systematically discouraged and blocked their achievement striving. But as the barriers to upward mobility are broken down, it will be necessary to help stimulate the motivation that will lead them to take advantage of new opportunities opening up.

## Extreme Reactions

But a word of caution: Whenever I speak of this research and its great potential, audience reaction tends to go to opposite extremes. Either people remain skeptical and argue that motives can't really be changed, that all we are doing is dressing Dale Carnegie up in fancy "psychologese," or they become converts and want instant course descriptions by return mail to solve their local motivational problems. Either response is unjustified. What I have described here in a few pages has taken 20 years of patient research effort, and hundreds of thousands of dollars in basic research costs. What remains to be done will involve even larger sums and more time for development to turn a promising idea into something of wide practical utility.

## Encouragement Needed

To take only one example, we have not yet learned how to develop $n$ Ach really well among low-income groups. In our first effort—a summer course for bright underachieving 14-year-olds—we found that boys from the middle class improved steadily in grades in school over a two-year period, but boys from the lower class showed an improvement after the first year followed by a drop back to their beginning low grade average. (See chart.) Why? We speculated that it was because they moved back into an environment in which neither parents nor friends encouraged achievement or upward mobility. In other words, it isn't enough to change a man's motivation if the environment in which he lives doesn't support at least to some degree his new efforts. Negroes striving to rise out of the ghetto frequently confront this problem: they are often faced by skepticism at home and suspicion on the job, so that even if their $n$ Ach is raised, it can

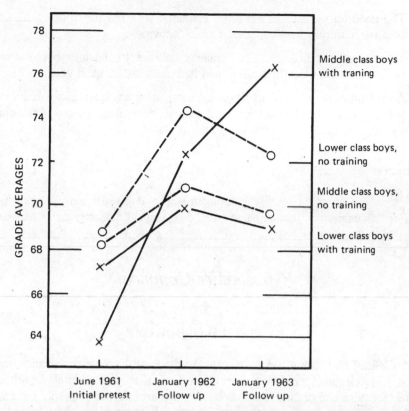

Figure 1. In a Harvard study, a group of underachieving 14-year-olds was given a six-week course designed to help them do better in school. Some of the boys were also given training in achievement motivation; or *n* Ach (solid lines). As graph reveals; the only boys who continued to improve after a two-year period were the middle-class boys with the special *n* Ach training. Psychologists suspect the lower-class boys dropped back; even with *n* Ach training; because they returned to an environment in which neither parents nor friends encouraged achievement.

be lowered again by the heavy odds against their success. We must learn not only to raise *n* Ach but also to find methods of instructing people in how to manage it, to create a favorable environment in which it can flourish.

Many of these training techniques are now only in the pilot testing stage. It will take time and money to perfect them, but society should be willing to invest heavily in them in view of their tremendous potential for contribution to human betterment.

---

## Learning Review

*Questions:*

1. Most people with _____ _____ are always setting _____ _____ for themselves, tasks to make them stretch themselves a little.

2.  The need for _____ is often confused with the need for _____ because both may lead to "_____" activities.

3.  The "_____ _____" training courses for businesspersons were designed to increase their nAch, and had _____ main goals.

4.  A method of developing achievement motivation has obvious applications in helping _____ countries; and also in developing more nAch among _____ _____ groups.

*Answers:*

1. motive A, challenging goals   2. power, achievement, outstanding   3. total push, four   4. underdeveloped, low income

---

# *Retrospective Comment*

✦

## BY DONALD D. BOWEN *

McClelland's contributions to our understanding of human motivation in his work on *n* Ach (need for achievement) have been truly monumental. As students of management and organizational behavior, we are inevitably deeply interested in the factors which cause people to accomplish and achieve. McClelland also recognized the importance of this issue and it has profoundly affected his more recent work:

> ". . . the man with high *n* Achievement seldom can act alone, even though he might like to. He is caught up in an organizational context in which he is managed, controlled, or directed by others. To understand better what happens to him, we must shift our attention to those who are managing him, to those who are concerned about organizational relationships—to the leaders of men." [1]

Thus, McClelland's more recent investigations have centered on the need for power, rather than *n* Ach.

McClelland's approach to power motivation may provide even greater insights into the behavior of organization members than his studies of *n* Ach have. He identifies a number of different types of power orientations, some of which may tend to generate negative consequences and some of which may lead to highly constructive outcomes. [2] Since he now more clearly than ever recognizes that what people will try to accomplish is largely determined by the constraints and stimuli provided in their organizational or social environment, his contributions

---

* Professor of Management, University of Tulsa.

in the future to our understanding of the management of organizations may well dwarf the substantial impact of his earlier work on *n* Ach.

# REFERENCES

1.  McClelland, David C., *Power: The Inner Experience.* New York: Irvington Publishers, 1975. P. 254.
2.  *Ibid.*

# 24

# *Goal Setting—A Motivational Technique That Works*

GARY P. LATHAM                    EDWIN A. LOCKE

## *About the Authors*

**Gary P. Latham** is Professor and Chairman of the Management and Organization Department in the Business School at the University of Washington. He is a Fellow in both the American and Canadian Psychological Associations, and was the 1985 recipient of the Burlington Northern Foundation Distinguished Scholar Award. He serves on the editorial boards of three scientific journals and he is the author of numerous articles in professional journals. He consults with organizations in both the United States and Canada and is formerly staff psychologist for Weyerhauser Company.

Professor Latham received his Ph.D. from Akron University in 1974, his M.S. from Georgia Institute of Technology, and his B.A. from Dalhousie University in Nova Scotia.

**Edwin A. Locke** is joint Professor of Business and Management and of Psychology at the University of Maryland, College Park, where he has taught for the

Reprinted, by permission of the authors and the publisher, from *Organizational Dynamics*, (Autumn 1979). © 1979 American Management Association, New York. All rights reserved. Figures 1 and 2 slightly modified at the request of the authors. Photo of Latham provided by Jones Photo Co.

past twelve years. He received his Ph.D. from Cornell University in 1964, his M.A. from Cornell, and his B.A. from Harvard. From 1964 to 1967, he worked for the American Institute for Research in Silver Spring, Maryland. Originally trained in industrial psychology, Dr. Locke is also a practicing psychotherapist. He is a Fellow of the American Psychological Association and a member of the Academy of Management. He has published more than 70 chapters and articles and two books, primarily in the area of work motivation and job satisfaction.

# PREVIEW

A. Since managers cannot change the basic personality structures of their employees, they must rely upon incentives to direct employees' efforts toward the achievement of organizational goals.
   1. Money is a primary incentive.
   2. Money alone does not always produce high employee performance; organizations may also use such incentives as participation in decision making, job enrichment, behavior modification, or organizational development.
B. Several studies and experiments have determined that workers who are given goals are more productive than those without.
   1. Employees who are assigned specific goals perform better than those who are given vague goals.
   2. Employees given highly challenging goals perform better than those with moderately difficult or easily attainable goals.
   3. Pay and feedback lead to improved performance only when they lead individual employees to set high goals.
C. Goal setting improves productivity by providing workers with several benefits.
   1. Difficult, yet attainable, goals increase the challenge of a job.
   2. Specific goals make it clear to the worker what he or she is expected to do.
   3. Goal feedback provides the worker with a sense of achievement, recognition, and accomplishment.
D. Several methods exist by which goals are established; different approaches work best under different circumstances.
   1. The fact that a goal is set is more important than how it is set.
   2. Participative goal setting is superior to assigned goals only to the extent that it leads to higher goals being set.
E. Research and experience suggest that the best results are obtained when three steps are followed in goal setting.
   1. First, goals should be set that are both specific and challenging, yet achievable. Goals can be derived from several input sources.
   2. Second, goal commitment should be obtained by providing instruction backed with positive support and absence of threats and intimidation. Success in achieving a goal and competition among employees in meeting goals can lead to greater goal commitment.

3. Third, support elements should be provided to ensure that employees have adequate resources required to accomplish goals.

F. Care must be taken in setting goals, since incorrect use of goals may cause, rather than solve, problems.

   1. If goals are unfair, arbitrary, or unreachable, dissatisfaction and poor performance may result.

   2. If goals are set without quality controls, quantity may be achieved at the expense of quality.

   3. Pressure for immediate results may cause employees to use expedient, but ultimately costly, methods which result in short-term improvements at the expense of long-term success.

   4. It is important to set performance goals in all areas; managers should not succumb to the temptation to concentrate only upon areas that are easily measured.

---

The problem of how to motivate employees has puzzled and frustrated managers for generations. One reason the problem has seemed difficult, if not mysterious, is that motivation ultimately comes from within the individual and therefore cannot be observed directly. Moreover, most managers are not in a position to change an employee's basic personality structure. The best they can do is try to use incentives to direct the energies of their employees toward organizational objectives.

Money is obviously the primary incentive, since without it few if any employees would come to work. But money alone is not always enough to motivate high performance. Other incentives, such as participation in decision making, job enrichment, behavior modification, and organizational development, have been tried with varying degrees of success. A large number of research studies have shown, however, that one very straightforward technique—goal setting—is probably not only more effective than alternative methods, but may be the major mechanism by which these other incentives affect motivation. For example, a recent experiment on job enrichment demonstrated that unless employees in enriched jobs set higher, more specific goals than do those with unenriched jobs, job enrichment has absolutely no effect on productivity. Even money has been found most effective as a motivator when the bonuses offered are made contingent on attaining specific objectives.

## The Goal-Setting Concept

The idea of assigning employees a specific amount of work to be accomplished—a specific task, a quota, a performance standard, an objective, or a deadline—is not new. The task concept, along with time and motion study and incentive pay, was the cornerstone of scientific management, founded by Frederick W. Taylor more than 70 years ago. He used his system to increase the productivity of blue collar workers. About 20 years ago the idea of goal setting reappeared under a new name, management by objectives, but this technique was designed for managers.

In a 14-year program of research, we have found that goal setting does not necessarily have to be part of a wider management system to motivate performance effectively. It can be used as a technique in its own right.

## Laboratory and Field Research

Our research program began in the laboratory. In a series of experiments, individuals were assigned different types of goals on a variety of simple tasks—addition, brainstorming, assembling toys. Repeatedly it was found that those assigned hard goals performed better than did people assigned moderately difficult or easy goals. Furthermore, individuals who had specific, challenging goals outperformed those who were given such vague goals as to "do your best." Finally, we observed that pay and performance feedback led to improved performance only when these incentives led the individual to set higher goals.

While results were quite consistent in the laboratory, there was no proof that they could be applied to actual work settings. Fortunately, just as Locke published a summary of the laboratory studies in 1968, Latham began a separate series of experiments in the wood products industry that demonstrated the practical significance of these findings. The field studies did not start out as a validity test of a laboratory theory, but rather as a response to a practical problem.

In 1968, six sponsors of the American Pulpwood Association became concerned about increasing the productivity of independent loggers in the South. These loggers were entrepreneurs on whom the multimillion-dollar companies are largely dependent for their raw material. The problem was twofold. First, these entrepreneurs did not work for a single company; they worked for themselves. Thus they were free to (and often did) work two days one week, four days a second week, five half-days a third week, or whatever schedule they preferred. In short, these workers could be classified as marginal from the standpoint of their productivity and attendance, which were considered highly unsatisfactory by conventional company standards. Second, the major approach taken to alleviate this problem had been to develop equipment that would make the industry less dependent on this type of worker. A limitation of this approach was that many of the logging supervisors were unable to obtain the financing necessary to purchase a small tractor, let alone a rubber-tired skidder.

Consequently, we designed a survey that would help managers determine "what makes these people tick." The survey was conducted orally in the field with 292 logging supervisors. Complex statistical analyses of the data identified three basic types of supervisor. One type stayed on the job with their men, gave them instructions and explanations, provided them with training, read the trade magazines, and had little difficulty financing the equipment they needed. Still, the productivity of their units was at best mediocre.

The operation of the second group of supervisors was slightly less mechanized. These supervisors provided little training for their workforce. They simply drove their employees to the woods, gave them a specific production goal to attain for the day or week, left them alone in the woods unsupervised, and returned at night to take them home. Labor turnover was high and productivity was again average.

The operation of the third group of supervisors was relatively unmechanized. These leaders stayed on the job with their men, provided training, gave instructions and explanations, and in addition, set a specific production goal for the day or week. Not only was the crew's productivity high, but their injury rate was well below average.

Two conclusions were discussed with the managers of the companies sponsoring this study. First, mechanization alone will not increase the productivity of logging crews. Just as the average taxpayer would probably commit more mathematical errors if he were to try to use a computer to complete his income tax return, the average logger misuses, and frequently abuses, the equipment he purchases (for example, drives a skidder with two flat tires, doesn't change the oil filter). This increases not only the logger's downtime, but also his costs which, in turn, can force him out of business. The second conclusion of the survey was that setting a specific production goal combined with supervisory presence to ensure goal commitment will bring about a significant increase in productivity.

These conclusions were greeted with the standard, but valid, cliché, "Statistics don't prove causation." And our comments regarding the value of machinery were especially irritating to these managers, many of whom had received degrees in engineering. So one of the companies decided to replicate the survey in order to check our findings.

The company's study placed each of 892 independent logging supervisors who sold wood to the company into one of three categories of supervisory styles our survey had identified—namely, (1) stays on the job but does not set specific production goals; (2) sets specific production goals but does not stay on the job; and (3) stays on the job and sets specific production goals. Once again, goal setting, in combination with the on-site presence of a supervisor, was shown to be the key to improved productivity.

## Testing for the Hawthorne Effect

Management may have been unfamiliar with different theories of motivation, but it was fully aware of one label—the Hawthorne effect. Managers in these wood products companies remained unconvinced that anything so simple as staying on the job with the men and setting a specific production goal could have an appreciable effect on productivity. They pointed out that the results simply reflected the positive effects any supervisor would have on the work unit after giving his crew attention. And they were unimpressed by the laboratory experiments we cited—experiments showing that individuals who have a specific goal solve more arithmetic problems or assemble more tinker toys than do people who are told to "do your best." Skepticism prevailed.

But the country's economic picture made it critical to continue the study of inexpensive techniques to improve employee motivation and productivity. We were granted permission to run one more project to test the effectiveness of goal setting.

Twenty independent logging crews who were all but identical in size, mechanization level, terrain on which they worked, productivity, and attendance were located. The logging supervisors of these crews were in the habit of staying on the job with their men, but they did not set production goals. Half the crews were randomly selected to receive training in goal setting; the remaining crews served as a control group.

The logging supervisors who were to set goals were told that we had found a way to increase productivity at no financial expense to anyone. We gave the ten supervisors in the training group production tables developed through time-and-motion studies by the company's engineers. These tables made it possible to determine how much wood should be harvested in a given number of manhours. They were asked to use these tables as a guide in determining a specific production goal to assign their employees. In addition, each sawhand was given a tallymeter (counter) that he could wear on his belt. The sawhand was asked to punch the counter each time he felled a tree. Finally, permission was requested to measure the crew's performance on a weekly basis.

The ten supervisors in the control group—those who were not asked to set production goals—were told that the researchers were interested in learning the extent to which productivity is affected by absenteeism and injuries. They were urged to "do your best" to maximize the crew's productivity and attendance and to minimize injuries. It was explained that the data might be useful in finding ways to increase productivity at little or no cost to the wood harvester.

To control for the Hawthorne effect, we made an equal number of visits to the control group and the training group. Performance was measured for 12 weeks. During this time, the productivity of the goal-setting group was significantly higher than that of the control group. Moreover, absenteeism was significantly lower in the groups that set goals than in the groups who were simply urged to do their best. Injury and turnover rates were low in both groups.

Why should anything so simple and inexpensive as goal setting influence the work of these employees so significantly? Anecdotal evidence from conversations with both the loggers and the company foresters who visited them suggested several reasons.

Harvesting timber can be a monotonous, tiring job with little or no meaning for most workers. Introducing a goal that is difficult, but attainable, increases the challenge of the job. In addition, a specific goal makes it clear to the worker what it is he is expected to do. Goal feedback via the tallymeter and weekly recordkeeping provide the worker with a sense of achievement, recognition, and accomplishment. He can see how well he is doing now as against his past performance and, in some cases, how well he is doing in comparison with others. Thus the worker not only may expend greater effort, but may also devise better or more creative tactics for attaining the goal than those he previously used.

## New Applications

Management was finally convinced that goal setting was an effective motivational technique for increasing the productivity of the independent woods worker in the South. The issue now raised by the management of another wood products company was whether the procedure could be used in the West with company logging operations in which the employees were unionized and paid by the hour. The previous study had involved employees on a piece-rate system, which was the practice in the South.

The immediate problem confronting this company involved the loading of logging trucks. If the trucks were underloaded, the company lost money. If the trucks were overloaded, however, the driver could be fined by the Highway Department and could ultimately lose his job. The drivers opted for underloading the trucks.

For three months management tried to solve this problem by urging the drivers to try harder to fill the truck to its legal net weight, and by developing weighing scales that could be attached to the truck. But this approach did not prove cost effective, because the scales continually broke down when subjected to the rough terrain on which the trucks traveled. Consequently, the drivers reverted to their former practice of underloading. For the three months in which the problem was under study the trucks were seldom loaded in excess of 58 to 63 percent of capacity.

At the end of the three-month period, the results of the previous goal-setting experiments were explained to the union. They were told three things—that the company would like to set a specific net weight goal for the drivers, that no monetary reward or fringe benefits other than verbal praise could be expected for improved performance, and that no one would be criticized for failing to attain the goal. Once again, the idea that simply setting a specific goal would solve a production problem seemed too incredible to be taken seriously by the union. However, they reached an agreement that a difficult, but attainable, goal of 94 percent of the truck's legal net weight would be assigned to the drivers, provided that no one could be reprimanded for failing to attain the goal. This latter point was emphasized to the company foremen in particular.

Within the first month, performance increased to 80 percent of the truck's net weight. After the second month, however, performance decreased to 70 percent. Interviews with the drivers indicated that they were testing management's statement that no punitive steps would be taken against them if their performance suddenly dropped. Fortunately for all concerned, no such steps were taken by the foremen, and performance exceeded 90 percent of the truck's capacity after the third month. Their performance has remained at this level to this day, seven years later.

The results over the nine-month period during which this study was conducted saved the company $250,000. This figure, determined by the company's accountants, is based on the cost of additional trucks that would have been required to deliver the same quantity of logs to the mill if goal setting had not been implemented. The dollars-saved figure is even higher when you factor in the cost of the additional diesel fuel that would have been consumed and the expenses incurred in recruiting and hiring the additional truck drivers.

Why could this procedure work without the union's demanding an increase in hourly wages? First, the drivers did not feel that they were really doing anything differently. This, of course, was not true. As a result of goal setting, the men began to record their truck weight in a pocket notebook, and they found themselves bragging about their accomplishments to their peers. Second, they viewed goal setting as a challenging game: "It was great to beat the other guy."

Competition was a crucial factor in bringing about goal acceptance and commitment in this study. However, we can reject the hypothesis that improved performance resulted solely from competition, because no special prizes or formal recognition programs were provided for those who came closest to, or exceeded, the goal. No effort was made by the company to single out one "winner." More important, the opportunity for competition among drivers had existed before goal setting was instituted; after all, each driver knew his own truck's weight, and the truck weight of each of the 36 other drivers every time he hauled wood into the yard. In short, competition affected productivity only in the sense that it led to the acceptance of, and commitment to, the goal. It was the setting of the goal itself and the working toward it that brought about increased performance and decreased costs.

## Participative Goal Setting

The inevitable question always raised by management was raised here: "We know goal setting works. How can we make it work better?" Was there one best method for setting goals? Evidence for a "one best way" approach was cited by several managers, but it was finally concluded that different approaches would work best under different circumstances.

It was hypothesized that the woods workers in the South, who had little or no education, would work better with assigned goals, while the educated workers in the West would achieve higher productivity if they were allowed to help set the goals themselves. Why the focus on education? Many of the uneducated workers in the South could be classified as culturally disadvantaged. Such persons often lack self-confidence, have a poor sense of time, and are not very competitive. The cycle of skill mastery, which in turn guarantees skill levels high enough to prevent discouragement, doesn't apply to these employees. If, for example, these people were allowed to participate in goal setting, the goals might be too difficult or they might be too easy. On the other hand, participation for the educated worker was considered critical in effecting maximum goal acceptance. Since these conclusions appeared logical, management initially decided that no research was necessary. This decision led to hours of further discussion.

The same questions were raised again and again by the researchers. What if the logic were wrong? Can we afford to implement these decisions without evaluating them systematically? Would we implement decisions regarding a new approach to tree planting without first testing it? Do we care more about trees than we do about people? Finally, permission was granted to conduct an experiment.

Logging crews were randomly appointed to either participative goal setting, assigned (nonparticipative) goal setting, or a do-your-best condition. The results were startling. The uneducated crews, consisting primarily of black employees who participated in goal setting, set significantly higher goals and attained them more often than did those whose goals were assigned by the supervisor. Not surprisingly, their performance was higher. Crews with assigned goals performed no better than did those who were urged to do their best to improve their productivity. The performance of white, educationally advantaged workers was higher with assigned rather than participatively set goals, although the difference was not statistically significant. These results were precisely the opposite of what had been predicted.

Another study comparing participative and assigned goals was conducted with typists. The results supported findings obtained by researchers at General Electric years before. It did not matter so much *how* the goal was set. What mattered was *that* a goal was set. The study demonstrated that both assigned and participatively set goals led to substantial improvements in typing speed. The process by which these gains occurred, however, differed in the two groups.

In the participative group, employees insisted on setting very high goals regardless of whether they had attained their goal the previous week. Nevertheless, their productivity improved—an outcome consistent with the theory that high goals lead to high performance.

In the assigned-goal group, supervisors were highly supportive of employees. No criticism was given for failure to attain the goals. Instead, the supervisor lowered the goal after failure so that the employee would be certain to attain it. The goal was then raised gradually each week until the supervisor felt the employee was achieving his or her potential. The result? Feelings of accomplishment and achievement on the part of the worker and improved productivity for the company.

These basic findings were replicated in a subsequent study of engineers and scientists. Participative goal setting was superior to assigned goal setting only to the degree that it led to the setting of higher goals. Both participative and assigned-goal groups outperformed groups that were simply told to "do your best."

An additional experiment was conducted to validate the conclusion that participation in goal setting may be important only to the extent that it leads to the setting of difficult goals. It was performed in a laboratory setting in which the task was to brainstorm uses for wood. One group was asked to "do your best" to think of as many ideas as possible. A second group took part in deciding, with the experimenter, the specific number of ideas each person would generate. These goals were, in turn, assigned to individuals in a third group. In this way, goal difficulty was held constant between the assigned-goal and participative groups. Again, it was found that specific, difficult goals—whether assigned or set through participation—led to higher performance than did an abstract or generalized goal such as "do your best." And, when goal difficulty was held constant, there was no significant difference in the performance of those with assigned as compared with participatively set goals.

These results demonstrate that goal setting in industry works just as it does in the laboratory. Specific, challenging goals lead to better performance than do easy or vague goals, and feedback motivates higher performance only when it leads to the setting of higher goals.

| Researcher(s) | Task | Duration of Study or of Significant Effects | Percent of Change in Performance [a] |
|---|---|---|---|
| Blumenfeld & Leidy | Servicing soft drink coolers | Unspecified | +27 |
| Dockstader | Keypunching | 3 mos. | +27 |
| Ivancevich | Skilled technical jobs | 9 mos. | +15 |
| Ivancevich | Sales | 9 mos. | +24 |
| Kim and Hamner | 5 telephone service jobs | 3 mos. | +13 |
| Latham and Baldes | Loading trucks | 9 mos.[b] | +26 |
| Latham and Yukl | Logging | 2 mos. | +18 |
| Latham and Yukl | Typing | 5 weeks | +11 |
| Migliore | Mass production | 2 years | +16 |
| Umstot, Bell, and Mitchell | Coding land parcels | 1–2 days [c] | +16 |

[a] Percentage changes were obtained by subtracting pre-goal-setting performance from post-goal-setting performance and dividing by pre-goal-setting performance. Different experimental groups were combined where appropriate. If a control group was available, the percentage figure represents the difference of the percentage changes between the experimental and control groups. If multiple performance measures were used, the median improvement on all measures was used. The authors would like to thank Dena Feren and Vivki McCaleb for performing these calculations.
[b] Performance has remained high for seven years.
[c] Simulated organization.

*Figure 1.* Representative field studies of goal setting

It is important to note that participation is not only a motivational tool. When a manager has competent subordinates, participation is also a useful device for increasing the manager's knowledge and thereby improving decision quality. It can lead to better decisions through input from subordinates.

A representative sample of the results of field studies of goal setting conducted by Latham and others is shown in Figure 1. Each of these ten studies compared the performance of employees given specific challenging goals with those given "do best" or no goals. Note that goal setting has been successful across a wide variety of jobs and industries. The effects of goal setting have been recorded for as long as seven years after the onset of the program, although the results of most studies have been followed up for only a few weeks or months. The median improvement in performance in the ten studies shown in Figure 1 was 17 percent.

## A Critical Incidents Survey

To explore further the importance of goal setting in the work setting, Dr. Frank White conducted another study in two plants of a high-technology, multinational corporation on the East Coast. Seventy-one engineers, 50 managers, and 31 clerks were asked to describe a specific instance when they were especially productive and a specific instance when they were especially unproductive on their present jobs. Responses were classified according to a reliable coding scheme. Of primary interest here are the external events perceived by employees as being responsible for the high-productivity and low-productivity incidents. The results are shown in Figure 2.

The first set of events—pursuing a specific goal, having a large amount of work, working under a deadline, or having an uninterrupted routine—accounted for more than half the high-productivity events. Similarly, the converse of these—goal blockage, having a small amount of work, lacking a deadline, and suffering work interruptions—accounted for nearly 60 percent of the low-productivity events. Note that the first set of four categories are all relevant to goal setting and the second set to a lack of goals or goal blockage. The goal category itself—that of pursuing an attainable goal or goal blockage—was the one most frequently used to describe high- and low-productivity incidents.

The next four categories, which are more pertinent to Frederick Herzberg's motivator-hygiene theory—task interest, responsibility, promotion, and recognition—are less important, accounting for 36.8 percent of the high-productivity incidents (the opposite of these four categories accounted for 19.1 percent of the lows). The remaining categories were even less important.

Employees were also asked to identify the responsible agent behind the events

| | Percent of Times Event Caused | |
| Event | High Productivity | Low Productivity |
| --- | --- | --- |
| Goal pursuit/Goal blockage | 17.1 | 23.0 |
| Large amount of work/Small amount of work | 12.5 | 19.0 |
| Deadline or schedule/No deadline | 15.1 | 3.3 |
| Smooth work routine/Interrupted routine | 5.9 | 14.5 |
| Total | 50.6 | 59.8 |
| Interesting task/Uninteresting task | 17.1 | 11.2 |
| Increased responsibility/Decreased responsibility | 13.8 | 4.6 |
| Anticipated promotion/Promotion denied | 1.3 | 0.7 |
| Verbal recognition/Criticism | 4.6 | 2.6 |
| Total | 36.8 | 19.1 |
| Pleasant personal relationships/Unpleasant personal relationships | 10.5 | 9.9 |
| Anticipated pay increase/Pay increase denied | 1.3 | 1.3 |
| Pleasant working conditions/Unpleasant working conditions | 0.7 | 0.7 |
| Other (miscellaneous) | — | 9.3 |

* N = 152 in this study by Frank White.

Figure 2.   Events perceived as causing high and low productivity *

that had led to high and low productivity. In both cases, the employees themselves, their immediate supervisors, and the organization were the agents most frequently mentioned.

The concept of goal setting is a very simple one. Interestingly, however, we have gotten two contradictory types of reaction when the idea was introduced to managers. Some claimed it was so simple and self-evident that everyone, including themselves, already used it. This, we have found, is not true. Time after time we have gotten the following response from subordinates after goal setting was introduced: "This is the first time I knew what my supervisor expected of me on this job." Conversely, other managers have argued that the idea would not work, precisely *because* it is so simple (implying that something more radical and complex was needed). Again, results proved them wrong.

But these successes should not mislead managers into thinking that goal setting can be used without careful planning and forethought. Research and experience suggest that the best results are obtained when the following steps are followed:

**Setting the Goal.** The goal set should have two main characteristics. First, it should be specific rather than vague: "Increase sales by 10 percent" rather than "Try to improve sales." Whenever possible, there should be a time limit for goal accomplishment: "Cut costs by 3 percent in the next six months."

Second, the goal should be challenging yet reachable. If accepted, difficult goals lead to better performance than do easy goals. In contrast, if the goals are perceived as unreachable, employees will not accept them. Nor will employees get a sense of achievement from pursuing goals that are never attained. Employees with low self-confidence or ability should be given more easily attainable goals than those with high self-confidence and ability.

There are at least five possible sources of input, aside from the individual's self-confidence and ability, that can be used to determine the particular goal to set for a given individual.

The scientific management approach pioneered by Frederick W. Taylor uses time and motion study to determine a fair day's work. This is probably the most objective technique available, but it can be used only where the task is reasonably repetitive and standardized. Another drawback is that this method often leads to employee resistance, especially in cases where the new standard is substantially higher than previous performance and where rate changes are made frequently.

More readily accepted, although less scientific than time and motion study, are standards based on the average past performance of employees. This methods was used successfully in some of our field studies. Most employees consider this approach fair but, naturally, in cases where past performance is far below capacity, beating that standard will be extremely easy.

Since goal setting is sometimes simply a matter of judgment, another technique we have used is to allow the goal to be set jointly by supervisor and subordinate. The participative approach may be less scientific than time and motion study, but it does lead to ready acceptance by both employee and immediate superior in addition to promoting role clarity.

External constraints often affect goal setting, especially among managers. For cxample, the goal to produce an item at a certain price may be dictated by the actions of competitors, and deadlines may be imposed externally in line with contract agreements. Legal regulations, such as attaining a certain reduction in pollution levels by a certain date, may affect goal setting as well. In these cases, setting the goal is not so much the problem as is figuring out a method of reaching it.

Finally, organizational goals set by the board of directors or upper management will influence the goals set by employees at lower levels. This is the essence of the MBO process.

Another issue that needs to be considered when setting goals is whether they should be designed for individuals or for groups. Rensis Likert and a number of other human relations experts argue for group goal setting on grounds that it promotes cooperation and team spirit. But one could argue that individual goals better promote individual responsibility and make it easier to appraise individual performance. The degree of task interdependence involved would also be a factor to consider.

**Obtaining Goal Commitment.**　If goal setting is to work, then the manager must ensure that subordinates will accept and remain committed to the goals. Simple instruction backed by positive support and an absence of threats or intimidation were enough to ensure goal acceptance in most of our studies. Subordinates must perceive the goals as fair and reasonable and they must trust management, for if they perceive the goals as no more than a means of exploitation, they will be likely to reject the goals.

It may seem surprising that goal acceptance was achieved so readily in the field studies. Remember, however, that in all cases the employees were receiving wages or a salary (although these were not necessarily directly contingent on goal attainment). Pay in combination with the supervisor's benevolent authority and supportiveness were sufficient to bring about goal acceptance. Recent research indicates that whether goals are assigned or set participatively, supportiveness on the part of the immediate superior is critical. A supportive manager or supervisor does not use goals to threaten subordinates, but rather to clarify what is expected of them. His or her role is that of a helper and goal facilitator.

As noted earlier, the employee gets a feeling of pride and satisfaction from the experience of reaching a challenging but fair performance goal. Success in reaching a goal also tends to reinforce acceptance of future goals. Once goal setting is introduced, informal competition frequently arises among the employees. This further reinforces commitment and may lead employees to raise the goals spontaneously. A word of caution here, however: We do not recommend setting up formal competition, as this may lead employees to place individual goals ahead of company goals. The emphasis should be on accomplishing the task, getting the job done, not "beating" the other person.

When employees resist assigned goals, they generally do so for one of two reasons. First, they may think they are incapable of reaching the goal because they lack confidence, ability, knowledge, and the like. Second, they may not see any personal benefit—either in terms of personal pride or in terms of external rewards like money, promotion, recognition—in reaching assigned goals.

There are various methods of overcoming employee resistance to goals. One possibility is more training designed to raise the employee's level of skill and selfconfidence. Allowing the subordinate to participate in setting the goal—deciding on the goal level—is another method. This was found most effective among uneducated and minority group employees, perhaps because it gave them a feeling of control over their fate. Offering monetary bonuses or other rewards (recognition, time off) for reaching goals may also help.

The last two methods may be especially useful where there is a history of labor-management conflict and where employees have become accustomed to a lower level of effort than currently considered acceptable. Group incentives may also encourage goal acceptance, especially where there is a group goal, or when considerable cooperation is required.

**Providing Support Elements.**   A third step to take when introducing goal setting is to ensure the availability of necessary support elements. That is, the employee must be given adequate resources—money, equipment, time, help— as well as the freedom to utilize them in attaining goals, and company policies must not work to block goal attainment.

Before turning an employee loose with these resources, however, it's wise to do a quick check on whether conditions are optimum for reaching the goal set. First, the supervisor must make sure that the employee has sufficient ability and knowledge to be able to reach the goal. Motivation without knowledge is

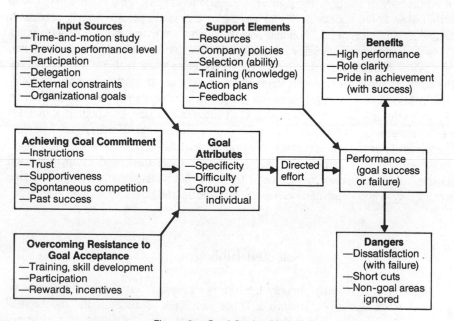

*Figure 3.*   Goal-Setting Model

useless. This, of course, puts a premium on proper selection and training and requires that the supervisor know the capabilities of subordinates when goals are assigned. Asking an employee to formulate an action plan for reaching the goal, as in MBO, is very useful, as it will indicate any knowledge deficiencies.

Second, the supervisor must ensure that the employee is provided with precise feedback so that he will know to what degree he's reaching or falling short of his goal and can thereupon adjust his level of effort or strategy accordingly. Recent research indicates that, while feedback is not a sufficient condition for improved performance, it is a necessary condition. A useful way to present periodic feedback is through the use of charts or graphs that plot performance over time.

Elements involved in taking the three steps described are shown in Figure 3, which illustrates in outline form our model of goal setting.

## Conclusion

We believe that goal setting is a simple, straightforward, and highly effective technique for motivating employee performance. It is a basic technique, a method on which most other methods depend for their motivational effectiveness. The currently popular technique of behavior modification, for example, is mainly goal setting plus feedback, dressed up in academic terminology.

However, goal setting is no panacea. It will not compensate for underpayment of employees or for poor management. Used incorrectly, goal setting may cause rather than solve problems. If, for example, the goals set are unfair, arbitrary, or unreachable, dissatisfaction and poor performance may result. If difficult goals are set without proper quality controls, quantity may be achieved at the expense of quality. If pressure for immediate results is exerted without regard to how they are attained, short-term improvement may occur at the expense of long-run profits. That is, such pressure often triggers the use of expedient and ultimately costly methods—such as dishonesty, high-pressure tactics, postponing of maintenance expenses, and so on—to attain immediate results. Furthermore, performance goals are more easily set in some areas than in others. It's all too easy, for example, to concentrate on setting readily measured production goals and ignore employee development goals. Like any other management tool, goal setting works only when combined with good managerial judgment.

## Selected Bibliography

A summary of the early (mainly laboratory) research on goal setting may be found in E. A. Locke's "Toward a Theory of Task Motivation and Incentives" (*Organization Behavior and Human Performance,* May 1968). More recent reviews that include some of the early field studies are reported by G. P. Latham and G. A. Yukl's "Review of Research on the Application of Goal Setting in Organizations" (*Academy of Management Journal*, December 1975) and in R. M. Steers and L. W. Porter's "The Role of Task-Goal Attributes in Employee Performance" (*Psychological Bulletin*, July 1974).

An excellent historical discussion of management by objectives, including its relationship to goal-setting research, can be found in G. S. Odiorne's "MBO: A Backward Glance" (*Business Horizons*, October 1978).

A thorough review of the literature on participation, including the relationship of participation and goal setting, can be found in a chapter by E. A. Locke and D. M. Schweiger, "Participation in Decision-Making: One More Look," in B. M. Staw's edited work, *Research in Organizational Behavior* (Vol. 1, Greenwich, JAI Press, 1979). General Electric's famous research on the effect of participation in the appraisal interview is summarized in H. H. Meyer, E. Kay, and J. R. P. French, Jr.'s "Split Roles in Performance Appraisal" (*Harvard Business Review*, January-February 1965).

The relationship of goal setting to knowledge of results is discussed in E. A. Locke, N. Cartledge, and J. Koeppel's "Motivational Effects of Knowledge of Results: A Goal Setting Phenomenon?" (*Psychological Bulletin*, December 1968) and L. J. Becker's "Joint Effect of Feedback and Goal Setting on Performance: A Field Study of Residential Energy Conservation" (*Journal of Applied Psychology*, August 1978). Finally, the role of goal setting in virtually all theories of work motivation is documented in E. A. Locke's "The Ubiquity of the Technique of Goal Setting in Theories of and Approaches to Employee Motivation" (*Academy of Management Review*, July 1978).

---

## Learning Review

### Questions

1. _____ are used by managers to motivate employees to make efforts to achieve organizational _____.

2. _____ is a widely-used form of goal setting for managers at various ranks in the organization.

3. _____, _____, but _____ goals lead to highest performance.

4. The two factors mentioned in the article that resulted in higher productivity by logging teams were _____ and _____.

5. Commitment to goals may be increased by _____ _____ and _____ _____.

6. To successfully achieve a goal, an employee must have not only motivation but _____ and _____.

*Answers:*

---

# Retrospective Comment

## BY GARY P. LATHAM

Since writing our article in 1979, we have worked independently and together to increase our understanding of four issues: the importance of participative versus assigned goals; the effectiveness of self-set goals; the relationship of one's self efficacy to one's goals and subsequent performance; and the effect of task complexity on the goal-performance relationship. Some of this work has been summarized in Locke and Latham (1984).

In 1986, we began a collaboration with Dr. Miriam Erez to identify why she has consistently found that participatively set goals result in higher performance than assigned goals. We, on the other hand, have found that when the difficulty level of the goal is the same, performance too is the same, regardless of whether the goal is assigned or set in a participatory manner. From a motivational standpoint, we found that the value of participatively set goals is that they can result in setting higher goals, hence achieving a higher performance than when a goal is assigned initially.

What is unique about our work with Dr. Erez is that this is one of the few times in science when "antagonists" have worked together to resolve contradictory findings. Initially we focused on the meaningfulness of the task, hypothesizing that, with boring tasks, participatively set goals result in superior performance than assigned goals. However, the data showed this was not the case. Both methods of goal setting proved to be equally effective with regard to a person's performance. We are continuing our work with Dr. Erez to discover an explanation for our differences. The three of us are in agreement that participatively set goals are an effective way of improving performance; we continue to disagree on the value of assigned goals.

Regarding self-set goals, Locke and I find that they are every bit as effective in the workplace as goals that are either assigned or set participatively. One of us has just completed a study where self-set goals proved to be effective in increasing the job attendance of unionized state government employees.

Our work on self efficacy—the belief that one can or cannot perform a specific task—showed that there is a positive association between self efficacy and the difficulty level of the goals one chooses, as well as one's subsequent performance. Our study on job attendance showed that training people in self-management skills increased attendance because it involved their self efficacy beliefs regarding their ability to overcome problems affecting their ability to come to work.

Our research on task complexity corroborates the work of others. As might be expected, goal setting is effective with all types of tasks over which the individual has control. The relationship between goal setting and performance, however, is strongest with straightforward tasks.

# REFERENCE

Locke, E. A. & Latham, G. P. (1984) *Goal Setting: A motivational technique that works.* Englewood Cliffs, NJ: Prentice-Hall.

# 25

# On the Folly of Rewarding A, While Hoping for B

## STEVEN KERR

### About the Author

**Steven Kerr** is Dean of Faculty and Research Professor of Management and Organization in the Business School at the University of Southern California. His Ph.D. is from the City University of New York. Before joining USC, he worked in the private sector and served on the faculty of The Ohio State University. He is a member of three editorial review boards, has chaired both the Organizational Behavior and Organization and Management Theory Divisions of the Academy of Management, and has been a member of the Academy's Board of Governors. He is the coauthor of two books and has written more than forty articles for scholarly journals.

Reprinted by permission of the author and the *Academy of Management Journal*, Vol. 18, (December 1975), pp. 769–783.

# PREVIEW

A. Most organisms seek information designed to identify those activities that
   are rewarded. These are the activities they then perform.
   1. An examination of costs and benefits, combined with what motivates an
      individual, determines what is rational for that individual.
   2. Behavior desired by the organization may not be personally rational for
      the individual.
   3. Numerous examples exist of reward systems designed that reward behavior
      the manager is attempting to discourage, while not rewarding desired
      behavior.
B. Several factors exist that may lead to the creation of a reward system that
   rewards undesired behavior.
   1. Fascination with objective criteria often results in measurement of unimpor-
      tant factors, while ignoring more important—but more difficult-to-mea-
      sure—factors. This may result in goal displacement.
   2. Overemphasis on visible behavior typically results in some desired behav-
      iors being unrewarded because they are not highly visible.
   3. Emphasis on morality or equity may prevent the establishment of a system
      that rewards efficient behavior.
C. Since individuals possess divergent goals, it is unlikely that managers and
   subordinates will always seek the same goals. Three possible remedies for
   this potential problem exist:
   1. The organization may seek to employ only those individuals whose goals
      and motives match those of the organization.
   2. The organization may attempt to alter employee goals to better conform
      to those of the organization through extensive training.
   3. Reward systems can be altered to reward desired, rather than undesired,
      behavior.

---

Whether dealing with monkeys, rats, or human beings, it is hardly controversial
to state that most organisms seek information concerning what activities are
rewarded, and then seek to do (or at least pretend to do) those things, often
to the virtual exclusion of activities not rewarded. The extent to which this
occurs of course will depend on the perceived attractiveness of the rewards
offered, but neither operant nor expectancy theorists would quarrel with the
essence of this notion.

Nevertheless, numerous examples exist of reward systems that are fouled
up in that behaviors which are rewarded are those which the rewarder is trying
to *discourage*, while the behavior he desires is not being rewarded at all.

In an effort to understand and explain this phenomenon, this paper presents
examples from society, from organizations in general, and from profit making

firms in particular. Data from a manufacturing company and information from an insurance firm are examined to demonstrate the consequences of such reward systems for the organizations involved, and possible reasons why such reward systems continue to exist are considered.

## Societal Examples

### Politics

Official goals are "purposely vague and general and do not indicate . . . the host of decisions that must be made among alternative ways of achieving official goals and the priority of multiple goals . . ." (8, p. 66). They usually may be relied on to offend absolutely no one, and in this sense can be considered high acceptance, low quality goals. An example might be "build better schools." Operative goals are higher in quality but lower in acceptance, since they specify where the money will come from, what alternative goals will be ignored, etc.

The American citizenry supposedly wants its candidates for public office to set forth operative goals, making their proposed programs "perfectly clear," specifying sources and uses of funds, etc. However, since operative goals are lower in acceptance, and since aspirants to public office need acceptance (from at least 50.1 percent of the people), most politicians prefer to speak only of official goals, at least until after the election. They of course would agree to speak at the operative level if "punished" for not doing so. The electorate could do this by refusing to support candidates who do not speak at the operative level.

Instead, however, the American voter typically punishes (withholds support from) candidates who frankly discuss where the money will come from, rewards politicians who speak only of official goals, but hopes that candidates (despite the reward system) will discuss the issues operatively. It is academic whether it was moral for Nixon, for example, to refuse to discuss his 1968 "secret plan" to end the Vietnam war, his 1972 operative goals concerning the lifting of price controls, the reshuffling of his cabinet, etc. The point is that the reward system made such refusal rational.

It seems worth mentioning that no manuscript can adequately define what is "moral" and what is not. However, examination of costs and benefits, combined with knowledge of what motivates a particular individual, often will suffice to determine what for him is "rational." [1] If the reward system is so designed that it is irrational to be moral, this does not necessarily mean that immortality will result. But is this not asking for trouble?

### War

If some oversimplification may be permitted, let it be assumed that the primary goal of the organization (Pentagon, Luftwaffe, or whatever) is to win. Let it be assumed further that the primary goal of most individuals on the front lines is to get home alive. Then there appears to be an important conflict in goals—personally rational behavior by those at the bottom will endanger goal attainment by those at the top.

But not necessarily! It depends on how the reward system is set up. The Vietnam war was indeed a study of disobedience and rebellion, with terms such as "fragging" (killing one's own commanding officer) and "search and evade" becoming part of the military vocabulary. The difference in subordinates' acceptance of authority between World War II and Vietnam is reported to be considerable, and veterans of the Second World War often have been quoted as being outraged at the mutinous actions of many American soldiers in Vietnam.

Consider, however, some critical differences in the reward system in use during the two conflicts. What did the GI in World War II want? To go home. And when did he get to go home? When the war was won! If he disobeyed the orders to clean out the trenches and take the hills, the war would not be won and he would not go home. Furthermore, what were his chances of attaining his goal (getting home alive) if he obeyed the orders compared to his chances if he did not? What is being suggested is that the rational soldier in World War II, *whether patriotic or not,* probably found it expedient to obey.

Consider the reward system in use in Vietnam. What did the man at the bottom want? To go home. And when did he get to go home? When his tour of duty was over! This was the case *whether or not* the war was won. Furthermore, concerning the relative chance of getting home alive by obeying orders compared to the chance if they were disobeyed, it is worth noting that a mutineer in Vietnam was far more likely to be assigned rest and rehabilitation (on the assumption that fatigue was the cause) than he was to suffer any negative consequence.

In his description of the "zone of indifference," Barnard stated that "a person can and will accept a communication as authoritative only when . . . at the time of his decision, he believes it to be compatible with his personal interests as a whole" (1, p. 165). In light of the reward system used in Vietnam, would it not have been personally irrational for some orders to have been obeyed? Was not the military implementing a system which *rewarded* disobedience, while *hoping* that soldiers (despite the reward system) would obey orders?

## Medicine

Theoretically, a physician can make either of two types of error, and intuitively one seems as bad as the other. A doctor can pronounce a patient sick when he is actually well, thus causing him needless anxiety and expense, curtailment of enjoyable foods and activities, and even physical danger by subjecting him to needless medication and surgery. Alternately, a doctor can label a sick person well, and thus avoid treating what may be a serious, even fatal ailment. It might be natural to conclude that physicians seek to minimize both types of error.

Such a conclusion would be wrong.[2] It is estimated that numerous Americans are presently afflicted with iatrogenic (physican *caused*) illnesses (9). This occurs when the doctor is approached by someone complaining of a few stray symptoms. The doctor classifies and organizes these symptoms, gives them a name, and obligingly tells the patient what further symptoms may be expected. This information often acts as a self-fulfilling prophecy, with the result that from that day on the patient for all practical purposes is sick.

Why does this happen? Why are physicians so reluctant to sustain a type 2 error (pronouncing a sick person well) that they will tolerate many type 1 errors?

Again, a look at the reward system is needed. The punishments for a type 2 error are real: guilt, embarrassment, and the threat of lawsuit and scandal. On the other hand, a type 1 error (labeling a well person sick) "is sometimes seen as sound clinical practice, indicating a healthy conservative approach to medicine" (9, p. 69). Type 1 errors also are likely to generate increased income and a stream of steady customers who, being well in a limited physiological sense, will not embarrass the doctor by dying abruptly.

Fellow physicians and the general public therefore are really *rewarding* type 1 errors and at the same time *hoping* fervently that doctors will try not to make them.

## General Organizational Examples

### Rehabilitation Centers and Orphanages

In terms of the prime beneficiary classification (2, p. 42) organizations such as these are supposed to exist for the "public-in-contact," that is, clients. The orphanage therefore theoretically is interested in placing as many children as possible in good homes. However, often orphanages surround themselves with so many rules concerning adoption that it is nearly impossible to pry a child out of the place. Orphanages may deny adoption unless the applicants are a married couple, both of the same religion as the child, without history of emotional or vocational instability, with a specified minimum income and a private room for the child, etc.

If the primary goal is to place children in good homes, then the rules ought to constitute means toward that goal. Goal displacement results when these "means become ends-in-themselves that displace the original goals" (2, p. 229).

To some extent these rules are required by law. But the influence of the reward system on the orphanage's management should not be ignored. Consider, for example, that the:

1. Number of children enrolled often is the most important determinant of the size of the allocated budget.
2. Number of children under the director's care also will affect the size of his staff.
3. Total organizational size will determine largely the director's prestige at the annual conventions, in the community, etc.

Therefore, to the extent that staff size, total budget, and personal prestige are valued by the orphanage's executive personnel, it becomes rational for them to make it difficult for children to be adopted. After all, who wants to be the director of the smallest orphanage in the state?

If the reward system errs in the opposite direction, paying off only for placements, extensive goal displacement again is likely to result. A common example of vocational rehabilitation in many states, for example, consists of placing someone in a job for which he has little interest and few qualifications, for two months or so, and then "rehabilitating" him again in another position. Such behavior is quite consistent with the prevailing reward system, which pays off for the number of individuals placed in any position for 60 days or more. Rehabilitation counselors also confess to competing with one another to place relatively skilled clients, sometimes ignoring persons with few skills who would be harder to place. Extensively disabled clients find that counselors often prefer to work with those whose disabilities are less severe.[3]

### Universities

Society *hopes* that teachers will not neglect their teaching responsibilities but *rewards* them almost entirely for research and publications. This is most true at the large and prestigious universities. Cliches such as "good research and good teaching go together" notwithstanding, professors often find that they must choose between teaching and research oriented activities when allocating their time. Rewards for good teaching usually are limited to outstanding teacher awards, which are given to only a small percentage of good teachers and which usually bestow little money and fleeting prestige. Punishments for poor teaching also are rare.

Rewards for research and publications, on the other hand, and punishments for failure to accomplish these, are commonly administered by universities at which teachers are employed. Furthermore, publication oriented resumés usually will be well received at other universities, whereas teaching credentials, harder to document and quantify, are much less transferable. Consequently it is rational for university teachers to concentrate on research, even if to the detriment of teaching and at the expense of their students.

By the same token, it is rational for students to act based upon the goal displacement which has occurred within universities concerning what they are rewarded for. If it is assumed that a primary goal of a university is to transfer knowledge from teacher to student, then grades become identifiable as a means toward that goal, serving as motivational, control, and feedback devices to expedite the knowledge transfer. Instead, however, the grades themselves have become much more important for entrance to graduate school, successful employment, tuition refunds, parental respect, etc., than the knowledge or lack of knowledge they are supposed to signify.

It therefore should come as no surprise that information has surfaced in recent years concerning fraternity files for examinations, term paper writing services, organized cheating at the service academies, and the like. Such activities constitute a personally rational response to a reward system which pays off for grades rather than knowledge.

## Business Related Examples

### Ecology

Assume that the president of XYZ Corporation is confronted with the following alternatives:

1. Spend $11 million for antipollution equipment to keep from poisoning fish in the river adjacent to the plant; or

2. Do nothing, in violation of the law, and assume a one in ten chance of being caught, with a resultant $1 million fine plus the necessity of buying the equipment.

Under this not unrealistic set of choices it requires no linear program to determine that XYZ Corporation can maximize its probabilities by flouting the law. Add the fact that XYZ's president is probably being rewarded (by creditors, stockholders, and other salient parts of his task environment) according to criteria totally unrelated to the number of fish poisoned, and his probable course of action becomes clear.

## Evaluation of Training

It is axiomatic that those who care about a firm's well-being should insist that the organization get fair value for its expenditures. Yet it is commonly known that firms seldom bother to evaluate a new GRID, MBO, job enrichment program, or whatever, to see if the company is getting its money's worth. Why? Certainly it is not because people have not pointed out that this situation exists; numerous practitioner oriented articles are written each year to just this point.

The individuals (whether in personnel, manpower planning, or wherever) who normally would be responsible for conducting such evaluations are the same ones often charged with introducing the change effort in the first place. Having convinced top management to spend the money, they usually are quite animated afterwards in collecting arigorous vignettes and anecdotes about how successful the program was. The last thing many desire is a formal, systematic, and revealing evaluation. Although members of top management may actually *hope* for such systematic evaluation, their reward systems continue to *reward* ignorance in this area. And if the personnel department abdicates its responsibility, who is to step into the breach? The change agent himself? Hardly! He is likely to be too busy collecting anecdotal "evidence" of his own, for use with his next client.

## Miscellaneous

Many additional examples could be cited of systems which in fact are rewarding behaviors other than those supposedly desired by the rewarder. A few of these are described briefly below.

Most coaches disdain to discuss individual accomplishments, preferring to speak of teamwork, proper attitude, and a one-for-all spirit. Usually, however, rewards are distributed according to individual performance. The college basketball player who feeds his teammates instead of shooting will not compile impressive scoring statistics and is less likely to be drafted by the pros. The ballplayer who hits to right field to advance the runners will win neither the batting nor home run titles, and will be offered smaller raises. It therefore is rational for players to think of themselves first, and the team second.

In business organizations where rewards are dispensed for unit performance or for individual goals achieved, without regard for overall effectiveness, similar attitudes often are observed. Under most Management by Objectives (MBO) systems, goals in areas where quantification is difficult often go unspecified. The organization therefore often is in a position where it *hopes* for employee effort in the areas of team building, interpersonal relations, creativity, etc., but it formally *rewards* none of these. In cases where promotions and raises are formally tied to MBO, the system itself contains a paradox in that it "asks employees to set challenging, risky goals, only to face smaller paychecks and possibly damaged careers if these goals are not accomplished" (5, p. 40).

It is *hoped* that administrators will pay attention to long run costs and opportunities and will institute programs which will bear fruit later on. However, many organizational reward systems pay off for short run sales and earnings only. Under such circumstances it is personally rational for officials to sacrifice long term growth and profit (by selling off equipment and property, or by stifling research and development) for short term advantages. This probably is most pertinent in the public sector, with the result that many public officials are unwilling to implement programs which will not show benefits by election time.

As a final, clear-cut example of a fouled-up reward system, consider the cost-plus contract or its next of kin, the allocation of next year's budget as a direct function of this year's expenditures. It probably is conceivable that those who award such budgets and contracts really hope for economy and prudence in spending. It is obvious, however, that adopting the proverb "to him who spends shall more be given," rewards not economy, but spending itself.

## Two Companies' Experiences

### A Manufacturing Organization

A midwest manufacturer of industrial goods had been troubled for some time by aspects of its organizational climate it believed dysfunctional. For research purposes, interviews were conducted with many employees and a questionnaire was administered on a companywide basis, including plants and offices in several American and Canadian locations. The company strongly encouraged employee participation in the survey, and made available time and space during the workday for completion of the instrument. All employees in attendance during the day of the survey completed the questionnaire. All instruments were collected directly by the researcher, who personally administered each session. Since no one employed by the firm handled the questionnaires, and since respondent names were not asked for, it seems likely that the pledge of anonymity given was believed.

A modified version of the Expect Approval scale was included as part of the questionnaire. The instrument asked respondents to indicate the degree of approval or disapproval they could expect if they performed each of the described actions. A seven point Likert scale was used, with one indicating that the action would probably bring strong disapproval and seven signifying likely strong approval.

Although normative data for this scale from studies of other organizations are unavailable, it is possible to examine fruitfully the data obtained from this survey in several ways. First, it may be worth noting that the questionnaire data corresponded closely to information gathered through interviews. Furthermore, as can be seen from the results summarized in Table 1, sizable differences

| Dimension | Item | Division and Sample | Total Responses | Percentage of Workers Responding | | |
|---|---|---|---|---|---|---|
| | | | | 1, 2, or 3 Disapproval | 4 | 5, 6, or 7 Approval |
| *Risk* *Avoidance* | Making a risky decision based on the best information available at the time, but which turns out wrong. | A, levels 1–4 (lowest) | 127 | 61 | 25 | 14 |
| | | A, levels 5–8 | 172 | 46 | 31 | 23 |
| | | A, levels 9 and above | 17 | 41 | 30 | 30 |
| | | B, levels 1–4 lowest | 31 | 58 | 26 | 16 |
| | | B, levels 5–8 | 19 | 42 | 42 | 16 |
| | | B, levels 9 and above | 10 | 50 | 20 | 30 |
| *Risk* *Avoidance* *(Continued)* | Setting extremely high and challenging standards and goals, and then narrowly failing to make them. | A, levels 1–4 | 122 | 47 | 28 | 25 |
| | | A, levels 5–8 | 168 | 33 | 26 | 41 |
| | | A, levels 9+ | 17 | 24 | 6 | 70 |
| | | B, levels 1–4 | 31 | 48 | 23 | 29 |
| | | B, levels 5–8 | 18 | 17 | 33 | 50 |
| | | B, levels 9+ | 10 | 30 | 0 | 70 |
| | Setting goals which are extremely easy to make and then making them. | A, levels 1–4 | 124 | 35 | 30 | 35 |
| | | A, levels 5–8 | 171 | 47 | 27 | 26 |
| | | A, levels 9+ | 17 | 70 | 24 | 6 |
| | | B, levels 1–4 | 31 | 58 | 26 | 16 |
| | | B, levels 5–8 | 19 | 63 | 16 | 21 |
| | | B, levels 9+ | 10 | 80 | 0 | 20 |

*Conformity*

| | | | | | |
|---|---|---|---|---|---|
| Being a "yes man" and always agreeing with the boss. | A, levels 1–4 | 126 | 46 | 17 | 37 |
| | A, levels 5–8 | 180 | 54 | 14 | 31 |
| | A, levels 9+ | 17 | 88 | 12 | 0 |
| | B, levels 1–4 | 31 | 53 | 28 | 19 |
| | B, levels 5–8 | 19 | 68 | 21 | 11 |
| | B, levels 9+ | 10 | 80 | 10 | 10 |
| Always going along with the majority. | A, levels 1–4 | 125 | 40 | 25 | 35 |
| | A, levels 5–8 | 173 | 47 | 21 | 32 |
| | A, levels 9+ | 17 | 70 | 12 | 18 |
| | B, levels 1–4 | 31 | 61 | 23 | 16 |
| | B, levels 5–8 | 19 | 68 | 11 | 21 |
| | B, levels 9+ | 10 | 80 | 10 | 10 |
| Being careful to stay on the good side of everyone, so that everyone agrees that you are a great guy. | A, levels 1–4 | 124 | 45 | 18 | 37 |
| | A, levels 5–8 | 173 | 45 | 22 | 33 |
| | A, levels 9+ | 17 | 64 | 6 | 30 |
| | B, levels 1–4 | 31 | 54 | 23 | 23 |
| | B, levels 5–8 | 19 | 73 | 11 | 16 |
| | B, levels 9+ | 10 | 80 | 10 | 10 |

*Table 1.* Summary of two divisions' data relevant to conforming and risk-avoidance behaviors (extent to which subjects expect approval)

between various work units, and between employees at different job levels within the same work unit, were obtained. This suggests that response bias effects (social desirability in particular loomed as a potential concern) are not likely to be severe.

Most importantly, comparisons between scores obtained on the Expect Approval scale and a statement of problems which were the reason for the survey revealed that the same behaviors which managers in each division thought dysfunctional were those which lower level employees claimed were rewarded. As compared to job levels 1 to 8 in Division B (see Table 1), those in Division A claimed a much higher acceptance by management of "conforming" activities. Between 31 and 37 percent of Division A employees at levels 1–8 stated that going along with the majority, agreeing with the boss, and staying on everyone's good side brought approval; only once (level 5–8 responses to one of the three items) did a majority suggest that such actions would generate disapproval.

Furthermore, responses from Division A workers at levels 1–4 indicate that behaviors geared toward risk avoidance were as likely to be rewarded as to be punished. Only at job levels 9 and above was it apparent that the reward system was positively reinforcing behaviors desired by top management. Overall, the same "tendencies toward conservatism and apple-polishing at the lower levels" which divisional management had complained about during the interviews were those claimed by subordinates to be the most rational course of action in light of the existing reward system. Management apparently was not getting the behaviors it was *hoping* for, but it certainly was getting the behaviors it was perceived by subordinates to be *rewarding*.

### An Insurance Firm

The Group Health Claims Division of a large eastern insurance company provides another rich illustration of a reward system which reinforces behaviors not desired by top management.

Attempting to measure and reward accuracy in paying surgical claims, the firm systematically keeps track of the number of returned checks and letters of complaint received from policyholders. However, underpayments are likely to provoke cries of outrage from the insured, while overpayments often are accepted in courteous silence. Since it often is impossible to tell from the physician's statement which of two surgical procedures, with different allowable benefits, was performed, and since writing for clarifications will interfere with other standards used by the firm concerning "percentage of claims paid within two days of receipt," the new hire in more than one claims section is soon acquainted with the informal norm: "When in doubt, pay it out!"

The situation would be even worse were it not for the fact that other features of the firm's reward system tend to neutralize those described. For example, annual "merit" increases are given to all employees, in one of the following three amounts:

1. If the worker is "outstanding" (a select category, into which no more than two employees per section may be placed): 5 percent

2. If the worker is "above average" (normally all workers not "outstanding" are so rated): 4 percent
3. If the worker commits gross acts of negligence and irresponsibility for which he might be discharged in many other companies: 3 percent.

Now, since (a) the difference between the 5 percent theoretically attainable through hard work and the 4 percent attainable merely by living until the review date is small and (b) since insurance firms seldom dispense much of a salary increase in cash (rather, the worker's insurance benefits increase, causing him to be further overinsured), many employees are rather indifferent to the possibility of obtaining the extra one percent reward and therefore tend to ignore the norm concerning indiscriminant payments.

However, most employees are not indifferent to the rule which states that, should absences or latenesses total three or more in any six-month period, the entire 4 or 5 percent due at the next "merit" review must be forfeited. In this sense the firm may be described as *hoping* for performance, while *rewarding* attendance. What it gets, of course, is attendance. (If the absence-lateness rule appears to the reader to be stringent, it really is not. The company counts "times" rather than "days" absent, and a ten-day absence therefore counts the same as one lasting two days. A worker in danger of accumulating a third absence within six months merely has to remain ill (away from work) during his second absence until his first absence is more than six months old. The limiting factor is that at some point his salary ceases, and his sickness benefits take over. This usually is sufficient to get the younger workers to return, but for those with 20 or more years' service, the company provides sickness benefits of 90 percent of normal salary, tax-free! Therefore. . . .)

## Causes

Extremely diverse instances of systems which reward behavior A although the rewarder apparently hopes for behavior B have been given. These are useful to illustrate the breadth and magnitude of the phenomenon, but the diversity increases the difficulty of determining commonalities and establishing causes. However, four general factors may be pertinent to an explanation of why fouled up reward systems seem to be so prevelant.

### Fascination with an "Objective" Criterion
It has been mentioned elsewhere that:

> Most "objective" measures of productivity are objective only in that their subjective elements are a) determined in advance, rather than coming into play at the time of the formal evaluation, and b) well concealed on the rating instrument itself. Thus industrial firms seeking to devise objective rating systems first decide, in an arbitrary manner, what dimensions are to be rated, . . . usually including some items having little to do with organizational effectiveness while excluding others that do. Only then does Personnel Division churn out official-looking documents on which all dimen-

sions chosen to be rated are assigned point values, categories, or whatever (6, p. 92).

Nonetheless, many individuals seek to establish simple, quantifiable standards against which to measure and reward performance. Such efforts may be successful in highly predictable areas within an organization, but are likely to cause goal displacement when applied anywhere else. Overconcern with attendance and lateness in the insurance firm and with number of people placed in the vocational rehabilitation division may have been largely responsible for the problems described in those organizations.

### Overemphasis on Highly Visible Behaviors

Difficulties often stem from the fact that some parts of the task are highly visible while other parts are not. For example, publications are easier to demonstrate than teaching, and scoring baskets and hitting home runs are more readily observable than feeding teammates and advancing base runners. Similarly, the adverse consequences of pronouncing a sick person well are more visible than those sustained by labeling a well person sick. Team-building and creativity are other examples of behaviors which may not be rewarded simply because they are hard to observe.

### Hypocrisy

In some of the instances described the rewarder may have been getting the desired behavior, notwithstanding claims that the behavior was not desired. This may be true, for example, of management's attitude toward apple-polishing in the manufacturing firm (a behavior which subordinates felt was rewarded, despite management's avowed dislike of the practice). This also may explain politicians' unwillingness to revise the penalties for disobedience of ecology laws, and the failure of top management to devise reward systems which would cause systematic evaluation of training and development programs.

### Emphasis on Morality or Equity Rather than Efficiency

Sometimes consideration of other factors prevents the establishment of a system which rewards behaviors desired by the rewarder. The felt obligation of many Americans to vote for one candidate or another, for example, may impair their ability to withhold support from politicians who refuse to discuss the issues. Similarly, the concern for spreading the risks and costs of wartime military service may outweigh the advantage to be obtained by commiting personnel to combat until the war is over.

It should be noted that only with respect to the first two causes are reward systems really paying off for other than desired behaviors. In the case of the third and fourth causes the system *is* rewarding behaviors desired by the rewarder, and the systems are fouled up only from the standpoints of those who believe the rewarder's public statements (cause 3), or those who seek to maximize efficiency rather than other outcomes (cause 4).

# Conclusions

Modern organization theory requires a recognition that the members of organizations and society possess divergent goals and motives. It therefore is unlikely that managers and their subordinates will seek the same outcomes. Three possible remedies for this potential problem are suggested.

## Selection
It is theoretically possible for organizations to employ only those individuals whose goals and motives are wholly consonant with those of management. In such cases the same behaviors judged by subordinates to be rational would be perceived by management as desirable. State-of-the-art reviews of selection techniques, however, provide scant grounds for hope that such an approach would be successful (for example, see 12).

## Training
Another theoretical alternative is for the organization to admit those employees whose goals are not consonant with those of management and then, through training, socialization, or whatever, alter employee goals to make them consonant. However, research on the effectiveness of such training programs, though limited, provides further grounds for pessimism (for example, see 3).

## Altering the Reward System
What would have been the result if:

1. Nixon had been assured by his advisors that he could not win reelection except by discussing the issues in detail?
2. Physicians' conduct was subjected to regular examination by review boards for type 1 errors (calling healthy people ill) and to penalties (fines, censure, etc.) for errors of either type?
3. The President of XYZ Corporation had to choose between (a) spending $11 million dollars for antipollution equipment, and (b) incurring a fifty-fifty chance of going to jail for five years?

Managers who complain that their workers are not motivated might do well to consider the possibility that they have installed reward systems which are paying off for behaviors other than those they are seeking. This, in part, is what happened in Vietnam, and this is what regularly frustrates societal efforts to bring about honest politicians, civic-minded managers, etc. This certainly is what happened in both the manufacturing and the insurance companies.

A first step for such managers might be to find out what behaviors currently are being rewarded. Perhaps an instrument similar to that used in the manufacturing firm could be useful for this purpose. Chances are excellent that these managers will be surprised by what they find—that their firms are not rewarding what they assume they are. In fact, such undesirable behavior by organizational members as they have observed may be explained largely by the reward systems in use.

This is not to say that all organizational behavior is determined by formal rewards and punishments. Certainly it is true that in the absence of formal reinforcement some soldiers will be patriotic, some presidents will be ecology minded, and some orphanage directors will care about children. The point, however, is that in such cases the rewarder is not *causing* the behaviors desired but is only a fortunate bystander. For an organization to *act* upon its members, the formal reward system should positively reinforce desired behaviors, not constitute an obstacle to be overcome.

It might be wise to underscore the obvious fact that there is nothing really new in what has been said. In both theory and practice these matters have been mentioned before. Thus in many states Good Samaritan laws have been installed to protect doctors who stop to assist a stricken motorist. In states without such laws it is commonplace for doctors to refuse to stop, for fear of involvement in a subsequent lawsuit. In college basketball additional penalties have been instituted against players who foul their opponents deliberately. It has long been argued by Milton Friedman and others that penalties should be altered so as to make it irrational to disobey the ecology laws, and so on.

By altering the reward system the organization escapes the necessity of selecting only desirable people or of trying to alter undesirable ones. In Skinnerian terms (as described in 11, p. 704), "As for responsibility and goodness—as commonly defined—no one . . . would want or need them. They refer to a man's behaving well despite the absence of positive reinforcement that is obviously sufficient to explain it. Where such reinforcement exists, 'no one needs goodness.' "

# FOOTNOTES

1.   In Simon's (10, pp. 76–77) terms, a decision is "subjectively rational" if it maximizes an individual's valued outcomes so far as his knowledge permits. A decision is "personally rational" if it is oriented toward the individual's goals.

2.   In one study (4) of 14,867 films for signs of tuberculosis, 1,216 positive readings turned out to be clinically negative; only 24 negative readings proved clinically active, a ratio of 50 to 1.

3.   Personal interviews conducted during 1972–1973.

# REFERENCES

1.   Barnard, Chester I. *The Functions of the Executive* (Cambridge, Mass.: Harvard University Press, 1964).

2.   Blau, Peter M., and W. Richard Scott. *Formal Organizations* (San Francisco: Chandler, 1962).

3.   Fiedler, Fred E. "Predicting the Effects of Leadership Training and Experience from the Contingency Model," *Journal of Applied Psychology,* Vol. 56 (1972), 114–119.

4. Garland, L. H. "Studies of the Accuracy of Diagnostic Procedures," *American Journal Roentgenological, Radium Therapy Nuclear Medicine,* Vol. 82 (1959), 25–38.
5. Kerr, Steven. "Some Modifications in MBO as an OD Strategy," *Academy of Management Proceedings,* 1973, pp. 39–42.
6. Kerr, Steven. "What Price Objectivity?" *American Sociologist,* Vol. 8 (1973), 92–93.
7. Litwin, G. H., and R. A. Stringer, Jr. *Motivation and Organizational Climate* (Boston: Harvard University Press, 1968).
8. Perrow, Charles. "The Analysis of Goals in Complex Organizations," in A. Etzioni (Ed.), *Readings on Modern Organizations* (Englewood Cliffs, N.J.: Prentice-Hall, 1969).
9. Scheff, Thomas J. "Decision Rules, Types of Error, and Their Consequences in Medical Diagnosis," in F. Massarik and P. Ratoosh (Eds.), *Mathematical Explorations in Behavioral Science* (Homewood, Ill.: Irwin, 1965).
10. Simon, Herbert A. *Administrative Behavior* (New York: Free Press, 1957).
11. Swanson, G. E. "Review Symposium: Beyond Freedom and Dignity," *American Journal of Sociology,* Vol. 78 (1972), 702–705.
12. Webster, E. *Decision Making in the Employment Interview* (Montreal: Industrial Relations Center, McGill University, 1964).

---

## Learning Review

*Questions:*

1. People seek to perform activities that are _____.

2. _____ goals are vague and general; _____goals are specific.

3. Examination of costs, benefits, and motivation results in determination by the individual of what is_____.

4. _____occurs when means displace original goals.

5. Several reasons explain why reward systems frequently reward undesired behavior. They include:
   (a) _____ _____;
   (b) _____ _____;
   (c) _____ _____.

*Answers:*

emphasis on morality or equity, rather than efficiency.
5. fascination with objective criteria, overemphasis on highly visible behavior,
1. rewarded; 2. Official, operational; 3. rational; 4. Goal displacement;

## *Retrospective Comment*

### BY STEVEN KERR

Two ironies are associated with "On the Folly of Rewarding A, While Hoping for B." The first is that perhaps it shouldn't have been published, since it was based on what turned out to be a false assumption. The assumption was that I had discovered some odd, atypical, dysfunctional reward systems—systems that reward behaviors the rewarder is actually seeking to discourage, while ignoring or even punishing hoped-for behaviors.

At first amused, then captivated by this paradox of circumstances I began what has turned out to be a ten-year investigation of organizational reward systems. Some of the results of this investigation have been published elsewhere (see Schneider and Schoorman, 1986), but the essential point is that there is nothing atypical about the examples described in "On the Folly. . . ." To the contrary, I have become convinced that *nearly all organizations* are afflicted with the problems I had earlier described.

The second irony, which I would emphasize more were I writing the article today, is that most people already know, and act on in everyday life, the principles that underlie the piece. For example, when we tell our daughter (who is about to cut the cake) that her brother will select the first piece, or inform our friends at the *start* of a meal that separate checks will be brought at the end, or tell the neighbor's boy that he will be paid five dollars for cutting our lawn *after* we inspect the lawn, we are using prospective rewards and punishments to cause other people to care about our objectives. Organizations are more complex, but the principles are no different.

The third of my two ironies (I said this was about ironies) is that the article was first refused for presentation at the Eastern Academy of Management; then barely accepted by the *Academy of Management Journal* when my good friend, Jack Miner, broke a tie between two reviewers. None of the critiques I saw denied the relevance of my content, but reviewers were mighty disturbed about the tone of the thing, and therefore questioned its appropriateness for an academic audience. A compromise was reached whereby I added a bit more of the great academic cure-all—data (the Table 1 you see in the article)—and the copy editor strangled much of the life out of my writing style.

## REFERENCE

S. Kerr, "Some Characteristics and Consequences of Organizational Reward Systems", in B. Schneider and D. Schoorman (eds.), *Facilitating Work Effectiveness*. Lexington, MA: Lexington Books, 1986.

# 26

## *The Effect of Performance on Job Satisfaction*

EDWARD E. LAWLER, III LYMAN W. PORTER

### *About the Authors*

***Edward E. Lawler, III*** received his B.A. from Brown University and his Ph.D. from Berkeley in 1964. He has taught at Yale University and at Michigan, where he was Professor of Psychology and Program Director in the Survey Research Center at the Institute for Social Research. He has been a visiting scientist at the Battelle Institute and has held a Fulbright Fellowship at the London Graduate School of Business. In 1978 he joined the faculty at the University of Southern California. Professor Lawler serves on the editorial board for five professional journals and is the author of over 100 articles and books, including *Managing Organizational Behavior* (Little, Brown, 1979).

***Lyman W. Porter,*** formerly Dean of the Graduate School of Management, is Professor of Management and Psychology at the University of California, Irvine. After earning his Ph.D. at Yale, he taught for eleven years at the University of California, Berkeley. Professor Porter is the author of six books and over 70 articles in the fields of organizational psychology and management. He is a

Reprinted from *Industrial Relations, a Journal of Economy and Society,* 1967, 7 (1), 20–28.

past president of the Academy of Management and of the Division of Industrial-Organizational Psychology of The American Psychological Association. He is a recipient of the Academy of Management's highest honor, the Scholarly Contributions to Management Award.

# PREVIEW

A. There is evidence indicating a low but consistent relationship between satisfaction and performance.
   1. It is not clear why this relationship exists.
   2. A relationship between satisfaction and performance has been accepted—and later rejected—in the past.
B. Job satisfaction is important to all organizations.
   1. A strong correlation exists between absenteeism and satisfaction.
   2. Job satisfaction has a low but consistent association with job performance.
C. Satisfaction and performance are caused by different factors, although they bear some relationship to one another.
   1. According to Vroom, good performance leads to rewards.
   2. Rewards lead to satisfaction.
   3. Thus performance is the cause of satisfaction.
D. Two types of rewards exist.
   1. *Intrinsic rewards* are given to the individual by himself or herself for good performance.
   2. *Extrinsic rewards* are organizationally-controlled rewards (such as pay, promotion, and status) which are likely to be imperfectly related to performance.
E. An empirical study conducted by the authors considered such factors as satisfaction and performance; satisfaction and effort; and intrinsic and extrinsic rewards.
   1. Job satisfaction correlated highly with performance.
   2. Satisfaction was more closely related to performance than to effort.
   3. Intrinsic rewards were more likely to be related to performance than were extrinsic rewards.

The human relations movement with its emphasis on good interpersonal relations, job satisfaction, and the importance of informal groups provided an important initial stimulant for the study of job attitudes and their relationship to human behavior in organizations. Through the thirties and forties, many studies were carried out to determine the correlates of high and low job satisfaction. Such studies related job satisfaction to seniority, age, sex, education, occupation, and income, to mention a few. Why this great interest in job satisfaction? Undoubtedly some of it stemmed from a simple desire on the part of scientists to learn more about job satisfaction, but much of the interest in job satisfaction seems to have come about because of its presumed relationship to job performance. As Brayfield and Crockett have pointed out, a common assumption that employee satisfaction directly affects performance permeates most of the writings about the topic that appeared during this period of two decades.[1] Statements such as the following characterized the literature: "Morale is not an abstraction; rather it is concrete in the sense that it directly affects the quality and quantity of an individual's output," and "Employee morale—reduces turnover—cuts down absenteeism and tardiness; lifts production."[2]

It is not hard to see how the assumption that high job satisfaction leads to high performance came to be popularly accepted. Not only did it fit into the value system of the human relations movement but there also appeared to be some research data to support this point. In the Western Electric studies, the evidence from the Relay Assembly Test Room showed a dramatic tendency for increased employee productivity to be associated with an increase in job satisfaction. Also, who could deny that in the Bank Wiring Room there was both production restriction and mediocre employee morale. With this background it is easy to see why both social scientists and managers believed that if job dissatisfaction could be reduced, the human brake on production could be removed and turned into a force that would increase performance.

## Previous Research

But does the available evidence support the belief that high satisfaction will lead to high performance? Since an initial study, in 1932, by Kornhauser and Sharp, more than thirty studies have considered the relationship between these two variables.[3] Many of the earlier studies seemed to have assumed implicitly that a positive relationship existed and that it was important to demonstrate that it in fact did exist. Little attention was given to trying to understand *why* job satisfaction should lead to higher performance; instead, researchers contented themselves with routinely studying the relationship between satisfaction and performance in a number of industrial situations.

The typical reader of the literature in the early fifties was probably aware of the fact that some studies had failed to find a significant satisfaction-performance relationship. Indeed, the very first study of the problem obtained an insignificant relationship.[4] However, judging from the impact of the first review of the literature on the topic, by Brayfield and Crockett, many social scientists, let alone practicing managers, were unaware that the evidence indicated how little relationship exists between satisfaction and performance.[5] The key conclusion that emerged from the review was that "there is little evidence in the available literature that employee attitudes bear any simple—or, for that matter, appreciable—relationship to performance on the job." (The review, however, pointed out that job satisfaction did seem to be positively related, as expected, to two other kinds of employee behavior, absenteeism and turnover.)

The review had a major impact on the field of industrial psychology and helped shatter the kind of naïve thinking that characterized the earlier years of the Human Relations movement. Perhaps it also discouraged additional research, since few post-1955 studies of the relationship between satisfaction and performance have been reported in scientific journals.

Another review, covering much of the same literature, was completed about the same time.[6] This review took a more optimistic view of the evidence: ". . . there is frequent evidence for the often suggested opinion that positive job attitudes are favorable to increased productivity. The relationship is not absolute, but there are enough data to justify attention to attitudes as a factor in improving the worker's output. However, the correlations obtained in many of the positive studies were low." [7] This review also pointed out, as did Brayfield and Crockett, that there was a definite trend for attitudes to be related to absenteeism and turnover. Perhaps the chief reasons for the somewhat divergent conclusions reached by the two reviews were that they did not cover exactly the same literature and that Brayfield and Crockett were less influenced by suggestive findings that did reach statistical significance. In any event, the one conclusion that was obvious from both reviews was that there was not the *strong, persuasive* relationship between job satisfaction and productivity that had been suggested by many of the early proponents of the Human Relations movement and so casually accepted by personnel specialists.

A more recent review of the literature by Vroom has received less attention than did the two earlier reviews,[8] perhaps because it is now rather generally accepted that satisfaction is not related to performance. However, before we too glibly accept the view that satisfaction and performance are unrelated, let us look carefully at the data from studies reviewed by Vroom. These studies show a median correlation of $+.14$ between satisfaction and performance. Although this correlation is not large, the consistency of the direction of the correlation is quite impressive. Twenty of the 23 correlations cited by Vroom are positive. By a statistical test such consistency would occur by chance less than once in a hundred times.

In summary, the evidence indicates that a low but consistent relationship exists between satisfaction and performance, but it is not at all clear *why* this relationship exists. The questions that need to be answered at this time, therefore, concern the place of job satisfaction both in theories of employee motivation and in everyday organizational practice. For example, should an organization systematically measure the level of employee satisfaction? Is it important for an organization to try to improve employee job satisfaction? Is there theoretical reason for believing that job satisfaction should be related to job behavior and if so, can it explain why this relationship exists?

## Why Study Job Satisfaction?

There are really two bases upon which to argue that job satisfaction is important. Interestingly, both are different from the original reason for studying job satisfaction, that is, the assumed ability of satisfaction to influence performance. The first, and undoubtedly the most straightforward reason, rests on the fact that strong correlations between absenteeism and satisfaction, as well as between turnover and satisfaction, appear in the previous studies. Accordingly, job satisfaction would seem to be an important focus of organizations which wish to reduce absenteeism and turnover.

Perhaps the best explanation of the fact that satisfaction is related to absenteeism and turnover comes from the kind of path-goal theory of motivation that has been stated by Georgopoulos, Mahoney and Jones; Vroom; and Lawler and Porter.[9] According to this view, people are motivated to do things which they feel have a high probability of leading to rewards which they value. When a worker says he is satisfied with his job, he is in effect saying that his needs are satisfied as a result of having his job. Thus, path-goal theory would predict that high satisfaction will lead to low turnover and absenteeism because the satisfied individual is motivated to go to work where his important needs are satisfied.

A second reason for interest in job satisfaction stems from its low but consistent *association* with job performance. Let us speculate for a moment on why this association exists. One possibility is that, as assumed by many, the satisfaction *caused* the performance. However, there is little theoretical reason for believing that satisfaction can cause performance. Vroom, using a path-goal theory of motivation, has pointed out that job satisfaction and job performance are caused by quite different things: ". . . job satisfaction is closely affected by the amounts of rewards that people derive from their jobs and . . . level of performance is closely affected by the basis of attainment of rewards. Individuals are satisfied with their jobs to the extent to which their jobs provide them with what they desire, and they perform effectively in them to the extent that effective performance leads to the attainment of what they desire." [10]

## Relationship between Satisfaction and Performance

Vroom's statement contains a hint of why, despite the fact that satisfaction and performance are caused by different things, they do bear some relationship to each other. If we assume, as seems to be reasonable in terms of motivation theory, that rewards cause satisfaction, and that in some cases performance produces rewards, then it is possible that the relationship found between satisfaction and performance comes about through the action of a third variable—rewards. Briefly stated, good performance may lead to rewards, which in turn lead to satisfaction; this formulation then would say that satisfaction, rather than causing performance, as was previously assumed, is caused by it. Figure 1 presents this thinking in a diagrammatic form.

This model first shows that performance leads to rewards, and it distinguishes between two kinds of rewards and their connection to performance. A wavy line between performance and extrinsic rewards indicates that such rewards are likely to be imperfectly related to performance. By extrinsic rewards is meant such organizationally controlled rewards as pay, promotion, status, and security—rewards that are often referred to as satisfying mainly lower level

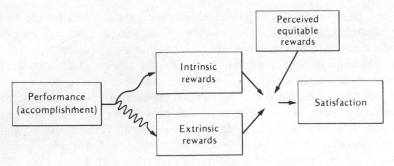

*Figure 1.*   The Theoretical Model

needs.[11] The connection is relatively weak because of the difficulty of tying extrinsic rewards directly to performance. Even though an organization may have a policy of rewarding merit, performance is difficult to measure, and in dispensing rewards like pay, many other factors are frequently taken into consideration. Lawler, for example, found a low correlation between amount of salary and superiors' evaluation for a number of middle and lower level managers.[12]

Quite the opposite is likely to be true for intrinsic rewards, however, since they are given to the individual by himself for good performance. Intrinsic or internally mediated rewards are subject to fewer disturbing influences and thus are likely to be more directly related to good performance. This connection is indicated in the model by a semiwavy line. Probably the best example of an intrinsic reward is the feeling of having accomplished something worthwhile. For that matter, any of the rewards that satisfy self-actualization needs or higher order growth needs are good examples of intrinsic rewards.

The model also shows that intrinsic and extrinsic rewards are not directly related to job satisfaction since the relationship is moderated by expected equitable rewards. This variable refers to the level or amount of rewards that an individual feels he *should* receive as the result of his job performance. Thus, an individual's satisfaction is a function both of the number and amount of the rewards he receives as well as what he considers to be a fair level of reward. An individual can be satisfied with a small amount of reward if he feels that it is a fair amount of reward for his job.[13]

This model would seem to predict that because of the imperfect relationship between performance and rewards and the importance of expected equitable rewards there would be a low but positive relationship between job satisfaction and job performance. The model also leads to a number of other predictions about the relationship between satisfaction and performance. If it turns out that, as this model predicts, satisfaction is dependent on performance, then it can be argued that satisfaction is an important variable from both a theoretical and a practical point of view despite its low relationship to performance. However, when satisfaction is viewed in this way, the reasons for considering it to be important are quite different from those that are proposed when satisfaction is considered to cause performance. But first, let us look at some of the predictions that are derivable from the model and at some data that were collected in order to test the predictions.

## Research Data

Usable data were collected from 148 middle and lower level managers in five organizations. One of the organizations was a large manufacturing company; the others were small social service and welfare agencies. As determined from the demographic data collected from each manager, the sample was typical of other samples of middle and lower level managers, with one exception—31 of the managers were female.

Two kinds of data were collected for each manager. Superior and peer rankings were obtained on two factors: (1) how hard the manager worked, and (2) how well the manager performed his job. Since a number of peers ranked each manager, the average peer's rankings were used for data analysis purposes. The rankings by the superiors and peers were in general agreement with each other, so the rankings met the requirements for convergent and discriminant validity. In addition to the superior and peer rankings each manager filled out an attitude questionnaire designed to measure his degree of satisfaction in five needed areas. This part of the questionnaire was identical to the one used in earlier studies by Porter.[14] It consists of 13 items in the following form:

The opportunity for independent thought and action in my management position:

     (*a*) How much is there now?
          (min)  1  2  3  4  5  6  7  (max)
     (*b*) How much should there be?
          (min)  1  2  3  4  5  6  7  (max)

The answers to the first of these questions (*a*) for each of the 13 items was taken as the measure of need fulfillment or rewards received. The answer to the second of the questions (*b*) was taken as a measure of the individual's expected equitable level of rewards. The difference in answers between the second and first of these questions was taken as the operational measure of need satisfaction. That is, the larger the difference between "should" and "is now" in our findings, the greater the *dis*satisfaction.[15]

The 13 items, though presented in random order in the questionnaire, had been preclassified into five types of needs that have been described by Maslow: security, social, esteem, autonomy, and self-actualization.

## Predictions and Research Results

Let us now consider two specific predictions that our model suggests. The first is that an individual's degree of need satisfaction is related to his job performance as rated by his peers and by his superior. A second prediction is that this relationship is stronger for managers than for non-managers.

The basis for this second prediction can be found in the assumed connection between rewards and performance. It seems apparent that most organizations have considerably more freedom to reward their managers differentially than they do their often unionized rank-and-file employees (unless the latter are on incentive pay plans). Even in a nonunionized organization (such as a governmental unit), management jobs generally offer the possibility of greater flexibility in differential rewards, especially in terms of prestige and autonomy in decision making. Management jobs also typically provide greater opportunities to satisfy higher order intrinsic needs. As the model shows, satisfaction of these higher order needs is more closely tied to performance.

**Satisfaction and Performance.**   Data collected from our sample of managers generally support the first two predictions. Job satisfaction (the sum of the difference scores for all 13 items) correlates significantly with both the superiors' rankings ($r = 0.32$, $p < 0.01$) and peers' rankings ($r = 0.30$, $p < 0.01$) of performance. Although the correlations are not large, they are substantially larger than the median correlation between satisfaction and performance at the level of rank-and-file workers ($r = 0.14$ as given in Vroom's review). It is possible that this higher relationship came about because we used a different measure of need satisfaction than has been typically used before or because we used a better performance measure. However, our belief is that it came about because the study was done at the management level in contrast to the previous studies which mainly involved nonmanagement employees. Neither our measure of job performance nor our measure of satisfaction would seem to be so unique that either could account for the higher relationship found between satisfaction and performance. However, future studies that use the same measure for both managers and non-managers are needed if this point is to be firmly established.

**Satisfaction and Effort.**   An additional prediction from the model is that satisfaction should be more closely related to the rankings obtained on performance than the rankings obtained on effort. The prediction is an important one for the model and stems from the fact that satisfaction is seen as a variable that is more directly dependent on performance than on effort. Others have pointed out that effort is only one of the factors that determines how effective an individual's performance will be. Ability factors and situational constraints are other obviously relevant determinants. It is also important to note that if we assume, as many previous writers have, that satisfaction causes performance then it would seem logical that satisfaction should be more closely related to effort than to performance. Satisfaction should influence an individual's performance by affecting his motivation to perform effectively, and this presumably is better reflected by effort than by job performance.

The results of the present study show, in fact, a stronger relationship between the superiors' rankings of performance and satisfaction ($r = 0.32$) than between the superiors' rankings of effort and satisfaction ($r = 0.23$). Similarly, for the

|  | Rankings by | |
| --- | --- | --- |
| Needs | Superiors | Peers |
| Security | 0.21[a] | 0.17[b] |
| Social | 0.23[a] | 0.26[a] |
| Esteem | 0.24[a] | 0.16[b] |
| Autonomy | 0.18[b] | 0.23[a] |
| Self-actualization | 0.30[a] | 0.28[a] |

[a] $p < 0.01$
[b] $p < 0.05$

*Table 1.* Pearson correlations between performance and satisfaction in five need areas

peer rankings there is a stronger relationship between performance and satisfaction ($r = 0.30$), than between effort and satisfaction ($r = 0.20$).

**Intrinsic and Extrinsic Rewards.**   The model suggests that intrinsic rewards that satisfy needs such as self-actualization are more likely to be related to performance than are extrinsic rewards, which have to be given by someone else and therefore have a weaker relationship between their reception and performance. Thus, the satisfaction should be more closely related to performance for higher than for lower order needs. Table 1 presents the data relevant to this point. There is a slight tendency for satisfaction of the higher order needs to show higher correlations with performance than does satisfaction with lower order needs. In particular, the highest correlations appear for self-actualization which is, of course, the highest order need, in the Maslow need hierarchy.

Overall, the data from the present study are in general agreement with the predictions based on the model. Significant relationships did appear between performance and job satisfaction. Perhaps even more important for our point of view, the relationship between satisfaction and performance was stronger than that typically found among blue-collar employees. Also in agreement with our model was the finding that satisfaction was more closely related to performance than to effort. The final prediction, which was supported by the data, was that the satisfaction of higher order needs would be the most closely related to performance. Taken together then, the data offer encouraging support for our model and in particular for the assertion of the model that satisfaction can best be thought of, as depending on performance rather than causing it.

## Implications of the Findings

At this point we can ask the following question: what does the strength of the satisfaction-performance relationship tell us about an organization? For example, if a strong positive relationship exists we would assume that the organization is effectively distributing differential extrinsic rewards based on performance. In addition, it is providing jobs that allow for the satisfaction of higher order needs.

Finally, the poorer performers rather than the better ones are quitting and showing high absenteeism, since, as we know, satisfaction, turnover, and absenteeism are closely related.

Now let us consider an organization where no relationship exists between satisfaction and performance. In this organization, presumably, rewards are not being effectively related to performance, and turnover in the organization are likely to be equally distributed among both the good and poor performers. Finally, let us consider the organization where satisfaction and performance bear a negative relationship to each other. Here absenteeism and turnover will be greatest among the best performers. Furthermore, the poor performers would be getting more rewards than the good performers.

Clearly, most organization theorists would feel that organizational effectiveness is encouraged by rewarding good performers and by restricting turnover to poorer performers. Thus, it may be desirable for organizations to develop a strong relationship between satisfaction and performance. In effect, the argument is that the less positive relationship between satisfaction and performance in an organization, the less effective the organization will be (*ceteris paribus*). If this hypothesis were shown to be true, it would mean that a measure of the relationship between satisfaction and performance would be a helpful diagnostic tool for examining organizations. It is hardly necessary to note that this approach is quite different from the usual human relations one of trying to maximize satisfaction, since here we are suggesting trying to maximize the relationship between satisfaction and performance, rather than satisfaction itself.

One further implication of the model appears to warrant comment. It well may be that a high general level of satisfaction of needs like self-actualization may be a sign of organization effectiveness. Such a level of satisfaction would indicate, for instance, that most employees have interesting and involving jobs and that they probably are performing them well. One of the obvious advantages of providing employees with intrinsically interesting jobs is that good performance is rewarding in and of itself. Furthermore, being rewarded for good performance is likely to encourage further good performance. Thus, measures of higher order need satisfaction may provide good evidence of how effective organizations have been in creating interesting and rewarding jobs, and therefore, indirect evidence of how motivating the jobs themselves are. This discussion of the role of intrinsic rewards and satisfaction serves to highlight the importance of including measures of higher order need satisfaction in attitude surveys. Too often attitude surveys have focused only on satisfaction with extrinsic rewards, such as pay and promotion, and on the social relations which were originally stressed by the human relations movement.

In summary, we have argued that it is important to consider the satisfaction level that exists in organizations. For one thing, satisfaction is important because it has the power to influence both absenteeism and turnover. In addition, in the area of job performance we have emphasized that rather than being a cause of performance, satisfaction is caused by it. If this is true, and we have presented some evidence to support the view that it is, then it becomes appropriate to be more concerned about which people and what kind of needs are satisfied in the organization, rather than about how to maximize satisfaction generally. In short, we suggest new ways of interpreting job satisfaction data.

## FOOTNOTES

1.   Arthur H. Brayfield and Walter H. Crockett. Employee attitudes and employee performance. *Psychological Bulletin,* Vol. 52 (September, 1955), 396–424.

2.   *Ibid.*

3.   Arthur Kornhauser and A. Sharp. Employee attitudes: Suggestions from a study in a factory. *Personnel Journal,* Vol. 10 (1932), 393–401.

4.   *Ibid.*

5.   Brayfield and Crocket, *op. cit.*

6.   Frederick Herzberg, Bernard Mausner, R. O. Peterson, and Dora F. Capwell. *Job attitudes: Review of research and opinion* (Pittsburgh: Psychological Service, 1957).

7.   *Ibid.,* p. 103.

8.   Victor H. Vroom. *Work and motivation* (New York: Wiley, 1964).

9.   Basil S. Georgopoulos, G. M. Mahoney, and N. W. Jones. A path-goal approach to productivity. *Journal of Applied Psychology,* Vol. 41 (1957), 345–53; Vroom, *op. cit.;* Edward E. Lawler and Lyman W. Porter, Antecedent attitudes of effective managerial performance. *Organizational Behavior and Human Performance,* Vol. 2 (May, 1967), 122–43. See also Lyman W. Porter and Edward E. Lawler. *Managerial attitudes and performance* (Homewood, Ill.: Irwin-Dorsey, in press).

10.   Vroom, *op. cit.,* p. 246.

11.   Abraham H. Maslow. *Motivation and personality* (New York: Harper, 1954). According to Maslow, needs are arranged in a hierarchy with physiological and security needs being the lowest level needs, social and esteem needs next, and autonomy and self-actualization needs the highest level.

12.   Edward E. Lawler. Managers' attitudes toward how their pay is and should be determined. *Journal of Applied Psychology,* Vol. 50 (August, 1966), 273–79.

13.   Lyman W. Porter. A study of perceived need satisfactions in bottom and middle management jobs. *Journal of Applied Psychology,* Vol. 45 (January, 1961), 1–10.

14.   *Ibid.*

15.   A third question about the importance of the various types of needs was also included, but the results based on it are not reported in the findings presented in this article.

---

## *Learning Review*

*Questions:*

1.   There is evidence indicating a low but consistent relationship between _____ and _____.

2.   Two kinds of data were collected in the research study reported in this reading: _____ and _____ rankings and _____ _____.

3.   Extrinsic rewards include _____, _____, _____, and _____.

4.  Job satisfaction would appear to be an important focus of organizations attempting to reduce _____ and _____.

5.  Lawler and Porter attempted to understand _____ job satisfaction should lead to improved performance.

*Answers:*

1. satisfaction, performance; 2. superior, peer, attitude questionnaires; 3. pay, promotion, status, security; 4. absenteeism, turnover; 5. why

---

# Retrospective Comment

✦

## BY EDWARD E. LAWLER, III

Despite the fact that a considerable amount of research has been done on the relationship between performance and satisfaction since our article was published, I don't feel it has been seriously outdated. Most of the points that are made in this article still appear to be valid today, and for that reason, I feel very good about having published this article. At the time we published it, I felt it was an important article because it reversed traditional thinking about the relationship between performance and satisfaction. That is, it argued for a reverse causal relationship. But in my mind, it did more than simply argue for a different kind of causal relationship. It specified some testable hypotheses about when satisfaction and performance should be related. Because it did this, it not only changed the way people think about the causal relationship between performance and satisfaction, it gave them a way of thinking about when the two should be related and when they should not. The latter point I think is particularly important since it got us away from thinking about a simple causal relationship and helped explain why these two variables are not always related. Perhaps the one thing that later research has shown is that our model is too simple. Many more factors than the ones we specified undoubtedly do influence the relationship between satisfaction and performance. In addition, research has suggested a more dynamic relationship between satisfaction and performance than seems to be suggested in this original article.

In summary, then, if I were doing the article again, I wouldn't change it dramatically, but I would probably emphasize the dynamic mutual influence of satisfaction and performance on each other, and the complexity of the issues involved.

# 27

## Coming to a New Awareness of
## Organizational Culture

### EDGAR H. SCHEIN

### *About the Author*

**Edgar H. Schein** received his undergraduate degrees from the University of Chicago and Stanford University, where he also earned his master's in Social Psychology. His Ph.D. is from Harvard. He is presently Sloan Fellows Professor of Management and Chairman of the Organizational Studies Group at the Sloan School of Management, Massachusetts Institute of Technology.

Professor Schein has extensive consulting experience in human resource planning and development, organization development, and related fields. His numerous books and articles are major contributions to the study of organization development, human resource management, career studies, and organizational culture. His most recent books are *Organizational Culture and Leadership* (Jossey-Bass, 1985) and *Career Anchors: Discovering Your Real Values* (University Associates, 1985).

# PREVIEW

A. Organizational culture can be defined in terms of a dynamic model of how culture is learned, passed on, and changed.
   1. Culture is the pattern of basic assumptions that a given group has invented, discovered, or developed in learning to cope with its problems of external adaptation and internal integration.
   2. The pattern of basic assumptions is the cultural paradigm on which the perceptions, thoughts, and feelings of organizational members are based.
   3. Culture exists in groups—sets of people who have shared significant problems, solved them, observed the effects of their solutions, and who have taken in new members.
   4. Basic assumptions inherent in a culture serve to stabilize the group and are highly resistant to change.
   5. Culture cannot serve its stabilizing function unless it is taught to new members.
B. Four approaches can be used in various combinations to decipher a culture's paradigm of assumptions.
   1. Interviewers can analyze the process and content of socialization of new members.
   2. Interviewers can analyze responses to critical incidents in the organization's history.
   3. Beliefs, values, and assumptions of culture creators or carriers can be analyzed.
   4. Interviewers and organization members can jointly explore and analyze anomalies, or puzzling features, uncovered in interviews.
C. Cultures may serve different purposes at different stages in the development of an organization.
   1. Culture serves as a source of identity and strength for young and growing companies. Little chance exists for successfully changing culture at this stage.
   2. In organizational mid-life culture may be changed, but not without consideration of all sources of stability. Managers must decide whether to encourage diversity of subcultures to promote flexibility, or attempt to create a more homogeneous, stronger corporate culture.
   3. Maturity or decline resulting from excessive internal stability which prevents innovation may be combatted by changes in culture. This is a painful process, however, and one likely to elicit strong resistance.
   4. Attempts at culture management strategies must begin by considering the organizational life cycle.

The purpose of this article is to define the concept of organizational culture in terms of a dynamic model of how culture is learned, passed on, and changed. As many recent efforts argue that organizational culture is the key to organizational excellence, it is critical to define this complex concept in a manner that will provide a common frame of reference for practitioners and researchers. Many definitions simply settle for the notion that culture is a set of shared meanings that make it possible for members of a group to interpret and act upon their environment. I believe we must go beyond this definition: even if we knew an organization well enough to live in it, we would not necessarily know how its culture arose, how it came to be what it is, or how it could be changed if organizational survival were at stake.

The thrust of my argument is that we must understand the dynamic evolutionary forces that govern how culture evolves and changes. My approach to this task will be to lay out a formal definition of what I believe organizational culture is, and to elaborate each element of the definition to make it clear how it works.

## Organizational Culture: A Formal Definition

Organizational culture is the *pattern of basic assumptions* that a *given group* has *invented, discovered, or developed in learning to cope* with its *problems of external adaptation and internal integration,* and that have *worked well enough to be considered valid,* and, therefore, to be *taught to new members* as the correct way to *perceive, think, and feel* in relation to those problems.

## 1.   Pattern of Basic Assumptions

Organizational culture can be analyzed at several different levels, starting with the *visible artifacts*—the constructed environment of the organization, its architecture, technology, office layout, manner of dress, visible or audible behavior patterns, and public documents such as charters, employee orientation materials, stories (see Figure 1). This level of analysis is tricky because the data are easy to obtain but hard to interpret. We can describe "how" a group constructs its environment and "what" behavior patterns are discernible among the members, but we often cannot understand the underlying logic—"why" a group behaves the way it does.

To analyze *why* members behave the way they do, we often look for the *values* that govern behavior, which is the second level in Figure 1. But as values are hard to observe directly, it is often necessary to infer them by interviewing key members of the organization or to content analyze artifacts such as documents and charters.[1] However, in identifying such values, we usually note that they represent accurately only the manifest or *espoused* values of a culture. That is, they focus on what people *say* is the reason for their behavior, what they ideally would like those reasons to be, and what are often their rationalizations for

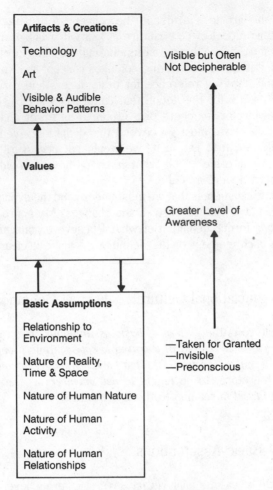

*Figure 1.*   The Levels of Culture and Their Interaction

their behavior. Yet, the underlying reasons for their behavior remain concealed or unconscious.[2]

To really *understand* a culture and to ascertain more completely the group's values and overt behavior, it is imperative to delve into the *underlying assumptions,* which are typically unconscious but which actually determine how group members perceive, think, and feel.[3] Such assumptions are themselves learned responses that originated as espoused values. But, as a value leads to a behavior, and as that behavior begins to solve the problem which prompted it in the first place, the value gradually is transformed into an underlying assumption about how things really are. As the assumption is increasingly taken for granted, it drops out of awareness.

Taken-for-granted assumptions are so powerful because they are less debatable and confrontable than espoused values. We know we are dealing with an assumption when we encounter in our informants a refusal to discuss something, or when they consider us "insane" or "ignorant" for bringing something up. For example, the notion that businesses should be profitable, that schools should educate, or that medicine should prolong life are assumptions, even though they are often considered "merely" values.

To put it another way, the domain of values can be divided into (1) ultimate, nondebatable, taken-for-granted values, for which the term "assumptions" is more appropriate; and (2) debatable, overt, espoused values, for which the term "values" is more applicable. In stating that basic assumptions are unconscious, I am not arguing that this is a result of repression. On the contrary, I am arguing that as certain motivational and cognitive processes are repeated and continue to work, they become unconscious. They can be brought back to awareness only through a kind of focused inquiry, similar to that used by anthropologists. What is needed are the efforts of both an insider who makes the unconscious assumptions and an outsider who helps to uncover the assumptions by asking the right kinds of questions.[4]

## Cultural Paradigms: A Need for Order and Consistency

Because of the human need for order and consistency, assumptions become patterned into what may be termed cultural "paradigms," which tie together the basic assumptions about humankind, nature, and activities. A cultural paradigm is a set of interrelated assumptions that form a coherent pattern. Not all assumptions are mutually compatible or consistent, however. For example, if a group holds the assumption that all good ideas and products ultimately come from individual effort, it cannot easily assume simultaneously that groups can be held responsible for the results achieved, or that individuals will put a high priority on group loyalty. Or, if a group assumes that the way to survive is to conquer nature and to manipulate its environment aggressively, it cannot at the same time assume that the best kind of relationship among group members is one that emphasizes passivity and harmony. If human beings do indeed have a cognitive need for order and consistency, one can then assume that all groups will eventually evolve sets of assumptions that are compatible and consistent.

To analyze cultural paradigms, one needs a set of logical categories for studying assumptions. Table 1 shows such a set based on the original comparative study of Kluckhohn and Strodtbeck.[5] In applying these categories broadly to cultures, Kluckhohn and Strodtbeck note that Western culture tends to be oriented toward an active mastery of nature, and is based on individualistic competitive relationships. It uses a future-oriented, linear, monochronic concept of time,[6] views space and resources as infinite, assumes that human nature is neutral and ultimately perfectible, and bases reality or ultimate truth on science and pragmatism.

In contrast, some Eastern cultures are passively oriented toward nature. They seek to harmonize with nature and with each other. They view the group as more important than the individual, are present or past oriented, see time as polychronic and cyclical, view space and resources as very limited, assume that human nature is bad but improvable, and see reality as based more on revealed truth than on empirical experimentation.

1. **The Organization's Relationship to Its Environment.** Reflecting even more basic assumptions about the relationship of humanity to nature, one can assess whether the key members of the organization view the relationship as one of dominance, submission, harmonizing, finding an appropriate niche, and so on.

2. **The nature of Reality and Trust.** Here are the linguistic and behavioral rules that define what is real and what is not, what is "fact," how truth is ultimately to be determined, and whether truth is "revealed" or "discovered"; basic concepts of time as linear or cyclical, monochronic or polychronic; basic concepts such as space as limited or infinite and property as communal or individual; and so forth.

3. **The Nature of Human Nature.** What does it mean to be "human" and what attributes are considered intrinsic or ultimate? Is human nature good, evil, or neutral? Are human beings perfectible or not? Which is better, Theory X or Theory Y?

4. **The Nature of Human Activity.** What is the "right" thing for human beings to do, on the basis of the above assumptions about reality, the environment, and human nature: to be active, passive, self-developmental, fatalistic, or what? What is work and what is play?

5. **The Nature of Human Relationships.** What is considered to be the "right" way for people to relate to each other, to distribute power and love? Is life cooperative or competitive; individualistic, group collaborative, or communal; based on traditional lineal authority, law, or chrisma; or what?

Source: Reprinted, by permission of the publisher, from "The Role of the Founder in Creating Organizational Culture," by Edgar H. Schein, *Organizational Dynamics,* Summer 1983 © 1983 Periodicals Division, American Management Associations. All rights reserved.

*Table 1.* Basic underlying assumptions around which cultural paradigms form

In this light, organizational culture paradigms are adapted versions of broader cultural paradigms. For example, Dyer notes that the GEM Corporation operates on the interlocking assumptions that: (1) ideas come ultimately from individuals; (2) people are responsible, motivated, and capable of governing themselves; however, truth can only be pragmatically determined by "fighting" things out and testing in groups; (3) such fighting is possible because the members of the organization view themselves as a family who will take care of each other. Ultimately, this makes it safe to fight and be competitive.[7]

I have observed another organization that operates on the paradigm that (1) truth comes ultimately from older, wiser, better educated, higher status members; (2) people are capable of loyalty and discipline in carrying out directives; (3) relationships are basically lineal and vertical; (4) each person has a niche that is his or her territory that cannot be invaded; and (5) the organization is a "solidary unit" that will take care of its members.

Needless to say, the manifest behaviors in these two organizations are totally different. In the first organization, one observes mostly open office landscapes, few offices with closed doors, a high rate of milling about, intense conversations and arguments, and a general air of informality. In the second organization, there is a hush in the air: everyone is in an office and with closed doors. Nothing is done except by appointment and with a prearranged agenda. When people of different ranks are present, one sees real deference rituals and obedience, and a general air of formality permeates everything.

Nonetheless, these behavioral differences make no sense until one has discovered and deciphered the underlying cultural paradigm. To stay at the level of artifacts or values is to deal with the *manifestations* of culture, but not with the cultural essence.

## 2. A Given Group

There cannot be a culture unless there is a group that "owns" it. Culture is embedded in groups, hence the creating group must always be clearly identified. If we want to define a cultural unit, therefore, we must be able to locate a group that is independently defined as the creator, host, or owner of that culture. We must be careful not to define the group in terms of the existence of a culture however tempting that may be, because we then would be creating a completely circular definition.

A given group is a set of people (1) who have been together long enough to have shared significant problems, (2) who have had opportunities to solve those problems and to observe the effects of their solutions, and (3) who have taken in new members. A group's culture cannot be determined unless there is such a definable set of people with a shared history.

The passing on of solutions to new members is required in the definition of culture because the decision to pass something on is itself a very important test of whether a given solution is shared and perceived as valid. If a group passes on with conviction elements of a way of perceiving, thinking, and feeling, we can assume that that group has had enough stability and has shared enough common experiences to have developed a culture. If, on the other hand, a group has not faced the issue of what to pass on in the process of socialization, it has not had a chance to test its own consensus and commitment to a given belief, value, or assumption.

### The Strength of a Culture
The "strength" or "amount" of culture can be defined in terms of (1) the *homogeneity* and *stability* of group membership and (2) the *length* and *intensity* of shared experiences of the group. If a stable group has had a long, varied, intense history (i.e., if it has had to cope with many difficult survival problems and has succeeded), it will have a strong and highly differentiated culture. By the same token, if a group has had a constantly shifting membership or has been together only for a short time and has not faced any difficult issues, it will, by definition, have a weak culture. Although individuals within that group may have very strong individual assumptions, there will not be enough shared experiences for the group as a whole to have a defined culture.

By this definition, one would probably assess IBM and the Bell System as having strong cultures, whereas very young companies or ones which have had a high turnover of key executives would be judged as having weak ones. One should also note that once an organization has a strong culture, if the dominant coalition or leadership remains stable, the culture can survive high turnover at lower ranks because new members can be strongly socialized into the organization as, for example, in elite military units.

It is very important to recognize that cultural strength may or may not be correlated with effectiveness. Though some current writers have argued that strength is desirable,[8] it seems clear to me that the relationship is far more complex. The actual content of the culture and the degree to which its solutions fit the problems posed by the environment seem like the critical variables here, not strength. One can hypothesize that young groups strive for culture strength as a way of creating an identity for themselves, but older groups may be more effective with a weak total culture and diverse subcultures to enable them to be responsive to rapid environmental change.

This way of defining culture makes it specific to a given group. If a total corporation consists of stable functional, divisional, geographic, or rank-based subgroups, then that corporation will have multiple cultures within it. It is perfectly possible for those multiple cultures to be in conflict with each other, such that one could not speak of a single corporate culture. On the other hand, if there has been common corporate experience as well, then one could have a strong corporate culture on top of various subcultures that are based in subunits. The deciphering of a given company's culture then becomes an empirical matter of locating where the stable social units are, what cultures each of those stable units have developed, and how those separate cultures blend into a single whole. The total culture could then be very homogeneous or heterogeneous, according to the degree to which subgroup cultures are similar or different.

It has also been pointed out that some of the cultural assumptions in an organization can come from the occupational background of the members of the organization. This makes it possible to have a managerial culture, an engineering culture, a science culture, a labor union culture, etc., all of which coexist in a given organization.[9]

## 3.   Invented, Discovered, or Developed

Cultural elements are defined as learned solutions to problems. In this section, I will concentrate on the nature of the learning mechanisms that are involved.

Structurally, there are two types of learning situations: (1) positive problem-solving situations that produce positive or negative reinforcement in terms of whether the attempted solution works or not; and (2) anxiety-avoidance situations that produce positive or negative reinforcement in terms of whether the attempted solution does or does not avoid anxiety. In practice, these two types of situations are intertwined, but they are structurally different and, therefore, they must be distinguished.

In the positive problem-solving situation, the group tries out various responses until something works. The group will then continue to use this response until it ceases to work. The information that it no longer works is visible and clear. By contrast, in the anxiety-avoidance situation, once a response is learned because it successfully avoids anxiety, it is likely to be repeated indefinitely. The reason is that the learner will not willingly test the situation to determine whether the cause of the anxiety is still operating. Thus all rituals, patterns of thinking or feeling, and behaviors that may originally have been motivated by a need to avoid a painful, anxiety-provoking situation are going to be repeated, even if the causes of the original pain are no longer acting, because the avoidance of anxiety is, itself, positively reinforcing.[10]

To fully grasp the importance of anxiety reduction in culture formation, we have to consider, first of all, the human need for cognitive order and consistency, which serves as the ultimate motivator for a common language and shared categories of perception and thought.[11] In the absence of such shared "cognitive maps," the human organism experiences a basic existential anxiety that is intolerable— an anxiety observed only in extreme situations of isolation or captivity.[12]

Secondly, humans experience the anxiety associated with being exposed to hostile environmental conditions and to the dangers inherent in unstable social relationships, forcing groups to learn ways of coping with such external and internal problems.

A third source of anxiety is associated with occupational roles such as coal mining and nursing. For example, the Tavistock sociotechnical studies have shown clearly that the social structure and ways of operation of such groups can be conceptualized best as a "defense" against the anxiety that would be unleashed if work were done in another manner.[13]

If an organizational culture is composed of both types of elements—those designed to solve problems and those designed to avoid anxiety—it becomes necessary to analyze which is which if one is concerned about changing any of the elements. In the positive-learning situation, one needs innovative sources to find a better solution to the problem; in the anxiety-avoidance situation, one must first find the source of the anxiety and either show the learner that it no longer exists, or provide an alternative source of avoidance. Either of these is difficult to do.

In other words, cultural elements that are based on anxiety reduction will be more stable than those based on positive problem solving because of the nature of the anxiety reduction mechanism and the fact that human systems need a certain amount of stability to avoid cognitive and social anxiety.

Where do solutions initially come from? Most cultural solutions in new groups and organizations originate from the founders and early leaders of those organizations.[14] Typically, the solution process is an advocacy of certain ways of doing things that are then tried out and either adopted or rejected, depending on how well they work out. Initially, the founders have the most influence, but, as the group ages and acquires its own experiences, its members will find their own solutions. Ultimately, the process of discovering new solutions will be more a result of interactive, shared experiences. But leadership will always play a key role during those times when the group faces a new problem and must develop new responses to the situation. In fact, one of the crucial functions of leadership is to provide guidance at precisely those times when habitual ways of doing things no longer work, or when a dramatic change in the environment requires new responses.

At those times, leadership must not only insure the invention of new and better solutions, but must also provide some security to help the group tolerate the anxiety of giving up old, stable responses, while new ones are learned and tested. In the Lewinian change framework, this means that the "unfreezing stage" must involve both enough disconfirmation to motivate change and enough psychological safety to permit the individual or group to pay attention to the disconfirming data.[15]

## 4. Problems of External Adaptation and Internal Integration

If culture is a solution to the problems a group faces, what can we say about the nature of those problems? Most group theories agree it is useful to distinguish between two kinds of problems: (1) those that deal with the group's basic survival, which has been labeled the primary task, basic function, or ultimate mission of the group; and (2) those that deal with the group's ability to function as a group. These problems have been labeled socioemotional, group building and maintenance, or integration problems.[16]

Homans further distinguishes between the *external system* and the *internal system* and notes that the two are interdependent.[17] Even though one can distinguish between the external and internal problems, in practice both systems are highly interrelated.

**External Adaptation Problems.**   Problems of external adaptation are those that ultimately determine the group's survival in the environment. While a part of the group's environment is "enacted," in the sense that prior cultural experience predisposes members to perceive the environment in a certain way and even to control that environment to a degree, there will always be elements of the environment (weather, natural circumstances, availability of economic and other resources, political upheavals) that are clearly beyond the control of the group and that will, to a degree, determine the fate of the group.[18] A useful way to categorize the problems of survival is to mirror the stages of the problem-solving cycle as shown in Table 2.[19]

The basic underlying assumptions of the culture from which the founders of the organization come will determine to a large extent the initial formulations of core mission, goals, means, criteria, and remedial strategies, in that those ways of doing things are the only ones with which the group members will be familiar. But as an organization develops its own life experience, it may begin to modify to some extent its original assumptions. For example, a young company may begin by defining its core mission to be to "win in the marketplace over all competition," but may at a later stage find that "owning its own niche in the marketplace," "coexisting with other companies," or even "being a silent partner in an oligopolistic industry" is a more workable solution to survival. Thus for each stage of the problem-solving cycle, there will emerge solutions characteristic of that group's own history, and those solutions or ways of doing things based on learned assumptions will make up a major portion of that group's culture.

| | |
|---|---|
| **Strategy:** | Developing consensus on the *primary task, core mission, or manifest and latent functions of the group.* |
| **Goals:** | Developing consensus of *goals,* such goals being the concrete reflection of the core mission. |
| **Means for Accomplishing Goals:** | Developing consensus of the *means to be used* in accomplishing the goals—for example, division of labor, organization structure, reward system, and so forth. |
| **Measuring Performance:** | Developing consensus on the *criteria to be used in measuring how well the group is doing against its goals and targets*—for example, information and control systems. |
| **Correction:** | Developing consensus on *remedial or repair strategies* as needed when the group is not accomplishing its goals. |

Source: Reprinted, by permission of the publisher, from "The Role of the Founder in Creating Organizational Culture," by Edgar H. Schein, *Organizational Dynamics,* Summer 1983 © 1983 Periodicals Division, American Management Associations. All rights reserved.

*Table 2.* Problems of extermal adaptation and survival

**Internal Integration Problems.** A group or organization cannot survive if it cannot manage itself as a group. External survival and internal integration problems are, therefore, two sides of the same coin. Table 3 outlines the major issues of internal integration around which cultural solutions must be found.

While the nature of the solutions will vary from one organization to another, by definition, every organization will have to face each of these issues and develop some kind of solution. However, because the nature of that solution will reflect the biases of the founders and current leaders, the prior experiences of group members, and the actual events experienced, it is likely that each organizational culture will be unique, even though the underlying issues around which the culture is formed will be common.[20]

An important issue to study across many organizations is whether an organization's growth and evolution follows an inherent evolutionary *trend* (e.g., developing societies are seen as evolving from that of a community to more of a bureaucratic, impersonal type of system). One should also study whether organizational cultures reflect in a patterned way the nature of the underlying technology, the age of the organization, the size of the organization, and the nature of the parent culture within which the organization evolves.

## 5. Assumptions That Work Well Enough To Be Considered Valid

Culture goes beyond the norms or values of a group in that it is more of an *ultimate* outcome, based on repeated success and a gradual process of taking things for granted. In other words, to me what makes something "cultural" is this "taken-for-granted" quality, which makes the underlying assumptions virtually undiscussable.

| | |
|---|---|
| **Language:** | *Common language and conceptual categories.* If members cannot communicate with and understand each other, a group is impossible by definition. |
| **Boundaries:** | Consensus on *group boundaries and criteria for inclusion and exclusion.* One of the most important areas of culture is the shared consensus on who is in, who is out, and by what criteria one determines membership. |
| **Power & Status:** | Consensus on *criteria for the allocation of power and status.* Every organization must work out its pecking order and its rules for how one gets, maintains, and loses power. This area of consensus is crucial in helping members manage their own feelings of aggression. |
| **Intimacy:** | Consensus on *criteria for intimacy, friendship, and love.* Every organization must work out its rules of the game for peer relationships, for relationships between the sexes, and for the manner in which openness and intimacy are to be handled in the context of managing the organization's tasks. |
| **Rewards & Punishments:** | Consensus on *criteria for allocation of rewards and punishments.* Every group must know what its heroic and sinful behaviors are; what gets rewarded with property, status, and power; and what gets punished through the withdrawal of rewards and, ultimately, excommunication. |
| **Ideology:** | Consensus of *ideology and "religion."* Every organization, like every society, faces unexplainable events that must be given meaning so that members can respond to them and avoid the anxiety of dealing with the unexplainable and uncontrollable. |

Source: Reprinted, by permission of the publisher, from "The Role of the Founder in Creating Organizational Culture," by Edgar H. Schein, *Organizational Dynamics,* Summer 1983 © 1983 Periodicals Division, American Management Associations. All rights reserved.

*Table 3.* Problems of internal integration

Culture is perpetually being formed in the sense that there is constantly some kind of learning going on about how to relate to the environment and to manage internal affairs. But this ongoing evolutionary process does not change those things that are so thoroughly learned that they come to be a stable element of the group's life. Since the basic assumptions that make up an organization's culture serve the secondary function of stabilizing much of the internal and external environment for the group, and since that stability is sought as a defense against the anxiety which comes with uncertainty and confusion, these deeper parts of the culture either do not change or change only very slowly.

## 6. Taught to New Members

Because culture serves the function of stabilizing the external and internal environment for an organization, it must be taught to new members. It would not serve its function if every generation of new members could introduce new perceptions, language, thinking patterns, and rules of interaction. For culture to serve its function, it must be perceived as correct and valid, and if it is perceived that way, it automatically follows that it must be taught to newcomers.

It cannot be overlooked that new members do bring new ideas and do produce culture change, especially if they are brought in at high levels of the organization. It remains to be settled empirically whether and how this happens. For example, does a new member have to be socialized first and accepted into a central and powerful position before he or she can begin to affect change? Or does a new member bring from the onset new ways of perceiving, thinking, feeling, and acting, which produce automatic changes through role innovation? [21] Is the manner in which new members are socialized influential in determining what kind of innovation they will produce? [22] Much of the work on innovation in organizations is confusing because often it is not clear whether the elements that are considered "new" are actually new assumptions, or simply new artifacts built on old cultural assumptions.

In sum, if culture provides the group members with a paradigm of how the world "is," it goes without saying that such a paradigm would be passed on without question to new members. It is also the case that the very process of passing on the culture provides an opportunity for testing, ratifying, and reaffirming it. For both of these reasons, the process of socialization (i.e., the passing on of the group's culture) is strategically an important process to study if one wants to decipher what the culture is and how it might change.[23]

## 7.  Perceive, Think, and Feel

The final element in the definition reminds us that culture is pervasive and ubiquitous. The basic assumptions about nature, humanity, relationships, truth, activity, time, and space cover virtually all human functions. This is not to say that a given organization's culture will develop to the point of totally "controlling" all of its members' perceptions, thoughts, and feelings. But the process of learning to manage the external and internal environment does involve all of one's cognitive and emotional elements. As cultural learning progresses, more and more of the person's responses will become involved. Therefore, the longer we live in a given culture, and the older the culture is, the more it will influence our perceptions, thoughts, and feelings.

By focusing on perceptions, thoughts, and feelings, I am also stating the importance of those categories relative to the category of *overt behavior*. Can one speak of a culture in terms of just the overt behavior patterns one observes? Culture is *manifested* in overt behavior, but the idea of culture goes deeper than behavior. Indeed, the very reason for elaborating an abstract notion like "culture" is that it is too difficult to explain what goes on in organizations if we stay at the descriptive behavioral level.

To put it another way, behavior is, to a large extent, a joint function of what the individual brings to the situation and the operating situational forces, which to some degree are unpredictable. To understand the cultural portion of what the individual brings to the situation (as opposed to the idiosyncratic or situational portions), we must examine the individual's pattern of perceptions, thoughts, and feelings. Only after we have reached a consensus at this inner level have we uncovered what is potentially *cultural*.

## The Study of Organizational Culture and Its Implications

Organizational culture as defined here is difficult to study. However, it is not as difficult as studying a different society where language and customs are so different that one needs to live in the society to get any feel for it at all. Organizations exist in a parent culture, and much of what we find in them is derivative from the assumptions of the parent culture. But different organizations will sometimes emphasize or amplify different elements of a parent culture. For example, in the two companies previously mentioned, we find in the first an extreme version of the individual freedom ethic, and in the second one, an extreme version of the authority ethic, *both* of which can be derived from U.S. culture.

The problem of deciphering a particular organization's culture, then, is more a matter of surfacing assumptions, which will be recognizable once they have been uncovered. We will not find alien forms of perceiving, thinking, and feeling if the investigator is from the same parent culture as the organization that is being investigated. On the other hand, the particular pattern of assumptions, which we call an organization's cultural paradigm, will not reveal itself easily because it is taken for granted.

How then do we gather data and decipher the paradigm? Basically, there are four approaches that should be used in combination with one another:

1. **Analyzing the Process and Content of Socialization of New Members.**    By interviewing "socialization agents," such as the supervisors and older peers of new members, one can identify some of the important areas of the culture. But some elements of the culture will not be discovered by this method because they are not revealed to newcomers or lower members.

2. **Analyzing Responses to Critical Incidents in the Organization's History.**    By constructing a careful "organizational biography" from documents, interviews, and perhaps even surveys of present and past key members, it is possible to identify the major periods of culture formation. For each crisis or incident identified, it is then necessary to determine what was done, why it was done, and what the outcome was. To infer the underlying assumptions of the organization, one would then look for the major themes in the reasons given for the actions taken.

3. **Analyzing Beliefs, Values, and Assumptions of "Culture Creators or Carriers."**    When interviewing founders, current leaders, or culture creators or carriers, one should initially make an open-ended chronology of each person's history in the organization—his or her goals, modes of action, and assessment of outcomes. The list of external and internal issues found in Tables 2 and 3 can be used as a checklist later in the interview to cover areas more systematically.

4. **Jointly Exploring and Analyzing with Insiders the Anomalies or Puzzling Features Observed or Uncovered in Interviews.**    It is the *joint*

*inquiry* that will help to disclose basic assumptions and help determine how they may interrelate to form the cultural paradigm.

The insider must be a representative of the culture and must be interested in disclosing his or her *own* basic assumptions to test whether they are in fact cultural prototypes. This process works best if one acts from observations that puzzle the outsider or that seem like anomalies because the insider's assumptions are most easily surfaced if they are contrasted to the assumptions that the outsider initially holds about what is observed.

While the first three methods mentioned above should enhance and complement one another, at least one of them should systematically cover all of the external adaptation and internal integration issues. In order to discover the underlying basic assumptions and eventually to decipher the paradigm, the fourth method is necessary to help the insider surface his or her own cultural assumptions. This is done through the outsider's probing and searching.[24]

If an organization's total culture is not well developed, or if the organization consists of important stable subgroups, which have developed subcultures, one must modify the above methods to study the various subcultures.[25] Furthermore, the organizational biography might reveal that the organization is at a certain point in its life cycle, and one would hypothesize that the functions that a given kind of culture plays vary with the life-cycle stage.[26]

## Implications for Culture Management and Change

If we recognize organizational culture—whether at the level of the group or the total corporation—as a deep phenomenon, what does this tell us about when and how to change or manage culture? First of all, the evolutionary perspective draws our attention to the fact that the culture of a group may serve different functions at different times. When a group is forming and growing, the culture is a "glue"—a source of identity and strength. In other words, young founder-dominated companies need their cultures as a way of holding together their organizations. The culture changes that do occur in a young organization can best be described as clarification, articulation, and elaboration. If the young company's culture is genuinely maladaptive in relation to the external environment, the company will not survive anyway. But even if one identified needed changes, there is little chance at this stage that one could change the culture.

In organizational midlife, culture can be managed and changed, but not without considering all the sources of stability which have been identified above. The large diversified organization probably contains many functional, geographic, and other groups that have cultures of their own—some of which will conflict with each other. Whether the organization needs to enhance the diversity to remain flexible in the face of environmental turbulence, or to create a more homogeneous "strong" culture (as some advocate) becomes one of the toughest strategy decisions management confronts, especially if senior management is unaware of some of its own cultural assumptions. Some form of outside intervention and "culture consciousness raising" is probably essential at this stage to facilitate better strategic decisions.

Organizations that have reached a stage of maturity or decline resulting from mature markets and products or from excessive internal stability and comfort that prevents innovation [27] may need to change parts of their culture, provided they can obtain the necessary self-insight. Such managed change will always be a painful process and will elicit strong resistance. Moreover, change may not even be possible without replacing the large numbers of people who wish to hold on to all of the original culture.

No single model of such change exists: managers may successfully orchestrate change through the use of a wide variety of techniques, from outright coercion at one extreme to subtle seduction through the introduction of new technologies at the other extreme. [28]

## Summary and Conclusions

I have attempted to construct a formal definition of organizational culture that derives from a dynamic model of learning and group dynamics. The definition highlights that culture: (1) is always in the process of formation and change; (2) tends to cover all aspects of human functioning; (3) is learned around the major issues of external adaptation and internal integration; and (4) is ultimately embodied as an interrelated, patterned set of basic assumptions that deal with ultimate issues, such as the nature of humanity, human relationships, time, space, and the nature of reality and truth itself.

If we are to decipher a given organization's culture, we must use a complex interview, observation, and joint-inquiry approach in which selected members of the group work with the outsider to uncover the unconscious assumptions that are hypothesized to be the essence of the culture. I believe we need to study a large number of organizations using these methods to determine the utility of the concept of organizational culture and to relate cultural variables to other variables, such as strategy, organizational structure, and ultimately, organizational effectiveness.

If such studies show this model of culture to be useful, one of the major implications will be that our theories of organizational change will have to give much more attention to the opportunities and constraints that organizational culture provides. Clearly, if culture is as powerful as I argue in this article, it will be easy to make changes that are congruent with present assumptions, and very difficult to make changes that are not. In sum, the understanding of organizational culture would then become integral to the process of management itself.

## FOOTNOTES*

1.  J. Martin and C. Siehl, "Organizational Culture and Counterculture: An Uneasy Symbiosis," *Organizational Dynamics,* Autumn 1983, pp. 52–64.

* The research on which this article is based was supported by the Chief of Naval Research, Psychological Sciences Division (Code 452), Organizational Effectiveness Research Programs, Office of Naval Research, Arlington, VA 22217, under Contract Number N00014–80–C–0905, NR 170–911.

Special thanks go to my colleagues Lotte Bailyn, John Van Maanen, and Meryl Louis for helping me to think through this murky area; and to Gibb Dyer, Barbara Lawrence, Steve Barley, Jan Samzelius, and Mary Nur whose research on organizational culture has begun to establish the utility of these ideas.

2. C. Argyris, "The Executive Mind and Double-Loop Learning," *Organizational Dynamics,* Autumn 1982, pp. 5–22.

3. E. H. Schein, "Does Japanese Management Style Have a Message for American Managers?" *Sloan Management Review,* Fall 1981, pp. 55–68;

E. H. Schein, "The Role of the Founder in Creating Organizational Culture," *Organizational Dynamics,* Summer 1983, pp. 13–28.

4. R. Evered and M. R. Louis, "Alternative Perspectives in the Organizational Sciences: 'Inquiry from the Inside' and 'Inquiry from the Outside,'" *Academy of Management Review* (1981):385–395.

5. F. R. Kluckhohn and F. L. Strodtbeck, *Variations in Value Orientations* (Evanston, IL: Row Peterson, 1961). An application of these ideas to the study of organizations across cultures, as contrasted with the culture of organizations can be found in W. M. Evan, *Organization Theory* (New York: John Wiley & Sons, 1976), ch. 15;

Other studies of cross-cultural comparisons are not reviewed in detail here. See for example:

G. Hofstede, *Culture's Consequences* (Beverly Hills, CA: Sage Publications, 1980);

G. W. England, *The Manager and His Values* (Cambridge, MA: Ballinger, 1975).

6. E. T. Hall, *The Silent Language* (New York: Doubleday, 1959).

7. W. G. Dyer, Jr., *Culture in Organizations: A Case Study and Analysis* (Cambridge, MA: Sloan School of Management, MIT, Working Paper #1279–82, 1982).

8. T. E. Deal and A. A. Kennedy, *Corporate Culture* (Reading, MA: Addison-Wesley, 1982); T. J. Peters and R. H. Waterman, Jr., *In Search of Excellence* (New York: Harper & Row, 1982).

9. J. Van Maanen and S. R. Barley, "Occupational Communities: Culture and Control in Organizations" (Cambridge, MA: Sloan School of Management, November 1982);

L. Bailyn, "Resolving Contradictions in Technical Careers," *Technology Review,* November-December 1982, pp. 40–47.

10. R. L. Solomon and L. C. Wynne, "Traumatic Avoidance Learning: The Principles of Anxiety Conservation and Partial Irreversibility," *Psychological Review* 61, 1954, p. 353.

11. D. O. Hebb, "The Social Significance of Animal Studies," in *Handbook of Social Psychology,* G. Lindzey (Reading, MA: Addison-Wesley, 1954).

12. E. H. Schein, *Coercive Persuasion* (New York: Norton, 1961).

13. E. L. Trist and K. W. Bamforth, "Some Social and Psychological Consequences of the Long-Wall Method of Coal Getting," *Human Relations,* 1951, pp. 1–38; I. E. P. Menzies, "A Case Study in the Functioning of Social Systems as a Defense against Anxiety," *Human Relations,* 1960, pp. 95–121.

14. A. M. Pettigrew, "On Studying Organizational Cultures," *Administrative Science Quarterly* (1979): 570–581;

Schein (Summer 1983), pp. 13–28.

15. Schein (1961);

E. H. Schein and W. G. Bennis, *Personal and Organizational Change through Group Methods* (New York: John Wiley & Sons, 1965).

16. A. K. Rice, *The Enterprise and Its Environment* (London: Tavistock, 1963);

R. F. Bales, *Interaction Process Analysis* (Chicago, IL: University of Chicago Press, 1950);

T. Parsons, *The Social System* (Glencoe, IL: The Free Press, 1951).

17. G. Homans, *The Human Group* (New York: Harcourt Brace, 1950).

18. K. E. Weick, "Cognitive Processes in Organizations," in *Research in Organizational Behavior,* ed. B. Staw (Greenwich, CT: JAI Press, 1979), pp. 41–74;

J. Van Maanen, "The Self, the Situation, and the Rules of Interpersonal Relations," in *Essays in Interpersonal Dynamics,* W. G. Bennis, J. Van Maanen, E. H. Schein, and F. I. Steele (Homewood, IL: Dorsey Press, 1979).

19. E. H. Schein, *Process Consultation* (Reading, MA: Addison-Wesley, 1969).

20. When studying different organizations, it is important to determine whether the deeper paradigms that eventually arise in each organizational culture are also unique, or

whether they will fit into certain categories such as those that the typological schemes suggest. For example, Handy describes a typology based on Harrison's work that suggests that organizational paradigms will revolve around one of four basic issues: (1) personal connections, power, and politics; (2) role structuring; (3) tasks and efficiency; or (4) existential here and now issues. See: C. Handy, *The Gods of Management* (London: Penguin, 1978;

R. Harrison, "How to Describe Your Organization," *Harvard Business Review,* September-October 1972.

21. E. H. Schein, "The Role Innovator and His Education," *Technology Review,* October-November 1970, pp. 32–38.

22. J. Van Maanen and E. H. Schein, "Toward a Theory of Organizational Socialization," in *Research in Organizational Behavior,* Vol. 1, ed. B. Staw (Greenwich, CT: JAI Press, 1979).

23. Ibid.

24. Evered and Louis (1981).

25. M. R. Louis, "A Cultural Perspective on Organizations," *Human Systems Management* (1981): 246–258.

26. H. Schwartz and S. M. Davis, "Matching Corporate Culture and Business Strategy," *Organizational Dynamics,* Summer 1981, pp. 30–48; J. R. Kimberly and R. H. Miles, *The Organizational Life Cycle* (San Francisco: Jossey Bass, 1981).

27. R. Katz, "The Effects of Group Longevity of Project Communication and Performance," *Administrative Science Quarterly* (1982): 27, 81–194.

28. A fuller explication of these dynamics can be found in my forthcoming book on organizational culture.

## *Learning Review*

### *Questions:*

1. Organizational culture can be defined as a dynamic model of how culture is _____, _____, and how it _____.

2. Organizational culture can be truly understood only by analyzing its _____.

3. A cultural _____ is a set of interrelated assumptions that form a coherent pattern.

4. The two types of situations where solutions to problems facing the culture are learned include positive _____ situations and _____ situations.

5. Groups face problems of external _____ and internal _____.

6. Culture influences the individual's _____, _____, and _____.

### *Answers:*

1. learned, passed on, changes; 2. underlying assumptions; 3. paradigm; 4. problem-solving, anxiety-avoidance; 5. adaptation, integration; 6. perceptions, thoughts, feelings.

# *Retrospective Comment*

## BY EDGAR H. SCHEIN

Since writing this article, I have expanded the ideas into a full-scale book entitled, *Organizational Culture and Leadership* (Jossey-Bass, 1985) and have found that the response to both the paper and the book has been very positive. Organizational culture seems to be a concept that is finding an important place in our conceptual frameworks.

# Name Index

✦

463

# Subject Index

✦